THE New Male
Sexuality

THE *New Male*
Sexuality

BERNIE ZILBERGELD, PH.D.

BANTAM BOOKS
New York   Toronto   London   Sydney   Auckland

THE NEW MALE SEXUALITY

A Bantam Book / July 1992

Library of Congress Cataloging-in-Publication Data:

Zilbergeld, Bernie.
    The new male sexuality / Bernie Zilbergeld.
       p.   cm.
    Includes index.
    ISBN 0-553-08253-1
    1. Sex instruction for men.   2. Sex role.   3. Masculinity
(Psychology)   I. Title.
HQ36.Z55   1992
613.9'6'081—dc20   92-1226
                                                  CIP

Published simultaneously in the United States and Canada

PRINTED IN THE UNITED STATES OF AMERICA

RRH   0 9 8 7 6 5 4 3 2 1

FOR IAN, WITH LOVE

and the hope that the boys and girls of your generation
will grow up to enjoy a safer, saner, more loving,
and more fulfilling sexuality.

Contents

THE New Male Sexuality

Introduction

THE *new* male sexuality? What in heaven's name could be new about sex, especially for men? Everyone knows that men are the essence of simplicity. They have only one sexual organ, which is hanging right out there in public view; nothing mysterious or complex about that! And it's clear what men want and what their main problem is: getting as much sex as they can.

I never subscribed to that bit of fantasy, but when I wrote *Male Sexuality* in the mid-1970s, I thought that I had explored the topic. Sure, I might someday do an update, covering medical and therapeutic advances in the treatment of male sex problems. But a whole book within fifteen years on the new male sexuality? The idea didn't occur to me, and if it had, I would have dismissed it as silly.

But reality intervened. Even before *Male Sexuality* was published in 1978, I was hearing about new issues from my clients. One of the most astonishing was that in a number of couples the woman was complaining that the man was far less interested in sex than she was. Who had ever heard of such a thing? Another surprise was the number of men who were having sex but not enjoying it. There was also increasing anger from women about men's unwillingness to relate the way the women wanted them to, and increased resentment and despair among men about what they perceived as women's insatiable demands for personal sharing. The world, as usual, was changing. It is these changes—in sex, men, relationships, therapy, and in society at large—that resulted in this book. Here, in somewhat overlapping categories, is some of what is new in our world and in this book.

1

SEX

"When I'm being honest with myself, I have to admit there's a lot about sex I don't know. It's not only not knowing more about women and what makes sex good for them. There's a lot about my own sexuality I haven't explored. I'm in my thirties, but I think my sexual knowledge is at the fifteen-year-old level."—MAN, 34

"My friends and I pretend we know a lot, but we don't. We just feed off each other's ignorance. We can't even talk honestly about sex. I think we're all good at getting ourselves off, but I doubt that any of us is a good lover."—MAN, 21

"I guess I'm lucky. I've never had a problem functioning or getting as much sex as I wanted. But I often wonder if this is all there is. I mean, sex is usually pleasant, sometimes very good. But it's never the kind of stuff you read about in books or see in movies. Am I missing something or is that stuff just media hype?"—MAN, 39

Can you imagine a conversation between your grandparents or parents on an early date in which one asked the other if he or she had been tested for a certain sexually transmitted disease? Or where they discussed how many sexual partners they had had and what kinds of things they had done with them? Or, when they finally got into bed (which might not have been until they were married), one asked the other how she liked to be stimulated or which intercourse position he preferred? Such discussions simply didn't take place in the past.

We view sex differently than our ancestors and even our parents did. While we agree with them that sex is powerful, potentially dangerous, and potentially wonderful, we differ from them in our sense of entitlement about sex. Most Americans now see sexual activity and pleasure as their natural birthrights, something we are free to do or not do when, how, as often as, and with whom we please. While we aren't in favor of people having sex in the streets or in front of children, we see no reason to keep it hidden behind closed doors. We want sex more out in the open than in the past, we want information about it to be readily available, and we most certainly don't want parents, government, or religious institutions to dictate our sex lives.

We are also aware of risks. While sexually transmitted diseases are as old as sex itself, we are the first generation in history to be confronted with the most deadly of these diseases. The specter of AIDS looms in the background no matter what we say, and even if our behavior doesn't change much, there's always a moment of hesitation, a sense that one may be risking one's life. AIDS has somewhat dampened the unabashed enthusiasm for sex so many of us experienced in the 1960s and '70s.

Our sense of entitlement to sexual pleasure and the fear of AIDS are not the only things that are changing sex. For the first time in history, women are now seen as equal partners: being as fully sexual as men, having the right to initiate as well as refuse, being able to orchestrate the process and suggest new ideas, being equally entitled to sexual satisfaction. The idea of sex as something a man "took" from a woman with the only goal being his satisfaction is as dead as the dodo bird in the majority of American male hearts. We want to make our partners happy in bed. For some men, equal participation in sex has been liberating. For others, unfortunately, it has only contributed to the pressure to perform that men have always felt.

There's also a nagging sense that the sex we know and have isn't as good as it could be. One reason involves gender-related differences. Men and women are not the same sexually, just as they are not the same in other areas. But many of us realize that we don't understand the differences and what to do about them.

Even aside from gender differences, there's a sense that something is not quite right with the models of sex dominant in our culture. There's too much emphasis on performance, too many unspoken rules, too much tension, too little time and ability to really get into it and be oneself and to explore new possibilities. Added to this is a feeling that the sex we know is too greatly focused on young people with new partners and new relationships, and not enough on how to make and keep sex enjoyable as we and our relationships age.

The traditional model of sex most of us were trained in focuses on male performance. The man has to make the right moves, has to get and keep an erection for as long as necessary, however long that might be, and, now that women are entitled to sexual satisfaction, also has to provide an ecstatic experience for his partner. Just how he's supposed to know what moves to make, how he's supposed to control an organ that often seems to have a mind of its own, and how he's supposed to know what his partner needs and wants are questions for which there are no clear answers. This model puts enormous pressure on the man to perform and leads to unnecessary anxiety and fakery of all sorts (pretending to be interested when he isn't, pretending to have knowledge he doesn't, and even pretending to have orgasms; women aren't the only ones who do this). For men, the traditional model of sex amounts to playing against a stacked deck. Maybe we need to start stacking the deck on our side.

Throughout the book I offer the elements of a new model of sex, one that emphasizes pleasure, closeness, and self- and partner-enhancement rather than performance and scoring. This model broadens the acts we usually think of as sexual and also how we go about them. Good sex doesn't have to be the traditional foreplay-intercourse routine. There are whole menus of choices that can give pleasure and fit the relationship and situation precisely. We need to know what the choices are and be willing to be flexible. This model has a lot to offer both men and women because it allows us to more closely integrate sex with the rest of our lives and values, to be free of unnecessary performance pressures and anxiety, to be more honest with ourselves and each other, and to feel better about what we're doing.

This new model is based on a growing awareness among both men and women that good sex is not something that just happens. Although reproduction may be natural, reproductive sex is not necessarily good sex. Conception can occur with rape or incest, with sex that lasts only three seconds and doesn't feel particularly good for either partner. Although there are still many people who think sex is or should be natural, with no need to think or learn or talk, this idea has been increasingly discredited. Good sex is no more doing what comes naturally than is an adult conversation. Whether we're talking about your behavior in the bedroom or boardroom, the athletic field, the concert hall stage, or most other places, an incredible amount of learning and effort has gone into it. Acting "naturally" in any of these places would be totally out of place, except for a three-year-old.

Adult spontaneity comes when you have integrated your learned behaviors (including feelings, attitudes, and thoughts) into a smooth sequence of acts that looks graceful to others and feels automatic or natural to you. Each of us daily does many things that seem totally natural yet at one time caused us all sorts of difficulties. If you want to improve your skills in intimacy or sex, rest assured that with enough time and practice the awkwardness and sense of artificiality will disappear and your new skills will feel absolutely natural.

A good lover is not someone who's just doing what comes naturally. Rather, he is a man who has learned and practiced a lot, who now feels relatively comfortable with his body, his values, and his skills, and acts in ways that maximize the chances of generating pleasure for himself and his partner. That is what he is and what you can be as well.

Since the new model of sex is based on pleasure rather than performance, **there is a new chapter on sexual arousal, the key to good-feeling eroticism.** And since so much of what inhibits us sexually has to do with what we think is right or normal, **there is a new chapter exploring the nature of sexual normality. Two additional new chapters explore sex among singles and how to keep sex good over the years. There is yet another new chapter on a topic hardly anyone touches upon but is of significant importance to men: how to initiate sex.**

MEN

"I think I'll someday look back and say this was an exciting time. But right now it's mainly confusing. Nothing seems clear or defined; it's like everything is up for grabs. There's no standard for being a man or woman, for how to relate, even for how to have sex. A little more clarity would be appreciated."—MAN, 42

"The world is becoming feminized. Women are the ones defining what the rules are in terms of love, sex, and everything else. I'm not even sure what it means to be a man anymore."—MAN, 47

A new consciousness has been stirring among some men in the last ten years. Although this is not an exact parallel to the women's movement of twenty or so years ago, there's no doubt that something is afoot. Many men, by themselves or in groups, are starting to question the values they were brought up with. They are asking what those values mean and what prices they exact; and more generally, what it means to be a man and, more personally, what kind of man they want to be.

This raises the question of whether there is indeed a "new man," a being we've heard a lot about from the media in the last ten years. The idea is that, basically in response to the women's movement, men have changed. They have become more what women want—more sensitive and understanding, more intimate, more involved in child-care and housework.

I believe there is some truth in this claim. There have been changes. We know that men are doing more housework than before and more child-care. And more men are taking seriously women's complaints about men not being intimate and sensitive enough. But, as always, the media exaggerate. A few years ago, there were so many stories about househusbands, men who took care of home and children while their wives went out to work, that you could easily get the impression that this was a major trend in modern society. Yet the fact is that very few men could be called househusbands by any reasonable definition.

I think it's closer to the mark to say not that a new man has arrived but rather that men today are struggling with a situation far more complicated and confusing than it was for their fathers and grandfathers, that men are subject to new pressures and messages, many of which conflict with the older rules.

Yes, a man should still be strong, but this should be balanced by sensitivity and restraint. Too much strength is now paradoxically seen as a defect, a sign of neurosis. The term *macho* is used today as often in a derogatory sense as in an admiring one. And a man has to be careful about the sensitivity, as well. Too much of it, however much that may be, can get him called wimp and weakling. Yes, a man should still be successful at work, but somehow he should also find time to relate to his partner and participate equally in child-rearing and household chores. Exactly where the time and energy will come from to carry out all these tasks is never explained. Yes, a man should still be a forceful lover. After all, women don't want wimps in bed. But in addition he should be tender and considerate, understanding his partner's desires and rhythms even though she may not speak them, and be willing to do whatever is necessary for her satisfaction. Yes, a man should still take the sexual initiative, and he should persevere even when he encounters slight or possibly feigned resistance. But he now needs to be able to differentiate possibly feigned resistance from a genuine rebuff, and he needs to be careful lest a sexual invitation he makes is construed as sexual harassment.

In addition to gaining a clearer understanding of these conflicting pressures, we are also gaining a better comprehension of how men get cheated in life and how much they suffer. We stunt the development of our boys as much as—in some ways even more than—we stunt the development of our girls, and boys are abused in at least as many ways as girls. In recent years, we have learned a great deal about what is done to young females and how this helps to account for the behavior and problems of adult women. A great deal of understanding and sympathy has been generated for girls and women, and I believe we have all become wiser and more compassionate as a result.

But not much has been said about what is done to boys and men. Males are still assumed, by themselves and by women, to have a better deal. They are the privileged ones, with all sorts of perks and power that women usually don't have, and they make more money and have more options in many areas. While many women are sympathetic and desire to learn more about men, there are also women who are anything but understanding. To them it's similar to hearing of the problems of the rich and famous. And many men themselves are unsympathetic. Because of their training, they don't want to be seen as complainers or as people with problems. They just want to get on with their lives, muddling through as best they can.

I suggest that it's not easy being a woman or a man and that our training and treatment of men has been as misdirected and harmful as our training and treatment of women. The pressures and problems are somewhat different, but both sexes get battered in the process.

Some Ways in Which Males Get a Raw Deal

• Although the arrival of a male child is generally greeted with more enthusiasm than the arrival of a girl child, males receive less nurturing from their parents, are later held to a stricter definition of appropriate gender-role behaviors, and are punished more often and more severely. After the initial celebration of the child's maleness, his self-esteem gets a daily pounding. The competitiveness that boys engage in and which is reinforced by parents and society scars the majority of boys and inhibits the development of a positive self-regard. Boys are far more likely than girls to be labeled as dyslexic, learning disabled, and hyperactive, and to have far more trouble in school. Although it is easy to sympathize with teachers, parents, and other students who have to deal with unruly boys, consider what it must be like for those boys who feel like failures in school.

• Boys must travel a more torturous route to consolidate their identities than do girls—because boys must give up their first love, their mothers, and identify with a male—but they have generally not been provided with loving and physically and emotionally present models. The lack of a loving, respectful relationship with their fathers is one of the greatest tragedies males suffer and in itself accounts for many of the problems men have relating to others and even themselves. Consider what it must be like to be a boy child and never know if your father loves or even likes you or, worse, but quite common, to believe in your guts that he does not.

• While there has been plenty of publicity about the fact that males commit about 90 percent of all violent crime, there has been little understanding that males are also the main victims of that crime. Potential violence is a fact of life for boys from the first day they encounter other boys. As one English boy put it, "The bigs hit me, so I hit the smalls—that's fair." Without making light of the violence men visit on women, it's a fact that males are three times more likely than females to be assaulted and three times as likely to be murdered. Consider what it must be like for most boys and men who know they can't run from a fight even though they are scared and ill-equipped for battle.

• Because we learn from an early age that manhood is conditional rather than absolute, males are in constant danger of losing their manhood and their identities. Not making the team, not being willing to fight, not performing in bed, losing a job—that's all it takes and our man no longer believes that he's a man. Women have no experience with and little understanding of this kind of threat.

• Males are the ones who are forced to suppress huge parts of themselves, the softer and vulnerable aspects. While this is usually heard as a complaint from women, there is little recognition of how men suffer because of it. They are the ones who aren't able to get hugged or comforted, who can't physically or verbally express the love they feel for male friends they may have known for half a lifetime, who can't find release and relief through tears, who can't openly admit fear and despair. While it's easy to sympathize with mothers who complain their husbands don't spend time with the children, up until recently men simply weren't allowed to participate fully in the joys of parenting. Their children and wives got cheated, but so did the men. While it's easy to sympathize with women who complain their men spend their weekends and vacations working, consider what it must be like to be one of those men, unable to let go of burdens and chores and simply play and have fun. And while it's easy to sympathize with women who complain their men don't talk about personal things, consider what it must be like to be one of those men, without the permission and experience to express their innermost thoughts and feelings.

• Males live fewer years than females and are more likely to commit suicide, to become dependent on drugs and alcohol, to become psychotic, to suffer from stress-related illnesses like ulcers and heart disease, and to be involved in serious accidents.

• Today's man is caught in a very peculiar position because the definition of love has become feminized. In the past, what men did—working to support the family, spending time at home, not running around with other women, not getting drunk too often, doing the kind of chores they could—was accepted as showing their love. No more. Now men are expected to show love the way women do, by sharing feelings and talking in a personal way. Since this definition derives from what women want and do, it's not surprising that men always come out on the short end. They are constantly criticized for what they don't do, and the ways that they do try to show their love are barely even recognized or acknowledged.

• The definition of sex itself is also on its way to becoming feminized. Sex in committed relationships is in; casual sex is out. Sex of long duration, with lots of foreplay and afterplay, is good; "zipless fucks," even though the term was coined by a woman, are bad. Gentle sex is in; hard-driving sex is out. Lusting after a variety of partners, especially young partners, is now considered a sign of immaturity or even mental illness.

But not all the rules have changed. Men are still the ones who have to initiate and perform and whose failure to perform is so obvious and painful. They are the ones who have to "give" their partners orgasms and satisfaction.

• Virtually everything men were trained to do and everything they think, want, and are has come under scrutiny and attack. A man who has followed the precepts taught by his parents, the mass media, teachers, coaches, and other authorities is now in the very strange position of hearing that everything he learned was wrong. The man who does not live up to the traditional standards of success and status is criticized. A woman executive I know had been dating a "kind and sensitive hippie type who does part-time carpentry." When I asked why she stopped seeing him a few weeks later, she proclaimed, "He was nice enough and a good lover, but then I thought, 'What am I doing with a guy who only works when he feels like it and lives in a one-bedroom cottage?' " But the man who climbs the ladder of success and pays the necessary prices is also criticized . . . for being a work-aholic; for not putting enough time, energy, and sensitivity into the relationship; for not wanting children or not spending lots of time with them; and so on.

• Because of the heavy pummeling they have received from women in their lives, from the media, and from therapists, many men are resentful and despairing. Whatever they do and everything they are is somehow wrong, bad, or inadequate. They believe they are willing to change, but it seems that they can't quite understand what is wanted of them or can't make the changes fast enough or can't make enough of them. The withdrawal by men that many women complain about is often no more than the manifestation of the men's just giving up. They can't deal with hearing of more things they are doing wrong, more ways in which they are incompetent. While this withdrawal hurts women, it also hurts men in a profound way because they know full well that withdrawal from conflict is itself the antithesis of what they've been taught about masculinity.

In the past, most jokes were at the expense of women. They were dumb blondes who didn't know anything, they couldn't balance a checkbook or put oil in a car, they were absolutely bizarre about sex, they talked all the time, and on and on. But the tides have changed. Now there's a ready explanation for what women do. If they're not good at math, that's because they were steered away from it in school and at home. If they're squeamish about sex, that's because they were raised by the double standard or sexually molested. If they want to talk, well, that's just normal; everyone should want to talk a lot.

The jokes these days are at the expense of men. They're dumb jocks who think with their dicks, all they care about is sports, work, and sex, they can't change a diaper, feed a baby, or remember a birthday or an anniversary or to pay a bill. And there are no good explanations or reasons for men other than the frequently heard "testosterone poisoning" or "what can you expect from a man?"

I am not trying to say that men suffer more or have it rougher than women. Both sexes suffer and pay enormous prices in today's world.

What I am saying is that men, too, deserve understanding, sympathy, and support. Their lot is not the bowl of cherries we have been led to believe. Unfortunately, men don't get much understanding because they have a hard time making a case for themselves, for expressing what's going on with them and how they feel about it. Which is exactly what we'd expect from people brought up the way we bring up our boys. I take up this subject in greater detail in **a new chapter on male socialization.** There, and in other parts of the book, I discuss the pressures and challenges men face in and out of bed. **In the last chapter, I deal with the crucial topic of how men can be the fathers for their own children that they themselves never had.** Not only is fathering crucial for children, but it is one of the best ways for men to find themselves.

RELATIONSHIPS

"Men and women need each other, but the hassle and pain are unbelievable. When I talk with a woman, I'm not sure we're talking the same language even when we use the same words. We mean different things, see the world differently, want different results. There's got to be a better way."—MAN, 34

Since the beginning of time, there has been widespread discontent among both men and women with male-female relationships. Today, there is a yearning for new ways of relating, ways that provide companionship, joy, personal development, and sexual satisfaction over the years but with less pain and tension. There is also a desire for new tools to negotiate and resolve the inevitable differences and conflicts that arise.

We have developed a better understanding of the ways in which relationships and sex affect one another. In the traditional model, they were two separate categories. This is still seen in the many books on relating and communicating that don't talk much or at all about sex, and in the many books on sex that don't talk much or at all about relating. Relationships and sex have a powerful reciprocal relationship. What goes on in the relationship can result in frequent, loving, exciting, and highly satisfying sex. It can also result in infrequent, boring, or nonexistent sex. Relationship dynamics can cause sex problems, help maintain already existing problems, and make problems difficult or impossible to resolve. On the other hand, good sex can make a relationship more harmonious and satisfying and help resolve nonsexual difficulties, whereas dissatisfying or dysfunctional sex can cause or worsen problems in the rest of the relationship.

It is high time to stop pretending that sex and relating are separate entities. Aside from masturbation, every sexual act takes place in the context of some kind of relationship. Whether that relationship lasts one evening or forty years, whether sex is its main purpose or almost incidental, it's still a relationship, and what happens in it heavily influences the kind of sex that will result, just as the quality of the sex heavily influences what will happen in the relationship.

Because of these considerations, **I devote significant space in this book to the nature of male-female relationships and how they can be improved.** Most of the methods I offer have to do with that modern buzzword *communication*, because communication or connection is the heart and soul of a relationship. I provide many ideas and techniques for the man who wants to improve his listening and expressive skills, as well as his ability to get what he wants in conversations without trampling on the rights of his partner. I take special note of the problems and objections men have about better communications and try to offer ways around them.

One specific tool that's new in this book is the large number of scripts, examples of how to talk to your partner about various issues, some sexual, some not. We men simply have not had enough examples in our own upbringing and in the media to know how to talk sensitively yet assertively about feelings, relationships, and sex. These scripts have been tested with many clients and all have worked a good percentage of the time. If a script says exactly what you want to say, you might use it word for word. If it doesn't quite fit who you are, how you feel, or how you talk, feel free to make changes.

NEW SOLUTIONS TO SEXUAL PROBLEMS

For those with sex problems, a wider array of effective treatments is now available than at any previous time in history. The sex therapy introduced by behavior therapists and Masters and Johnson in the 1960s and early '70s has proved its worth, and there are also new and beneficial mechanical and medical methods. One way or another, there's hope for almost everyone with a sexual problem. The last section of this book is devoted to suggestions and exercises for overcoming the most common male sex problems, and much of the rest of the book offers advice for improving sex.

Some of the material on resolving sex problems was covered in *Male Sexuality*, but it has been updated and new material and suggestions are offered. Among the new items in this book:

- Two chapters on what has become the most common and vexing sex problem for couples: differences in sexual desire.
- A chapter on getting our minds, easily our most powerful sex organ, on our sides, using methods developed by athletic trainers and world-class athletes as well as therapists.
- Suggestions for increasing sexual arousal, the power that fuels sexual functioning and joy.

- New material on the medical side of sex problems and new medical treatments.

This book is based on many of the themes and much of the material in my *Male Sexuality*, but it is by no means just an update. That book was taken apart, rethought, and rewritten, and a great deal of new material was added. A number of sex therapists, researchers, and educators were kind enough not only to read drafts of the chapters in this work, but also to suggest what new material should be added and what could be deleted from the old work.

I have written this book for any man or woman who wants to know more about the sexual development, thoughts, feelings, behavior, and potential of men. It's for those in relationships and those not, those currently having sex with a partner and those who aren't. It's for those who want information, those who want advice and exercises on how to make sex better, and those who want help in resolving sexual problems.

Although this is a self-help book—that is, it contains suggestions and exercises for making changes in your life—some people's situations are such that they need competent professional help. This applies particularly to those in relationships overflowing with hostility and those who may have a physical basis for the sexual difficulties they are experiencing. Even in such cases, this book isn't likely to get in the way. It may resolve the problem or, if not, it may give some assistance, perhaps by pinpointing exactly what the problem is. The reader may still want to consult a professional after using what I present or even at the same time. In several places in the text, I suggest which readers may need professional help.

This may be a good place to explain how my own programs, the suggestions and exercises in this book, were put together. I have been working with people on sexual and relationship problems for twenty years (eight years in a large sex clinic at the University of California, San Francisco, and twenty years in private practice). I have worked with men individually and in groups, with couples, and with women individually. All of the suggestions and exercises are things I use regularly in therapy. They have been tested time and again by me and other therapists (and many in research studies as well) and only those that have proved themselves are included here. But of course in therapy I give my instructions orally rather than in writing. To make sure that my written instructions were clear and comprehensive, I have over the past few years given clients drafts of exercises and chapters that are in the book. This was very instructive. Often what was clear to me wasn't clear to clients, often my organization was an obstacle rather than a help, and often I forgot to include matters about which they had questions. I learned from the comments of all these clients and rewrote accordingly.

One way in which my programs differ from other self-help materials I've seen is that they include more exercises and more instructions on how to do them, which means more pages to read and more ideas to digest. I hope you won't be daunted by this. One reason for the failure of many self-help materials is that insufficient information is given on what to do and how to do it. Some writers, for example, devote only a few paragraphs or pages to gaining ejaculatory control or overcoming erection problems. Some don't even give exercises, instead offering only a few general ideas. It's often unclear how frequent a certain thing should be done or even what that thing is. And often there's no mention of problems that may come up and how to deal with them.

I assume these abbreviated approaches work for some people, but they certainly don't work for many others. Having more exercises and more instructions does not necessarily mean my program takes longer. Instead, it means there are more options to choose from and more details about what to do, what to be aware of, and what problems might develop.

HOW TO USE THE BOOK

My guess is that there are two general types of readers of this book: those who mainly want information and those who want help making sex better or overcoming problems. I wish I could say that the first group should read only certain chapters whereas the second group should read others. But that's not how it is. Because there is a great deal of overlap between topics and chapter headings, there is an advantage to reading the book straight through no matter what you want to get out of it. I realize that those who feel an urgency about resolving a problem may tend to zoom right in on the chapters that deal with their problem, but that is a mistake. The book is structured so that you'll do best by reading through the early chapters (1 through 18) before doing any of the self-help exercises.

Those who want to deal with a problem should be warned: reading alone rarely changes behavior or resolves problems. You need to follow the suggestions and do the relevant exercises if you want to make changes. I provide further discussion of how to undertake a self-help program in Chapters 19–26.

SOME WORDS ON MY USE OF WORDS

In some sense there are no such entities as men and male sexuality. There are only individual men and only the sexuality of individual men. But there is a need to generalize at times, and this book is one such occasion. Obviously much of what I say does not apply to all men and some of it applies only to certain groups or types of men. For example, when I deal with assertiveness, my main interest is helping those men who need to be more direct and persistent. But this does not mean I think all men need to go in this direction. Some would do better to ease up and allow their partners more space. I make frequent use of qualifiers such as *many, some, men often,* and so on, but to do that in every sentence becomes boring and I hope unnecessary. I ask for your understanding. In saying "men do" or "men say," I don't mean to imply that every single man in the world, or even in America, does or says that thing. The same applies to generalizations about women.

When I talk about the other person, the one you're relating to or having sex with, I use a number of terms synonymously: *partner, lover, spouse, wife,* and *mate.* Just because I use *wife* or *spouse* does not mean I think you are or should be married to her.

My examples and language reflect my own heterosexuality and that of the vast majority of men I have worked with. Much of the material and most of the techniques apply equally to bisexual and homosexual men. All men in this culture are socialized into the same models of manhood and sexuality, and all men—indeed, all people—have similar problems in communicating and relating. And sex problems and their treatments cut across sexual orientations. Gay readers, however, will have to translate some of my words into language more appropriate to their own situations.

My writing also reflects a lesson I've learned in many years of trying to help clients and students change their perceptions and behavior. The lesson is that, although book reviewers and some readers dislike repetition, it is crucial to learning. So don't be surprised when you run into the same ideas time and again. The repetition is deliberate. Reading the same idea with a small change in wording or from a slightly different angle really does expedite learning. And in a few places in the self-help chapters, I have described exercises very similar to ones already given in other chapters. The only reason for this is so that you won't have to turn to another chapter to read those exercises.

TAKING GREATER CONTROL OF OUR LIVES

Although men often give the impression of being in control of their lives—that's the impression men are supposed to convey—and although women often believe this impression and envy it, I have been amazed over the years by how many men feel exactly the opposite. In bed and out, they feel buffeted like leaves in a strong wind. They often aren't getting what they want. They often feel powerless to affect the course of their work, their relationships, and even what happens in sex. One cause of sadness for me in the last two decades is that the great debates about taking charge of one's life have been conducted almost entirely by and for women. They are the ones who've been working to redefine traditional concepts of gender and sexuality itself. I'm not sad about what women are doing—I think it's great—but about the fact that more men haven't been doing the same. It goes against our grain. We're too busy performing to take time to think about such issues; these issues involve how we feel about things, something we have always been warned to stay away from; and we don't want to be whiners and complainers, we don't want to admit to problems we don't have ready answers for.

Nonetheless, we men have a lot to gain from taking greater control over our lives. We don't have to be at the mercy of our genitals or hormones or the sex-role scripting we were brought up on. We don't have to forgo the incredible joys and benefits of parenting and truly loving relationships. We don't have to put up with boring, joyless, or dysfunctional sex. We can develop personal styles, relationships, and sexual patterns that more closely fit our own values, preferences, and interests; that more closely fit our human selves. For those who are willing to make the effort, that's what this book is about.

_____ _1_

The Making of Anxious Performers

"I hear girls had it rougher, but you couldn't prove it by me. Growing up was the pits. Incredible pressures all the time, everywhere. Had to do well in school, had to do well in sports, had to maintain my manly image and couldn't walk away from a fight, and later had to do well with girls and pretend I knew all about sex and was getting it regularly. I often wished the whole world would just go away and leave me alone. I don't know what I would have done, but it couldn't have been any worse."—MAN, 36

"It took me half a century to realize that I'd been living a half life, that I had buried important feelings and parts of myself. I was a shit father and husband. Not abusive or anything like that, but I wasn't even home most of the time. Aside from money and fixing things around the house, I didn't contribute anything. Only when my grandson arrived did I make a shift. With him, I am a whole person. I can love him, cuddle him, listen to him, and really talk to him. Sounds funny, listening and talking to a four-year-old, but it's true. His expression of emotion has allowed me to unblock my own feelings. I'm sad that my wife died before I could be a real partner to her. I'm sad that I didn't give more to my own children and that I missed out on so much."—MAN, 54

MAKING THE MAN

Men in our culture walk a thin line. Like their fathers and grandfathers, they must be sure their behavior conforms to what is considered manly. It takes very little—maybe as little as one failure or one sign of weakness—to lose one's place in the charmed circle of men and to be called "lady," "woman," or "pussy"—all signifying a non-man or less than a man. But if a man isn't a man, what then is he? The answer most men seem to believe is: Nothing at all. For their identities are inextricably linked to their gender role.

The concern of being considered a non-man keeps men in a state of almost perpetual vigilance and anxiety. It also makes for a certain inflexibility. If the results of changing one's behavior can be so dire as a loss of identity, one doesn't take change lightly. There is nothing new about this situation for men; it has existed in Western societies for hundreds of years. What is new is that the traditional definition of masculinity has come under scrutiny and attack and that the messages men get have become quite confused. Men are still supposed to exhibit all the manly virtues, but now they should also be sensitive and emotionally expressive, attributes that used to be considered feminine. Being a man has become more difficult than ever before.

What follows is, in my mind, not a pretty story. It shows how we transform male babies into adult beings who are somewhat less than human, who are cut off from huge portions of themselves, the parts that have to do with caring, nurturing, and expressing, who must wear a suit of armor almost all day and night, and who in a very real sense are only pale reflections of who they might be. At least in the old days, they were heavily rewarded for succeeding at being who society wanted them to be. But in recent times, men have come under unrelenting criticism for being who they were trained to be and for not being who they were discouraged from being. The cry is heard on media talk shows, in countless books and articles, in therapy offices, and in bedrooms and kitchens throughout the land: "Why aren't men more interested in relationships, why aren't they softer, why don't they express feelings, why aren't they more interested in household chores and childcare?" The questions are of course not really questions, but accusations.

But why should men be these ways? Where did they learn to focus on relationships, to express emotion, to be interested in children? The answer is: Nowhere at all.

By the age of three or so, boys and girls are aware that they are not just children—they are boy children or girl children, and these distinctions are extremely important. Later learning is always filtered through their gender-colored lenses. Even such neutral-seeming activities as cooking, soccer, and math are influenced by these lenses. Very early on, the child has a notion that soccer and math are things boys are interested in, while cooking is for girls. These notions are easily modifiable at early ages—a boy whose father takes pride in his culinary skills may well conclude that cooking is for males—but the point remains that everything is seen in terms of gender. This is especially true for areas such as sexuality, which is always and everywhere seen in gender-linked ways; in every culture, the rules for male and female sexual behavior are different.

What a culture teaches its boys and girls is dependent on its images of men and women, what it wants these youngsters to grow up to be. Although in recent years we have been reevaluating what we want from men and women, the traditional definitions still exert a very strong pull. A number of researchers have found that a small number of characteristics comprise most of what we expect from our men: strength and self-reliance, success, no sissy stuff (in other words, don't be like women), and sexual interest and prowess. Here's a description from a Harold Robbins novel: "This was a strong man. . . . The earth moved before him when he walked, men loved and feared him, women trembled at the power in his loins, people sought his favors." That may seem a bit outdated, but here's how a recent Sidney Sheldon novel describes the hero: "He was like a force of nature, taking over everything in his path." In a 1989 novel titled *Sophisticated Lady*, we read of the hero (who had, of course, a "tall, powerfully built body"): "Just standing there, he radiated a quiet kind of strength and authority. . . ." And it goes without saying that he was a very successful businessman. He's the modern version: less raucous, more sophisticated, but still strong and successful. Over and over, the descriptions of admired men in books and movies convey, implicitly or explicitly, strength, power, and independence.

Of course there are contrary images: weak men, passive men, and general bunglers like Dagwood Bumstead. But we know they aren't what's wanted, that their bungling is precisely what makes them funny. Real men don't behave like this.

Little boys and little girls are certainly not the same—boys, for example, are on the average more active and aggressive—but they are more similar than adult men and women. Boys, like girls, are playful, warm, open, expressive, loving, vulnerable, and all the other things that make children so attractive. But when we look at adult men, we may wonder what happened to all these wonderful qualities. As adults, men display them to a far lesser degree, if at all. A lot of their best stuff has been trained out of them. In addition, some of their worst and most dangerous tendencies—toward aggressiveness and even violence—have been overdeveloped.

Although I emphasize the role of learning or socialization in the discussion that follows, I do not mean to imply there are no biological differences between the sexes. There certainly are. Nature had different purposes in mind for males and females and programmed them accordingly. Nonetheless, the training given to boys and girls is strikingly different and has an important influence. While we may not be able totally to undo a genetic disposition, we can shape it to some extent. It is probably true, for instance, that males are genetically more aggressive than females, but how frequently and in what ways aggressiveness is manifested are significantly influenced by societal messages boys and men get about it.

For the last seven years I've been involved in helping to raise a boy named Ian, who is now eight. He and his friends are nothing like any man I know. Expressing feelings? No problem. When I've hurt his feelings, Ian doesn't beat around the bush: "Bernie, you hurt my feelings and that isn't very nice." When we go into a room that contains strangers, he takes my hand and says: "I'm scared. You know how shy I am." He has no trouble saying he's sad or apologizing when he has offended someone. He cries, he laughs, he smiles in a way that lights up the sky for everyone around, and he literally jumps for joy.

Little boys present a huge problem for all societies, because the societies don't want men to be like these boys. The question is how to make these open, expressive boys who wear their vulnerabilities and fears on their sleeves into strong, decisive performers who will be able to do whatever the society deems manly. We may think it's cute for a young boy to say, trembling, "I'm scared a monster is gonna get me," but we don't want a twenty- or thirty-year-old to act that way. Instead, we want him to deny his fear ("Monsters don't scare *me!*") and announce he's going to kick some monster ass.

Training in masculinity begins as soon as the child is born and continues for the rest of his life. By the age of six or seven, important lessons have already taken hold. An image of this process comes from a scene in a recent novel about a shooting at an elementary school. There was the usual mass confusion, shots, and a dead body being carried out; in short, a trauma. How did the kids react? A "little girl burst into tears. A chubby boy, five or six, cried. The boy next to him was older, maybe eight. Staring straight ahead and biting his lip, straining for macho." Between the ages of five and eight, he has learned lessons about being male. He will not cry, maybe never again. Nor will he show fear or dependency or tenderness, and he may not even be able to ask for directions when he's lost. He will lose his ability not only to show feelings, but also to experience and know them. He won't understand why his girlfriend or wife just wants to cuddle, to hear his fears and express hers, simply to talk.

You can see the results of men's training everywhere, and such examples serve to reinforce the training for all men who observe. One football-highlights TV show I saw in the fall of 1990 focused on New York Giants coach Bill Parcells, who coached his team that Sunday despite suffering from "painful kidney stones." (The very fact of working while in great pain itself conveys a powerful message regarding what a man is.) As Parcells talked to reporters after the game, his discomfort was obvious. A reporter yelled out, "How do you feel, Bill?" Since it was apparent how he felt, all that was required was that he give a few words to his pain. But his response was this: "I'm going into the hospital tomorrow morning and I'll probably be there a day or two." Feelings? What's that? The message that men watching the show will take away is as clear as the pain that Parcells felt but couldn't put into words.

An important ingredient of the socialization of boys is the message "Don't be like a girl." Since females of all ages are the softer ones—the people who express feelings, who cry, who are more people oriented—not being like them is an effective way to suppress the softer side of males. Girls and women are allowed far greater leeway. *Tomboy* has nowhere near the derogatory punch of *girl* or *sissy*. Girls can play boys' games and with boys' toys, wear boys' clothes. But can you imagine what others will call a boy after the age of four or five who wears a dress or plays house or with dolls?

The primary focus of males and females is very different. Connection to others is the name of the game for females of all ages, even in their play. Dolls (the typical plaything of girls) are more conducive to intimacy training than the toy trucks and weapons boys get. You can cuddle a doll, comfort it, feed it, talk to it, sleep with it. But what can you do with a fire truck that has anything to do with relationships?

Ask little girls about their best friends, and this is what you get: "Janie is my best friend because we talk and share secrets." Research shows that girls spend much more time than boys in one-to-one interaction with their friends, in what one researcher called "chumships." Boys go in a different direction. They learn that the primary thing in life is doing or performing in the world out there, not in the family in here. When little boys are asked about their best friends, their answers usually are about activities: "Robert is my best friend because we play baseball and do lots of other things." Much more so than girls, boys spend time in large groups, often playing games. By the ages of six or seven, the differences that plague adult couples are already in evidence. The boys stress action and the girls talking.

These separate emphases set the stage for huge problems in adult relationships. Both men and women say they want love and intimacy, but they mean different things by these terms. Women favor what has been called face-to-face intimacy: They want to talk. Men prefer side-by-side intimacy: They want to do.

In almost all societies, femininity is given by having the right genitals. Masculinity or manhood is not. It is conditional. Having the right genitals is necessary but not sufficient. As Norman Mailer put it: "Nobody was born a man; you earned your manhood provided you were good enough, bold enough." In his book *Manhood in the Making*, anthropologist David Gilmore notes a recurring notion

> that real manhood is different from simple anatomical maleness, that it is not a natural condition that comes about spontaneously through biological maturation but rather is a precarious or artificial state that boys must win against powerful odds. This recurrent notion that manhood is problematic . . . is found among the simplest hunters and fishermen, among peasants and sophisti-

cated urbanized peoples; it is found in all continents and environments.

It is assumed that girls will grow up to be women simply by getting older, but boys need something special to become men. Thus, most societies have had special rituals, usually difficult and painful, sometimes life-threatening, that boys had to go through before they themselves and the rest of the group considered them to be worthy of the name of men. The good thing about these rituals was that once one had navigated his way through them, one's manhood could never again be questioned. Others might question your competence or attractiveness, but not your masculinity. At least that much was safe.

Western societies long ago got rid of these rituals. But in the process, something valuable was lost and men were left in a perpetual state of anxiety. Now one's manhood was always on the line. One deviant act was all it took for your manhood to be questioned. Maybe you really weren't good enough or bold enough, maybe you didn't have what it took. This is why men walk the thin line I mentioned earlier.

Early on the boy gets the idea that he can't be like the person who means the most to him, his mother. No longer is it acceptable to bask in her warmth and nurturance, except occasionally, and no longer is it possible to think that he, as she did, will someday give birth to babies. She's a woman, and he can't be like her or any other woman. In effect he's wrenched away from the closest relationship he's had and may ever have. In most primitive societies, boys were also wrenched away from Mom, but they were entrusted to the care of one or more men who guided their development. In our society, there is no such arrangement.

There is only Dad, or whoever is playing that role for the boy. It is from him that the boy will learn his most important lessons about masculinity. Unfortunately, that relationship is rarely nurturing or positive in our society. Fathers are often not physically present and when they are, often are not emotionally present. Physical affection, emotional sharing, expression of approval and love—these are the human experiences that very few boys get from their dads. It is a tragedy of the greatest magnitude for men not to have been respected, nurtured, loved, and guided by their fathers.

Martial arts expert Richard Heckler recalls what happened when he was a child and his sailor father returned from a yearlong cruise:

I felt proud of him, proud that he was my father, proud that after not seeing him for a year and not even sure what he looked like, I still had a father. He came up to me and extended his hand in his stiff, formal way. "Hello son. Have you been taking care of your mother and sister while I was away?" I was nine years old and I wanted him to hold me and have him say that he loved me. But he didn't then or ever. . . .

What boys do get from their dads, if anything at all, is reinforcement of macho tendencies (Dad much more than Mom is the one who teaches the necessity for toughness) and the necessity for performance and achievement. Therapist Terrance O'Connor relates this story:

I was struggling in my first year of high school. My father had just given me holy hell for the scores I had received on a standardized test. I felt terrible. In my room, I went over the results again and again. . . . Suddenly I realized that the numbers were raw scores. They needed to be converted. I was astonished. In percentiles, my scores were in the nineties. Vastly relieved, I rushed out to show my father. "Then why in hell don't you get better grades?" he yelled. It was a dagger in my heart. Never a word of love. Never a word of praise. Back in my room, teeth and fists clenched, I said a prayer: "Dear God, never, never, never, let me grow up like that son of a bitch."

This is not to blame our fathers, who were only doing what was done to them. Nonetheless, the wounds opened by this lack of care run deep and are rarely healed. And few men can find ways to express this primal pain and to heal the wounds. If you want to see grown men cry, give them a safe setting and get them talking about their fathers. That's all it takes.

Because the boy is wrenched away from his first real intimate relationship, does not get to experience one with his father, and is taught a body of attitudes, beliefs, and behaviors that are in fact not conducive to intimacy, he will arrive at adulthood quite unprepared for the requirements of a mature relationship. The point is simple and frightening: The socialization of males provides very little that is of value in the formation and maintenance of intimate relationships.

Since so much of male training is in opposition to female qualities, males come to believe that these qualities, and therefore femaleness as a whole, are strange and inferior. The result is the development of a habit of not taking women seriously. Although a man may dearly love a woman and want very much to be considerate, fair, and respectful, he has years of training pulling in the other direction. Women are icky, weird, and disgusting; they're weak and dependent rather than strong and independent as he's supposed to be; they're overly emotional and not logical; they're at the mercy of their hormones (as if they were the only ones with hormones and cycles); and, well, they just don't see things the way men do. Since the boy had to break away from his mother and feminine ways to establish his masculinity, there's also a fear of once again coming under the domination of a woman. To be in this situation is too much like childhood, when he was a non-man. The last thing any man wants is to be "pussy-whipped" or "henpecked" because that's a clear indication that he's not man enough to keep "the little woman" under control. This, too, often leads men, no matter how much they love their partners, to be not quite able to treat them as full human beings with equal rights. This inability to take women seriously can cause much friction in adult relationships and negatively affects sex itself, as we will see later.

Since strength and self-reliance are the primary goals we have for our males, they are trained to mistrust and dislike the more vulnerable and expressive side of themselves. When the boy watches the adults around him, he sees that men are very different from women. Men are rougher and gruffer, they don't express many feelings, they don't talk about personal matters, they don't touch the way women do, and they're admired and rewarded for accomplishments that have nothing to do with what he loves in his mother.

Boys are rewarded for "toughing it out," "hanging tough," not crying, not being weak. By the time Ian was four, he was using the words *tough* and *strong* in an admiring way. By the time he was five, *wimp* and *sissy* had entered his vocabulary as negative terms for males. Sometimes when he was angry at me, he would explode, "You're just a wimp."

Part of being tough is not getting or needing the loving touching that all babies get. Parents stop touching their boys early on; it seems somehow feminine or treating him like a baby or sissy. Girls, on the other hand, continue to be touched and hugged. We end up with women who understand touch as a basic human need and like to touch and be touched as a way of reinforcing contact and demonstrating affection; men, in contrast, lose sight of their need for touching except as a part of roughhousing or sex.

Boys learn that competition is an aid in proving oneself. If you're as good as or better than other males, then at least you're some kind of man. Maybe not the man you could or should be, but at least you're not out of the running.

Most of us experienced no choice: We had to demonstrate our masculinity no matter how ill equipped and ill prepared we felt. In his essay "Being a Boy," Julius Lester captures the agony so many of us felt. Comparing himself to girls, he says:

> There was the life, I thought! No constant pressure to prove oneself. No necessity always to be competing. While I humiliated myself on football and baseball fields, the girls stood on the sidelines laughing at me, because they didn't have to do anything except be girls. The rising of each sun brought me to the starting line of yet another day's Olympic decathlon, with no hope of ever winning even a bronze medal.

Competitiveness turned out to be one of the uglier manifestations of male upbringing. First, because so few of us could win and therefore feel good about ourselves. After all, how many boys can excel at baseball, basketball, and football? And what are the others supposed to do? Countless men have stories to tell about how humiliated they felt as boys when they weren't successful on the athletic field, couldn't even do well enough to be chosen when teams were selected. They felt bad not only because they didn't get to play, but because their very personhood or manhood was questioned.

Second, competition is antithetical to intimacy. As psychologist Ayala Pines points out, in competition the question is "Who's on top?" or "Who's in front?" In intimacy the question is "How close are we or do we want to be?" Closeness is tied to openness, how much we can share of ourselves. But it's difficult to be open if you have a competitive mental set, for the fear is that what is revealed can be used to the other person's advantage.

Because of the emphasis on strength and self-reliance, men have trouble admitting to unresolved personal problems. It's not that problems don't come up, but you handle them, solve them, master them without help and without complaint. That's a large part of what being tough and independent—of being a man—means.

Like so many of the other ideas that men learn, this one puts them in a bind. What is a man supposed to do when he's confused, when he's frightened, when he needs help? Almost by definition, if he acknowledges his confusion or fear and asks for help, there's something wrong with him. He's not as tough as he ought to be. If, on the other hand, he doesn't acknowledge what's bothering him and get help, he may literally make himself sick and do worse at the task he's working on. On a mundane level, this belief results in the ridiculous behavior of men driving around endlessly in their cars because to stop and ask for directions would suggest they need help, which they do.

Many men do not acknowledge their worries and fears to their partners. They simply try to handle everything on their own. I have been involved in many cases where the man was confronted with a major crisis that involved his whole family—the possible loss of a job or a move to another part of the country—but didn't say a word about it to his partner. She knew something was wrong because of the man's distance or irritability, but feared upsetting him by bringing it up: "I told you everything is fine. Leave me alone!" Yet, if she doesn't bring it up, she has to suffer with the man's behavior and may blame herself as well.

Not being able to talk about problems works against intimacy. As linguist Deborah Tannen points out, women use such "troubles talk" as a way of getting support and maintaining connection. But men aren't used to expressing their own problems or having to deal with anyone else's, so while troubles talk can be a wonderful way to maintain closeness between two women, it often doesn't work very well between a man and a woman.

Another consequence of being unable to express problems is that men often don't get what they need. They are slow to admit to illness and other physical problems, and they are even slower to admit to emotional distress. And the idea of needing to go to an expert for help in dealing with personal or relationship problems is anathema to many of them. Men are changing in this respect—more men, for example, are coming to therapists' offices—but the change is slow, and men are still nowhere near as willing as women to admit to personal problems.

It's not easy for boys and men. It's not easy to give up the warm, tender side of themselves. It's not easy to squelch feelings of dependency, love, fear, and anxiety. It's not always easy to be posturing, pretending to be more knowledgeable, more self-reliant, more confident, and more fierce than you really are. There are many times when a man feels fearful or defeated and wants nothing more than to be held and comforted, just as his mother held and comforted him long ago. But he can't get it. He can't admit his feelings and he can't ask to be held. And that is very sad. Like some men, he may choose to drown his feelings in alcohol or sex; at least in sex he will get some body contact and a distraction from his feelings. But neither the alcohol or the sex is the same as real physical and emotional comforting. Too bad he can't get what he really needs and wants.

It's not easy to always have to perform and succeed, whether on the athletic field, in the boardroom, or in the bedroom. Although the whole process has been romanticized, the fact is that boys and men often make themselves sick and crazy in getting ready to perform. It's not unusual for athletes to throw up in locker rooms before competition (romanticize that if you can) and to get themselves into a murderous rage that under any other circumstances would rightfully be considered psychotic. This process, by the way, is often called "getting it up." It's not easy for a man to go into a sexual situation believing that everything rides on how well he performs (especially with a part of himself that he can't control), but what else is he to do?

Being a male is like living in a suit of armor, ready for battle to prove himself. The armor may offer protection (although it's not clear against what), but it's horribly confining and not much fun. In fact, fun is exactly what it's not. Maybe this is why so many men take to alcohol and other ways of deadening themselves. And it may help explain men's fascination with sports.

In sports many of the usual prohibitions on males are lifted. A man can be as emotional and expressive about his favorite team and players as he wants. He can cheer them on with unabashed enthusiasm and what might even pass for love. He can be ecstatic and jump up and down when they win and he can feel despair and weep when they lose. Playfulness and creativity are allowed. He can dress up in ridiculous hats and shirts, make up posters and poems and songs, and just be plain silly. There's even a lot of physical contact: back- and butt-slapping, shoulder- and arm-touching, and hugging. And one can express anger without much risk, cursing a bad call, a decision, or a mistake. Sports is one of the few places where men can safely become boys again, where they can drop the facade of Mr. Uptight-and-in-Control and just play. Sports, whether watching or participating, is one of the few places that adult men display the expressiveness and playfulness of Ian and his friends. Is it any wonder they love it so?

LEARNING ABOUT SEX

> "Through no fault of my own I reached adolescence. While the pressure to prove myself on the athletic field lessened, the overall situation got worse—because now I had to prove myself with girls. Just how I was supposed to go about doing this was beyond me. . . . Nonetheless, duty called, and with my ninth-grade gym-class jock-strap flapping between my legs, off I went."—JULIUS LESTER

Between the ages of eleven and fourteen, children enter puberty. The brain signals the pituitary gland to increase its production of growth hormones and, in males, of testosterone. One of the first outward signs of puberty is a spurt in the rate of physical growth, unmatched since the first few years of life. During the next few years, in boys the penis and scrotum enlarge to adult size, facial and pubic hair appear, and sperm and semen are manufactured. By the age of fifteen or so, boys (and girls as well) are capable of sexual reproduction. And they feel differently than before, trying to get accustomed to their new bodies, trying to make sense of new sensations they experience, trying to deal with the hormonal gush. Testosterone in boys and estrogen in girls make a crucial difference, causing the boys and girls to seek each other out, but also propelling them along the separate paths already well developed.

Before they start having sex with partners or even themselves, boys know that sexual interest and prowess are crucial to being a man. The message permeates our culture. Here's how the hero of a romance novel thinks of himself: "He was, after all, a very physical man with a highly active sex drive. He enjoyed women, all kinds of women. . . ." All kinds: apparently short ones, tall ones, young ones, old ones, fat ones, thin ones, smart ones, dumb ones. He likes to get it on and presumably isn't too particular with whom. Can't be a hero if you don't have a highly active sex drive. When Jerry Brown was governor of California, one of the biggest questions concerned his sex life. That he didn't seem to have one was intolerable. The whole state felt greatly relieved when we learned he was going out with Linda Ronstadt.

It's interesting that in the liberated '90s we still have a double standard for males and females regarding sex. Boys will be boys, after all, and how can you be against a boy sowing his wild oats? We tend to admire males who get around. No one I know thought any the less of John F. Kennedy after learning that he had bedded almost every woman in town; in fact, most men I know seemed to think more of him. But although women are no longer expected to be virgins, God help any of them who has had sex with too many men, however many that might be.

Since sexuality is such a crucial component of masculinity, males feel pressured to act interested in sex whether or not they really are. They have to join in the jokes and banter. "Getting any, Fred?" "Oh yeah, more than I know what to do with." And they have to face the derision of their peers if they're still—God forbid—virgins at the advanced ages of eighteen or twenty-three. This is a great setup for faking, lying, and feeling inadequate.

Perhaps no one has captured the angst of boys' sexual learning better than Bill Cosby in an article he wrote about his first sexual nonexperience. Believing that other boys are doing what he isn't, Cosby asks his girlfriend if she'll have sex with him. She agrees to do so next Saturday, at which point Cosby realizes he has a problem: He doesn't know what sex is or what to do.

I'm trying to ask people questions about how they get some p-u-s-s-y. And I don't want guys to know that I don't know nothin' about gettin' no p-u-s-s-y. But how do you find out how to do it without blowin' the fact that you don't know how to do it? So I come up to a guy and I say, Say man, have you ever had any p-u-s-s-y? And the guy says, Yeah. And I say, Well, man, what's your favorite way of gettin' it? He says, Well, you know, just the regular way. And I say,

Well, do you do it like I do it? And the cat says, How's that? And I say, Well, hey, I heard that there was different ways of doin' it, man. He says, Well, there's a lotta ways of doin' it, you know, but I think that . . . you know, the regular way. . . . I say, Yeah, good ol' regular way of gettin' that p-u-s-s-y.

As he continues his ruminations on the way to the girl's house, Cosby shows how well he has learned that a man should be able to do it all on his own.

So now, I'm walkin', and I'm trying to figure out how to do it. And when I get there, the most embarrassing thing is gonna be when I have to take my pants down. See, right away, then, I'm buck naked in front of this girl. Now, what happens then? Do you . . . do you just . . . I don't even know what to do . . . I'm gonna just stand there and she's gonna say, You don't know how to do it. And I'm gonna say, Yes I do, but I forgot. I never thought of her showing me, because I'm a man and I don't want her to show me—I don't want nobody to show me, but I wish somebody would kinda slip me a note. . . .

And here's an account from a man twenty years younger than Cosby who attended high school in a wealthy suburb.

It was horrible. I was consumed with sex, masturbating at least once a day, and trying to figure out where I stood and what I should be doing. I was always checking out other guys' cocks in the locker room and the toilet. It didn't do a lot for my self-esteem to notice that everyone else's was bigger than mine. Everybody was talking about getting laid and I thought I was the only one who wasn't. I was so scared the other guys would find out I was a virgin. My friend Ronnie saved me from despair when he told me that he was also a virgin despite all his talk. He said it was just a game and you had to pretend. That made me feel better and I started bullshitting, too. I got quite good at it. I never said enough to get me in trouble, but I managed to give the impression that I was getting quite a bit and the girls thought I was heaven-sent. Something else, too. Ronnie laughed when I told him I had a small dick; he said he thought mine was bigger than his. Ronnie made things better, but that whole time was still horrible. It was a relief to finally have sex with a girl, but the overall situation didn't get much better. I always thought some other guy could have done it better or longer or something and been more of a thrill to the girl. I wish Gallup had come to our school and done a poll. My guess is he would have discovered that at least half the guys were lying and that almost all of them thought they had the smallest dicks and the least experience and were the worst lovers.

The sex that adolescent boys learn about is totally penis centered. The focus is narrow-mindedly on what can be done with their frequent erections. But this penis orientation has to do with more than just immediate pleasure and release. Boys are aware, even if only vaguely, that having and using erections has something to do with masculinity. Popular literature abounds with statements linking the two, phrases about a woman grasping or feeling "his throbbing manhood" or reaching for the "essence of his masculinity." And it goes even further: She reached for *him*, or she grasped *him* gently, the *him* in both cases referring to his penis. From a recent novel: "Her hands left my neck and scrambled at my fly. More fumbling, eyes closed. Then she located me." What she located, of course, was his penis. This creates an incredible confusion between personhood or identity and one's sexual organ. No wonder men get so perturbed when their penis isn't the "right" size or doesn't operate according to spec. No penis, no person.

The sex that boys learn about is also largely impersonal. Although this message may serve one of Nature's goals (for men to spread their seed as widely as possible regardless of love or commitment) and therefore be programmed into men, there is no shortage of cultural messages to reinforce the idea. For example, one of the characters in Irving Wallace's *Guest of Honor* is the secretary of state. He's approached by the president's adviser for a favor requested by the first lady. "I'd do her any favor, if she'd do one for me. I'd love to fuck her." And then: "Not that I care for her that much. I just have a hunch she'd be fun between the sheets."

The message is clear: For men, sex doesn't have to be connected to anything except lust, and it doesn't matter much toward whom it's directed. A boy may have fantasies about girls in his classes, his friends' mothers, neighbors, girls or women in the street, movie and TV stars, and anyone else. The female in his fantasies is simply a tool to gain release. And then to do it again, and again, and again. Next time it will probably be a different female. And he certainly doesn't have to like the girl to want to have sex with her. This is clearly demonstrated in an old practice where teenage boys have sex with unpopular girls they despise and wouldn't be seen with in daylight. It's enough if she'll give the boy sex. At these early ages, we can see the start of the male split between love and sex. Sex is a thing unto itself for adolescent boys, cut off from the rest of life and centered on their desire for physical release and the need to prove themselves.

Girls go in a different direction. Perhaps because their genitals are internal and less obvious and obtrusive than boys', their attention isn't constantly drawn downward. Probably of greater importance is that nature had a different task in mind for women than for men (to find a mate to help to care for and raise the children they produced). Although in recent years girls have started masturbating earlier and more frequently than in the past, the percentage of girls who do masturbate is far smaller than the percentage of boys. And the girls who do masturbate don't do it as much as boys of the same age.

Teenage girls aren't as focused on physical sex as boys. "Getting off" in itself isn't nearly as important to them. Girls' sexuality is channeled or filtered through personal connection. They want to have sex with Prince Charming or Mr. Right in the context of a relationship. The idea of a group of girls getting together to have sex with Joe Dork just because he's willing to put out is almost unthinkable. More so than men's, women's first sexual experience with a partner is likely to be with someone they love. And women are far less likely than men to seek sex for its own sake. It's not surprising that when Lonnie Barbach and Linda Levine asked women what qualities make for a good sexual experience, relationship factors were mentioned most often. "Women talked about the security, comfort, and sharing that took place in the emotional relationship as being necessary prerequisites for good sex."

Here we see a male-female difference that persists into adult life. For women, sex is intertwined with personal connection. For men, sex is more a thing in itself, an act to be engaged in with or without love, with or without commitment, with or without connection. Although in surveys men agree with women that the best sex occurs in loving relationships, much more so than women they'll take it any way they can get it.

That the sex boys learn about is performance oriented goes without saying. What else could it be for a person who has already had over a decade of training in becoming a performance machine?

It's Two Feet Long, Hard As Steel, Always Ready, and Will Knock Your Socks Off: The Fantasy Model of Sex

"I learned so much crap about sex as a kid that it took most of the rest of my life to unlearn it and come up with something better. It's still hard to believe how much hassle I caused myself and what a poor lover I was in my early years. I wish I could apologize to every woman I was with before I shaped up."—MAN, 49

WHEN I started working with men with sex problems over twenty years ago, I was immediately struck by the absolutely fantastic beliefs they held. They seemed to believe, for example, that they needed a penis as big and hard as a telephone pole to satisfy a woman, that male and female orgasm were absolutely necessary, that intercourse was the only real sexual act, that good sex had to be spontaneous, without planning or talking, and that it was a crime against humanity if a man had any questions, doubts, or problems in sex. As I reflected on these beliefs, I was shocked to realize that my clients weren't the only ones who held them. I shared many of them myself, and so did most men who weren't clients, and many women as well.

Where, I wondered, did we get these messages? They weren't taught in most sex courses or in sex books by professionals. I was making the mistake, of course, of assuming that most knowledge about sex comes in formal ways, from courses and books. But before boys and girls get to sex courses and books, they already have had years of learning about the subject.

Whether we know it or not, whether it's intended or not, sex education goes on all the time, from the day we're born until the day we die, with an especially heavy dose coming during puberty. Long before we are exposed to the realities of sex, our heads are filled with all sorts of nonsense. Every time we tell or listen to a sexual joke, watch a movie that depicts sexuality explicitly or implicitly, read a novel or see a television program that involves sex or adult relationships—at all these times and many others, we either learn something about sex or, more likely, something we already believe is reinforced and strengthened.

The messages get through because of our basic insecurity about sex and our sensitivity to any information about it. Whether we are trying to learn anything or whether we are aware of having learned anything is irrelevant. Most men, I suspect, would deny that they are affected by all the positive references in jokes and novels to large penises and the denigrating references to small ones. I suggest, however, that these references do indeed have a cumulative effect and help explain why so many men feel their own penises are inadequate. Many of the things that we believe are natural, real, or "the way it is" are in fact absorbed in this way but, because of our insistence to the contrary, are resistant to change or even examination.

The hunger on the part of children for sex information is not sufficiently appreciated. Like Bill Cosby, we want someone to slip us a note, or a whole bunch of notes.

When I was in high school, sex education was a flourishing concern even though there was no official course. The younger guys would be all ears as the older guys told us their versions of sexual reality. Only years later did I realize that, whether deliberate or not, what they said was absolute garbage. Novels with sexual passages—*Peyton Place*, *The Amboy Dukes*, and some of Harold Robbins's early books—were passed around regularly. We read for titillation as well as information, of course, but the information we got was widely inaccurate. Getting better information was virtually impossible. One day in biology, for example, we received new textbooks, the first we had seen with translucent plates, each showing one bodily system. When all the plates were stacked up, you were supposed to have a view of the whole physical body, from the skeletal structure on out. All of the boys immediately turned to where they thought the reproductive organs would be and there was a huge sigh of disappointment. In 1959 there were no reproductive organs in these biology texts. My brother was in the class and later that day he sadly said: "I was all set to check out the penis department, to see if I was OK, and there was nothing. Sure is hard to figure out anything."

Because all the media portray essentially the same sexual messages, it's virtually assured that all men and women will learn the same model of sex, although, to be sure, the messages are filtered through the different gender training males and females have undergone. What is picked up from one source is reinforced by the others. Even if you never read a book or saw a movie, you'd still learn the model. It pervades our culture. Our friends learned it (and you probably learned a lot from them), our parents learned it, and so did everyone else.

The sexual messages conveyed in our culture are the stuff of fantasy, of overheated imaginations run wild, and that's why I call them collectively the fantasy model of sex. It is a model of total unreality about how bodies look and function, how people relate, and how they have sex. The main actors in this model are not actually people, but sexual organs, especially the penis. These penises are not like anything real but instead are, according to historian Steven Marcus, "magical instruments of infinite powers." The men these penises are attached to are not exactly average either. They are always well-built and muscular, even if they're over sixty and even if they do nothing but shuffle papers all day. They are usually tall, with "strong, intelligent" faces, they "radiate power," most are extremely successful at work, and sexual energy oozes from every pore.

The women in fantasyland are incredible. With beautiful faces, sensuous lips and hips, lustrous hair, slim bodies, full breasts always pointing outward and upward, and long, shapely legs you wouldn't believe. It might be thought that the combination of slimness and big breasts would create a problem of balance; but fear not, none of the women ever keel over. And these women are mainly young, meaning in their twenties or early thirties. The few older women we encounter, except for those who are someone's mother, don't look half their age and could pass for college sophomores. For instance: "She was a month away from her fortieth birthday and looked thirty, even on a bad morning."

Regardless of age, these women have some interesting features. Barbara, in John Gardner's *Secret Houses*, is, well, kind of perfect: "As she leaned over him, he noticed that her hair, like her breasts, stayed in perfect order." Wouldn't do to have any hairs or breasts flopping about. Her breasts are worth another few words. They "remained the same whichever way she turned. They did not even seem to flatten when she was on her back, as some girls' did." Ain't life wonderful?

Another interesting feature of women in fantasyland is that they are seriously into sex. They go around with dripping panties, are ready for action at a moment's notice, and can express their desires as some men have always done: "That's right, honey, eat me, hurt me, talk dirty to me, and fuck me. That's all I want." Unless they're virgins, foreplay is not something they need much of. Orgasms, dozens of them, come quickly and easily to them.

Some women complain that this emphasis on perfect female forms is a male conspiracy, but the women created by female writers—for example, most of those who write romance novels—also tend to be young and physically perfect. The fantasy model is equally hard on men and women. The male bodies, organs, and performances are just as far out of reach for the ordinary man as the female bodies and performances are out of reach for the average woman.

Here's a little passage from a Harold Robbins novel that sums a lot of the action of the fantasy model. Try to keep in mind that this book is not only not pornographic by any of the usual definitions, but for decades has been available at many drugstores and supermarkets; Robbins is one of the best-selling authors of fiction in the world. He, along with other popular writers like Henry Miller, Norman Mailer, Mario Puzo, Sidney Sheldon, Erica Jong, Judith Krantz, and Jackie Collins—all of whose books have sold millions of copies and all of whom share some rather interesting ideas about sex—may be far more influential sex educators than Masters and Johnson and Dr. Ruth.

The man in the story is a wealthy businessman and the woman is his wife's dressmaker, whom he has just met. He got aroused and asked her how much. She indicated she wanted to open a small shop, and he said, "You've got it." With that for introduction and foreplay, we begin:

> Gently her fingers opened his union suit and he sprang out at her like an angry lion from its cage. Carefully she . . . took him in both hands, one behind the other as if she were grasping a baseball bat. She stared at it in wonder. . . .
>
> [After placing his hands under her armpits and lifting her in the air] he began to lower her on him. Her legs came up, circling his waist, as he began to enter her. Her breath caught in her throat. It was as if a giant of white hot steel were penetrating her. She began to moan as it opened her and climbed higher into her body, past her womb, past her stomach, under her heart, up into her throat. She was panting now, like a bitch in heat. . . .
>
> [He then lifts her off him and throws her onto the bed.] Then he was posed over her. . . . His hands reached and grasped each of her heavy breasts as if he wanted to tear them from her body. She moaned in pain and writhed, her pelvis suddenly arching and thrusting toward him. Then he entered her again.
>
> "My God," she cried, "my God!" She began to climax almost before he was fully inside her. Then she couldn't stop them, one coming rapidly after the other as he slammed into her with the force of the giant body press she had seen working in his factory. She became confused, the man and the machine they were one and the same and the strength was something she had never known before. And finally, when orgasm after orgasm had racked her body into a searing sheet of flame and she could bear no more, she cried out at him: "Take your pleasure . . . Quick, before I die!"
>
> A roar came from deep inside his throat. . . . she felt the hot onrushing gusher of his semen turning her insides into hot, flowing lava. She discovered herself climaxing again.

You may be wondering what's wrong with this kind of material. Isn't it more exciting and more fun to view, read about, and fantasize about perfectly built people and flawless performances than about real people? I admit it can be great fun to get away from the shortcomings and hassles of real life and imagine only perfection. That's one of the main purposes of fantasy. But there is a problem. Because we don't have any realistic models or standards in sex, of what is customary or even possible in the real world, we tend to measure ourselves against these fantasies. We often don't remember that what we're comparing ourselves to is for the most part unattainable by human beings. We usually aren't even aware that we're comparing ourselves to anything. We just know that we feel bad because our equipment and performances aren't what we wish they were.

In a society that doesn't give realistic models of sexuality, where else would people go for standards? It's rare, for example, to read of or see an average-looking couple having sex, so we end up feeling inadequate about our own bodies and our partners'. It's rare to read about or see a couple having the kind of sex that is possible in the real world, so we feel bad about our less than cataclysmic experiences. It's rare to read of or see a couple discussing a sexual problem, so we learn that sex problems don't or shouldn't exist, and we fail to learn how to deal with them when they do occur.

We compare ourselves to what we've learned, and almost everyone feels that they've come out on the short end. No matter what kind of equipment you have, no matter what partner, no matter what you do, no matter what the results—none of it equals what you heard and read about. Good sex is always somewhere else with someone else.

The myths generate huge amounts of anxiety and bad feelings about ourselves and our partners. They help create sex problems and make resolving them difficult, they bring misery to relationships and individuals, and, in general, they make good sex hard to come by.

Virtually all of the men and women I've talked to over the years who say they have good relationships and good sex report that they had to unlearn or give up a number of harmful notions and replace them with ideas that were more realistic and constructive. The purpose of this chapter is to give you an opportunity to look at some of the main destructive myths men hold about connecting and sex.

MYTH 1: WE'RE LIBERATED FOLKS WHO ARE VERY COMFORTABLE WITH SEX

Beginning with the sexual revolution of the 1960s and '70s, the idea has spread that we have overthrown and overcome the prudishness and inhibitions of our Victorian ancestors. Sexual pleasure is our birthright, and we don't much care what our religions or churches or parents say about it. We're going to do what we want with whom we want, and we're going to enjoy it. In other words, we are fairly calm about and accepting of sex. This view is now held by many people, especially men.

This belief is reinforced by media portrayals of erotica. Everyone in movies and books seems so comfortable with sex. No woman is concerned with her weight or the state of her breasts, thighs, or hips, or about her ability to lubricate and be orgasmic. No man is concerned about the size and hardness of his penis or his sexual endurance. No one questions his ability to provide a mind-blowing experience for himself and his partner. Everyone is comfortable with everything: vaginal, oral, and anal sex, sex with and without drugs, sex in public places, sex with several partners at the same time, and sex without protection against pregnancy and disease. In fact, people in fantasyland are usually so comfortable that it doesn't make any difference whether the partners even know each other. In the Harold Robbins story I quoted earlier, the man and woman had barely exchanged a dozen words; he didn't even know her name until ten seconds before sex. But, hey, no problem! Once they decide to have sex, everything is just fine. And this is far from the only example in popular literature where people who don't know each other, haven't exchanged a word, and maybe don't even like each other just do it and have a wonderful time.

While I'm not saying that greater comfort with impersonal sex is a desirable goal, it certainly would be nice if we were more comfortable with our bodies, our sexual organs, and sexuality in general than we are now. But it seems quite clear that we have not quite reached nirvana yet. I have yet to meet a man or woman who I think is totally comfortable with sex, and that of course includes myself. We all seem to have hang-ups of one kind or another.

How else could it be in a society where parents are still very uncomfortable with their children playing doctor with the boy or girl next door and with, God forbid, their children's masturbatory behavior? How else could it be in a society where even supposedly liberated parents still protect children from movies that show more or less explicit sexuality? We allow our children to see violence in all its ugly faces—the average fifteen-year-old has seen more bombings, shootings, and knifings on television than most soldiers see in actual combat—but we draw the line at erotic pleasure. What messages do you think get across? Kids aren't stupid. They get the point: There's something wrong with sex. As the children grow up, they also learn that sex is pleasurable. But if you scratch the surface you often find the earlier belief, that there's something wrong with sex.

If we're so accepting of sex, why is there so little decent sex education in this country? And how come so few of us can talk about it with our partners? And how come so many of us feel so bad and guilty about our own self-stimulation? And how come so many of us have trouble consistently and effectively using protection against disease and unwanted pregnancy?

In her book *Erotic Wars*, Lillian Rubin notes that although sex is now openly discussed and displayed, it's a different matter in our private lives. "There, sex still is relegated to a shadow existence, and silence is the rule. There, the old taboos still hold: sex is a private affair, something we don't talk about, not with friends, often not even with lovers or mates."

Believing that we are so liberated about sex leads to arrogance and narrow-mindedness. It makes it difficult to examine our own knowledge and attitudes, to see and appreciate our own ignorance and discomfort. And this makes it hard to change our behavior.

MYTH 2: A REAL MAN ISN'T INTO SISSY STUFF LIKE FEELINGS AND COMMUNICATING

In the last chapter we saw that men don't have much practice discerning their feelings or talking about them. Women want to talk, men want to do. She can't understand why he doesn't say more about how he feels and isn't more interested in her personal expressions. He can't understand why she wants to talk so much and why she doesn't want to just get down to sex or whatever else he wants to do.

Because men have trouble directly expressing feelings except for sexual ones, they tend to get sneaky. In one scene in the movie *Three Men and a Baby*, Tom Selleck asks his woman friend to spend the night and the subject of feelings comes up. She says: "I thought sentiment made you uncomfortable." His reply: "I can handle it, as long as it's disguised as sex."

A man in a research study spoke for a lot of men when he said: "What it really comes down to is that I guess I'm not very comfortable with expressing my emotions—I don't think that many men are—but I am pretty comfortable with sex, so I just sort of let sex speak for me." A woman in the same study gave what I think is the perfect response to him: "Sex is his one and only way to be intimate. But how close can you get to someone who only communicates with his cock?"

Talking is important in sex. One reason it's important is so you can protect yourself. Sex has always been a risky activity, and these days the ante has been upped considerably. I'm talking not only about AIDS, but about all the sexually transmitted diseases. And of course unwanted conception is still very much with us. In order to protect yourself against all the complications of sex, you have to be able to talk. At the very least, you need to be able to say, "Wait a sec, I've got to put this rubber on."

Another reason for talking is that it leads to better sex. People who have good sex all say that you need to be able to talk about it. To speak your preferences and desires (that is, your feelings), to ask for changes, and so on. This is one of the main keys to sexual happiness.

The ability to talk is also important in another way. In many relationships, there's less sex than the man wants precisely because his partner feels the absence of connection. He doesn't listen to her or talk to her, so she feels estranged and isn't receptive when he comes on to her.

MYTH 3: ALL TOUCHING IS SEXUAL OR SHOULD LEAD TO SEX

Boys and girls learn different things about touching, and men and women use touch in different ways. Women tend to see touching as a goal in itself; that is, they hug in order to hug, not in order to get someplace else. For men, touching is more often a means to an end; hugging is a part of the foreplay to sex.

As a result, misunderstandings and conflicts over touch are common.

SHE: Why can't we just touch sometimes without having to go on to sex?

HE: But touching turns me on and I want sex. What's wrong with that?

Touching is a more fundamental human need than sex. Studies with monkey babies have shown that those who aren't touched grow up to be damaged emotionally and behaviorally. They don't behave like normal animals and, interestingly, they don't have sex. Studies with human babies have shown something even more dramatic: Without touching, babies tend not to survive.

Touching soothes us, makes us feel loved and supported, makes us feel good. Readers in their late and middle years may recall how wonderful it felt when they were hospitalized (which in general didn't feel good at all) and got a nightly back-rub from a nurse. As one who had several such experiences, I remember thinking that those back-rubs did more for me than most of the medicines I was receiving. Unfortunately, nurses' back-rubs have gone the way of the horse and buggy, and many patients feel worse as a result.

The idea that touching is sexual is so deeply ingrained that many men don't consider having physical contact unless it is part of or going to lead to sex. Women complain about not getting as much touching as they want, but they aren't the only ones being deprived. Men need touching, if only they knew it, and cheat themselves as well. If sex isn't possible—because of illness, a sexual problem, or something else—touching becomes even more important as a source of support and bonding. But many men don't see this and distance themselves physically from their partners in times of trouble.

There are many times when all we need is a hug or to be held. It's ridiculous to go through a whole sexual act to get that. And we go through other acts as well to get touched. Many women point out a hidden purpose for the wrestling that men often engage in with their children. As one puts it clearly: "He can't ask for a touch or a hug, not from me or the boys. So he wrestles with them and with me. Seems like a lot of sweat and effort just to get a hug. Must be terrible to be a man." What she didn't say but is equally true is that he's teaching his boys to be just like him. They don't see a man getting his touching needs met directly, so they'll probably end up having to wrestle or have sex to get a simple hug.

This myth robs us of the joys of "just" touching, it confuses us as to what we want, and it puts pressure on us to be sexual whenever we touch or are touched.

MYTH 4: A MAN IS ALWAYS INTERESTED IN AND ALWAYS READY FOR SEX

As I indicated in the last chapter, sexual interest and activity are part of the model of manhood we learn. A real man is someone who's always interested in sex and ready for it. Here's an example from a novel about a man's needs: "Ike Vesper had had his fill of girlie magazines. Ten weeks without a woman was nine weeks and six days too long." Poor baby! And from another novel:

> Now all Alexis wanted was to be inside a woman. Nothing gave him more pleasure than fucking women, in every way. He had all three of them, going from one to the other in every position imaginable. Juju begged to be sodomized and the two women prepared her, for Alexis's sheer size would have ripped her apart had she not been helped. Before he left the bed he had filled each of them with his sperm.

Having to be ever-eager for sex makes it difficult for a man to refuse a sexual invitation. If someone within five miles is interested in sex, far be it from him to say no. Not being able to say no leads to trouble, because there's nothing more likely to result in a sex problem than having sex when you're not interested.

> A young man came to see me years ago about an erection problem. He was telling me about his latest failure, a woman he had been with a few nights before. I asked him to think back if he really wanted to have sex with her. He thought about it awhile and then admitted he didn't. I asked what he would have preferred. He said his muscles were sore from moving furniture that day and a back-rub would have been really nice. So I asked why he didn't ask her for one. He looked at me as if I was crazy and blurted out: "How could I have asked her for a back-rub? It was our first date. I hardly knew her!"

Since that story was published in *Male Sexuality*, a number of men I've seen have said that reading it made them think about themselves. They realized there were times when they wanted physical affection (usually having to do with getting comfort) but had problems getting it without having sex.

Both of us had tears in our eyes as one man relayed what happened when he lost his job. "I felt utterly crushed. I'd been riding on top of the world for several years, pulling in more bucks than I imagined possible. I felt so proud about giving my family that great new house and all the other goodies. And now we were going to lose it all. I felt like a nothing. I realized later that what I needed was for my wife to take me in her arms and hold and rock me, just like my mother used to do. To let me know she loved me and that things would be okay. But I didn't know this then. All I could think of was to have a few drinks and go home and make love with her. The sex wasn't bad, it helped, but I know it would have been better had I not had the drinks, but just told her what happened and let her hold me."

The reality is that no one is always interested in any one activity. Of course there are times when a man would rather read or sleep or walk or talk or be comforted than have sex. Too bad it's so hard to admit this.

This myth also puts tremendous pressure on young men to be sexual as early as possible. But why should a boy get into sex if he isn't interested or ready? Some young men won't be ready to have sex with a partner until they're out of college. Too bad they and their friends can't see there's nothing wrong with this.

If you aren't ready to talk to someone about sex and if you aren't ready to ask them for a back-rub or a hug, you're definitely not ready to have good sex with them.

MYTH 5: A REAL MAN PERFORMS IN SEX

You've got to have good equipment and you've got to use it right. Sex isn't mainly for enjoyment or to express love or caring or lust, it's mainly to prove that you're a man. This performance orientation explains why men are so much into measurements. If sex is to enjoy and express personal feelings, then you just do and enjoy. But if you're into proving something, then you have to know how you measure up. How big is it, how long did it last, how many orgasms were there? The performance orientation also explains why some men brag about sex to their friends. What's the point of a great performance if no one knows about it?

The quote from Harold Robbins earlier in the chapter is one kind of great performance. Here's another one, from Erica Jong's best-seller *Parachutes and Kisses*:

> He heaped the pillows in front of her for her to lean on, and cupping her breasts, he took her from behind, ramming her harder than before. Her cunt throbbed, ached, tingled. She screamed for him to ram her even harder, to smack her, to pound her. . . .
>
> Never had she so surely met her sexual mate—a man who never tired of fucking, who liked to fuck until the point of soreness and exhaustion, a man who had as few hang-ups about sweat and smell and blood as she had. . . .
>
> She had never come before in this position—but when she did, it was as if thirty-nine years of comes were released and she howled and growled like an animal—whereupon he was aroused beyond containment and he began to come with a pelvis and cock gone wild, pounding her fiercely, filling her with come. . . .

Whew! I get tired just reading this stuff.

One fascinating fact is that fictional accounts of sex almost invariably depict male *performance* and female *pleasure*. He *acts* (rams, pounds, thrusts, bangs) and she *feels* ("unbearable pleasure," "overwhelming joy," "delirious ecstasy," "a sublime moment of climax in which all the stars in the heavens seemed to explode in her mind"), the usual male-female dichotomy. Although she sometimes performs (she too can thrust and bang), it's rarely clear what he feels and experiences. It's as if his feelings and pleasure are beside the point.

Now let's look at the main performance specifications.

MYTH 6: SEX IS CENTERED ON A HARD PENIS AND WHAT'S DONE WITH IT

The adolescent male's fixation on his penis remains constant throughout life. When men think of sex, they think of what they can do with, or what can be done to, their erections. That's what it's all about. And not any old penis or erection will do. Men have a set of specifications for what's required.

Size: Penises in fantasyland come in only three sizes: large, extra large, and so big you can't get them through the door. "Massive," "huge," and "enormous" are commonly mentioned in fiction. "She reached inside his pants and freed his huge erection." "He was so big that she could not reach her fingers all around him." Sometimes we get numbers: "She swears that her Italian singer's cock is over ten inches long." In Mario Puzo's *Godfather*, Sonny Corleone's main claim to fame is the possession of the biggest cock in the known universe. Here's the experience of one of his many lovers with it: "Her hand closed around an enormous, blood-gorged pole of muscle. It pulsated in her hand like an animal and almost weeping with grateful ecstasy she pointed it into her own wet, turgid flesh." And this is what happens in Harold Robbins's *Dreams Die First* to women who witness the unveiling of a male model appropriately called King Dong: "I've seen them go absolutely glassy-eyed and come right in their pants the minute he takes out his tool."

Not only are penises huge to begin with, they can get still bigger during intercourse. "She wailed in hot flooding ecstasy. It went on and on, one climax after another, and as Craig's penis lengthened unbeliev-ably, his semen erupting within her, she wailed again, this time in unison with him." With that penis expanding the way it was, it's no wonder everyone was wailing.

Hardness: These organs that might be mistaken for phone poles are not mere flesh and blood but "hard as steel," "hard as a rock," or a "diamond cutter." Something that could cut a diamond, the toughest substance in the world, must really be hard. One wonders whether we're talking about making war or making love with these tools. There is, of course, no joy in a penis that's sort of hard, semihard, or "only 70 percent" erect.

Activity: These rocklike monstrosities manifest an excess of exuber-ance, for they are forever leaping, surging, springing, and, in general, behaving in a manner that might be considered dangerous for objects so large and hard. Two examples from novels: "He sprang swollen into her hand" and "She captured his surging phallus." Sounds like that one almost got away. Nowhere does one read of a penis that quietly moseyed out for a look at what was going on before springing and crashing into action.

The desired penis functions automatically and predictably, just like a well-oiled machine. It should immediately spring into full readiness whenever its owner decides he will use it. If you're dancing close with someone, your penis should be fully erect, pressing mightily against your pants and making its presence clearly felt. If a woman unzips your fly, your erection ought to spring out at her. If you kiss, well, here's how one novel put it: "The lingering kiss [the first one that day, it should be said] induced an immediate erection." The way some men talk about it, I have the impression they think their penises should stand fully erect if a woman even says hello to them.

Automatic functioning means that the penis should function regardless of any other considerations. Neither rain, nor snow, nor sleet shall keep the almighty penis from its appointed rounds. No matter if you're sick or well, tired or fresh, preoccupied or fully present, if you like your partner or not, if you're angry or not, if you're anxious or relaxed, or if you've gotten any stimulation or not—your penis should immediately come to full attention and do its manly thing.

Penises in fantasyland are also distinguished by their ability to last. They can literally go all night. The admiring wife in one novel: "With Dax it's like having a machine gun inside you. It never stops shooting and neither does he." In one scene, she and Dax have intercourse and both have orgasms (naturally). Immediately after: "She looked at him in surprise. 'You're still hard,' she exclaimed, a note of wonder coming into her voice. She threw her head back . . . as he thrust himself into her again."

The clear message to men and to women is that a man showing up at a sexual event without a rock-hard penis is as inappropriate as a carpenter showing up for work without his hammer and tape measure. You simply can't leave home without your stiff dick. Almost needless to say, these requirements make men feel inadequate about the size and power of their penises and under a bit of pressure to have and keep erections.

MYTH 7: SEX EQUALS INTERCOURSE

Both men and women learn that the main thing in sex is intercourse, and for most of us the two terms are synonymous. Almost all resources that deal with sex—medical books, textbooks, popular books, and articles, as well as erotic materials—treat sex and intercourse as if they were the same. Kissing, caressing, and manual and oral stimulation of genitals are all fine, but mainly as preliminaries to the ultimate: having the penis in the vagina. The very term we use to describe these other activities—foreplay—indicates their lowly status relative to intercourse. They are presumably important only as means to that main event.

This is silly. Since the goal of the vast majority of sexual encounters is not conception, there is no good reason why they have to include or end in intercourse, unless that is what the participants desire. There is no "normal" or "natural" way for sex to proceed. There are lots of possibilities, most of which do not include intercourse. These are discussed in the next chapter.

But we men continue to expect and press for intercourse. Although women in general are more likely to enjoy other aspects of sex, many of them also demand intercourse even though they may not be orgasmic with it.

Insisting on intercourse as a necessary part of sex—the only real way to go—creates a number of problems. One is that it reinforces our performance orientation and makes it difficult to enjoy other aspects of what's going on because we're so focused about getting to intercourse. In this way we rob ourselves of pleasure and of fully experiencing the stimulation necessary for an enjoyable sexual response.

Because intercourse requires some kind of erection (not as much as most men think, but still some hardness), making it a mandatory part of sex reinforces our anxiety about erections. And this, not surprisingly, is likely to result in erection problems.

I'm not against erections or intercourse. If it were up to me, you'd have as many as you wanted. But the absolute need to have them causes lots of problems. When the penis doesn't operate as we want it to, many of us get upset and refuse to have sex at all. If we can't do it the "right way," why do it at all? Should we deprive ourselves of all sexual pleasure because we can't do sex one particular way? Does this make any sense?

Say a man is fortunate enough to have a Mercedes, a car he gets a lot of pleasure from. Then his luck changes and he has to sell the car. What would we think if he refused to drive any other car or take public transportation? If he said, "If I can't go the right way, I won't go at all"? Wouldn't we consider him silly or even mad? Suppose he finally came to terms with taking buses or driving another car, but his wife refused to go with him because she considered a bus or Toyota "settling for second best"? Wouldn't we think her a bit rigid in her thinking?

Yet when it comes to sex, people behave in these peculiar ways all the time. Some men who have trouble with erections stop having sex altogether. Others are willing to try sex but give up as soon as it's clear they're not going to get hard. Still others will do other things—for example, stimulate their partners by hand or mouth—but still feel terrible because they didn't have an erection. And some women whose partners are having erection problems do the same. "I don't want to get myself all worked up and be left hanging." But he'll satisfy you some other way. "It's not the same. I'd rather do without."

There's nothing wrong with wanting a Mercedes and erections and intercourse. But there's also a lot to be said for flexibility. In fact, it's one of the hallmarks of maturity.

MYTH 8: A MAN SHOULD BE ABLE TO MAKE THE EARTH MOVE FOR HIS PARTNER, OR AT THE VERY LEAST KNOCK HER SOCKS OFF

There has been an important change in men's view of their role in sex in the last twenty-five years or so. It used to be that scoring was all that mattered. Any man who got a lot of sex could consider himself success-ful in the sex department. But now we are much more focused on the pleasure of our partners. You can't consider yourself a good lover unless you give your partner an earthshaking experience.

Here is an example of what a man should be able to bring about:

> Then Jeff rolled on top of her and was inside of her and it began again, more exciting than before, a fountain spilling over with unbearable pleasure, and Tracy thought, *Now I know. For the first time, I know.*

Sometimes it's more than purely physical. In the novel *Nightwalker*, the beautiful Grey has sex with martial-arts expert Khan (who, of course, had a "large, rigid penis [that] was formidable"). This was not a one-shot affair: "He took her time after time. When she thought she could bear no more, he took her again." And there was variety: "He was gentle, softly stroking, coaxing, his soft lips teasing, then suddenly he was again demanding, hard, plummeting the very depths of her passion." The outcome: "She was all woman now, spirit truly touched by the earth-shaking revelations her body had revealed. . . . There were no words to describe the intensity of her feelings."

But another popular author found the words: "Alix felt as if she had been thrown into a fire, felt as if her bones were melting. She could not catch her breath. She had never felt such overwhelming pleasure." Once her bones start melting, you know you're doing it right.

If you're in doubt, she'll probably tell you. In a novel by Irving Wallace, a man receives the ultimate accolade from his lover: "You're good, Ezra, very good. You're the best I know. You're spoiling me for all other men." And a woman in one of Harold Robbins's books: "You're the most man I ever had."

In fantasyland, sex is always the best, the greatest, the most wonderful. The earth always moves.

One result of this myth is added pressure on a man to perform. Not only does he have to get it up and keep it up, he also has to use his tool, and everything else he has, to give his partner a mind-blowing experience. And, of course, no one ever tells him exactly how he's supposed to accomplish that.

This belief has another unfortunate consequence. It can make it difficult for a man to feel good about a sexual encounter that consists primarily of being pleasured by his partner. Sometimes, when the woman is not aroused and the man is, she can engage in intercourse or some other act for his pleasure. As long as she feels good about what she's doing and there's no coercion, I don't see anything wrong with this, just as I don't see anything wrong with a man stimulating his partner for her satisfaction when he isn't in the mood for something for himself. This practice can be quite helpful in a relationship where one partner wants sex more frequently than the other.

But because of the idea that sex isn't complete unless the woman has convulsions, many men disparage such activities as "servicing" and say they aren't interested. So the man may deprive himself of the sex he could have had and feel frustrated, annoyed, or angry. The woman may also be in a bad place. What she was able and willing to provide isn't good enough, and now she's got an upset partner. Should she just accept that, or should she try to force feelings that aren't there or even fake them? This kind of stuff does not make for happy relationships.

MYTH 9: GOOD SEX REQUIRES ORGASM

It has always been accepted that the goal of sex for men is their own ejaculation/orgasm. I've never seen or read of a sexual experience that didn't include clear indication that the man had "come," "finished," "shot his load," "exploded inside of her," and so on.

And now women have to have orgasms as well. It is rare these days to view a sexual scene in a movie or read of one in a book that doesn't include at least one per experience. Ever since Masters and Johnson's research showed that some women are capable of multiple orgasms, these have become the rage, and expectations have soared. "One climax after another" is a common way of putting it in novels. Here's one happy woman: "Deeper, harder, faster, until she cried out again, barely recovered from her first overwhelming orgasm before she was thrust into her second." Any man who can't generate at least a dozen or so orgasms in his partner is hardly worth considering.

There's also concern about the type of orgasm that women have. In fantasyland, they are quick and furious. Women have orgasms "instantaneously" or "almost before he was fully inside her," always accompanied by screams and a thrashing of limbs. "With three violent thrusts he brought her to orgasm" is one example, as is "Within seconds they reached orgasm simultaneously."

The equating of sex with orgasm has become so common that the reaction of a number of readers to calling this a myth has been one of incredulity: "Now he's really gone off the deep end. What's the point of sex without a climax?" What's the point indeed? And what's the point of dinner without dessert? Or a baseball game without a home run?

The point is simple. With or without an orgasm, with or without dessert, with or without a home run, the sex, dinner, and game go on. There's interesting stuff to be had, if only you can pay attention and not get upset because it doesn't have the ending you want.

I have nothing against orgasm. If it's in the cards and can happen without making someone miserable, then enjoy it. But what's the point of twisting oneself into a pretzel in order to have an orgasm? Many men try to force their own orgasms by thrusting wildly and calling up every fantasy they can think of. Although it surprises many people when I say this, more than a few men I've talked to have faked orgasm. They felt bad about doing this, but they didn't want their partners to know they hadn't come. Besides, they had no idea of how to stop the activity without an orgasm.

Men also put pressure on their partners to have quick, loud orgasms so they, the men, will be able to feel good about themselves. No wonder that faking orgasms on the part of women hasn't gone out of style. Even if she has a real one, she may feel pressured to fake several more, or to make it more dramatic than it really is. What's the point of doing this to one's partner?

Actually, there are several points or reasons, all understandable but still harmful. One reason has to do with the male focus on specifications and indicators. Now that women are supposed to enjoy sex—which is understood as, we men are supposed to make it enjoyable for them—how do we know they enjoyed it? We need a clear sign, and orgasm is the clearest sign we can think of. The reason that orgasm is a better sign than her saying she enjoyed it has to do with our own experiences. Since many men (unfortunately) don't get much out of sex aside from orgasm, they assume the same is true for their partners. Men I've questioned about this come up with similar responses: "It just doesn't make any sense. How can you enjoy sex without orgasm? That's like saying you enjoyed a joke without hearing the punch line."

All of this is foolishness. There can be good sex that doesn't include orgasm for either partner, that results in orgasm for only one partner, in which the woman has only one orgasm, and that has less than house-shaking and bed-breaking orgasms.

MYTH 10: MEN DON'T HAVE TO LISTEN TO WOMEN IN SEX

Despite the increasing emphasis on giving women a good time in bed, there is also a contradictory myth that men can do whatever they want regardless of what the woman says.

One form of this myth is that females don't necessarily mean it when they say no to sex and that it pays to push on regardless of their protests.

In popular novels and movies, it's common for a man to be rewarded for not taking a woman's rebuff seriously. He forces himself on her, and somewhere along the way, she gets into it and they both have a wonderful time.

A quote from a piece of pornography from Victorian England sums up the idea:

> He pressed me in his arms. "Robert, let me go—where are you drawing me—you will make me fall. Oh! what do you mean—don't push your knees there—don't attempt to raise my dress. Robert, what are you about—I won't let you—take it away—you must not do it—Oh! Oh!—you are hurting me—Oh, my! what are you pushing in—yes, I do feel it—hold me in your arms—yes, I like that—you may fuck me, Robert, as hard as you like."

Literary luminaries such as Norman Mailer and D. H. Lawrence convey the same message. The hero in Mailer's *American Dream* overpowers his maid and is rewarded by her telling him, "You are absolutely a genius, Mr. Rojack," and "I love you a little bit." The words Lawrence puts in Lady Chatterley's mind are even worse because they confirm specifically what many men want to believe: that women secretly want what they say they don't, that a man should press on despite protests, and that there's nothing to feel bad about:

> She had needed this phallic hunting out, she had secretly wanted it, and she had believed that she would never get it. . . . What liars poets and everybody were! They made one think one wanted sentiment. When what one supremely wanted was this piercing, consuming, rather awful sensuality. To find a man who dared do it, without shame or sin or final misgiving. If he had been ashamed afterwards . . . how awful!

While some men are concerned only with their own desires and don't care if the woman says no, most men are genuinely confused. They want sex, she says no, and they aren't sure what to do. This can be on an early date, when the couple has never had sex before, or it can happen after they've been together a long time. Some of the confused men will, of course, back off. But others will be guided by the message of the fantasy model and assume that things will turn out well if they persist. Once started on this path, it may be difficult to turn back even after it becomes clear that the woman really doesn't want to go on. Rapes on dates and in marriages are far more common than many of us think.

Another form of this myth is that it doesn't make any difference even if she really means no. Under certain circumstances, a man has the right to force himself on a woman. This notion seems to stem from a very old idea that women are only things or property and a man can do with them whatever he wants. One study found that teenage males (and a significant minority of teen females) believe that a man has the right to force sex on a woman if she starts to have sex but changes her mind, if she has "led" the boy on, or if she has gotten him sexually excited. Over a third of the boys agreed it's okay to force sex if he has dated a girl for a "long time."

Given the double messages conveyed by the media and by some women, it's understandable that men might be confused. Despite this, we need to take women seriously. If a woman says no to sex, it's fine to ask what's going on. Maybe there are some problems or issues that can be worked out, another example of why talking is important. But the reality also is that it's not OK and not legal for a man to force himself on a woman sexually. Not even if you try to rationalize it with that old bit of nonsense that women really want to be raped. I've never met a woman who wanted to be raped, and I don't know anyone else who has either. Having sex with a woman against her will is rape, a particularly heinous crime, and it doesn't make any difference if you're living with her or married to her, if you're up to your eyeballs in alcohol or some other drug, if she has gotten you excited, or even if you believe she's led you on.

Yet another form of this myth concerns sexual preferences. Because of the great male emphasis on penises, which is reinforced in all erotic literature, most men think that's all that's necessary to satisfy a woman. So when a woman says she wants some other kind of stimulation, many men don't hear so well. The fact is that the majority of women are not sexually satisfied solely by means of the thrusting penis. They need direct clitoral stimulation, something a penis is not well suited for.

The not listening applies to more than just what kind of stimulation is appropriate. I have witnessed countless arguments over the intensity of stimulation (with the woman usually wanting a softer touch than the man) and the timing of genital stimulation and the beginning of inter-course (with the woman usually wanting to delay genital stimulation until she's more aroused and intercourse until she feels truly ready for it).

We men need, I believe, to take women more seriously. We need to listen to and understand them, to hear their suggestions and complaints. Not to do so makes everything more difficult—our own lives, our relationships, and, yes, even sex.

MYTH 11: GOOD SEX IS SPONTANEOUS, WITH NO PLANNING AND NO TALKING

Fantasyland sex is spontaneous. People get turned on to each other and one thing leads to another, as we like to say. Of course, one or both partners may have been thinking about sex beforehand, hoping for it, anticipating it. And the partners may hint, flirt, tease, and seduce. But apparently it's not okay to talk openly and plan together for sex.

A quote from the best-selling author Jackie Collins illustrates part of this myth. A man and woman who don't know each other and who have barely exchanged a dozen words start having sex: "There was nothing awkward about their lovemaking. He entered her smoothly and she moved with him as if they had been together many times before. Instinctively she knew his rhythm and he knew hers." Isn't that nice? Nothing was awkward and each "instinctively" knew the other's rhythm and presumably desires as well. Just like in real life, right? Later, as the man recalls the experience, he thinks this: "No corny lines or bullshit. Just wonderfully uninhibited silent sex." The message is clear: Discuss-ing sex, or even getting to know one another—all this is "corny lines or bullshit." Only silent sex is real and meaningful.

This shows why fantasy sex is so popular. It feeds into the childish fantasies we all carry around, where people instinctively know what the other wants and willingly provide it, where there are no serious prob-lems, where we can have whatever we want and all we want of it.

We have no trouble planning dates, dinners, vacations, and social events. Few people show up at airports, laden with suitcases, asking, "Do you have planes going to any interesting places today?" Rather, they plan their vacations, and no one seems to suffer because of this. And few people have any problems discussing what to do about dinner tonight.

Do you want to eat in or go out? Early or late? Chinese, Mexican, Italian, or what?

But because we still view sex, even in marriage, as not quite all right, we'd rather sneak our way into it—and call it spontaneity. Planning sex usually involves talking about it, something that makes most of us very uncomfortable. So the less we plan and the less we talk about it, the less real it seems and the less embarrassed we have to get.

We pay heavily for our desire for spontaneity. Because of a lack of planning, we often have less sex than we want. Our spontaneous invitations often get rebuffed because of insufficient time or energy. Because we don't want to plan and talk, we often fail to use necessary protections against disease and conception. Yet another price is that sex often isn't as good as it could be if we were willing to plan for it (by making time, anticipating it, setting the appropriate mood, and so on).

If you want more sex, safer sex, and better sex, you might want to rethink whether spontaneity is really crucial. And while you're thinking, keep in mind that planning does not rule out spontaneity. Couples who have good sex talk about it and plan for it, and also take advantage of spontaneous opportunities.

MYTH 12: REAL MEN DON'T HAVE SEX PROBLEMS

In fantasyland there are no sexual problems or difficulties. It's all perfect and wonderful, just like in a fairy tale, which is exactly what it is.

It's as if sex problems don't exist. Despite the fact that millions of American men and women have sexually transmitted diseases—herpes, chlamydia, and genital warts, to name only the most common—no one in popular fiction has them, so there's no discussion of how to tell a partner about them and how to manage a sex life to avoid infecting others.

The avoidance of discussing sex problems, especially men's sex problems, is unfortunate because it plays into the larger fiction discussed in Chapter 1: that men don't have personal problems of any kind. Because having personal problems means a man doesn't have it all together, men are much less willing than women to acknowledge such difficulties and much less willing to get help for them. The whole thing gets magnified dramatically when it comes to sex. It's bad enough for a man to have a

problem of any kind, but for "his manhood" not to be in perfect order—
that's an incredible blow. The usual case when a couple comes in for sex
therapy is that even if the problem is primarily the man's, he's there only
because the woman dragged him in. He doesn't want to acknowledge
the problem, just wants the whole matter to go away. Needless to say,
this just makes the therapy more difficult and the chances of a successful
outcome less likely.

The reality is that men have as many personal problems as women,
including problems with sex. But because it's so fraught with meaning if
a man has a difficulty, he's in an incredible bind. Not being able to
acknowledge it means he can't try to resolve it on his own or with his
partner. She knows there's a problem but can't get him to talk about it,
which puts her in a bind as well. This kind of situation drives women
crazy. If she doesn't do anything, the problem remains. If she keeps
bringing it up, she risks feeling like a nag. It doesn't take long before the
partners are distant and the relationship deteriorates; in some cases, it is
destroyed. This is sad, because in the vast majority of these cases the
problem could have been easily dealt with, if only it could have been
confronted.

These and similar myths have made men and women anxious, created
problems and dissatisfactions, and made resolution of existing problems
more difficult. But we are not stuck with these destructive notions. We
can reject them and put in their place more realistic and more constructive ideas. In the process, we can make our sex lives a true reflection of
our values, feelings, thoughts, and the best interests of ourselves and our
relationships, rather than trying to measure up to ridiculous standards
set by others. In the rest of the book, you'll have numerous opportunities to examine and modify beliefs that may be creating problems in your
sex life.

SEXUAL
REALITY

_____3

What Is This Thing Called Sex?

"Sex! Everything connected with it. People spend more time thinking, worrying, agonizing over it than all the rest of the woes of man put together. Nothing so drives people—men, women— off the rails. I sometimes think God had begun to doze, was excessively fatigued, hadn't worked it out properly, when he put that part in place."—WILLIAM BRINKLEY

"I used to think I was a hot stud in college and knew everything about sex. Turned out that I knew very little: just get her hot, stick it in, hump away, and come. Took me a while to find out sex is a lot more than that."—MAN, 31

THE main problem with the fantasy model of sex is that it holds up standards that are for the most part unattainable by human beings and probably not desirable even if they could be reached. But because people take the model as a standard against which to measure their own behavior and feelings, as defining normal, they not only end up feeling inadequate but they also miss the obvious. They don't ask if they're getting what they want and if their erotic activity in fact enhances their pleasure, self-esteem, and relationship.

In many ways, the sex people actually have doesn't differ that much

65

from the sex any animals have. And that's depressing, to think that what you're doing isn't much different from what a mouse or chicken or monkey does. And in some ways, lower animals have it better. They may not have long-lasting intercourse, but at least they aren't sneaky about their matings and apparently they don't feel guilty about what they do, and I doubt they worry about their performance. In a reproductive sense, it doesn't make much difference, of course—just whatever gets the job done. But humans are capable of so much more.

The model of sex I discuss in this chapter and that will take me most of the rest of the book to illustrate is more distinctly human and more intimate than what we've had before. It's a sexuality in which *people* interact and relate, not just genitals; in which deceit and coercion play no part; in which what's between your ears is as important as what's between your legs; in which you can plan for sex and talk about it before, during, or after the actual events; in which you can change directions or stop at any point. The goals of this intimate model of sex are pleasure, closeness, and self- and partner-enhancement, not performance or conquest.

This is a freer and better-feeling kind of sex. It's freer because you have more options; you and your partner can select from whole menus of possibilities how to express your sexual feelings and are no longer limited to just the old foreplay-followed-by-intercourse routine. You can even decide not to plan or talk or be intimate; in other words, part of this new sex is the option to have sex in the old way. It's more enjoyable because it's understood that pleasure rather than performance or obligation is the goal; you don't *have* to do anything, and there's permission to be yourself and get what you want and need. You can be loving, playful, silly, lusty, or whatever else you want. You can have affection without sex, sex with or without affection, or none of the above. You're freer to enjoy yourself because of all the choices and because most of the worry is taken away: The emphasis on talking and planning allows you and your partner to protect yourself against unwanted consequences.

The freedoms gained in the sexual revolution allow us to create a smarter, more enjoyable, more exciting and satisfying, and more humane sexuality. Unless we want to continue paying the prices that sex has exacted from the beginning of time (bad feelings, unnecessary anxiety, dysfunctions and dissatisfactions, unwanted conception, debilitating and even fatal diseases), maybe it's time to try something different.

GOOD SEX

Although good sex is often defined in terms of specific behaviors and specific body parts, feelings are paramount. And this is as true for men as for women. Even though men tend to think and talk in terms of activities—"I'd like to fuck [or, make love to] her"; "I'd like her to give me head"—it seems clear that what's really wanted is the feelings these actions will produce. They will make him feel sexy, excited, satisfied, manly, powerful, and so on.

Good sex is not about using any particular organ, following any particular script, or doing any particular act. Rather, it has to do with the emotions generated by whatever you and your partner do. The best definition I've heard derives from an idea of San Francisco sex therapist Carol Ellison and goes like this: YOU'RE HAVING GOOD SEX IF YOU FEEL GOOD ABOUT YOURSELF, GOOD ABOUT YOUR PARTNER, AND GOOD ABOUT WHAT YOU'RE DOING. IF LATER, AFTER YOU'VE HAD TIME FOR REFLECTION, YOU STILL FEEL GOOD ABOUT YOURSELF, YOUR PARTNER, AND WHAT YOU DID, YOU KNOW YOU'VE HAD GOOD SEX. As such, it need not include intercourse or any other specific act or sequence of acts, it need not include orgasm, and the event can take anywhere from a few seconds to several hours.

Certain things, however, are excluded. Any kind of coercion, for example. If coercion is used, whether physical or psychological, at least one partner is not going to feel good during and after the activity. The same is true for deception. I would make a similar point for impulsive sex that goes against one's interests and values. If you don't want conception to occur, yet take no measures to protect against it, you're going to worry and feel bad afterward. I wouldn't call that good sex.

Let's take an example from another area, driving. If you believe the ads on TV, a good drive consists of quickly shifting through the gears and getting your car to do 150 miles an hour. Given the condition of today's roads and traffic, it's a mystery where you could do this—on most roads these days you're happy if you can get up to 20 mph—but it's clear that lots of people buy the fantasy, always looking for a place to "open it up."

Even assuming you could safely drive at 150 mph, it would still only represent one kind of good drive. Suppose you took a leisurely drive through the country, looking at the sights and smelling the scents. Couldn't that be a good drive? Or suppose you took a drive with a friend and had a stimulating conversation. Wouldn't that constitute a good drive? And wouldn't it also be a good drive if during it you worked out a problem in your head, had an interesting fantasy, or enjoyed listening to the radio? And what about the unlikely circumstance where there was little traffic and good weather and you simply got to your destination without hassle. Might that not be a good drive as well? Isn't it also possible to have a good drive or trip by letting someone else do the driving, by car-pooling, or taking a bus? You could also consider using a bicycle rather than a motorized vehicle. Couldn't that be a good drive— as well as good exercise?

Just as there are lots of ways to have a good drive and lots of kinds of good meals and good experiences, there are lots of ways to have good sex.

Before getting to sexual options, let's take a closer look at what they're alternatives to, the traditional sexual script.

THE PRIMACY OF INTERCOURSE

As I mentioned when discussing sexual myths, almost everyone seems to believe that intercourse is what sex is mainly about. Even people who consider themselves liberated and are comfortable with many different sexual acts feel cheated if intercourse isn't part of the routine. This goes for women as well as men. Since most sex problems in both men and women tend to occur more often, or only, during intercourse, a common technique in sex therapy is to ask couples to engage in sex but refrain from intercourse for several weeks. Needless to say, sex therapists expected and got serious resistance to this idea from many men. What we didn't anticipate, but got anyway, was just as serious resistance from many women, including women who had never had orgasm during intercourse and didn't expect to.

Although there's no doubt that social conditioning plays a role in reinforcing the belief that intercourse is *the* sexual act, common sense requires us to acknowledge that the desire for sexual intercourse is also, perhaps mainly, caused by something else. Intercourse is the only way to reproduce the species, and reproducing the species is nature's main interest. All of us, women and men, are programmed to want intercourse. That much is fact, and it is folly to ignore or deny it.

Culture follows nature, at least in the most important areas. While political and religious authorities often are uncomfortable with anything sexual, no reproduction means the whole enterprise will soon go out of business. So while many authorities through history have been unable to stomach the idea of masturbation, homosexuality, or oral or anal sex, they always make provision for heterosexual intercourse under certain circumstances.

Most people, of course, do not think they want intercourse because they are following nature's programming or in order to produce more of the faithful or more soldiers or customers. Their desires are always experienced in more personal terms.

> A woman says this about intercourse: "It's not as exciting as oral sex or a vibrator, it's certainly not orgasmic, but I feel incomplete without it. It's just something I have to have." A man puts it differently: "I love when she goes down on me. My orgasms in her mouth are unbelievable. I even love a quick hand job. But there's something special about intercourse. A sense of having her, possessing her, that I only get when my penis is in her vagina and I come inside of her."

Because of feelings like these, and also because of the sexual conditioning we're given, the standard sexual script is simple: foreplay (which may include oral or manual stimulation of genitals, and the main purpose of which is usually thought to be getting the woman ready for what is to follow) and then intercourse.

And it seems so natural, which of course it is, and makes so much sense. After all, he has a pole, she has a hole, so it seems only natural that the pole should go in the hole. This can also be seen in seemingly more sophisticated ways, having to do with the merging of the yin and the yang, the merging of bodies and maybe souls. There's also the silly thing that humans do with possibilities: They always make them into imperatives. Since a man can get hard, he ought to get hard. Since we can stick poles in holes, we ought to; otherwise there's something wrong.

Although from an evolutionary standpoint, there is good reason for us to desire intercourse, there is a lot wrong with intercourse as an imperative, having to have it and seeing everything else as second best. The problems with intercourse as the main course can be grouped into six categories:

1. Since intercourse demands some kind of erection (not as hard as most men think, but still some hardness), it puts tremendous pressure on a man to get erect. The pressure would be less if the man could just will himself erect, as many men wish they could. But the penis is not subject to this kind of control.

Bad feelings result if the man doesn't get and stay erect. He feels inadequate and less of a man, a very heavy burden indeed. And the woman often feels that his "failure" is a comment about her: She's not sexy or skillful enough to get him hard. What is the point of all this self-inflicted misery?

2. Women are also put in a difficult situation. Thanks to Sigmund Freud and thousands of writers of pornography, it was assumed that both men and women would climax in intercourse. But the majority of women require direct clitoral stimulation and do not climax solely by means of intercourse. Thanks to the women's movement of the 1960s and '70s and the advent of sex therapy in the 1970s, this fact got lots of exposure and women were given permission and encouragement to get the kinds of stimulation they needed. Many men and women, however, continue to believe that women should somehow climax during intercourse and feel bad when that doesn't happen.

3. Intercourse as generally done takes more time and effort than some other sex acts, and also, as already noted, puts more pressure on both partners. This means that there is less sex than might be the case if other sexual activities were given equal significance.

4. It's also a fact that many sex problems occur mainly or only during intercourse. Many men who ejaculate very quickly in intercourse, for instance, can enjoy manual or oral stimulation for much longer.

5. The emphasis on erections and intercourse fails to take into account our aging population, people with various kinds of illnesses and disabilities, and couples in which the woman is in the last stages of pregnancy or has recently given birth. Many people in these groups have difficulties with erections or intercourse and don't fit the traditional sexual script very well. What are they supposed to do about sex?

6. Intercourse is also the most dangerous sexual act. One huge risk is pregnancy itself. I realize, of course, that Mother Nature would

have a tough time with that one. She did not foresee a time when reproducing the species would be the least of our problems; we already have more people than we know what to do with. Conception is the goal only a tiny proportion of times men and women get together sexually. Disease is another problem. Although it's true that most sexually transmitted diseases can be transmitted orally, the main risk is intercourse. Why are we so intent on emphasizing a sexual act that can be so risky?

Given the stage we've reached in our historical development, given that pleasure and relationship enhancement are what we want from sex rather than reproduction, to some extent it's fair to say that we have to go against Nature's design. But not by much. After all, while giving primacy to intercourse, she also built us to feel great pleasure with masturbation, with oral sex, and with lots of other kinds of stimulation. In addition to genitals, she gave us hands and mouths and tongues and lots of sensitive skin all over. Consider for a moment the fact that no matter how large your penis is, even if it's twelve inches long and four inches around, that represents only a fraction of your total body area. Why should great feelings and great pleasure be limited to this tiny portion of your anatomy? And Nature gave women a clitoris, an organ that has nothing to do with reproduction and whose only function is sexual pleasure. Interestingly, she put the clitoris in a place that makes it difficult for a penis, thrusting or not, to stimulate it. Maybe she thought that other kinds of sex than intercourse should be part of the plan.

I believe that the fairest interpretation of Nature's plan these days is that it allows humans the freedom to choose how to enjoy sex. We can choose to enjoy it alone or with a partner; and with a partner we can choose from a whole menu of options.

The more you accept the idea that there are many ways to give and receive sexual pleasure, that erections, intercourse, and even orgasm are nice but not necessary, the more frequent and better sex you will have. Since you'll be putting fewer demands on your penis, it will be free to do its best, and you'll be able to enjoy a wide variety of sexual activities, including intercourse.

*   *   *

"Other things can be fun, but it doesn't feel like making love unless we have intercourse." That's to be expected, because traditionally making love has been a synonym for intercourse and not for other kinds of sexual activity. I suggest, however, that *making love has to do with feelings rather than with specific acts.* People can feel very loved and loving with all sorts of acts, many of them not even sexual. If you can allow this idea to be your guide—that it's the feelings rather than the acts that define making love—I think you'll agree. If your partner lovingly caresses you all over your body or lovingly stimulates your penis with her hand or mouth, why can't that be as much a lovemaking as intercourse?

SEXUAL OPTIONS

I'm not suggesting you never have intercourse with an erection. Whenever you and your partner are agreed that's what you both want, that's what you should have. But you'll have more sex, and probably more fun and satisfaction as well, if you're willing to consider other options like the following:

- Flirting with your partner although you both know nothing physical can take place now.
- Flirting with another woman although you both know nothing physical will ever take place between you.

"Flirting is OK, but it's not the same as physical sex." Of course it isn't. But that doesn't mean it can't feel sexual and be the source of great pleasure. Why not just enjoy the feelings?

"Flirting is OK as far as it goes, but it doesn't go far enough. I'm afraid I'd get all worked up and get frustrated." I guarantee that no one has ever been taken to a hospital emergency room because of sexual frustration. Don't worry. You won't explode. Why not allow yourself to enjoy the good feelings and then let them subside? Or, if you know you and your partner will be together later, why not let the flirting start your juices flowing and build the turn-on?

- Bathing your partner, or she you, or both of you bathing each other.

Take your time and remember that getting clean is not the main purpose.

- Receiving a sensuous massage from your partner that does not include genital stimulation.
- Receiving a sensuous massage that does include genital stimulation.
- Giving a sensuous massage to your partner that does not include genital stimulation.
- Giving a sensuous massage that does include genital stimulation.
- One of you treating the other to a session of toe sucking, which can be followed by genital stimulation or not. If you've never done this, it may sound very strange, but I know people who swear it's delightful.
- A variation of the preceding point is finger-licking and sucking. This too may sound weird to those who haven't done it, but giving it a try won't cost you much.
- Kissing and hugging followed by rubbing your bodies and pelvises together while clothed (called "dry-humping" when I was growing up). You can be creative regarding where you do this: in alleys, stairwells, elevators, up against walls, in parked cars, and so forth.
- Dirty dancing, which is dry-humping on a dance floor.
- What used to be called petting—kissing and hugging and fondling breasts and genitals while clothed or partially clothed. Petting and dry-humping remind many adults of sexual activity in their adolescence, when that's all they could do. But many adults have told me how deliciously wicked and sensual they feel when doing these things now. And I've observed more than a few couples in airplanes and in parking lots having great pleasure with them.
- Kissing and hugging followed by your partner stimulating you orally.
- Kissing and hugging followed by you stimulating your partner orally.
- Kissing and hugging followed by your partner stimulating you by hand.
- Kissing and hugging followed by you caressing your partner by hand.
- Your partner caressing you by hand or mouth without any kissing or hugging.
- You doing your partner by hand or mouth without any kissing or hugging.

"My partner and I often do oral and manual stimulation as part of foreplay. But it would seem strange for one or both of them to be the main course." The strangeness comes from your idea of what "real" sex is. But that idea can change. Why can't manual or oral stimulation, as well as some other items mentioned later, be the main course sometimes? You might find you enjoy a more varied menu.

"It seems unequal if I'm getting all the pleasure or if she's getting all the pleasure." Who said that you have to be equally excited or derive equal pleasure? It is often the case, even in intercourse, that one partner is more excited and gets more out of it than the other. What's wrong with you getting most of the goodies sometimes? What's wrong with her getting most of the goodies at other times?

"Your-turn, my-turn kind of sex seems so artificial and unnatural." The traditional model of sex is a reciprocal one. While she's kissing your neck, you're kissing her neck or fondling her breasts. While you're touching her clitoris, she's touching your penis. And then you both participate in intercourse. But who says it has to be this way? Suppose she does all the "work" while you just sit or lie back and enjoy? Can't that also be a loving or passionate or caring experience?

The main problem with the reciprocal model is that your attention is always split. One moment you're focusing on the stimulation you're getting, the next moment on the stimulation you're giving. This has its benefits, of course, but because of the split attention, you're never able to focus in on your own pleasure for long.

The main advantage of the taking-turns kind of sex is that the receiver can just receive, focusing only on pleasure, without also being concerned about giving anything in return. This allows a deep focusing-in, a total concentration on sensations and feelings, that often results in a powerful experience.

"But it seems so mechanical or clinical when the only action is her doing me." There are at least two possible reasons for the sense that what's going on is mechanical or clinical. One is that anything different than the traditional model of reciprocity feels funny simply because it's not familiar. So it's possible the bad feelings are coming from you. They will diminish or vanish as you accept the idea that there's nothing peculiar about what you're doing and there is nothing sacred about reciprocity or intercourse.

Another possibility is that your partner is acting in a mechanical or clinical way. Maybe she doesn't like what she's doing, feels anxious about it, or maybe she's just spacing out when stimulating you, and you're picking up on this. You might want to talk to her about your perception and ask what's going on with her.

The important thing to remember is that there's nothing inherently mechanical or clinical about my-turn, your-turn sex.

- You masturbating while your partner holds and touches you.

"Masturbation is something I do myself. I don't see it as something to do with a partner." Of course. That's part of our traditional model. In partner sex, you touch your partner and she touches you, but no one touches himself or herself. But why not? Why can't touching yourself be part of what you do with a partner? Masturbating with some kind of partner participation is just another way of having good sex.

Many men say their most intense orgasms come through masturbation. The reason is simple: No one knows or can know your body as well as you do. I realize that intense orgasms are not the only reason to have sex. There are many other rewards as well. But what's wrong with masturbating with partner involvement and giving yourself an incredible climax?

"The idea sounds fine, but I'm shy about touching myself with her watching." Many men (and women as well) feel this way at first. Fortunately, all it takes is the courage to do it once or twice. The shyness and embarrassment usually evaporate quickly. By the way, most women like watching their partners masturbate; it's a turn-on. As one woman put it: "I enjoy it because I love to see a man doing something loving for himself."

- You masturbating while your partner tells you an exciting fantasy, perhaps over the phone.
- Your partner masturbating with her hand or a vibrator while you hold and touch her.

- Your partner masturbating while you tell her an interesting fantasy, perhaps over the phone.
- One of you orally or manually stimulating the other one who is talking on the phone with someone else. The third party, the one on the other end of the telephone line, does not know what is going on. Several people have told me it can add to the excitement if the third party is someone in authority: a parent, teacher, coach, or employer.
- Each of you masturbating while you lie side by side or facing one another (so you can see each other's faces).
- During any sexual activity, change what you do with your eyes. If you usually keep them closed, open them. If you usually have them open, close them. Experience the difference. A man in his fifties who had never kept his eyes open during sex until I suggested it to him gave this report: "It opened up a whole new world. It was a fantastic turn-on to watch our bodies together and to see the changes in her body movements and facial expression as she got more aroused."
- Your partner uses a finger or two to massage your perineum (the area between the scrotum and the anus) or anus, or inserts a well-lubricated finger into your anus during any other sexual activity. Although as children we were all warned away from the anal area, it is richly endowed with nerve endings and a source of great erotic pleasure to many men (and women).
- Intercourse with no foreplay. This is usually called a quickie and most often is done for the man's pleasure. But many women like it for themselves. A woman reader of an earlier draft of this chapter added these words to this option: "It's quick fun before a class or dinner. I recall sitting in class with heat coming off my body, my crotch still wet and tingly, and me with a huge grin and a secret. It was wonderful!"

"I occasionally did this when I was dating and enjoyed it. But when I brought it up with my wife, she said she wasn't interested because it was too one-sided, with the woman getting nothing out of it." It sounds like your wife feels she's been shortchanged sexually or fears she might be. Further discussion might help, especially if you listen carefully to her concerns. Like any sex act, or any kind of act, quickies can be unfair to one or the other party. But it doesn't have to be and shouldn't be. Respect for the partner and the willingness to reciprocate, though not necessarily the same day, are critical. Perhaps there are some things she'd especially like for you to do in sex. Your willingness to do them might help change her mind about quickies.

- Intercourse without much of an erection.
- Your partner stimulating your soft penis with her hand or mouth.
- Intercourse of a different kind. Instead of having the penis in the vagina, it's between your partner's breasts, which she squeezes together and holds in place to provide friction for your penis. If the fit allows it, the tip of your penis could go in and out of her mouth. Another possibility is to move your penis between her closed thighs.

I hope it goes without saying by now that all of the above acts can be enjoyed with or without orgasm. Too many people don't enjoy sex because they're so focused on the Big O that's supposed to happen and then get upset when it doesn't. Orgasms are nice and I'm all for them, but you can have lots of pleasure without them.

Remember, as long as you feel good about yourself, good about your partner, and good about what you're doing or have done, that's good sex.

EXPRESSING DIFFERENT FEELINGS IN SEX

So far we've been talking about options involving different activities. But there is also another kind of option having to do with the main feeling that's expressed in sex. Sexual activity with a partner can be a fine way to express a number of feelings. These days, it seems that the main goal of both women and men in this regard is to connect deeply to another person we care about. And there are times when a couple really makes love. What they do is a reflection of the deep feelings they have for each other, and the result is an openness and bonding that lasts for hours or days, regardless of what they actually did sexually. Individual boundaries may diminish or disappear, and it really feels like a unity or oneness, or "we-ness," as if two people have merged and become one. You can't plan for this kind of sex and you can't make it happen. But if you really care about one another and are open to yourselves and each other, sometimes it just happens. And when it does, it makes everything right, like the sun suddenly appearing on a dark and rainy day.

But good sex can be far more than an expression of loving feelings. In the old days, women complained that men were rough and quick; apparently the main feelings the men expressed were their own lust and desire for gratification. But men have changed, as have women, and now a frequent complaint is that men are too timid, too careful, too unassertive and unpassionate. My experiences working with men tend to support this idea. Many men are really hanging back in sex.

There's nothing wrong with expressing love and caring through sex; it's a great vehicle for showing these feelings. But there's also nothing wrong with expressing lust in sex, or fun, or other feelings. If sex is a vehicle for only one kind of feeling, you'll be limited in the amount of sex you have—you can only be sexual when, say, you feel loving or only when you feel lustful. Also, expressing only one kind of feeling in sex can lead to boredom.

Many couples differentiate between at least two kinds of sex: making love (gentle, concerned with expressing romance, caring, and love) and fucking (more passionate and expressing only desire).

Too much sensitivity can inhibit passion.

Writer Myron Brenton relates the story of Allan, a law student in love with his partner Marie. He was always soft and gentle, holding himself back in sex for fear of hurting her. While on vacation, he met a seductive, teasing woman who finally managed to get him in bed with her. Not caring much about her, and feeling angry toward her, he thrusted hard and vigorously when they had intercourse. He expected to be criticized for this and was surprised when she said it was terrific. When Allan returned to school, he decided to try this kind of sex with Marie, even though he feared she might not like it. Her reaction was to ask why they hadn't always made love like this.

Passion and love are far from all the emotions that can be expressed. Good sex can also be playful, fun, and even silly. For the most part we're talking about differences in perspective and feeling rather than different activities. You may do the same things while making love, being playful, or fucking. But you do them with a different attitude and spirit.

A long-married woman told me that one of the aspects of sex with her husband that she most appreciates is the silliness. "After all," she said, "the whole thing—the positions and all—is pretty ridiculous to begin with. It sometimes reminds me of being a child and engaging in explorations of my own and friend's bodies. I feel so secure with my husband that I can let that little girl's silly side come out. It's great fun."

Some couples sometimes revert to baby talk during sex; some enjoy teasing and being teased.

One of the most memorable experiences I had wouldn't even fit most people's definition of sex. My girlfriend and I were in bed one afternoon. Just as she was guiding my penis into her, she came out with phrases she had gotten from a book of pornography she had looked at earlier that day: "Stick that huge, hard cock into my hot and juicy pussy. I want to feel all twelve inches of you, filling me up, fucking and thrusting as hard as you want, spilling gobs of seed into me." We both broke up into gales of laughter, and I fell off of her. We laughed and laughed for what seemed like hours. Every time we tried to talk, we started laughing again. There was no intercourse, no other sexual activity, and no orgasm for either of us. But it was an incredibly wonderful experience that I recall vividly and lovingly over twenty years later.

Sex can also be a great tension-reliever. We have all sorts of nostrums for reducing stress—everything from physical exercise to meditation to various drugs—but sex is one of Nature's best ways to feel relaxed.

I know a man who usually gets tense before he has to give a public talk. He's tried beta-blockers and other pills, relaxation tapes, and other remedies, but the one that works the best, with no side-effects, is an orgasm produced by his partner's hand or mouth. How does she feel about it? I asked her: "Absolutely fine. I'm happy to be able to do this for him. And he reciprocates when I need it, usually when I have trouble falling asleep."

Of course this won't work if your anxiety is about sex itself. But for stress related to work and other matters, it's often quite useful.

Although some people have trouble with this one, I also believe it's fine to express anger through sex—provided, of course, that this doesn't happen all the time, that it's okay with both partners, and that the anger doesn't turn to violence. Physiologically, anger and sexual arousal are quite similar. Both excite the nervous system. While it's true that some people can't even think about sex when they're angry, let alone do something about it, others find that anger—regardless of its source— can serve to heighten the sexual experience. Recall that anger at his new partner was partly what caused Allan, the law student mentioned on page 78, to let go and find a new way of being sexual. This isn't unusual. Some couples report their best sex occurs in the midst of an argument.

Anger is a strong emotion and should be treated with caution. Nonetheless, anger is a fact of life and it can be used to enhance one's sex life.

The most important thing about expressing different feelings is that the partners have to agree on what they're doing. It can lead to confusion, frustration, and other negative feelings if one partner is fucking while the other is trying to make love, or if one wants a stress-reliever or sleeping potion while the other has something else in mind. Clear communication is a must.

I hope you'll go over the ideas in this chapter and share them, or at least the ideas that appeal to you, with your partner. While I certainly haven't covered all the possibilities, I hope I've made you aware that sex isn't any one thing and isn't confined to any one script or routine. With skin all over our bodies, with hands, mouths, breasts, penises (hard or soft), clitorises, vaginas (wet or dry), anuses, and with incredibly powerful and creative minds to work with and lots of different emotions that we can experience, we have lots and lots of possibilities.

Of course, there's no rule that you have to like all the options. Some may not appeal to you and some may not appeal to your partner. But I hope that at least a few of them will sound attractive enough to both of you to warrant a bit of experimentation.

When I was in high school, there was a saying that some guys would take sex any way they could get it. That remark wasn't exactly a compliment, referring as it did to guys who were totally nondiscriminating regarding whom they had sex with and how they went about it (often with a good deal of pressure and deceit and a total lack of responsibility). But it can be seen in a different, more positive way. As long as the goal of sex is pleasure for both you and your partner and there is no deceit or coercion, taking it any way you can get it is a pretty good way to go. You'll have more sex and better sex if you're open to a number of possibilities.

4

What Is This Thing Called a Penis?

"You would think I'd know better. I mean, I'm well educated and have read a lot about sex. But I still believe that I'd be more attractive to women and a better lover if my penis was an inch or two longer and an inch wider."—MAN, 28

"My big wish is that my cock were exactly like my hand. If I told it to stand up, it would stand up. If I told it to lie down, it would lie down. Why can't I have the same control over my penis that I have over all my other appendages?"—MAN, 50

IN this chapter I discuss the issues about penises that have been of most interest to the men I've worked with. I've been surprised to discover over the years how ignorant many men are about this organ that means so much to them. Some basic knowledge can be helpful. I won't bore you with irrelevant details, but I will discuss what penises are, what can reasonably be expected from them, and what happens to them as they age.

Let's start with how we think and feel about our penises.

TOWARD A FRIENDLIER AND MORE REALISTIC VIEW OF OUR PENISES

To say the least, we men have mixed feelings. Our penises are very important to us. They are the main distinguishing characteristic between us and women, and they are a source of great pleasure. But there's often a sense of unease or discontent with our organs. We fear that they may not be up to snuff in terms of size, power, and predictability. Control and predictability are crucial to us, yet in sex we are dependent on an organ that often seems to have a mind of its own, totally beyond our attempts to direct it. This does not feel right or good. We fear that, sooner or later, it is going to disappoint and embarrass us.

Some men are on friendly terms with their penises. They like them for the pleasure they provide and see them as a kind of friend, sometimes even giving them pet names. Other men, however, are in a state of near war with their cocks. They speak cajolingly, angrily, or threateningly to them: "Come on, please, you can do it, yes you can"; "You better come through for me, you son of a bitch"; or "I'll break your neck if you don't get hard." This kind of self-talk is often caused by the penis's failure to do what its owner wants, or fear of such a failure. Whatever the reason, it is not conducive to friendly relations.

Being on better terms with our penises is made difficult by the common terms we have for them—cock, prick, rod, tool, ramrod, hard-on, dick. These words sound harsh and do not contribute to a sense of warmth, gentleness, or friendliness. They fit right in, of course, with the view of penises in fantasyland, always throbbing, thrashing, banging, ramming, thrusting. You'd think a penis was a weapon of war rather than an instrument of pleasure and love.

This depiction is neither realistic nor useful. We need something more accurate and helpful. Consider that the penis is very soft. Even when fully erect, the skin is velvety soft and smooth. Consider also that the penis spends the vast majority of its time in a flaccid state, just lying there all crinkled up and cuddled against the body. Even the fabled adolescent penis spends most of its time just resting.

In addition, we should take into account the age-old idea that penises have minds of their own. A man usually comes to this conclusion when he feels aroused and ready for sex but his penis isn't cooperating. A useful way of looking at this situation is to ask, "Why won't it cooperate?" or better still, "What does it need that it isn't getting?" I used to ask men with erection problems to take the role of their penis and write a letter or essay giving its point of view. The results were quite revealing. Often the penis complained mightily about not getting what it needed (a relaxed owner, a booze-free environment, proper stimulation, and so on) and resented the demands being made on it. An example:

> You never pay attention to me unless you want something, and then you want it exactly when you want it, and get angry and threaten me unless I comply. Half the situations you get into scare the hell out of you and that scares me. I'm not at my best when I'm scared. I want you to know that unless you pay more attention and give me what I need, like more appealing and less frightening situations, you're getting zilch. And that's that!

It may sound strange to hear that penises have needs and can get frightened. But real penises are far more vulnerable and frail than the robotlike machines in the fantasy model. They do have needs. Just as athletes have long known that their muscles and systems work better under certain conditions than others (having to do with rest, nutrition, exercise, temperature, and so on), we now know that penises and sexual systems do the same. In Chapter 6, I'll talk more about what you and your penis need.

It will pay you to start thinking of your penis as the human organ it is. The more you can regard your penis in a gentler and more humane way, the more you take care of it, the better relationship you'll have with it and the more it will behave as you want. And when your penis doesn't do what you want, it pays to listen carefully. It's trying to tell you something.

PENIS ENVY

Sigmund Freud, the founder of psychoanalysis, had a theory that girls and women were dissatisfied with their own genitals and envied men their penises. They wanted them, too. I have yet to meet a woman who wanted to have her own penis (except on camping trips), although many like to borrow one from time to time. As a woman friend once put it: "Why would I want a thing like that hanging between my legs? I'd be afraid I'd sit on it."

I think, however, that Freud was partly right about penis envy. It exists, but only in males. Almost every male seems to envy someone else's penis. He wants one that's longer, wider, harder, with more staying power, and he assumes that some other man, or lots of other men, have one just like that.

One reason we are so unhappy with our penises is the superhuman expectations we have learned. Having repeatedly read and heard about gargantuan, hard-as-steel ramrods, our own real penises don't seem like much. How can anything real seem adequate compared to the telephone poles we read about?

And most heterosexual men have never seen another erect penis, or at least not a typical one. The ones we are likely to have seen, in pornographic movies and magazines, are not representative. The producers of these films conduct broad searches for the biggest phalluses in existence. Given the absence of reasonable standards, there is good reason for us to wonder about the adequacy of our own organs.

HOW LARGE IS ENOUGH?

Like all other physical characteristics, penises do differ in size and shape. As indicated in Figures 1 and 2 on pages 86 and 87, some are longer, some shorter; some are broader or wider, some narrower; some curve or bend to the right, some to the left, some not at all; some point upward when erect, some downward, some just straight out. Although penises differ in size, there is less variation among hard penises than among soft ones because a smaller soft penis will increase more in size during erection than a larger soft penis. Nonetheless, there is still some variation and there's nothing that can be done about that.

Men almost invariably assume that a bigger penis is better and is what women prefer. Women think much less about penis size than do men. The vast majority of women I've talked to could not recall a conversation about sex with women friends where penis size was even mentioned. When I questioned these women about size preference, they gave surprising answers. There are, to be sure, a few who said they like very large

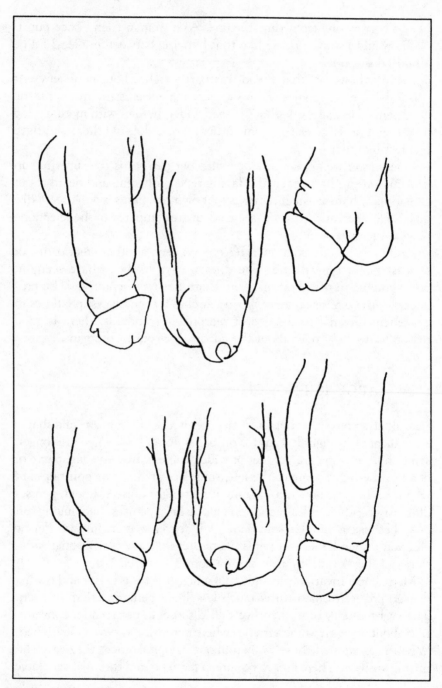

Figure 1: Flaccid penises

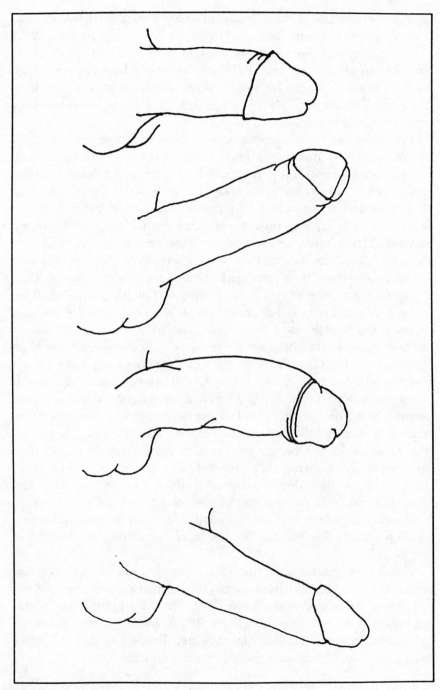

Figure 2: Erect penises

penises, which give them a "filled-up" feeling in intercourse. But the vast majority of women I've talked to do not desire large penises. Here's what a thirty-seven-year-old woman had to say: "The penises in my fantasies are always very large and thick, but in real life a large penis can be hard to take. I'm much more orgasmic with an average-size penis; a large one is distracting. The old adage 'It's not the meat but the motion' most definitely applies."

I've also talked to a number of men with very large penises. You'd think they'd be quite content, because they're the ones who measure up to the fantasies of most men. Surprisingly, many of these men are anything but happy. Most of them say they wish they had smaller organs. They complain about women gasping—not in ecstasy, but in horror—when they first lay eyes on their outsized organs. Some women have refused to have intercourse with them at all, and many have refused to do oral sex on them, fearing they would choke. And some of these men said they often have to be careful when having sex lest they do hurt their partners. Sometimes living up to a fantasy isn't all it's cracked up to be.

Most women I've talked to prefer average-size penises, and that's nice, because that's what most men have. But what about smaller-than-average penises? It's true that some men's erections are shorter than average (which is about five and a half or six inches long) and some are less thick than others. While it may be difficult to believe, such variations really don't make much difference. As already indicated, most women aren't half as interested in penis size as men. But when I've pressed women to talk about smaller-than-average penises, several said the guys they knew who had such penises were terrific lovers. Perhaps to compensate for what they considered an inadequacy (their small penises), these men developed their skills at touching, kissing, and caressing. But this does not mean you have to get a Ph.D. in sex if your penis happens to be on the small side. Most women said that a small penis was fine because "it's the man that counts, not the size of his penis."

If you have trouble accepting your penis, you might want to spend some time considering what it would take to make it acceptable. After all, this is the only penis you'll ever have. There are no penis transplants and there is no way to make what you have larger. I realize there are advertisements in magazines claiming that Product X or Y will make your penis larger. You can waste your money on such things if you want, but your penis will remain as it is. Is there any chance you can just accept it and move on? I guarantee you that the size and shape of your penis is not what makes for a good lover.

THE PARTS AND HOW THEY WORK

Before going further with the penis, let's take a quick look at the internal sex organs; these are the testes, epididymis, vas deferens, seminal vesicles, prostate gland, and urethra. The testes produce sperm and the hormone testosterone. The vas deferens are two firm tubes that extend from the testes to the prostate gland. Sperm travel through the tubes from the epididymis and are stored at their upper ends until they mix with the secretions of the seminal vesicles and prostate just prior to ejaculation. The secretions of the prostate comprise about a third of the seminal fluid or ejaculate, giving it its whitish color. The sperm actually account for only a tiny fraction of the ejaculate, which explains why a man who has had a vasectomy still ejaculates about the same amount of fluid as before the operation.

The urethra is a tube running from the bladder through one of the spongy tissues in the penis and ending in a slit in the head of the penis. Both urine and seminal fluid travel through it, but not at the same time. The prostate surrounds the urethra where it leaves the bladder, and prostate problems such as inflammation or enlargement can cause urinary difficulties.

The external male genitalia consist of the penis and the scrotum, the latter containing the testes. Despite what many people think, the penis contains no striated muscle tissue, the kind that can be enlarged with exercise. There is also no bone in the penis, giving the lie to the term *boner*, which many of us used as teenagers. Most of the penis is filled with two large cylinders of spongy tissue surrounded by a tough fibrous covering. In a healthy male, the spongy tissues become engorged with blood during sexual excitement, causing the penis to expand. As the spongy tissues fill with blood, they push against the fibrous sheath, making the penis hard. This is quite similar to what happens when you fill a tire with air. As air fills the tube (comparable to the spongy tissues in the penis), it pushes against the tire, which limits the expansion. So the tire gets hard, just as your penis does. As the spongy areas in the

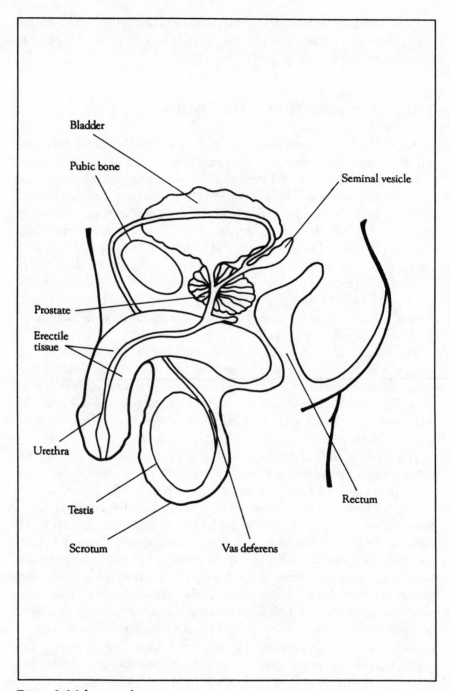

Figure 3: Male genital anatomy

penis expand with blood and press against the sheath, the flow of blood out of the penis, through very small veins, is reduced.

In terms of sensitivity to stimulation, most men find the heads of their penises to be the most sensitive. This is not to say that the rest of the penis is insensitive, merely that for the most pleasure, the head of the penis should be included in whatever stimulation is done. Many men also like their scrotums stimulated—touched, rubbed, held, licked, or squeezed (though not too firmly)—during sex. Another area of sensitivity for many men is the perineum, the area between the scrotum and the rectum.

SEXUAL RESPONSE

In their pioneering work, *Human Sexual Response*, Masters and Johnson described the physiological changes a man goes through during sex in terms of a sexual response cycle arbitrarily divided into four phases: excitement, plateau, orgasm, and resolution. This part of their work has been widely popularized and accepted.

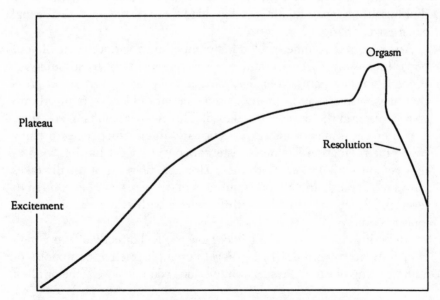

Figure 4: Male sexual response according to Masters & Johnson

Masters and Johnson's sexual response cycle suffers from a number of problems, some of which they noted in their book but which have been neglected by those who summarize their findings. Many men's (and many women's) sexual responses do not fit neatly into the Masters and Johnson scheme, and some people have asked what was wrong with them for not fitting the model.

I think Kinsey was more on target: "There is nothing more characteristic of sexual response than the fact that it is not the same in any two individuals." There is no right or normal way to have a sexual experience. Your response is the result of a complex interaction among many variables, including, for example, your age, your physical and emotional state, how turned on you are, what your partner does, and how you feel about her. Lots of types of response cycles are possible, as shown in Figures 5 and 6.

The main physical changes that occur during a sexual experience are the result of vasocongestion, the accumulation of blood in various parts of the body. Muscular tension increases and other changes occur. With orgasm, the muscular tension is released or discharged and blood flow resumes its normal or nonsexual pattern, but these phenomena happen even without orgasm, though more slowly.

A sexual response begins when you receive some kind of sexual stimulation: a touch, smell, sight, thought, fantasy, or anything else that has erotic meaning for you. Provided that you are open to a sexual experience, changes commence.

An increased volume of blood is pumped into various parts of your body, increasing their size and often their sensitivity to stimulation. Aside from your penis, your lips, earlobes, and breasts are other areas that may be so affected. An increased amount of blood is pumped into your penis, and the outflow is reduced. This is what results in erection.

Full erection may or may not occur early in an experience. In many young men, erection is almost instantaneous; they get hard as soon as they get any stimulation. With increasing age, however, it usually takes longer to get hard, and direct stimulation of the penis may be required to reach full erection. There is nothing wrong with either the shorter or longer route.

All bodily changes are reversible. How you feel directly affects what's happening to you physically. If you get bored, distracted, or anxious, or aren't getting optimal physical stimulation, you may lose some or all of

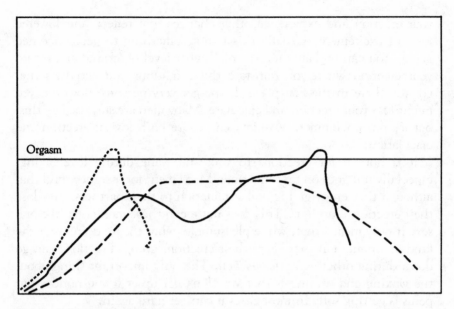

Figure 5: Male Sexual Responses

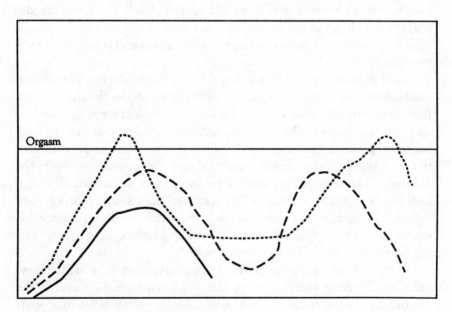

Figure 6: More Male Sexual Responses

your erection and experience other changes that reflect your lowered level of excitement. Usually this is not something to get concerned about. You can probably return to a higher level of arousal and regain your erection when you reinstate the conditions and activities that got you there in the first place. If you get very nervous, however, you might lose your erection and ejaculate. Many men are surprised by this, but it's not uncommon. Anxiety can cause both loss of erection and ejaculation.

It is normal for erections to wax and wane during lovemaking, especially if it goes on for some time. Many men, for instance, find that although they enjoy giving oral stimulation to their partners, they lose their erections during it. This does not mean these men don't like oral sex. It only means that, while pleasurable, what they're doing isn't the kind of stimulation that keeps their erections going. Erections can go down during other activities as well. The only important thing about the waxing and waning is that you don't get upset if you notice your penis is getting soft. In most cases it can get hard again.

The scrotum and testes undergo some interesting changes during sex. The skin of the scrotal sac thickens and contracts, while the testes increase in size because of the engorgement of blood. The testes are also pulled up within the sac until they press against the wall of the pelvis. This elevation of the testes anticipates ejaculation and is necessary for it to occur.

Ejaculation is a spinal reflex that releases the muscular tension that has built up and reverses the flow of blood in the body, draining it away from the penis and other engorged areas. Two distinct steps are involved in ejaculation. First, the prostate, seminal vesicles, and vas deferens contract, pouring their contents into the urethra. The sperm mix with the secretions of the seminal vesicles and the prostate to form the ejaculate. The contractions are the beginning of ejaculation. To you, it feels like "I'm going to come" or "It's coming." Masters and Johnson have called this "ejaculatory inevitability." Since the ejaculatory process is already in motion, ejaculation is inevitable. Nothing can stop it once the point of inevitability has been reached.

During the second step of the ejaculatory process, which follows immediately after the first step, the fluid is propelled through the urethra by contractions of the pelvic muscles. The semen may spurt several inches or even feet beyond the tip of the penis, or it may just ooze out. The force and amount of ejaculate expelled are determined by a number of factors, including your age and the length of time since the last ejaculation.

Ejaculation is a total-body response, not just something that happens in the crotch. Respiration, blood pressure, and heartbeat increase as the man approaches ejaculation, usually peaking at the moment of ejaculation. Involuntary muscle contraction and spasms may occur in various parts of the body, including legs, stomach, arms, and back.

Although many people use ejaculation and orgasm synonymously, I find it is useful to draw a distinction between them. Ejaculation is the physical part, the propulsion of seminal fluid. Orgasm is the peak feeling in sex. This peak feeling usually occurs in men during ejaculation, but not always. Sometimes there is no peak feeling and sometimes that feeling comes long before ejaculation. Some men don't have a lot of feeling when they ejaculate, and some men have lots of peak feelings, with and without ejaculations. There is no good and bad, right and wrong, about any of this.

What would happen if you got very excited, had an erection, but for one reason or another did not ejaculate? Many men believe that this would lead to the condition commonly called "blue balls" or "lover's nuts": discomfort, pain, and soreness in the testes. This belief is easy to understand: The fantasy model of sex invariably includes orgasm for the male, and the implication seems to be that its absence would be disastrous.

In fact, it is not disastrous. There may be soreness or pain, but this is rare. You might want to think back over your sexual experiences and see if this is true for you. Be sure to include all instances where, whether with masturbation or with a partner, you got very aroused and did not ejaculate. How many times was there pain? Probably very few, although those are the ones we tend to remember. It is not necessary to ejaculate every time you have sex. It's nice when it happens, but there's no reason to try to force it. You and your partner will probably feel better stopping while you are still feeling good. Working at producing an ejaculation has a way of making sex tedious and usually doesn't succeed anyway.

After ejaculation, your body starts to return to where it was before the sex began. Blood flows out of your penis and it returns to its nonerect state. The rate at which this happens depends on many factors and varies with each occurrence. Sometimes your erection may go down immediately, while at other times it may stay relatively firm for many minutes after ejaculation. Blood pressure, pulse, and breathing rates gradually return to their prearousal levels. The scrotum and testes descend to their normal position. A thin film of perspiration may appear over much of your body.

When there has been excitement and no orgasm, resolution usually takes longer. The muscular tension and accumulation of blood are released more slowly than when there has been an ejaculation. Because of this, you may feel a bit congested in the pelvis and perhaps a little tense or jittery. If there is pain, a short period of rest will help, or perhaps you'll want to stimulate yourself, or have your partner stimulate you, to ejaculation.

After ejaculation, many men experience feelings of lassitude and deep relaxation. For some this immediately leads to sleep, often to the chagrin of their partners. Women usually prefer a continued connection—holding, cuddling, relaxed talking, and so on—which some call afterplay. Most men I've worked with have found they can become comfortable with these activities if they desire to do so. And sometimes, of course, sleep is just the right thing to do.

WHAT DOES AN ERECTION MEAN?

Many men, and women as well, assume that an erection means the man wants sex. If only life were that simple. Of course an erection may mean the man desires sex, but it also may mean nothing of the kind.

Consider that during rapid eye movement (REM) sleep, the part of sleep in which we dream, males—from one-day-old infants to men ninety and older—usually have erections. This means three to five erections a night, each lasting from a few minutes to an hour. Does this mean all men want to have sex three to five times a night? While they're asleep? We really don't know why these erections occur or what they mean, but studies have been done in which the men were awakened during their dreams and asked what they were dreaming about. Sex isn't one of the main topics.

Consider that males often have erections at times when they will tell you they're not interested in sex. Teenage boys, for example, have erections in class when they're trying to concentrate on the classroom material, when walking down the street not thinking about sex, and on many other occasions. This causes embarrassment and frantic efforts to hide the bulge behind books, packages, and jackets. I played football in high school and invariably had an erection when "The Star-Spangled Banner" was played before each game. Did that mean I wanted to make love to the flag, to someone in the band, to one of the cheerleaders? I guarantee that sex was the farthest thing from my mind at the moment.

To make things even more complex, consider that erections can be produced by certain kinds of fear (while other kinds of fear can prevent erections). There have been a few reported cases of men being forced at the point of a knife or gun to have intercourse with one or more women. This isn't the kind of rape we usually hear about, but the evidence is clear that the male victims did get erect and were able to have intercourse. Erections are not only produced by positive, loving, or lusty feelings.

An erection means only that your penis is hard. Whether or not you *want* sex has to do with how you feel, how excited you are. Whether or not you *should* have sex has to do with your appraisal of the situation, what your head tells you. You may have an erection and you may be wonderfully turned on, but if your head reminds you that the woman in question is your best friend's or boss's wife, or that you have no protection against disease or unwanted pregnancy, you may want to think carefully about what to do.

WHAT DOES LACK OF ERECTION MEAN?

Just as many people confuse erection with an interest in sex, they also confuse lack of erection with a lack of interest. Women are especially likely to make this error and to personalize it. If you don't have an erection in a sexual situation, your partner may well assume that you're not turned on to her or that she doesn't know what to do to turn you on. It's possible, of course, that she's right. Maybe you're not aroused by her at the moment or ever, or maybe she's not doing what you'd like.

But most of the time lack of erection in a sexual situation means something else entirely. Let's say you are excited beyond belief by your partner. Your heart and mind very much want to have sex with her. Your penis does too, but unbeknownst to you there is a problem: perhaps because of arterial blockage not enough blood can get into the penis, or perhaps the blood isn't staying there because it is leaking out through the veins in the penis. The situation won't make any sense to you or your partner. You're hot to trot and your penis isn't cooperating. Unless you get a urological examination, you'll stay confused.

The problem need not be physical. Perhaps you're concerned about your sexual performance or about something at work. The more important it is to you to perform well and please your partner, the higher the anxiety will be. If the anxiety is strong enough, the penis won't be.

I hope it's clear that not having an erection doesn't necessarily mean you don't want sex. You may want sex a great deal, but something is getting in the way. I will turn to what that something may be in a moment.

OBSTACLES TO ERECTION

It should be clear by now that erection requires that a whole constellation of things be right. Your nervous and vascular systems have to be capable of responding properly and your emotions have to be capable of aiding, or at least not impeding, the process. Anything—physical or emotional—that gets in the way of sufficient blood getting and staying in the penis can cause problems with erections.

Medical Conditions

It used to be thought that erection problems were almost always in the man's head—that is, caused by psychological factors. But we have learned in recent years that this isn't the case. Many erection problems are the result of disease or drugs by themselves or in combination with emotional factors.

Any disease that interferes with blood getting to the penis, with blood being kept in the penis, or with the nervous system's control over the blood-flow process may cause erection problems. Any kind of blood-vessel disease, such as hardening of the arteries, can be a big problem simply by preventing sufficient amounts of blood from flowing into the penis. A number of medical conditions are known to affect the nervous system's ability to control blood flow or the ability of blood to get into and stay in the penis. Hormonal imbalances, diabetes, heart disease, multiple sclerosis, spinal cord injuries and back problems, injuries to the pelvis, and alcoholism are some of these conditions.

Just because you have hardening of the arteries or any of the other problems mentioned above does not necessarily mean that they are the cause of your erection problems. Such problems may also be caused by anxiety and other emotions. But it is important to determine what's going on. A visit to your physician—or better yet, to a urologist who specializes in sexual problems—is in order to discuss your situation. See Chapter 23 for more information about whether you need a urological consultation and what it can offer you.

Drugs

The penis can be affected by anything taken into the body. For example, drugs you take for depression, anxiety, high blood pressure, and many other conditions, as well as for recreation, can affect the penis. The effect is usually negative. In the Appendix, I list a number of common drugs that can adversely affect sexual functioning.

If you're taking any of the listed drugs, or for that matter any drugs at all, and are having erection problems, you should talk to the doctor who prescribed the medicine and see what can be done. And you should tell any professional you see about your sex problem—family doctor, urologist, or sex therapist—what drugs you are taking.

Emotional Factors

We've already seen that physical factors can hinder the blood flow required to get an erection. And so can psychological factors. Anxiety about performance (concern about whether or not you'll get or maintain an erection) has been the one most discussed in the media and is probably the most common one. But other feelings also enter in. Anger, for instance, no matter who it's directed at, can block your ability to get hard. So can the absence of a feeling, the lack of arousal. If you're not turned on, perhaps because you're highly anxious, because your mind is preoccupied with something else, or because you are angry at your partner, this may be enough to prevent stimulation from translating into erection.

THE PLEASURES OF THE SOFT PENIS

Penises do not have to be hard to produce pleasure. A soft penis has just as many nerve endings as a hard one and is therefore capable of generating good feelings. Whether exactly as enjoyable as an erect penis is difficult to say. Although the number of nerve endings doesn't change, it's possible that the engorgement of the hard penis with blood amplifies the sensations. Some men say it's more pleasurable to be stimulated with an erection and some men say it doesn't make any difference. And it's also possible to have an orgasm with a soft penis.

You already know how much pleasure can be gotten from the stimulation of a soft penis. Think about it for a minute. Have you ever started a sexual experience, alone or with a partner, without an erection? How did it feel as you or your partner stimulated your soft penis? Didn't it feel good? And it probably didn't feel as good as it could because you or you and your partner were focused on making it hard and were therefore anticipating what was to come rather than what was happening at the moment.

There are two reasons for taking more seriously the pleasure that can be yielded by a flaccid penis. One is that doing so takes some pressure off it to get hard. And the fewer demands put on a penis to behave in certain ways, the better it will function. The other reason is that it simply gives you more options. You can enjoy sex without an erection. And your partner will know she can give you pleasure without your having an erection.

It's also possible to have intercourse with a soft penis. But be warned: This only works if both of you are comfortable with the soft penis, if you're not going to get upset if it doesn't get hard, if you're willing to experiment with different positions, and if you can talk about what's happening. It sometimes happens that once you start having intercourse, your penis will get harder. If that happens, it's fine. And it's also fine if it doesn't.

A number of men have been surprised by my earlier statement that orgasm is possible without a full erection. Nonetheless, it's true. Erection and orgasm are separate entities and not dependent on each other. Just as you can have an erection without an orgasm, so, too, you can have orgasm without erection.

FEMALE SEXUAL ANATOMY AND RESPONSE

I know I said this chapter was about penises, but this seems a good place to say a few things about female sexual functioning. Although male and female genitals develop from the same basic structures, they end up looking quite different. The external genitals of a woman are illustrated in Figure 7 on page 102. Of course, women's genitals, just like men's, differ in many ways—size, color, placement—but the figure will do for our purposes.

The clitoris is unique in having no function other than giving sexual pleasure. Men have nothing quite like it, since the penis also serves as an organ of elimination. Aside from that, however, the penis and clitoris are similar. Even though the exposed part of the clitoris is small, it is as richly endowed with nerve endings as the head of the penis and is therefore very sensitive to stimulation.

The clitoris is for most women the site of their most intense pleasure. When women masturbate, they typically do so by rubbing on or near the clitoris (the clitoris is so sensitive in many women that they prefer stimulation to the right or left of it rather than actually on it). Rarely do they insert anything into the vagina. By now it is widely accepted that clitoral stimulation is what leads to orgasm in most women.

Some men don't like this idea. They, like Freud, believe that the vagina should be the core of female pleasure and that women should have orgasms in intercourse, just like men. Freud thought that in a mature woman the sensitivity of the clitoris was somehow "transferred" to the vagina. Just how this magical transformation was supposed to take place was something he never bothered to spell out. But his theory was sufficient to make many women feel inadequate because this metamorphosis did not occur and they could not have so-called vaginal orgasms.

The clitoris rarely gets direct stimulation in intercourse. It is difficult for a penis to be in the vagina and touching the clitoris at the same time. To accomplish this in most positions would require an L-shaped penis, which became extinct at the same time as the dinosaurs. The clitoris does, however, receive indirect stimulation in intercourse. As the penis moves in and out of the vagina, it tugs on the vaginal lips, which are attached to the hood of the clitoris. But this stimulation is insufficient to produce orgasm in most women.

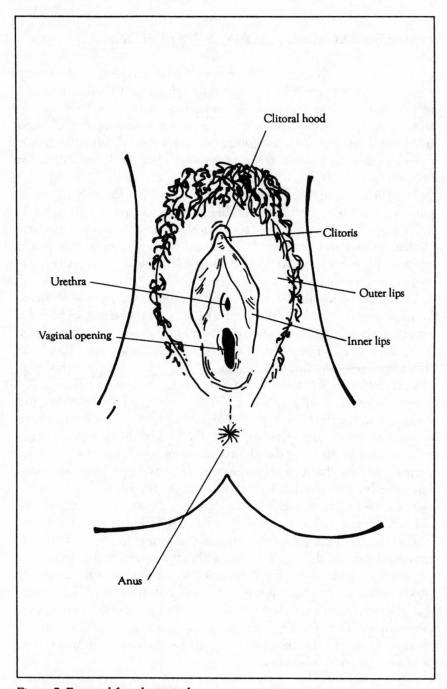

Figure 7: External female genitals

The clitoris can be stimulated in a more direct fashion by rubbing it against the man's pubic bone. This can be achieved with the woman on top position if she leans forward far enough and also with the man on top position if the man positions himself high enough so that his pubic bone presses against his lover's clitoral area. This practice, advocated in older marriage manuals, was called "riding high." Clearly, pubic bone clitoral stimulation is possible, but such contact is often difficult to maintain during intercourse. Even if maintained, it does not necessarily provide sufficient stimulation to allow the woman to orgasm.

If the woman wants to orgasm in intercourse, one option is to have her or her lover stimulate her clitoral area with a finger or two during penile thrusting. This is generally easier than riding high or any other alternatives.

The outer lips of the vagina are covered with pubic hair. The inner lips are closer to the vaginal opening and are usually closed. When the woman spreads her legs or is aroused, they part, exposing the urethra and vaginal opening. Both the outer and inner lips are sensitive to touch in most women, although such stimulation in itself is unlikely to produce orgasm.

Although I've already made a number of statements about what is and is not likely to lead to orgasm, I should add a qualification. Erogenous zones and orgasms vary from woman to woman. While a significant minority of women do not find breast stimulation arousing, there are some who can orgasm solely from such stimulation. There is also a small number who can orgasm solely by means of fantasy.

While often thought of as a hole, the vagina is actually a potential, rather than a real, space. In the unaroused state, its walls are relaxed and touch each other. When sexually excited, the walls balloon out, forming a real space. The space will accommodate itself to fit snugly around whatever object is in it, from the smallest penis to a baby's head.

While the erotic sensitivity of the vagina differs from woman to woman, the outer third of it, the part closest to the entrance, contains the most nerve endings and probably the only nerves in it that are sensitive to touch. The inner two-thirds are insensitive to touch, but are sensitive to pressure and stretch in many women, and the thrusting and distention that occur during intercourse can be very pleasurable for them.

Women who have no-hands orgasms in intercourse (no hands meaning no simultaneous finger stimulation of the clitoris) seem to do it in one of two ways. One way involves pressing the clitoral area against some part of the man, usually his pubic bone. The other way is solely through vaginal responsivity. These women describe having hot spots or particular areas of sensitivity in their vaginas. When thrusted against, these spots generate orgasms. Three researchers caused a stir a few years ago when they gave a label to this sensitive area, the G-spot, and suggested it was a true anatomical structure like the clitoris or nipple. Unfortunately, the evidence for an anatomical structure is shaky unless we want to say that any very responsive place is a G-spot. The vaginally sensitive women I've talked to locate the spot in different places in the vagina. Whether it makes any sense to use the term G-spot remains to be decided, but the important point is that some women are definitely responsive in their vaginas and do orgasm solely through the thrusting of intercourse.

Most of what was said earlier about sexual response in men also applies to women. As do men, women have many different ways of having a sexual experience. When a sexually meaningful stimulus is present, an increased volume of blood is pumped into various parts of a woman's body—including, but not necessarily limited to, the pelvis, breasts, lips, and earlobes—increasing their size and sensitivity to stimulation. Vaginal lubrication begins soon after blood starts flowing into the pelvic region. It is produced by the vaginal walls in a process similar to sweating.

There are many parallels between the assumptions we make about erections and their lack in men and vaginal lubrication or its lack in women. Profuse lubrication does not necessarily mean a woman is highly aroused, and little or no lubrication is not necessarily a sign of lack of arousal. A thirty-six-year-old colleague who read this chapter in draft form wrote the following:

I don't think men know enough about what lubrication does and does not mean. They assume lubrication means the woman is turned on and vice versa. This is NOT TRUE! There are times in my menstrual cycle when I'll be wet all the time and other times when my secretions will be minimal, regardless of how turned on I am. And, to make it more confusing, sometimes I'm dry on the outside when aroused but quite moist inside.

There's also something she didn't mention. Women differ tremendously in how much they usually lubricate. Some women lubricate so profusely that they often have the wet panties pornographic writers love to mention. Most women lubricate somewhat less, and other women lubricate very little no matter what time of month it is or how aroused they are. And because lubrication is linked to hormonal levels, it can be very sparse or absent in a woman who has recently given birth, who is nursing, or who has reached menopause—no matter how turned on she is.

The best way to determine what lubrication or its lack means is talking about it. And whatever you do, don't make the mistake so many men do of assuming that a woman is ready for intercourse just because her vagina is wet. She may be, and then again she may not be.

The flow of blood to the sexual tissues causes them to enlarge. The breasts, clitoris, and inner and outer vaginal lips puff up. The vagina starts expanding and lengthening at the same time. As stimulation continues, the outer two-thirds of the vagina narrows, creating what Masters and Johnson call the "orgasmic platform."

As blood flows into it, the clitoris expands in a process similar to penile erection. It always increases in diameter, but only in some women does it also get longer. As stimulation continues, the clitoris retracts under its hood. It may no longer be visible and is often difficult to find. This can come as a great surprise to a man who is stimulating it and now wonders where on earth it went. There's no need to look for it because you probably won't find it. Even though not visible, however, the clitoris continues to respond to stimulation of the area around it.

During a woman's sexual experience, increased muscular tension may be evident: in the face, hands, thighs, abdomen, or almost any place. There may also be involuntary contractions or spasms in the pelvis, buttocks, and elsewhere.

As with men, all these changes are reversible. If the woman is distracted or gets anxious, her emotional excitement will drop, accompanied by physical changes reflecting the lesser degree of arousal. This is nothing to get concerned about. Reinstating the conditions and activities that led to the higher level of arousal will probably have the same effect again.

Orgasms in men and women are similar both physically and emotionally. The main physical difference is that men ejaculate and women apparently do not. The reason for the qualifier *apparently* in the last sentence is that several sexologists, the same people who brought us the G-spot, have recently claimed that at least some women do ejaculate. Exactly how many women do this and exactly what they ejaculate are not questions that can be answered definitively at this time. Emotionally, men and women describe orgasm in similar terms. There is tremendous variation among individual men and individual women, and among different orgasms in the same person.

The physical changes that occur with orgasm also occur without it in both women and men, but more slowly. Not orgasming is not a tragedy for either sex. Emotionally, however, it can be something else, depending on the woman's perceptions. If she feels good about the relationship and believes her partner is interested in her satisfaction, it's usually no big deal if she doesn't have an orgasm today. On the other hand, if she feels that the man cares only about his own satisfaction and isn't willing to do anything for her, there will be problems.

In many women orgasm is accompanied by contractions of the pelvic muscles, contractions that you may feel if your finger or penis is in the vagina. While some sexologists feel these contractions are the defining characteristic of female orgasm, others argue that orgasms without noticeable contractions are not only possible but common. I side with the second group. Orgasms, like so much else in sex, follow no absolute pattern. There may be evident pelvic contractions or there may not. Only your partner knows if she has had an orgasm.

Men's orgasms are easier to figure out because we tend to assume that ejaculation means orgasm. If you see the white stuff, that means he came. Since most women don't expel anything, how can you know? Many men are troubled by not having definitive evidence of their partner's orgasm. In fact, it is one of their most common questions about female sexuality: How can you tell if she came? The only way to determine for certain is to ask her. But a lot depends on the circumstances and how the question is asked. Some women respond angrily or anxiously because they feel they are being tested or put in a position of having to prove themselves. In a stable relationship, it should be possible to tell your partner that you're interested in her satisfaction and want to know when and how she orgasms. But in newer relationships, perhaps the best question is something like "Is there something I can do for you?" Or maybe a simple statement that you are interested in her satisfaction and would be happy to hear about anything she wants.

But beware of becoming too involved with the issue of her orgasms. She didn't hire you to be her sex therapist. As I discuss in detail in Chapter 9, women like men who give them what they (the women) need and want, not men who give them what they (the men) want them to want or think they should want. Women, more than men, tend to evaluate sex in terms of feelings rather than performance. If a woman feels good about what happened, whether or not it included an orgasm, let her keep the good feeling.

The issue of how many orgasms a woman can or should have has become salient since Masters and Johnson demonstrated that some women in their laboratory could have more than one orgasm in a relatively short period of time with continued stimulation. As is typical, a possibility got turned into an imperative, with the result that some men are trying to force their lovers to have strings of orgasms and some women are feeling inadequate because they can't even have one orgasm or can have only one.

The fact is that while some women—and we have no idea how many—can have multiple orgasms, many cannot, and even many who can are often satisfied with just one or even none. If your partner likes to have several orgasms in one session, that's nice, but no nicer and no more proof of anything than if she has only one or none on a particular occasion. The only reason for having more than one orgasm is that it feels good and right at the time—unless you or she is training for the Orgasm Olympics.

As far as is known, most men do not have multiple orgasms. They experience a period after ejaculation during which no amount of stimulation will produce either erection or ejaculation. In teenage boys, however, this period can be extremely brief. Whether the refractory period most men experience is necessary is not something that can be answered conclusively at present. There is evidence that at least some men can learn to have multiple orgasms similar to women's. But the current situation is that most men do not have them.

The last part of a sexual experience is basically the same in men and women. It is simply a return to the unaroused state. The swelling in the genitals and other areas decreases as blood flows away from them, the muscles become relaxed, and the organs and tissues return to their normal positions. This process occurs more quickly if there has been an orgasm than if there has not. Sometimes, if there has been high arousal and no orgasm, the return to the unaroused state can take more than a few minutes and there may be some discomfort. Masturbating to orgasm can bring relief, if it is desired.

THE PENIS THROUGH THE LIFE CYCLE

Like all parts of the body, the penis changes as it ages. The truly young penis—in babies and grade-school boys—is basically a sleeper. True, it gets hard during dreams and at other times, especially when stimulated, but it doesn't do much otherwise except for resting and urinating.

The adolescent penis is another story altogether. It is rambunctious and rowdy; it gets hard all the time and at the most inappropriate times. The problem for many teenage boys is not getting it up but trying to keep it down. The writer Julius Lester recalls just how ubiquitous and embarrassing the adolescent penis can be:

> God, how I envied girls. . . . Whatever it was on them, it didn't dangle between their legs like an elephant's trunk. No wonder boys talked about nothing but sex. That thing was always there. Every time we went to the john, there it was, twitching around like a fat little worm on a fishing hook. When we took baths, it floated in the water like a lazy fish and God forbid we should touch it! It sprang to life like lightning leaping from a cloud. . . . I was helpless. It was there, with a life and mind of its own, having no other function than to embarrass me.

The teenage penis is often very stiff and hard. The idea that penises are hard as steel comes from the adolescent penis. Even though they aren't hard as steel, they often feel like they are. The adolescent penis seemingly wants to explode to orgasm every few minutes. It comes, and ten minutes later it's hard again and wants to come again. And what orgasms these are. The force is explosive and the pressure is immense; large amounts of semen fly across the room. And if the owner doesn't stimulate himself to orgasm, then it happens all by itself in wet dreams.

The adolescent penis is the penis at its ultimate power. From here on until the end of life, there is a gradual tapering off. Never again will it be so quick to get hard, so stiff, never again will the orgasms be so explosive and the need for them so insistent. There will also be a loss of independence over time. The adolescent penis needs little or nothing from the outside. It gets hard on its own, without needing physical or other kinds of stimulation. As it ages, it will require more stimulation of various sorts.

Although what I have described about the adolescent penis is typical, there are some that don't fit this picture. Some teenage boys have illnesses or injuries that make erection difficult or impossible to get or maintain. And some have difficulties because of strong feelings such as anxiety, guilt, or disgust.

The penis in young adulthood, approximately twenty to thirty-five, is similar to the adolescent penis, but signs of mellowing may already be present. The frequency of masturbation tends to drop, and wet dreams may be less common. Some men in this age group notice that their penises are not as hard when erect as they once were and that they require direct stimulation to get hard.

As the penis enters midlife, say around ages forty to fifty, some changes are obvious. It may require physical stimulation, either from its owner or his partner, to get hard. It may not get as full or as firm as before. It is easier for it to lose its hardness and, once lost, the hardness may be more difficult to regain. Men often notice and worry about the angle of erection. The erection that in younger years pointed up may now just stick straight out; the one that in previous times stuck straight out may now, though stiff, point slightly down. In most cases, these are just normal changes and nothing to get excited about. The need for orgasm is less pronounced. The force of the ejaculation is less, as is the amount ejaculated. Attending to the penis's conditions becomes more important.

The changes continue as the penis reaches its fifth, sixth, and seventh decades. Men frequently comment that it's not as hard as it used to be. Physical and mental arousal are much more critical. Things that before usually produced erection—seeing one's partner undressed, kissing and hugging, even watching X-rated movies—now may not do so. Penises at this age often take longer to ejaculate and they don't need to ejaculate every time. Every second or third time is fine.

Ejaculation is much less powerful. Semen may seem to seep out instead of shooting out. And once a fiftyish-, sixtyish-, or seventyish-year-old penis ejaculates, it may be days before it can get hard again.

Many men at this age decide they're over the hill as far as sex goes, or that they need some help. Getting help is realistic for some, but for others all that's needed is the understanding that just because something isn't the way it was twenty, thirty, or forty years ago doesn't mean you can't use and enjoy it. A raging erection that points at the ceiling and that won't quit is not necessary for good sex. After all, many men in their sixties enjoy walking, jogging, and dancing even though they can't move as fast or as far as they did when they were thirty. The senior penis can still give and take pleasure, even though it's not the same as it was decades ago.

As sex therapist Leslie Schover points out, some men do fine with their less-than-Herculean erections until confronted with a new situation: for example, sex with a new partner after a divorce or the death of a spouse. The same erection is now considered inadequate.

The changes I've described gradually continue until the end of life. Like the rest of physical functioning, the erection and ejaculatory processes become less efficient. **But the penis and the rest of the body *never* lose their capacity for pleasure.** There are men in their seventies, eighties, and even nineties who enjoy sex. As do their partners. According to many women I've spoken with, the owners of penises often develop qualities as they age that more than make up for the declining powers of their penises. These women say that older men are attractive sexually because they are more open to emotion and generally more loving, more patient, not as quick on the trigger, and often more sensuous.

The big problem for penises is that they've had a bad press. Perhaps it's more accurate to say that they've had a misguided press. The adolescent penis is the one that's idealized and idolized in the popular media, and it's also the first penis males have sexual experience with. Many men expect a penis of any age to act like the adolescent one.

In other areas we don't have these outrageous expectations. When it's old timers' day in baseball, we don't expect Joe DiMaggio and the other stars of yesterday to hit and run and pitch the way they did before. And we don't expect a forty-year-old man to run as fast as he did when he won the 100-meter race in the Olympics. But almost every man expects his penis to behave the way it did when he was seventeen or, just as bad, the way he wishes it had behaved when he was seventeen.

To the extent that we can get rid of these ridiculous expectations, accept the penis that we have, meet its needs, and like and enjoy it for what it is—to that extent we can give and receive erotic pleasure as much as we want and for as long as we want. And that, I suggest, is what it's all about.

5

Am I Normal or What?

"Sex is always on my mind. I think about it ten, twenty, or more times almost every day. Is that normal?"—MAN, 24

"My lover thinks I'm abnormal because I want sex almost every day. I think she's a little strange because she could do with once a week or less. Is either of us, or both of us, nuts?"—MAN, 34

"My wife says it's not natural for me to want anal sex or to experiment with bondage, and I guess I'm not sure myself. Is wanting these things OK?"—MAN, 47

"I'm concerned because although I love my wife and we have good sex, I often imagine sex with other women, even when I'm making love to her."—MAN, 55

BECAUSE sex is shrouded in secrecy and loaded with anxiety, people often have questions about whether they are okay. The main concern seems to be whether what they are—or are not—thinking, feeling, and doing makes them different, abnormal, or even weird. This apparently is the main reason for the popularity of books like the Kinsey and Hite reports and others that give statistical data about sex. Readers can check to see if they are in the same ball park, sexually speaking, as others of their gender, age, and so on.

In earlier times, part of this issue was easier to address, at least in terms of official mythology. Medicine, in league with religion, had long lists of thou-shalt-nots, activities said to be sinful, abnormal, and un-healthy, and only a very short list of what was acceptable. Masturbation, perhaps the most common sexual activity, was definitely not on the approved list. In 1758, a prominent Swiss physician, S. A. Tissot, published a book called *Onania, or a Treatise upon the Disorders Produced by Masturbation*. Needless to say, this was not a celebration of the pleasures of self-love. The idea that masturbation could lead to insanity was promulgated for over two hundred years. The main supporting evidence was the observation that inmates in mental asylums mastur-bated. Therefore, it was clear that masturbation must have led to their insanity. Science was not well developed at this time, and the necessity of having control groups hadn't yet taken hold. No one thought of determining the masturbatory practices of those not in mental institu-tions. In any case, the apex of the ideas of masturbatory insanity and sex as disease-producing was reached in 1882 with the publication of *Psy-chopathia Sexualis* by Richard von Krafft-Ebing, one of the world's lead-ing psychiatrists at the time. He reached the conclusion that not only masturbation but all nonreproductive sexual activity was sick, bad, and abnormal.

Similar nonsense was promoted in America. Benjamin Rush, the father of American psychiatry, proclaimed in the early years of our nation that masturbation (which he called "self-pollution") caused poor vision, memory loss, dizziness, epilepsy, and a host of other disorders, including psychosis. In the middle 1800s, a Sylvester Graham led one of the first health-food crusades in this country. He thought that bad health was related to sexual excesses such as intercourse more than once a month, masturbation, and erotic dreams, all of which were caused by eating rich and spicy foods. These foods "increase the concupiscent excitability and sensibility of the genital organs." The antidote he prescribed was a vegetarian diet of plain and boring foods, one key element of which was coarse, whole-wheat flour. Although you probably never heard of Mr. Graham, you have undoubtedly tasted a processed and sweetened version of his attempt to reduce sexual excess—the graham cracker.

Graham wasn't the only nut rolling around in nineteenth-century America; many others were also concerned about curbing sexuality.

John Harvey Kellogg gained a reputation both as a nutritionist and a sexual adviser. He thought sex the ultimate abomination and remained chaste even in marriage. Masturbation was the worst sin of all, "the vilest, the basest, and the most degrading act that a human being can commit." In his view, it led not only to the usual stuff like tuberculosis, heart disease, epilepsy, dimness of vision, insanity, idiocy, and death, but also to bashfulness in some people, unnatural boldness in others, a fondness for spicy foods, round shoulders, and "acne, or pimples on the face." Kellogg introduced a number of foods designed to promote health and decrease interest in sex, one of which he called Corn Flakes. The rest, as they say, is history.

In the Victorian period, it was thought that men had an excess of sexual feeling and desire, which they needed somehow to control, and no decent woman had any. No one should have sex outside marriage, certainly not girls and women, and certainly no one should take things in hand and commit the unholy act of self-abuse. All sorts of measures were taken to prevent masturbation in boys and girls—it seems that the devil was busily tempting many decent folks—and to punish those who succumbed to temptation. Sex with partners of the same sex, a practice that apparently has existed since the beginnings of human history, simply was not spoken of. Within marriage, men and women were supposed to have only the kind of sex that might lead to conception; this usually meant missionary-position intercourse. And that was that. It was assumed that men wanted sex more than their partners but wouldn't get too much because of their partners' reluctance. Presumably no one, except for the seriously deranged, was having a lot of sex.

What people actually did during the period from Tissot to Krafft-Ebing and Kellogg did not exactly match official ideology. We know homosexuality existed, that prostitution and pornography flourished in England and America, that about one-third of births in colonial America resulted from premarital conception (the Pilgrims weren't half as puritanical as we make them out to be), and that affairs were not unheard of. Masturbation apparently was widespread, as it always has been in human history. It's probable that the main effect of the official ideology was not to change behavior but rather to make people feel guilty, anxious, and bad about what they did.

Needless to say, things have loosened up a bit since then, both publicly and privately. Now almost everything goes and is considered acceptable. A majority of boys have had intercourse before they are out of high school, and a large minority of girls. Although man-on-top intercourse is still the most popular position, every other imaginable position has been tried and many couples regularly use some of them. Anal sex, or sodomy, considered quite depraved in the past, is now an act that about 30 percent of couples have tried and that some do regularly. Another great sin of the past, oral sex, has become quite common; it is a regular part of many couples' sex play. And that ultimate abomination, self-abuse, is engaged in not only by those without regular partners but also by those with. Surveys in the last twenty years also find that a fair number of couples engage in light bondage. As for how often sex takes place, a lot depends on the age of the participants and the duration of their relationship. Sylvester Graham and John Kellogg would certainly do cartwheels in their graves were they aware that a great many people these days have intercourse more than once a month, many of them even more than once a week.

Most experts now believe that the existence of rigid rules regarding sexual normality is itself a kind of sickness. A large reason for this attitude is our knowledge of the incredible range of sexual thought, feeling, fantasy, and behavior. Some people, for example, think about sex a hundred times a day, every day, and others can't remember when they last had a sexual thought. The same is true about behavior, although, to be accurate, I should say I've never heard of anyone having sex a hundred times a day. It's true that there are only so many convex and concave surfaces on the human body, and only a few protrusions and orifices, but people have been very creative with what they have to work with.

There's actually very little basis for saying that this or that activity, this or that frequency, is bad or abnormal unless it causes harm to a person or a relationship. And it's clear that most of the harmful effects proclaimed by people from Tissot to Kellogg were nothing but rationalizations for their abhorrence of sex in any form. There's little or no basis to maintain that sex with someone of the same sex is sinful or sick (unless you take certain religious teachings as the ultimate sexual authority), that sex before marriage is abnormal or harmful (unless you're not using protection and therefore risking unwanted pregnancy or disease), that masturbation is wrong in or out of marriage (unless it's causing a problem for the relationship), that anal sex is bad (unless you're not using protection and therefore risking getting a disease), or sex five times a day is harmful or bad (unless it's preventing you from getting to school or work).

Of course, there are still folks who are put off by sex, especially by any kind of sex that does not meet their personal notions of acceptability. Nonetheless, these days sexual tolerance is the rule rather than the exception, both among experts in human relations and sexuality and among the general public.

THE ABNORMALITY OF NORMALITY

"We all want desperately to be normal about sex. Well, it is normal to have sexual questions, concerns, and problems."
—JOSHUA GOLDEN

In the fantasy model of sex, we men have been led to believe that we should have active hassle- and problem-free sex lives, that we should be able to function more or less automatically, and that we and our partners should be quite pleased with the erotic side of our lives, just as it is for people in movies and books. Supposedly, this is normal or usual. But in fact it is not. Most of us, at least some of the time, have questions, doubts, and concerns. Sex is often not hassle-free. Sex is often not as frequent or as joyful as we think it should be.

Concerns about performance and anxiety about sex aren't supposed to be normal. But they're common, perhaps universal, in men. Jim Brown, perhaps the greatest running back in the history of American football, had a reputation as a lover that rivaled his reputation as a ball carrier. In his autobiography, *Out of Bounds*, he complains that even his friends thought he was a superman in bed. But, says Brown, "I was never Superman. I had the same doubts about performing up to expectations that they did." If even Jim Brown, with all his experience, had anxiety about his sexual performances, maybe it's understandable that the rest of us would too. And there's evidence that we do.

After interviewing 125 men of all ages for their book *What Really Happens in Bed*, Steven Carter and Julia Sokol concluded that "all men have sexual anxieties." More specifically:

Young men are anxious that their inexperience will show; they are also typically anxious about premature ejaculation and whether they know enough about female anatomy. Middle-aged men are worried that their erections are not as firm, or quickly achieved, as they were when they were in their late teens and early twenties. Older men worry that erections are less frequent, less firm, and more temperamental.

In *The Hite Report on Male Sexuality*, Shere Hite reports that a majority of her seven thousand respondents had concerns about getting and keeping erections and ejaculating too quickly. This confirms my own findings at talks and workshops. When I ask how many men have had concerns about performance more than a few times, at least half the men in the group raise their hands. There is good reason to believe, therefore, that **there's nothing abnormal or unusual about men being anxious about sex.**

Another place where our ideas of normality are way off base concerns sexual problems. Such problems, most of us think, are rare and hardly the norm. But is that really the case? A review of community studies by Ilana Spector and Michael Carey found that about 7 percent of men have chronic erection problems while about 37 percent suffer from chronic rapid ejaculations. The same review found that about 5 percent of men have difficulty ejaculating with their partners and about 16 percent complain of low sex drive. That's a lot of men with problems, especially since some difficulties—such as a sex drive that's grossly discrepant from that of one's partner's and dissatisfaction with sex even though there aren't any functional problems—weren't even considered in the studies done.

To add to this, we need to recall that most men *occasionally* don't function as they desire: They come too quickly or they can't get or maintain erections some of the time. Carter and Sokol, mentioned above, found that "most" of the men they interviewed "have experienced performance failure." In Shere Hite's large sample of men, 65 percent answered yes when asked if they had ever had difficulty having an erection when they wanted one, and 70 percent said they had ejaculated more quickly than they had wanted on at least one occasion. I hope the point is clear. **Sex problems are normal and typical.** I know, I know, all of your buddies are functioning perfectly and never have a problem. If you really believe that, I have a nice piece of oceanfront property in Kansas I'd like to talk to you about.

In case you're wondering about women, Spector and Carey found that about the same proportion of women as men have chronic or sporadic problems with sex; these include difficulties getting aroused and having orgasm, painful intercourse, and low desire. For both men and women, it seems, sex problems are not unusual. While I grant it doesn't feel good when you have a problem, it's just part of the human condition. Welcome to the human race.

WHAT ABOUT HOMOSEXUALITY?

Many people believe, often quite rigidly, that man-woman sex is the only normal or right kind. To them, sexual activity between same-sex partners is abnormal, sick, and sinful. While it is true that homosexual behavior is not the norm in any society, homosexual feeling and activity is found in just about every society we know of. No matter how repressive the society and no matter how horrible the punishments meted out to those who are attracted solely or mainly to those of the same sex, some minority of men are attracted to other males.

The heterosexual/homosexual dichotomy is actually too simple to describe the real world. Research indicates that a fairly large number of men who consider themselves heterosexual have had at least one sexual experience with another male sometime during their lives, and that an even larger group of men who consider themselves heterosexual have had erotic fantasies about men. And of course there are men called bisexuals who have sexual thoughts about and activity with both men and women.

All of this is by way of saying that it is not a matter for concern if you've had sexual feelings for or fantasies about men, or even sexual activity with them. Unless such things are causing a problem in your life, they aren't problems. And unless you take the Bible as the last word on sexual normality, there is no basis for saying that there's anything wrong or sick about any of it.

It *is* a problem that American men have been indoctrinated in a system of beliefs that strongly condemns not only the practice of homosexuality but any strong positive feelings toward other men. Because we are so frightened of homosexuality, we tend to suppress our feelings of affection for other men and our desire to hug, touch, or hold them (notice that women engage in these behaviors with other women without becoming lesbians). This is one of the reasons it is difficult for us to have truly close friendships with other men. And because of our strong negative feelings about love and sex between men, we tend to treat homosexuals as if they were an alien race instead of people who are very much like ourselves except for whom they have sex with.

WHAT ABOUT MASTURBATION?

Although the dictionary definition of masturbation is stimulation of the genitals by means other than intercourse, I use the term as most people do, to refer to sexually stimulating oneself. Common synonyms include "playing with yourself," "self-pleasuring," and "self-stimulation."

Playing with oneself is one of the most common sexual acts. Little children do it—at least until their parents shriek at them to stop—and it has been found in every society studied. In America, the vast majority of boys start masturbating sometime during puberty and most of them continue to pleasure themselves for the rest of their lives. Estimates are that about 70 percent of married men sometimes stimulate themselves (and a similar percentage of married women).

Although there is nothing abnormal or unnatural about self-pleasuring, most of us feel ashamed or guilty about it. It seems selfish and too explicitly sexual (you can't pretend you're doing it for anyone else's benefit or for anything but *sexual pleasure*), and hints of immaturity. A real man, we think, would be able to find a partner to have sex with rather than being left to his own devices. If he already has a partner, then why on earth would he want to have sex by himself? A married man in his fifties expressed his concern like this:

> I'm embarrassed about this, but I've masturbated once a week or so all through my marriage. It's not that Grace leaves anything to be desired. She's a wonderful sex partner and rarely turns me down. But there are times when it just seems easier to do it myself. This isn't taking anything away from what we have together, it's just a separate thing. I think she'd be shocked and hurt if she found out and I wouldn't know how to explain myself.

It's understandable that masturbation should make us feel uneasy. Sex by oneself for one's own pleasure—where even the pretense of trying to conceive didn't exist—was always at or near the top of the worst sexual abuses in Western cultures, the mere mention of which was enough to send religious and medical "experts" into a state of hysteria. The terms they used to refer to the act—"self-abuse," "self-pollution," and "the solitary vice"—reflect their attitude. It was only about thirty years ago that the American Medical Association and the Boy Scout Manual dropped their opposition to masturbation. Although virtually all medical and psychological experts today consider the activity quite normal, we aren't that far removed from the days when it was considered anything but normal.

Despite its reputation, masturbation actually has a number of uses and benefits.

- It's fun, one of the small pleasures of life. What's wrong with making ourselves feel good?
- In masturbation you don't have to look your best, and, as Woody Allen put it, it's sex with someone you love. You don't have to concern yourself with anyone else's feelings, desires, or goals. You can do whatever you want for as long or as short a time as you like and get whatever you want out of it. Partner sex, while certainly having advantages of its own, does require that we carefully attend to the desires of our partner and synchronize our behavior with hers, and that's not something one always wants to do.
- Self-pleasuring is an excellent way to learn how you like to be touched and stimulated, not only on your genitals but elsewhere as well. This information can then be given to your partner, thus enhancing your sex life together.
- Even if you're committed to partner sex as the best way of satisfying your erotic needs, there may be times when you don't have a partner or the partner you do have isn't available because of illness, fatigue, or something else. Why deny yourself sexual pleasure at such times?
- As I discuss in detail in the latter part of the book, masturbating in certain ways can help overcome sexual problems such as erection difficulties and rapid ejaculation.

The only sense in which masturbation can be said to be bad is when a man regularly uses it as a substitute for sex with his partner. That is, whenever he feels sexy he satisfies himself and rarely or never wants sex with his partner. Understandably, the partner may feel less than ecstatic about this state of affairs. Usually, something else is involved. The man is unhappy about either the partner or relationship, about himself or about sex with her.

Because most of us still feel somewhat uneasy about masturbation, we try to hide it. When a man is walked in on by his partner while masturbating, instead of simply acknowledging what he is doing, he often denies it. "Nothing, just dozing" or "I had an itch [or ache] in my penis and was just scratching [examining] it." Yeah, sure. How much better and easier if he could just say what he was doing.

It's possible the woman may not feel good about what he's doing, just as he feared. She may feel that her attractiveness or skillfulness is inadequate if he masturbates even though she's available.

Such feelings need to be talked about. They stem from our culture's narrow view of sex. As I try to show throughout this book, the only rules necessary for good sex are consent (if you're doing it with someone else, they must agree to the activity), honesty (don't say things that aren't true), and responsibility (it's not right to make babies when you don't want them, to spread disease, or to behave in ways that are disrespectful of your partner). Aside from these things, anything goes. It's perfectly fine to masturbate even though you have a sexual partner, it's fine to masturbate in her presence or with her participation, it's fine for the two of you to masturbate together, and it's just as fine for either of you to stimulate yourself during an erotic encounter together. Just because you have a partner who's available to have oral sex or intercourse or any other sexual activity doesn't necessarily mean you'll always want to engage in that activity with her. There are times when you may simply prefer to stimulate yourself despite your partner's availability.

OK, you say, so masturbation is fine, but what about "excessive masturbation"? This is a common concern.

I recently got a call from a young physician who wondered if he was masturbating too much. It turned out he was doing it several times a day, every day, for a total of twenty to twenty-five times per week. Statistically, this is extreme. But, in answer to my questions, he revealed that: his health is fine; he's generally satisfied with his life, work, and marriage; his penis isn't sore or bruised and he has no problem ejaculating alone or with his partner; and he has sex with his wife two or three times a week, a frequency they're both content with. There was no way I could determine that his frequent self-stimulation was interfering with any aspect of his life. Highly sexed? Definitely. Sick or weird? No. I've talked to men who were masturbating much less than this doctor, sometimes as infrequently as once or twice a week, who also wondered if they were doing too much.

As far as I'm concerned, the same rules apply to self-stimulation as to any other sexual activities. If whatever you're doing isn't hurting you, your partner, or your relationship, why not just enjoy yourself?

WHAT IS NORMAL SEXUAL DESIRE OR ACTIVITY?

This is a very sensitive topic for both men and women. Bad feelings and name-calling are typical when someone feels his partner wants too much or too little. If she wants less, she's frigid, withholding, unloving, neurotic, and a sexless bitch. If she wants more, she's oversexed, a slut, a tramp, neurotic, and a demanding bitch. As Kinsey put it, a nympho-maniac is anyone who's having more sex than you are. All of these terms are simply ways of saying that you don't like your partner's level of interest. Instead of putting it that way, our frustration and anger result in name-calling and put-downs. In effect, we're saying she's abnormal and ought to shape up.

In answer to the question of what is normal sexual desire, we don't know—unless all you want is a purely statistical report on how often people demographically similar to you have sex. It's not even clear that the question makes any sense. What is normal eating desire or activity? We don't know that either. Most people eat meals three times a day and have a few snacks as well. Some people eat only two meals a day and a few eat only one. And there are also people who eat small meals every two or three hours, never having what the rest of us would call a regular meal. We judge not the eating but the results. If you're not obese or anorexic, your arteries aren't clogged, and your health is good, you're

OK whatever it is you're doing about eating. And, unlike sex, eating is necessary for your survival.

I think we need to judge sexual interest and activity, as we do eating, by the results. If it's not causing a problem in your life or relationship, whatever you're doing is OK. We know there are huge variations. Some couples have sex several times a day, every day. Most couples have sex less frequently. Believe it or not, there are also men and women, not all of them priests and nuns, who've never engaged in partner sex.

I was consulted on a nonsexual matter by a couple in their forties a few years ago. When they noticed all the sex books in the bookcase, they told me their story, "just so you'll know that people can be happy without sex." Both realized from adolescence that they differed from their peers because of a lack of sexual interest. They dated and experimented with sex, their experiences confirming their differences. Each decided to try to find an opposite-sex counterpart. The woman found one and married him, but he turned out to be alcoholic and they soon divorced. The man kept looking, and one day they found each other. They have been married almost twenty years and not once have had sex. They are physically affectionate and sleep in each other's arms, but there has been no genital touching. My impression was that they were indeed well matched in most areas, loving, and quite content. Although this couple is not typical or normal statistically, they are not unique, and there's no basis I can think of to view their situation as harmful or problematic.

In my opinion, sex—however defined—is not necessary for survival or for a good relationship. And if you are having sex, a large amount is fine and so is a moderate or a low amount.

A widespread problem these days is the inability of couples to agree on how often to make love. In most of these cases there's no basis on which to say that one partner's desire is abnormally high or the other's abnormally low, but there's plenty of basis to say that the discrepancy is causing huge problems in their relationship. I deal more with this issue in Chapters 25 and 26.

WHAT ABOUT THE USE OF EROTIC MATERIALS?

The use of erotic pictures, books, and other materials is hardly new. Even in Victorian England, one of the most sexually repressive societies in history, pornographic books and magazines were quite popular. With the advent of movie-making, erotic movies, often called stag films, appeared. More recently, with the proliferation of VCRs, it has become convenient and common for individuals and couples to watch sexy videos in their homes.

A controversy has raged over erotic materials for a long time. Many religious authorities object to them because they tend to incite sexual arousal, which of course is their purpose. Some feminists object to them, claiming that these materials treat women as objects and cause violence against them. But as other people have pointed out, erotic materials do not discriminate against women: They objectify everyone. Sexual organs and acts are all they focus on. As for violence, the vast majority of erotic films and other materials contain none. You are far more likely to see murder and rape and other kinds of mayhem in PG-13 or R-rated movies than in those rated X. (There is, to be sure, a very small segment of the erotica market that caters to those who are aroused by the combination of violence and sex. But these materials are easy to avoid.)

It's difficult to see how the use of erotic materials can be considered abnormal or sick. It's apparent that most males use them at some times in their lives. How many boys and men can honestly say they've never looked at *Playboy* or *Penthouse*, never read an erotic book or viewed an erotic movie? And millions of women regularly read romance novels that often are hard to differentiate from hard-core sex books. Erotica is not without risk. It can cause the development of unrealistic expectations about ourselves, our partners, and sex itself. But if you remind yourself not to confuse fantasy, which is what erotica is, with reality, I think its use is mainly beneficial. Erotic materials usually turn people on, and often these aroused people want sex with themselves or their partners. How is that bad?

The use of erotic materials is similar in many ways to the use of sexual fantasies. In the case of fantasies, the representation of sexual events is internal; with erotica, it's external—you're reading, hearing, or watching someone else's fantasy, which, of course, may not only turn you on but also start your own fantasies going.

WHAT ABOUT FANTASIES?

Many questions about sexual normalcy have to do with fantasies. A sexual fantasy is *any* mental representation of *any kind* of sexual activity. Many fantasies are like a movie. That is, they tell a story and move from beginning to middle to end. An example would be imagining meeting a woman at a conference, taking her to your room, kissing, fondling, engaging in oral sex, followed by intercourse. But fantasies need not be so full-blown or elaborate. You may, for instance, just imagine one act— a kiss, oral sex, or intercourse—or one feeling, such as orgasm.

A number of men I've seen in therapy at first denied they ever had sexual fantasies (women are even more likely to deny such fantasies). On closer examination, however, it turned out they all did. The reason they thought they didn't was that their fantasies were not fully formed "movies." They were more like fleeting images; just a quick look at a breast or crotch or an activity. But these qualify as fantasies by any reasonable definition.

Sexual fantasies are entirely normal for human beings. Our minds are constructed so as to be able to represent internally any aspect of the world we choose, and this includes things that don't really exist out there. We can imagine what our lives would be like if we were billionaires, even though we aren't. We can imagine sex with our favorite movie star or the girl next door, even though we've never had sex with either of them and aren't likely to.

How we use our minds varies considerably. Some people's fantasies are mainly positive, while other people's are mainly negative. Some people spend a lot more time with their fantasies than others, and usually their fantasies are more elaborate. Some people are willing to fantasize about things that others aren't. They find it pleasurable to fantasize about sex with their partners, other people's partners, animals, and all sorts of combinations. Other people have trouble with such fantasies. They think it's wrong to fantasize about sex at all, about certain kinds of sex, or sex with certain people.

Fantasies serve several purposes. One is that they are an inexpensive entertainment that usually makes us feel good. Even though we're not likely to ever have sex with fourteen Playboy bunnies at the same time, or even sequentially, it can feel very good to imagine doing so. Another purpose is turning us on, really an extension of the first purpose. Whether or not you're fantasizing about sex with your partner, what goes on in your imagination can arouse you to the point that you'll want sex with her or that you'll be more passionate when you see her than otherwise might be the case.

Sexual fantasies can also be used therapeutically. Imagining an arousing activity can be helpful in the midst of sex. If you notice your arousal or erection flagging during erotic activity, conjuring up a favorite fantasy may make a difference. Imagining a sexual activity that you haven't tried but think you might want to can give you a better sense of how you might go about that, and if you really do want to do it.

Despite the fact that fantasizing about sex comes so naturally and easily to human beings, and despite the helpful purposes it serves, sexual fantasies have not enjoyed a good press in Western culture, which, of course, has traditionally been predominantly antisexual. The biblical injunction "One who looks at a woman lustfully has already committed adultery with her in his heart" sums it all up.

Part of the problem with our culture is that it doesn't make a clear enough distinction between imagining something and actually doing it. The fear has been that if you fantasize about having sex with a neighbor, you'll actually do it. There is at least a grain of truth in this. Fantasy can serve as rehearsal for behavior. Imagining the same thing repeatedly may motivate you to try it out. But in most cases this isn't much of a problem. Real-life obstacles and your own values help keep the fantasy where it belongs—in your head.

People who feel guilty about their fantasies need to remind themselves that there is a big difference between imagining doing something and actually carrying it out. There is no law against imagining forcing someone to have sex with you, and there are both men and women who enjoy this kind of fantasy. Doing it in reality, however, is another matter entirely. There is also nothing wrong with fantasizing about protection-free, worry-free sex with strangers. In the real world where sexual diseases are commonplace and where conception and bad feelings occur far more often than anyone would wish for, you ought to take the necessary precautions.

Fantasies can also be helpful in determining what you might want in the real world. Perhaps there are some elements of your imagery that you would like acted out. Some men I've worked with, for example, have had fantasies about "zipless fucks"—no words, not much foreplay, just silent, passionate, and no-strings-attached fucking. In a number of these cases, they were able to talk to their partners about the fantasies and act them out, much to everyone's satisfaction. To take another example, some men and a great many women have very romantic sexual fantasies: exotic settings, candle-lit dinners, sunsets, many words and touches of affection, only gradually getting into very caring yet passionate love-making that goes on for what seems like hours. And many of these people were able to live out these fantasies and were happy as a result.

Please don't assume that I mean you should act out everything in your fantasies. I don't mean that at all. Just because you enjoy imagining being whipped and dominated by a woman does not mean you'll actually enjoy the reality of it. Use your common sense and consider whether this is something you'd really like to try and if you're willing and able to go through it. The real world often exacts prices that fantasies do not. Having sex with your wife's sister may make for a wonderful fantasy. The reality, however, could be quite costly.

Despite the anti–sexual fantasy position of our culture, most males have and enjoy erotic mental productions. It's typical for boys and men to have fantasies when they masturbate. And from the studies that have been done, it's typical for men and women to fantasize about sex at all sorts of times. But there are still many questions and doubts.

A professional man consulted me because of guilt about his fantasies. Although he loved and was turned on by the woman he lived with, during lovemaking he often had fantasies of sex with other women. He felt bad about this, as if he weren't being true to his partner. He felt much better after we discussed the subject and I loaned him several collections of fantasies, which make it quite clear that many men and women fantasize about other people while having sex.

Some men readily accept that no matter how much they love and are turned on by their partner, they will continue to be turned on by and have fantasies about other women. But other men, like the man just mentioned, have trouble with this. It can help if they understand that being aroused by other women is typical for men. In fact, I've rarely encountered a man who said he was not turned on by other women and did not have fantasies about sex with them.

Although I can't prove it, I believe that it goes even further than this. My impression is that after the newness of a relationship wears off, most of our sexual turn-ons do not come from our partner. Yes, you may still get greatly aroused by her, particularly if she says or does a certain thing, but I think chances are good that much of the passion you feel and that leads you to want sex with her is evoked by other women or situations. There are many, many attractive women in the world, and you'll run into lots of them through the media and in real life: You'll see them on the street, in your office, on the bus or train or plane, in the restaurant, and so on. There's nothing wrong with getting sexually excited by seeing, hearing, or smelling a woman other than your partner. This is not the same, I hasten to add, as actually doing something sexual with these other people.

Since it's a fact of life that a great many of us get turned on by other people—that the phenomenon is natural, if you will—there doesn't seem to be any point to getting upset about it. As I show in Chapter 16, we can use the arousal generated by other women to better our sex lives with our partners.

Studies of sexual fantasies have found a wide variety of presentations. There are some differences between men and women in the types of fantasies they have most often. As you might expect, men more frequently imagine sex with strangers, sex with more than one person, and forcing a woman to have sex with them. Women more frequently imagine romantic settings and being forced to have sex. There is no basis for saying that any of these fantasies is abnormal or unhealthy.

There is an enormous range regarding the frequency of sexual fantasizing, just as there is an enormous range regarding the frequency of any sexual behavior. Some men have sexual fantasies many times each day, while others can go for weeks without one. Some men have asked me if they fantasize too much. "My mind always has something sexual going on in it," was how one young man expressed his concern. It was piqued after learning that his girlfriend rarely thought about sex or had erotic images. He wondered if he was weird. He was reassured after I explained that in general males have more erotic thoughts and fantasies than women (which is what we'd expect in a society that encourages male sexuality but until recently has discouraged female sexuality) and that the frequency of his fantasies didn't seem unusual. My experience is that people to whom sex is a priority have lots of sexual thoughts and fantasies. As long as the fantasizing isn't interfering with your relationship, your work, and the normal chores of life, I can't see how it is a problem.

Some couples find it very arousing to share fantasies. That is, the partners tell each other what they fantasize about, either when they're actually having sex or at other times. These couples not only report increased excitement but also a feeling of greater closeness. As one man put it:

> You might think it would make me jealous, hearing her fantasies about sex with other men. But it doesn't. It makes for an incredible turn-on. It also makes for incredible love. I feel closer to her knowing that she trusts me enough to tell me these secrets, things she's never told anyone else. Now I can also share some of my fantasies with her and that makes for even more closeness. I've never trusted any other woman that much.

Despite what I've said, don't rush off to tell your partner your latest fantasy. While the sharing of fantasies can be wonderful for some couples, it is not without risk. Some women are not comfortable with such goings-on. They may feel hurt, insulted, rejected, or jealous if you report imagining sex with someone else. There are also your own feelings to consider. Would you really be comfortable hearing that your partner imagines sex with men more handsome, more muscular, with greater charm or more money or power than you? Realistically assess both your possible reactions and those of your partner before you conclude that sharing fantasies is a great idea. If you should decide to go ahead, do it gradually. Start with a fantasy that is least threatening; for example, one that includes her or of having sex with the girl you first had sex with. Don't get into the fantasies of sex with her best friend, or your neighbor, or with whips and chains, until you feel it's reasonably safe to do so.

All in all, I think sexual fantasies are a natural, healthy, and pleasurable part of life. They're free, readily available, and rarely have side effects that can't be dealt with. It's almost like you can't not have them, so it makes sense to make yours as useful and enjoyable as possible.

THE QUESTION IS NOT IF IT'S "NORMAL," BUT IF IT'S A PROBLEM

Although "normal" is basically a statistical term (what's typical or average), in ordinary usage it has a judgmental and moralistic connotation. That is, there's something wrong with you if you're not doing what most other folks are doing. This connotation mainly serves to increase our anxiety and bad feelings and therefore makes clear thinking and productive decision-making more difficult.

If what you want or do makes your life difficult or sets you and your partner at odds, then there's a problem, regardless of how typical your action may be. The incidence of quick ejaculations among young men, for example, is so high that it could easily be considered normal or typical; we're talking about millions of men here. But that doesn't mean that it's not a problem for these men or their partners. Another example concerns the widespread practice of oral sex. If you want to go down on your partner or have her go down on you and she wants no part of either, that's a problem regardless of how common these activities are.

Another example of a widespread practice that is a problem for some people concerns the use of alcohol and drugs in sex, especially among singles. It's not unusual for singles to meet and mingle in bars and at parties where they ingest alcohol and other drugs. While I'm not suggesting there's anything wrong with a social drink to help one relax, it often goes far beyond this. Drugs cloud the brain and often make for destructive sexual decisions resulting in bad feelings, unwanted conception, and disease. And heavy use of alcohol and other drugs over the long run can result in serious loss of sexual appetite and erectile ability. Just because a practice is so widespread that it could be considered normal doesn't mean it's healthy or wise.

There are several ways in which sex can be a problem.

If it's illegal: These days you're not likely to get in trouble with the law about sexual acts done in private with consenting adults. But peeping into other people's windows, exposing yourself, trying to force your attention on women who aren't interested, and anything sexual with children can most certainly lead to the jailhouse. If you're doing any of these things, then you definitely have a problem and should get competent help.

If it's driven or compulsive: Some men's (and some women's) sexual behavior is compulsive. That is, the man feels out of control; he has to fantasize about sex virtually all the time, has to masturbate or have sex with his partner twice each day, or has to have sex every time he can and he doesn't care who it's with.

> A man I saw some years ago felt he had to have sex three times each and every night with his partner. He didn't feel he had any choice in the matter; he just had to do it. He had already lost several relationships because of this and was about to lose another. As the woman put it: "This is ridiculous. I'm so sore I can't sit down, and I'm so tired I can't stay awake at work."

The trendy term of *addiction* has recently been used to characterize such men. Although I have some problems with that term, there's no doubt that compulsive sexual behavior exists and is a source of great suffering for those so afflicted. These men need good professional help.

If it gets in your way: If you are consumed by sexual feelings, fantasies, or behaviors to the point where you can't engage in the usual kinds of social intercourse or can't focus on your work, that's clearly a problem. There are cases where a man felt driven to masturbate five or more times a day. Aside from getting a sore penis, he's also likely not to be able to do his work. The major problem for many of those men who feel their sexual behavior is compulsive or addictive is precisely that it gets in the way of getting on with the other important aspects of life.

If it creates problems with your partner: If whatever you're doing or not doing causes conflicts with your partner and harms your relationship, then obviously it's a problem. This could be the situation when, for example, your partner very much wants you to go down on her but you consider such behavior unseemly or disgusting. Or when she wants much longer foreplay than you feel is reasonable or even doable.

Another kind of difficulty that occurs in couples is when, for example, you *always* require a special something in order to get turned on.

One woman whose live-in lover could rarely get sexually aroused unless she wore spike heels said this: "It feels like he's in love with the shoes, not with me. Given how he carries on about them, I think he should find a nice pair of shoes to marry." I know of one couple where the man introduced bondage and dominance games early in the relationship. The woman didn't mind, in fact thought them an interesting twist, but as time went on she turned off completely when she realized the man couldn't get aroused without these activities. She then felt that he was "sick and abnormal."

Men who always use the same fantasy to get aroused (for example, the partner has to be nineteen and has to have a certain build) may condition their turn-on to that type of partner and be unable to get aroused with anyone else. This, of course, can create serious problems in the real world. Similarly, fantasies involving coercion are common among both men and women, but they can become troublesome if you fantasize only about forcing someone to have sex with you. You may be conditioning yourself to get aroused only when coercion is involved, and that will create havoc in a relationship. As long as you enjoy a variety of fantasies, there's no problem.

There are often disagreements in relationships over preferences or conditions that almost no one would consider strange or abnormal. For example, you may feel most sexy in the mornings and prefer that time for lovemaking, but your partner may feel as strongly about evenings. Because of the conflicting preferences, you and your partner are going to have to work out an accommodation. It's important to understand this point. **Just because you and your partner don't have the same preferences or don't agree on when and how sex is to occur does not necessarily mean that anything is wrong with either of you.** It usually means only that the two of you have to negotiate a reasonable solution to your differences.

Fantasizing can sometimes be bothersome in a relationship. For example, let's say that during lovemaking you trip out on a fantasy, and although this increases your arousal and you're having a great time, your partner feels alone and neglected. She doesn't know you're fantasizing, she only knows that although you're having sex with her, you don't seem present. She may not voice her complaint as I have. Instead, she may say that she has trouble getting aroused or maintaining the excitement, or has problems having orgasm. It may only be with further exploration that she can come up with the feelings I've suggested.

Although it seems far more common for women to feel lonely and left out in sex, it happens for some men, too. The reason appears to be the same. The partner gets more involved with her fantasy than she is with you. Regardless of who feels left out, something needs to be done. It helps considerably if the one doing the fantasizing can admit it. There's no need for apologies or feeling bad, just a need to see what's going on and what could help.

Another kind of problem that can arise in a relationship is when the woman gets upset about a man's fantasies or erotic materials. Does his use of them indicate he no longer finds her attractive or desirable? In such situations, a good discussion about her concerns and his feelings is required.

Returning to where we started, with what's normal and what's not, my advice is to forget about the question as much as you can. Focus instead on how you feel about your sex life. If it's not as good as you want, use the information and exercises in this book to make it better. If there are serious problems, decide if the book is enough or if you also need professional help.

_____ 6

Your Conditions for Good Sex

"It doesn't seem right. I know women need fuzzy feelings, the right atmosphere, and appropriate kinds of stimulation. But guys aren't supposed to be like that. We're supposed to be able to get it up and go to it regardless of anything."—MAN, 21

"It's so obvious it's almost laughable that I didn't see it before. I function better and enjoy more when I'm rested, haven't had anything to drink, and I'm not thinking about work. Wish I'd realized this thirty years ago."—MAN, 52

As we saw in the last chapter, what we usually think of as sexual normality isn't normal at all. It's a fantasy, one we could well do without. There's yet another aspect of normality that needs discussion, one so important that it deserves its own chapter.

The fantasy model of sex, the basis for many of our notions of what is normal, dictates that men be able to function and presumably enjoy without any special requirements. Regardless of who you're with, how you feel, and what's going on between you and your partner, you should be able to do your job.

But the fact is that we all have requirements or conditions. We're accustomed to hearing them from women. In older times a familiar

134

condition was "I can't have sex with you because we're not married." A newer version is "I don't know you well enough" or "I can't have sex with you because you're not interested in a relationship." These women were just stating a necessary condition for them to be able to participate in or enjoy sex. And many of us have heard other ones as well. For instance: "I don't feel like having sex when we've barely been civil all week" or "For me to be able to orgasm, I need this [or that] kind of stimulation."

Certain frames of mind, attitudes toward partner and self, physical and mental stimulation, and a number of other things influence how much we want sex, how aroused we get, how much we enjoy it, and how well we function. And these things are as true for men as for women. Jim Brown put it in his usual blunt way: "Every dick, including mine, has a mind of its own. I never felt like I could fuck any woman, any time. My sexuality hinged on the woman and the situation." Despite what we have been taught, it is not strange or unusual for men to have requirements that need to be met in order to have good sex.

If you want better sex or to resolve a sexual difficulty, determining your conditions is imperative. **If I were asked what's the most important single thing a man (or woman) could do to have better sex, my answer would be: Find out what you need and want and make sure to get those things (consistent, of course, with not trampling on your partner's needs).** Which is just another way of saying that you should meet your conditions. In a very real sense, most sex therapy, most books and workshops on sexual enhancement, and much of the rest of this book can be seen as helping you to determine what you need and how to get it.

Conditions is a very simple idea. A condition is anything that maximizes the chances of reaching a desirable goal: increasing or decreasing sexual desire, getting more aroused, enjoying sex more, delaying ejaculation, getting or keeping erections. When I say anything, I mean exactly that: time of day, how tired or energetic you are, how sick or well you are, how you feel about yourself, how you feel about your partner, what you do, what she does, how much privacy there is, or anything else that makes a difference to you.

It's not surprising that we should have sexual conditions—we have conditions in almost all areas of our lives. Take work, for example. I do my best writing in a dimly lit, totally quiet room with no one else around. Just me and my computer. With this arrangement, I get into a kind of trance and just buzz along. I don't do as well in a library or other public place because I tend to get distracted by the goings-on around me. I know a free-lance writer who is just the opposite. For months she tried writing at home alone and got nothing done. She needs lots of people around, ringing telephones, and so on. The noisier and busier it is, the better she concentrates and the more she does. Her way isn't better than mine and mine isn't better than hers. We just have different requirements.

Even with as mundane an issue as getting a good night's sleep, many people have conditions. Some need a firm bed, six pillows, total darkness, and a temperature that would make me freeze. Others have a different pattern. And so it goes in almost every aspect of life. Some people function better socially in large gatherings, others in small groups. Some do better with male teachers or therapists, others with female. Some people get their best workouts in the morning, others in the evening. All these preferences are conditions.

Conditions can range in importance from absolute necessities to druthers, things you'd prefer to have but can also live without. For the free-lance writer mentioned earlier, working in a noisy, busy place is essential. My requirement for a solitary, quiet place is not absolutely necessary, but it's more than a simple preference. I can get work done in a library if I have to, but I'm not at my best.

In a sexual situation, a condition is anything that makes you more relaxed, more comfortable, more confident, more excited, more open to your experience. Put differently, a condition is something that clears your nervous system of unnecessary clutter, leaving it open to receive and transmit sexual messages in ways that will result in a good time for you.

Despite the importance of conditions, many men have trouble accepting the concept. Conditions remind us that we're not robots, that we're flesh-and-blood human beings with feelings and vulnerabilities. This flies in the face of not only the fantasy model of sex but also most of our training in masculinity. We have no trouble understanding that women have all sorts of needs and preferences. That's how women are. But it just doesn't seem right to us that men should be the same. This is one of the main ways we're supposed to differ from women. We grit our teeth, disregard our feelings (or try to will the ones that are necessary), and do our jobs, including the job of sex. Just give us an available partner, and one way or another we'll be able to have good sex with her.

Because of this attitude, we feel ashamed of any needs and wants we have and try to hide them or pretend they don't exist. But this is destructive. Men are just as human as women, even though we try hard not to show it, and have as many requirements. It is perfectly acceptable to be yourself, to have your own desires, anxieties, concerns, and style. They should not be viewed as deficiencies. Conditions are expressions of our uniqueness and constitute a large part of who we are sexually.

Brad, a man of thirty-six, came to see me with the complaint of "being dysfunctional in bed." It turned out that he occasionally lost his erection or ejaculated very quickly. After doing the Conditions Exercise that I give later in this chapter, we determined that his "dysfunction" occurred only when he felt that his partner, Lee, didn't care for him.

Lee did not immediately express her complaints and dissatisfactions, but saved them up until she exploded in twenty- or thirty-minute tirades in which she vented all the complaints she had collected since the last diatribe. When an explosion occurred, Brad came away feeling unloved. She, on the other hand, felt much better after having gotten everything out and often wanted to make love immediately afterward. When Lee came on to him, Brad was aware of feeling terrible, but he was so anxious to "regain her love," as he thought of it, that he tried to go along. And that's when he lost his erection or came fast.

He wasn't any happier when I explained it was entirely natural for this to happen given how sad he was feeling (because of his idea that he had lost the love of the woman who meant so much to him) and how much anxiety he had (about regaining her love). His first comment is typical of men: "But I shouldn't let that stuff get to me." It took a while for Brad to learn that it's natural in human beings for "that stuff"—powerful emotions—to get to you. Once he accepted that, we found a solution for his problem.

In their attempt to function like "well-oiled machines," men overlook what they already know: that machines themselves have conditions, including being well oiled. When we're made aware of these needs, we don't get upset, we just fulfill them. For example, we accept that a car doesn't run without gas. If our car runs out of gas, we may get angry with ourselves for forgetting about this, but we don't get angry at the car for needing gas. Computer dealers report that they receive many calls from customers complaining that a printer or display doesn't work. The most common reason is that the customer forgot to turn the display or printer on. The callers may feel stupid for forgetting to flip the ON switch, but they don't kick the printer for needing to be turned on. Yet many men kick themselves for not being able to function sexually even though they aren't turned on.

Rob complained of sometimes not feeling much in sex and being unable to get erect. When we compared such times with times when everything worked out, it was clear that the difference was arousal. When he felt interested and excited, he functioned fine and enjoyed. When these feelings weren't present, he often couldn't get erect or, even if he did, the experience didn't feel very good. In answer to my question of why he was making love when he didn't feel like it, he gave the typical response—he did so in order not to disappoint his partner.

Much like Brad, Rob felt he shouldn't be deterred by his feelings. "Why can't I just jump-start my penis and sexual feelings if I'm not already in the mood?" was how he put it. Simply, because a man is not a car. Sometimes one can get into the mood by doing the right things—for example, touching one's partner and being touched in return, engaging in loving or erotic talk—and sometimes not. But Rob needed to learn that he couldn't force a mood or feeling and also that it was foolish to proceed in the absence of arousal.

The idea of jump-starting feelings appeals to men because jump-starting is a synonym for willing or forcing, and men have had lots of lessons about being able to force or will things. But it simply does not work in sex. You can't will or force an erection, and you can't will or force erotic feelings. Feel free to try it if you're not sure what I'm saying is correct. What often does work, however, is to figure out what it would take to get turned on or erect (for instance, "If I was feeling more awake and rested [or more sober]") and put that requirement in place. And that's exactly what fulfilling one's conditions means.

For some men, determining and fulfilling their conditions is crucial from the onset of their sex lives. For others, conditions and even preferences don't seem important until later. At first, usually in their teens, twenties, and thirties, they were always or usually aroused, functioned well, and had a good time. Many men, especially when they are young, function automatically, without regard for particular conditions; some of them can function fine even without being aroused. It's not that they don't have needs or conditions when younger, it's just that they can function despite not fulfilling them, much as a young person can function reasonably well without getting as much sleep as he needs. As he ages, however, not getting enough rest will take a heavier toll.

With regard to sex, something often happens—the man and his relationship get older, a sexual experience goes badly, he suffers from job stress or something else—and the system is disrupted. Once this happens, automatic functioning usually cannot be restored, at least not the way it was before. The man has to pay attention to factors he once could ignore. As time goes on, of course, and these factors become a regular part of his thought and behavior, his functioning will become less self-conscious and more automatic. But it will now include some conditions he had previously ignored.

Here are a few common sexual conditions that men have reported to me.

- Feeling connected and close to your partner. Although this is often considered mainly a requirement of women, many men need it as well. If you're not feeling connected to her, if either one of you is feeling angry or distant, you may need to do something about it before you can have good sex. I deal with ways of being close and connected in Chapters 10 to 14.
- Absence of strong anxiety about performance. You either feel confident about how you'll do or you know that you won't have to pay any great price if things don't go as anticipated.
- Feeling safe with your partner, which often is just another way of saying you don't feel anxious. You know that whatever you do and whatever happens, it will be OK with her.
- You know you'll get what you need from her in terms of attitude, response, and stimulation.
- Not feeling tired, ill, preoccupied, or under the influence of too much alcohol or other drugs.

- Feeling positive about the situation before it even starts. You're interested, you know she is, and you're both looking forward to a fun time.
- Feeling turned on, aroused, sexually excited. Aside from the absence of performance anxiety, this is probably the most important condition for men. If you want to learn more about this crucial quality and how to increase it, turn to Chapter 16.

Physical stimulation requires discussion. In the fantasy model, men don't require any physical stimulation other than seeing or kissing their partner. They are immediately excited and their penises immediately stand to attention and are ready for action. This matches the adolescent experience of many males: They didn't require any stimulation at all. But this often changes after adolescence. Not only men in their fifties and sixties but also many men in their thirties and forties require direct penile stimulation to get and stay hard and also to get emotionally excited. This is not a "problem," it's just life. If you find you require direct penile stimulation, or any other kind of stimulation, then get it. And make sure you get the kind that feels just right to you.

Foreplay—defined as erotic stimulation preceding intercourse—is usually considered something the man does to get the woman ready for intercourse. And it's certainly true that many women complain they don't get enough of it and many men complain that women want too much. But it turns out that many men need it, too, although sometimes it takes an extreme situation to determine this.

Many years ago when I was a horny student, and long before anyone had heard of AIDS or even herpes, I met a woman at a conference. There was an immediate attraction, and we were soon making out and pawing each other in the hotel lobby. Unfortunately, it couldn't go any further because I had to catch a plane. A few days later she called to invite me to her home several thousand miles away. We were going to finish what we started.

She greeted me at her door wearing only a T-shirt and big smile. She immediately led me to her bedroom and without any further ado took off her shirt, got on the bed with her legs apart, and told me to take her. I still recall my thoughts: "My God!, a fantasy come true. But some words, hugs, or kisses would be nice." I tried for the kisses, but she turned her face away and immediately guided me into her. I had an erection because I was young at the time and had been thinking of her ever since her call. So we had intercourse, during which she rejected all my attempts to kiss; although I ejaculated, it wasn't very pleasurable. And it didn't get better on subsequent occasions.

I asked her about kissing. Her words shocked me: "I really don't like kissing or touching. I just like to fuck." In response to my question about the necking we had done at the hotel, she said she was willing to do it there because we didn't have time for anything else and it was clear I enjoyed it. "But here we can screw and don't have to do other stuff."

I felt as if I had landed on a strange planet. I'd never heard of women like this. I didn't even know any men who felt like that. Although in the past I had sometimes complained about the lengthy foreplay some women wanted and had fantasies about wild women who just wanted to screw, this experience demonstrated that *I* needed foreplay, too. I hadn't yet formulated the idea of conditions, but already I had come up with one of my own. I could function without it, but it wasn't fun (now that I'm twenty-five years older than I was then, I'm sure I couldn't even function without it). In fact, it was so little fun that I cut my trip short and never saw the woman again.

Of course, one can take the position that I'm a wimp, that a real man would have exploited this incredible opportunity to the full. I admit that this idea occurred to me and, as soon as it did, I started to feel bad about myself. But, fortunately, I rejected it in favor of another formulation that has aided me through the years and also been of assistance to some other men.

That idea is that **a real man is *not* someone who can live up to other people's standards and expectations. Rather, he is someone who knows who he is and goes after what he wants and needs, even if some of those wants and needs are not on Harold Robbins's, Arnold Schwarzenegger's, this or that woman's, or anyone else's approved list.** I realized I could have gotten some mileage from male friends by telling them about this wonderful week in another city where I screwed this incredibly attractive woman fifty times without one second of foreplay. But then I recalled that it wasn't wonderful, not even good. I didn't want to get any mileage from that story. It really was okay that I liked kissing and hugging and wanted to feel connected to the women I slept with.

I'm not saying it was easy. A number of times, usually when I was feeling lonely and horny, I was tempted to feel bad about what had happened with this woman. If only I'd accepted her restrictions, I could probably still be in touch with her and occasionally see her for sex. Why did I have to be so damned particular! Any other guy would have been more than delighted by what she offered. What kind of man was I, anyway? But as the months went by, I more and more accepted that it was fine to be myself. And that was fortunate, because a little over a year later, I was put to the test.

As hard as it was for me to believe, I met another woman who wouldn't kiss. She was married, but she and her husband both played around. (I should mention that this was in the late 1960s, at the height of the sexual revolution.) She had nothing against kissing, but part of the deal she had with her husband was that although they could merge genitals with other folks, they couldn't kiss them. I was very attracted to this woman and had been extremely flattered by her suggestion that we have an affair. But as soon as these words were out of her mouth, I realized I had heard this tune before and it wasn't my song. Apparently taken aback when I said I needed to think about what she said, she added this: "Guys come on to me all the time. Any other man would jump at the chance."

I struggled for three days. On the one hand, I couldn't believe my good luck. This was another male fantasy come to life: no relationship, no commitment, and no foreplay, just sex. On the other hand, I couldn't believe my bad luck. Another woman who didn't kiss. Was I willing to turn down all the kinds of sex she offered just because of a silly thing like kissing? I recall thinking that other guys would think me crazy and say I was acting like a girl. Nonetheless, it didn't feel right, and I told her. She was clearly shocked and also deeply hurt by the rejection. She had put it all on the line and had been rebuffed. Because of this, I believe, she got nasty: "Not much of a man, are you?"

I was hurt by what she said and again went through some doubts about what kind of man I was. But my main feeling was one of sorrow. Sorrow that I had not been able to accept her offer and sorrow that I had hurt her so much. Within a few days I was feeling something else: a clear sense that she was absolutely wrong in her accusation, that what I had done was sure indication that I was on my way to becoming the kind of man I wanted to be.

Time of day is another matter that doesn't receive as much attention as it deserves. Particularly for older men, but also for some not so old, the when of sex is as important as the how.

Wendall, sixty-four, was distraught when he came to see me. He had been celibate for almost six years after his wife's death and had almost given up on finding someone with whom to share the rest of his life. But in the last few months he had been seeing Emma, a woman he met at church. Everything was fine except for his inability to get hard with her. Although Emma accepted him as he was and said it wouldn't stand in the way of them being together, he felt it wouldn't be right to marry her unless he could have intercourse.

As we compared sex with his late wife and with Emma, two differences came to light. His wife used to stimulate his penis with her hand during most of their sex play, and Emma rarely did and never for long. The other difference had to do with time. In their later years together, most of the lovemaking with his wife had been in the morning. Because Emma had several times said she was "a night person," Wendall never initiated sex with her except at night.

Wendall had been vaguely aware of both differences before he talked with me, but he didn't give them the weight they deserved. His penis was clearly a morning person and required sustained, direct stimulation. He was somewhat surprised: "You mean that's all it would take, sex in the mornings and some hand work from her?" I said I couldn't be sure, but it was certainly worth a try. He left the session a bit skeptical but promising he would talk to Emma about trying the new regimen. Three weeks later he called to say that although his penis wasn't as young as it used to be, the new routine had worked well enough for them to have enjoyable intercourse several times.

Your conditions may or may not be similar to the ones I've mentioned above, but that's not the point. What *is* important is that you find out what you need and then get it.

Before offering an exercise that can help you determine your specific conditions, I want to mention a difficulty you may encounter. Like Brad, Rob, and myself, you may find yourself coming up with things you wish weren't true. Your conditions may strike you as strange, unmanly, old-fashioned, or something else you don't like. Despite this, it is best to write them out and give some thought to them. The vast majority of times, one's conditions are acceptable to one's partner. In general, conditions are much easier to accept and fulfill than to change. With the exception of the rare instance where your conditions involve harm or pain to you or your partner, chances are excellent that, no matter how new or unusual they seem to you at first, you can learn to accept and meet them.

Since what follows is the first exercise I offer in this book, a few words about exercises may be helpful. Although reading itself can provide you with new information, years of experience with different kinds of self-help materials and psychotherapies has shown that *doing something*, even just writing lists or keeping a diary, is essential for making the kinds of personal changes most people want to make. And that's why I offer exercises.

The best way to deal with an exercise is first to read it carefully one or more times, along with the material that comes before and after it, and make sure you understand what is required. If, after doing this, it seems that an exercise might be useful to you, then just follow the directions.

In this exercise, I use the example of increasing arousal (passion, excitement). But it can be done with any other sexual issue: increasing sexual interest, delaying ejaculations, having and maintaining erections, experiencing more pleasure, and so on. All you need to do is substitute the appropriate word or phrase for arousal when reading and doing the exercise.

EXERCISE 6–1: CONDITIONS

Compare two or three sexual experiences in which you were highly aroused with an equal number where you were much less aroused and list all the factors that differ between the two groups. An example might be: "High arousal—I was rested, felt close to Cindy, wasn't pre-occupied with work, wasn't in a hurry. Low arousal—I was distant from Cindy (one time we had been in a battle for over a week), was preoccupied and in a hurry (once I was so involved in a sales talk I had to give the next day that I kept going over it in my mind while I was caressing her and couldn't wait to get back to my typewriter), or was exhausted (like that time I had just flown in from Europe and had crossed five or six time zones; I was totally out of it)." The items in the high-arousal list are your conditions. It's important to be as specific as possible. If you have not had any high-arousal experiences, or it is difficult to recall them in sufficient detail, use your imagination and list those things you think would be necessary and helpful to be more turned on.

Whether you use real-life comparisons or your imagination, consider all these areas: your physical health; amount of anxiety or tension; use of alcohol and other drugs; how much time you felt you had; whether you were preoccupied with other matters; fears about performance, pregnancy, and disease; your feelings about your partner, especially closeness, anger, or resentment; your feelings about yourself; your confidence that you would not be put down no matter what happened.

When you have finished with your list, put it away for a day or two, then reread it and see if there is anything you want to change. Now go through each item and reword it so that it is specific enough to be put into practice.

Let's say one of your items is "Need to make love earlier. After 10 P.M. I'm tired and into my work mode, thinking about what I'm going to do at the office tomorrow." So what has to happen to make love earlier? Two obvious possibilities come to mind. One is that you talk to your partner and let her know that having sex earlier will make it easier for you to get turned on and result in more pleasure for both of you. The two of you may then need to think about how and when lovemaking can take place. A second possibility is that you decide for yourself how to initiate sex earlier. For example: "When I get turned on at work, I can call Jan and let her know. If she's up for sex, we can send the kids out to play when we get home, and then take them to McDonald's."

An alternative way of doing this exercise is simply to make a list, over a period of days or weeks, of things you'd like in sex that you're not getting. You should consult both your erotic fantasies and past experiences with your current partner or with others. Are there things you used to do that you miss? Are there things in your fantasies that you'd like to try?

The importance of being specific in your conditions cannot be over-emphasized. If they are worded too vaguely, you won't be able to put them into practice. Take all the time you need to determine what your conditions are and how you can fulfill them.

Mario, an ambitious and hardworking lawyer in his midthirties, was troubled by sporadic rapid ejaculation. I worked on the exercise with him, and this is what we came up with.

Need to feel Sue wants to have sex with me. I sometimes feel she's just doing it to please me and that makes me tense, which in turn makes me come fast. I'd know she wanted sex if she initiated it, if she said she wanted it, if she physically and verbally indicated her enjoyment, or if she played an active role in physically stimulating me.

Need to know she won't be upset if I do come quickly. Only way I can get this is to talk with her and see if it's OK to come fast sometimes.

Need to be more relaxed before and during sex. Taking care of the first two items on this list will help, as will listening to a relaxation tape or taking a long, warm bath after I come home from work.

Need to be more focused on how aroused or nervous I am during sex. Then I can make the adjustments needed to last longer. A good way to do that is to focus solely on my own pleasure, what I'm doing and feeling. Have to keep in mind to focus on me, not her.

This is a good list, because it is comprehensive and indicates not only what things are needed but also considers ways of getting them.

Here's another list, this one from a man whose main goal was simply to enjoy sex more:

I want to be able to express my "adventurous" ideas, but in order to do that I'd like to know she's not put off when I do it. She's told me it's OK, but sometimes she gets what I take to be a funny look— like when I suggested she tell me one of her fantasies while we were having sex—that makes me feel ashamed and wish I had kept my mouth shut.

Also I'd like to know that she's not put off by my expressions of pleasure. As I've become more open, I've started to do things that sometimes surprise even me. Like the other night when she was giving me head, I totally got lost in it and realized later that I had panted like crazy and screamed at the top of my lungs. I think it's OK with her, but I'd feel better if I knew for sure.

As this man's situation shows clearly, just knowing your conditions may not be enough. You may have to talk with your partner to determine her feelings about certain activities and expressions or to ask her to do or not to do certain things. I discuss effective ways of expressing your needs and desires in Chapters 8 and 12.

BETTER SEX

_____7

On the Road to Better Sex

"Had enough bad love. I need something I can feel proud of."
—ERIC CLAPTON

"**T**HIS **is starting to sound complex. Why can't sex be simple?**" Sex is simple . . . for simple creatures with limited goals. Our primate cousins, for example, apparently have sex mainly to induce male ejaculation and conception. Their sex is very brief, a few thrusts and it's all over, but effective in its narrow aims. We humans could have the same kind of simple sex if we were willing to settle for the same modest ends.

But most of the time we want a lot more. In fact, our goals are quite expansive. We want to satisfy ourselves and our partners (and that satisfaction may be defined differently at different times by each individual), to bring us closer together (to _make_ love), to validate our sense of masculinity and femininity, to reflect and generate feelings of excitement and passion, and for some people, to produce a mystical experience. And all this may be in addition to creating orgasms and perhaps even a new life. This is asking quite a bit from what looks like a simple physical activity. A lot is wanted; a lot is at stake. When things reach this level, we are very far from doing what comes naturally and equally far from something that's easy and simple.

The desire to have sexual intercourse is wired into us, but we are equipped with the tools, both physical and mental, to have a more interesting and more elaborate kind of sexuality. Developing and using

151

those tools, adding the embellishments that make human sexuality so much more fascinating and satisfying than that of other animals, is the product of intention, effort, and learning. We have already started on the road to better sex in the first section of the book. The chapters in this section continue on that path and focus more directly on what is required. In the rest of this chapter, I address what I consider to be the six major requirements for having good sex. The first three have already been covered. The others require discussion.

THE REQUIREMENTS FOR GREAT SEX

1. Accurate information about your own sexuality, your partner's, and about sex itself. This means getting away from the myths and unrealistic expectations discussed in the first section of the book and being able to learn about your own sexuality and that of your partner.

2. Having or developing an orientation based on pleasure (arousal, love, lust, and fun) rather than performance. In other words, holding to some version of the definition of good sex given in Chapter 3, and being willing to work and focus on arousal (excitement, passion—the key to good erotic feelings).

3. Having the kind of relationship in which good sex can flourish. Whether your relationship lasts for an afternoon or forty years, its dynamics have a significant influence on the quality and quantity of sex. Relationship issues are typically seen as something more important to women than to men—and they certainly are very important to women—but, as we shall see, they are also crucial to men. A major aspect of having a good relationship is being able to deal with differences of opinion and conflicts quickly and effectively. Sex usually suffers when there is tension, hostility, or distance.

4. Being able to communicate verbally and nonverbally about sex. Perhaps the most important component of a good relationship is the ability to communicate. Regarding sex, you need to be able to express your wants and don't wants, your questions and concerns, and your pleasure, and you need to be able to listen to and understand what your partner is expressing. You also need the capacity to discuss conflicts and problems with your partner and work toward mutually satisfying solutions.

One reason you need to be able to communicate is that sex with another person involves physical coordination of a kind that's rare anywhere else. Let's compare masturbation with partner sex to illustrate this point. Our bodies are the most sophisticated feedback systems ever built. When you touch your own body, the process is automatic, self-correcting, and extremely efficient. Continuous feedback between your penis, your brain, and your hand allows the brain automatically to move your hand to achieve the results you want.

Now let's consider your partner stimulating your penis with her hand. Suddenly, things are much more complex. Your feedback mechanism still works—you know to what extent you're getting what you want—but your friend isn't part of it. To include her in the feedback loop, you must bring into awareness and put into words what by yourself was done without words and without awareness. "Move your hand up . . . too far . . . down a bit more . . . that's right, and a little harder . . . a little faster . . . that's good . . . oops, harder now . . . faster . . . that's great," and so on. You even have to tell your friend when to stop stimulating, because she may stop sooner than you want or not soon enough.

This is complicated business, and the complications increase with other acts. In oral sex, for instance, you may have to inform your partner that her teeth are hurting you, that she should apply more or less pressure with her mouth and hand (assuming that she's also using her hand), or that you want her to take more of your penis in her mouth. With a partner, you may want—and she almost certainly wants—certain kinds of stimulation that you ordinarily can't or don't do by yourself (hugging, kissing, expressing feelings orally, and so on). With her, you may also want certain feelings to develop aside from sexual arousal, and their development may require the expression of certain attitudes and behaviors. With masturbation, you can do it or not do it, or start and abruptly change your mind, stop, and do something else. With a partner, you have to inform her of what is happening. And since the two of you won't always be in agreement as to what should or should not be done, there has to be a way of expressing and dealing with the discrepant desires. Partner sex also carries baggage that masturbation usually does not. If you decide not to masturbate today or for the next ten weeks, or if you decide to masturbate every single day, it's unlikely that issues of love, desirability, or adequacy come into play. It's no big deal whatever you do. But with a partner, things are a bit different. Being able to talk, listen, understand, and negotiate are absolutely essential.

5. Being assertive about your own desires and able to focus fully on your own pleasure and also being exquisitely sensitive to your partner and able to give her what she wants. I know, it sounds like a contradiction, but it really isn't.

Being only self-centered or only sensitive does not work. The man who only goes after what he wants and pays little attention to his partner will end up alone or with a very unhappy partner. The man who focuses solely on his partner's desires will not get what he wants and therefore be unhappy. And his partner may also be dissatisfied because she senses that no matter how sensitive he is to her needs, he's not expressing or fulfilling his own.

In days of old, sex was mainly an act of male assertiveness. Having an orgasm inside a woman was what he wanted, and it was far from clear what she might want or what he might be able to do for her. Many men didn't think women wanted anything in sex but engaged in it only because they wanted something else that sex could bring—conception, a steady boyfriend, a happy husband—or because they had been tricked into it. For men who weren't cads, the main aspect of sensitivity was not harming the woman; in other words, treating her gently and using protection against pregnancy and disease.

The view of women as nonsexual came under attack in the last century and increasingly in the twentieth century until it was finally accepted that women were indeed sexual creatures. Men should strive not only for their own satisfaction but also for their partners'. Since men were still seen as more sexual than women, and since they had more leeway to gain experience, it was their task to introduce women to the joys of sex.

The research of Kinsey and later Masters and Johnson added influence to this view. Women were capable not only of enjoying sex but also of orgasm, maybe more orgasms than men. Men ought to give them their due. This was an important step forward, but one result is that men felt more pressured to perform because somehow the message was that they had to "give" their partners orgasms. Some men became so focused on ensuring their partners' pleasure that they forgot about their own.

In the new male sexuality I hope we are constructing, the satisfaction of both partners is paramount. The man has to assert his own wants and preferences, but also be sensitive to his partner's. It is not his job to give her orgasms, but it is in his interests to understand her desires and to fulfill them to the best of his abilities.

Being assertive and self-focused entails knowing your conditions, going after them, and thoroughly involving yourself in your own pleasure. You want sex now, so you try to interest your partner. You like to kiss this way, so that's what you do. You like to touch her breasts that way, so you do it. You like intercourse in such a position, so that's what you go for. And while doing these things, you're immersed in your sensations and experience, fully present and alive to what is happening. A good lover is assertive in these ways. He knows what he wants, or is willing to find out, and he goes after it without apology or guilt.

But a good lover is also sensitive to his partner's needs. You notice if she doesn't seem interested in exactly what you want or suggests something else, and you're flexible enough to try to combine both of your desires to make for a mutually satisfying experience. And you don't use guilt or other types of coercion to get what you want. A good lover is attentive to his partner's breaths, sounds, and movements and notices what works and doesn't work for her. He also listens carefully when she says what she likes. If she doesn't spontaneously voice her likes and dislikes, he asks. Bad lovers don't ask, don't listen, and don't remember.

A good lover takes the time and energy to use his knowledge to make sure his partner enjoys sex as much as he does. He also knows that sex isn't necessarily over when he's satisfied. Maybe she wants something more. A good lover would not be open to the charge a woman made about her new boyfriend: "He's one of these selfish or unconscious men. When he comes, it's all over. I have to go, 'Knock, knock, can I have a turn, too?' " A good lover is also sensitive enough to not pressure his partner to perform to boost his ego.

It *is* difficult, perhaps impossible, to be both sensitive and self-absorbed at the same time. The trick is to be able to be both, but at different times. If you want her to go down on you, for instance, ask her to. That's being assertive. But if she says no, accept the no with good grace and find out what else you two can do. If she never wants to stimulate you orally and that kind of stimulation is important to you, talk to her about it and see if something can be worked out. If she wants you to go down on her, listen to her request and do as she wants, say you don't feel like it now, or tell her what your objection is and work something out. If you want her to initiate more, you say so, but you also listen sympathetically if she tells you why this is difficult.

There can be times when sex is mainly for her and others when it's mainly for you. If it's for you, then get into your self-absorbed mode and get exactly what you want. If it's for her, then focus entirely on what she wants.

Of course there are other times when it's mainly for both of you. This requires some shifting back and forth. Perhaps you like to kiss her breasts quite hard but she likes that only after some softer touching and kissing. So you could do it the way she wants until she's ready for you to do it your way. If she likes slow and gentle intercourse and you prefer it fast and furious, you could do it her way for a while, then your way. Or there can be occasions when intercourse is done her way, other times when it's done your way. Perhaps your favorite intercourse position is from the rear or with you on top. Your partner enjoys these positions but they are not her favorites. Nonetheless, she's happy to use them mainly for your pleasure. She adjusts herself to your pace and tries to give you everything you want. You should accept her gifts and make it as pleasurable as possible for yourself. Perhaps her favorite position is her on top. Now you should accommodate yourself to her rhythm and try to give her everything she wants.

We have already started on the self-centered side by determining your conditions in Chapter 6. The next chapter deals with how to get them met and how to be assertive in your communications. Then there is a chapter on what women want. In those chapters and in most of the ones that follow, I switch back and forth between the two poles of sexual happiness: assertiveness and sensitivity. I realize it's a bit of a balancing act (both for you as reader and me as writer, as well) for all of us in real life. But it is a balancing act that must be mastered if we are to have truly wonderful sex.

6. Understanding, accepting, and appreciating sex differences. Perhaps the main reason that being sensitive to your partner is difficult is that she is not only a separate and unique human being, and therefore in some respects not like you, but also because the two of you belong to different cultures.

Of course, one of the greatest attractions women have for us is that they are different. They are small where we are large, soft where we are hard, curvy where we are flat, and they have an orifice where we have a protrusion. But they differ from us in other ways as well, and these differences often drive us crazy, and does the same to them. Since the beginning of time, men and women have been exasperated and frustrated in trying to understand and deal with each other.

Men complain: Why are women so emotional and such nags? Why do they want to talk so much? Why are they so weird about sex? What in God's name do they want? Is there any way to satisfy them? From women come a different set of grievances: Why are men so withholding? Why are they so focused on sex and so unromantic? Why can't they remember a birthday or anniversary? From both men and women come the cry: "Why can't they be more like us?" The common phrase "the war of the sexes" indicates the strength of our feelings.

One could easily get the impression that men and women are totally different, as this man's statement implies: "If the first space visitor arrived from Mars, and was male, I'd have more in common with him than with any woman on Earth." In fact, because we are all humans, we are more similar than different. We all breathe air, sleep, eat, eliminate, use language, think, and feel. If it were possible to quantify everything, we would probably conclude that women and men are 90 percent similar. But it's that remaining 10 percent that causes all the trouble.

Even in something as fundamental as the use of language, there are differences between the typical man and the typical woman. Sex therapist Victor Barbieri sums it up this way: "Men and women use the same words but speak different languages." As Deborah Tannen demonstrated in her *You Just Don't Understand*, the definitions of even simple terms like talk and conversation depend heavily on whether you are a she or a he. And clearly men and women don't necessarily have the same things in mind when they use words such as *relationship, love, sex*, and *intimacy*.

We saw in Chapter 1 that girls and boys specialize in different areas. Boys learn to achieve and perform in the outside world, while girls get more practice dealing with feelings, communicating, and relating.

We also saw that males and females come to sex from different perspectives—girls approaching via love and sensuality, boys more from lust and a desire to prove themselves. While men and women both want love and sex, they have separate styles of loving and being sexual.

It is these separate styles that justify thinking of men and women as representing different cultures and that result in no end of misunderstandings, confusion, and conflicts. Here is a common example:

> HE: "Everything between us was so tense after our spat on Sunday. I thought if we made love, things would get better."
>
> SHE: "How can we make love? We haven't talked in days."

The differences between the sexes affect our perceptions and understandings of ourselves, our partners, and our relationships and can make us feel bad about all three. It helps enormously to understand and accept these differences. The more you understand and accept your male tendencies, the better and less guilty you'll feel. The more you understand that your partner is acting as she is not because she wants to thwart you, not because she's neurotic, and not necessarily because of anything you've done, but simply because this is the way women tend to be, the better you'll feel both about her and about yourself.

I now turn to some of the main differences between men and women that can lead to misunderstandings and conflicts. Please keep in mind that I do not believe and am not saying that one way is better than another. The point is to promote understanding, not to pass judgment. There are, of course, exceptions to every single item. But the existence of an exception, or even many of them, does not necessarily invalidate a rule.

• *Men have a distinctive style of expressing love.* A man feels he is showing love by working to support his partner, spending time with her (watching TV, playing tennis, walking, taking trips, or whatever), having sex, giving her help and advice when she has problems, and doing chores like fixing the car and the back door. This type of loving has been given the label "side-by-side intimacy." With the exception of sex, it's the same kind of closeness men have with one another. Shared activities, not personal discussion, is the main theme. Women, on the other hand, prefer what has been called "face-to-face intimacy," where personal sharing is the main theme, and this is what they do with their women friends.

Given who men are, it's not surprising that they haven't been articulate about what they're doing, but they can put it into words when pushed. A forty-eight-year-old accountant had this to say after his wife complained he never said he loved her and didn't share his feelings:

> What's so important about words? Words are cheap. It only counts when you put your money where your mouth is. Every tax season, the busiest time of my year, I spend several evenings doing taxes for all of her relatives and several of her friends. I barely know some of these people and some have complicated returns. I don't get a cent for this. I don't want to do their taxes. I wish they'd get their own accountants. I do them only out of love for my wife. Why can't she understand that's what love is?

My own father was another example of this male style of loving. Although not a tough guy, he found it difficult to express affection physically and with words to his children. When I was a rebellious student, we once had an argument about the need for and value of work. He had worked hard his whole life in his small clothing store; it required his attention fifty-five to seventy hours a week and he once went twenty-one years without a vacation. I assumed that he worked so much because he enjoyed it. At one point, I made the mistake of saying that to him. His angry retort still brings tears to my eyes.

> I see that going to college hasn't improved your understanding of people. You think I like doing this lousy work six, seven days a week, never having a day off, never being able to leave for an hour to have lunch? I hate it. I wouldn't wish this on a dog. If I had my way, I'd never go inside that store again. I do it only because I love your mother and you children and I want you to have a decent life.

I don't know if my father expressed this to my mother in this way before she died, but I hope so. What he did, and what so many men do, is out of love, but women often don't understand it that way.

In one study, when a man was told to increase his affectionate behavior toward his wife, he washed her car. He was surprised to discover that neither his wife or the researchers viewed the car washing as an affectionate act. I have related this story in a number of talks and always gotten the same reaction: Virtually all of the women in the audience have a good laugh and it's clear most of them believe the man is a dumbbell. What they fail to see, however, is that he's expressing love as he knows how to do it. Within his mental/emotional framework, it makes sense. I'm sure he had better things to do than wash her car, and washing it was a genuine act of affection. And I'm sure his wife liked having a clean car. But to her it was a favor, not an act of love.

Another example is a recent cartoon. A man is saying to a woman: "I told you I loved you when we were married twenty-eight years ago. Have you forgotten already?" There are lots of men who have a similar attitude. Like the accountant and my father, they believe what they do is more important than what they say.

Men don't understand "this constant need for reassurance" (women wanting to hear "I love you") and this continuing desire to talk about feelings. Men want to get on with life and "not talk it to death." They see women's desires not as attempts to be loving and get closer but as irrelevant, trivial, or nagging. Women, on the other hand, can't understand why their men aren't more forthcoming about their feelings and with words of affection. The result is frustration for everyone. Women feel deprived and taken for granted; men feel badgered and inadequate.

In earlier times, men's style of love was more accepted. But in our time, the female definition of love has triumphed. It is accepted by women, by the popular media, and by mental health experts as being the only real love. Face-to-face intimacy is the standard against which men are judged and, not surprisingly, they come out on the short end.

I don't have any ready solutions for this huge discrepancy in the way men and women define love. But clearly both sexes need to understand the validity of both sides. Men have to understand the value of personal talk and sharing feelings. But men also need to articulate and stand up for their style of loving. Sharing activities, including sex, can also be healthy and beneficial. The advice and practical help men offer their partners is not to be sneered at. Given who men are, having sex with their partners often is a real act of love, one of the best ways they know to give love.

The problem for men is that because how they feel and what they do is so foreign to women, they need to explain themselves. The man who washed his wife's car, for example, needed to realize that she might not see it as an act of love and find a way of explaining what washing the car meant to him. This probably would have been difficult for him, but certainly not impossible.

Before getting to the specifics of men's style of sex, I want to share several ideas with you. We men have taken a lot of heat in recent years for our attitudes about sex. We are told that we are obsessed with sex, especially sex without love and commitment, that we push too hard for it and in inappropriate ways both in new and old relationships, and that we pout when we don't get what we want. Such attitudes, we are told, are immature and maybe downright sick. But I think the criticisms themselves are wrongheaded and destructive. Males can't help having their attitudes, which are probably due at least as much to physiology as to learning. Sex, after all, is life-affirming, and there's no point in feeling bad about that.

Sex is not only life-affirming, but life itself. I find it fascinating that so many people who take such great joy and pride in the birth of a new child find it so hard to acknowledge, let alone celebrate, what made that new life possible. But a sperm-shooting penis in a vagina is exactly what it took. If we felt better about sex, we might find male attitudes easier to accept.

I think there's a lot to be admired in men's, especially boys' and young men's, attitude toward sex. They are wonderfully curious, enthusiastic, and exuberant about it, and they're willing to pay enormous prices to pursue the subject.

A number of times, I have watched a group of two, three, or four boys at a bookstore looking at *Playboy* or *Penthouse*. The only word that comes to mind to describe what I saw is *charming*. There's something truly wonderful about it, a lot of what I'd call good energy. I rarely sensed any disparagement of women. The same was true in my high school days when we boys passed around novels with explicit sexual descriptions. Desire, curiosity, and great enthusiasm, but really no ugly feelings toward girls or women. With testosterone virtually running our minds and bodies, we wanted to learn everything we could about the doing of sex, and we looked forward with great excitement and anticipation to the acts themselves.

What does present a problem is that the girls these boys pair up with are coming from a different place. While most boys report mainly positive feelings about their first sexual experience—at least relief that they finally had it—many girls don't feel so good about it. It's as if sex happened to them while they were thinking of something else. The boys feel good because they got something they wanted. The girls, on the other hand, don't feel as good because they aren't sure they wanted to do what they did. Perhaps it is true, as so many parents and others have charged, that we ought somehow to stop boys and young men from putting so much pressure on girls and young women. But there's an equally valid case to be made for allowing females to take a more lively interest in sex. Why should girls and women who are sexually active have to worry about their reputations, when boys and men don't? But making this kind of change assumes that we really believe willing participation in sex is life-affirming and healthy.

• *Sex is very important to men.* Males spend more time thinking, dreaming, and fantasizing about sex than females. They start to mastur- bate earlier and they do it more often. Many of them are willing to pay for sex and some will even use force to get it, neither of which is common among women. In Shere Hite's survey of male sexuality and in a number of other studies, men's major sexual complaint was that women didn't want sex as much as they did. In the Hite survey, this complaint held regardless of age and whether the men were single or married.

In general, sex seems less important to women. They aren't consumed by it, get along easier without it, and can even shut off interest at times. While men not in relationships complain constantly about missing sex, many women who aren't in relationships hardly think of sex at all. A woman I know once complained after a period of months without a relationship that she was so touch-deprived she could hug a tree. No man who was deprived of physical contact with a woman for months would put it quite like that.

• *For men, sex has intrinsic value.* Both men and women prefer sex in a loving relationship. But men also tend to view sex as a good thing in and of itself, regardless of whether it's part of a loving relationship or if the participants have any other feelings for each other. For most women, sex devoid of some kind of relationship and close feelings is not appealing.

In one study, 85 percent of the college women surveyed said emotional involvement is a prerequisite for engaging in sex "always" or "most of the time," whereas 60 percent of the men said "sometimes" or "never." In response to being asked what would be the primary reason for refusing to have sex, all of the women answered "too soon in the relationship" or "not enough love/commitment." Forty-six percent of the men said they would never refuse to have sex.

Even more impressive data come from a study of responses of college students to sexual invitations from strangers. Male and female confederates of the experimenters approached members of the other sex on campus with these words, "I've been noticing you around campus. I find you to be very attractive." This was followed by one of three questions: "Would you go out with me tonight?" "Will you come to my apartment tonight?" or "Would you have sex with me tonight?" Fifty percent of both males and females who were approached agreed to go on a date. Only a few women agreed to go to the male confederate's apartment, and not one agreed to sex. But over 70 percent of the men who were approached—almost three out of four—agreed to have sex.

This difference is well illustrated in comparing pornographic books and movies, written primarily by men and which women rarely buy or see, with erotic romance novels, written primarily by women and which men rarely buy or read. In the material men like, plots are flimsy and character development and relationships virtually nonexistent. Pornography focuses on orifices, organs, and positions. But romance novels are about love and romance. There is sex, sometimes spelled out graphically, but sex with love, not just the conjunction of body parts.

- *Men use sex as a way of getting close (of showing love).* This sounds like a contradiction to the point above, but both are true. Sex can be only a physical expression for a man, with little feeling except the erotic behind it, but it can also be a way of being loving or of trying to get closer and deeper. Many men report that they do feel loving during and after sex, and some say they are able to be more emotionally expressive after sex. And many men, as in the example given earlier, will try to use sex to close the gap after a period of estrangement.

This, of course, is different from how women usually go about things. For them, talking, touching, and feeling close come first, then maybe sex. It can help a man to understand that this is women's preferred style, and maybe he can even say something about it ("I know you'd probably like to talk now, but I think I would feel more like talking after making love").

• *Men sexualize all sorts of situations and behaviors.* Because sex is so important to men, they tend to see sex and sexual invitations everywhere, often much to the surprise or even shock of the recipients of their attentions. Many women are amazed at how often men—whether strangers, friends, or even lovers—take a friendly hug, a revealing outfit, a sexual joke, or agreement to go on a date as meaning they want sex.

Although women are often quite aware of their effect on men, at other times they seem totally unconscious of it. For a man, cleavage, a short shirt or tight sweater, or a jiggle under a shirt is absolutely riveting. We cannot not look, cannot not get aroused. And then many men make a leap. They tend to project their own feelings onto potential partners. If a woman looks sexy to a man, if she turns him on, and especially if she's dressed or acting in a way he takes as provocative, he assumes that she is feeling sexy, too. She must be interested; otherwise, she wouldn't have worn what she's wearing or act the way she's acting, because obviously she must be aware of the effect it is having. In reality, it often turns out that she is *not* feeling sexy.

Men need to understand that how a woman looks to them and the effect she is having on them may have nothing to do with how she feels.

• *Men tend to get aroused by aspects of female anatomy that they see.* Although the human species generally depends heavily on sight, and although women are also capable of being aroused by what they see, this is more common with men. Male fantasies, for example, include more visual content than do female fantasies, and men tend more to focus on minute details of their fantasized partner's physical appearance.

One young and articulate woman put quite clearly the differences between men and women:

I've gotten to know about men from my older brothers and three boyfriends and, I swear, we're from different planets. They see a pair of legs or boobs they like and that's it. They're turned on and ready to go. They don't care if she's a nice person, if they like her beyond what they see, or if they'd want to be with her longer than screwing would take.

I'm not like that and neither is any woman I know. Sure, I can get interested and enthusiastic if I see a good-looking guy, but the interest isn't mainly sexual. I like some male bodies better than others, but there's no kind of body or body part that in itself can make me want sex. I have to get to know the man and see what else is there. If I keep getting stuff I like, then I start to turn on.

Women are far less likely to be aroused by, or even interested in, naked male bodies than men are by naked female bodies. *Playgirl* and *Viva* (now defunct) found out that their women readers simply didn't have much interest in pictures of men with their penises hanging out.

I realize that in recent years women have enjoyed going to clubs where men engage in stripteases for them. But women go for different reasons and have different reactions than men. It's true the women have a good time. But for them it's a "fun night out with the girls" (a phrase that came up in almost every report I heard) that has very little to do with sex. None of the women I talked to got sexually aroused. One woman said: "It was wonderful, very entertaining, hooting and hollering and being coarse." In response to the question of whether she got sexually aroused, her surprised response was, "Why would I?" This is not the answer one would expect from a man at a strip show.

Perhaps because of their visual orientation, men generally prefer young, physically attractive women. In sexual materials that appeal to men, the women are almost without exception young and beautiful. Women seem more flexible with respect to age and physical characteristics. In romance novels, for instance, the hero is often older, sometimes much older, than the woman. Other qualities, such as those that indicate the man might be a good mate and provider, seem more important.

• *Men are more likely to be sexual initiators.* Simply put, men go after sex and in a variety of ways. They're willing to put up with rejection, to pay for it (prostitution and massage parlors), to lie and sometimes use force, and to take on commitments and responsibilities they might not really want in order to get it. In virtually all cultures we know of, and in every era, men initiate and women accept or reject.

Without male initiations, there is much less sex. Lesbian couples, for example, have far less sex than heterosexual couples. It's not necessarily that lesbians want less sex—in one study of sex in different kinds of couples, over 80 percent of the lesbians said they wished there was more sex—but it can be difficult to get without a man going after it.

Men complain regularly that women don't initiate sex enough. But it helps to realize that women may feel less comfortable than men in doing this. It is certainly true that women send out signals that they are available and interested, but women are far less likely to actually say they want sex or to make a physical move that says the same thing.

One of the main sources of the anger and resentment that men have against women has to do with what the men perceive as sexual withholding. This is one place where many men feel quite powerless. They believe that sex is good—after all, God, Nature, or some other powerful entity put it into place—and that women make them jump through too many hoops and suffer too many rejections in order to get it. Men don't like to feel like beggars, and although they have learned to deal with rejections over the years, they don't particularly like being rejected. And it all seems so pointless and stupid to them. Why turn down an invitation for a good time?

• Men tend to view sexual arousal as a runaway train; once in motion, it should not be stopped or deflected until it reaches its destination. Males get very upset when they are not allowed to find culmination (partner sex finishing in orgasm) after becoming aroused. Some nasty scenes occur with men claiming that women have led them on when the women have wanted to stop the sexual events from progressing further or when they haven't wanted to have sex at all. Some of the male statements are undoubtedly intended to play on the woman's guilt and to manipulate her into doing more than she wants. But whether or not there is such an intention, there does seem to be a strong male attitude of "If you don't want to play, you shouldn't look or act like you do" or "Don't start anything you don't intend to finish."

Women tend to have a somewhat different attitude. They do not feel the same urgency about sex. Many are accustomed to being aroused without orgasm and many feel sex is, or should be, a process that can be interrupted by either party at any point.

• Men tend to get aroused quickly. Given a sexual stimulus, men will say sooner than women that they are ready for explicit sexual activity. For many men, erection is all they think they need. As soon as they have one, they're ready for intercourse or some other sexual act. For women, however, being lubricated does not necessarily mean a readiness for intercourse or even genital touching. This difference commonly leads to problems with the man pushing for genital fondling and even intercourse before the woman feels interested or ready.

• *Men are goal-oriented in sex.* As mentioned earlier, women tend to see sex as part of a larger context. The emotional context is crucial, but another important component of this context or process is touching. They like touching of all sorts. It's a way of expressing many things—caring, support, love, lust—and they like to be touched here, there, and everywhere. They tend not to like immediate and exclusive concentration on genitals. In a study of sexual fantasies, women were much more likely than men to focus on nongenital caressing and touching and much more likely to take their time getting to explicit sexual activity. Women see no reason for hurrying through a pleasurable experience. If it feels so good, why not prolong the pleasure?

Women are perturbed that touching is so often seen as sexual by men. As one woman put it: "I'd like to just snuggle sometimes without him thinking we have to go on to sex. Why do men take every kind of physical contact as a sexual advance?"

Men are a bit different in the touching department. They often view touching as merely a means to an end, and go for the genitals and orgasm as quickly as possible. A lifelong bachelor summed up this difference like so: "I've concluded that in sex women are more interested in the foreplay and afterplay, while men, or at least this man, is more interested in what happens between those two events."

Sometimes it seems to women that men are focused on orgasm to the exclusion of all else. Although today's woman tends to like orgasm as well, it's not the be-all and end-all for her that it is for a man, and she can enjoy sex without it. But many men can't accept this—largely, I think, because they themselves don't enjoy sex much except for orgasm.

It's not that men don't enjoy touch—after all, many men adore having their backs and necks rubbed—but in sex they often just forget about it in their haste to get down to business and orgasm. But this is an area in which change is relatively easy. Many men have learned to touch more and to enjoy it more.

• *Men tend to orgasm quickly and easily.* One reason that men like sex so much is that their gratification—defined here as having an orgasm with a partner—is virtually assured. Only a small number of men have problems having orgasm in partner sex. For women, on the other hand, difficulties reaching orgasm are the main sexual complaint.

Part of the discrepancy is explained by the fact that the traditional script, where intercourse is the main event, favors men. This is a way in which men come easily, but most women do not. However, this does not explain the whole situation. Even with oral or manual stimulation, men orgasm more quickly and easily than women. It's almost comic that so many women fear taking too much time, while so many men fear not taking enough.

• *Men don't necessarily want to be emotionally or physically close after sex.* Although this seems to be changing, there still is a difference between men and women. For some men, the problem is that they aren't sure what to do. They have a script for sex, but not for after sex. Others are uncomfortable with so much closeness. For others, it's more the case that since sex was all that was wanted, now that it's over there's no point in hanging around. For women, however, since sex is usually seen as part of an emotional connection, the connection should continue after sex is done.

• *Men are concerned with sexual performance.* It makes sense that those who see sex as a performance should worry about not being able to perform adequately. This is not to say that women don't also have sexual worries. They do. But women have a different perspective than men. They tend not to see sex as primarily a performance, despite the pressure for them to perform in certain ways, to lubricate and have orgasms, and they have fail-safes—artificial lubricant, the ability to have inter-course even when not aroused, and the ability to fake orgasms—that most men don't.

By and large, men don't have any fail-safes. The lack of erection is obvious, as is quick ejaculation. Given who men are and what they learn, it's not surprising they are greatly concerned about performance and greatly distressed by the lack of it.

It can help men to realize that most women are less concerned about a man's performance than they are to his reaction to it and to her. Women are more likely to get upset about the man's negative reaction to a performance problem (anger, guilt, constant apologies, withdrawal) than to the problem itself.

• *Men are interested in a variety of sexual partners for the sake of variety.* This notion is well captured in the old saying, "So many women, so little time." I recently had lunch with a colleague who has an incredibly gorgeous and sexy wife. We got to talking about what we fantasize about, and this is what he said: "It sounds crazy, but I always fantasize about other women, even fat women and old women. They don't have anything she doesn't have except one thing: They're not her." It's hard for a man to see an attractive woman without wondering what she'd be like in bed and without wanting to find out. Many prostitutes and call girls report that a significant portion of their clientele consists of happily married men who come to them only for some variety. And men are more likely than women to have affairs, and not necessarily because something is lacking at home, except for a variety of partners. Men are more promiscuous even in their fantasies. In one study of college students, 32 percent of the males, but only 8 percent of the females, reported that they had had sex with over one thousand different partners in their fantasies. Men also are far more likely than women to switch partners during a fantasy.

• *Men don't like to admit to sexual problems, especially their own.* Women are much more ready to admit ignorance, to find fault with their own behavior, and to look for ways of making things better. Compare women's magazines with men's. The women's magazines have articles on improving sex and fixing problems in virtually every issue. *Playboy* and *Penthouse* almost never have such articles. Since so much rides on a man's being good, or at least adequate, in sex, it's very difficult for men to hear they have a problem in this area.

A lot of these differences are things that both sexes have taken heat about. Women are often criticized by partners for their relative lack of interest, not initiating enough, wanting too much foreplay, and taking too long to get aroused or to orgasm. Men have been scolded for every single item on the list. I think the criticism is unfortunate and gets us nowhere. In a sense, everyone is doing what comes naturally, whether naturally be defined as what's built in or what's been learned over the years.

While it is true that we have to learn to accommodate to each other, I don't think blame and accusations or feeling guilty is going to help. We have to feel good about ourselves to have decent relationships and sex. A man should not have to feel guilty for looking at or fantasizing about younger women, for desiring sex without love, or anything else that he is or feels. But neither, on the other hand, should he denigrate his partner. It's fine if you have fantasies about the college girl next door, but it's something else if you make comments about her in front of your lover that imply your lover is inadequate. It's fine if you sometimes want a quickie—perhaps you can arrange it with your partner—but it is not fair to complain that you can't have them all the time or that she takes too long to turn on.

The male ways of expressing love and sex are really OK. And so are the female ways. The better we understand and feel about ourselves and each other, the more likely we will be able to make the changes we desire in our sex lives and elsewhere.

---8

The Power of Asserting Yourself

"I know I'm supposed to be able to assert myself—that's what men do, right?—but I've never been good at it."—MAN, 33

"I'm fine at the office and in public. No trouble saying what I want. But at home, especially in bed, it's like I'm mute. I don't know what I want and can't express it even when I do."—MAN, 42

"All my life I've gotten into trouble because of my pushiness. People get turned off by how I try to get my way."—MAN, 64

"My problem is that I'm aggressive but not assertive. I let things slide for a long time and then explode in rage and bitterness, which is quite difficult on those I do it to."—MAN, 47

BEING able to express and go after what you want—meeting your conditions—is an absolute essential if you want good sex. This is supposed to be something men are skilled at, but I've not been impressed with the ability of men to get, or even to express, what they want in personal relations.

Of course, no one ever gets everything he wants, and all of us must compromise and sometimes do things we aren't thrilled with. But an

171

assertive person expresses his desires and tries to get what's right for him. He does not regularly go along with a situation not to his liking or express his anger in inappropriate ways.

I have certainly seen men act aggressively, intimidating and bullying their partners. They sometimes get their way, of course, but they cause immense damage to their relationships and aren't happy with what they get; they recognize at some level that it wasn't given freely. Although most onlookers would agree that these men have lots of power in their relationships, I have yet to meet one who felt powerful. They often feel just the opposite, powerless.

> Hank comes on very strong. He doesn't ask, he demands. His girlfriend often has sex with him—and does other things as well— when she doesn't want to, because there doesn't seem to be a choice. The result is that she's turned off sexually and has been seriously thinking of leaving. And Hank isn't happy with the sex he's been getting. He wants a more enthusiastic partner. Yet he has difficulty understanding that the way he expresses himself is a turnoff to her.

Other men are sensitive and empathic, but they are not strong or assertive. They don't seem to have much energy, enthusiasm, or skill for getting their own needs met. They are similar to aggressive men in that they feel no sense of control in their relations with women.

> Roger often wanted sex with his wife, but he rarely got it because he carefully considered her mood and situation before suggesting it to her. If she seemed tired or busy, if she said she had a rough day, if she was reading a book or watching TV—if any of these things was the case, he didn't initiate sex. Needless to say, Roger felt frustrated a lot of the time. Even when he had sex, he didn't get what he wanted. He accepted whatever his wife offered and never brought himself to tell her that he wanted something else.

To help you determine if you need help with assertiveness, consider the following questions:

- Can you tell your partner that you need more time for yourself (to be with your friends, read, exercise, or whatever)?

- Can you tell her you want to spend more time with her?
- Can you let her know that you'd like to spend your next vacation differently than you have in the past?
- Can you let her know about something she's done or not done that upsets you?
- Can you let her know that you are not in the mood for sex even though she is?
- Can you let her know clearly when you do want sex?
- Can you tell her that you don't want intercourse but would like some other form of sex?
- Can you indicate clearly exactly what kind of acts and stimulation you want?
- Can you let her know that certain feelings are getting in the way of your sexual interest, arousal, or functioning?
- Can you ask her how she likes to be stimulated?
- Can you say clearly that you want to stop in the middle of a sexual event?
- Can you initiate a conversation with her about things in your sex life that you'd like to be different?
- Can you maintain your point of view when she disagrees with it?
- Can you, when there is disagreement, understand the validity of her position as well as your own and work toward a resolution that satisfies both of you?

If you answered yes to some or all of these questions, I have another one for you. Can you say and do these things in ways that do not leave her feeling blamed, disliked, humiliated, or undesirable? If you can honestly answer yes, you are one of the fortunate few. These are situations that men find difficult to handle. If you have trouble with any of these items, you could benefit from developing your assertiveness skills, to get more of what you need and not go along with things that make you uncomfortable, and to do so in ways that do not intimidate or crush your partner.

Assertiveness is not rudeness, bullying, or aggression. Being assertive does not mean that you won't consider your partner's needs or satisfy her. It does mean, however, that you are going to pay serious attention to your own needs. It does mean that you will express your desires directly and try to get what you want.

So often in sex today the situation is that each partner is focused primarily on satisfying the other one. Each is looking out for the other, and neither is taking care of his or her own needs. A lot of mind reading and guesswork is involved. No one wants to appear selfish, which we've all been taught is a very bad thing. While such altruism may sound virtuous, the result is usually somewhat less than satisfying for both participants. If both could start paying more attention to getting their own needs met—a little selfishness, if you like—sex would be much better for both.

When people become more assertive, they tend to get more of what they want and to be happier as a result. One additional benefit in sex is that more assertive people are more turned on, which feels good not only to themselves but to their partners as well.

THE ISSUE OF ENTITLEMENT

Some men don't feel they have the right—that they are entitled—to get what they want. This has been said before, but usually about women. The fact is that many men have exactly the same problem. Part of this comes from the performance or work ethic: A man is someone who does what he's supposed to do. No one said that taking time for yourself or enjoying yourself was part of being male. Now that we have a new rule in sex—the man's primary job is to satisfy his partner—there's an additional reason to focus on her enjoyment rather than your own.

You have every right to be assertive. You have every right to try to get your relationship as you want it and to try to have sex when you want, where you want, and how you want—provided, of course, that you go about this in ways that honor your partner and allow her to have her own preferences and opinions.

If you think this sounds self-centered or selfish, ask yourself why. Why don't you have the right to say what pleases you? What's selfish about that? What's wrong with a man telling his partner that he'd like to go out more (or less) with friends, that he'd prefer to vacation in the mountains this year instead of Hawaii, that he'd like sex on the floor (or on the sofa or in the car), that he'd like this kind of stimulation or that?

See if you can get yourself into a mind-set where you realize that being assertive is not only not bad, it's good for you, your partner, and your relationship. In the traditional model of masculinity, assertiveness was a given; it was assumed a man would stand up for himself and get what he needed. I think this is one part of the old model we need to keep. There's very little to say against it and a great deal in its favor. Notice that many women are trying to be more assertive. I think that's good for them and for us. But we need to respond with our own assertiveness. That way, each of us can look out for himself or herself and the other, thus creating assertive and healthy relationships.

"I JUST CAN'T DEAL WITH HER"

An important reason that men aren't assertive in their relationships is that they simply don't know how to deal with their partners. Here are two examples.

> No matter how I put it, whenever I say that I want something, she takes it as a criticism and cries. I can't handle that, so I try to comfort her and get things back to where they were. I either forget what I was trying to get or just give up on it.

> My impression is that when I've asked for something, she starts talking about something she's not getting. I feel criticized and am happy to drop the whole subject before we get into a fight.

Many of the men I work with hadn't even tried to get what they wanted. They feared the consequences illustrated in these examples and didn't want to risk finding out if they were right.

Notice that underlying both of the statements is the fear that being assertive will make matters worse. There's no question that going after what you want can make matters worse, at least for a while. But there's no necessary link here, no reason assertiveness *has* to make things worse, and certainly no reason why things should usually get worse.

"BUT I DON'T KNOW WHAT I WANT"

A great many men, in discussing assertiveness, come up with this: "I don't know what to ask for; I don't know what I want." My response is that's an interesting kind of statement to be making about yourself, saying that you don't know what you'd like to do tonight or on your day off, where you want to travel, what kind of sexual stimulation provides you the most pleasure. If you don't know the answers to the questions, you can find them. All you really need to do is pay attention and use your mind. Try different things (in your mind, if you can't try them in reality without great cost or effort) and see what feels best. That's all there is to it.

Regarding sex, you can also use your imagination to help determine the kinds of things you might like. What kinds of acts and stimulation do you use in your favorite fantasies? Do you want to try any of these with your partner? Try different things with her. You can touch her here and there, this way and that way, and get her to do the same for you. You can try this act and that one. You can try it in the living room, the dining room, the kitchen, and the hallway. Find out what you like best.

"BUT MEN ARE ALREADY TOO SELFISH"

Some women object to my thesis that men need to be more assertive. Their argument is that men are selfish and always get what they want while they (the women) don't get anything. I think the problem is that we're talking about two different groups. There's no question that some men are too self-centered, too aggressive and demanding, and barely even recognize that their partners also have needs. Hank, whom I mentioned a few pages back, is one of these men. They need to learn to be more sensitive to their partners and become more assertive rather than aggressive. But there's also no question that a great many men like Roger are far less assertive than is good for them. Both the Rogers and Hanks of this world can benefit from becoming more assertive and either less passive or less aggressive.

TAKING CARE OF YOURSELF

Asserting yourself is part of a larger idea: being good to or taking care of yourself. We men are always so busy doing our tasks and performing that we rarely take sufficient time to get what we need and enjoy, and this is directly related to the problems we have in relationships and in sex.

The following exercise will give you the opportunity to do some things that please you.

EXERCISE 8-1: DOING THINGS YOU ENJOY

This week do one or two things that you really want to do and that are fun for you. The only criteria are that you enjoy them and they not be work-related. They may or may not involve other people.

Here are some examples of what some men did with the exercise. Jake loved spending time with his two girls, although he rarely did so because he "didn't have the time." So he took them on a picnic on Sunday, followed by a children's movie. He had a ball. After years of not reading mysteries and science fiction because "they were a waste of time" (even though he really enjoyed them), Lou bought some books and started reading. Bernard took a week off from work and went alone to visit a friend in Florida with whom he had served in the army; he had long wanted to make this visit, but didn't because he felt it wasn't fair to leave his wife for a week. James, who loved children although he didn't have any, volunteered for a community organization that helped tutor disadvantaged kids.

Your activities may or may not be similar to these examples. As long as you enjoy them, you're doing the right thing.

Do one or two enjoyable things per week as long as you follow the programs in this book. I hope you'll continue taking time for yourself long after you have forgotten this book.

ASSERTING YOURSELF WITH YOUR PARTNER

The next exercise, developed by sex therapist Lonnie Barbach, is the best I know to help you learn to assert yourself in a variety of situations.

EXERCISE 8-2: YES'S AND NO'S

Yes's: A Yes involves attempting to get something you want from someone, which you ordinarily would not allow yourself to ask for. The assignment lies in the request, not the response. Even if your request is rejected, you have done a Yes by asking. Examples of Yes's are: asking someone to give or loan you something, like a ride, a book, record, or money; asking someone to spend time with you or listen to something you want to say; asking for a certain type of date or sexual activity.

No's: A No is a refusal to do something that you don't want to do but ordinarily go along with. If you habitually loan money to a friend not because you want to but because you fear what he will think of you if you refuse, turning him down would be a No.

We all do many things we don't want to do. Some of them are necessary since the consequences of not doing them are serious (like not paying your bills). But there are many other things we don't like that we don't have to put up with. The No's will give you an opportunity to turn some of them down. Being able to say no is crucial in sex: Going along with things you don't like in sex is one of the best ways not to get turned on and to lose interest in the whole subject.

Before doing Yes's and No's, it's a good idea to read the next section on principles of assertive communication.

SUGGESTIONS FOR DOING YES'S AND NO'S

1. Do two Yes's and two No's the first week, then three of each per week. As you do them, you'll discover what is easy and what is difficult. Since there is no benefit in endlessly repeating easy items, gradually include more difficult ones.

2. Start with items that are easy, even trivial, and gradually work up to ones that are more difficult. Since sex is a hard issue for many men, don't do sexual Yes's and No's until you are comfortable doing them in other areas.

3. Use your common sense. There are situations in which the consequences for being assertive may be serious. Don't get too assertive if an armed thief demands your money.

4. Continue doing Yes's and No's until you feel confident of being able to get what you want in sex. This may take anywhere from four to twelve weeks. Since this exercise takes only a few minutes a week, it is simple to do while you continue with other exercises in the book.

POSSIBLE PROBLEMS

1. You try to do too much too soon, the most common problem in doing this exercise. Remember to start with relatively easy items. Since this is an important exercise, do it in a way that will allow you to progress and feel good about it.

2. **You feel bad about being rejected. You will undoubtedly get turned down some of the time when doing Yes's. If you are getting rejected almost every time, this means you are asking for too much or from the wrong people, or in such a way that defeats your aim.**

3. **You feel guilty about being assertive. For most men, guilt diminishes in frequency and intensity as they get more practice using their assertive skills. It can also help to reread the section on entitlement on page 174.**

The Yes's and No's exercise will provide you with many chances to try different approaches to getting what you want and evaluate their effectiveness.

PRINCIPLES OF EFFECTIVELY ASSERTING YOURSELF

I realize my list of principles is long and some of them are not easy to apply. Nonetheless, the more of them you can incorporate into your communications, the better your chances of getting what you want.

1. *Determine what your goal is or remind yourself of it* before you say anything, or anytime you realize the discussion isn't going well. Knowing that your goal is to reestablish harmony with your partner after a spat or to have more sex will help keep you on track and away from war games and other side issues that will get you nothing of what you want.

2. *Treat the person you're talking to with kindness and respect.* This means not making demands, not calling her names, and not demeaning her in any way. People are much more likely to be able to hear your side and do what you want when they feel treated fairly.

3. *Don't talk when you're angry.* This is a controversial point. Many therapists encourage people to get their anger out whenever possible. But, as Carol Tavris documents in her wonderful book *Anger*, unleashing anger doesn't work. When people talk in anger, they say provocative and stupid things and therefore encourage the listener to respond in kind. War games are quickly established and everything goes to hell in short order.

You have every right to talk about what's bothering you, but you have a much greater chance of being heard and getting all or some of what you want if you wait until you're not in the heat of anger and can talk civilly. Until then, it's best to keep your mouth closed, which, I hasten to add, is not the same as sulking.

4. *If you want to discuss a problem or make a complaint, ask permission to do so.* "I'd like to talk about what happened at the dinner. Is that OK?" Or, "I didn't like something that happened yesterday. Is this a good time to bring it up?" If this isn't a good time for the other person, ask when would be.

5. *Start off on as positive a note as possible.* "I love you," "I love making love with you," or "We have a good marriage." It's a lot easier for your partner to hear a complaint or criticism if you've started with something more positive.

6. *Show your understanding of and empathy for the listener's position to whatever extent possible.* "Given what happened with Tim [her last boyfriend, who left her because of sexual incompatibility], I can understand your reluctance to talk about sex. I know it's difficult and scary. But I think we have to go into this." The more she feels her position is understood, the less need she will have to explain, defend, or justify herself.

7. *Focus on your feelings and desires rather than hers.* "I'd feel more loved if we had more sex" instead of "You never want sex" or "You don't like sex." This is the "I language" that's been promoted so vigorously by communication experts in recent years. Saying "I feel this" and "I'd like that" is less likely to make the listener feel defensive than statements such as "You do this" and "You're responsible for that."

8. *Talk about what you want instead of what's wrong or what you don't want.* You may have to mention what you don't like, of course, but it's important not to get stuck on it because doing so can make the listener feel blamed. The quicker you can get to what you'd like in the future and the more you focus on it, the better the chances of having a reasonable conversation and getting what you want.

Another way of stating this idea is don't blame and don't accuse. One clue to accusations is the frequent use of *you* followed by absolutes: phrases like *you never* or *you always.* Try to avoid them. Another clue to blaming is telling your partner what she thinks or feels in a negative way; for example, "You're afraid of intimacy," "You don't care about me," or "You're being irrational." Moralistic judgment or name-calling is yet another clue to blaming. Watch for words like withholding, compulsive, hysterical, neurotic, sick, prude, slut, and so on. Blaming and accusing almost invariably lead to counter-charges and defensiveness, exactly what you don't want.

Another kind of blaming is bringing up the past. If you're complaining about your partner being late yesterday, there's no need to remind her that she was also late for your first date twelve years ago.

9. *Criticize the behavior that upsets you, what she does, rather than her personality or who she is.* It's much easier to hear "I get angry when you come late" than "You're an irresponsible person." It should always be clearly stated or implied that while you like or love her, you dislike a certain behavior. Of course, if it is her personality, who she is, that's bothering you, maybe you shouldn't be together.

Stick with one complaint or problem at a time. People find it easier to hear about one thing they're doing that upsets you than two or three or twenty things. The more different complaints or problems you bring up at a time, the greater the chance that your partner will feel overwhelmed and get defensive.

10. *Make it your problem rather than hers as much as possible.* It's usually a matter of perspective anyway, so why not express the perspective that's most likely to get her to listen? You may think that her lateness is a crime against humanity that would bother any sane person. But that's not the case. I know people whose partners are frequently late and it doesn't bother them at all. They take the behavior into account and bring something to read or even come late themselves. So you can use this information to make your presentation more effective. "I'd like to talk about your coming late to things. I don't know why, but it bothers me terribly [this is what I mean by making it your problem rather than hers]. I get upset when you're not here within five or ten minutes of when you said you'd be. And I go absolutely crazy when you're not here within half an hour. Is there anything we can do about this?"

Her willingness to hear you can also be increased significantly if you acknowledge your contribution to the problem (and chances are good that you did make one). Take the situation where you want to stop the name-calling the two of you have been engaging in. You might say something like "I know it wasn't right [wasn't fair, didn't help matters] to call you frigid."

11. *Be as specific as possible about what you want.* "I'd like more sex, although it doesn't always have to be intercourse" instead of "I'd like

more loving." Generalities mean different things to different people. Being specific promotes understanding.

12. *Offer alternative solutions.* If more than one thing might do it, list them. "Sometimes maybe you could just get me off quickly if you're not in the mood for intercourse, but I'm also up for quickies for both of us or petting." Having options makes the listener feel she has some control. If she doesn't like one of them, she can choose something else.

13. *Be clear how important the matter is to you.* "This means a great deal to me." This prevents the listener from thinking that the matter is trivial and doesn't have to be attended to.

14. *Indicate what you're willing to do to help.* "I'm willing to reciprocate if you tell me what you'd like." This makes it a joint effort and can make the listener feel more agreeable.

15. *Be clear that this is not a nonnegotiable demand.* Rather, it's part of a process between the two of you to work out something that's bothering you. You want to hear her reaction and see what can be done. "I want to hear your reaction" or "This is the best I can come up with now. Maybe you have some better ideas." Nonnegotiable demands make the listener feel caught in a power struggle, which will result in power plays directed at you. The more she feels that her reaction is wanted and that this is a process of trying to find a suitable solution, the more receptive she'll be.

16. *Ask for her understanding of what you've said.* Not a word-for-word repetition, but a summary of the important points. "Before you give your reaction, can you tell me what you heard? I want to make sure we agree on what we're talking about." A great deal of conflict is caused by different perceptions of the issue at hand. That is, what you said is that you want more sex, maybe once or twice a week; what she heard is that you want sex every day. Following as many of the rules given here as possible and getting her understanding of what you said will help reduce these misunderstandings.

"Something bothers me about these items. They're too nice, too considerate. I thought assertive meant being strong and really socking it to her. But you're very concerned about her feelings and reactions."

Assertiveness is not about blowing your stack or having a temper tantrum. If you're so angry that you want to explode at your partner and don't care about consequences, be my guest. Just be aware that you're going to have to pay for what you say. But whatever you do in this vein, it's not assertiveness. Being assertive is about effectiveness, about maximizing the chances of getting what you want. It is strong in that it directly puts forth your desires, but it is also considerate because by being respectful, understanding, and willing to negotiate you are far more likely to get what you want.

EXAMPLES OF ASSERTIVE COMMUNICATION

You Want Your Partner to Stop Complaining About You in Public

When the two of you are alone, you might say something like this: "I enjoy going out with you [starting with a positive statement], but I have a concern. Is this a good time to talk about it [asking permission to continue]? I really dislike it when you criticize me in front of Roger and Chris [saying what bothers you]. I don't think our finances are any of their business and I don't like airing our problems in public. I realize you may be frustrated because I haven't been eager to listen to your complaints at home [showing an understanding of her position and taking responsibility for your actions]. But I want to change that. I want to hear what's bothering you and I promise I'll listen and respond [saying what you're willing to do to help], but please, not in front of other people."

You Want to Work Something Out Regarding What Your Partner Tells Other People About You

Given that women frequently talk to their friends about intimate matters, it's understandable that your mate might share information about you or the two of you. But given that men don't tend to share this kind of information, it's also understandable that you might not like it. As one man put it: "It feels like a betrayal. What goes on between us is private and none of anyone else's business. But now I find that her best friends know all about what goes on between us, even in the bedroom."

What's needed is a compromise that honors her desire to share with her confidantes and your desire for privacy.

Here's one opening statement that could work: "I'd like us to figure out something better about what you tell your sister about me [stating the problem as a collaborative effort]. I know it's good for you to talk to her and I understand your right to do that [empathizing with her position]. But I feel bad about it. It's upsetting to think that anything I say or do isn't private. That your sister might know, without my choosing to tell her, about my deepest thoughts and feelings. It makes me feel like not telling you certain things because I'm afraid you won't keep them to yourself [clearly stating the problem from your point of view]. I don't have a solution, but I think we have to come up with something [indicating you don't have the answer but want to work one out with her]."

You Want to Figure Out What Your Partner Expects from You

Following her requests for more personal expression, you've made a concerted effort to be more expressive and believe you've made big strides. Nonetheless, she continues to complain. You're tempted to say: "What the hell do you want from me! You say I don't talk enough, so I try my best and talk more, and you continue to be on my case about it. Will you ever be satisfied?" This guarantees she'll be defensive and that things are going to get worse.

Here's a better way: "I'd like to talk about your expectations about my expressiveness. OK [getting permission]? I agree with you that I needed to say more about what's going on with me and I've worked very hard at it for the last few months. I believe I've made a lot of progress. But you still criticize me for not speaking up. That troubles me. I don't know if you don't notice the changes I've made, if the things I do say aren't exactly what you want, or if your expectations are different from mine. I'd like to get your perspective on this." You're now asserting yourself in a way that most people would find easy to listen to. Instead of attacking her, you're asking for a better understanding of what's going on with her.

You Want to Stop Feeling Neglected and Have More Time with Your Partner

YOU: "Honey, I need to talk to you about something I'm feeling, OK? I'm feeling very neglected lately. I know you love me [your acknowledgment of her love will probably prevent her from having to defend it], but it seems like you don't have much time for me. I know your job and school take up lots of time and energy, but I feel left out. I mainly see you when you're too tired to go out, too tired to talk, too tired for sex. Is there anything we can do about this? Maybe scheduling one night a week when I'd have you all to myself with no homework and no calls to return." This is a concise statement of the problem from your point of view. It says clearly what you're feeling, shows an understanding of her position, and suggests a possible solution for her consideration.

You Want More Time Alone

Balancing time together and time alone is tricky for many couples. Individuals vary considerably, with some needing more alone time and some needing more togetherness, and it's usually the case that the partners in a relationship don't have exactly the same requirements. Making the necessary adjustments and compromises takes both assert-iveness and consideration. Here's how a conversation might start if you've decided you need more time alone and you're concerned about your partner's reaction:

YOU: "I'm having a problem I'd like your help with [making it your problem and asking for help, good ways of disarming defensiveness]. I realized I'd like to go fishing by myself, but I'm concerned you'll hear that as negative, as meaning I don't want to be with you."

HER: "Well, I do."

YOU: "I was hoping there's a way I could talk to you about it so you wouldn't take it that way. Last week I saw some kids fishing. Reminded me of how much I used to enjoy it. After a few hours being by myself in the sun, I used to feel so peaceful and relaxed. I was sad that I haven't been fishing in years, that I haven't had that wonderful feeling. I'd like to have it again." Given the non-threatening way you have put this, it's going to be difficult for her to feel angry or negative about the request.

You Want to Feel Better About Oral Sex

YOU: "I'd like to talk to you about a problem I'm having with sex [making it your problem]. OK? I know you don't like to swallow my come [acknowledging her position], but I feel terrible when you immediately grab the towel and spit it out. It makes me feel dirty and rejected. I'm not asking you to swallow [saying this will probably prevent her from having to defend her unwillingness to swallow], but I'd like to work out something that wouldn't feel so bad."

You Want More Feedback in Sex

YOU: "We've kidded around about how quiet you are in sex, but there is something about it that bothers me. Is this a good time to bring it up? It doesn't bother me that you're not a screamer, I don't need that, but I don't think I'm being as good a lover as I could be because I'm not getting the feedback I need. It's hard for me to tell if you're enjoying what I'm doing or if I should do something else. So I often feel confused, not sure if I should continue or change. Is there any way you could let me know how what I'm doing affects you?"

You Want More Immediate Feedback in Sex

YOU: "I would enjoy sex more if I felt you really wanted me and really got off on what we're doing. I know you've told me many times how much you enjoy our lovemaking, but I'd like something different. I'd like to hear how much you're en-joying it when we're actually doing it, I'd like to feel and hear your pleasure. Some of the things you've said out of bed would mean even more to me if you said them in bed. And I wouldn't mind some of the sounds and movements you make when we're dancing."

You'd Like Your Partner to Initiate Sex More Often

YOU: "I think our sex is pretty terrific. But it would be even more terrific for me if you initiated more often. I can't describe how exciting that feels, that my woman wants me and is coming after me. Is there something we can work out about this?"

You Don't Know Exactly What You Want. All You Know for Sure Is That You've Been Feeling Out of Sorts and Want to Talk

YOU: "I've been feeling out of it—kind of down, not really excited about anything or even interested—the last week or so. It
would help if I could ramble on a bit about what's going on. OK
with you?"

Being assertive means directly going after what you want in appropriate
ways. It means avoiding the extreme position of being so passive and
compliant that you don't get your needs met and also avoiding the other
extreme of being so overbearing and aggressive that you trample over the
rights of others. The middle position of assertiveness, however, is by no
means a thin line. There are many, many ways to express appropriately
what you want and what you don't want, and you can find those that feel
most comfortable and work best for you and your mate.

9

How to Be a Good Lover for Your Partner

HAVING considered how you can go after what you want, I now turn to the other crucial issue: giving your partner what she wants. Since I don't know your partner, however, I have to deal with women in general.

Fortunately, I have found over the years that a great many women agree, at least in general terms, as to what makes a man a good lover. For this book, I thought I would interview about one hundred women on this matter (asking two open-ended questions: What makes a man a good lover? and What makes a man a poor lover?). But I stopped after only thirty interviews because the information I was getting was so redundant. Not only did these women in large part agree with one another, but their answers were similar to the ones Lynn Stanton and I obtained in a survey we did for *Male Sexuality* more than twelve years ago. And the information from both studies was similar to what I had heard in the sex and couples therapy I had done in the last twenty years and in workshops and other settings. In what follows I report on the attitudes, characteristics, and behaviors that are most appreciated by women and are most likely to satisfy them.

**HOW TO BE A SEXUAL FAILURE:
SUREFIRE TURNOFFS**

Sexual failure is easy to come by. Following all or even a few of these rules will guarantee a bad experience. Using the rules consistently will guarantee that no one will think you're a good sexual partner.

- Having the proper attitude is crucial. This attitude is that women are not to be respected or taken seriously. Don't listen to her, don't tell her about yourself, and put her down whenever possible. Regarding sex, just do your own thing and don't worry about what she might want.
- With a new partner, don't use or say anything about protection against conception and disease.
- Out of the blue, with no connection established, say something like "Wanna do it?" or "How about a roll in the hay?"
- Be as gross as possible with a partner who doesn't like such behavior or whose attitude about it you don't know: "I wanna fuck your brains out" or "Suck my cock."
- Don't let a negative response get in your way. Everyone knows that a woman really means yes when she says no. Just go on with the business at hand no matter what she says or does.
- Stay as far away as you can from tender, loving gestures and words. Gentle touches and statements like "I love you" are only for women and wimps.
- Be sure you haven't bathed for at least a day or two. Not having shaved and brushed your teeth also helps.
- Don't waste time with kissing and touching nongenital areas, but go immediately for the important parts, her breasts and crotch.
- If you have any kind of problem (getting it up or keeping it up, for example), try to hide it from her. This won't work, so you need a backup plan. When the problem becomes manifest, blame her: "This never happened with anyone else."
- Act as if you're in a hurry and she's taking too long.
- Make it clear that the only point to this whole effort is for you to get your penis inside of her as quickly as possible and then to come as quickly as possible.
- Don't listen to any suggestions or directions she gives. If your partner should indicate she needs clitoral stimulation, tell her that no other woman you've been with has needed it.
- Get her to stimulate you orally and then refuse to reciprocate.
- Since it's well known that women like pain, use lots of force in whatever you're doing. Squeeze her breasts hard. If you do her orally, rest your teeth against her clitoris or actually bite it. If you're using your finger, apply as much pressure as you can on her clitoris.
- Keep your excitement to yourself. Don't let on with words, sounds,

and movements that you're enjoying the proceedings. Keep as quiet as possible, especially when you come. Otherwise, she might get the impression that she turns you on.

- Pressure her to have an orgasm so you can feel good about your abilities. If she tells you to discontinue stimulating her or says she doesn't need an orgasm that day, act insulted and tell her she's behaving like a traffic cop.
- As soon as you've come, stop and ask her, "Dijacome?" Whether she has or hasn't, pressure her to assure you that you're the greatest stud she's ever been with. "Did the earth move for you?" and "Am I the best, or what?" are two possibilities. Whatever she says, roll over and go right to sleep or get up, get dressed, and go do something important, such as turn on the TV.

WHAT WOMEN WANT

As you read the following material, please keep in mind that I am not trying to provide a blueprint for satisfying women. No two women are exactly the same. But the following points are ones that many women agree with. Most of them are covered in greater detail in other chapters in the book. Discussing them with your partner can be beneficial. Even if she doesn't agree with some of the items, you will learn what's true for her and that's the only important thing.

- Attend to the nonsexual aspects of your relationship. Whether it's a new or an established relationship, make sure you are indeed relating. Work out disagreements and conflicts and get the good feelings going and keep them going in the rest of your life; sex will be much better. This business of relating is extremely important to women, most of whom can't have good sex without it. As a forty-two-year-old woman said to her husband in my office: "If I'm not feeling good about you or our relationship, the door to sex is closed." She did not mean this as a threat, just as a statement of fact.

- Be there. This is the old '60s idea of "Be here now." Whatever you're doing, do it. If you're talking to a woman at a party, look at her. Don't let your eyes keep roaming around the room as if you're searching for someone better. If you're having a talk or getting affectionate, don't turn on the television or keep glancing at a magazine. If you're being affectionate or sexual, don't bring up extraneous matters. Talking about sports or business does not work in the bedroom, although I've been surprised to hear how many men bring up these subjects.

> "Men are superbly attentive when they first meet you. But after we're an item, their attention span seems to reduce to four seconds except when they're working or watching sports. It's infuriating to try to talk to someone who's glancing at the TV or a paper."
> —WOMAN, 32

> "I like a man who's all there when we're together, especially in bed, really focused on us and what we're doing. I don't like guys who space out and I don't know where they are. It's like they're marching to a different drummer, and since I have no knowledge of the drummer or the beat, I feel totally abandoned. They can drum their own song when they masturbate. When they're with me, I want a duet."—WOMAN, 44

• Let her know how you feel about her. What about her do you find beautiful, striking, attractive, exciting, or sexy? Many women weep when they tell their friends or therapists how long it's been since their men paid them a compliment. The lesson is obvious. And when feelings of affection, caring, and love come up—before, during, or after lovemaking—express them.

> "I guess I know Rolph appreciates and loves me, and it's obvious he depends on me a lot, but it wouldn't hurt to have him say it once in a while."—WOMAN, 37

> "I know men are different. Sometimes they get hot and any hole in the world would do. I don't mind that Clint sometimes acts like this, but I'm grateful that most of the time he makes it personal. It's me in particular he wants to touch, me in particular he wants to be inside of. I couldn't deal with it if it was always the impersonal way."—WOMAN, 48

• Listen to her and take her words seriously, especially when she says no and when she requests a change in what you're doing. If she says she doesn't want sex tonight, or that she doesn't want to do a certain thing, make sure to guide your behavior accordingly. If she says she doesn't want you to blow in her ear, then stop blowing and make sure to remember her preference. Many women feel they don't get listened to sexually (and generally), and it drives them crazy. "I told him a hundred times I don't like him blowing in my ear, and here he is doing it again!" If there's a big conflict about what she says—for example, if blowing in ears is very important to you—then understand what she's saying, tell her your thoughts, and see if something can be worked out. But don't pretend you didn't hear her. Learn to listen; better yet, learn to enjoy listening.

Whatever you do, absolutely abide by her sexual rejections. If she says she doesn't want sex now, it's fine to try to persuade her. But this must be tempered by an ability to hear her rejections and back off. Women are enraged by men who can't take a no seriously and graciously.

> "When my husband is hot to trot, he just keeps coming on. First he tries verbal persuasion and, if that doesn't move me, he escalates: I don't love him, I don't care about his needs, that kind of thing. If that doesn't do it, he gets demanding—I have a duty to have sex with him—or tries the old his-work-will-suffer-if-he's-carrying-around-all-this-tension routine. If none of this succeeds, he stops talking to me for a week. I really hate this shit."—WOMAN, 35

> "I love sexual invitations. They make me feel desired and great. But it has to be understood that I'm free to accept, amend, or decline. With my first husband, it was never that way. There were no invitations, just demands, and, boy, did he get pissed if I didn't want to go along."—WOMAN, 41

> "I like a partner who can be sensitive to my needs while still being true to his own. I like to have my requests listened to and to not be forced into doing things I don't want. In short, I like an equal relationship rather than a one-sided one."—WOMAN, 39

• Learn to enjoy nonsexual touching and sensuality. Be willing to hug and snuggle without going on to sex. The words of a forty-one-year-old single woman ring in my ears as I write this: "Hey, if a guy can't snuggle, what's the point of having sex with him?" Experiment with bathing together, foot rubs and back-rubs, stroking and brushing hair, and so on. Your partner will appreciate it, and you'll probably find you like it as well.

> "I go for sensual guys, the ones who enjoy kissing (and not just passionate kisses), holding, hugging, and caressing. I love to touch and to be touched and I just can't be with a man who can only slap you on the back or fuck you. With a guy like that, being fucked is exactly what it feels like, and I don't need that."—WOMAN, 25

> "Affection is what I crave. Touching is important *all* the time."
> —WOMAN, age unknown

• Be honest, or, to put it differently, do not misrepresent yourself. Despite the fact that many men have lied to get sex, it is not acceptable, at least not to any women I've talked with. It's not OK to say you've had a vasectomy when you haven't, that you'll use a condom when you won't, that you love her when you don't, that you're disease free when you're not or don't know if you are, or that you're not married when you are.

Lying in order to have sex comes from the childish idea of conquest—scoring (getting a woman into bed) no matter how or what the cost. If you're not the right person for her, why not just accept that fact and move on? If the circumstances aren't right for her now, why not see what can be honestly done about them or just wait for another opportunity?

> "I want a man to level with me and let me make up my own mind. A number of men have lied, especially about not being married or involved with anyone else, and I always felt had when I found out. It's a terrible feeling. On the other side, last year on vacation I made it with a married man I met in Paris. I was charmed by him, especially his honesty. I thought it out after he told me he was married and decided I wouldn't mind spending the next two weeks with him. We had a great time."—WOMAN, 38

> "Honesty is crucial. I will never, repeat, never, see a guy again if I learn he's lied to get me in bed."—WOMAN, 25

• Take responsibility. Women appreciate men who take an interest and participate in the preparations and protections that make good sex possible. It's as much your responsibility as hers to get the children to bed, to ensure privacy, and to make sure that no unwanted conception occurs and that no disease gets passed on.

> "Some men act like they're doing you a big favor by giving you their cock for a while, so everything else is up to me. I no longer put up with that. A good lover shares the load. He asks or says something about contraception and if we decide I'll use something, he takes an interest in it and helps pay for it."—WOMAN, 31

> "That's one of the main things that attracted me to my husband. He was one of the first men I'd been with who brought up protection and had condoms with him. After I decided to go back on the pill, he offered to pay. When I asked why, he said that since I was taking them for our mutual pleasure, he wanted to do his part. Can't help but like a guy like that."—WOMAN, 40

• Start slow and gentle and away from the genitals. Aside from the rare circumstance in which the two of you are burning with desire and want nothing more than to rip off each other's clothes and get right to it, it pays to start in a more leisurely manner. Much more so than men, women like starting away from breasts and genitals and gradually working up to these areas. Learn to enjoy touching and kissing hands, arms, faces, backs, necks, and shoulders, and to be gentle about it. This is another way of saying that you should learn to initiate lovemaking in ways that are seductive to you and your partner.

> "I absolutely cannot tolerate men who go for my breasts or crotch right away. What does it take to get them to understand that's not a turn-on to me or any other woman I know? None of us are prudes by any means, but we like to move gradually into sex, not be smashed into it."—WOMAN, 36

• Express yourself sexually. Although men are supposed to be the big talkers when it comes to sex, many women say their partners rarely say or express much of anything. A great many women say that after years of being with the same men, they have no idea of what they like most in sex or if they even enjoy it. As surprising as it may sound, hundreds of women have told me that their men are so unexpressive in sex that the only way they know he's had an orgasm is when he stops moving.

So learn to express yourself. If you've been missing your lover and thinking about how much you want to kiss her, fondle her, make love with her, or whatever, tell her.

If you don't know what you like or like best, experiment and find out. I can't tell you how many women complain that they can't find out what their lovers want in sex.

> "I like for men to tell me what feels good to them and what they like for me to do sexually. It not only helps me know what to do, but it also makes it easier for me to tell them what I like."—WOMAN, age unknown

> "I try to find out by asking, but no matter what I do all he says is, 'It feels great.' It's like talking to my five-year-old; no matter what I ask, the answer is always 'Fine.' I'd like to know specifically what he most likes and doesn't like."—WOMAN, 39

Many women interpret this lack of a differentiated response to mean that the man is withholding information or that he isn't interested enough to give a relevant answer. So pay attention and express your desires and pleasure. If you like what she's doing to you right now or what she did to you yesterday, tell her. Use words, sounds, and movements to convey your enjoyment.

If you have sexual concerns, speak about them as well. Perhaps you're concerned because sex has become so infrequent or because it seems routine. Say so, and maybe the two of you can work something out.

• Take rejections gracefully and without rancor. Good lovers get rejected a lot. Your partner isn't always going to be interested in what you're interested in, and that's just a fact of life. If she's absolutely not interested in anything sexual right now, then so be it. No reason for withdrawing and pouting. There will be other opportunities.

> "I think most men need to go to an ear doctor. They have incredible trouble hearing when a woman says no to sex. I like guys who can hear no as well as other things I say."—WOMAN, 21

"Jack is a much better lover than he used to be. One way he's changed that's wonderful is that when he wants something I don't, he no longer tries to make me feel guilty. He either gives up on it or tries to interest me in something else. That's made a huge difference."—WOMAN, 55

• As already noted, be sensitive to her desires, both in and out of bed, and assertive about yours. A good lover does both. Since so many women need a relationship that feels close in order to enjoy sex, you might want to attend carefully to the following chapters that deal with relationship and communication issues.

• Take it any way you can get it. There's nothing wrong with wanting something—a new position or practice, for example—but don't get so caught up in it that you can't enjoy something else. If she doesn't want to have intercourse now, see what she is willing to do. If she doesn't want to swallow your come, see if you can enjoy oral sex without that. And if you can't have intercourse or you don't last a long time, see what else can be done. Stay flexible and be open to the possibilities.

• Don't force her to have an orgasm or to perform in any other way.

"I like a man who is being himself and lets me be who I am. That's a good lover. But some guys have a program they need me to follow. I can't quietly enjoy sex, I have to scream obscenities and carry on like women in porn movies. I don't like that kind of pressure; it makes me feel like a trained seal."—WOMAN, 40

Another way of stating this point is: Let her define her own satisfaction. Many of the women I interviewed angrily reported that some men wouldn't believe them when they said they enjoyed sex without orgasm. So the women have to put up with extra stimulation they don't want.

"Although I'm embarrassed to say it, I fake orgasms all the time. I tried being honest in the beginning and told him that I can often enjoy sex without orgasm. But he doesn't believe it. He has no problem having intercourse for endless periods of time and he won't come until I do. I don't like to keep on when I'm sore and it's no fun anymore. Since there's no way of stopping him without having an orgasm, I've become an actress."—WOMAN, 30S

• Whatever else it is, sex is for fun and a good time. No matter what happens, make sure it ends with good feelings. Even if things don't go exactly as you or she hoped, that doesn't mean you have to create a disaster. There's always another time. Make sure this encounter ends on a positive note. In other words, lighten up and have fun.

"Bob is the first man I've ever been with where sex is always good. No matter what happens or doesn't happen, no matter if he comes or I come or we both come or no one comes, we always have a good time. I can't tell you what a relief and pleasure this is after some of the experiences I had when I was single."—WOMAN, 41

"I like for men to regard sex as a fun thing, not as something real heavy."—WOMAN, age unknown

• Be adventurous and imaginative. Feel free to suggest new ways and places. If you want to do something in the backyard, in the shower, or on the beach, say so. I was surprised at how many women I interviewed brought this up: They want you to bring up fresh ideas. If you'd like her to reciprocate, let her know.

"Jimmie is great at coming up with ideas for something different. Half the time they don't work out, but it's a gas anyway. Once he wanted me to blow him in the car when we were driving to Sacramento, so I bent over and set to work, totally forgetting that we have a sunroof. It was fine until this truck driver starting honking his horn and pointing at us. I was so embarrassed I thought I was going to die. But then we laughed all the way to Sacramento."—WOMAN, 38

"I love playfulness and rule-breaking in lovemaking. Nothing sacred or orderly or sequential, just experimenting and the shared closeness it brings."—WOMAN, age unknown

• Stay awake and present after sex is officially over, at least sometimes. All the women I interviewed spontaneously mentioned the importance of togetherness after the genitals are spent. They want to cuddle, to talk, to stay connected in some way, at least for a moment or two. Even if the sex was planned as a quickie, it's important to take a little time to stay connected. Otherwise, the woman is likely to believe that, having gotten what you wanted, you no longer have any interest in her, a feeling that is certain to lead to trouble.

> "Going to sleep right away is OK sometimes, but usually I need a little loving after sex. I want to savor the experience. Makes me feel very close and peaceful in a way that sex itself doesn't."—WOMAN, 28

> "For me, the buildup and the afterwards are at least as important as the actual sex. It's just a wonderful sense of connection that I have to have."—WOMAN, 42

• Confront problems, especially your own. If some aspect of sex is problematic, don't pretend it doesn't exist. If you've lost your desire or are having trouble functioning, talk about it with as little blame as possible and do what's necessary to resolve it. If getting outside help seems necessary, then get it.

> "I don't mind if a guy has problems. Hell, we all do, and I've got my share. What I can't stand, though, is when he pretends that he doesn't or tries to blame them on me. I want to say, 'Hey, be a man. Say what's what and let's see what we can do about it.' "—WOMAN, 27

> "The only time that men's sexual problems become real problems is when the man uses it as a way of distancing himself from me by withdrawing or berating himself, refusing to accept my acceptance of the situation."—WOMAN, 52

• Inject some romance into your lives now and then. Candle-lit dinners, mood music, getting dressed up for a night on the town, celebrations of birthdays and anniversaries, and other such things can add a special something. Be aware, however, that romance has as much or more to do with how you act as with what event you arrange or what gift you bring. The women I talked to said men are more romantic during courtship than after the relationship has been established. So if you're wondering how to be more romantic, consider what you'd do if this were a second or third date, or how you'd act if you had but one night to spend with the most desirable woman on earth.

> "I think women are generally the more romantic ones and more likely to arrange quiet dinners and get-togethers. But I like a man who occasionally does the same, who says sweet nothings, who makes me feel special and loved, maybe cooks something he knows I like."—WOMAN, 35

> "I think most men are into romance by the numbers and that takes away from the meaning, at least for me. Like you see all these men lined up at candy stores on Valentine's Day; it's like a duty. Bruce is different. He remembers my birthday for sure, but it's the other things he does that are so special. Like one day last week, he came home, took me in his arms, looked in my eyes, and said he wanted me to know I was the best thing that ever happened to him. I thought I was going to melt. It meant so much. We ended up in bed and it was one of the most loving times we've ever had."—WOMAN, 39

EAT WHAT? THE IMPORTANCE AND JOYS OF ORAL SEX

No discussion of how men can be good lovers is complete without mention of oral sex. In the old days, putting your mouth on someone else's genitals was considered one of the ultimate abominations, right up there with self-abuse and anal sex. No self-respecting person would get his face or mouth on or near someone's filthy genitalia. Of course, many men liked to have someone's mouth on their penises, but apparently in Victorian times that was difficult to get except with prostitutes.

Oral sex is now in vogue, mainly because it feels so good and perhaps also because it's a lot safer than intercourse (less risk of passing on disease and no risk of pregnancy). We men know how good it feels when it's done to us. But not all men have been willing to do the same for their partners.

"Cunnilingus" is the official term for licking a woman's genitals, but it's more commonly called "going down on her" or "eating pussy." It is important for a number of reasons. Many women derive great pleasure from it and want it. For many women it's their main or only way of having orgasm. Many women also feel it's a particularly loving thing for a man to offer. Yet another reason is that women want reciprocity. If they suck your penis, they want you to lick their clitoris.

Some men have said they'd like a manual on how to do oral sex on their partners. Space limitations preclude such an endeavor, and there's also the fact that women differ so much that whatever I said would be true of some and untrue of others. Nonetheless, a few points can be made.

If you're willing to experiment with oral sex, one thing to remember is that although the clitoris is the general area you want to stimulate, many women's clitorises are too sensitive to take direct stimulation. That is, they want to be licked around it (sides, top, or bottom), but not directly on it. And of course women differ in the kinds and intensity of stimulation they prefer. The only way to determine what your partner likes best is to be guided by her reactions or to talk with her.

Although pornographic accounts of oral sex often talk about putting your tongue in her vagina, the action usually is on the outside, not the inside. That is, the man uses his tongue and lips (not teeth, however) around the clitoris and the outer lips. Some women enjoy the man putting a finger or two in their vaginas while he's licking the clitoral area, but putting a tongue inside the vagina is less common. This information may be helpful to men who have concerns about the smell of the vagina.

Speaking of which, a scent does exist, but it varies greatly from woman to woman and from time to time. Some men like the smell, some don't. It may help to keep in mind that unless your partner has a vaginal infection or poor hygienic practices, her odor shouldn't be so strong as to offend you. This is especially true when you consider that your mouth isn't in the vagina and your nose is quite far away. If you have your tongue on her clitoris, your nose will be above it, probably in her pubic hair, several inches from the vagina. Of course, pubic hair has its own fragrance (in men as well), but many men find it less objectionable than vaginal odor.

If there are concerns about odor or anything else regarding oral sex, why not talk to your partner about them? Perhaps washing before sex—

which many couples consider essential whether or not oral sex is on the menu—will help, or a dab of perfume in the general vicinity.

As with all sexual acts, it's important to get feedback on how your partner reacted to your licking her clitoral area. Unless she shows with words and acts that this was the greatest thing since the invention of chocolate, you might want to ask what she liked best and least. If she's able to give specific answers, it can cut down on a lot of guesswork.

One complaint I've received from a number of women who like oral sex is that they often feel lonely during it. Although the genital stimulation is terrific, there's no body to kiss, hold, or hug. Given the nature of the act, of course, it's a bit difficult to lick your partner's genitals and simultaneously hug her or kiss her mouth. But it can help not to get so involved with her genitals that you forget the rest of her. If it's agreeable to both of you, you can use your free hand or hands to hold her hands, stroke her belly or breasts or, depending on your exact positions and the length of your arms, touch and stroke her face and hair.

Many of the men I've talked with very much enjoy and are aroused by giving oral sex to their partners. And some of them take particular pride in how skillfully they use their tongues and the pleasure they provide. One man put it like this:

> When I first went down on a woman years ago, it was a duty, something I thought I had to do to give her pleasure. But I've gotten to enjoy it very much myself and have perfected my abilities. Although I don't get off with it, it's one of the most enjoyable acts in my repertoire. Thank God for tongues and clitorises.

Here is the report of another man about oral sex with his wife of seven years:

> I love eating her. She has her best orgasms this way, and I get something that's wonderful but hard to put in words. When my tongue is on her clit and we're holding hands and I can feel her orgasms, sometimes it's like we become joined, like I'm a part of her. It's an incredible feeling. We have a variation that's awesome. While I'm licking her, I reach a hand up and she sucks on one of my fingers, like she was giving me a blowjob. I'm licking her, she's sucking me. Wow! I can't tell you how good that feels.

_____10

What Is This Thing Called Connection and Who Needs It Anyway?

"Talking is the major way we establish, maintain, monitor, and adjust our relationships."—DEBORAH TANNEN

I HOPE it's clear by now that a man's sex life can be greatly improved by developing his willingness and ability to communicate or connect. This is not only what women want but also what almost all experts say is essential for good sex.

I think, however, that there's a lot more to it than just more or better sex. Men have a great deal to gain by becoming more expressive. Here are some of the benefits you might derive.

1. *More of what you want, more in control of your life, and better feelings in general.* A great many men are not getting their needs met in their relationships and in sex, either because they aren't sure what those needs are or because they can't express them appropriately. Not getting one's needs met leads to frustration, anger, and a sense of hopelessness. It can make a world of difference to be able to express yourself and have some control over your relationship.

Often when a couple comes to therapy, the man says he doesn't have any needs—he's just here because of his partner's complaints. But at some point, I'm able to help him look more closely at himself and it turns out there are all sorts of things he's missing. One man, for example, was very dissatisfied with his career. But he put off discussing this with his wife and doing anything about it because he feared she might not be supportive. So he continued to do work he disliked and felt very discouraged about ever being able to change. When he finally was able to talk to her, she was both understanding and supportive. Another man had some ideas about adding spice to his sex life but for years didn't bring them up with his lover because of a vague anxiety that she might not agree. The partners of such men are often shocked at what they hear: "I had no idea you felt like this. Why didn't you tell me sooner?" If you want to get more of what you want, good communication is essential.

2. *Better health.* There's a host of evidence that we men keep too much bottled up inside and pay for it with unnecessary stress and stress-related diseases and problems.

3. *An improved relationship.* Your partner will probably appreciate what you're doing and be happier as a result. Women complain more about their men's unwillingness to talk and listen than about any other thing. Fully 98 percent of the several thousand women in Shere Hite's study *Women and Love* said they wanted "more verbal closeness with the men they love." Specifically, "they want the men in their lives to talk more about their own personal thoughts, feelings, plans and questions, and to ask them about theirs." Almost every single woman I've talked to, in therapy or out, agrees.

When you do relate more, not only will you have the satisfaction of making your partner happier but you'll also reap the many benefits of being with a more contented person. Also, you and your partner will probably understand each other better and be able to work out some difficulties that previously seemed insurmountable. This will allow you to feel close and hassle free more of the time and avoid some of the blowups you've had in the past.

4. *Avoidance of serious relationship distress.* When people in relationships feel unable to connect easily and comfortably, the results are almost always unpleasant and sometimes dreadful: irritability, angry blowups, constant tension, affairs, and even separation or divorce.

When men don't listen or talk, the results can be shattering. Here's one example.

Brian had been married to Sharon for twelve years. The relationship wasn't the same as it was at the beginning, but Brian thought it was solid. Then he came home one day to find a note saying Sharon had moved out and wanted a divorce. Brian felt as if he had been hit by a thunderbolt. When he came to see me a week later, he kept repeating that he had no idea Sharon had been so unhappy. He was absolutely shocked at her leaving. As he talked, it became clear that Brian hadn't been paying attention. Sharon had countless times expressed her dissatisfaction: her desire for more time together and better communication and, in the last few years, for marriage counseling. Brian had heard her complaints—he was able to tell me about them—but they hadn't registered.

Brian isn't alone. In one study of divorce, fully 25 percent of the husbands were surprised when their wives said they wanted a divorce.

Because of the way men have been trained many of us are almost unconscious in our relationships. If you want a decent relationship and sex, it's important you learn not to be unconscious, that you learn to listen to the complaints and suggestions you get and to express your own.

5. *A better position from which to work on and resolve any sex problems you or your partner have.* Almost all sex therapists agree that before a couple can work productively on a sex problem, they need to feel close and get their relationship in as good an order as possible. Otherwise, trying to resolve the sexual problem can be difficult or impossible.

6. *Increased ability to deal with other people.* Many men report that the skills in these chapters have benefited them in dealing with their children, with people at work, and with relatives and friends.

I hope I've said enough to spark your interest. We men have a lot to gain from improving the ways we connect with the people we love. I realize that the process of accomplishing this will take time and effort and you'll feel awkward and uncomfortable at times. I wish I had a way around this, but I don't, and neither does anyone else. But from my experience, both personal and professional, I'm fully convinced the costs are well worth it.

In this and the following chapters on relating, I use both sexual and nonsexual examples. If you've understood what I've said earlier about the association between good sex and good relationships, you know why the nonsexual illustrations are here.

WHAT EXACTLY IS CONNECTION OR COMMUNICATION?

There are many ways of connecting or relating to those we care about, but the two most important—talking and listening—are the ones I'll spend the most time on in this section and are also the ones men have the most trouble with. The term that covers both of these has become one of the main buzzwords of our time: *communication*. Unfortunately, this term is used so often in so many ways that it is no longer clear what it means, so let's pin it down.

The Kind of Talking That's Required

Many women complain that men "don't talk," but of course they do. Often they talk more than women. The crucial issue is not the amount of talk, but what's talked about and how.

The kind of talk that's necessary for a good relationship and good sex is of the personal kind that conveys information about how the speaker perceives, thinks, and feels about matters of importance and relevance such as himself, his partner, their relationship, their sex, their jobs, and so on. Some examples: my desire to have sex in the morning rather than the evening, your desire that we do more things together, my feeling pressured because of your attempts to get me to open up more, my complaint that you don't give me enough feedback when we're making love, your complaint that I talk so much during sex that you're distracted from your feelings.

Men often leave the personal part out and engage in what linguist Deborah Tannen has called "report talk," talk designed solely to present new information. Instead of saying, for example, "I'm worried there might be war in the Middle East (because my son might be drafted, I might be drafted, innocent lives will be lost)," they might simply report, "Looks like there's going to be war." While the latter may have some interest to the listener, it isn't giving any personal information about the speaker's hopes, fears, or concerns.

We men are good at talking about sports, politics, money, and things (cars, computers, and so on), but we haven't had much practice with personal talking. The kinds of friendships we've had with other males since childhood revolve around activities rather than personal sharing. There's nothing wrong with this, of course, except that often the relationship goes no further than the activity itself.

Many men who do business or engage in sports together often know almost nothing about the lives of their "friends." Their togetherness focuses on what they do, not on who they are. Not long ago, I learned that a psychologist I frequently talk to about professional issues had been separated from his wife for over a year without my knowing about it. Personal matters never came up in our conversations. A more dramatic example comes from a forty-six-year-old acquaintance:

> Terry, a friend my age, died suddenly of a heart attack a few years ago. Recently, his mother died. His sister reported that at the wake several of her father's closest friends, men he played golf with almost every day, asked why Terry wasn't there. "Because he's been dead two years," she snarled. Talk about jaws dropping—including hers when she realized that Dad had never told his friends that his only son had died.

Talking from the heart may be new to many of us, but we can learn.

WHY MEN HAVE TROUBLE CONNECTING

Here are some of the main complaints and problems men have with connection and my responses to them.

"I've heard this before from women I've been involved with. It seems like you and they want to turn life into an endless talkathon."

It sometimes seems as if women want to do nothing but talk, but I've never found that to be the case in reality. I agree that life consists of a lot more than just talk, and I also know that some couples talk too much and in destructive ways. My main point, and that of the women I've heard from, is that men need to be able to listen better and talk more effectively about what's going on with them. How *much* you should talk depends on you and your partner.

Another thing to consider is that the reason women talk more than you want is usually because they feel they are not being heard. So they just keep trying over and over. One way to get less talk is to listen better right away.

"I feel it's unfair, that you're taking her side. Why can't she learn to understand me better? Why can't she see that my offering advice when she has a problem, fixing things around the house, having sex, or just watching TV together are acts of love?"

I think it would be wonderful for her to know you better, to understand how you feel when you give advice, make love, or watch TV together. But to accomplish this, you're going to have to tell her. And that's exactly what she wants and what I'm suggesting.

"But I'm not very good at talking about my feelings. I don't even know what they are half the time."

It's true that most men don't have as much experience talking about feelings and personal ideas as women, so we're bound to be awkward about it at first. But so what? This isn't a contest to determine who's better at talking. It's important that men understand this. Talking is not another performance, another way of proving yourself. Rather, it's an option to exercise as you see fit for making your life better. As you do more talking and listening, you'll get better at it and feel more comfortable doing it.

And try not to worry about not knowing what's going on inside you. No one always does. One of the great things about personal talking is that it often leads to interesting discoveries and clarifications. For example, you may know only that you feel out of sorts, but have no idea why. Talking about how you feel and what's on your mind may lead to greater clarity.

"I can see the importance of talking. I envy the way my wife talks to her women friends; they have a closeness that I've never had with anyone. But I grew up in a family where the men never said anything. All action, no words. I'm discouraged about learning to be different."

Many men feel the same. Can they learn as adults things that women have been practicing since they were toddlers? The answer is yes.

Talking and listening are skills that can be learned. What's needed is lots of practice. And while practice doesn't necessarily make perfect, it sure makes better.

Another thing to keep in mind is that many men have talking and listening skills they aren't even aware of. I've often been impressed with how well men listen at work. They really hear when a customer says he's interested in style but that cost is paramount. And they often follow carefully the intricacies of a report or marketing plan that's presented. These men are often articulate at work as well. They take information from various sources and express it so others can understand. Yet many of these same men don't follow and can't remember a minute later what their lover said, and they have nothing to say when she asks "What do you feel about that?" These men need to transfer the communication skills they use at work into their private lives (more about this later).

"I have some feelings I don't want my wife to know about; for example, that I still lust after other women."

No one said you have to tell her everything. No one could possibly tell another person everything that he feels or that passes through his mind, and there's no reason to try. I'm not suggesting a new tyranny to the effect that you should tell your lover everything that goes on inside you. That's no better than the old tyranny that you shouldn't tell her anything. What I'm proposing is that you have the option to talk about what you want to. You're the one who decides whether a certain feeling or idea gets expressed. If you think it would help you, her, or the relationship, express it. If you think it wouldn't help or might hurt, keep it to yourself.

"I understand intellectually how talking can help. But it never seems to help with us. Whenever we try to talk about our problems, one or both of us gets angry and everything goes to hell."

This is a common problem in many relationships and very discouraging to both partners. It's also the main complaint men have about connection. They are very sensitive to the risks of communication and don't want to make things worse.

The problem, however, is not inherent in communicating but in how it's done. When people attack and blame and accuse, things are going to get worse, usually very quickly. What's needed is learning how to communicate in more constructive and less destructive ways, which is really the subject of this section.

"I don't want to listen to my wife. She comes on like a crazy person: screaming, crying, exaggerating, lying, blaming me for everything in the world. I can't take it."

This is a common theme among men. They say they'd be willing to listen if conversations were reasonable and calm, but they can't put up with "hysterical outbursts." I can't guarantee that better communication can be developed (that depends on a number of things, especially what kind of shape your relationship is in), but there's probably a good chance it can be. It's almost certainly worth your time and energy to carefully go over the rest of material in this section, all of which is devoted to developing better and more reasonable communication.

"Some of the stuff my partner talks about is boring to me. I find it hard to listen to time and again."

It may help to tell her your feelings about listening to certain subjects. For example, if you're bored and frustrated at listening to the troubles she's having with her sister for the thousandth time, you can let her know. Making such a statement—tactfully, I hope—would be an assertive way of expressing yourself.

"I don't want my lover to think I'm a wimp. I'm concerned she will if I tell her about all my fears and doubts."

No man wants to be thought a wimp, and no woman wants to be with one. We men are caught in an unfortunate bind. If we don't talk about weaknesses and failures and fears, we're emotionally constipated. But if we do, we run the risk of being considered weak and unmanly.

I have nothing against men being strong, and neither does any woman I know. But being strong does not mean being other than human. All of us have feelings, all of us have doubts, concerns, and fears, all of us have areas of vulnerability. Even Samson and Achilles, perhaps the strongest of men, had their vulnerable spots. Strength has to do with being able to acknowledge who you are and the feelings you're having, and being able to deal with them. Pretending not to be sad or not to be afraid isn't strength; it's a lie that makes us look like robots and that turns women off. It helps to realize that it's normal and perfectly okay not to know everything, not to be able to do everything, not always to be confident. It's really okay to be who you are. And if your partner sometimes has trouble dealing with this, you can talk about and deal with that as well.

I once worked with a man who had been seeing a woman for several months. Whenever something was broken at her apartment—a door that didn't close properly, a toilet that didn't flush—she asked him to fix it and he tried. The problem was that he didn't know how to fix these things any better than she did, but feared she would view him as unmanly if he told her. The result was a lot of confusion on her part (why did it take him so long to make what she assumed was a simple repair?) and incredible pressure on him to do what he couldn't do. With my help, he finally told her that he didn't know how to fix things and when he had similar problems at his place, he called a handyman. She was surprised, since she had assumed that all men were handy around the house, but she soon got over that and didn't think any the less of him.

"If I start speaking my feelings, other guys, particularly those at work, will think less of me."
Let's assume you're right, that the men you know would think less of you if you expressed your feelings. So don't express them when you're around these men. Once again, it's important to remember that **we're talking about having choices; the ability to express feelings when you want to, the ability to keep quiet when you want to.** If you believe that expressing a doubt or weakness to someone at work would be used against you, don't do it.

Many men have said they wish they could be more open with other men outside the workplace and that other men would be more open with them. It's hard for men to do this, because we're used to competing with each other and fear that anything we say will give the listener an advantage over us. So we end up with men who've known each other for many years really not knowing anything about each other. Although they call one another pals, buddies, and friends, they know nothing about what makes them tick. Once you've had more practice in sharing thoughts and feelings, you may want to be more open with one or two men you like. That decision is up to you. But feel free to apply whatever safeguards you think necessary.

Yes, there are good reasons why men hesitate about connecting, but I believe they are by far outweighed by the advantages. If we want to be more fully human, if we want better relationships with our lovers and children, and if we want better sex, I don't think we have much choice.

WAR GAMES: THE MAIN OBSTACLE TO GOOD COMMUNICATION

Aside from the reluctance many men have to communicate about personal matters, the greatest obstacle to good communication is a number of methods or tactics (used by both men and women) that I refer to collectively as war games. The extent to which couples often resemble soldiers in combat is tragic. The tools of war are not conducive to healthy, happy relationships.

Attack and Defend

The essence of war is defending ourselves and attacking the enemy, and this is how many couples conduct themselves as soon as there is disagreement. We feel wronged and get busy defending our own actions and attacking our partner's. This means at least several things: that we don't listen empathically and hear what's being said, that we lose sight of the only important fact (that someone is unhappy and that the relationship is suffering as a result), that we get diverted into legalistics (who really did or said what), and that in the process we create more distance and anger, thereby hurting both people and their relationship.

The basic structure of these discussions is like this:

PERSON A: "You did [or did not do] X."
PERSON B: "That's not true. Here's what really happened."
A: "Not so. It happened the way I said it did."
B: "No way! I'm right."
A: "The hell you are. I am!"

The content of these discussions can be almost anything: if someone arrived late and by how many minutes; whether someone actually said X or Y and how many times; whether someone agreed to do something and, if so, what; who lost the money, keys, shampoo, and so on.

Here's an example of this structure in action:

You and your partner are sleeping in this Saturday morning for the first time in a long while. At ten o'clock your buddy Roger calls to ask if you'd like to play tennis. You say yes and hang up. Much to your amazement, your partner starts crying and yells: "You don't love me. You never want to do anything with me. All you care about is your stupid tennis."

You feel angry and defensive. So you reply: "And all you care about is criticizing me. Whatever I do is wrong. And it's not true that I never do things with you. We went out to eat just two days ago and we went to your sister's last month. What the hell's wrong with you anyway?"

HER: "Nothing's wrong with me. But something is certainly wrong with you. Oh sure, we went out to eat. With everybody from your damn company and all their friends. We never do anything together, just you and me. You're always too busy. Yet you're never too busy to play tennis or watch football on the tube."

YOU: "How can I love you if you're always criticizing me? I don't know what you want. You were the one who encouraged me to watch my weight, but now you get angry if I exercise. You're never satisfied."

HER: "Maybe you're right. Maybe you're not the man for me. I can't go on like this."

Terrific! One or two statements more, and we're going to be talking about divorce.

If you listened empathically, you might realize that your partner is lonely and upset. It seems to her that you don't love her because although you usually have time for tennis, you don't seem very interested in doing things with her. She misses being with you. And she's frustrated because she's tried to bring this issue up with you a number of times, but you didn't want to listen. Her feelings have been building for some time and what happened this Saturday was just the last straw.

But she's not the only one with complaints. You also feel distance in your relationship. But to you, the main problem is that she always seems to be on your case. The more critical she is, the less you want to be with her. But you're also sad because you miss her company.

Unfortunately, there haven't been any productive conversations about the complaints on either side. She has tried, but you didn't want to listen because you felt you were going to be criticized again. You didn't try to express your complaint because you're not used to doing that and you're discouraged about ever being able to satisfy her.

Despite the good reasons for not talking, it is necessary that the two of you do talk. The main issue is not about the legalities (whether in fact you are always ready to play tennis and never want to spend time with her); it rarely is. The main issue consists of the negative feelings—the unhappiness and alienation—each of you is having. That's what needs attention. Getting into who really did what is only an unfortunate distraction. The problems you are having cannot be resolved at that level, can't even be productively discussed at that level.

Problems in relationships invariably involve feelings. Someone feels misunderstood, slighted, hurt, ignored, put upon, treated unfairly, not cared for, not appreciated, or not loved. These feelings are what cry out for attention (and that's perhaps the main reason that men need to be better at expressing feelings). But what so often happens is that we get sidetracked into defensiveness and legalistics.

Defending yourself and attacking your partner does not work, pure and simple. One's defense of oneself hardly ever persuades the other person. Even if she has to grant the point you make, she doesn't grant the issue. Whether or not you persuade her on some small point or she persuades you, the usual outcome is further attacks and counterattacks, with more and more distance and bad feelings. It really doesn't make any difference if you were ten minutes or two hours late. What does matter is that your partner has feelings about your lateness that need to be addressed.

But what about truth and right? What about when you know for certain that she did so say X or did so do Y? This may come as a surprise, but it doesn't make any difference. In the first place, in most relationship conflict, truth cannot be established. No one will ever know for sure how late you or she was, no one will ever know who really said what in the car last Sunday. Most of the time there isn't one truth. There are only different perceptions, interpretations, positions, and opinions. And no one can persuade the other. She will go on believing that you responded "angrily" to something she said, while you'll go on believing you weren't angry. In the second place, even if truth could be established, even if twelve angels were to swear that you are correct and she isn't, it will not help the situation one iota. In fact, it may even make things worse.

Beware of establishing the truth of your position, beware of being right and making her wrong—this is death to a relationship. A relationship is not a courtroom or battlefield, or at least it shouldn't be. The fewer conversations of the defensive kind you have, and the quicker you get out of them once they've started, the better off you and your relationship will be.

When you realize that you're defending yourself or fighting over how late you were, you should understand that things are getting out of control. Once you understand that, you may be able to do something about it, the details of which I get into in the following chapters.

All other war games are some variant of attack and defend. I briefly discuss some of the most common ones below.

Monstrify Your Partner

Although it is common to attack and hurt the people we love, so common that it seems entirely "natural," we have a need to justify the behavior in our own minds. To do this, we engage in a mental process for which I have coined the ungainly term *monstrification*. We make a monster or demon out of our partner. This is similar to what goes on in real war. We have to make monsters out of the other side, to see them as less than human. They are not real people like ourselves but cruel savages, godless commies, dirty Japs, gooks, and so on, out to kill and enslave us. Once we get into this frame of mind, it's easy to justify killing them.

We do something similar when we get into a conflict with someone we care about. We tend to see her not as the woman we care about and who cares about us, but in terms of the feelings we're having at the moment. So we perceive her as uncaring, nasty, cruel, out to hurt us, and gloating over our misery. Here are some responses I got when I asked men in therapy how they saw their partners in the midst of a struggle: "a brutal bitch," "a heartless sadist," "a nagging, whining bitch who'd like to cut my balls off," "a woman whose only purpose is to nail me to the wall," and "a vicious devil who delights in my suffering."

Once you believe that this is who you're dealing with, it's easy to justify almost any behavior. You can attack, cause pain, and punish her with impunity. And this is how love comes to look more and more like war. Unless you want your relationship to resemble a battlefield, you need to understand the process of monstrification and how to abort it, about which I say more in Chapter 12.

Sulk and Destroy

A great many people, especially men, deal with relationship distress by withdrawing and sulking for hours or days. Their silence is a noisy one. Without saying much—or anything at all—they manage to convey that the partner is to blame for their suffering. Their partners are devastated by this behavior. They are being held culpable, yet there is nothing they can do. They often don't even have a clue about what the problem is, and there's no one to talk to or negotiate with. Many women have said there's nothing worse than this kind of behavior. It destroys love and relationships.

Women usually feel they are being punished. The man is in effect saying, "This is what you get for criticizing me. I won't talk to you for a week. See how you like that!" This may make her reluctant to bring up complaints in the future, because she doesn't want more sulking. While this may look like a good outcome, it is far from that. She may tend to keep her criticisms to herself, but the complaints will not go away. Emotional and sexual distance between the partners will be the result.

Although there is little doubt that some men intend to punish their partners by sulking, it's also true that many men withdraw because they simply don't know what else to do. They feel overwhelmed by what their partner says, they feel hopeless about finding a solution, and they feel outclassed in trying to talk to her (or they feel they can't get heard). Withdrawal seems like the only reasonable path.

I can think of only one time when withdrawal is reasonable, and that's when the man feels he's losing control of himself and that he may get violent if the confrontation continues. Almost anything that prevents violence is a good solution, at least for the moment. But momentary withdrawal (similar to the time-outs I discuss in Chapter 12) is not the same as sulking. It's one thing to say, "I'm starting to lose it and need a break from this," and come back in an hour or so to resume the conversation in a better frame of mind. It's something else again to hang around morosely for a week and not say a word.

Sulking is similar in many ways to guerrilla warfare. Like a guerrilla army, the sulker lets you know he's there—who could ignore his noisy but silent accusations?—and takes a heavy toll, but when you go to confront him and deal with the issues, there's no one there.

Like attacking and defending, sulking doesn't work in relationships. I grant that the temptation to do it can be great. Withdrawal may seem like the only way to deal with what you perceive as a hopeless situation, and there can also be satisfaction in seeing your partner suffer as a result of it, but the cost to the relationship is too heavy to bear for long. I believe we men have to learn better ways to deal with relationship problems.

Finding Allies

Just as countries at war form alliances to increase their power, lovers enlist the aid of other people, often authority figures, to increase their leverage. Instead of just saying that I'm upset by something you did, I let you know that my best friend, your best friend, my mother, my thera-pist, or even your mother agrees that you were wrong.

> A woman friend told me that she and her lover have been engaged in a conflict for months. He has lots of free time and wants to spend more of it with her. But she has two young children to take care of and a very demanding job. She would like to spend more time with him, but just doesn't have any. Now he has enlisted the aid of his therapist. He tells my friend that his therapist says that she is afraid of intimacy, that she's running from real love. Does this alliance with the therapist gain him anything? Maybe the satisfaction of feeling that he's right, but the effect on my friend is that she feels she's being ganged up on and is getting very angry.

This is one typical response for those who feel overwhelmed by alli-ances. Another typical response is for them to get their own allies. "I don't care what *your* therapist says, *my* therapist [friend, mother, who-ever] thinks you're a schmuck!"

Real progress, right? It's bad enough that you and your partner can't resolve a conflict. Bringing in allies may seem like a good idea at the time, but it doesn't help. The number of allies mushrooms, and so does the anger and the distance between the partners. Best to leave alliances to those fighting real wars.

Going for the Jugular or Nuking Them

In real war, what one wants is to deliver the knockout punch or the killing blow, the act that will so devastate the enemy that they will be unable to continue the struggle. Most people would agree that using the equivalent of a nuclear weapon on someone you love is unconscionable, but in the midst of a struggle we often lose this perspective and go straight for the jugular.

And we are in a unique position to do it. We know our partner's most vulnerable points, all the things she is most ashamed of and that are most hurtful to her. Having already made her into an enemy unworthy of fair play, we launch our most destructive assault. Her weight or age, her too small or too large breasts, her failure to complete college or to succeed in a particular endeavor that was important to her—anything and everything that will shame, hurt, and humiliate her are brought up in the ugliest way possible.

The results of nuking them are predictable. Either the partner is so devastated that she withdraws in hurt and the whole relationship goes on hold for days, weeks, or even longer. Or she responds in kind and now you're both devastated. In either case, not only is there more than enough hurt to go around, there's also a loss of trust.

Even if there is a moment of satisfaction in knowing you have decimated your partner, these kinds of victories remind me of old King Pyrrhus. In 279 B.C. he defeated a Roman army, but with such staggering losses that he was moved to say, in effect, "One more victory like this and we're done for."

I trust my main point is clear. Attacking and defending belong on the battlefield, not in the bedroom or the living room. **If you bring the weapons of war into your home, you, your partner, and your relationship will all end up as casualties.**

Another point should also be clear. Despite what many books and some experts claim, achieving good communication isn't the easiest goal in the world to reach. It is difficult to listen and to express yourself well. It's also difficult for two human beings to relate in ways that are supportive, respectful, helpful, fun, and that honor both of them. That's just the way it is, and so far no one has found an easy way out. The great French writer Jean-Paul Sartre spoke for the feeling we all have at times, when he said, "Hell is other people." That puts in a nutshell just how difficult it can be to deal with others and how often it goes awry. But what Sartre forgot to add is that an even greater hell for most of us is not having other people. And when everything comes together and clicks, we could just as easily say that heaven is other people (or at least this one other person).

Perhaps one of the most important things that lovers can do is understand and sympathize with the difficulties they're both having with what they're trying to do. Empathic listening and free expression of thoughts and feelings allow us to gain a deeper understanding of ourselves and our partners. It almost always demonstrates that no one is being intentionally cruel, that no one is trying to thwart the other, and that no one gains when the other is unhappy. It allows us to see with crystal clarity just how hard it is to be in a close relationship and to find contentment. To the extent we can be in touch with these realities and commiserate with each other about the difficulties, we can obtain for ourselves and give to our partners a deeper love and support than is otherwise possible.

It's past time that we men started along this path.

WHAT IF THESE METHODS DON'T HELP?

Although the suggestions in the next three chapters have been highly effective for a number of couples, they don't work for everyone. Some degree of goodwill and a willingness to make things better is required, but not all couples and not all individuals have these qualities. It's also the case that some individuals and couples do better in face-to-face contact with a professional than by using a book. If you're in a relationship, I think it is best to discuss the changes you'd like to make with your partner. If she would prefer consulting with a professional rather than, or in addition to, using a book, the two of you have some talking to do. If talking about what changes should be made is impossible or too difficult, you can simply select the ideas that seem relevant and use them as you see fit; the same is true, of course, if you're not in a relationship.

It's important to give your new behaviors a fair trial. Don't expect great changes in your partner or the relationship after a day or two. If you believe you've listened better, expressed more, been more tactful, and so on, for a month or more, and nothing good has come of it, you should seriously consider professional help. See if your partner will go with you to a therapist who deals with relationship issues. That's the best choice, because relationship problems are most effectively dealt with in couples therapy. If she refuses this offer and the two of you can't find a way of getting to a more harmonious place on your own, you might want to go to a therapist yourself to explore your options.

_____11

How to Be a Better Listener

"Most times at work, I'm all ears and all there when someone talks. I know I need the information. But at home, my ears go off duty and I'm in kind of a haze. We've had incredible fights where Jan says she already told me this or that several times and I have absolutely no memory of it. I'm sure she's right, that I just haven't heard what she said."—MAN, 39

"I don't want to be a traitor to my sex, but I'm convinced women are better listeners than men in relationships. I've seen it with myself and with my friends. Just last week I saw it with my friend Walt. He was telling me about an argument he had with his wife, where he denied saying something she claimed he said. I know she was right because I was there when he said it to her. Men don't even listen to themselves."—MAN, 55

PEOPLE in relationships complain all the time about not being heard. Women are the chief complainers, but "My wife doesn't understand me" *is also common.* Many children have the same complaint about their parents and say that's why they no longer talk to them. I often have the experience of listening to a couple talking or arguing, and it's clear that neither partner understands what the other is saying. She says A but he hears B. So he responds to B, which she never said, by saying C. She's confused (because it has little or nothing to do with the point she

220

started with) and upset (because she's not getting her point across). So she may try again. But now there may be anger in her voice, which will make it harder for him to hear accurately, and he may well be upset because she isn't responding to what he said. And on and on it goes, with lots of heat and no real connection.

You can learn to be a better listener. Being a good listener can make a critical difference not only in your relationship and sex life, but in every single aspect of your life that involves other people.

The main obstacles to good listening are the war games discussed in the last chapter. But there are several other barriers and problems that apply particularly to men.

• *Not realizing listening is important.* No one ever said that listening to women is an important part of masculinity, so we tend to discount it. We feel free to listen with less than full attention when our partner is trying to tell us something.

• *Assuming—and fearing—that understanding is the same as agreeing.* Some men believe that if they say they understand what their partner says, she'll take that to mean that they agree. That isn't the case at all. You don't have to agree with your partner. It's often the case in relationships that the partners don't agree and, sure enough, the lack of agreement can cause problems. But usually these can be ironed out. What's important is hearing and understanding. People are usually receptive to working out an arrangement if they feel understood. If they don't feel understood, they aren't receptive to much of anything because all their energy is tied up in trying to get understood or in dealing with their feelings about not being understood.

• *Not understanding the emotion that's expressed.* Communication consists of at least two parts: content (what is said) and affect (the feeling[s] behind it). Because we men haven't been trained to give much importance to feelings, we're more likely to get the content and miss the affect, meaning that the speaker will not feel understood. The feeling is usually more important than the content.

Let's say your partner is feeling neglected. Ideally, she would just say so. But that's not always how it goes. So without mentioning neglect, she accuses you of having an affair. Her sense of neglect is the issue, but it's easy to miss that and get caught up in defending yourself against the accusation. The problem is that proving you aren't having an affair will settle nothing. She'll still feel neglected.

• *Judgmentalism, criticizing the speaker's feelings or position.* Your partner says her boss takes advantage of her generosity, and you tell her she's overreacting or that the situation isn't as bad as she thinks. Now she's got to persuade you that it's exactly that bad.

Another example of judgmentalism is commenting that her feelings aren't logical, perhaps because she expresses two seemingly contradictory emotions. But feelings have their own logic. It's common to have contradictory feelings. Love and hate come quickly to mind. One can experience both of these emotions at the same time toward the same person, especially a parent, child, or spouse. Feelings aren't neat and clean like a balance sheet or a syllogism.

• *Trying to fix things rather than just listen.* Since men are trained to be problem-solvers, when we hear of a difficulty we immediately set out to make it right. It's hard to remember that there's often nothing to fix. Your partner may just want a listener. It's common for a woman to say, "I just wanted to tell him about a problem I'm having. But before I even get it all out, he's already got four things for me to do to make it better. I don't need him to solve my problems. All I wanted was a sympathetic ear."

This does not mean you have to give up advice-giving entirely. Offering practical advice is something many men are good at and many women appreciate. But it's crucial to listen carefully first. Once the speaker has gotten it all out, she may ask for advice. She may be especially interested in what you have to say now that she believes you have all the essential information.

The key to effective listening is empathy, the ability to understand what's being said from the speaker's point of view. This requires that we try to get into her shoes and see it from her perspective, not from our own. You might want to recall an experience where you expressed something and the other person seemed to understand exactly what it was like for you. Wasn't that a powerful experience and didn't it give you a feeling of OKness and freedom? The OKness results simply from having the understanding. Humans need that. The sense of freedom

---

HOW *NOT* TO LISTEN

Following these rules is guaranteed to enrage your partner and to cause serious damage to your relationship.

1. Let her know you don't want to listen. Tell her that you have better things to do, that you don't want to hear the same old stuff again, or ask, "Do we have to talk about this?"

2. When you do get around to listening, do it halfheartedly. Keep glancing at the TV or at a newspaper as your partner talks. This will let her know that you aren't interested and are hoping she'll finish as soon as possible.

3. Interrupt frequently with irrelevant questions and topics. This will reinforce her sense of not being taken seriously.

4. Make lots of judgments about what she's saying. Tell her she's having the wrong feelings, that she's not being logical, that she's misread the situation, that she's handling it wrong, and so on.

5. Give unrequested advice. Tell her exactly what she should do to resolve the problem.

---

comes from not having to defend or justify what you've said. It's been accepted, which frees you to explore the issue further, to come up with solutions, or just to leave it alone. That's what everyone wants.

RULES OF EFFECTIVE LISTENING

1. Remember that your one and only job while listening is to understand *her* experience, feelings, attitude, or point of view. While listening, your point of view is not relevant. You can express your side later if you want, but only after you've understood what she is saying.

2. Give her your full attention. Turn off whatever is on—radio, stereo, or TV—put away any materials you have in your hands, and look at your partner (very important, because it gives her a sense of being listened to and helps cut down on anger and defensiveness).

3. Ask questions to encourage her, help her along, and also to gain clarification for yourself. For example, you might say: "How did you feel about that?" "What happened next?" When we are asked questions about an event we are relating, it not only helps but also assures us of the listener's interest. Asking questions about her experience can also defuse tension and hostility. Most of us are accustomed to hearing denials and angry statements when we're lodging a protest or criticism; anticipating such responses adds to our anxiety and anger. But when we are greeted with something like "Can you say more about what I did that upset you?" a lot of the negative feelings evaporate.

But it's not always necessary to ask questions. An "Oh?,", "I see," "Ummm," or gestures like nodding your head or touching the speaker are among other ways you can assure her of your attention and induce her to continue.

4. Try to understand the feeling behind what she's saying as well as the content. She may tell you directly (for example, "I'm so angry [or upset or disappointed or sad]") or you will get clues from what she says, her tone of voice, and her demeanor. If you're not sure what emotion she had or has, ask: "How did that make you feel?" or "What was that like for you?"

5. Demonstrate your understanding. One way is simply by acknowledging her feelings: "I can see why you're so angry" or "That's really frustrating" or "That's so annoying." It's important that you acknowledge the feelings *she's* having, not the ones you're having. If you talk about your feelings at this point, you're taking attention away from her, and that will probably make her upset. Another approach is to summarize what you heard her say, including the feeling(s) she's having.

There's no question whatever that these rules are hard to follow. Even the best listeners don't always apply all of them. Despite that, they are important. The more of them you use, and the more often you use them, the better listener you will be.

Here's an example of how *not* to do it:

HER: "I'm so upset, I feel like quitting my job. Fred got on my case because the Jones report wasn't done today, even though it's not due till next week."
YOU: "Fred's an asshole, and you should tell him what to do with his report."

This is risky, because you're unnecessarily interjecting yourself into her situation. She may not think Fred's an asshole and may resent your giving advice she hasn't asked for. You are not seeing the situation from her perspective.

Another way of *not* doing it would be like this: "I'm sure Fred will realize his mistake and it'll all be OK tomorrow." This doesn't work because the hidden message in your statement is that she's having the wrong feelings: She shouldn't be upset because everything will be OK. This is not likely to make her feel understood.

Here's a better way:

HER: "I'm so upset I feel like quitting my job."

YOU: "You really are upset—what happened [simply acknowledging her feeling and encouraging her to continue]?"

HER: "Fred got on my case because the Jones report wasn't done today even though it's not due till next week."

YOU: "That's enough to upset anyone [validating her feeling]."

HER: "It wouldn't have been so bad except that he did it in front of Lucy and Jane. It was embarrassing to be scolded in front of them."

YOU: "Wow. That really made it worse [again, just acknowledging what she's saying]."

HER: "Yeh, it was pretty bad. But I feel a little better now" (followed by a silence).

YOU: "Have you thought what you want to do about this?" [This question gives her encouragement to express any plans she's considered, but it also allows her to say that she's been too upset to consider what to do.]

HER: "I think I need to talk to Fred. Usually he's fine but he gets so stressed out by deadlines that he loses it and acts like an ass. . . . Yeah, I definitely need to talk to him about this."

YOU: "Sounds like you have a plan [acknowledging her plan]."

In this example, you didn't seem to do a lot. Yet chances are she'll feel it was a good discussion and will be grateful to you for listening. She got something off her chest and decided on a plan of action. You helped facilitate it without judgments, without interference, without giving advice. What you did may have been what allowed her to clarify what she's really upset about (that Fred embarrassed her in front of her colleagues) and to decide what to do about it.

Some people wonder why it's OK for the woman to call Fred an ass but not OK for the man to call him an asshole. The reason is simple: It's her show; she can call him anything she wants. But it's not your job to tell her what Fred is or isn't.

The best way to become a better listener is to practice listening as often as possible, employing the above rules as much as you can. Opportunities for listening are usually close at hand. Someone is always trying to say something to you: your lover, child, boss, colleague, a customer or client, someone sitting next to you on the plane or bus, and so on.

EXERCISE 11–1: LISTENING

Time Required: Varies, but rarely longer than a few minutes

When you feel like it, but at least twice each day, make it a point to really listen. It might be when you know someone is going to talk to you—a client is coming in at ten to discuss a problem, your partner says you need to talk—or when someone has already started talking to you. Your goal is simply to try to understand what is said from the speaker's point of view. So just put on your listening hat and apply the principles suggested earlier. Be sure to check the accuracy of your understanding by reflecting it back to the speaker.

If you belong to the group of men mentioned in the last chapter, those who listen better at work than elsewhere, you want to discover how to transfer your work skills to a different environment. When you're going to listen to someone not connected with work, find a way of getting into your best listening mode. There may be some behavior connected with your work-listening mode that you can use: Perhaps you have a way of clearing your mind of other things. If so, then do the same mind-clearing before listening to your lover or child. Another way is simply to tell yourself "I want to listen to June the same way I listen to our largest customer." These aids may seem awkward at first, but they get much more comfortable and effective with regular practice.

The results of this exercise can be astonishing. One man said that after years of what he considered nagging, he finally understood what his lover meant by wanting more intimacy and recognized the legitimacy of her request. Another man reported a new understanding of his ten-year-old son: "I'd never before really heard what he was trying to tell me about math. I just thought he was lazy. But it turns out he feels incredibly stupid and inadequate with numbers. No matter how hard he tries, he doesn't do well and he feels like giving up in despair." Many other men report having new understandings of their partners and developing increased closeness as a result.

LISTENING TO COMPLAINTS

Now suppose your partner has something critical to say about you. This is where lots of men have trouble. Who wants to hear complaints and bad news? Your answer is probably "no one." That's understandable; I feel the same way. But I also know it's smart to listen to bad news.

Even though it doesn't feel good at the moment, a complaint or criticism is a gift. Instead of taking her love or sex elsewhere, your partner is sticking with you, alerting you to a problem, and handing you an opportunity to rectify it. Many of our best-run businesses have learned to look at complaints in this way and require their top executives to spend time each month reading letters of complaint and taking phone calls from those with problems. Most relationships would benefit from a similar policy.

There's one other thing about complaints and criticisms you should be aware of, because it can help take the sting out of them. Most of them are based on a compliment. If your partner complains that you're not spending enough time with her, the hidden compliment is that she wants to spend more time with you. If she complains there isn't enough sex, she's saying she wants to make love with you more often. If she complains that you're not lasting as long as she'd like in intercourse, that means she wants you inside of her longer. These are serious compliments, even though they may come across as something else.

LISTENING TO AN ANGRY PARTNER

"What am I supposed to do when she's shrieking and making it sound like I'm the worst bastard who ever lived?"—MAN, 49

One of the toughest issues for men to deal with is the anger of their partners. It used to be that women didn't express anger much, at least not directly. But that has changed. Many women now feel free to vent their anger, and their men often feel overwhelmed and helpless.

The major problem for men, I believe, is their feeling of discouragement and hopelessness when dealing with an angry partner. They feel that nothing they can do will make any difference. Yet my experience suggests there's a great deal that can be done. I hope you're willing to experiment with the following suggestions.

When people are angry, they usually want to be heard and understood. What they don't want is criticism in return, denial of their perceptions or feelings, or attacks on their position or personality. So one helpful practice is to avoid adding fuel to her fire. It's bad enough that she's so angry about whatever it is, but in most of these situations the man gives her more to be angry about by getting into war games. Simply by not attacking her, not defending yourself, and not withdrawing, you help keep her anger where it belongs—on the specific behavior or issue that set it off.

But what else can you do? A great deal. Many of the tools given in this section can help. Anything conciliatory will be of benefit. Asking questions, for example, is an excellent way of disarming anger. Rather than slamming back at her or withdrawing (both of which can be taken to indicate a lack of interest in her feelings) you can ask her to tell you more: "I'm sorry you're so angry. Could you say more about what I did that upset you?" Another resource is empathy, showing that you understand what she's saying. Yet another is to agree with what you can agree with. Sincere apologies are yet another. All of these approaches are elaborated on in the chapters that follow.

I can't guarantee that her anger will immediately evaporate if you use some or all of these methods. It probably won't. She'll still be angry over whatever it was, and you may have to hang in there until she calms down. But you won't be making matters worse, and your conciliatory gestures will help her de-monstrify you and deal more constructively with what's troubling her.

NAGGING

One of the most common complaints men have about women is nagging. "She's always on my case"; "She's always ragging on me"; "She's the biggest nag since my mother"—these are the words men use to register this behavior that bugs the hell out of them.

The best way I've found to look at this issue is to understand that nagging represents usually desperate attempts on the part of women to get heard and understood. The woman wants her man to understand her feelings, to discuss an issue, to make certain agreements, or to live up to ones he's already made.

The men usually feel overwhelmed. They work hard, they're tired, and they don't want to hear about something they're doing wrong or that needs work. Unfortunately, there may not be a good alternative. The best way to prevent nagging is not to let things reach that point—that is, to listen to what your partner has to say and to deal with those things that can be dealt with, no matter how difficult that may be. If she says, for example, that sex has become boring, you might want to swallow your pride and do your best to find out what she means. And then decide with her what should be done about it and do it.

Another good way to prevent nagging is to live up to your agreements. If you make agreements you don't keep, you can be sure that nagging is what you're going to get.

Yet another way to prevent nagging is to be willing to get outside help for the problems the two of you can't solve on your own. There are lots of kinds of help that may be required. Some couples I've seen needed to hire extra child-care or housecleaning services; neither the woman or the man could do any more, and the only good solution was getting someone else to help. Other couples needed financial advice. Yet others needed psychotherapy or sex therapy.

Men are much less willing to go for psychological help than women. It's difficult for a man to acknowledge that he has a relationship or sex problem that he can't resolve on his own. One dramatic case comes to mind as I write this.

I once saw a couple in which the woman had been begging the man to get help for his very quick ejaculations for over fifteen years. During the first years of their marriage, he wouldn't even hear her complaint. There was nothing wrong except in her imagination. Then he acknowledged a problem existed, but it was hers: If she didn't take so long to come, his lasting longer wouldn't be an issue. By the time he finally came to grips with reality and they came to therapy, it was almost too late. Her anger had built to such a point that she was never able fully to let go of it even though he was now eager to get the help he had so long resisted.

As I talked with this man, he mentioned time and again how difficult it was to live with such a nagger. What hadn't occurred to him in fifteen years was that his behavior gave her no choice. If he had simply admitted the problem and sought help, there would have been no reason for nagging.

My best advice is to not be like this man. Don't cause your spouse (and yourself) to suffer for fifteen years just because you don't want to hear about a problem. Sooner or later you're going to have to deal with it, so you might as well skip the suffering and get right to it.

If you think your partner is a nag, why not ask yourself what she's talking about? If you have any doubts you have it right, why not ask her?

> YOU: "I'm concerned about the housework business. You keep bringing up that I don't do my share and I barely hear you anymore. It's not good for us. Would you please tell me exactly what you want and let's talk about it?"

Let's say she says something like this: "John, I'm worried about us. We seem to be drifting apart." That should set off bells or lights in your head. She's saying the relationship is in trouble. You may feel like hell and want to run away but, believe it or not, you're being handed a gift.

Here's one way *not* to handle it effectively. "Look, I know I've been busy. But things will be better after the Christmas season. You'll see." All you're doing is shutting her up and making light of the complaint. The only sure things anyone will see are her increasing anger and a worsening of the problem.

Here's an even worse way. "Damnit! I'm tired of your telling me something else is wrong. Just leave me alone." I won't even comment on that one except to note that it's quite common. But suppose you actually said it and later realized you were wrong. No need to feel embarrassed or alone. Many of us have done it. What you need to do is admit your mistake and tell her you'd like to listen. "I made a mistake last night when you said we were drifting apart. It scared me, and I blew up. I'm calmer now and would like to hear what you have to say."

YOUR CONDITIONS FOR EFFECTIVE LISTENING

It's important to understand that you can be a better listener under certain circumstances than others. You need to determine how you can listen best and take steps to get what you need. Most people, for example, find they don't listen well when they're tired, angry, or in a hurry. So they need ways of saying this isn't a good time.

> I know we need to talk, but I'm too bushed to give you my full attention. Could we talk about this in the morning?

> I want to hear what you have to say, but I'm so pissed about what happened at work I really can't concentrate. Can you wait until I've taken a bath and calmed down?

Suppose you'd like to listen to your partner but she talks in ways that make that difficult. Maybe you need to tell her something like this:

> I know you're upset and I really want to hear what you have to say. But it's very difficult for me to listen when you call me names and belittle me. I promise I'll listen attentively if you're willing to tone that down.

If she can't or won't stop, you have every right to call a time-out (see Chapter 13). When the two of you regroup and are calmer, assure her of your desire to listen, but let her know the circumstances under which you can hear best.

LISTENING TO SEXUAL COMPLAINTS AND FEEDBACK

It's not easy for men to listen to sexual complaints. We like to think that we're good lovers, so anything suggesting we're not hits us where it hurts. But at the same time, it's necessary that we do learn to listen. Let's say your partner tells you that you come too fast. It's important that you hear what she's saying instead of your own fantasies or nightmares, for example, that "I'm a bad lover"; "I'm not man enough for her"; or "She's going to leave me." Hearing such things will probably cause you to become upset and defensive. So you reply with something like, "Well, if it didn't take *you* a week to come, it wouldn't be too fast." Now everyone is hurt and angry, and we're heading for trouble.

A better way would be like this: "That's upsetting, but tell me more about it." You want to find out all the specifics about her complaint and what she wants.

> HER: "I've never had an orgasm with intercourse and assume I never will. So it's not that. But I really like having you inside me and I feel frustrated that you're in and out so fast. I'd like it to be longer."
>
> YOU: "Let me be sure I understand. Although you're not looking to have a climax that way, you're frustrated that we don't have longer intercourse."
>
> HER: "That's right. It feels so good I want it to go on longer."

Now that you understand the gist of her comment, you can try to get more information.

> YOU: "When you say longer, what do you mean?"
>
> HER: "That's hard to say. I don't even know how long it usually lasts now. It feels like only two or three minutes but I'm not sure that's accurate. I don't know, maybe twice as long as now."

This is crucial information that you learned only because you were able to hear and understand what she said earlier. It may be that what she's saying sounds fine to you. In that case, you need to let her know:

> YOU: "That sounds reasonable. I'd like that too."

Now the two of you need to talk about how to reach the goal you've agreed on. It's equally important to let her know if you don't agree or don't think change is possible.

> YOU: "I'd love to be able to last longer, but I've been coming fast all my life. When I was with Joan, I went to a shrink for over a year and it didn't help. I don't know what to do."

Your statement, as discouraging as it sounds, leaves the door open for further discussion. For example, she may want to bring up going to a therapist who specializes in this kind of problem. Or maybe you have something to offer:

> YOU: "This book I'm reading has exercises that the author says have been helpful. I'll show them to you if you like. Maybe they can work."

Let's turn to the subject of listening to sexual feedback, which may or may not be a complaint. Many men appreciate hearing what their partners like and don't like in sex. It saves them the effort of making assumptions and wondering if they have it right. But some men get into a snit because they feel bossed around. As one man said: "It's always a little slower, a little more gently, do this and do that. It's like she's directing traffic." These men often take the woman's suggestions as criticisms and feel bad because what they were doing wasn't right.

Many women are perplexed about giving sexual feedback. They know they need to say what they want, but they fear hurting their partner's feelings. It's immeasurably easier for them when the partners encourage and welcome information. It's much harder when what they say is not received well. The partner of the man quoted above had this to say: "He doesn't know what I like, but he doesn't seem to want to learn. I tell him in the most gentle ways I know, but he takes everything as a criticism. What am I supposed to do?"

Men have been trained to believe that they should somehow know what a woman needs in bed. If they don't, that's a negative statement about their masculinity. But, like all the other myths, this is ridiculous. There is no way of knowing how to please a partner without learning from her. No matter how many women you've had sex with and no matter how many books you've read, the only way to know what this partner wants is from her.

Some men who've heard this have objected, saying they had experiences where what they did was exactly what the woman wanted. Other men have reported stories from partners who said that a former lover knew exactly what to do. I don't deny that it sometimes happens like this: The man's style and preferences match exactly or very closely the woman's and all is fine, as if by magic. But you need to understand that this is rare, just as it's rare to meet someone whose taste in food or leisure activities is exactly the same as yours. In most cases, sexual and otherwise, learning is necessary.

Feedback is something to be thankful for. When your partner tells you to touch her like so, or that she likes this or that, she's telling what she needs for a good sexual experience *with you.*

If she's speaking in ways that make it hard for you to hear—because she's coming across as derogatory or blaming, for example—it's perfectly acceptable to let her know how you could listen better.

With that exception, however, you have no choice but to get over your feelings of being criticized and listen. Unless you listen carefully to what she says and act accordingly, the chances of good sex are seriously diminished. Most of the women I interviewed spontaneously mentioned that listening to, understanding, and acting on the woman's suggestions are important aspects of being a good lover. That's what they want rather than a man who can anticipate their every desire or who automatically knows what they prefer.

If you're not sure you understand what she wants, having a longer talk about it and getting a demonstration can be of great help.

GETTING A DEMONSTRATION

Let's say your partner wants longer kisses or a particular way of being touched. Although you may be able to repeat back her words exactly, you may still not know what she means. For example, your understanding of *long* or *gentle* may be very different from hers. It happens all the time. The woman tells the man to touch her more softly. He shows his understanding by saying, "You want a softer touch," then proceeds to touch her in a way that is soft by his definition but not by hers.

Even the seemingly simple word *kiss* can present problems. There are many different kinds of kisses, and it's by no means guaranteed that you have the same kind of kiss in mind when your partner says she'd like more kissing. Is she talking about a peck on the cheek, an affectionate kiss, an all-out passionate kiss? It's important not to assume that just because she said, "More kissing," and you repeated back, "More kissing," that the two of you are talking about the same thing. You may be, but then again you may not be.

Asking for a demonstration is very helpful, which is what the next exercise is about. I use the example of kissing because the first few couples I used it with were having trouble with kissing, but the exercise works well with many activities: genital and nongenital stimulation, hugging, holding, intercourse positions and movements, and even back-rubs.

EXERCISE 11–2: KISSING (OR WHATEVER) SEMINAR

Time Required: 2 to 10 minutes

Tell your partner you'd like help with kissing because she's been complaining about it. "I'd like to learn to kiss the way you want, but I need help. Would you tell me exactly what you want and then show me? I want to get this right."

Listen to her explanation and check your understanding by summarizing what you hear her say. When she agrees that you have it, have her kiss you that way. (If the issue is touching rather than kissing, you can have her demonstrate on herself as well as on you. You can also have her guide your hand with hers when you touch her.) Then you do what she's been doing and ask for feedback. Use that information when you try again. Don't expect to have it perfect right away. Pay attention and take your time.

The exercise should probably not last more than 10 minutes. End it when you're both feeling good, even if you still haven't mastered what she wants. You can always arrange another seminar later.

POSSIBLE PROBLEM

You can understand and do what she wants, but it's not what you want. Kissing her way is not your favorite way. One possibility is to try it her way for a time—say, a few weeks—to see if you get to like it more. If not, the two of you may want to agree to have more my-turn, your-turn sex, where sometimes it's done mainly for her and sometimes mainly for you. When it's done for her, you kiss her way. Another possibility is to kiss both ways during sex, sometimes her way, sometimes yours.

LISTENING TO REPORTS OF SEXUAL ASSAULT

By now it should come as no surprise to hear that millions of American women have been victims of incest, molestation, or rape. These assaults are a leading cause of sexual problems in women. If your partner was a victim, it's important to be able to listen to her if she wants to talk about it. Of course, she probably won't tell you if you're not already a good listener.

You may well find that her story stirs up all sorts of feelings in you, but it's crucial not to let them overpower you. This is definitely one time where her feelings are far more important than yours. What you mainly need to do is listen, encourage her to say as much as she wants, and be supportive.

Whatever you do, do not explicitly or implicitly criticize her behavior now or in the past. In the matter of rape, for example, you may believe that she shouldn't have gone out with that guy in the first place, shouldn't have been walking in that area alone at night, or should have fought back harder, but do everyone a favor and keep these assessments to yourself. Even if it could be shown that your views are somehow correct, expressing them will do nothing to help the situation. She's had a horrible experience and needs you to be there for her. Don't give advice unless it is requested, don't make judgments, and don't try to fix her. You are not her doctor or sex therapist, and you shouldn't try to be. If she needs professional assistance, she should get it from a professional. It is also counterproductive to get crazy and threaten to kill the man who assaulted her. Such macho posturing works only in the movies. Besides, if you get angry, she'll be torn between dealing with her own feelings and dealing with yours. She was the one who was assaulted. Don't take the attention away from her by getting carried away with your feelings.

You'll need all the empathy you can muster to just be there with her. It's possible that talking will bring back strong feelings and she may shake, scream, or cry. Try not to assume that you have to do anything about her feelings and behavior. The only thing you can do, aside from listen, is to hold her, if she wants to be held, and assure her of your love and support. If she doubts her desirability, you can assure her of it, but that's all. If at some point she wants to be alone, then let her be alone.

It may well be that she'll want to talk about what happened a number of times, not just once. It's also possible that something accidental or seemingly trivial will bring back the bad feelings for her.

I know of one woman who had been raped and sodomized years before she met her current boyfriend. She had counseling to deal with her trauma and had discussed it several times with the boyfriend. Apparently everything had been dealt with. Yet one day when they were attempting rear-entry intercourse, his penis accidently touched her anus. That one touch brought back all the old feelings and she turned on her lover as if he were the rapist, cursing, punching, and kicking him. After recovering from his shock, he held her so she couldn't continue assaulting him and kept telling her he was he and not the rapist. He got through to her after a moment and her rage changed to fear and sadness. He held her and listened for a long time. And that's about all anyone could have done.

If it turns out that you can't listen anymore because you're getting close to overload, you need to let her know. For instance: "I'm sorry you feel so bad. But I'm getting overwhelmed. Could we just hold each other for a few minutes? Then I think I'll be able to listen again."

If you keep two words in mind—understanding and support—you should do fine.

_12_

Expressing Yourself

"My girlfriend says she wants me to express my feelings more and I don't think I'm opposed, but I'm not sure I really know what she means."—MAN, 24

"I undertook the process of learning to express my feelings to please my wife. It wasn't always easy, yet I'm glad I did it. I know myself better, I'm closer to my wife and my interactions with her are much smoother."—MAN, 54

ASSERTING yourself, which we've already covered, is one way of expressing yourself. When you assert yourself, you are not only expressing preferences, what you want and don't want, but you may also be saying more: You want X because it makes you feel loved or wonderful; you don't want Y because it makes you feel sad or neglected. Nonetheless, some ways of expressing ourselves aren't necessarily associated with being assertive.

Despite what some people think, it's not true that men don't have or express feelings. They do. Men can get very emotional—excited, enthusiastic, sometimes ecstatic—about sex, closing a deal, winning the woman of their dreams, and cheering on their favorite athletic team. They also can get very emotional—upset, gloomy, angry—when their team loses, when they don't make the big deal or win the woman, and when they don't get sex. But basically a man sees himself as someone who is in control of himself, including his feelings, and he doesn't let them carry him away. And certain feelings, he has learned, aren't acceptable for him at all:

- Those related to caring and love or their lack. These are difficult because they make the man seem or feel dependent on women. Men are, of course, exceedingly dependent on their relationships with women (in many ways more so than women are dependent on relationships with men), but it's hard for us to admit it because of what we've been taught about masculinity.
- Those suggesting weakness, including fear and hurt. These strike at the strength that's supposed to be the essence of masculinity. No man wants to feel—or have others think—that he's confused, overwhelmed, intimidated, or feels neglected or despondent. There is no end of stories of men being called wimps, sissies, girls, and pussies by other men because they manifested any of these feelings.

Because anger is one of the few feelings men believe they can have, it's often a mask for other feelings, especially such as feeling hurt or neglected, that suggest weakness. It's much easier for men to deal with anger than with these other emotions.

The result of the prohibition on experiencing and expressing feelings is that men often lose track of them. That is, they don't know when they're feeling love or sadness and they don't get much practice expressing most of their emotions. Strange things can happen when one doesn't feel or express much.

Rod, a forty-four-year-old executive, is an extreme example. He learned as a child that expressing any emotion was unacceptable and became a virtual robot. He says he has never been angry; neither has he felt love or strong sexual arousal. In situations that would make almost anyone angry, he feels "mildly annoyed" or "slightly irritated." He's attracted to women in a vague sort of way but has all manner of problems with them and with sex. He sometimes doesn't get erections. When he does, he usually can't ejaculate. Whether he ejaculates or not, there isn't much feeling. Then there are the physical problems. His blood pressure is off the charts even though there's no family history of high blood pressure and even though he exercises and eats carefully. His exercise program is often on hold, however, because he's had back and neck problems for many years as well as stomach pain. And he's always having accidents when walking, running, and driving.

Though Rod's situation is extreme, it gives some clues as to what can happen when emotion is constantly blocked.

Because men are not trained to be aware of emotion, many of us don't notice feelings even though they may be apparent to observers. In my practice, it happens many times that a woman says her man is feeling a certain way (angry, irritated, fearful, or even joyful) and the man denies it. I don't want to imply that women are always correct in their reading of men's feelings—that is not the case—but I do know, after having gone over hundreds of such situations, that very often the men come to realize that they were indeed feeling as their partners said they were. In sex, a partner often picks up on the man's anxiety before the man himself does.

If determining your feelings is difficult, attending to the two main indicators of emotion—what's going on in your body and what's going on in your head—can be very helpful. Therapists and partners usually pick up on body language. When a client clenches his fists and maybe his teeth as well, I suspect he may be angry even if he denies it. I can't be certain, of course, but if he consistently manifests this behavior when a certain topic comes up, I know it's worth asking him to consider what he's feeling. Let's say you know that in certain situations your heart is pounding, your neck, back, or shoulders feel tight, your stomach is tight or upset, your hands are sweating, or that you're holding your breath or breathing shallowly. These things in themselves don't necessarily indicate emotion—maybe your heart is racing because you've been exercising, maybe your stomach is upset because of something you ate. But if these phenomena, singly or in combination, occur regularly in certain situations, ask yourself what emotion might be behind them. The examples I gave above are common signs of anxiety, fear, and anger. A trembling lip may indicate anxiety or, in conjunction with tears welling up, perhaps sadness.

Your mind is also full of clues about what you may be feeling. Research in the last twenty years strongly suggests that to a large extent emotion is generated and maintained by our thoughts. You may not be aware of being anxious, sad, or depressed, for instance, but if you're having thoughts of losing someone important to you or failing at an important task, you should ask yourself what emotion you might be having. Recurring images of hurting someone may indicate anger, hurt, rage, or frustration.

The examples I've given so far have to do with what most people consider negative emotions. But positive feelings are also indicated by your mind and body. If your usually tight neck muscles are not tight when you engage in a certain activity or are with a certain person, if your body feels light and generally good, or if you usually have positive thoughts and pictures about that person or activity, that may be a sign of relief, comfort, enthusiasm, joy, or even love.

WHERE ARE YOU?

In order to help to get a better idea of where you are and what you want to do about knowing and expressing emotion, consider the following questions: Do you know what you're feeling much of the time? When a lover or therapist asks what you're feeling, do you usually know, or are you at a loss? If you were asked the question of what you're feeling right now, while watching a movie, before, during, or after sex, or during a disagreement with your lover, would you know or be able to find out? Has a woman friend or lover ever told you that you're not in touch with your feelings or that you don't express them?

FEELINGS: PERMISSIBLE AND OTHERWISE

To further help determine if you need help getting in touch with your feelings, expressing them, or both, I have compiled a list of feelings, grouped in several categories. While not exhaustive, it does contain a number of ways of referring to the most common emotions. A useful activity is to go over the emotions on the list and try to recall a time when you felt each of them. Don't worry if you haven't felt some of them or if there seem to be redundancies; a number of the items are synonyms. Are you experiencing a variety of feelings, or are most of them in just one or two categories? If you're not experiencing a variety, you may want to do some work on getting in touch with more of your emotional world.

Then go through the list again, and for each emotion you recall having, ask yourself if you expressed it directly in words to anyone—for example, "I'm feeling distant from you"; "I'm feeling pressured and overwhelmed"; "I feel strong and confident"; "I love you." Calling someone names because you were angry or not speaking to them because you were upset does not count. If you haven't directly expressed any of the feelings other than anger, you have some work to do. If there are several categories of emotion that you haven't felt or expressed, you may want to expand your emotional capabilities. The same is true if you tend to be one-sided—that is, feel and express only positive emotion (strength, joy, confidence, and so on, but never fear, confusion, resentment, or sorrow) or only negative emotion (depression, insecurity, neglect, worry, and so on, but never happiness, satisfaction, affection, optimism, and so forth).

Feelings having to do with anger

Annoyed	Pissed off
Bitter	Resentful
Furious	Upset
Irritated	

Bad about self

Crushed	Hopeless
Defeated	Inadequate
Discouraged	Incompetent
Helpless	Insecure

Distanced

Alienated	Cold
Aloof	Disconnected
Bored	Put off

Fear/anxiety

Anxious	Panicked
Concerned	Scared
Horrified	Terrified
Intimidated	Uneasy
Nervous	Worried

Guilt/shame

Apologetic	Mortified
Embarrassed	Remorseful
Humiliated	Sorrowful

Good about self

Confident	Optimistic
Encouraged	Proud
Hopeful	Strong

Hurt

Betrayed	Jealous
Disappointed	Offended
Envious	Pained
Insulted	

Joy or happiness

Contented	High
Cheerful	Pleased
Delighted	Terrific
Ecstatic	Up
Glad	Wonderful

Left out

Abandoned	Neglected
Alone	Rejected
Ignored	Unloved
Lonely	

Love/affection

Caring	Loved
Close	Loving
Connected	Warm

Sadness

Blue	Low
Depressed	Melancholy
Down	Unhappy
Gloomy	

Sex

Aroused (or	Passionate
not aroused)	Sensual
Desirable	Sexy
Horny	Turned on
Hot	(or off)

Others

Ambivalent	Hassled
Appreciative	Overwhelmed
Confused	Pressured
Frustrated	Put out

GETTING IN TOUCH WITH EMOTION

Learning about your feelings is basically a matter of paying attention to your inner world. The simple exercise that follows can help.

EXERCISE 12–1: LOGGING FEELINGS

For the next two or three weeks, carry a small notebook or some index cards in a shirt or jacket pocket wherever you go. As many times as possible during each day—at least eight to ten times—ask yourself what you are feeling. Jot down in your book the day and time, the stimulus for the feeling, if you know what it is, and the feeling(s). Since no one but you is going to look at your notes, feel free to use whatever shorthand you like.

An entry in your book might look like this: "Mon 10 A.M.: Read that Bob died of heart attack. Feeling sad. Also scared: He was my age."

For best results, vary the times and places you check into your feelings. Make sure you check your feelings before and after sex and before and while you spend time with your children. You might also want to take in some movies or plays. Actors and directors are masters at manipulating emotion. They want to get you to feel pride, anger, sympathy, fear, sadness, and many other feelings. Since they are working at evoking feelings in you, this is a good way to check on your range of emotions.

If you don't know what you're feeling or aren't sure, take a moment and see what happens. You might want to consult the list of feelings given above; it's almost certain you're feeling at least one of them. Don't settle for "nothing," "don't know," or "neutral." These are not feelings. Make a guess.

Because men often use anger to conceal other feelings, ask yourself this when you feel hostile: "What would I be feeling if I wasn't angry?" Push yourself to come up with an alternative feeling. I can almost guarantee there's one there, probably having to do with hurt or pain. And make sure it's not a synonym for anger, like "mad" or "pissed off."

Beware of several traps. Feelings usually consist of only one word, as on the list above. If your expression of feelings consists of more than a word or two, check to make sure you're really talking about feelings. If your sentence would make as much sense if started with "I think," then you're *not* expressing feelings. But use your statement to uncover the feeling. If what you said was, "I feel my wife should assert herself more at work" (which is *not* an expression of feelings), this may mean that you feel sad because it seems your partner is being taken advantage of on the job or that you're frustrated because you can't help her there.

Another trap is to assume that feelings are exclusive. You may feel several things, some of which seem contradictory. There's nothing wrong with that. List all the emotions you're experiencing at the moment.

After a week or two, take a few minutes to go over the feelings you've written down. Do you experience a wide range of emotion, including the feelings that men have trouble with? Do you basically have the same feelings all the time? What kinds of feelings are missing from your list?

ALTERNATIVE VERSION

If the exercise as given is hard to do because you usually aren't aware of feelings, try the following. Whenever you have a few seconds to spare, just ask what is going on in your head (thoughts and images) and in your body (tight muscles, any kind of tension or upset), and take a guess what emotions are being manifested; looking over the list of feelings given above can aid in this endeavor. Try not to worry about being wrong. You will make incorrect guesses some of the time, everyone does—but the process tends to be self-correcting. As you mull over the emotions and the people and situations that evoke them, you'll be able to fine-tune your perceptions. You may realize you are more hurt than angry about what someone said or more anxious than sexually aroused with a certain person. Regularly noticing what your mind and body are doing and considering what feelings are there are excellent ways of getting in better touch with yourself.

FEELING STATEMENTS

In order to talk about feelings, we want to do more than just label them. We want to create statements about them. These statements include not only the name of the emotion but also what it and the event that evoked it mean to you. Using the same example as before, here's how a feeling statement about it might go (with the feelings italicized):

It *scared* the hell out of me that Bob died. We went to college together, and he was my age. Really hit me: Life doesn't go on forever. Made me very *concerned*. I haven't been taking care of myself. I'm carrying at least twenty extra pounds. The *fear* is motivating. I'm going to call my doctor for an appointment right now.

I'm also *sad*. I wasn't that *close* to Bob, but he seemed like a nice guy. Very sensitive and kind. It's *sad* to think he's no more. I'm *sorry* I didn't get to know him better. It's been typical of me to get close to the go-getters and not pay much attention to those like Bob who are more people-oriented. But the sadness I'm feeling suggests that I *miss* having friends like Bob, guys who aren't going to set the world on fire but who are decent and interested in me as a person, not as an account.

A feeling statement can be more or less elaborate than this illustration. But it must contain more than the simple "I'm sad" or "I'm feeling down." Sometimes, however, you may not know more than what you're feeling. In that case, it can be worth it to put out something like this to your partner or a friend: "I've been feeling very sad and low the last few days and have no idea what it's about." Of course, this is itself a feeling statement. If you're open to an exchange, it's possible that the questions of the listener may help you figure out what's going on.

EXERCISE 12–2: CREATING FEELING STATEMENTS

Here you want to develop a statement about your feelings, something that you might want to express to others.

Go over several of the notes from the preceding exercise and create feeling statements about them, as in the illustration I just gave. Your statements don't have to be as elaborate as that one, but they should have at least a few sentences in them.

You can also practice creating feeling statements when things come up in your life. Everything from the trivial to the monumental can serve your purpose: for example, someone cutting you off on the highway; a piece of good or bad news in the mail; a news event; the promotion, marriage, divorce, or death of someone you know. And make sure to go over some recent activities you did with your partner—making love, planning or taking a trip, dealing with a disagreement, and so on—and create feeling statements about each.

The more you practice identifying your feelings and creating statements about those feelings, the more comfortable you'll feel doing this and the more ready you'll be to express these statements to your partner when you choose to do so.

TO EXPRESS OR NOT TO EXPRESS

Being more aware of your feelings is useful in itself, because it helps you zero in on what's going on with you in a way that no amount of thinking can do. But since our primary concern here is with connecting with another person, the question now is when to express your feelings to your partner. All the rules are simple common sense. What purpose will be served by telling her? By not telling her? What harm or benefit may result to you, to her, to the relationship? For example, if your partner has bought a piece of clothing on sale that cannot be returned and you don't like it, clearly no purpose is served by telling her, so it's probably best to keep your dislike to yourself.

Expressing Negative Feelings

You may believe, like many men, that you are being virtuous by not expressing negative feelings to your partner. You don't want to burden her with your anxieties, concerns, complaints, doubts, and so forth. While that's an understandable sentiment, there's also another perspective. Chances are excellent that your partner is picking up that something is wrong. But she doesn't know what's going on and is probably thinking that your mood is the result of something she's done. If that's true, she can't do anything about it because you're not talking. Even if it isn't true, she's still in a funny place that isn't helping her or the relationship any. She can't get close to you and she doesn't know what's going on. There's also the point that it may help you to share what's on your mind. Just talking about a painful experience or feeling can make you feel better. And perhaps she can do or say something to comfort you. This is how people get to know one another better and share their lives. According to psychologist and marital therapist Dan Wile, this is what true intimacy is: each of you telling the other the main things that are on your mind and in your guts.

Expressing Positive Feelings

With positive feelings, there's not as much to think about. It's rare, for example, that expressing appreciation, affection, excitement, happiness, joy, love, or passion carry much risk. We're talking about your partner now, of course, not the boss's wife. Ayala Pines's research into what she calls "marriage burnout" demonstrates that the more that appreciation is expressed in a marriage, the less burnout there is. If you're not expressing such emotions to your partner, you really need to ask yourself why.

It's amazing how often a woman will complain about not hearing something such as "I love you" or "You look terrific" and the man will respond with "But I do love you" or "You certainly did look terrific." But why didn't he say it spontaneously? Why should the woman have to fish for compliments and expressions of love? The rest of this discussion assumes that you do love and care about your partner but just aren't expressing the feelings directly. If you don't like or love your partner, or are so angry with her that you're not even sure, you probably need to get competent professional help or a new partner.

Human beings need to be appreciated and complimented. We all need our daily quota of strokes. When we don't get enough, we are often irritable and out of sorts. When we do get enough, we're more pleasant to be with, more amenable to working things out, and can endure a great many things that otherwise would have us climbing the walls. Yet it's amazing that both at home and at work so many of us—men and women—feel unappreciated, unnoticed, and unliked.

If you have trouble expressing compliments or words of love, the next two exercises can help.

EXERCISE 12–3:
EXPRESSING APPRECIATION OR COMPLIMENTS

Spend some time over the next week thinking of things you like and appreciate about your partner and jot them down. Most of the time you won't actually have to do any thinking; you'll be aware of saying things to yourself like "I'm glad to have her help with X," "She really looks great," "She's such a joy," "She's got a great sense of humor." Write these thoughts on a piece of paper.

At the end of the week, go over your list and ask yourself how many of these thoughts you expressed in words to her. Be careful with this. Many men believe they've expressed a compliment when in fact all they did was say it to themselves. Make sure you actually said it to her. If there are compliments you didn't give to her, would you be willing to express more of them? What would it take?

If you're willing, just do it. Not all at once, but when it's appropriate. For example, if you appreciated the help she gave on some task, even if that was two weeks ago, why not tell her now? If she looked beautiful when you went out last weekend, why not tell her now? If you appreciate her intelligence, decisiveness, humor, mothering skills, cooking, or anything else, why not just say so?

Give yourself a goal of giving her a specific number of compliments in the next three days, maybe two or three of them. Keep track of how many you give and what they were.

Then ask yourself what good feelings you have about her that you're not letting her know about. If there's no compelling reason for your silence, see if you're willing to break it.

It's a good idea to check whether your compliments are limited to just one area.

The girlfriend of a client recently asked him if he could say something nice about her that didn't have to do with her looks or sexual abilities, which he has effusively praised. Although there are many other things about her he admires and likes, he hadn't mentioned them. He was wondering if he should stop mentioning her looks and sexual skills; he didn't want her to feel he was treating her as a sex object. My take on the situation, confirmed by her, was not that she minded the compliments he was giving—she loved them—but only that she also wanted to hear about other qualities he liked.

Women adore being treated as sex objects, but they detest being treated as *nothing but* sex objects. Feel free to compliment her looks and sexual competence, but make sure to mention other qualities as well.

You should do this exercise every week for a month or so, until you get into the habit of expressing your positive feelings.

Now to the famous phrase "I love you." Few words mean as much to a woman, yet a great many women claim they don't hear it at all or as much as they'd like. What's fascinating about this is that, upon hearing the complaint, the men usually respond immediately with "But of course I love you." The problem is not lack of love but lack of expression.

EXERCISE 12–4: SAYING "I LOVE YOU"

For the next week, every time you feel that you love your partner, tell her. If she's not there, call and tell her. If you can't reach her, tell her later: "I was in a meeting today but had a hard time concentrating. All I could do was think of how much I love you." Another option is to write your feelings down on a piece of paper and leave it where she'll find it. Don't get fancy: "I love you" or "I adore you" is all that's needed. Other phrases, such as "I'm so glad you're in my life" or "Marrying you was the best thing I ever did," will be taken as synonyms for "I love you" by some women but not by others.

If you can't do what I've suggested above—that is, tell her you love her—then write your feelings on a piece of paper when you have them. Do this for several weeks, and at the end of each week, go over what you've written. Then close your eyes and imagine yourself telling her these things. Many men find that after a week or two of this, it's much easier to express their love directly to their partners.

In some relationships, whether or not the man is expressing compliments and words of love, he feels that he's not receiving as many of them as he wants. He feels neglected, unappreciated, taken for granted, unloved, or something of the kind. If this is true for you, you might want to do something about it. For example:

I agreed last week with what you said about me not sending out enough positive and loving messages to you. And I've been trying to say more of the positive things I feel. But I realized that I'm in the same boat as you and would also like some compliments. I often feel taken for granted. Like when I got your sister's car ready for her trip. That was a pain in the butt and took my whole Sunday. I only did it for you. Your sister said thanks, but I don't recall your saying anything. I felt really bad, as if you didn't care about all the trouble I had gone through to do something you wanted. When I do something like that, I'd like some appreciation. A hug and a thank you would mean a lot.

GETTING IT OUT OF YOUR HEAD

Much of what I've been saying in this chapter can be summarized as getting your feelings out of your head or body and making them public. As I mentioned earlier, men frequently have been thinking or feeling but not expressing what their partners want to hear. So most of the time it's not a question of finding things to say but simply getting out what's already there.

A related issue has less to do with feelings than with just keeping your partner up to date with what's going on in your world. Here's one example of what often happens.

Tracy calls John at work, a regular practice of hers that he usually welcomes, and starts telling him about something that happened that morning. A moment later, John screams at her to stop bothering him and hangs up. Both of them were quite upset when they came to see me. John explained that the day was frantic. Two of his largest clients were visiting and a report was due before closing. He viewed Tracy's call as intrusive and insensitive. The truth was that Tracy was typically very considerate of John's time and work, but he hadn't said a word to her about how that day was special. If he had only told her, she wouldn't have called.

The kind of contact we're talking about here is usually far less difficult and weighty than what we've already discussed. But it's important, because not maintaining it results in unnecessary upset and arguments. When something changes in your schedule or in your mind that might affect your partner, why not tell her?

WHAT ABOUT TEARS?

Crying is a natural way of expressing feelings associated with losing someone or being reunited with someone we thought we had lost or might lose. I suspect that when someone doesn't cry at certain times—for example, on learning of the death of a loved one—some serious suppression is going on. While I don't think one has to cry to be a good person, I do believe that being able to do so is one sign of being in touch with and able to express certain feelings.

All babies cry, and it's not unusual for five- or six-year-old boys. But you don't see many ten-year-olds cry and it's rare in the popular media to see or read about a male of any age crying. The message, although perhaps delivered earlier, starts getting through around ages seven and eight: "Big boys don't cry." The message often comes from parents, but also from peers and is certainly reinforced by them. An eight-year-old boy who cries during a game or at school is going to find out very fast that such behavior is unacceptable. It's fascinating and quite sad to watch eight- and nine-year-old boys when they are hurt, disappointed, fearful, or in grief. You can see the tears well up and the lips trembling, but you also see them fighting back the tears, trying not to look at you, biting their lips and, as Jonathan Kellerman so aptly put it, "straining for macho."

And that's all it takes for many males. They may never again cry, not when a friend or their parents die, not when they return from a war to see their wives and children after years of absence, not even when they are so sad or lonely or heartbroken that they're thinking of killing themselves.

You can unleash the ability to cry if you want to. What's required is to remove the blocks that have been put in the way. Being in a safe setting, or with a safe person, makes a great difference. Many men, for example, have cried for the first time in many years when they participated in encounter groups popular during the 1960s and '70s or in group therapy or in men's groups. Many men have cried for the first time in years when they were in a relationship where they felt very safe. They knew it was acceptable to cry in such places, that they wouldn't be put down or considered less manly for doing so.

What these men accomplished in groups and relationships can be done on one's own by deciding that crying is okay and by looking at how you stop yourself from doing it. When the tears want to come out, what are you doing to stop them? A common obstacle is fear—not only of not being manly, but also of not being able to stop crying if you start. Since men aren't accustomed to their own tears, they often fear being overwhelmed by them. That fear is not realistic. You usually can stop the crying when you want or, even if not, you do get cried out and it stops of its own accord.

Here is one man's account. He decided, in his forties, that not being able to cry made him an incomplete human being. He felt bad that he hadn't cried when his mother died a few years earlier. He had felt sad and desolate but was aware at the moment that he wouldn't let himself cry. He set himself the task of sitting home one night and thinking about his mother. If the tears were there, he wanted to let them out. They were, and he did:

> This is the first time I've cried since I was a baby. It was frightening at first. It felt like a tidal wave of tears, and I thought I might drown in it, but I made an amazing discovery. Crying actually feels good. It's a way of handling sadness, and you feel better as a result. I somehow feel more complete about my mother than I have before. She was very good to me and a wonderful person. It's fitting that her son cried for her. When I feel like crying in the future, I'm going to let it happen. No more stomping down the tears like I've done all my life. If someone doesn't like it, that's their problem.

Another man, in his thirties, made this report:

> The last time I remember crying was when I was eight or nine and my Little League team lost a big game. After that, I not only didn't cry myself but became part of the macho police and made fun of other guys who cried. But a few years ago when Ellie and I almost

split up and then decided to stay together, I just started weeping like a baby. I was surprised and embarrassed, but I thought about it later and felt, What's the big deal? I'm not any less a man for it. Crying is okay. Since then I cry a lot, at least for a man. I cry when I'm sad, I cry when I'm happy, and you wouldn't believe the stupid movies I've cried at. And when we had our son, when Ellie was holding him for the first time, I just wept and wept. I'm not sure what I was feeling, it felt like ten different things, but it was wonderful.

EXPRESSING YOURSELF SEXUALLY

Many women I've talked with complain that men don't express their sexual passion and pleasure. Even women who didn't have this as a primary complaint could recall one or more lovers who fit this category. The specific complaints ranged from men who didn't initiate sex with passion and enthusiasm to those who didn't express pleasure during sex and, perhaps most surprisingly, those who were so quiet during orgasm that their partners weren't sure if they had come.

My take on all this is that it has to do with the general flattening of affect in men because of what we've been taught. We learn that any expression of emotion is suspect, and any indication of being carried away by feelings is even worse, so we tend not to let ourselves get carried away. As a result, many of us keep a tight rein on all our feelings. Even though sex may feel great, and orgasm may feel terrific, we tend not to let it show. This is unfortunate in at least two respects. First, we cheat our partners. By not letting them know how much we desire and enjoy them, we rob them of feeling desirable and knowing how much pleasure they bring us. Second, we rob ourselves, because the expression of desire and pleasure can add to our own arousal and enjoyment.

Many of us are unaware of how inhibited we are in these areas. I have watched many times while men listened in disbelief as their partners reported they didn't feel desired (even though the men initiated sex) and didn't feel the man enjoyed sex. These men were simply unaware of how little they let their feelings show.

One way to check into how expressive you are in sex is to ask your partner. Does she know when you're really hot for her? Does she know how much you enjoy making love with her or when she does a certain thing? Is she aware of how much you enjoy your orgasms?

Another way of checking is to look into yourself. When you desire her, are you letting all of your desire show or are you doing some heavy editing? An example of editing would be feeling "I really want her" but saying only something like "Would you like to make love?" Why not show her and tell her what you're actually feeling?

And during sex, are there any feelings, sounds, and movements that you're bottling up?

One man whose partner complained about his inexpressiveness told me this when we were alone: "I know there's a lot I'm keeping to myself. I really do enjoy sex, but I'm afraid I'd sound like a squealing pig if I let it all show. This doesn't quite fit my image of myself, and I'm not sure how well she'd accept what I might do." What he didn't know was that his wife had a lover before him who did let it all hang out and she loved it. "I loved seeing him so uninhibited and out of control," she said, "and it made me feel so powerful, that I was the source of all this pleasure."

I have never heard a woman complain that her lover was too uninhibited, that he made too much noise, that he expressed too much pleasure. When you think about it, it's clear that we love to see others express pleasure, especially when we're the source of it. We delight in babies who squeal and squirm with joy when we touch them. We delight in how excited our dogs get when we come home and pet them. And most men delight in women who are "wild" and "uninhibited" lovers. There may be a moral here.

If you want to be more expressive in sex, just attend to the difference between what you're feeling on the inside and what you're exhibiting on the outside. If there's a sound, a word, a movement that wants to come out, why not let it? If you have concerns about how your partner might react, why not discuss this with her first? As you express more, I'm sure you'll find that your and your partner's enjoyment will increase. Decorum has its place, but not in the bedroom.

Speaking of which, let's consider words that you don't find in the Sunday newspaper. Many people find that so-called dirty words such as *fuck, cock, prick, pussy,* and *cunt* sometimes more accurately express their feelings than polite terms and also serve to heighten arousal. As I mentioned before, you may not want to *make love* every single time you have sex. At times, you may want to *fuck* or *screw*. The use of four-letter words isn't for everyone, and it pays to be cautious in new relationships, but you never know until you try it or at least think about it. If your partner doesn't like such words, you two need to talk. A number of men have told me about situations in which their partners were shocked or disgusted the first time the man mentioned wanting to fuck, to eat pussy, or to have his cock sucked. But in almost all these situations, the woman became more accepting after the man explained why he used the language he did and what it meant to him. And, to be fair, I've also heard reports where it was the woman who introduced the man to the pleasures of using plain words in the bedroom.

And don't forget about talking about sex after it's over, minutes later and even days later. Such talk provides guidance to your partner and can help the good feelings continue long after the act is over. The kinds of expression can vary from general comments about what went on to more specific feedback:

Saturday morning was special. You're terrific.

I feel so good and so close to you. I love making love with you.

That was wonderful. I especially liked it when you licked my nipples the same time you were playing with my penis.

I keep thinking about last night. It was great. I'd like a repeat performance ASAP.

Of course, "I love you," if sincerely meant, is never out of place.

Regular practice with the exercises and ideas in this chapter can make a dramatic difference in how well you express yourself and the quality of your relationship. Men have a lot to gain by being more expressive.

13

Tools for Dealing with Conflict

"We're grinding each other up into mulch each time we fight. There's got to be a better way."—MAN, 35

CONFLICT is an inevitable part of close relationships. How it is handled determines to a large extent how well a relationship and sex go. In this chapter I discuss a number of ideas and methods that can help keep conflict to a minimum and from getting out of hand. I have given examples of most of them in the previous chapters, but I want to get into more detail now. They aren't panaceas—unfortunately, there are no panaceas—and they cannot by themselves undo the effects of years of neglect, distress, and abuse. But these suggestions can help cut down on war games and stop discussions from getting out of hand.

Keep two things in mind whenever you deal with or think about your partner and while you read the following material. One is your overall goal with her, which I'll assume is something like having a loving relationship. The more you focus on this goal, the less you'll give in to temptations to berate, criticize, and monstrify her.

The second thing to keep in mind is that even though it may not seem that way, you always have choices. No matter how badly certain conversations have gone in the past, no matter how upset you've gotten when

257

she said or did a certain thing, it doesn't have to be this way now. You can choose to listen more empathetically, to greet a complaint of hers with a question for more information rather than a countercomplaint, to phrase your comments in a more constructive way, to call a time-out when things are going badly. These choices are always available, and every important change starts with making one different choice. The smoker decides not to have a cigarette after dinner, the drinker not to have a drink before. If you pay attention, you'll notice many opportunities for doing things in ways that will help you reach your goal.

REGULAR SUMMIT MEETINGS

The first tool is the most general and also one of the best for preventing conflicts: a regular time for having discussions. A major problem in relationships is feelings, complaints, and issues that don't get dealt with. They get swept under the rug but continue to cause trouble. It can help immeasurably if couples have a definite time each week where each partner feels free to bring up anything he or she wants. This prevents anything from festering for more than a week.

The first thing to do is schedule a regular time for the meeting, a time when you won't be interrupted or in a hurry. Most of the couples I've worked with have chosen a time on Sundays, but any day is fine. At least thirty minutes should be allotted. Either partner can start, but a modified talk-and-listen format should be followed (see the next section). It helps if only one issue or problem is discussed at a time. Finish with item A, then go on to item B, and so on. When one person is finished, the other starts.

It's fine to bring up problems and negative feelings, but it's important not to ignore the good things that happened. This is especially true in relationships when one or both partners don't regularly express compliments and affection. If you felt grateful to your partner for something she said or did, you should make a point of telling her during a summit.

It also helps if each person says what he or she wants done about something negative that's been brought up. If, for example, you are upset that your partner spent more money on the rug she bought than you wanted, what do you want? An apology? to return the rug? a promise to check with you on future large expenditures? or what?

Here is an abbreviated example of how a summit meeting might go:

A: "First, I want to say how much it meant to me when you talked so long and kindly to my mother on the phone. I know you don't like her and you did it only for me and I really appreciate that." [Because this statement is a short compliment, there's no need for B to say what he heard.]

"Now I have two other things. One is I was upset when you didn't leave a note about Bill's message. Because you weren't here when I got home and I went to bed early, I didn't get the message until the next morning. I feel a duty to call him back the same day but couldn't because I didn't know he called. In the future, I'd like for us both to write down phone messages and leave them on the fridge, even if we think the other one will be here in a few minutes and we'll just tell them. Can you agree to that?"

B: "Both of us should write down all messages and post them on the fridge [indicating that B has understood A's point]. Yes, it's a good idea. And I'm sorry about Bill's message. I really blew that one. How about I take you to dinner tonight to make up for it?"

This example may seem too easy because there was no disagreement. That is possible, but it's also true that when couples regularly have meetings to air feelings and resolve conflicts, disagreements tend to become less common. Partners learn that they can talk and be understood and that problems can be worked out. If this is not the case, further work with the ideas and exercises in this section or a visit to a therapist is required.

There's no question that such meetings help most couples. The problem is that some couples, even in the face of overwhelming evidence of the effectiveness of the meetings, often start skipping them because of other events that come up. The best way to prevent this outcome is for both partners to commit themselves to have the meetings once a week come hell or high water. It's best if the meetings are held at the same time each week. But sometimes that's hard to do; for example, when you get an important invitation that conflicts with the meeting time. In that case, set a specific new time for the meeting as soon as you realize you can't have it at the regular time.

ENSURING UNDERSTANDING

In previous chapters I've given numerous examples of informal ways of ensuring understanding ("Let's see if I understand what you're saying . . ." or "I hear you're upset because . . ."). But understanding is most important when the issue is crucial or when tension is already present. People feel less belligerent and more accommodating when they believe they are heard and understood. This exercise can help.

EXERCISE 13–1: TALK AND LISTEN

When either of you have something important you want the other one to hear and understand, make an appointment to say it. The time need not be right now; you can arrange to do it later, when you are both reasonably relaxed and free from interruption.

The speaker (let's say it's you) should stick to one point and should speak for no longer than three minutes. This may sound short, but it isn't if you stick to one issue. It helps, of course, if you go over your thoughts in advance to ensure the presentation is as clear and concise as possible. The more you stick to the rules of assertive communication discussed in Chapter 8, the better things will go. It's especially important that you speak from a position of "This is how I see it [feel about it, recall it, think we should handle it]" rather than in a way suggesting the incorrectness or impropriety of any other point of view.

Your partner has only one job: to understand what you're saying from your point of view. She is not to interrupt unless she needs clarification, and she is not to respond.

Let her know when you're done. She is then to summarize your main point in a sentence or two to show her understanding (e.g., "I hear you feel neglected because I was out at meetings every night last week. You think that means I'm losing interest in you."). If you believe she has correctly understood you, let her know. If not, restate your main point and have her reflect back her new understanding. Continue in this way until you are satisfied that she understands. Try not to be picky, however. Understanding means only that she can correctly summarize your main point, not that she can repeat verbatim all that you said.

If she wants to respond to what you said, use the same format with you now in the role of listener. You may want to take a short break between your statement and hers. And remember that understanding does not require or imply agreement. It's enough that you understand each other's positions. When that's the case, the two of you will be able to go on to try to reconcile your differences.

Say a conversation is getting heated and you believe your partner hasn't understood your position. You might want to say something like this: "I think things are starting to get out of hand, and I don't want us to have a fight. I'm not sure I've expressed my feelings well on this business. How about we take a little break and then we can each take a few minutes to present our positions without interruption? Or we can do it now if you want." If the two of you have already talked about the exercise, you can simply say you'd like to do the talk-and-listen thing.

Virtually every couple who has used this exercise regularly has reported significant gains in understanding and goodwill.

DE-MONSTRIFYING YOUR PARTNER

Although in the midst of a struggle it may feel to you that your partner is a sadistic witch out to cause you pain, you need to remind yourself that's not who she really is. She's probably pretty much the same as you—a loving, caring person who's hurting and not expressing herself very well. It's a safe bet that she's in as much pain and feeling as confused, as upset, and as hopeless as you. It's very difficult for one partner to feel good when the other is suffering. And while it's not rare for one partner to try to get back at the other one, that's invariably because of some sense of feeling wronged.

It can be of enormous benefit to check back over major conflicts and recall how you saw your partner. If you usually saw her as the basically good person she is, there's no problem and nothing to be done. But if you tend to make a demon out of her, that can be changed. It's very difficult to want to listen and talk straight to someone you view in negative ways. It's much easier to resolve conflict if you perceive her as someone you love and who loves you even though she doesn't happen to agree with you right now, and as someone who also wants to find a solution to the problem.

The best way I know to see your partner's behavior in perspective is through empathy, through trying to understand her situation. Let's say it's true that she was ranting and raving the other day after you didn't have an erection with her. She called you impotent and said she wanted to have an affair. You felt horrible and angry. You may be focusing on the feelings you had and be seeing her as an incredibly cruel witch out to destroy what the two of you have. But ask how this usually loving and supportive woman could have reached the point where she'd say such things. This is not a question that many of us stop to think about, but it can be enormously helpful.

Let's say you know she's insecure about her attractiveness. Perhaps a hard penis is her main way of knowing that she's desirable; without that sign, she may doubt herself. Since you've had erection problems for some time, the two of you have been over this before and generally she's been able to take things in stride, which itself is a sign of just how understanding and supportive she usually is and a point you should focus on. But she's been feeling shaky lately, both because her work isn't going well and because you haven't had an erection in several weeks. Isn't it possible that when you didn't get erect last Tuesday, that was just the final straw? She needed a boost to her ego and was hoping your erection would do it for her. When that didn't happen, she felt ugly and unwanted and blew up. To the extent that you can understand her situation, you'll be far less angry and upset. Maybe you'll even be able to be supportive of her.

It can also help to directly manipulate the picture of her you have in your mind. When you're feeling she's cruel, evil, out to get you, and so on, you're probably picturing her as looking like that kind of person: perhaps her face contorted with rage or snickering over your unhappiness. Try changing the picture. Envision her as she usually looks and see if that doesn't make you feel better.

Whenever you're thinking of your partner in an ugly way—when you're taking a time-out from a conflict, when you feel she's deliberately out to get you, when you're in the middle of a tense situation with her—check how you're seeing her and make the changes that seem appropriate.

One more thing that may help you see your partner as she truly is and cut down on demonizing her is to look directly at her when the two of you are talking. When you look at her, even if she's angry, chances are good you'll notice that this is someone you really care about and who is in pain. This can help stop or at least mitigate the monstrifying process.

GIVE HER THE BENEFIT OF THE DOUBT

Another way of saying that you can de-monstrify your partner is to give her the benefit of the doubt. That is, assume she did what she did for good and sensible reasons rather than because she was trying to hurt you. Try to develop the mind-set that your partner is a good, loving, and caring person who wouldn't deliberately try to make your life miserable. I realize this might seem hard to do at times, but here's an example of how it can be done.

> John got furious with his wife for what he considered her extrava-gant tendencies—that is, when she spent more money on clothes for herself than he thought necessary. At such times he perceived her as totally unconcerned about their hard-earned money and the things he wanted to spend the money on. Since he felt she didn't care, he would go into a rage and scream obscenities. John needed to tell himself certain things when Stella came home with new clothes. First was that the Stella who bought the clothes was the same "sweet Stella"—his words for her in happier times—whom he loved, not some crazy spending machine totally out of control. Second was that her job, unlike his, required her to dress well, a fact he knew but often lost sight of. Third was that she did care, and manifested her concern by shopping only during sales and by buying what in fact were relatively inexpensive items.
>
> John practiced making these statements to himself, at first in my office while relaxed, then at home with Stella when she made smaller purchases, and later with her when she went on a major shopping expedition. By continually reminding himself that she was doing the best she could to save money and still meet the clothing requirements she faced at work (the net effect of the three self-messages he gave himself), over time he was able significantly to reduce his negative feelings about her purchases and to be much more understanding.

We should try to show the same understanding and tolerance of our partner's behavior that we'd like her to show to us. We usually think there is justification for our own acts. Why not grant the same for the acts of the women we love?

UNDERSTANDING AND FORGIVING YOUR PARTNER

You may believe that your partner has said or done something so heinous that you're entirely justified in your ugly feelings toward her or that you just don't know how to let go of them. It's possible you may need to forgive her before you can move on. We don't hear much about forgiving these days, but I have found it to be wonderfully beneficial. Basically it means saying: "Even though I don't like what you did or said, I'm willing to let go of my hurt, my anger, and my desire to get back at you. I want our relationship to work, so I want to let bygones be bygones and to get on with our lives."

Unfortunately, it may not be that simple. You may find that you can't simply forgive, that you need something from her in order to forgive her.

Take as much time as you need to consider what it would take for you to be able to forgive. Maybe you need an apology, or that she explain in detail why she did what she did so that you can understand it better, or that she promise not to say or do it again. Or it may be something else entirely. Whatever it is, write it down and put it away for a few days. Then come back to what you wrote and see if it still sounds right. Then spend a few moments imagining that she does what you want. How do you feel about that? Can you then forgive her and let go of the feelings you've been carrying? If the answer is no or if you're not sure, consider again what you need to forgive her. Maybe there's something else.

Forgiving is usually easier if you can understand the action from her point of view. This exercise can help.

EXERCISE 13–2: UNDERSTANDING AND
DEFENDING WHAT YOUR PARTNER DID

The idea behind this exercise is very simple. You are going to act as your partner's defense attorney. She is on trial for the behavior that bothers you (something she said or did). You are her attorney and have to persuade the jury (really you) that what she did was, if not right, at least reasonable and understandable. You are to make as strong a case for her as possible. Although it may be hard to believe right now, the stronger the case you make for her, the better it will be for you.

You will need lots of empathy to do the exercise properly. You must set your own feelings aside and see the situation as much as possible from her point of view. And you can feel free to interview her to get information about how she saw the situation and how she felt.

The main mistake people make with this exercise is being cavalier about it. Doing it properly will take over an hour and perhaps several hours. You want to marshal all the evidence and put together a strong case for her. When you have all this in order, there are three options for presenting it: Write or type the argument; speak it into a tape recorder; or present it orally to her or a third party, such as a friend (said presentation should be at least one page long or take several minutes to give orally).

The material on page 262 of this chapter explaining how "this usually loving and supportive woman" could have said the cruel things she did when you didn't have an erection is an example of the kind of defense I'm talking about here.

No one I've presented this exercise to has been enthusiastic at first. But it's a powerful technique that does result in changed attitudes.

AGREE, AGREE, AGREE

In any relationship there will be disagreements about certain issues that need to be worked out. But it's an infallible rule that the more agreement that there is, the easier it will be to solve the problem. In many cases, the real issues don't even get dealt with because the partners get into conflict about peripheral matters.

Look at what so often happens. Say your partner's very upset, claims you don't love her, and accuses you of having an affair. Let's say you're innocent of the charge. Since she really blasted you, you probably come on just as strong. "That's the stupidest thing I've ever heard. I'm either at the office or here. When the hell would I have time for an affair?"

The real issue, I suspect, is not about affairs. My guess is that she's concerned about the way you've been relating to her. Maybe you haven't shown much interest in spending time or having sex with her. She's worried about what this means and may be angry as well. So instead of saying, "I'm worried about us. We seem to be drifting apart," she accuses you of having an affair. Since you're being attacked, you defend. And you know you're right: You're not having an affair and you tell her so.

But now she's in a bad situation. It would be terrific if she could realize she didn't say exactly what she wanted to and make a U-turn. But maybe she can't. So she may feel that she has to defend her accusation. She may therefore reply that she doesn't know where you go on Sunday mornings when you say you're playing golf, or what you do on all those trips to Boston. What kind of business are you doing there, anyway? You may now feel you have to deny her accusation once again and perhaps account for your time in Boston.

But let's say you caught yourself and decided to try something different. Is there anything in what she's saying and implying that you could agree with? It makes no sense to agree to an affair if you're not having one, but are there reasons for her to think that you might be having one? In other words, can you understand what's going on with her? Suppose you said this to her: "I can understand why you think I might be having an affair. We haven't been close lately." In effect, this amounts to agreeing with her concerns. Imagine the effect on her. She doesn't have to defend or prove anything. Now she can get to what's troubling her. And you haven't lost anything. Rather, you've gained an opportunity for a serious conversation with your wife about what's going on in your marriage.

Take another example. Your partner says: "I'm sick of this. You never do your share around the house." A typical defensive reply would be to tell her she's wrong and enumerate all the household tasks you've recently done. Then she may feel forced to deny them ("Like hell you take out the garbage every week; you took it out only once last month") or claim that you still don't do as much as she does ("Big deal! So you take out the garbage. Do you know what I do every week?"). We are clearly headed for an unpleasant experience.

But suppose you decided to try something different and said this in response to her first statement: "I know I usually argue with you about this, but you're right: I don't do as much as you." This will probably stop her in her tracks. Now you can have a useful conversation about household chores, a common source of disagreement between couples.

I'm suggesting you seriously consider agreeing with your partner's complaints and criticisms and thereby allow the two of you to get to the serious issues. Don't allow yourself to get hung up on and defensive about whether you "never" do X, "always" do Y, or even about her choice of words. Since she's probably angry or upset, you can bet her words won't be tactful or precise.

"I object. This is the weirdest thing I ever heard. Why should I agree with my partner if she's wrong?"

I understand that what I'm saying can sound very strange. It sounded strange to me when I first heard of it years ago, and I was reluctant to hear more. I was especially concerned because it seemed as if I were being asked to lie. It helped me to understand that was not the case.

The real request is to find something in your partner's criticism that you can agree with. Maybe it seems surprising, but there almost always is something. No matter how outrageous her statements, no matter how exaggerated, there's usually a kernel of truth somewhere there. In the illustration above of the man charged with having an affair, he wasn't in fact having one. But he had been very distant from his wife, so there was reason for her to think that maybe he was. He did not agree that he was having an affair, which would have been a lie, but rather to understanding how she could think he was, which was true.

Many people find it easier to agree with feelings than with content. After all, if your partner says she feels X, Y, or Z, there's little room for disagreement. Acknowledgment of her feelings can help. "You're really upset with me"; "You're angry about what happened tonight."

Even better is if you can validate her feelings: "I understand why you feel that way"; "I can see why you're so disappointed"; "You have a right to feel that way."

Probably best of all is if you can validate her feelings and some of the content as well. "You're right. I was nasty to your sister. I can see why you'd be upset."

Although I've ranked these kinds of agreement in terms of good, better, and best, all are helpful. Any agreement is better than no agreement, and the greater the agreement, the less the chance of defensiveness and arguments.

Go over some arguments you've had with your partner and consider when you could have agreed with something she was saying. Then think over some complaints she's likely to make in the future. This isn't difficult. Most people can determine in advance what their partner will soon criticize. Then decide how you could agree with at least some of what she's saying to make for a more constructive discussion about the issue.

Therapist Dan Wile makes the important point that trying to find a way to agree is useful because it counteracts our natural tendency in such situations to distort in the direction of disagreeing. Agreeing with what you can agree with focuses on the similarities between you and your partner rather than on the differences. This can put both of you into a more relaxed and positive frame of mind, so you can better work on what you truly disagree about.

U-TURNS

In driving, a U-turn consists of turning around and going back the way you came after realizing you were going the wrong direction. In conversations, a U-turn is slightly different; here you head off in any new direction once you realize that the way you are going is leading to trouble.

Anytime you are aware that one of you is being defensive, getting sidetracked by issues of right and wrong, or that the conversation is getting out of control, consider a U-turn. A U-turn has the advantage of allowing the discussion to continue without interruption. If it works, you may not need a time-out (discussed later).

A U-turn can be almost anything that puts the conversation back on a better plane. One example is what we just covered, to stop defending yourself and agree with the portion of your partner's comments that you can agree with. Apologizing for something you did is another kind of U-turn, as is apologizing for being defensive just now.

Let's look at an example, taken from a conversation that took place in my office. The man was trying to say that his wife's sexual excitement had decreased, but this is how he put it: "She used to be a screamer. I mean, you could hear her blocks away. And then it suddenly stopped. Ever since then, nothing."

> HER: "That's not true. I never screamed." [Instead of focusing on the main issue—her decreased passion—she gets caught up in a word he used. He now feels the need to defend the use of that word and everything gets off the track.]

HIM: "Of course you did. You were a real screamer. You can't deny that."

HER: "I most certainly can. I'm not a screamer!"

A U-turn could have easily turned the situation around.

HIM: "Well, I guess I picked the wrong word. What I meant is that you used to be much more excited in sex than you are now."

HER: "Sure. There was a huge change."

Now we're dealing with agreement and can go on with the conversation. But this was almost lost as they started to get into a dispute of whether or not she used to scream. It's sad, as in this case, when lovers get into conflict over trivia and can't see that they agree about the major issue.

Here's another example of using a U-turn. Weeks ago you agreed to stop grabbing your partner's breasts in sex and to be more gentle. But just now you forgot and grabbed, and she got furious.

HER: "I can't trust a word you say. You promised not to grab and you're still doing it. You don't give a damn about my feelings [she's upset and is being provocative]."

YOU: "Christ, I blow it one time and suddenly I'm the worst person in the world." [Sure enough, you got pulled in and are defending yourself.]

As soon as these words are out of your mouth, you realize you're heading for an argument. So you try a U-turn: "I'm sorry, you're right, I totally forgot myself. I can see that you would be upset about it." Chances are good that this U-turn will turn the conversation around. Now the two of you can have a calmer discussion about the nongrabbing policy and the deviations from it that are certain to occur.

APOLOGIZE

Just as there is incredible power in agreeing with your accuser, there is incredible power in apologizing for something you did wrong or for the hurt you caused. But many of us men have difficulty saying, "I'm sorry."

We've had little permission to acknowledge errors and to apologize. It makes us feel weak and less manly, and that's unfortunate.

If apologizing is hard for you, you might want to consider doing something about it. When you feel you were wrong, when you feel you hurt someone, you should draft an apology in your mind, rehearse it, and then consider if you want to give it. No matter how awkward you feel, I think you'll be pleased with the results. And try to remember that there is nothing wimpy about apologizing. It takes a strong person to be able to say he's made a mistake or feels bad for what he's done.

Apologies are often parts of agreeing with your partner ("You're right, I was late; I'm sorry") and making U-turns ("I'm sorry I got so defensive; I can understand why you're angry").

Although it's essential to be able to apologize for your behavior, there is at least one circumstance where an apology not only won't satisfy your partner but may actually inflame her further. This occurs when you continually do the same offensive thing and continually apologize for it. She will correctly believe that you're just using apologies as a way to contain her anger, which, of course, will make her angrier. This is one good reason not to agree to anything you can't or won't follow through with, a subject to which I now turn.

KEEP YOUR AGREEMENTS

Often the outcome of a conversation is that you agree to do or not to do something. If you do make an agreement, you need to do what you agreed to, which is one good reason not to agree to anything unless you're certain you can and will do it. (If you don't want to do what your partner requests, you need to be assertive and state your position; then the two of you need to see what can be worked out.) Many battles erupt between partners because one of them did not do what he said he would. Most of these battles could have been prevented.

The rule is the same in business and in relationships: Don't agree to anything unless you're certain you can and will do it. There are a number of reasons all of us sometimes fail to keep our agreements: not understanding exactly what you agreed to do, forgetfulness, and time conflicts. But men have another: They often agree just to stop the conversation, to "get her off my back." While this is understandable, it's going to cause trouble, because she's going to be even more upset when he doesn't keep the agreement.

So if you're asked to do something, first make sure you understand exactly what that something is. The best way is to check your understanding with her. If the two of you agree on what's to be done, take a minute to imagine yourself doing it. In her presence or not, imagine yourself doing exactly what the two of you have been talking about. Then you need to seriously consider whether you can and will do it. And also whether you need any help in doing it. All of this will take time, anywhere from a few seconds to minutes or longer. But it's important to take the time you need. When you talk to her about your thoughts, you should close the discussion with a summary of what the agreement is. This is handy to prevent misunderstandings. Here's an example of the whole process:

> YOU: "I find myself a little bit at a loss. I agree with you that it's your body and I shouldn't touch you in ways you don't like. So I'll do my best not to touch your breasts roughly. But I can't guarantee never to do it. What feels rough to you comes from a strong feeling of lust. I'm not sure I can always catch this impulse before I grab you."

Depending on what she says, you might want to ask for her help:

> YOU: "I think I can do it most of the time. But there may still be a few times when I don't catch myself in time. I may already be squeezing your breast before I remember. It would help me a lot to know that you're not going to get upset if that happens occasionally. Maybe you could just remind me of what I'm doing."
> HER: "I'm willing to call your attention if you forget occasionally, but I want to know that you're taking this seriously."
> YOU: "I am. I want to touch you the way you like. I'm going to follow through on this and I appreciate your willingness to remind me if I forget."

You're right if you think she's going to be watching your progress with this, especially the first few times. You need to take whatever measures are necessary to make sure you carry out your agreement. Little aids can be a big help—for example, writing a note in your appointment book about what you agreed to do, or even putting a similar note on the bathroom mirror or on the nightstand next to the bed. Another aid is mental rehearsal. The more you imagine yourself touching her breasts the ways that are acceptable to her, the better the chances that's exactly what you'll do.

You can count on it, however, that you won't always remember. Rather than assuming this won't happen, it's best to plan how to deal with it when it does, which is what the man in the example tried to do.

CALLING TIME-OUT

It makes no sense to continue with conversations that have parted company with sanity. If all else fails and the conversation is getting out of hand, you can always call time-out to stop the craziness from escalating further. This signals that the two of you need to take a break and get into a better frame of mind before continuing. It can do a lot to prevent conflicts from getting unmanageable.

If you like the idea of calling time-out when things are getting out of hand, you should discuss it with your partner and get an agreement to use it. Either of you can say, "Time-out," whenever you feel that discussion is turning into argument. The harder part is for the other partner, the one who didn't call time-out, to stop talking or screaming immediately. But this has to be done for the procedure to work. Once time-out is called, there is no more talking. Each of you does something to calm down: take a walk, do some work, think things over, or whatever you like. When you're feeling better, you should consider how you might say what you have to say in more constructive ways.

Although it's impossible to say exactly how long time-outs should last, they should not go on interminably. An hour or two works well much of the time. The sooner the two of you can reconnect and become more harmonious, the better for all concerned. Often it's best to do what's necessary to feel close again, which may mean tabling discussion of the troublesome issue for a while. Once the two of you are feeling close, you can get back to it.

The main problem with time-outs that I've noticed is when one partner regularly expresses himself and then calls time-out before his partner can respond. Needless to say, she feels this is unfair and gets even angrier.

It's a good idea while taking a time-out to calm yourself down and employ some of the suggestions made earlier in this chapter. Try to understand your partner's position, try to see her as the person you love and who is hurting, and consider what you can agree with in what she's saying.

CONSIDER WRITING A NOTE

Things can get to the point where discussion is impossible. Bad feelings arise whenever a certain subject is broached, and fights quickly ensue. Or perhaps you believe that you haven't been able to express adequately something important. If either of these things is happening in your relationship, writing a note may help.

The primary advantage for the writer is that you get to say exactly what you want to say precisely as you want to say it. You can write as many drafts of your statement as you want, perhaps getting help from a friend or therapist, until it's exactly as you want it. And you don't have to be worried about getting distracted and forgetting to include something, or getting upset because of your partner's response and saying things you'll later regret. Yet another advantage, and perhaps somewhat of a task as well, is that you can anticipate your partner's objections and address them without the risk of getting into a squabble over them. Additionally, as you draft the note, you may discover that *you* haven't really thought through the issue clearly, that *you've* been getting side-tracked by peripheral issues, and so on. It's a good opportunity to reexamine the problem in a less pressured environment.

The main advantage to your partner is that she gets to read your note at her leisure and can mull it over without having to respond immediately. That can greatly cut down on defensive behavior.

There is one potential shortcoming of notes that you should be aware of. When we talk, a great deal gets communicated aside from the words. Tone, inflection, facial expressions, and body posture can soften or strengthen the words. On paper, the words are all you get. What in a conversation would have been expressed by a look or a tone needs to be put into words in a note. So if you're not being critical or if you're feeling love or sadness or whatever, remember that the reader of the note won't know it unless you expressly say so.

You don't have to be a writer to write the kind of note I'm talking about. Literary elegance is not what it's about. Clarity of expression and consideration for how to best say what you want to get across are. The less fancy and eloquent you try to be, the better.

The best way I know of writing a note is to take some uninterrupted time, get a fix in your head of what you want to say, and then just write (with pencil, typewriter, computer) without stopping to make any corrections or changes. Just get it all out. Later on, you can go over what you've written as many times as you desire, keeping in mind the rules of assertive communication on pages 179–183, and make all the changes you want. When you've pretty much gotten the note as you want it, make sure to put in an introductory comment about why you're sending a note. Here is an example of the first few lines of a note written by a client of mine to his lover:

> Dear Marcy:
> I love you dearly and want more than anything for our relation-ship to continue. I think we're good for each other in most of the important areas, but I need a change in sex. Since we haven't been able to talk about this without getting into fights, I'm trying writing. I'd be happy to hear your response, in person or in a note, as soon as you're ready.

It seems best not to be present when your partner reads your note. Let her choose how and when to respond.

"I liked what you said earlier about asserting yourself, but now you seem to be contradicting yourself. Understand your partner, agree with her criticisms, apologize to her—just give in and make nice to her. It all sounds so weak and wimpy."

I agree it can sound like that, and that many men have trouble with these parts. You're not the first to see it this way. The important thing, I think, is not so much how something sounds but how well it works. There is a great deal of power in these methods. My experience is that following the ideas in this and the preceding chapters does *not* reduce assertiveness or result in men's feeling weak or wimpy. On the contrary, men report feeling stronger because they have more control over conver-sations that they previously felt helpless to influence. They also report more harmonious and satisfying interactions with their lovers. Whatever doubts remain, I would ask you to put it to the test. Give these methods and ideas a trial for a fair period of time—say, a month—and then come to your own conclusions.

I like the ideas in this and the preceding chapters not only because they work so well but also because of the powerful meta-message they send to your partner. You are in effect saying: "I care so much for you and what we have that I'm willing to do what's hard for me, to tell you what goes on inside of me. I'm also willing to listen to what's going on with you, even when it hurts and even when you talk in anger and exaggerate, and to try to work problems out. I'm willing to apologize when I've wronged or hurt you, and when I say I'll do something, you can count on it." This is a very caring, very loving kind of message that can't help but result in better, more satisfying relationships. Such sentiments are also, I think, the mark of a civilized human being.

_____14

Touching

"I wasn't touched much as a child, even by my mother. My father only touched when he spanked. The result is that I don't touch my wife or kids much. It upsets her, and I'm sure it's not good for the kids. I know touching is good; I like it when they touch me. But it isn't easy. I have to keep reminding myself to touch and hug them."—MAN, 41

"When I met Anna, I wasn't into touching at all. The only times I got touched was in sex and at the barber's. She opened up my eyes. I found I like to touch and be touched; it makes a difference in how I feel."—MAN, 36

"We still have sex sometimes, even though it's difficult because of my medical problems and hers. But touching is the main physical thing we do, touching of all sorts, and it means a lot. It makes us feel close and keeps the loving feelings alive."—MAN, 71

ALTHOUGH the word _sex_ usually conjures up images of genital-to-genital contact, our hands and lips are usually more active in sex than our penises. Hand-to-skin (as well as lip-to-skin) contact usually precedes more explicitly sexual activity. If that touching does not go well, there may not be any further activity. Many women report that if they don't like how a man touches and kisses, they figure they won't like sex

276

with him either and therefore terminate the proceedings then and there. And even during explicitly sexual acts, the hands are usually busy. Touching is crucial if you want to be a good lover. But touching is also important in other ways as well.

Unfortunately, our culture is ambivalent about both sex and touching. Since touching is an integral part of sex, and since we're confused and ambivalent about both activities, it makes sense that we would tend to confuse them. We have sexualized touching to the point where all but the most superficial types of touch (handshakes, pats on the back) are thought to be sexual invitations.

A number of observers of the American scene have claimed that most of us, especially males, suffer from sensory starvation, a lack of nonsexual touching, and that we are unaware of how damaging this state of affairs is. Touching is a vital human need, from infancy through old age. Studies of a wide variety of animals, including humans, have demonstrated that without touching, the animals tend to die in infancy (this goes for humans as well) or grow up to be quite peculiar in all respects.

Although it seems that America has become a more touching society in the last twenty years, it still has a long way to go. And before the last twenty years, there wasn't much touching at all. I've been amazed at how many clients can barely recall even a few instances of physical affection between their parents. As usual, the exceptions prove the point. I have a friend whose parents have always been affectionate. They often hold hands, hug, and touch each other. When other people see this, or hear my friend's report about it, they are amazed. Common reactions are: "They must really be in love," "God, I never saw my parents hug at all," and "I didn't even know if my mom and dad liked each other."

If the child does see his parents touching, it is often followed by embarrassment or by their going off to the bedroom, telling him they don't want to be disturbed. And the media, from which he learns so much, reinforce the message. People hug, then kiss, then they have sex. Slowly but surely, the child acquires the societal understanding about touching: It is sexual.

Boys fare worse in this drama than girls. Females of all ages get more touching than males. Mother and father know the masculine model and fear that too much "mothering" may make sissies of their sons. And even mothers, who are much more in tune with the need for touch than fathers, may fear that their sons may interpret touching as sexual and that this may lead to psychological difficulties. So the boy is weaned early from such "childish" or feminine practices.

Fathers, having lived in a culture that is terrified of affectionate physical contact between males, don't touch their sons much after infancy. Since it is the father the boy will emulate, a powerful lesson is transmitted by this lack of touching. The boy also does not see other males touching.

Boys learn that physical contact is acceptable only in sports, in roughhousing, and in sex. There are no taboos on touching if you are playing football, wrestling, boxing, or in some other way being rough. One cause, as well as result, of this notion can be seen in the way fathers handle their sons. They often seem uncomfortable just holding or cuddling their boys, being more at ease when throwing them around or engaging in mock wrestling bouts. Since roughness is what we learned, it's no surprise that we often show affection by being rough, by wrestling with our lovers and playfully punching our friends. And it's no surprise that we're often rough in sex, less gentle than our partners would like.

The equating of touch and sex also gets in the way of physical contact between both same-sex and other-sex friends. Men who have been friends for twenty years are often afraid to touch one another because that might suggest sexual interest to someone. And to touch a woman friend might be construed as sexual by her, by you, and by God knows who else. The link between sex and physical affection even works to keep lovers from touching each other. Since touching is seen not so much as a thing in itself but as the first step toward intercourse, many people won't touch unless they feel ready and willing to "go all the way."

The taboo on touching except as a part of sex confuses us about what we want and how to get it. Ashley Montagu, author of the classic study *Touching*, says that "it is highly probable that . . . the frenetic preoccupation with sex that characterizes Western culture is in many cases not the expression of a sexual interest at all, but rather a search for the satisfaction of the need for contact."

Because girls are allowed much more freedom to express and explore their desire for physical contact, they learn to differentiate their needs for support, comfort, validation, and connection from the need for sex. In fact, given the way girls are brought up, sex is the one need they have trouble noticing and expressing. Boys, of course, go in the other direction. Wanting sex is legitimate, even encouraged, while wanting to be held or loved is unacceptable.

These needs do not disappear in boys and men. They simply go underground and get reorganized and relabeled. Wanting a hug or to feel close to another sounds too feminine, but wanting sex is the epitome of masculinity; and in sex you can get some of these other things as well. After years of practice, the man just never feels a need for closeness or comfort or support. All he wants is—sex. Whenever he feels something that might be called warm or close or loving, he reads it as indicating a desire for—sex.

While this may seem like a brilliant feat of engineering, the result too often for too many men has been a confusion about what they want and therefore an inability to meet many of their needs. One place where this is especially evident is in relations among men. Many men are realizing that they want something from other men: closeness, understanding, support, and so on. But as soon as they start getting any of these things, they often pull back in fear and sometimes come into therapy to discuss their "latent homosexual feelings." This is especially true of men who have engaged in some physical contact with other men and found it pleasurable. Because of the link between sex and touching in their thinking, they decide that what they really want from other men is sex and, because that is unacceptable to them, they should just stay away from any physical contact with men. What they fail to see is that touching need not be sexual, any more than feelings of love or closeness or caring need to be sexual. One can hug or cuddle a man, women, or child, or even an animal for that matter, and not have sex.

But can't touching lead to sexual feelings and erections? Of course it can, but that in itself doesn't mean a lot, nor does it imply a necessary course of action. Erections can be caused by lots of things that do not necessarily indicate a desire for sex. Your erection need not run your life. The following story has been very helpful to many men who were concerned about what it meant if they got sexually aroused or erect when touching or being touched by another man.

As a teenager, John frequently rode on buses. The vibrations of the bus, sometimes combined with adolescent sex fantasies, often produced arousal and erection. Despite the sexy feelings and the erection, John somehow managed to contain himself and never became a bus-fucker.

Even if your feelings about someone are clearly sexual, you don't have to act on them. It is possible for all of us to be turned on by many different people and things. I've talked to men who became aroused and erect while stroking a child or pet, and to some who were aroused while listening to music or watching a sunset. And neither they nor you have to do anything about such events except appreciate and enjoy the good feelings.

It is becoming clear that men need different things from different people. They need men as well as women, and many feel incomplete unless they can also relate to people much older as well as those much younger than themselves. It seems a great tragedy if we separate ourselves from those we want to be with because of our fears about what being close and touching imply. They need indicate nothing more than what they obviously are, and I don't mean sex.

Men need physical affection as much as women, but many men don't get as much as they need. This is partly the result of not knowing when they want touch and partly of not knowing how to get touched even when they know they want it.

Ask yourself if you're getting as much touching—holding, hugging, kissing, cuddling, massaging—as you'd like. Ask your partner the same question. If either of you wants more, you have some work to do.

Touch can do all sorts of things. It's one of the best sources of comfort known to human beings. When you're feeling defeated or crushed, when something terrible has happened, being held or getting a hug won't necessarily solve the problem, but it sure can make you feel better. Some men have trouble accepting a comforting touch or hug, perhaps because it reminds them of when they were small and comforted this way by their mothers. Some men even push women away when they try to hug or hold them. If you are in this category, you might want to consider accepting a hug next time it is offered. It really can make a difference, can make you feel you have the other person's support, understanding, and love. Touching can also be a great facilitator of conversation. When someone is talking about something difficult for them, a brief touch on the hand or arm can help them continue.

Touching between parent and child is extremely important. Children need to be touched, and hugged, and so do parents. You might want to ask yourself if you're touching your children, whatever their ages, as much as you want and as much as they want. If you think more would be better, why not gradually increase the amount?

THE SECRET OF PLEASURABLE TOUCH (AND SEX AS WELL)

Much of the touching we do, even with lovers, is perfunctory and meaningless. A man kisses his wife as he leaves for work, for example, but his mind is elsewhere and he could just as well be kissing the lamp. Often in sex there's a similar situation. The man is hugging his partner or kissing her, but his mind is on what he hopes will come next, not on what he's doing now.

The only secret to pleasurable touching and sex is to be fully present, to be alive in the moment, even if the moment lasts only a few seconds. The difference is immediately noticeable. When you're really present, the touch means something, no matter how brief it may be. When you're not present . . . well, you're just not present. You can't experience something if you're not there when it happens.

Being present takes no more time than being absent. But to be fair, I need to say that it will take a bit of effort to change how you touch, at least for the first few weeks. If you want, just decide that tomorrow when you kiss your partner good morning or good-bye or whatever, you will focus on what you're doing for the few seconds it takes. Let go of your concerns about work or whatever else may be on your mind by focusing on the feel of your lips on hers or on how your bodies fit together in the hug. Focus on your body, on the sensations and feelings evoked by the touch. And do this with the ideas and exercise offered in the rest of the chapter. In the underground science-fiction classic of some years ago, *Stranger in a Strange Land*, the heroine is asked what she means about Michael being such a great kisser. Her answer says it all: "Mike doesn't have any technique . . . but when Mike kisses you he isn't doing *anything* else. You're his whole universe . . . and the moment is eternal because he doesn't have any plans and isn't going anywhere. Just kissing you. It's overwhelming."

SELF-SENSUALITY

Touching oneself can be an important step in becoming a more sensuous person. I know you're not supposed to do this—it's not nice—but you might want to consider it. Taking a warm bath, rubbing yourself gently (or even not so gently) with a washcloth or towel, can be a nice way to treat yourself. The same is true for rubbing body lotion or oil onto your hands and arms, legs, or your whole body. You may get aroused while doing this and want to go on to stroking your penis, but it's not necessary.

Touching things can also help develop sensuousness. Many of us don't even notice or experience the objects we touch almost every day. Yet being aware of what we're doing can add to our sensual abilities and yield pleasure. An orange feels different from a peach, leather different from silk or cotton, wood different from vinyl. When you want to, pay attention to what you're touching, touch it in different ways, and allow yourself to experience the sensations.

PROFESSIONAL MASSAGE

One of the nicest things a person can do for himself is get a professional massage. It's relaxing and refreshing. In many other countries, this idea is taken for granted. Athletes and many other people routinely get massages. In America, however, we are so confused about sex and touch that massage is often a synonym for a blow job or some other sexual activity. Needless to say, when I say massage I mean *massage* and not sex.

If you've never experienced a professional massage, you might want to treat yourself. (This is also a nice gift for someone you care about.) Find yourself a reputable nonsexual masseuse or masseur and make an appointment. If you have any qualms about this, take the shortest appointment he or she gives; for example, a half hour rather than an hour, or one hour rather than two hours.

An added benefit to professional massages is that it can help increase your awareness of the possibilities of touch. You can transfer this knowledge to touching yourself and your partner. I'm not implying, by the way, that you need to become an expert at massage or that you should mainly be a student when you get a professional massage. The main thing to do is experience and enjoy, but you'll learn anyway, without even trying.

BEING SENSUAL WITH A PARTNER

There are many ways of touching and being sensual with your partner, a few of the more important ones I discuss here.

Hugging and Holding

If you and your partner agree there should be more hugging and holding, just get to it. Every day, devote a few moments to holding one another. It will help if the two of you have a brief talk in which the ground rules are established. The most important thing is that both of you understand that touching need not lead to sex. Each of you should feel free to touch when you want without feeling that you may therefore be required to do something that you're not in the mood for.

There's nothing wrong with going on to sex if both of you agree that's what you want to do, but there's also nothing wrong with just touching.

Scratching

Scratching isn't a very sexy or sensual term, but many people enjoy having their backs scratched, and this is a nice thing lovers can do for each other.

Touching Your Partner's "Things"

No, I don't mean those things! What I have in mind here are items like her clothes and her hair. Hugging or touching her when she's wearing a silk shirt or dress is different than touching when she's wearing something else or nothing. Pay attention, and you'll notice and experience the differences. And what about her hair? Have you ever really touched and stroked it, just to experience the feel of it? If not, why not give it a try? Many women have told me it's a treat when their lovers brush their hair for them. You might want to consider doing this if your partner is up for it.

Washing Your Partner

Being bathed caringly is something all of us experienced as children, and we took it as a loving act. Unfortunately, many of us never got to experience that again. What about washing your partner slowly and lovingly while you're in the shower or tub and having her do the same for you? If you want to go all out, you can do it just as it is done for children. One of you, let's say it's you, runs the bath and maybe adds bubble bath or lotion as well. Then slowly and with care you wash her. After that, you dry her, maybe also applying powder or lotion. Keep in mind that getting clean is only the secondary purpose of the bath; showing care and love is the primary one.

A Slow Hand, and a Gentle One As Well

Women routinely complain that men are too hurried and too rough in their touching. If you believe this complaint might apply to you, you can consider what you want to do about it. For most people, the kinds of touch that convey love, support, closeness, and understanding are gentle and slow. This is not to say there aren't times when a quick or firm touch isn't appropriate. But most of the time, soft and slow is where it's at. You have nothing to lose by starting out this way.

Body-Rubs

A body-rub is simply you touching, stroking, or massaging some or all of your partner's body (except for the genitals). There are two basic formats. In one, you touch her for your own pleasure; she will intervene only to let you know she doesn't like what you're doing. In the other format, she touches you as you direct her to, but you don't touch her back. Many men have trouble with this one, because it involves a more passive role than they are accustomed to. Aside from giving oral instructions, however, you're just supposed to lie back and enjoy the stimulation. You may find that you're also touching her. Try to resist that impulse. Most of us men are already good at being active. We need to learn also to be more passive, just to accept pleasure without giving anything in return at the moment.

I have found that body-rubs work best if they are not considered medicinal—that is, if they aren't the deep muscle manipulation that often goes under the name massage and is usually used for muscular aches and pains. If you want your partner to massage your sore shoulder, that's fine, but it's not a body-rub.

If you have a sexual problem, body-rubs are an excellent first step to take before you begin the partner exercises to resolve the problems that are described in Chapters 22 and 24. They are also an excellent first step in learning how to be comfortable in telling your partner how you like to be stimulated.

EXERCISE 14–1: NONGENITAL BODY-RUBS

Time Required: 15–20 minutes each

In both steps of this exercise, one of you gives a light, stroking body-rub to the other. How light depends on individual preferences, but you should avoid the heavy, kneading type of rubbing usually done for sore muscles and in some kinds of massage.

You will need a warm room, a comfortable place for the receiver to sit or lie, and a lubricant (hand lotion, massage oil, or talcum powder).

First you must decide who will give and who will receive in a given session. The receiver is not to touch or do anything else to or for the giver, except as specified in the instructions.

Since the receiver may not feel like doing anything active after the session, it's best not to plan to have two sessions back to back. Wait at least half an hour between sessions.

One goal of both steps is to allow you to experience touching and being touched without any other ends in mind. The giver should focus on his touching and the receiver on the sensations produced by being touched.

The other goal is for both of you to make each experience as positive—relaxing, pleasant, pleasurable—as possible. *Sexual arousal is not the goal of this exercise.* It sometimes happens, and it's fine if it does, but that's not what we're looking for. The exercise is not a prelude to anything. It is simply what it is.

In each step there is a clearly designated giver and receiver, with different roles to play. These distinctions are important and should be adhered to. After each step, spend a few minutes talking about what the experience was like for each of you. Say what you liked most and least about it, what the main feeling was, and also indicate any difficulties you experienced. This talking is useful for learning how to communicate better about physical preferences; include it after every session, and be as specific as possible.

Step A: The receiver, the one who is going to be touched, is in complete control. He asks for the body-rub and gives directions on how and where he wants to be touched. The giver simply follows the directions.

The receiver should use this opportunity to discover what kinds of touching he most enjoys. You can ask for anything at all except genital touching. Try new things and places even if you aren't sure you will enjoy them. If you've ever wondered how it would feel to have the areas between your toes touched, or the backs of your knees, or anything else, now is the time to find out. Make sure you are getting precisely what you want, no matter how many times you have to explain or demonstrate to the giver.

Since 15 to 20 minutes isn't enough time to do a whole body, you should focus on one area, such as face or feet or perhaps your whole front, from scalp to toes. Take your time and get into the sensations. The receiver is the one who calls time.

The giver should do everything that is asked so long as it is not obnoxious or uncomfortable for her. She should feel free to ask for more specific instructions if needed.

Step B: The giver initiates the exercise and touches, strokes, and rubs his partner for his own pleasure, doing whatever he wants. The receiver should accept what is done without comment unless there is discomfort or pain, in which case she should ask the giver to do something else.

The giver should use this opportunity to explore his partner's body with different types of touch, pressure, and rhythm. Touch where and how you want to *for your own pleasure.* It's important *not* to try to give the receiver a good time or to turn her on. Give yourself a good time. I emphasize this point because many men have trouble with it, focusing their efforts on giving the partner a good time rather than themselves. Do whatever is necessary to follow the directions.

Spend no more than 20 minutes on this. The giver is the one who calls time.

When time is up, remember to face each other and give a few moments of feedback to your partner on what the experience was like for you.

After you have done the body-rubs a few times as they are described, feel free to experiment. Some couples make them a regular part of their lives, a treat to be enjoyed when they have a few minutes free and want something physical but not sexual. Some couples use them as a means of stress management because they find getting a body-rub is a wonderful way to relax. Some couples use them as a transition activity that takes them from work or chores to sexual activity. The body-rub helps them let go of what they were doing before and helps open them up to an erotic experience. And many people find that what they learn in doing body-rubs—giving directions regarding the physical stimulation they want, accepting and focusing in on physical stimulation without doing anything in return at the moment, following a partner's directions for desired stimulation, and touching a partner for one's own pleasure—transfer quite nicely and easily to more erotic activities.

I am not prescribing touching as a panacea for all your ills or as a compulsory ritual that should be followed whether you like it or not. Rather, I see touching as a very important human need, one you should be free to fulfill in ways and with people of your own choosing. It won't change the world and it won't solve all your problems, but it will probably make you feel better and bring you closer to the people you love. Men need touching as much as anyone else, and there is no good reason to deprive yourself in this area.

Get in touch with those you care for. Stay in touch. Literally.

_____15

Initiation and Seduction

"It is not enough to conquer; one must know how to seduce."
—VOLTAIRE

"Having to initiate sex is one of the worst parts of being a man. It feels like an enormous burden. I'd just like to turn the whole job over to women—they're the ones who control if and when sex happens anyway—and be done with it."—MAN, 36

"I'm never sure if I know the best ways to get sex started. Is it best to use words, not use words, or what? I always think there's something about this subject I don't know."—MAN, 21

How well sex goes is often determined in the first few moments or even before the fact, yet initiating sex is a topic that receives little attention. Men have traditionally been given the job of getting the ball rolling, especially in new relationships, and yet have been given no training in how to do it. Some men don't particularly like the job, some of them— whether they like it or not—don't handle it well, and some have trouble dealing with their partner's initiations.

If initiation covers all ways of getting sex started, then seduction constitutes one kind of initiation. Exactly how it differs from initiation isn't easy to say. Perhaps the best thing is to note that seduction may involve more effort and time—more salesmanship—possibly because your partner is not immediately agreeable to what you have in mind. Seduction includes many forms of persuasion and influence.

In some circles, seduction and its synonyms such as *lure* and *entice* have bad reputations because it's thought that the woman is being tricked and will be harmed or wronged. This makes sense. In the old days, sex was something men had to extract from women. So they coaxed, cajoled, and lied. And often the woman did come to harm by having her feelings hurt, getting a disease, or getting pregnant.

Although such consequences still occur, generally things are different now. Most women enjoy sex and want to have it in the right circumstances. Interestingly, many of them complain that men know nothing about seduction and enticement. A woman in her twenties whom I interviewed had this to say:

> To me, seduction is putting some thought into sex, doing something special and memorable for another. Maybe candles, special foods, bubble bath, or something like that. I like doing such things for a man and I sometimes do, but I haven't met a man yet who does them for me. To them, sex is more like let's get down to business.

Are these women saying they want to be lied to, bullied, and led into harm's way? Of course not. But they are saying they want, at least sometimes, to be led into sex. They want some convincing, some persuasion, some salesmanship. Not the salesmanship common in the selling of cars, but salesmanship of a sweeter, gentler kind.

Seduction and the other terms I've used, including *initiation*, come under the broader heading of *influence*. We all influence and try to influence one another all the time. I want to influence you to come to my party, hear my talk, buy my book. You want to influence me to go to a movie with you or to try your favorite Chinese restaurant.

Life as we know it is inconceivable without creatures trying to influence each other. There's absolutely nothing wrong with doing it. There are, however, better and worse ways of influencing others. If I tell you I love you when I don't, just to get you into bed, that's not so good because it's a lie. But if I suggest in words or action that putting down your book and getting into bed with me will feel good to both of us, that's a different story.

SEXUAL INVITATIONS AND CONSENT

One way around the problem of what terms to use is to think in terms of invitation. Inviting someone to join us in an activity (a walk, a meal, a show, and so on) is an action we all take frequently in many areas of our lives. Invitation sounds nice to most of us—we like to get invited to things—and it doesn't carry any of the negative connotations of *seduce* and *lure*.

I think the term *invitation* can add some needed perspective to sex, particularly because of the issue of consent. The basic goal of all invitations is similar: to obtain the other person's consent to engage in the activity. We may actually want more than this, of course. We may want them to be enthusiastic and excited about engaging in the activity with us. But consent is usually the minimum we can settle for. We seem to understand that the activity cannot occur without the consent of both parties. Sure, we feel free to make the event sound more attractive if they seem reluctant—"The movie got very good reviews" or "We can stop at your favorite restaurant for a bite before the show"—but we generally don't push too hard. It's rare to hear that a man tied up his wife and carried her to a ball game, or threatened his lover with all sorts of dire consequences if she wouldn't go to a movie he wanted to see. And it's unusual for a man to pout for a week because his sweetheart didn't want to go to a restaurant he wanted to try.

I am fully aware that there is a vast difference between having meaningful sex and seeing a movie; nonetheless, I think the flexibility most men show in regard to responses to their nonsexual invitations might serve them well in sex. Men who think of their sexual initiations as invitations (whether or not they actually use the word) and realize that consent must be obtained, as with all invitations, don't get into trouble. And women, as already indicated, favor this approach. Although I use all the typical terms of initiation synonymously, the idea of invitation and consent is always implied.

There are at least three important elements in sexual initiation. First is your willingness to extend an offer of something exciting to come: the actual invitation or seduction. Second is your willingness to be rejected, a topic I cover later in this chapter. And third is the building of arousal. Initiations and arousal are closely tied—you want to gain your partner's consent and interest, and at the same time you want to build or maintain both of your excitement levels. Despite the connection between seduction and arousal, I separate them for purposes of discussion and take up arousal in the next chapter.

THE INVITATION OR ENTICEMENT

What we really want to do when we issue a sexual invitation is to arouse the other person's interest, desire, and hope. Your partner is watching TV, sitting next to you, or perhaps hugging you. You want to arouse sexual interest in her and the hope of a better time than what she's having now.

So how can one go about this seduction business? There are no blueprints, because people are so different. What appeals to one may turn off another altogether. Whatever works is fine so long as there's no deception involved and no one gets hurt. But there are a few principles that help most of the time.

It's obvious that any means of seduction has a better chance of succeeding if each of you feels good about the other. If there's been distance, coldness, or hostility, the chances of any sexual initiation working are diminished. So take care that connection has been established.

The most effortless and most concise way is simply to ask if she wants to make love. Of all the alternatives, this involves the least amount of seduction. You're simply asking a question. The enticement has to come from her mind. If she's in a similar state of mind or recalls that sex with you is usually enjoyable, that may be enough for her to say yes. But since you're not giving her mind much to work with, it also may not be enough.

It's important to consider language and gestures. Pornographic accounts of sex often involve the man's grabbing his partner's crotch or saying something subtle like "You seem overdue for a good fuck." Such approaches are not always ineffective. If a couple agrees on them, obviously they can work. But as I've pointed out, some women find such language a turnoff and detest the grabbing of their breasts and crotches. You especially want to avoid such things in a new relationship.

The other ways all involve some salesmanship. You try to show and tell her why making love is a good idea. You want to make sex with you sound appealing by creating attractive thoughts and pictures in her mind and enjoyable sensations in her body. Say you know your partner likes her neck and shoulders rubbed. You could come up behind her while she's reading and start rubbing her neck and shoulders the way she likes. You're trying to move her away from the book into either the physical realm (the sensations produced by your rubbing) or a different cognitive realm (imagining what further touching might be like). If she responds—say, by putting down the book and focusing on what you're doing—you could, after a bit, kiss her suggestively or move your hands in a more suggestive way. You could also do it verbally: "I love touching you. And there's a lot more I'd like to touch."

Use words and physical but nongenital stimulation, starting slowly and gently. Words are powerful, and so is physical stimulation. Together, they are even more powerful. And you have nothing to lose by starting with tenderness.

Music can also be an effective aid. Romantic music in the background was a sexual aphrodisiac known to our parents and grandparents. In a survey of readers of *Cosmopolitan*, 78 percent of the women said music was a turn-on. Many kinds of music work—Bach, Frank Sinatra, Ravel, early Beatles, and Bruce Springsteen. Almost any kind of music is appropriate, including hard-driving rock or soul, depending on your tastes and feelings at the moment. And don't forget about dancing. A slow dance to appropriate music, holding each other close, can be a wonderful way to start sexual feelings flowing.

Kissing is very important to most women, and many seductions need involve little more than kissing. It's often good to start easily, with small, light kisses, gradually working your way into longer, more passionate kisses that include tongues as well as lips. I've yet to hear a woman complain that her man kissed too much.

In the last few paragraphs I several times mentioned starting slow and easy. I should say more about this. The women I interviewed, and those I've talked to in therapy, are almost unanimous in desiring a slow approach to sex. Of course there are times when both of you have gotten steamed up doing something else and now want nothing more than to rip your clothes off and get right to it. But these occasions are infrequent. At all other times, you have nothing to lose and a great deal to gain by taking your time. As one woman told me:

I like a man to approach me slowly and gently, inviting me with touches and words, gradually drawing me into a sexual place. I can't stand when he grabs me or comes on fast or hard.

One aspect of seduction that's extremely important yet often overlooked is making your partner feel special. She wants to feel that it's *she* you want. The last thing she wants to feel is that anyone would do, but she's the only one around. There are many ways to make her feel special. One way is to use little gifts. Flowers, a poem you wrote for her, a book by her favorite author—these and any number of other tokens of love and appreciation can go a long way to making her feel special and moving the two of you into a loving space. I'm not suggesting you need to bring a gift every time you want sex—that would be ridiculous—but rather that an occasional gift to express your feelings for her can mean a great deal.

Another way of making her feel special we've already covered: doing something that she particularly likes, like rubbing her neck. Yet another way is to comment on some aspect of her being or action. For example, "I love kissing *you*," "*Your* eyes are so gorgeous," "*You* have such soft skin; I love to touch it," or "*You* look so beautiful when *you* come. I just can't get enough of it." I trust it's understood that these statements should be made only when they're true. Perhaps they are things you've often thought but haven't verbally expressed. A different kind of comment has to do with what you were thinking about: "As I was driving home, I had a warm thought about our lovemaking the other night [which in effect means, and comes across, as making love to *you*]. Can I interest you in a repeat performance?" Or maybe something like this: "I had a hard time settling down to work today. I kept thinking of how much I like to kiss *your* breasts. I could see myself doing it, could almost taste them."

The italicized words in the examples above—the *yous* and *yours*—are the important ones. These are the words that make her feel important and special.

Another aid in seduction is reminding your partner of a particularly good experience the two of you had. This brings into her consciousness the words, pictures, and sensations that can generate a desire to have sex with you now. "While coming home tonight, I recalled the time on the beach in Maui. Remember? We started kissing on the beach, and kissing and kissing. We hardly made it back to the motel with our clothes on."

SEDUCTION NO-NO'S

There are several things best be avoided in seduction. They either lessen the chances of success or destroy trust and the ability for future connection. A number of the points made in Chapter 7 are relevant, and there are a few more that apply particularly to initiations.

- Telling lies or using any kind of coercion.
- Not ensuring privacy. There's nothing like a ringing phone, a blaring TV, or the sudden appearance of a child or roommate to dampen sexual ardor. Women seem more distractable than men. I've heard many accounts of sex where the man had a good time but his partner couldn't focus because of the ringing phone or the noise of the TV or radio. Keep in mind that your partner may not be able to tune out the Celtics game as easily as you can.
- Irrelevant conversation. Sexual seduction basically consists of making a world inhabited only by the two of you and shutting out the real world. Bringing up sports ("The Mets lost again today"), business ("We're working on a really big deal") or children ("Mary looks tired today") is not appropriate and should be avoided.
- Initiating constantly. Here's how one woman put it: "I hate it when he keeps asking and asking, incessantly, never-endingly. I hate it when he asks so often that I never have a chance to recover some libido and ask him."

Initiation and seduction can begin before you're even together by using phone calls, notes, and letters. Let's say you feel turned-on at work. Why not call your partner and tell her so or leave a message on her answering machine? And include some suggestions about what you'd like to do when you are together again. If you're at home and she's not, you could leave a note in a prominent place, such as on a pillow, on the bathroom mirror, or on the refrigerator. (Be careful what you say in a note or leave on an answering machine, however, if there's a possibility that someone else, adult or child, might get to it before the one it is meant for.) If you're out of town, suggestive phone calls and letters are almost always appreciated and can set the stage for wonderful lovemaking when you're reunited.

Cards put out by Hallmark and other companies can serve a useful function. This wasn't the case years ago when the cards sounded as if they were written by someone from another planet. But these days there are many wonderful cards that may exactly express your feelings. There are loving cards, playful cards, suggestive ones, and out-and-out raunchy ones. If you find one that says precisely what you want to say, why not use it? If one comes close but isn't exactly right, make it right by adding a few words of your own.

The purpose of calls, cards, notes, and letters is the same as actual physical seduction: to set the stage, to get juices flowing, to induce a state of mind or mood. You could call your partner from work and say something like this:

I've been thinking about you, about what we did Sunday morning [you're making her feel special by thinking about her and you're turning her mind to the good experience you had on Sunday]. Just can't get it out of my mind. I want you again, same way. Can I interest you in a hot time on the sofa after work? [Assuming a positive response,] Good, I'm looking forward to seeing you around six. I can't wait.

Assuming you both remember Sunday morning with good feelings and you both agree on what's to happen this evening, the stage has been set. Both of you will be looking forward to getting together. The seduction is largely done. The juices have been set in motion and with almost no effort—just recalling Sunday and anticipating tonight— you'll each almost automatically keep things moving along. When you get together, you should both be at close to boiling and should have a marvelous time.

Talking about sex on the phone—phone sex, as some call it—can be much more exciting and elaborate than in the example above. Some people find it highly arousing to get into the details of what they did or what they're going to do. "I'm going to start by kissing your toes and running my tongue slowly between them, then gradually working my way up your leg, until I'm kissing and licking the back of your knees. Then, slowly run my tongue up and down the inside of your thighs. . . ." One partner can do all or most of the talking, or both can participate equally. It can result in extraordinary arousal.

Sex goes best if the partners are in the same mind-set at the start or are aware of the different states of mind they are in and make plans to deal with them. But this is not always the case.

What more often happens is something like this:

Bob has been turned-on all day, ever since meeting the attractive new buyer in his office. He's had a tingling in his groin and has enjoyed a number of erotic fantasies. When he comes home, he can't wait for dinner to be over and the baby to be put to bed. As soon as that's done, he comes on strong with his wife, Carol. But she's not feeling sexual at all, having been preoccupied all day with a problem at work and then having had to feed the baby and get him ready for bed. One possibility is that Carol just says no to Bob. This makes him angry and resentful.

Another possibility is that Carol accepts Bob's overture, hoping she can get turned on quickly. While he's trying to get inside her, she's trying to develop a little turn-on. Bob may get inside her and have an orgasm, but she may feel used.

A better outcome would be one of the following.

A. Bob calls Carol from work to share his turn-on and see if they can agree to an erotic get-together later on. If she's interested but mentions the difficult day she's having, Bob could offer to help her relax—for example, by taking care of the baby so she can have time to unwind, or by giving her a back-rub. He could, of course, make the same offers at home even if he hadn't called her earlier. In either case, he's doing what he can to help her get in the mood if she's so inclined.

B. If Carol shows any interest but it's clear that he's far more turned on than she is, he could offer physically or verbally to take his time getting her aroused. In a variant of this, he could ask her to get him off now and then he'll take his time doing the same for her. In yet another variation, if Carol simply isn't up for a whole sexual experience, Bob could simply ask her to do something for him— manually, orally, or with intercourse. In this case, it's clear to both that the experience is primarily for him and there's no requirement she get aroused.

C. If Bob and Carol are comfortable sharing fantasies, he could tell her what got him so turned-on and they could use this information to turn Carol on more or to get Bob off.

What's good about A, B, and C is that Bob and Carol agree where they are and what's going to happen. No one feels hurt, used, or angry.

Most men and women agree that it's best to initiate sex with the feelings you have at the time—playful, loving, or erotic. If you're feeling particularly loving toward your partner, your actions and words should be consistent with that feeling: words of care, love, and appreciation and soft touches. You want the sex to be an expression of the deep feelings you have for each other. If lust is where it's at—you want to fuck rather than make love—let your words and actions show it. The same is true if your main feelings are playful. Then play and have a good time.

It's also OK to express other feelings in sex. One that people tend not to think about is the desire to escape. As I mentioned earlier, sex often provides a wonderful escape from the cares and routine of everyday life. If you're in need of a big escape, you and your partner can set up a whole fantasy world and do whatever you want.

Once things are under way, you might want to consider sensually undressing your partner. This used to be a common practice, but it seems to have been left behind by the sexual revolution. Yet it's a wonderful means of arousal, and women love it. Fully 95 percent of the 106,000 women who participated in a survey done by *Cosmopolitan* said they like their partners to undress them before sex. You just lovingly (or lustfully) remove her clothes, one item at a time, while commenting on the beauty of the now-revealed parts and kissing and fondling them. Here is another opportunity to make your partner feel special: Those are *her* breasts, belly, buns, legs, and so on that you're talking about and that are turning you on.

(A woman who read that paragraph wrote in the margin that although it rarely happens, it gives her a very nice feeling and a sense of being deeply cared for when the man helps her to get dressed when sex is over and they're not going right to sleep. I checked this out with a number of women and they all liked the idea.)

One kind of initiation not yet covered involves wanting your partner to do something she's never done before and may have fears about. The three main topics that come up are oral sex, anal sex, and different intercourse positions. What seems to work best is simply to bring up your desire, following the rules of assertive communication discussed in Chapter 7. Here is an illustration of how such a conversation might start.

I'd like to talk about anal sex. I know you aren't thrilled by the idea. The one time you tried it with your husband was a disaster and I can understand your being scared by the idea. But it's important to me, I guess because I've never tried it and want to see what it's like. I wonder if you'd be willing to experiment with me, taking it very slowly and gradually. In fact, we wouldn't even start with a penis. Just using my pinky, very well lubricated, and only on the outside. I promise, word of honor, that we will stop whenever you want to for any reason. You will be in complete control.

If talking is difficult or if it has resulted in unresolvable conflicts, putting your thoughts in a note to her might help.

IF YOU WANT TO LEARN MORE ABOUT SEDUCTION

Let's say you still feel you don't know enough about seduction. Maybe you aren't sure the things I've mentioned will work with your partner, or you've tried some of them and they don't work. Why not ask her how she likes to be enticed into sex? For example: "What kinds of things put you in a sexual mood?" or "How would you like me to approach you for sex?" She may come right out and tell you. If she's shy, she may need some coaxing. But it's also possible she doesn't know. You can help her find out by suggesting she consult her fantasies. How does she get into sex in them? And what kinds of things in movies and books turn her on?

REJECTION

One of the big problems men have with initiation is the possibility of rejection. And it's real. You will get rejected many times. Your partner will not always be up for what you want. Sometimes she may not be up for anything sexual, or even personal, at all. There's no way around this. But some men are so fearful of rejection that they won't initiate unless they have strong indications they will be accepted.

I mentioned a man like this, Roger, on page 172. Unless his wife gave strong and clear messages that she was receptive to sex, he wouldn't initiate no matter how horny he felt. Needless to say, Roger felt frustrated a lot of the time. As we talked about this in the presence of his wife, she exploded: "This is ridiculous and I wish you'd stop reading my mind. So what if I've had a bad day? Sex is a way of making a bad day good. So what if I'm watching TV? Make me a better offer."

That's what many women would say. And you need to decide whether protecting yourself against rejection is worth the price it entails: less sex than you want and perhaps less of other things as well, because those who fear sexual rejection tend to fear other rejection also.

Imagine being rejected. This shouldn't be difficult, since you certainly have been rejected before and know what it's like. Go into the gruesome details. Feels pretty bad, right? Then ask what you're telling yourself. Are you saying to yourself that because your partner didn't want sex when you did that she doesn't love you, doesn't desire you, and that you're inadequate and a failure? If so, ask yourself if that's really what her rejection means. Chances are excellent it means none of these things.

Then ask yourself what you're missing by not initiating more. Get into the details of what you're missing. And when you're ready, make your decision. Is it better to keep on protecting yourself against rejection or is it better to get rejected more? If you're willing to get rejected more often and therefore get more sex and other good things as well, you might want to reread the beginning of this chapter to learn more about initiation and seduction.

And while you're considering all this, I'll tell you a not very well kept secret. Anyone who focuses on rejection isn't getting much out of life. People who succeed—whether in sex, relationships, business, politics, or something else—focus on success and not on failure. They know they'll fail a good portion of the time, but what's important to them are the successes. Each success can make you forget a score of failures.

The traditional male role entails lots of rejections—socially, sexually, and otherwise—because men are supposed to get things moving and that, by definition, will result in failure and rejection a large portion of the time. I don't know about you, but I think this is one of the features of the male role that's worth keeping. If you aren't being rejected, you probably aren't putting yourself out there much and aren't getting as much as you could out of life.

WHAT ABOUT WHEN SHE INITIATES?

Some men complain that their partners don't initiate often enough and love it when they do. And some men have trouble with this. The main problem seems to be their concern that they won't be able to deliver what the partner wants. If he's not in the mood and isn't sure if he can get in the mood and get his penis working, he fears failing her. This is another example of how thinking of sex as performance gets us into trouble.

It helps to understand that a sexual invitation isn't a test of your masculinity, your sexual prowess, your love for your partner, or a demand that you perform. It's just an invitation.

How should you handle the situation? Basically the same way you should handle any invitation, whether your partner asking if you want to go to the beach or out to eat, or someone else asking if you want to listen to or give a talk: Consider your feelings and see what you want to do.

It's possible that when your partner initiates, you not only don't want to have sex with her, you don't want to do anything with her. Maybe you're preoccupied with something, maybe you're busy, maybe you're tired. Whatever the reason, you want to be alone. You have every right to this preference and should announce it: "That's a nice invitation, honey, but I'm preoccupied with this report. I'd like to be left alone until I've worked it out." If you're just not interested in sex, why not say so? "I'm really not feeling sexy right now. But I'm up for some cuddling [or a walk or talk] if you want." She may well be disappointed, but it's perfectly acceptable. It's a different story, of course, if you always or almost always have a reason for not wanting sex.

Suppose the situation is that you aren't opposed to the idea of sex, it's just that you're not sure if you can get turned on and if your penis will function. Why not simply tell her what's going on with you?

I don't think I can get very excited. But I'd love to make you happy. What would you like?

I'm not turned-on now but I'd like to be. Why don't you do some work on me?

You seem like you need something to happen real soon. I'm happy to go down on you. Would you do the same for me later?

I don't know if I can get turned on or not. Let's get into bed and see what happens. If I don't get turned on, I'll do you.

Almost needless to say, these conversations will go better if you and your partner have talked about sex beforehand, especially about the sexual options discussed in Chapter 3. The situation you want to have regarding seductions, the best one I know, is that your partner feels free to initiate anytime she wants and so do you.

_____16

Sexual Arousal

"Being turned on is the best feeling in the world. Even better than orgasm because orgasm is an ending while turn-on is a beginning. Makes me feel totally alive and awake."—MAN, 34

"I think arousal is what it's all about. I love feeling sexually excited and I love my partner feeling it. Her turn-on pushes mine even higher and mine does the same for hers. An incredible spiral of greater and greater passion."—MAN, 46

WHEN people talk about "getting it up" in regard to sex, they usually mean the man's getting his penis up. But there is another kind of getting it up that is more important for men, and women too. I'm referring to getting your arousal up. Arousal, a feeling that is also called excitement, passion, lust, turn-on, and horniness, is what powers erections in men, lubrication in women, and orgasm in both. Arousal is also most of what makes for a sexual experience that feels really good.

EXACTLY WHAT IS AROUSAL?

Arousal is like love; even though we know what each one is, neither is easy to define. Let's start with what arousal is not. It definitely is not the same as the overwhelming excitement described in the popular media, which can make all of us feel inadequate. Even at the peak of passion, few human beings have felt that their bones were melting, or that they were floating in paradise, or that they were experiencing a tidal wave of unbearable pleasure. Arousal is also not the same as an intellectual interest in sex. For example, if you say to yourself, "Gee, it's been six weeks since I had sex," but don't feel any excitement, you're not aroused.

The most important thing arousal is not is erection. The two often go together—arousal is usually what makes your penis get hard—but they are best thought of as separate. You may, for instance, wake up in the morning with an erection but without any excitement. That means only that you have an erection and are not turned-on. And just as it's possible to have an erection without being aroused, it's also possible to be very sexually aroused and not have an erection (because fear, anger, another feeling, or a medical condition is getting in the way). Some men with erection problems say that erections accompanied by lust feel different from those without the feelings. When there's no turn-on, the erection seems like an anomaly, not at all connected to you. When there's an erection and arousal, you feel more connected to your penis; it's part of who you are as a total person at the moment. If you want to keep sex as good as possible and prevent erection problems, don't attempt to use your penis unless you are turned-on. If you are already having trouble with erections, this becomes an absolute rule.

Let's go to what arousal is. Above all, it has to do with things you sense and feel. One way of looking at it is that your body (and mind) is on, as in "all systems go." One man put it this way: "My heart was racing, my body was tingling, and I was raring to go." Not as extreme as having your bones melt, but pleasurable nonetheless. Terms frequently used to describe arousal, aside from the synonyms already given, include *warmth* or *heat* (as in "I was hot"), *tingling, blood rushing, heart pounding, wild, wanting to have her, to touch her, to be inside her.* Arousal is almost always described in positive ways; it feels good. Think of an activity in your life that most excites you: skiing, tennis, running, sex, closing an important deal, or whatever. Then recall a specific example of that activity when you were even more excited than usual. Take a moment or two to get into the details of how you felt. It's as if you're all fired up, your attention is narrowly focused, the blood is rushing through you, and you feel fully alive and terrific. That's what I mean when I say arousal or turn-on, even though we're talking about the high end. I wouldn't expect that you'd be that aroused every time you went skiing or had sex. But the extreme end does offer a good way of defining the idea for yourself.

I hope you don't get upset if you discover that you get more excited by something other than sex. That's not unusual. You may never get as wild in sex as when you learned you were accepted by the college of your choice or as you do when closing a million-dollar deal. But if you feel your sexual arousal is not as high as it could be, you can do something about it.

Now recall a time when you were very sexually aroused. You were really hot for it and really into it. You could feel it in your pelvis (whether or not you had an erection) and elsewhere, maybe in your heart or stomach. This is what we're talking about.

Now let's try something different. Does an attractive woman ever turn your head, as the old saying had it? That is, when you see a woman you consider sexy or attractive on the street, at work, in a movie or on television, do you ever get a kind of sexual urge, a tingling somewhere in your body, or do you ever have sexual thoughts about her? Maybe you imagine a long, deep, and soft kiss with her, or her lips around your penis, or her legs wrapped around you in intercourse. These feelings and ideas are signs of sexual arousal.

When people are highly aroused, they are narrowly focused. Their attention is devoted to what they're doing and going to do. So one way of telling how aroused you are is by asking how distracted you are by extraneous matters. A person who's distracted in sex by common outside noises (barking dogs, backfiring cars, the normal creaking of houses, and so on) is probably not very aroused. A person who's repelled or disgusted by a partner's varicose vein, or hair in a place he doesn't think there should be hair, or similar items is probably not very aroused. When you're excited, you either don't notice these things or they don't bother you much because you're too focused on something else.

DIFFERENCES BETWEEN DESIRE AND AROUSAL

Although desire for sex and arousal are often used synonymously, I think clarity is served by making a distinction between them. I use desire to mean wanting to have sex. You desire to, want to, do something sexual.

It's easy to understand wanting sex when you're already aroused. But it doesn't have to be this way. You could also want to have sex for other reasons. Perhaps your partner gets irritable and provokes a fight unless she has sex twice a week. Since she's starting to get irritable and you want to avoid a fight, you initiate sex. But what you really desire is to avoid trouble; having sex is merely the means to this end. There are men and women who want lots of sex even though they have trouble getting aroused. One reason for their high desire is the hope that if they keep working at it, they'll figure out how to get turned on.

It also works the other way. There are people who get easily and highly aroused in sex, but don't want much of it. This sounds strange, but it really isn't. A man in this category may feel that sex is a distraction from other things—usually work—that have a higher priority. Or he may believe that too much lovemaking makes him more committed or vulnerable than he wants to be. Or possibly he is using his ostensible lack of interest to get back at his partner for real or imagined wrongdoing.

To keep matters as clear as possible, I use desire to mean only that you have an interest in sex, whether or not you're aroused. A high level of desire simply means you want sex a lot. Arousal, on the other hand, is how high you get when you anticipate sex or engage in it.

RATING DEGREE OF AROUSAL

Although not necessary, it can be helpful to learn to rate your degree of arousal. The best way I know to do this is to recall the time when you felt most excited in sex, whether it was last night, last week, or twenty years ago. Try to recall exactly how exciting that was. And assign that degree of excitement a 10. At the other end of the scale, we need a 0, a time when you felt no arousal at all. Any occasion when you weren't thinking about sex or having any sexual feeling will do.

Now you have anchored your scale at both ends. You might want to assess your average degree of arousal in sex. Go over in your mind the last three or four times you had sex and rate your arousal for each. This can be a bit tricky, because your arousal probably varied during each experience. The most intense feeling was during or just before orgasm. A good way around this is *not* to include orgasm or the seconds just before it. Rate arousal based on how you felt before orgasm was imminent.

Although I always feel some concern when making judgments based on numbers, I'll do it anyway. If your usual arousal is less than 7 on a scale of 10, and certainly if it's less than 6, you might want to consider following some of the suggestions in this chapter. If your arousal is generally 5 or less, you should definitely attend to them. There's an excellent chance you can increase your excitement and enjoy sex more.

One wonderful feature of arousal is that it is responsive to direct effort; it's fine to work on increasing it, to try to make it higher. I mentioned earlier that trying to get and maintain erections can lead to problems. There's too much pressure put on the penis, and its response may be the opposite of what you want. In general, however, this danger does not exist with arousal. So feel free to focus on arousal during sex and at other times and to consider what might intensify it. The more you can work on increasing and enjoying arousal during sex, and the less you try to force your penis to do anything, the more fun you'll have and the more functional you'll be.

I now turn to some ways of increasing arousal, all of which work for some men. You should read them over and experiment with those that seem relevant to you.

CONDITIONS

As mentioned in Chapter 6, determining and meeting your conditions is essential. Certain conditions will allow higher arousal than others, and the absence of these conditions may make arousal impossible.

Because Randy had been badly stung by the derogatory remarks his ex-wife had made about his masculinity and sexual abilities around the time of their divorce, he was wary about getting serious with another woman. At the same time, however, he sought women's company and their bodies. But either he had difficulty getting an erection or he ejaculated very quickly. It soon become clear that he was very tense with these women, whom he saw only once or twice, and not the slightest bit aroused. This is not a good foundation for enjoyable or even functional sex. As we did the Conditions

Exercise in Chapter 6, he realized that in order to get aroused, he needed at least three things: to be less tense with a partner (which necessitated knowing her much longer than a few hours), to like and be attracted to her, and not to feel such tremendous pressure to prove that his wife was wrong about his sexual prowess. It took several months to meet these conditions, but once that happened he started enjoying sex again.

It will pay you to do the Conditions Exercise in Chapter 6 if you haven't already done so.

GETTING THE BEST PHYSICAL STIMULATION

One of your conditions may be getting certain types of physical stimulation. If so, it's important that you be able to express what you want.

First, however, you may need to find out what you want. Many men have little idea of what they like in sex and dismiss the question with a blanket "it all feels good." If you think it all feels the same, you can do a lot to improve your sex life by challenging that notion. It's inconceivable that a hard touch feels exactly as pleasurable as a soft touch, or that long kisses feel exactly the same as pecks on the cheek. The problem, I think, is that we men are so busy performing that many of us haven't taken the time to determine what pleasures us the most. If you want to find out more about what feels best to you, get your partner to do different things. You can also try touching yourself in different ways during masturbation. Focus in on the sensations and see how you feel. That's all there is to it. Doing this over a period of weeks will give you more information about what you like.

However you discover what you like, you may still need to express your desires to your partner. Even if she was there when you realized you like her to hold your balls when she strokes your penis and during intercourse, this does not mean she's going to know you want her to hold your balls right now or that she should hold them tighter. Only you can let her know. Rereading the chapter on assertiveness will help you be more forthcoming about your desires.

If you already know what kinds of stimulation you like, you might want to consider showing her, often more effective than simply telling her. The Kissing Seminar Exercise (page 235) will give you some pointers. Another possibility, if you're comfortable with the idea, is to masturbate in her presence so she can see how you like to be touched.

I have no idea how common this is, but in my practice at least, many of the men have wanted their partners to hold or stroke their balls during love play or intercourse. As one man reported: "It's incredibly arousing, but also something else. It's very friendly and warm. Makes me feel really accepted." But many of these same men hadn't been able to tell their partners. The word *balls* just wouldn't come out. And the synonyms—*scrotum, testes, sack*—were unacceptable to them. I'm not sure why *balls* was so hard for them. Perhaps it had less to do with the term itself and more to do with how personal they thought it was to ask for such a thing and how vulnerable it made them feel.

In all of these cases except one, the men learned how to express their desires. In most cases, we used a lot of repetition of the word—you're right, the clients sat in my office and said "balls" over and over, a good way of draining away the excess meaning the term carried for them— and mental rehearsal of expressing the wish to the partner. After they were more comfortable because of the mental rehearsals, we did role-playing in the office, where the man would pretend his partner was next to him and ask to have his balls stroked.

If you're feeling inhibited or awkward about expressing your desires, rereading Chapters 8 and 12 will help you to feel entitled to express yourself and give you permission to do so. You should start with requests that seem easy or small to you. If it feels very difficult to tell her how to stroke your penis, try a suggestion or two the next time she rubs your back. Then try something a bit more difficult. Gradually work your way up to expressing all of your desires for physical stimulation. At each step of the way, it will probably make you more comfortable if you rehearse what you're going to tell her several times in your mind before you actually do so.

The most important suggestion for expressing your desires is to put it positively and avoid the impression of blaming your partner for not doing it right. In other words, say what you want, not what you don't want. The following will definitely *not* work: "That's too light. I've told you I want a firmer touch. Why can't you remember!" Here's a better way: "A little harder . . . harder yet . . . that's it, just like that, feels great." This will be even more effective if you reinforce it later, after sex is over, with a comment like this: "I really enjoyed the stronger touch today. Thanks."

Try not to assume that she'll remember what you want the next time. If she doesn't, no need to get upset. Not doing it just right does not mean she didn't listen or doesn't care. More likely, it means only that it's difficult for her to change her habitual way of touching. Just remind her by saying "harder" again. You may need to do this many, many times.

Men and women I know who are good lovers give feedback like this all the time, even to partners they've had for many years. It's no big deal to them, just an integral part of lovemaking and getting exactly what they want.

FOCUSING ON SENSATION

In talking to thousands of people over the years about what they think about during sex, it's clear that many of them are light-years away from what's going on. Some are thinking about work, tomorrow's schedule, or sports. Men who have trouble delaying their ejaculations often focus on something other than sex deliberately, hoping that this will help them last longer. This tactic sometimes works, but I wonder what's the point of having sex if you're not there and not enjoying it. Such an approach seems mainly to reinforce what we don't need reinforced: joyless encounters where the only goal is performing well, no matter what the cost. In general, not focusing on what's going on will decrease arousal and make sex less enjoyable. Focusing, on the other hand, will amplify the sensations, make them feel better and more intense, and increase arousal.

Focusing on sensation means exactly that. You put your attention in your body where the action is. When you're kissing, keep your mind in your lips. This is *not* the same as thinking about your lips or the kiss; just put your attention in your lips. When your partner is touching a part of you, put your attention in that part. When your penis is being touched or when you are having intercourse, put your attention inside your penis; be aware of the fit between the penis and whatever is around it, pressure, texture, temperature, and wetness.

I have noticed that when I ask men to focus, some of them screw up their faces and grit their teeth. They're working very hard. When I ask about this, they usually say this is how they concentrate. Focusing need not and should not be hard work. The tension generated by trying too hard does not help. See if you can focus in a relaxed way. No pushing or shoving, just gently moving your mind, your attention, to where you want it.

A problem with focusing is that our minds tend to wander. There is no cure for wandering minds—that's what minds do—but practice will help yours wander less often. What you need to do is gently bring your attention back to where it belongs as soon as you're aware that it has drifted off.

Some men find it helpful to move back and forth between focusing on sensation and focusing on a fantasy. That's fine and often very arousing. You can also shift between focusing on sensations and focusing on feelings. You may be aware of how good it feels when your partner is touching your penis and then may shift into focusing on your feelings of love for her. That's fine, too.

EXPRESSING COMPLAINTS AND CONCERNS

Sex therapist Bernard Apfelbaum makes the important point that in sex we all try to be as positive as possible and to cover up any complaints or problems. If it doesn't feel good kissing your partner because she has bad breath, we try to ignore the odor and continue with the kissing. If we feel pressured by our partners to have erections, we do almost anything to avoid telling her about this.

Apfelbaum goes on to say that expressing the negative feelings—doubts, fears, concerns, complaints—can be very liberating. It can allow you to feel more in control of your life and to get more aroused. It is important, of course, that what you say be put in a way that will be possible for your partner to hear. Blaming and accusing statements will cause trouble and decrease everyone's sexual arousal.

One man I saw with erection problems was making progress by refocusing on sensation when he started to feel anxious in sex. Then I suggested the effectiveness of this strategy could be increased if he also told his partner about the anxiety when he felt it. His report about it is instructive.

I used to internalize the anxiety. But keeping it inside seemed to make it stronger. Tuesday I externalized it by telling her, and it was amazing. I felt free of it and it was easy to refocus on sensation. My penis behaved like a champ. I like this idea and will continue with it. It makes me feel more in charge of what's going on.

That may seem too easy, because although he was expressing a concern, it was about his own anxiety and wasn't in any way critical of his partner. So let's take a more difficult example, your sense of pressure from her to get an erection. Whether or not the pressure is truly coming from her, what you know is that you feel some urgency coming from somewhere that you get hard, and this is making you anxious. Here's a way you might express it, in this illustration when you're not in the middle of sex:

YOU: "I'd like to talk about sex. OK?"

HER: "Sure."

YOU: "Ever since I failed to get hard on our trip, I've felt tremendous pressure to have an erection when we're in bed. It makes me tense and I can't even pay attention to what we're doing. I know a lot of it comes from me. I feel rotten about disappointing you and not doing my part. But lately I feel that some of this pressure is coming from you. My impression is that you're as tense as I am and it's like you're demanding that I get hard. That's how it feels when you're using your hand on me. Is there anything to what I'm feeling?"

There's probably a good chance she'll agree with your impression. It makes sense that she'd be feeling anxious. She wants the problem resolved and, perhaps more important, she doesn't want to feel that you're not hard because you aren't turned-on to her or that she's not stimulating you in the best ways. If this is the case, the two of you are now in a position to decide what to do to relieve the tension.

EXPRESSING PLEASURE

While expressing concerns can clear the way to feeling more arousal, expressing pleasure with words, sounds, and movements can amplify the good feelings and get you more turned-on. It will probably also excite your partner, and her increased passion will undoubtedly do the same for you. I discuss this issue in detail in Chapter 12, so I will do no more than underscore it here as a means of increasing arousal. The more you express your excitement and pleasure, the more turned-on you will feel.

SIMMERING

Virtually all of us, including many who say they aren't turned-on very much, experience surges of sexual energy during the day. Unfortunately, we don't do anything with these feelings. This was brought home to me when I saw a couple in which the woman was complaining about the relative lack of sex.

> The man said he wasn't turned on much. I knew he worked in a large store in downtown San Francisco and asked if he ever had a sexual impulse during the day. He replied: "Sure, lots of times. You ought to see some of the women who come in the store." I then asked what he did with those feelings: "Nothing. They just sort of go away."

But why let these bursts of sexual arousal disappear? Why not use them? I taught this man about simmering, a simple but effective technique that sex therapist Carol Ellison and I developed some years ago. It's a way of hanging on to and developing your spontaneous sexual urges through the day, which can result in more arousal and better sex.

EXERCISE 16–1: SIMMERING

Time Required: A few minutes a day

The next time you're aware of a sexual feeling, hang on to it for a few seconds. Get into the experience by imagining what you'd like to do with that woman you see on the street or on TV, or by recalling in greater detail that fantasy or memory of a good experience. Whatever you're imagining, get into it. Imagine the touch of her lips, hands, breasts, vagina, or whatever. Feel the texture, the temperature, the way your bodies connect. In other words, run your own X-rated movie of what you want to do. Continue this for a few seconds, or even longer if you prefer. Then let the image fade away.

An hour or two later, close your eyes and get back into the image again for a few seconds. You can imagine exactly what you did the first time or change the experience any way you like.

Continue in this way every hour or two during the day, whenever you have a few spare seconds.

One way to enhance the simmering is to do a few Kegels (see pages 319–320) while you're imagining your scene.

The last step in the simmering exercise is to incorporate your real partner in the fantasy if she's not already included. You can do this when you're on the way to meet her—say, driving back home from work. Start the imagery with what you'd like to be doing with the person who started the simmering, then fade her out and put your partner into the fantasy. Might you enjoy doing the same things or something similar with her? Develop this idea any way you like. When you get home with your partner, you'll probably be highly aroused and ready for a good time.

Unless your partner is almost always ready for sex—which probably means she already knows about simmering—it's smart to include her in your thinking. A short phone call is all that's required. This way, you'll both be ready to go when you get together, or at least you'll be aware of what obstacles may exist.

Simmering should become a regular part of your life. People who consider themselves sexy and have good sex lives do it all the time. It does not get in the way of doing your work or interfere in any way with your life. But it does make you feel good and keep your sexual feelings flowing, ready to blossom when the time is right.

If you find that you don't have many surges of sexual energy to simmer with, carry around a small notebook in your pocket or some 3 × 5 cards for a week or two and write down each instance of such an impulse (rating it on a scale of 0 to 10) and the stimulus. An example would be: "10 A.M., Mon., 7, tall redhead in store." Almost every man I've worked with who has done this for a week or more discovered that he was indeed having sexual impulses. He just hadn't been paying attention before.

USING FANTASY

Simmering is one way of using fantasy to increase arousal. But there is at least one other important way: fantasizing during sex with a partner, something many people do. The fantasies can increase arousal and therefore help maintain erections and intensify orgasms.

If you haven't been fantasizing during sex, you might want to try it. Whenever it feels appropriate or useful, conjure up in your mind an especially arousing image and stay with it as long as you like. For further information about sexual fantasies and their use, read the rest of this chapter and also Chapter 5.

The only risk is the one mentioned in Chapter 5. If you focus entirely on the fantasy each time you make love, your partner may notice that you're not attending to her and therefore feel lonely and left out. If that's the case, you'll probably need to learn to switch between paying attention to her and focusing on your mental images. Most people find this fairly easy to learn.

USING EROTIC MATERIALS

There are a number of erotic materials that can help increase arousal. These include magazines such as *Playboy*, *Playgirl*, *Penthouse*, and *Forum*; popular and pornographic novels; R- and X-rated videos for the VCR. Unfortunately, many of us feel a bit embarrassed about using these materials. "Why do you buy *Playboy*, sir? Do you like looking at the naked women?" "Not at all. I barely look at the pictures. I buy it to read the short stories." Sure you do.

Even if your initial feeling about erotica is negative, you might want to give it a try. Many people who thought they couldn't stand reading or looking at this stuff found out that they got turned-on anyway. The question of why this is so need not detain us here. The point is simply that reading, viewing, or listening to erotic materials can increase your arousal, can add a spark to your lovemaking.

But, as with everything else, it's important to let common sense be your guide. If you always use these materials, they will themselves become boring. And if your partner is new to them or shy about them, you need to take her feelings into account and proceed slowly and only with her permission. You would certainly do well to start with the softest-core stuff and not with the raunchiest. A selection from a romance novel or D. H. Lawrence may do more for her, and be more acceptable, than a hard-driving pornographic account. There are now also many collections of erotica written by women, and erotic films made by women, that may be more to her taste, and perhaps yours as well.

Many women are more turned-on by love than sex, so love poems and literature may be a more promising field to explore for the purpose of arousing your partner. Her greater excitement may well have the effect of turning you on more. And if you're willing to check out the kinds of things that arouse her, she may be more willing to explore those that do the same for you.

ROLE-PLAYING

One very powerful way of increasing arousal is through role-playing or the acting out of fantasies.

Many years ago I was involved with a woman who sometimes would drop into a role in the middle of sex. She would suddenly say something like, "You haven't been a good boy today, so you're not going to get any." Since what we can't have is infinitely more exciting than what we can, my passion immediately skyrocketed, even though I knew she was only acting. I fell into step and would start apologizing and begging. She would repeat her refusal and give in gradually. "Well, okay, since you apologized, you can touch my pussy, but that's it. Just a touch." This would progress through steps including "You can put it in but only halfway. Not an inch further" and "Okay, your behavior is getting better, so you can put it all the way in, but no moving at all." It seems ridiculous on the written page, but I assure you the effect was real and powerful.

There are infinite possibilities as to what roles or games to play. You can get ideas from erotic literature, movies, and your own fantasies.

There is one common kind of role-playing that deserves special mention. When one person (let's say it's your partner) pretends to resist—to not want to have sex or engage in a certain activity—it is crucial that certain rules and signals be worked out beforehand and strictly adhered to. She has to know in her guts that if she really means *no*, *stop*, or *not yet*, and expresses it, you will understand and immediately comply. Trust has to be taken for granted.

Don't ignore your own fantasies. I find that many men are quite creative in their own minds but don't follow up on their ideas for a number of reasons. If your mind throws you an idea that really turns you on, consider it. If it is not likely to harm you or your partner, and not against either of your values, maybe there's some way you could try it out.

> I recall one man who got very aroused by fantasies of having sex on an airplane on one of the frequent trips he and his lover took. He hadn't thought about putting it into practice because he couldn't figure out how both of them, being large people, could even fit into the toilet on a 747, let alone do anything there. After he finally mentioned the fantasy to me, I asked why it had to be in the toilet. His incredulous response was, "In the aisle?!" No, not in the aisle; that would get him arrested. But on the night flights they frequently took, there are usually rows of empty seats and you can move the armrests out of the way. The session ended on that note and nothing more was said about the matter for a month. But when they returned from a cross-country flight, they happily reported that the armrests could indeed be moved. They haven't yet managed intercourse, but they did some other interesting things and were pleased.

RESISTANCE, FEAR, AND UNCERTAINTY

Some degree of resistance can heighten arousal (and desire as well). One problem in long relationships is that sex is too easy. You can pretty much have it when and how you want. Although this is convenient, it can lead to boredom. Contrast this to the situation most of us were in when we were younger and dating. There was resistance from our family and society (you're not supposed to be doing this) and maybe from a partner as well (we shouldn't be doing this yet). Most people agree that such resistance increased arousal.

This is why being sexual where you're not supposed to be (say, in the bedroom next to your parents' when you and your girlfriend are visiting them, or in a public place like a parking lot or an airplane) is so exciting. This is also why role-playing where your partner pretends to be uninterested or resistant in some way can be so exciting. Violating prohibitions and overcoming obstacles makes our blood boil, so to speak.

Uncertainty plays a role as well. In the role-playing example I gave above, for example, my partner was pretending to resist, one result of which was that I wasn't sure how far I would actually get. The lack of certainty helped drive my arousal off the charts. Not being sure of the outcome is also what makes sports and gambling so exciting. Although at its extreme end this idea can have disastrous consequences (as in compulsive gambling and in sex where the only important thing is the conquest and not the actual lovemaking), it is highly beneficial to many couples as a way to increase excitement.

Anxiety can also heighten passion. Although anxiety can have serious negative consequences for sexual functioning, at least one kind of fear—the fear of being discovered—can actually make us more aroused. This plays a part when we have sex in public places. You have to be careful with this, of course. If you have sex in a bedroom or bathroom of someone else's home where a party is going on and are discovered, you will have to live with the consequences. But if you can lock the door and make sure no one knows for sure what you're doing, you may find your arousal breaks all your records.

One couple I interviewed regularly used resistance, uncertainty, and fear of discovery to enhance their lovemaking. Whenever they went to a party, for example, they'd look for a room—bathroom, bedroom, pantry, basement—where they could have a quickie. They dressed appropriately, with clothes that allowed easy access to the genitals and usually with neither of them wearing underwear. Once in the room of their choice, they'd do a role-play. A favorite scene was where they pretended they were strangers and he was trying to seduce her while she resisted (and sometimes they reversed roles; she came on to him but he was reluctant because his "wife" was in the next room). To heighten what was already a very high turn-on, either or both might say that they thought they heard someone coming, someone turning the doorknob, the door opening slightly, etc. This may or may not be your cup of tea, but I know this couple has had a passionate sex life through their twenty-two years of marriage and neither one has had an affair.

THE ISSUE OF GUILT

Some men (and women, too) feel guilty when fantasizing about sex with someone other than their actual partner, or following some of the other suggestions in this chapter. This is almost invariably due to rigid childhood teachings about sex. "What would my mother think!" is how one man expressed his resistance to watching an erotic film. Other men have taken too literally a religious teaching about adultery ("It's like I believe imagining sex with another woman is equivalent to actually having sex with her"). Still others aren't clear exactly what the problem is, but they experience negative feelings when breaking the rules they were taught long ago.

Fortunately, guilt about sex seems to be on the wane in our society. Younger people I've worked with seem to have much less of it than their parents. But it still afflicts many.

There are several things you can do about guilt. One is to talk to someone about it: your sex partner, a close friend, or a therapist. Your discussion should include how you feel when you do the forbidden thing and what rule you're breaking. Guilt invariably involves breaking a rule, one of those "Thou shall not's"—Thou shall not play with oneself, thou shall not think about sex, thou shall not watch dirty movies, and so on. Also bear in mind the thoughts and feelings you as an adult have about the rules. No matter how well intentioned your parents or the religious advisers who taught you the rules, does it make any sense that an adult of your age should not be able to decide for himself whether to fantasize, read erotic materials, and watch erotic films?

A second suggestion is to consider the possible advantages in breaking the rules by doing the forbidden behaviors. They might include giving you more pleasure, helping you function better in sex, giving more pleasure to your partner, enhancing your relationship, and so on. Keep in mind that breaking the rules, doing "forbidden" and "dirty" things, can heighten arousal significantly. Perhaps this is what Woody Allen had in mind when he said: "Is sex dirty? Only if it's done right."

My last suggestion is to start breaking the rules gradually. This should be easier after you've followed the first two suggestions and will give you a chance to see how you feel now and whether the advantages of fantasizing or whatever outweigh the guilt feelings.

ENHANCING ORGASM

Since orgasm is just the extreme form of arousal, everything in this chapter can help make it more intense.

If you believe your orgasms aren't as exciting as they could be, if they are significantly more intense with masturbation than in partner sex, or if a partner has mentioned that you seem unexpressive or to be holding yourself back, be aware of what you're doing the next few times you orgasm. Some men do seem to be keeping themselves in check by restricting their breathing, movements, and sounds. If this is true of you and you want to do something about it, start letting yourself be a bit more expressive. Focus on the pleasurable sensations and let your body move as it desires, let yourself breathe (very important under any circumstances), and let some sounds come out. Don't try to let go of all your controls at once. Make small changes in one area at a time. If embarrassment is an issue, you might want to start being more expressive in masturbation before you do so with a partner. Gradually relax more of your controls and see if you aren't experiencing fuller orgasms.

Another method for increasing orgasm intensity (and sexual feeling in general) is by strengthening the pelvic muscles by doing the Kegel Exercise, named for the man who invented them. I have been using this exercise with clients for almost twenty years and have received numerous reports of greater sensation in the pelvis (including the penis), greater desire and arousal, and more powerful orgasms.

EXERCISE 16–2: KEGELS

Time Required: A few minutes a day

First you need to get in touch with your pelvic muscles. The best way of doing this is to pretend you are in danger of urinating or having a bowel movement but that you need to control this until you can reach a toilet. The muscles you squeeze to hold things in are the ones we are interested in.

The exercise itself is quite simple. Start by squeezing and releasing the muscles 15 times, twice each day. Don't hold the contraction; just squeeze and let go. At first, you may also be squeezing your stomach and thigh muscles. A few days of practice should allow you to isolate the pelvic muscles and squeeze only them. You can do the exercise unobtrusively anywhere: while driving a car, watching TV, reading the paper, during a meeting, and so on. It works best if you pair the exercise with a daily-occurring event—for example, each time you get on the freeway ramp or each time you read the paper. That way you'll automatically do them whenever the event occurs.

Gradually increase the number of squeezes until you're doing about 75, two times each day.

When you reach that number, you may want to do a variation: instead of immediately releasing the contraction, hold it for a count of three, then relax and repeat. These are a bit more difficult. Work up to about 50 of these long Kegels. If you like, you can do one set of short Kegels and one set of long Kegels each day.

Continue doing Kegels for at least six weeks. Results usually aren't noticeable for a month or more. As you continue with them, they will become automatic and require no conscious attention or effort.

Squeezing your pelvic muscles when you're having an erotic fantasy, when you're being sexually stimulated, and when you're having intercourse can increase pelvic sensation and help turn you on. Some men have reported squeezing and holding the contraction just before orgasm. They say it holds off orgasm for a few seconds and makes it more powerful. Feel free to experiment as you see fit.

More than anything else, arousal is what drives good sex. It *is* the spark. It is also the cornerstone of a sexuality based on pleasure rather than on performance. If you want more exciting and more satisfying sex, go for greater arousal.

_____17

Sex and the Single Man

"I'm the guy all girls' parents warn them against. I know someday I'll get married, have children, and be faithful. But what I want now is sex with every attractive woman I meet. I just want to get my fill and move on. It's fun and it's also an ego thing. My problem is that I've met only a few women who feel the same. Most of them want some kind of relationship, some hope for the future. I don't like to hurt them, but the situation is set up so that someone has to lose. If I'm honest, I won't get as much sex as I want. If I pretend I'm more interested in a relationship than I really am and then disappear, she gets hurt. I wish there was a way to be honest and still get what I want."—MAN, 33

"The disease thing is a real bummer. It's sort of there in the back of my mind, that I could end up sick or dead because of one night of sex, but I usually don't do anything about it. I don't like rubbers and I hate getting into conversations with women I hardly know about what disease she or I might have and who we've had sex with."—MAN, 29

"While I was married, I didn't think much about the singles world. It seemed like it was on another planet. Now that I'm divorced, I feel like a babe in the woods. Women are much more sophisticated than they used to be. They talk about sex easily and all of them come off as experts in oral sex and anal sex—who would have imagined that!—and five hundred positions of intercourse. And I'm so scared of AIDS and all the other bugs that I'm not sure I really want sex."—MAN, 46

321

IN some ways, the dating scene has changed dramatically in recent years. There are new ways of meeting Ms. or Mr. Right. Singles organizations, dating services complete with videos and other high-tech accoutrements, and personal ads have become popular alternatives or supplements to the old ways.

Since the sexual revolution, there's also a new attitude about sex. It is no longer the let's-do-it-even-though-we-don't-know-each-other's-name-yet notion of the 1960s and '70s, but there is a strong sense of entitlement about sexual activity and pleasure. The vast majority of dating men and women expect sex to be part of their activity within a few dates. The sense of freedom and entitlement about sex, however, has now been complemented by a new sense of fear about it. We're finally getting the message that sex isn't risk free. There's also a feeling among many people, men as well as women, that sex ought to make sense, that it ought to fit into one's life and values in a reasonable and positive way. What that way is, however, isn't always easy to determine and is bound to be different for different people.

It's now far more acceptable for dating couples to talk about sex before having it, especially about protection against disease and pregnancy. It's not that everyone is doing it, or even a majority of couples, only that it's no longer unusual. These talks can also include what turns each of you on and what kinds of things you especially enjoy and any problems that either is having. It's also more acceptable than, say, ten years ago, for dating couples to put off getting into sex for a time. No longer do you have to have sex by the third or fourth date to feel OK about yourself. I see all these trends as positive and hope they continue.

There are changes in our views not only of sex, but also of relationships. There is a kind of wariness about getting involved that didn't exist a generation or so ago. More and more young men (and women) come from homes where it was apparent that their parents' marriages, whether or not they ended in divorce, left a great deal to be desired. And there are large numbers of men (and women) dating who themselves have suffered through unhappy marriages and divorce. Although surveys indicate that most men and women do want to commit themselves to a relationship, and although the marriage statistics clearly indicate that the institution of marriage is flourishing, there exists a kind of jadedness and caution that is new.

Despite the changes regarding how and where to meet people and the new concerns about sex and relationships, there is a great deal of continuity. Males and females still dream of finding Ms. or Mr. Right, whether for a lifetime, the next few months, or only for tonight; they still wonder where to meet that special person and if they have enough to offer to attract and keep him or her; and, sexual revolution or not, they still wonder when to get sexual and what that means. Most of the questions and issues that concerned singles twenty and even forty years ago still concern us today.

THE IDEA OF GRADUAL INVOLVEMENT OR TAKING IT SLOWLY

There's no question that a great many problems that plague daters result from rushing into things and not taking the time to reflect on how you feel and what you want. A simple example is when you ask out a woman you've never met and don't know (you've gotten her name from a friend) for an extended date, say for Saturday night or an all-day outing. If the two of you don't hit it off, you're both going to be miserable. There's all that time looming in front of you, and you don't want to be there. This is also a convenient and destructive way of getting into sex. You don't know what to do with all that time available, so you resort to something you're comfortable with, your sexual routine. The problem is that you're likely to feel worse afterward rather than better.

The whole process of dating can and should be one in which you take your time getting to know someone, reflecting after each encounter what you feel about her and what you want from her. This allows you to stay within your zone of comfort and to make the best choices for yourself. I know it doesn't sound half as romantic as love or lust at first sight, but it makes a lot more sense for people who've gotten beyond letting their eyes, hearts, or penises run their lives. By the way, what I'm saying is relevant not only if you're looking for your one and only, but even when you're just looking for someone to spend a few nights with.

I've been a voyeur at the many professional conferences I've attended over the years, taking a lively interest in who shacks up with whom and with what results. One thing that's always amazed me is how often a man hits on a woman, makes an immediate decision to spend the night with her if he can, succeeds in his quest, and then can't stand the sight of her the next day, nor she of him. I've stood right next to several of these men the next day when the women they spent the night with walked by—which could hardly be avoided since they were going to the same meetings—and watched them tighten up in anxiety or disgust. The reaction of the women didn't seem any better.

Even if all you want is a night or two of fun, you can still take a little more time getting to know her and determining if you really want to spend those nights with her. I'm not a prude and I have nothing against a night or two of pleasure with someone new, provided you both understand what the rules are. But if you feel like hell when you wake up next to her the following morning and wish you were elsewhere, what's the point? Better, I think, to put a little more time and effort into getting to know her before getting into bed.

I very much like the idea of coffee dates or gradual involvement that I introduced in *Male Sexuality*, which is just a structured way of taking your time. At a conference or on a vacation, this means only that even if you are smitten by a woman, you don't try to rush her into bed, or let her rush you. Better just to have a drink together, or a meal or walk or talk, then separate for a while so you can consider how you feel about her. If all the thoughts and feelings are good, then by all means arrange to see her again. But then back off once again for reflection.

A first date should be time-limited, no more than an hour or two. If you like her, it will be easy to arrange a longer get-together for the next time. If the two of you don't hit it off, you haven't lost much and you don't have to worry about how to fill up endless hours.

Needless to say, the gradual-involvement-contact idea implies that you should take your time becoming sexual with a new partner. As I hope will become clear in the rest of this chapter, there's a great deal to be gained from this approach and almost nothing to lose.

THE QUESTION OF HONESTY IN DATING

A huge problem in the singles life is that many people get hurt because of different expectations about what being together or having sex means. Men often feel that they have to lie to get sex. They think they can't simply say, "You turn me on and I'd like to spend the night with you." So they have to concoct stories about wanting a relationship even when they don't.

It can help to realize that not every woman is looking for a big-time relationship. There are many women who would be happy to spend the weekend or week with you without any promises of more to come.

If you're honest about your desires, you will certainly be rejected some of the time. Some women you're interested in will not have sex with you if that's all you want. But you'll also get what you want some of the time and you won't have to feel bad afterward. I suggest honesty.

If you're at a conference or at Club Med and you only want company for the night or week, why not say so? "I get lonely at these meetings. It's much nicer if I can find someone to spend my free time with." Or, "I'm just taking a week to get away from it all. And I'm looking for someone who wants to enjoy the time with me."

The same kind of honesty can be used in more common dating situations. If you're not looking for a big-time relationship, but are wanting some company, why not just say so? "I've only been divorced six months and that whole business has taken a lot out of me. I'm not ready to settle down again but I enjoy company and want to have a good time." Suppose she asks if you think you'll ever want to get married again? An honest answer might be: "I really don't know. It's going to take me some time to sort out the whole business about love and marriage."

HONESTY AND SEXUALLY TRANSMITTED DISEASES (STDs)

What to do and say about STDs is a big issue. If you know you're disease free, you might want to find out if she is. If you know you've got something, what are you going to do about that?

Surveys show that many men, and women as well, don't tell new partners about their diseases and don't do anything to prevent infection. For what it's worth, I think this is immoral, immature, irresponsible, and probably illegal as well. How would you feel if you had sex with a woman and it turned out that you had contracted herpes, genital warts, or some other disease from her? I'll bet you'd be furious, and you'd have every right to be. So how do you think she'd feel if the tables were turned and she got something from you?

I think partners owe it to themselves and each other to (1) use condoms and spermicide every single time they have intercourse and (2) to be completely honest about any diseases they have. This is simply basic human decency. This is what we owe one another if we want to live in a humane, civilized society.

Once again, of course, rejection rears its head. Yes, it's true that if you tell a new friend that you have a disease, she may not want to have sex with you even with a condom or even though you know that you're not infectious right now. That's just the way it is. It's her right to make the decision, just as it's your right to decide what you want to do if she has a disease.

"But why do I have to tell her I have herpes [or genital warts, or whatever]? Wearing a condom will protect her."

Condoms are not 100 percent effective. Nothing is. Even with a condom, she might get what you've got. She's the one who needs to make the decision, not you. By not giving her the relevant information, you're ensuring that she can't make an informed decision. You're robbing her of a basic human right, the right of informed consent.

If you have something to tell your friend, just tell her. There is no best time, place, or method, which is another way of saying that any time (before sex), place, or way is acceptable. Here is an example: "This is difficult but there's something I need to tell you before we go away for the weekend. I have genital herpes. It's not active now and I wouldn't have sex when it was, and I always use a condom, but I wanted you to know."

What about the situation where you're disease free but want to know about her? This can be a bit difficult, and I disagree with a lot of the advice from experts in recent years regarding this question. Many of them suggest interrogating your about-to-be sex partner. I have nothing against asking, but I'm convinced that you can't have total faith in the answers. First of all, some people will say they're disease free when they're not. Second, some people aren't aware they have a disease. So even if she tells the truth as she knows it, it may not be accurate.

Feel free to ask if you want, but use protection in any case. Condoms aren't perfect, but they're a lot better than nothing. Condoms used with generous amounts of spermicide aren't perfect either, but they are even safer than condoms without spermicide.

Speaking of condoms, you should consider in detail ahead of time exactly how you're going to get a condom into the act. How are you going to bring up the subject, what are you going to say, and what are you going to do? Working out a routine and rehearsing it a number of times in your mind will help ensure that you actually do what you want to do. Having condoms available in a number of places will also help. You can always carry some in a shirt or jacket pocket (but *not* in a wallet or glove compartment, please, because the heat there can destroy latex), and have a few in your usual place for lovemaking, say a bedside nightstand.

Another question has to do with how many sex partners you and she have had. A number of men and women these days use this question as a way of getting information about disease. It's not a particularly good question because the number of partners doesn't reveal much about disease. You can be disease free even though you've been to bed with two hundred partners, and you may have caught a disease from the only partner you've had.

But suppose you're asked how many women you've had sex with. A recent survey indicates that some men and women lie by underreporting. Women feel pressured to do this because they fear being thought loose. And these days some men feel pressured to underreport for the same reason and also because a large number of partners implies the possibility of disease.

So what to do? Here again I believe honesty is the best policy. There's little point to pretending to be someone you're not, because sooner or later your friend is probably going to find out who you really are. If she isn't going to like that person, it's best to find out as soon as possible. And it doesn't help the development of trust, a crucial component in any decent relationship, when people start lying to each other.

HONESTY AND MULTIPLE PARTNERS

A number of women have had rude shocks thinking they were in an exclusive relationship only to find out their new partner was sleeping with one or more other women as well. Men are often shocked by how the women react, as in this example from a thirty-two-year-old man:

Women are impossible! I try to be honest, but there's no satisfying them. Since Tammy and I have been seeing each other about twice a week for a month and have been to bed several times, I thought it was time to tell her that I'm also seeing Rita. She went right through the roof. Went on and on that I should have told her sooner, before we had sex. Then she kicked me out and said not to call. What am I supposed to do—show up at the first date with a detailed description of how I spend my time?

The issue here, as with the others we've dealt with earlier, has to do with informed consent, the kind and amount of information new partners owe one another so that each can make the best decisions. A lot depends on the situation. If you meet someone at Club Med or an out-of-town meeting and it's clear that today or this week is all you have to give each other, marital status and relationship intentions and patterns may not be relevant. It's different if you're dating someone close to home.

Exactly when do you say what's what? There's no universal answer, but I think earlier usually works better than later, and before sex is better than after. Not only is sex still a more important decision for women than men, but there's also the matter of STDs. If you're not telling her that you're sexually involved, you are withholding information that many people consider important. Some women say that they would have held off having sex with the man had they known he was sleeping with other women. Others say they would have gone ahead anyway, but the fact that he didn't say anything about his other relationship makes them wonder if he can be trusted. This kind of question does not bode well for the formation of a good relationship.

"Once again, it seems you're siding with women rather than with men. You're not recognizing the power struggle that goes on. If I was honest about my intentions or how many women I'd slept with, I'd rarely get laid. Women are more honest because it's more acceptable to say you're looking for everlasting love than you just want sex tonight. Since a lot of guys want unencumbered sex, we have no choice but to tell tales."

You make a good point. The old power struggle between the sexes still exists, with men often pushing for as much as they can get and women often holding out for as little as they can give. And I don't have a ready answer for exactly how men and women should act in these circumstances.

But my concern is to protect men as well as women. My own experience with men corroborates that of other researchers: although they usually feel sexually satisfied after casual sex, men also report feeling "empty," "hollow," and "wasted" afterward. The negative feelings are exacerbated when they know they have misled or hurt their partners. Regret also enters in. In talking about these experiences, men often say they have to stop having them, they need to find a relationship or turn over a new leaf. I have been impressed with the similarities I hear when men talk about casual sex and when they talk about getting drunk. Both experiences feel good when they're happening, but then there's a terrible feeling the next day.

What I'm suggesting is that men find ways of getting what they want that allow them to feel good not only during but also after. For the majority of the men I've worked with, this has meant greater honesty so that their partners also feel good.

DON'T SAY YOU'LL CALL HER IF YOU AREN'T SURE YOU WILL

Speaking of honesty, women are confused and enraged by men who say they'll call and don't. My understanding of the man's position is this: He's either sure he will call or won't call, or he's not sure. If he thinks he will, he's just being honest. If he's not sure or knows he won't, he's using the promise that he'll call as a solution to a potentially unpleasant situation. He doesn't quite know how to say good-bye or good-night. "I'll call you" offers an easy way out. This isn't unusual. Telling little white lies is acceptable and common in many social situations.

The problem arises when she wants you to call and takes your promise seriously. She's looking forward to hearing from you and seeing you again. When you don't call, she feels disappointed and upset, and then angry. "Why did he lie to me?"

Once again, I think some kind of honesty is a better policy. I don't think it's necessary to say anything unkind or to get into a hassle. At the very least, though, if you're not positive you're going to call her, don't say you will. If you don't promise to call and then you do, that might be a nice surprise for her.

If you find yourself in the awkward position of having said you'll call and then realizing you don't want to, it is probably a good idea to call or, better yet, write a short note. For instance: "I enjoyed our date last week, but after thinking about what you said, I don't think we should get together again. You said you wouldn't be ready to settle down for a long time, and I'm looking for a steady relationship now." If it's something potentially more embarrassing or hurtful—you just don't care that much for her or she's not as ambitious, smart, or pretty as you want—a little white lie can be used: "I enjoyed our time together but realized later that the chemistry just isn't there" or "I think we're just too different to make it as a couple." This way, you're doing what you want, not seeing her again, but you haven't left any loose ends or bad feelings.

Not saying you'll call when you aren't sure you will is just one example of being honest and not making false promises. Although honesty isn't always the best policy—there are some circumstances where it's best to keep one's mouth shut—it should be the first policy we consider.

SUPPOSE YOU'RE A VIRGIN

Despite the common myth that all males over the age of eighteen or nineteen are sexually experienced, there are in fact many men in their twenties and some in their thirties, forties, and even older who have never had sex with a partner. Although the reasons vary—shyness, fear of women, fear of sex, or fear of closeness, not feeling a need to have an intimate relationship or sex, being preoccupied with work or other things—one thing these men have in common is a sense of inadequacy because they haven't had sex with a partner. When they decide they'd like to become sexually intimate with a woman, they often feel conflicted about a number of things, one of them being what they should say about their situation. They feel women will be turned off by their lack of experience, but at the same time don't want to lie; even those who have considered the possibility of lying fear their lack of experience will show.

Yet again, I think honesty is the first thing to consider. It's not necessary to announce, "Hi, I'm a virgin," but if it becomes appropriate or if you're asked a relevant question—such as "What have your past lovers been like?"—why not tell the truth? It's doubtful that your new friend is going to be horrified by your response. And if she is, you don't need her anyway. Although I can't guarantee it will happen to you, some women find a male virgin interesting.

Some men are virgins because their attempts at intercourse haven't worked out (ejaculation before insertion or inability to get or maintain an erection) and they've given up. If this is true for you, the material in the rest of this chapter and in Chapters 22 to 24 may help. Surrogate therapy (at the end of Chapter 24) is another possibility.

For some men, the problem is that they are very shy and find it extremely difficult to meet women or to ask them out. Although dealing with this issue is beyond the scope of this book, there are several good works on shyness and developing social skills available. A therapist can also help.

If the reason for your virginity is a fear of women or the closeness that sex might bring, you should consider professional therapy. Most of the time these problems can be worked out and you can learn to enjoy a close relationship.

Whatever the reason for your virginity, try to remember that it's not a disease or something you have to be ashamed of. It's just a fact, and if that fact bothers you, there are a number of options that can help get you what you want.

SEX FOR THE FIRST TIME WITH A NEW PARTNER

The first time a couple has sex is a poignant moment. Two people come together to share an experience and themselves, often in conflict or confusion within themselves, and perhaps with differing goals and expectations. Each hopes for at least a tolerable experience and fears a humiliating one, each yearns for acceptance and fears something less. Both are concerned that they will be found wanting in some way: that their bodies, behaviors, or personality will be compared to some superior standard and be found inadequate.

Men usually feel responsible for how the lovemaking goes. They wonder if they can do all they believe they should do: get the partner interested and aroused, get and maintain lasting erections, and provide the kind of ecstasy they assume their partners desire. They hope their performance will be, if not fantastic, at least passable.

Their partners often go through very similar types of questioning and agonizing. The woman wonders if the man will find her body attractive, if she'll be able to please him, and if he will find sufficient interest and pleasure to want to return.

It's totally understandable that people should be uneasy when they have sex with someone new. Even in these so-called liberated times, sex still means something special. It's not something you do with just anyone. In sex you allow a unique access to yourself—to your nudity, to the feel and smell and taste of your body and its fluids. And it can go even further. You may allow access to your emotions, at least to your interest and excitement. In doing so, you run the risk that this may be the start of real contact with the other person, a kind of intimacy, with all the possibilities and dangers that intimacy implies.

Because of the tension that accompanies first-time experiences, they are often unsatisfactory. Many men do not get or maintain erections, or they come quickly and then feel bad about these "failures." Other men function adequately but don't derive much pleasure. A great many women do not have orgasms the first time they have sex with a partner, a fact for which many men blame themselves. A woman I know says that the first few sexual encounters with a new partner are so bad she considers them "throwaways." The only reason she engages in them, she says, is that she can't figure out how to get to the fifth or sixth time—and good sex—without going through the first and second times.

It doesn't have to be this way. Although there is no way of dissipating all the strangeness and tension involved in first-time experiences, there are ways of making them better and more satisfying, with far fewer "failures" and bad feelings.

No Sex Before Its Time

The single most important point is this: **Don't rush into sex; go slowly and get into sex only when you're comfortable with your partner and your conditions are met.** This is the notion of gradual involvement applied to sex. There's no good reason to rush into sex on the first or second date, or even on the fifth or ninth date. Sex should occur only when you and your partner feel comfortable with each other and really want to engage in physical intimacy. This is especially true for men who've had problems in sex.

In case you're wondering how women feel about this idea, I'm happy to tell you that the vast majority of women I've talked to over the years have agreed that taking one's time getting to sex is what they prefer.

If you've read Chapter 3, you know there are lots of things you and your new friend can do besides the old foreplay-intercourse routine. As your comfort with each other develops, you could, for example, engage in more intimate forms of touching (hugs, kisses, massages, necking, petting, sleeping together, dry-humping, hand jobs, and so forth). There's certainly no shortage of activities.

It's clear from everything we know that sex goes best if it's done when both partners feel it's what they want. If one or both feel pressured into the activity, it will be something less than wonderful. It's well known that women often feel pressured into having sex. What's not so well known is that so do men. Men feel pressured by their notions of manhood: A man should make sexual advances very quickly in a relationship and a man should never rebuff the sexual advances of his partner.

Of particular relevance here is what you can do if your new partner pushes for sex before you feel ready. This situation is no longer unusual. A woman may make a sexual advance because she truly wants sex with you or because she's trying to deal with the insecurity generated in her because you haven't made one. Regardless of her motives, you're going to have to do something.

Probably the most common choice is to go along regardless of how you feel. I don't recommend this because it can easily lead to bad sex and bad feelings. Far better to get into your assertive and expressive mode and let her know how you feel. Here are two examples of what you might say:

I'm flattered you want me to stay the night. I've enjoyed our times together and am very turned on to you. But getting into sex this fast doesn't work well for me. I'd like us to take our time, getting to know each other better, and get to sex when it feels right for both of us. Can you understand what I'm saying?

I'm a little shy and it takes me a while to be comfortable enough to have sex. But I really enjoy you and want to spend more time with you. Does the idea of [insert activities you want to do, such as trading back-rubs, doing more kissing and petting, and so on] tonight do anything for you?

Suggestions for Sex with a New Partner

- Get to know her and give her the opportunity to know you. Give yourself time to determine if you really want sex with her.
- Be sensual with her before being sexual. Hold hands, hug, kiss, snuggle, or do anything else that feels good. Always stop when you want to, when you feel anxious, or when you get a signal from her that she wants you to stop.
- Do whatever is necessary to feel comfortable with her and get your conditions met. You might want to talk with her about both your expectations and hers. You might also want to talk about the kinds of physical contact you enjoy. Establish a habit of discussing your preferences and try to get her to do the same. This will serve you well when you become sexual with her.
- Always stay within your comfort zone. Refrain from activities that make you tense.
- Consider a session or two of massage or body-rubs before you get to sex.
- You might also want to consider *sleeping* or taking a nap with her, which can be a nice and cozy way of getting more comfortable. It's possible that sleeping together might lead to sex, which is fine if that's what feels right at the time. But make sure your conditions are met and that sex is what you want. If not, just sleep.
- Have a talk with her about protection against conception and disease before you get anywhere near genital contact. It's a mistake to assume that this is the woman's responsibility. Since both of you will have to deal with any consequences that occur, it's the responsibility of both partners.
- When your conditions are met, when you are aroused, and when you want to, feel free to engage in the sexual activities you like (as long as she also likes them). Keep in mind what was said about sexual choices. Intercourse isn't required. If you have had erection or ejaculation problems in the past, it is best not to have intercourse the first few times you are sexual with her. Do other things that feel good to both of you.
- Give feedback about your experiences with her. Tell her—during and after sensual and sexual activity—what you like and don't like,

and encourage her to do the same. This telling should, of course, be done gently and with tact. Doing this eliminates guesswork and misunderstandings, thus helping both of you to know each other better.

- Express your feelings. If you have feelings that get in the way of your sexual responsiveness or your ability to relate to her in any way, you would do well to discuss them with her. It will help her to know you, and it may totally or partially resolve the problems.
- Don't do anything you don't want to do. If she suggests sex before you feel ready for it, let her know how you feel, no matter how difficult this may be. You need to stand up for yourself. If she suggests activities that aren't your style, let her know immediately: "I'm sorry, but I really don't want your dog in bed with us." Take care of yourself.
- Keep intake of alcohol and other drugs to the absolute minimum you can tolerate. The last thing you need is some chemical screwing up your mind and nervous system.

IF YOU'RE HAVING ERECTION OR EJACULATION PROBLEMS

No one envies a single man with a sex problem. It's a difficult situation to be in. Different men react in different ways. Some don't date at all; better to go without love and without sex than to be humiliated. Others date lots of women but only for brief periods. As soon as they think sex might come up, they find someone else to go out with. Still others try to have sex. Sometimes everything works out and the problem is solved. But this isn't typical. The problem recurs and the man is devastated (whether or not his partner is). And there are still other men who try to fix the problem before dating by using self-help books or going to therapy.

There are several things a single man with a sex problem needs to keep in mind. Perhaps the most important is that having a sex problem doesn't make you an undesirable person. It just means you have some-thing that needs work, no different from any other problem. Because men with sex problems tend to do a lot of negative and destructive self-talk, it's important to read and master the information in Chapter 21. It also does you no good to keep away from women. Believe it or not, this will tend to make the problem worse.

There are several options. One is to have surrogate therapy for the problem (see pages 475–478). Another option, probably the one most frequently chosen, is just to date and see what happens. Some men with erection problems find that getting into sex slowly with a partner who really turns them on is helpful. After a few times with her, the problem seems to have disappeared, and often it has. These men can benefit from following the suggestions I give in this chapter. Unfortunately, this method is not likely to help a man with long-standing inability to control the timing of his ejaculations or with a long-standing erection problem.

Still other men won't go out, at least not beyond a second or third date, until they believe they've done something to resolve their problem. The twelve suggestions given above on sex with a new partner will help, as will doing the appropriate masturbation exercises in Chapters 22 and 24. And so will the following suggestion.

Consider Telling Your New Friend About the Problem

If you're like most of the men I've seen in therapy, this idea will make you uncomfortable. Despite that, there are a number of good reasons for thinking about it. Before I get into them, however, let's dispense with one piece of silliness. I'm *not* at all suggesting you introduce yourself like this: "Hi, I'm Fred and I have an erection problem." That's not the way to do it. But somewhere on an early date (but not the first one), when it looks like the two of you are moving toward becoming sexual, you can find an opportunity to tell her.

One advantage to telling her is that you'll eliminate the women whom you fear the most and whom you shouldn't be with in the first place: those who, for whatever reasons, can't handle the problem. The last thing you need is to be with someone who's unsympathetic or even hostile to your situation. Telling her before you get anywhere near a bed will ensure that you don't end up with such a person. Of course, it may feel very bad that this woman you're so attracted to says she doesn't want to see you again. Just keep telling yourself that there are plenty of other women you'll be attracted to and who will not be put off by your problem.

The other side of this advantage of telling is that you'll feel a lot better. You won't have to try to hide the problem if she already knows about it, and you'll know you're with someone who can deal with it. The men I've worked with who have told women they're dating about their sexual problems have felt incredibly relieved. For example:

I feel wonderful! I was scared to death before I told Jane about my situation. I was sure she was going to tell me to get lost. But she was wonderful. Said there were plenty of things we could do without an erection and she was looking forward to doing them. I can't tell you how good I feel!

It's understandable that men are very uncomfortable with the idea of telling a woman they're attracted to and don't know very well that they have a sex problem. The main reason is fear of rejection. As one man put it: "Oh, that's just terrific. Here we are just getting to know each other, just starting to think what sex together might be like, and I'm supposed to say, 'By the way, I can't get it up.' Talk about raining on a parade. It makes perfect sense that she'll tell me to get lost."

It is possible that she will tell you to get lost. The chances are probably small—most women I talked with will not react like that—yet they are real. But you have to realize that none of the options are good. To tell her is difficult and you may end up rejected. But not to tell her isn't exactly a bed of roses. You'll be worried about her finding out—and how is it possible that she won't?—and about her reaction to the discovery. This worry will make it harder for you to enjoy sex and to function as you'd like. And if you get rejected in bed, it may be much more difficult to deal with than if you got rejected before you had sex.

I recall a client, Frank, who was rejected after he told a woman he was dating about his erection problem. He felt totally devastated and assumed no woman would want him. I said that her rejection of him was her problem, not his, and that there was probably some good reason why she couldn't cope with this kind of problem. But he wasn't satisfied. He assumed that she was representative of all women. Since it was clear that he would feel better if he understood why she had rejected him, I suggested he call her and ask.

He did. He opened the conversation by saying he respected her wish not to see him again, but he was very hurt by what she said and wanted to understand her reason. So she told him. She had been with a man for ten years who had an erection problem, refused to get help for it, and often blamed her for its existence. She had become almost phobic about erection problems and simply couldn't be around a man who had one.

Frank felt a lot better after talking to her. He was disappointed she didn't want to see him again, but understanding her reason made it easier for him to accept the idea that not all women would reject him.

Despite his disappointment, Frank clearly did the best thing for himself. Can you imagine what would have happened if he hadn't said anything but had gotten in bed with her and not gotten hard?

It's important to realize that getting rejected doesn't decrease your worth as a human being, a man, and a lover one bit. You do have a problem, but it's resolvable under the right circumstances. If she decides she can't deal with it, that's because of something in her. The woman who rejected Frank provides one reason why someone might not be able to deal with your situation. Perhaps a more common one has to do with her insecurity. In talking with women over the years, I've often raised the question of what they would do if a man they were attracted to mentioned a sex problem before they had sex. The vast majority of the women said it wouldn't be an issue as long as he took responsibility for the problem and would be willing to get help if it didn't clear up on its own.

But a few said they wouldn't be able to see him again. One articulate woman put it like this:

I know it isn't fair. But to me, him not getting hard would mean I wasn't sexy or skillful enough. I know that's my own button, but it would be too much for me to handle. I'm sure I could cope if he developed an erection problem after we'd been together awhile. But at the start, when I'm so insecure anyway and so worried about my effect on him, I just don't think I could deal with it.

It's clear that she has the same fear of rejection you do. Your not getting erect seems to her like you are rejecting her.

Although I reported earlier that no man has reacted positively to my idea of telling potential partners about the problem, a great many of them ended up doing so. After considering the options, they realized this was the one that made the most sense.

So how did they go about this? The story of one client, Charles, offers some ideas.

He dated lots of women in the months after his divorce, but only once or twice each because of his fear that sex might come up and he would be humiliated. Finally, feeling he couldn't go on this way, he came to see me. When I brought up the idea of telling a woman about his problem, he tenaciously resisted. There was no way, he said, he was going to announce to a woman he barely knew that he was impotent. I questioned him about the term *impotent* and suggested we look at the facts. He had no sexual problems in his life until the last two years of his marriage, a time in which he and his wife were constantly at war and which wasn't conducive to his sexual functioning. He often had morning erections and always with masturbation. He wasn't impotent, but because of a number of failures to get or stay erect with his wife toward the end of the marriage, he was fearful that he wouldn't get hard with a woman. He felt a little better after this conversation. But the idea of telling Janet, a woman he had been out with once and who he was quite interested in, was frightening.

I suggested that since none of the options open to him were terrific, the only question was which of them was the least bad. He said he'd think about it. The next time he saw Janet, he told her. Here's his report:

"I realized that I had to tell her. I couldn't go on dropping women after only one or two dates. It was only making my fears worse. So I thought about how to bring it up. I realized we'd both been recently divorced and had talked a little about that during our first get together. Since I see my problem as a consequence of a failing marriage and then the divorce, I realized that I could bring it up during another discussion about divorce.

"I had planned to steer the conversation toward the subject of divorce the next time I saw Janet, but I didn't have to. She did by mentioning that one outcome of the divorce is that she's more guarded around men. I saw my chance and dove in. Told her I'm also more guarded and I've also got another consequence to deal with. With great difficulty I explained my erection problem. I was almost afraid to look at her while I was talking. But I did look at the end and she was smiling. Said she didn't see it as a big problem. People who care about each other can do lots of fun things that don't require erections."

If you think the problem is transient, here's something you can say: "It takes me a few times with a new woman to get comfortable enough so my penis feels it can do its stuff."

The same kinds of things can be said if your problem is rapid ejaculation, depending on whether the difficulty is transient or long-term. If you know from experience that your control will get better after a few more times, you can say: "I usually can last a lot longer after I've been with someone a few times." If the problem is chronic, you need to say something different.

What to Do When a Problem Occurs

When a problem occurs—whether or not you've spoken to your new partner about it and whether or not you've ever had this problem before—you should probably say something. Suppose you come fast in intercourse. Why not say something like this: "I was so excited, I couldn't control myself. I'd like you to feel as good as I did. Tell me what you like."

Let's take the same scenario but make one change. Instead of coming fast, you don't get an erection. Your partner uses her hand and her mouth on you, but to no avail. Chances are good that her efforts, as well intentioned as they are, will only make things worse because you'll feel under even greater pressure to get hard. This will be especially true if you sense, accurately or not, that her main concern is not giving you pleasure but only getting you erect.

There are several ways to handle this situation, but perhaps the best might go like this. You recognize you're tense and probably won't get hard. So you stop her from trying to stimulate you and say something like this: "He's [referring to your penis] shy the first time and I don't think he'll come out to play tonight. How can I make you feel good?"

Alternative: "I just realized I'm a little tense. I don't think I can get hard. Let's do something else."

I've suggested these kinds of statements to hundreds of men and have some idea of their reaction. The first response is fear: They've never heard anyone say something like this. They aren't sure it's okay to do so; they aren't sure they could do it. But after a bit of time, sometimes only a few minutes, they usually agree that making one of these statements would be better than the alternatives. Then the second and perhaps even more fearsome reaction comes in: "Suppose she doesn't like what I say and criticizes me or gets upset?" The chances of this happening are not great, but neither are they nonexistent. She might not like it. So let's tackle that.

Suppose she says: "That's so disappointing. I was looking forward to having you inside me." You could respond like this: "I was looking forward to it too. But look, I've still got a hand and a pretty wicked tongue. Wanna play?"

But suppose, you may be asking, she says no, she's no longer in the mood. OK, suppose that happens. It's not a tragedy. Just another fact to consider. Here's a way to deal with it: "I'm sorry you're so disappointed. Here, let me rub your back. That often helps me when I feel disappointed." Or (as you put your arms around her): "Maybe holding each other will help relieve the disappointment."

Do Not Apologize for the Problem or for Yourself

Although I think it's smart to tell a partner ahead of time about a problem and to acknowledge the problem when it occurs, it is *not* wise to apologize for it or for yourself. Men with sex problems feel bad because they "can't deliver" and tend to feel guilty and apologetic about everything. Continuing apologizing for the problem may help relieve their guilt for the moment, but it does nothing to endear them to their partners. It's difficult to be with someone or find him attractive if he seems to be apologizing for his existence.

My best advice is: Do not apologize for your physical appearance, your mental abilities, your personality, or your sexual history or performance. It's bad enough if you don't like any or all of these things. Apologizing will only call attention to them and get her to dislike them too. No one likes to be with a wet blanket. If you're terrible and life is terrible and everything is terrible, and that's all you can say, you should consider sitting home alone and not inflicting your misery on others.

Better yet, consider changing your perspective and feeling and acting more positively. Yes, you have a problem, but it is soluble. Explain it, acknowledge it when it occurs, have a good time in spite of it, and get on with resolving it.

Keeping the Spark Alive in Long Relationships

"We've had an active sex life for over forty years. Of course it isn't the same as it was when we first met. It's more affectionate and friendly than passionate these days, and nowhere near as frequent, but it's there and still a great source of love and comfort to both of us."—MAN, 69

"After eight years, I lost interest in her sexually. I fantasized about other women and had affairs. Finally it occurred to me that I didn't want to live like that and that I could have better sex with Gwen. It was really up to me. So we started to work on it and have continued for the last ten years. I'm sure you can tell by my smile that it's going well."—MAN, 45

RECENTLY there has been a huge interest in the possibilities for good sex over the years with the same partner, what might be called "romantic lust." Many people believe in monogamy, but they wonder if good sex can be part of it. In the 1960s and '70s, many folks tried out the alternatives, everything from spouse-swapping to full-scale orgies, and discovered the results achieved were somewhat less than the results advertised. And we've had some uninvited and unsavory guests show up at the sex parties, guests like chlamydia, herpes, and

343

AIDS. These guests themselves make one hope that romantic lust is possible.

The message has long been that marital sex wasn't anything to get excited about and that we should therefore introduce some variety into our lives. The sexual model portrayed in the popular media, the fantasy model, rarely deals with good sex over the long run. Rather, the primary focus is on sex in new relationships. Boy meets girl (said boy and girl, it should be noted, may be married to other people), they get it on, and it's terrific. But little is said about what happens after five, ten, or twenty years of togetherness, after the pitter-patter of little feet is heard in the house, and after neither partner is as svelte as he or she once was. How many books and movies can you think of that illustrate in detail satisfying sex among older men and women, among those who've been together for more than three years, among those with the aches and disabilities that accompany life beyond middle age? The fact that so much media time is devoted to extramarital sex itself implies that whatever it is that's going on in long relationships, it is sorely lacking.

Those who are married always seem to think the real action is somewhere else. Erica Jong puts it this way:

> What *was* it about marriage anyway? Even if you loved your husband, there came that inevitable year when fucking him turned as bland as Velveeta cheese: filling, fattening even, but no thrill to the taste buds, no bittersweet edge, no danger.

Philosopher Corliss Lamont has a similar perspective. In an article titled "How to Be Happy—Though Married," which in itself conveys an interesting message, he says the following:

> Many married couples find a certain monotony in monogamy; what they may need, as a sort of safety valve, is some diversity in love-making. To limit the supreme sexual experience to just one member of the opposite sex for an entire lifetime represents an unreasonable restraint. . . .

Is sex in long relationships really as bad as we've heard? Obviously it is for some couples. But "some couples" is not the same as couples in general. This may surprise you, but I have been unable to find any evidence to support the notion that for most people, sex in long relationships is less free, less functional, less satisfying than sex among the unattached or sex in affairs.

The results of a number of surveys strongly suggest that married men and women have more and better sex than anyone else. In one study, it was found that men and women have *less* variety and *less* experimentation in affairs than in marriage and that women were far more orgasmic with their husbands than with lovers. If we look at subjective satisfaction, studies find that both men and women are more satisfied with marital sex than outside flings. In a survey conducted by Louis Harris for *Playboy*, twice as many married men (66 percent) as single men (33 percent) report being "very satisfied" with their sex lives.

I suggest that the only proper conclusion is that, for most people, fulfilling eroticism is the result of time, familiarity, and a good deal of effort and cooperation. I do not mean to suggest that most sex in long relationships is wonderful or thrilling, merely that for most people it is at least as good and probably better than the alternatives. To be fair, I must admit that the sex in many marriages leaves a lot to be desired. There is a lot of dysfunctional, unsatisfying, and boring sex in many relationships. One of the main reasons, of course, is that many of these relationships themselves leave a lot to be desired. But there is hope for those who want better sex and are willing to do something about their marriages.

The main argument against good sex in the long run is what's called the Coolidge Effect, based on a story about President Calvin Coolidge. According to this story, the president and his wife were given separate tours while visiting a farm. Mrs. Coolidge saw a rooster mounting a hen and asked how often this happened. The answer was many times each day. "Please tell that to the president," she said. When the president was informed of the rooster's performance, he inquired whether it was with the same hen. "Oh, no," was the answer, "a different one each time." "Tell that to Mrs. Coolidge," replied the president.

There is no doubt that fresh flesh turns us on, especially men, and it's usually the men who determine how much sex there is in a relationship. There's something about a new person, full of mystery, that excites us. And there may also be something about the "conquest" of a new person that means a lot to some men. It's easy to get aroused with a new partner. Studies with cattle have shown that a bull will at some point quit having sex with a partner and just lie down, apparently exhausted. But put a new receptive female into the cage, and up he jumps, ready for action again. Many human males are like that too.

Another way of looking at the Coolidge Effect is that we tend to take for granted what we have and lust after what we don't, and this applies especially to men. You may have had unbearable lust for this woman when you first met her. You couldn't get her out of your mind and you would have done almost anything to get her into bed. And once you did, you couldn't get enough of her. At least for a few weeks or months. But now you've lived with her for years, you know her body, her preferences, her idiosyncrasies, and you can have her whenever you want. Playing with your computer, watching TV, or just going to sleep often seem more appealing. But that new woman in the front office sure seems interesting.

One way to have a better sex life over time with the same partner is to do whatever is necessary to combat the taking-her-for-granted syndrome. A number of the suggestions I give later can help in this regard.

It also helps to understand that sex does change over time with the same person. Frequency usually decreases significantly, although how much it decreases is largely under your control if you want it to be. The other important change has to do with lust. As the man I quoted at the head of the chapter mentions, sex over time tends to become less passionate and more affectionate and friendly. This doesn't mean there can't be times, even after you've been together twenty or more years, when sex is highly charged and exciting; following the suggestions I give below and also in Chapter 16 can aid in the endeavor. In general, however, lust is not as high as it is at the beginning of a relationship. Being able to accept this fact and being willing to explore the tender, friendly, and affectionate aspects of sex is crucial.

I once knew a man who couldn't do this. Although he was married, he was with a different woman almost every time I saw him. Finally, unable to contain myself any longer, I asked what was going on. His explanation: "The highest feeling in the world for me is being in lust. I love the first few weeks of a new relationship when I'm totally consumed with a woman. I want to be with her all the time and I want her every minute. We do it in bed, in the car, in elevators, in other people's offices, everywhere. We do regular, oral, anal, quickies, longies, anything and everything." What happens? I wanted to know. "The fire just burns itself out," was his answer. "I don't have the same lust, I don't look forward to seeing her. I find someone else to recapture the great feelings."

Obviously a man like this will not be happy or have good sex in a long relationship. One has to be able to accept that the kind of overwhelming and consuming passion that exists early in a relationship cannot last forever. It can be rekindled at times, but for most folks the erotic feelings tend to mellow.

There are, however, many things that can make for satisfying sex over time. Over the course of many years, I have interviewed a number of couples who said they had good sex. What I learned from these couples I then taught to my clients. The ideas and techniques that worked best are what follow.

• **Prioritizing,** which means a commitment to making sex good. People who prioritize see sex as a critical area and they're willing to do what it takes to make time for it and make it as fulfilling as possible. Putting sex high on the list has implications. It may mean, for instance, that if you get turned on while cutting the grass or working on a report, you put the lawn mower or pencil on hold while you take care of other business. It may mean that you sometimes are late to work, classes, or meetings. It may mean that you arrange vacations just for the two of you, without children or friends. It may mean you turn down the requests of relatives to stay at your place for extended periods. It may also mean that you keep track of how sex is doing and make corrections if it's not what you want. You don't simply forget about the subject and wake up twenty or thirty years later with the realization that sex has been bad or nonexistent most of your life.

Prioritizing is especially important for men because they usually determine how much sex there is. They are the ones with the easy rationalization for not having sex—work: preparing for it, doing it, being exhausted from it. They also often delude themselves into thinking that sex would be better and more frequent if only they had a younger, slimmer, sexier, less inhibited partner. That could be true, of course, but in most cases sex can be more frequent and more satisfying with the same partner if only the men are willing to put some time and energy into it.

• **Timing.** Good sex flourishes only when there is time for it. In many relationships the partners spend little quality time together. When they are together, they're often dealing with bills, children, and chores. When they go out, they often go with others. They don't do what they did when they were courting: spending lots of time together without distractions. There have to be some changes for couples like this to have good sex and it may have to start simply by having some dates, which, of course, requires that they give a higher priority to intimacy.

Vacations, time away from home, can help. The majority of couples I've talked to, regardless of almost anything else, have more and better sex on vacation than at other times. So one way to keep sex alive in a relationship is to plan numerous vacations, at least some of them just for the two of you. This does not mean you have to spend tons of money. A vacation can be just for a night or two in a neighboring town. The important thing is that you get away from home and all the work and tensions that accumulate there and into a situation that allows you to focus on love and lust.

Timing also means at least two things that lots of people consider a contradiction, though it really isn't. First is that you plan and make time for being together and for sex. Second is that you seize the times that come up spontaneously. I have yet to talk to a couple who had good sex over the years who didn't do both.

• **Relating,** meaning a commitment to keeping the relationship in good shape. Although there is no lack of stories about "the only thing that was good for us was sex," these tales tend to be told by those who are divorced. Most satisfying sex occurs in good relationships or, more accurately, in relationships that are good much of the time.

No union is good all the time—there are always ups and downs, and even periods of terrible strain—but fulfilling sex is more likely when there is closeness, liking, and caring, and much less likely when coldness, anger, and sulking prevail. One characteristic of satisfied couples is that although they disagree and argue and have periods when they can't talk to each other, as do all couples, they recover quickly. They tend not to sulk or carry around anger for long periods. They find ways of breaking the negative spiral, of ending disputes, or of being close in spite of unresolved differences. They do not go for long periods without having good times and without being close.

• **Isolating,** the ability to isolate sex from at least some of the negative vicissitudes of everyday life. I've already said that happily sexed couples don't carry anger around for long periods and that their sex lives suffer when they feel distant from each other. But isolating is yet another side of the picture. At times they can have good sex even though the rest of life is not going well.

They know how to put things aside and have a good time. If they've planned to go out for a night on the town, and if they happen not to like each other when that night comes around, they usually manage to put the negative feelings aside for at least a few hours, enabling them to have a good time and good sex, which, not surprisingly, often resolves the problems or makes resolution easier.

This is very different from what happens in other relationships. A couple is driving to San Francisco for dinner and the symphony, something they've looked forward to for months. Yet on the way over, one of the partners brings up a complaint about the other and soon they are heavily into war games. The chance for closeness and enjoyment is lost, which means that each is going to resent the other for creating this result, and that will drive them yet further apart.

Couples who are committed to enjoying each other physically make their relationship as good as they can and, when it's not so good, know how to detach themselves from the bad parts.

• **Separating,** by which I mean not spending all your time with your partner. This may seem like a contradiction to what I said earlier about needing to spend time together, but it isn't. You need both. A number of people have reported how much they wanted sex with their partners when they were apart and how good the sex was when they finally got together.

I'm not suggesting that you make a special trip to China for a month just so you can have hot sex when you get back home. But I am saying that time apart from your partner may not be a bad thing. You don't have to take her on every business trip you make, nor she take you on every one of hers. And maybe it isn't so bad for you to go off camping or fishing with the guys for a few days or take a trip alone to visit your parents or a friend.

Here is one woman's experience with these separations:

> Rob is gone more than I'd like on his business junkets, but they've had the effect of keeping our love life better than any other couple I know. I miss him when he's gone, especially his physical presence, and that quickly turns into missing him sexually. And the same happens for him. I can't tell you how many times we've done unspeakable things in the airport parking lot or on the way home in the car. When we do make it straight home, we usually have a very steamy session in bed. It's great.

• **Touching.** People who have good sex over time tend to be sensual. They understand the importance of hand-holding and hugs and kisses that are not perfunctory. They may also take baths and showers together, where they do more than just get clean, and they may massage one another, and not just because someone has a sore shoulder.

Touching literally keeps the couple in touch, communicates love, and keeps erotic feelings simmering, thus making a transition to sex relatively smooth when the partners want to go that way.

• **Romancing.** Sexy couples believe in wooing, courting, and seduction. They know the importance of surprise, tenderness, compliments, and all those special little things. They comment on how lovely, sexy, or wonderful the partner looks, they give a little touch as they pass the partner's chair, they occasionally arrange romantic dinners or picnics, they remember birthdays, anniversaries, and other special events, they bring little presents and surprises.

As an example of this, a woman told me about being at a party where a beautiful model was present. She was very moved when her husband, whom she was sitting next to, rubbed her thigh and whispered, "She's gorgeous, but I want you." And we've all heard scores of stories about how much it meant for someone to get flowers or a small gift with a special meaning.

• **Anticipating.** This is related to romancing but not exactly the same. Some couples are very creative. They know how to use the mind to keep erotic feeling alive. I think of a number of couples who've told me that when one of them gets turned on at work, that one will call the other one and make a date for later on. Usually both parties spend a lot of the rest of the day anticipating what will happen after work and getting themselves into a very sexy state of mind.

A man told me that one day at work, apropos of nothing, he received an unsigned note, but obviously in his wife's handwriting, that said: "Handsome man, if you're up for a night of grand passion, meet me at the Fairmount at 8." Enclosed was a key to a hotel room. He didn't get much work done that day.

A woman told me her birthday present from her boyfriend one year was a calendar with her birthday circled. Within the circle was a brief description of the erotic delights she would receive. The same date was circled for each of the other eleven months, and for each a different scenario was depicted. She says it was a very good year.

Contrast this to the lot of many couples, where the only anticipating comes after one says, "Wanna do it tonight?" I think you'll agree there is a difference.

If you or your partner take one of those separate trips I mentioned earlier, there is a lot you can do in your own minds and by phone and mail to get the anticipatory juices flowing.

• **Playing.** People who have good sex over the years seem not to take sex all that seriously, or maybe I should say somberly. They play at it rather than work at it. They have fun.

Couples who have good sex over time are adventurous in a childlike way. They play at exploring their own and each other's sensitivities, and they are willing to try out new things, although I hasten to add that this does *not* mean they try out every new fad that comes along. It's not so much how many different activities and positions they try, but their attitude as they do whatever they do. Many new things don't work—it isn't really that easy, after all, to have intercourse in the bathroom of a 747 or even to get two people into that tiny a space—but they have fun finding this out. They have a healthy sense of humor about the whole business. All of the people I talked to had stories of events that others make into tragedies—contraceptives that couldn't be put on or in, or gotten off or out, beds that creaked or broke, misunderstandings and miscommunications, and even parents and children walking in on them—but their response was a good laugh.

Playing at sex also means not having rigid rules about it, being tolerant for what it is and what it can give. These couples really do take sex any way they can get it rather than having to have it a certain way. This is especially important over the years, because passion isn't always immense and because age and illness take a toll. Men don't always have full erections or erections at all, they don't always have orgasms, and women may not lubricate as well or as much and they too may not have orgasms each time. These couples don't go into hysterical overdrive when they don't function perfectly but instead they use what they have to enjoy themselves.

These people know that Murphy's Law is always in effect, but that doesn't stop them from enjoying themselves, which, when you think about it, is the best and only revenge against Murphy.

• **Feeling,** which refers to a willingness to allow sex to have many expressions and faces, reflecting and expressing different emotions. Sometimes it's a tender lovemaking; at other times, it's an almost brutal fuck, where the only feeling is unalloyed lust; at other times it's just light fun and games. On occasion, sex can even be the expression of angry feelings. Sometimes it's mainly for the pleasure of just one partner, sometimes for the other, sometimes for both. It may last only a minute or two, or it may go on for hours. Depending on the dominant feeling, on some occasions there may be soft moans and words of endearment, on others there may be screams and obscenities.

Couples who engage in this kind of variety are cutting a broad swath. They don't have to go elsewhere for a quickie, or more physical sex, or more loving sex, or anything else. They aren't left thinking that they could do, say, be, or feel something different with someone else. They can do, be, feel, and say whatever they want right where they are. Contrast this with the situation of many couples, where the mood and feelings in sex usually remain the same. It's always serious, always tender and loving, always lusty, or always fun and giggles. Even fun and giggles get boring if that's all you ever get, and the same is true of lust.

• **Talking.** This is what I think of as oral sex: opening one's mouth and saying something. Every survey I'm aware of has found a strong positive correlation between this and sexual satisfaction. It's not that people who have good sex over time always talk about it or even that they talk about it a lot. It's simply that they have the option of talking about sex when there's something to be said. This prevents the kind of story that a therapist told years ago.

> A couple married for some years came to see him. They hadn't had good sex in a long time. When the therapist asked them to give a typical scenario, about the second thing the man said was that he put his tongue in his wife's ear. The therapist asked if he enjoyed doing that, and the man said yes. He guessed that his wife also enjoyed it, at which point she yelled, "You know, I hate that and I've hated it for eighteen years." Too bad she didn't discover oral sex until they were in the therapist's office.

Talking about sex gives one opportunities to change patterns, resolve problems, and basically just to remain on friendly terms about the whole issue. It also gives what is extremely important over time—feedback and reinforcement—so both partners feel good about what they're doing.

• **Sharing.** By this I mean talking about fantasies and sexual turn-ons. Not everyone does this, to be sure, and it is *not* necessary, but many couples find that it adds spice over the years. Sharing can mean watching erotic videos on the VCR, a practice becoming increasingly common among married Americans, reading sexy books together, or looking at erotic magazines; it can also mean sharing erotic fantasies. I think one needs to approach this area with caution because partners can sometimes react angrily or jealously when you say you fantasize about sex with her sister, her best friend, or the family dog. But despite the need for caution at the start, talking to people who do share these turn-ons with their partners tells me there's a lot to be gained here.

As you can see, there really isn't any secret at all to keeping sex alive in long relationships. The above ideas are obvious and relevant. The problem is that many people, left to their own devices, don't even think of them or are unable to put them into practice. They feel too guilty about being firm with their kids, they feel bad when they're not working, they don't know how to be romantic or seductive, they don't remember to touch. And they rationalize their unsatisfying erotic lives with the thought that that's just the way it has to be. That's the tragic part. But the positive side is that people can and do change. If good sex over time is important to you, you can employ some of these ideas and make at least some of the changes you want.

With couples who are willing to put in some time and to learn some new ways of doing things, the prospects are excellent. I've shared the ideas in this chapter with many couples, and it's clear that a change in even a few of these areas can make a significant difference. Some people I know experienced a large improvement in sexual contentment just by committing themselves to spend every Saturday afternoon together, with no visitors, no calls, no television, and no work. The same result was obtained by other couples simply by arranging more vacations. Almost anyone can have more satisfying sex over the years if they are willing to put some of these ideas into practice.

THE EFFECTS OF CHILDREN ON SEX

A number of studies have shown a decrease in sexual satisfaction from the birth of the first child until the last one leaves home. Children are hazardous to good sex unless you are aware of the difficulties and prepared to deal with them. Since men usually have not had much experience with children until they have their own, they are the ones who are usually taken by surprise.

Trouble can begin long before a child even exists. If there are difficulties conceiving, you may end up in the awkward situation of having sex on demand, when the woman is most fertile. It doesn't make any difference if you're interested or aroused—if today is the day, then you have to do it (that is, ejaculate inside of her). This practice produces serious tension and often, not surprisingly, sexual difficulties. Many men have reported being unable to get or keep an erection or to ejaculate. If they get upset about this, the condition can become chronic.

While having sex on demand is anything but ideal, the process can be navigated with a minimum of misery and risk if a few simple ideas are kept in mind, all of which come down to making the sex as enjoyable as possible. Just because you have to have sex tonight doesn't mean you have to see it as drudgery. After all, you're choosing to go through this in order to achieve a desired goal. So view it as your choice rather than an order from the doctor's office. Use humor to break the tension. It's healthy and fun to joke about your situation.

> One couple I know had an incredibly difficult time of trying to get the woman pregnant. They soon realized that if the tension continued to mount, they would end up hating sex and each other. So they started playing games with it. One of them, for instance, would write an official-looking note to the other from "Gestapo Headquarters" requiring that they engage in sexual intercourse that night for the good of the "Fatherland and the Führer." Other directives came from one set of their parents or the other. Sometimes these notes contained detailed and explicit directions on what they were to do. The couple reported that they often got turned on writing or reading these "orders."

And do what you can to get your conditions met, to get yourself interested and aroused. Since the main demands are on the man—he's the one who has to get erect enough to have intercourse and aroused enough to ejaculate—pull out all the stops and go for everything you've ever wanted. Act out your fantasies, use videos and reading material that appeal to you, try different positions and places.

If a problem occurs with erections or ejaculating, try to take it in stride. It's natural and understandable that such problems should result now and then, given the circumstances. Remind yourself that it's no big deal. All it means is that you're human.

When the baby arrives, there are other complications. Your partner may not be interested in sex for a long time afterward. This can be the result of the malaise or depression many women experience after giving birth, of the incredible demands of caring for an infant, or of the fact that many women experience a satisfaction from mothering that rivals what they experience in sex. Given that infants have peculiar schedules and sleeping habits, it's possible that *your* erotic interest may not be high either. Another possible complication is that your wife may be so involved with baby that you feel abandoned by her, hardly the kind of thing to stimulate sexual desire.

The best solution I know of for these matters is just to stay in touch with your feelings and your partner. No matter how erratic things get around the house, make sure to take time to stay in touch. Don't withdraw or bury your feelings. On the other hand, don't criticize her for doing what has to be done. Use the rules of good communication discussed in earlier chapters to say what's what with you. And, no matter how young the child, try to get the two of you away from the child for at least a few hours as often as possible.

That point remains crucial for as long as there are children in the home. Parents who have good sex have found it necessary to carve out and protect private times for themselves. They make it clear from the outset that, barring emergencies, there are times when they are not to be disturbed. They put a lock on their bedroom door or in some other way let the little people know that they want to be alone. One man related the following story.

> One of my earliest memories is of a sign that my father hung on the bedroom door when he wanted to be alone with Mom. It was the first thing I learned to read. I remember my older sister explaining it to me. "Do Not Disturb" meant that we were not to knock on the door, make loud noises near it, or get into fights when it was up. When I got older, my sisters and I vaguely understood that when we saw the sign, Mom and Dad were "doing it." I think having the privacy was not only good for them but also gave my sisters and me a beneficial lesson about the importance of privacy and sex in marriage. We're the only people I've met who know for sure that their parents had a sex life after they were born.

Parents who have good sex do not spend every waking moment with the children, even when the kids are very young; they hire help to take care of young kids or the housework so that they themselves aren't too tired for sex; and they sometimes get away for a weekend or longer without the children. Parents who have good sex also work to liberate themselves from the fear that they are damaging their children if they act lovingly in front of them or if they make love while the children are awake. There's nothing wrong with a passionate kiss that the kids can see, nor with a sexy touch or pinch. It won't hurt the children at all to know their parents love and have the hots for each other.

THE EFFECTS OF AGING AND DISEASE

The longer you're together, the older you're going to be and the greater the chance that one or both of you will be afflicted with a physical disability. That's sad, but it's just a fact of life. What is worse is that our culture focuses obsessively on youth. It regards aging not as a natural and inevitable process, full of possibilities and challenges as well as limitations, but rather as a dread disease to be fought against and staved off as long as possible by all the resources of modern technology. As a result, a great many men and women who no longer consider themselves young feel unattractive, unwanted, and inadequate.

This is especially true in sex because the mass media present so few examples of older and not perfectly healthy people having and enjoying sex. Older men who are interested in sex are considered "dirty old men" or "old lechers" and are accused of "carrying on," "acting like children," and even of "running around with loose women." While a younger man with the same interests might be called a stud or just a healthy guy, we don't even have a nice name for older men who like sex. And there is no name at all for older women interested in sex. Apparently they don't exist. The message conveyed is clearly that sex is only for the young, the beautiful, the acrobatic. Old folks need not apply.

There is no question that many men feel very bad and apologetic for being old or for not being as healthy as a twenty-year-old. They feel especially bad because their sexual functioning doesn't meet the specifications of the fantasy model.

It is a fact, as I explained in the earlier discussion about the penis through the life cycle, that our sexual organs, like all other human organs, undergo changes as they age. They become less efficient. Erections, for example, are more difficult to obtain, not as rigid as before, and, once lost, more difficult to regain. But this does not mean that men lose their interest in sex as they age, that they lose their ability to function in a variety of ways, or that they lose their ability to enjoy erotic activity.

Many people in their fifties, sixties, seventies, and beyond who've been together for many, many years still have good sex; it's also a fact that many people with heart disease, diabetes, arthritis, rheumatism, and various kinds of cancer and other serious illnesses still have good sex. The sex they have does not fit the fantasy model and it is often different from the kind of sex they had earlier in their relationship. These couples have to make adjustments to accommodate their physical abilities.

The only important point, as far as I'm concerned, is this: **If the intention is present, if you're willing to expend some time and effort, and if you're willing to experiment with sexual options, it's almost a certainty you can come up with at least several ways of making good love no matter what disabilities you or your partner have and no matter how long you've been together.**

This is true for one simple reason. No matter how long you've been with the same partner and no matter what the situation, your mind is still capable of doing its magic. You can still use it to tell you what's important, to make plans, to show feelings, to fantasize and do something about the fantasies, to teach you how to structure your life to get more of what you want, to remind you how to play and touch, and to motivate you to make the changes you desire. Our most powerful sexual instrument is not between our legs, but rather between our ears. As long as you're willing to use that incredible sexual tool, you can have exciting and satisfying eroticism with the same partner for a lifetime.

Here's what one man had to say about sex in his thirty-two-year marriage. Although he doesn't mention it, he had suffered from heart disease for several years and had heart surgery three years before I talked to him.

> We don't have as much sex as we did the first year we were together, but it's not much less and it's as pleasurable and loving as ever. We had some rough times when the kids were young, but we rarely let more than a week or two go by without some lovemaking. As the children got older, frequency increased and reached its present level about the time the oldest boy left for college. We're not kids anymore and the arteries have hardened somewhat. My erections aren't as good as they used to be and I don't always climax when we make love, but we have something very good. We know and love

each other, can ask for and do anything we want, and have trust and comfort. Our sex life is extremely satisfying and I couldn't ask for anything more.

AFFAIRS

The longer a relationship goes on, the greater the possibility that one or both partners will have sex elsewhere. People have been engaging in affairs (sex outside marriage or another relationship that violates an explicit or implicit commitment to monogamy) for as long as there have been relationships. Although different surveys come up with different figures, it appears that over 50 percent of men have at least once had sex outside their relationships and between 35 and 40 percent of women.

As much nonsense has been said and written about affairs as most other sexual topics. Religions view them as sinful, and many therapists see them in a similar way. According to this position, extra-relationship sex is certain to damage the primary relationship and is also a symptom of just how distressed that relationship already is or how damaged the person committing the adultery is.

The main conclusion I've come to is that affairs vary in every conceivable way and no one theory or conclusion fits all of them. Everything I've read about affairs is true . . . for some of them; but nothing I've read is true of all. I know of some affairs that have gone on as long, and in a few cases even longer, than the marriage or primary relationship. Others are one-shot events, never to be repeated and perhaps the partners never seeing one another again. Some involve regular contact, whether once a week, once a month, or once a year. Others are much more sporadic, catch as catch can.

The reasons people enter into affairs also vary considerably. Sometimes the reason is that with the outside lover they get something important they're not getting in their relationship. That something can be sexual (the excitement of sex with a new partner, more sex, less-hassled sex, and so on) or nonsexual (greater acceptance or even adoration and a lack of criticism, better conversation, or just more fun). Sometimes an affair is a way of striking back at a partner for his or her own affair or some other real or imagined wrongdoing. Sometimes an affair is a way of checking out the market or one's desirability when one is thinking of leaving the primary relationship.

Other reasons have nothing to do with the relationship: for example, a way to pass time or get comfort on a business or professional trip (as one man put it, "just a way of getting through the night in a strange city"). Still other reasons may be seen as a negative comment about the primary relationship but aren't seen that way by the man; for example, wanting to have sex with a younger woman or with any new woman. Since human beings are complex creatures, I suspect that most affairs occur for a combination of reasons.

Men are more likely to have affairs as a way of getting sexual variety (meaning a variety of partners and not necessarily a variety of positions or acts), whatever their feelings about their primary relationship, and seem better able than women to keep their involvement limited to the purely physical. Women, on the other hand, are more likely to be looking for, or to find regardless of what they were looking for, a complete relationship. While these statements seem to be generally true, I've known men who've fallen in love with their outside partners and women who have been able to keep their outside involvements very limited.

The consequences of extramarital sex also vary greatly. While it's true that they can be horrendous, this is not always the outcome. Some affairs, usually the ones that aren't discovered, don't seem to have hurt the primary relationship at all, and there are even a few in which a case can be made that they probably helped.

I know of one situation, for instance, where the marriage is strong in most respects but the man is continually frustrated because he can't discuss his work, which is very technical and very important to him, with his wife. She just doesn't have the background or the interest to understand it. For almost as many years as he's been married, he's been having an affair with a woman colleague who is also married. Their attraction is more intellectual than physical. They meet two or three times a year at professional conferences where they excitedly discuss their work. This excitement often becomes sexual, and they end up in bed. The man claims that the affair has helped his marriage. Because he knows he will get together with his friend within a few months, he doesn't have to push his wife to be more interested in and comprehending of his work than she wants; it takes the edge off of his frustration, so he doesn't take it out on his wife. All this may sound like an easy rationalization, but I've talked with this man about the affair many times over a number of years and I believe what he says.

I also know of couples where the affair was the result of dissatisfaction with the marriage and the affair was what made it possible to work on the marriage and get it to a better place.

A man had an affair after years of constant arguments and feeling constantly criticized by his wife. With his outside partner he didn't feel criticized and had very few arguments. In thinking about this, he realized that it wasn't primarily because his lover was less critical or argumentative than his wife. The main reason seemed to be that he was different with her. He didn't start conversations with his fists clenched, waiting for the inevitable argument to start. And he was much more considerate of and attentive to her. He concluded that if he could behave this way with his wife, their relationship would be more harmonious. This turned out to be more difficult than he anticipated and he ended up coming to therapy with me to get help, but he was able to change, and his marriage did get better.

Affairs are also used by some to resolve what seems to be an irreconcilable desire discrepancy in the primary relationship. The man wants a lot more sex than his partner does. So instead of pushing her to have more than she wants or to participate without enthusiasm, he gets sex elsewhere when he can.

Sex in affairs can differ from sex elsewhere. One reason of course is a new partner, which usually carries with it great excitement. But sex partners differ in other ways as well. A man who doesn't function well with his regular partner, or doesn't enjoy sex much with her, may find better functioning and greater enjoyment on the side.

I recall one man who rarely wanted sex with his wife and often lost his erections with her. With new partners he wanted sex all the time and functioned much better. The difference in this case was relatively simple. His wife was inhibited and passive; she waited for him to initiate, didn't do anything to stimulate him, and didn't express her own pleasure in ways he could understand. His affairs were with more active and less inhibited women. He didn't want to leave his wife, but when he wanted better sex, he sought out a new woman.

Being with a new partner may also mean there's none of the tension and bad feelings that exist in many long relationships, thereby allowing the man to function better and enjoy more. And there are also those magical times when a man hooks up with a woman who fits him perfectly. His usual sexual repertoire is just what she wants, and vice versa. It can feel like magic and it can also be misleading. For a relationship to work over the long run, there has to be a good fit in a number of important areas. Each of us could find someone with whom we fit better than our regular partners in this or that area. But whether we could have a better total relationship with them is questionable. With such a charged issue as sex, some people assume that because it works, everything else will also work. But many have learned to their horror that this is not always true. Here's one man's report of his experience:

Sex was so perfect for us I assumed we would be the perfect couple and left my wife to be with her. It was terrible. As long as we stayed in bed, everything was fine. But once we had more time together than we could spend screwing, it quickly became clear that we had nothing else. No common interests, nothing much to talk about, nothing we could agree on. The sex was great and I still think about it now and then, but I'm grateful my wife allowed me to come back.

Yet sex with an outside partner isn't necessarily better. Because of the newness of the partner and because of the man's knowledge that he's doing something he's not supposed to do, the situation can be charged with anxiety and guilt. A number of men have reported that they functioned less well or enjoyed less with an outside lover than with their regular partners.

In considering whether or not to have an affair, men frequently get overly involved with the fantasy elements (like how exciting it will be) and tend to overlook the hassles. Since affairs involve deception, there are always hassles. Even if it's only a one-night event on a business trip, you may have to explain why you didn't answer the phone at midnight or why, when you did, you were breathing so hard or seemed so unfriendly. You have to be careful where you make phone calls from, what charges you put on your credit card, and who sees you with your new friend. Speaking of which, I can't forget one California man's shock when his wife's sister walked into an elevator in a hotel in New York where he and his lover were locked in passionate embrace. "Who would have thought her sister would be in New York and in the same hotel?" Who indeed? And you may have to explain to your primary partner why you're not up for sex after being away for a week or where you got this idea to spray-paint her nipples with raspberry syrup and then lick it all off. The epidemic of sexually transmitted diseases presents another problem. If you're having an affair, you'd best be an expert on the practice of safe sex.

Anticipating the excitement of an affair is fine, but it helps to understand that with affairs there are always costs, some of which may be quite serious. If you're not willing to take the risks and pay the prices, perhaps you need to think carefully before you act.

In many cases where the man is committed to the relationship but seeks something with another women that he's not getting at home, which may or may not be primarily sexual, my impression is that he hasn't tried very hard to get what he wants from his primary partner. Although I have no way of knowing for sure, my guess is that many of these men could have succeeded had they been more assertive and persistent. A couple I saw is instructive.

The man started an affair with a woman he knew casually after she mentioned how much she enjoyed giving oral sex. His live-in lover found out about it and the two came to therapy. In explaining why he had the affair, the man said that he loved oral sex and didn't feel he could get it with her. She was incensed. It was true, she said, that she never initiated oral sex, because she didn't feel very skillful at it. But she had nothing against it and had no idea that it was important to him. She swore that he had never even asked for a blow job. He sheepishly agreed.

Since affairs can be costly, it makes sense to try very hard to see if you can get your needs met at home before going elsewhere.

Men used to feel quite free to engage in their own affairs but viewed with absolute terror the thought of their wives' going outside the marriage. Given the more liberated times in which we live, most men no longer feel the necessity to divorce their unfaithful partners or to shoot them and their lovers. However, there is often still a great deal of pain and damage to the man's self-esteem. My experience is that if a relationship is worth preserving, it's worth preserving despite the partner's affair; the man's pain can be healed and the damage to his self-esteem repaired.

One thing we can be sure of is that affairs will always be with us. No matter how much moralizing against them, no matter what punishments are meted out, no society and no group has ever been able to stop them. Which is the same as with other taboo or restricted sexual activities such as masturbation, oral and anal sex, and homosexual sex. Just because you or your partner have had or are having an affair doesn't necessarily mean that you're sick or she's sick or the relationship is in serious trouble. One or more of these things may be true, or they may not. As they say, it all depends. And just because the affair of you or your partner is discovered does not necessarily mean that your relationship has to end or be a horrible one. Here, too, it all depends.

Should You Tell Her About an Affair?

Some men attempt to deal with the guilt they feel about affairs they have had or are having by confessing to their partners. Although my bias is toward the greatest amount of openness a relationship can bear, my experience with couples has pushed me to counsel caution in this situation.

I have many times been asked to put the pieces back together after the man had an attack of honesty and told his partner about an affair. The results with these couples have been mixed. In some cases we got things back on track, but in others the news of the affair itself had such harmful results that the relationship did not survive. In a few other cases, the couple stayed together—for their own reasons, neither partner could leave—but it was never good again. Some of the partners were never able to get over their sense of betrayal and never able to reestablish the trust needed for a stable relationship. Every time the man went out of town, was late for a get-together, or seemed equivocal about where he had been or what he had been doing, the woman got suspicious and angry. She felt bad about having these feelings and the man felt he was walking on eggshells. This is not a good formula for a happy relationship.

I would think long and hard before telling a partner about an affair. My impression is that most of the men I've seen have focused mainly on how much better *they* would feel after having confessed to their partners. They realized their partners wouldn't exactly be thrilled by the news and feared the explosion, but they failed to consider the possible long-term consequences. Sometimes not telling can be an act of kindness as well as smart.

If you believe telling is the best course, don't do it impulsively. Sit on the decision for at least a week or two and consider it from all angles. Better yet, talk the matter over with a friend or relative you trust or a qualified therapist, and deal not only with your desire to tell but also with your guilt. If you conclude that you should tell your partner, understand that there will almost certainly be more to it than "I had an affair and I'm sorry and will never do it again." Be prepared to hear lots of feelings and questions and for lots of listening and talking.

OPEN MARRIAGES

While an affair by definition involves a violation of relationship rules, open marriages allow outside sex by consent. In some couples the partners believe that monogamy is impossible or not worth the effort and agree that each is free to have sex with others within certain boundaries. The purpose of such open relationships is to allow for sexual variety without the sneaking and cheating that affairs involve. I have no idea how many couples have open marriages. The number is certainly smaller than those who have affairs, though probably larger than most people think. Unlike those in open relationships in the 1970s, many of whom widely proclaimed their virtues and were happy to discuss them with anyone, the people I've talked to in recent years have been discreet. They feel that what they do is their own business and they have no need to advertize it or convert others.

There's no question in my mind that such arrangements work well for some people. But it's folly to assume they can work for everyone or that they're uncomplicated for anyone.

I met Nick and Evie after they had been together more than twenty years. They had come of age in the 1960s and believed that monogamy for life was neither possible nor desirable. They agreed when they were dating that each was free to have sex with others provided they certain rules were followed: no sex with people the other one knew, reporting that one was seeing someone and giving any other information that was requested, and using protection against disease and pregnancy. The arrangement worked reasonably well for a number of years although, not surprisingly, jealousy reared its head a number of times and had to be dealt with. As far as I could tell, Nick and Evie had a good relationship in most respects and their sex together was good. They were imaginative lovers, they incorporated into their repertoire ideas they got from other partners, and each of them got aroused by hearing of the other's outside adventures.

They came to see me because it looked as if their system was breaking down. Nick had been having what he called a midlife crisis for months. He had lost enthusiasm for his work and felt bad about himself. Evie, on the other hand, was just coming into her own. The small business she had started years ago had taken off, she felt good about herself and life, and she was regularly having sex with another man. Nick wasn't much interested in sex lately but, since Evie was the only one he felt could comfort him, he got very upset when she was out with the other man instead of being home with him. Evie felt that Nick was indulging himself and being unfair. She was willing to break dates and stay with him when there was an emergency, but she felt a ten-month emergency was a bit much.

The resolution in this case did not involve changing their open relationship, which Nick didn't want to do anyway. He got into therapy to deal with his issues, part of which included his re-establishing two friendships he had let drift over the years. This gave him someone to talk to aside from Evie. He also had to deal with his envy of her success. As he started feeling better about himself, their relationship improved. When I last saw them several years ago, they were basically content and still continuing with their arrangement.

Nick and Evie provide just one more example that, whatever approach one takes to sex, it is rarely simple or hassle free. Their way worked for them, despite the temporary setback that brought them to me, but it would not work for many other couples.

The real question is not whether there can be good, satisfying sex over the long run. It's obvious from what some couples do that it's possible. The only question is whether you and your partner want to make it happen for yourselves.

I close this chapter with the story of a man whom I knew for only a few minutes, because it so clearly illustrates that even if sex has not been good over the years, it's never too late. After attending a talk I gave on sex in marriage, he asked for my card and called the next day: "I'm calling to tell you how important your work is and to encourage you in it. I wish I had heard someone like you fifty years ago."

> After four decades of what he thought was good sex with his wife, Abby, Kip stopped initiating because his erections had become much more difficult to achieve and, even at their best, not very hard. While not being interested in the alternatives that a urologist he consulted offered—a penile implant or penile injections—he wanted something because he missed the physical closeness with his wife. When he read an article about manual and oral sex in a women's magazine at the grocery store, he realized there was more to sex than he had imagined. His sex life with Abby had been totally conventional: a short period of foreplay, intercourse until he came, some snuggling, and then sleep. They had never done oral sex, and foreplay was limited to getting him hard and her wet. They had not once talked about sex. He bought the magazine and asked Abby to read the article. He was so embarrassed he had to leave the house while she read. When he returned, with difficulty they started to talk.
>
> "I was shaken with what I heard. Abby is very tactful, but the essence of what she said was that sex hadn't been all that great for her over the years. She didn't get enough touching to get aroused and, as far as she knew, never had a climax. I felt terrible, but she said she was interested in experimenting with what was suggested in the article.
>
> "So we started, red-faced with embarrassment, like two old virgins. We started calling things by their names, we started figur-

ing out and saying what we liked. Things got easier as we had more practice. We made many discoveries. I found I could feel pleasure and climax even with a soft penis. I was surprised to discover that I liked doing her orally. She liked it, too. Would you believe? At the age of sixty-six, she had her first climax. That did both of us a lot of good. We now have what both of us think is wonderful sex. What we do may be a bit offbeat for most folks our age. We even got a vibrator that we occasionally use on her. But what the hell, we're having more fun than we ever did. It's a damn shame that people aren't given this information when they're young."

After listening to this man's report, I asked why he had come to my talk. His reply: "I like to keep up on the latest developments. Never can tell when I'll learn something I can use. Look what one magazine article did!"

RESOLVING PROBLEMS

_____ *19*

What to Do Until You
Resolve the Problem

"Everything has gone to pot. The tension about sex has infected
every part of our lives. We don't touch anymore, we don't have fun,
and both of us blow up at the slightest pretext. I feel bad all the
time and I'm sure she does too."—MAN, 42

LET'S face it: It's no fun to have a sex problem, and the prospect of
having to follow my suggestions and exercises isn't the most exciting
idea you've ever heard. You have my sympathy. Over the years, I've
followed various meditation, athletic, dietary, medical, and therapeutic
regimens myself, and I think I know what you're feeling. I did very well
with some of those programs, less well with others, and failed completely
with a few. But during the whole process I learned something important:
I did best when I made the programs fun. When I had to rely on
willpower alone and grit my teeth to do something, I didn't do very well.
In fact, it didn't take long before I was off that program altogether. I also
did best when I understood clearly what I was doing, why I was doing it
and stuck to a schedule.

I'm not a card player and my idea of a big bet is a dime, but I like the
idea of playing with a stacked deck—that is, getting everything you can
on your side and as little against you as possible. I'm continually amazed
at how many people are willing to play *against* a stacked deck. They don't

do the proper thinking and planning ahead of time. They plunge into a self-help program with almost no premeditation and then just as quickly stop it. This is why most people who join health clubs show up only a few times and are never heard from again; why most people don't stay on diets very long; and why many homes have all sorts of equipment, ranging from computers to exercise bikes and rowing machines, that was used only a few times. Whatever you do, don't stack the deck against yourself.

To work productively on a sex problem and maximize the chances of a successful outcome, you must meet three general requirements: (1) If you're in a relationship, you have to get it in as good a shape as possible. (2) You have to understand what will be asked of you and to make the necessary arrangements. (3) You have to get your mind working with you instead of against you. These three topics are covered in this and the next two chapters, respectively. Following the suggestions in them will help you stack the cards in your favor.

Estrangement is a frequent problem in couples who are having sex problems, although sometimes the sex problem itself causes estrangement. Partners blame themselves and each other, and they stop touching and feeling close. Frequently the woman is angry at the man for not being willing to get help sooner. In other cases the estrangement predates the sex problem or is independent of it; the couple is angry and distant for reasons besides sex.

Regardless of what is causing the distance and hostility, you must reestablish closeness and cooperation before you can undertake productive work on sex. A great deal of the time I spend with couples in sex therapy—especially at the start—is not devoted to sex. Rather, it involves getting them to stop the blaming of themselves and each other and in repairing the damage caused by that blaming, the withdrawing, and the fighting. If you don't have a therapist to help you in these ways, you can follow the recommendations in the rest of this chapter.

If you think all is well in your relationship and that nothing extra is required of you in this respect, check this with your partner. Make sure she agrees that you're ready to do the exercises. If things are not so good, read through the material and see which of it you want to apply. And feel free to use any other ideas you have for making your relationship better.

ENDING HOSTILITIES

If you and your partner have been in a virtual state of war, a cessation of hostilities has to be instituted before anything else can be done. You can undertake this task on your own: Stop withdrawing or attacking and resume civil relations.

In order to do this, you'll probably have to do the forgiveness and demonstrification exercises in Chapter 13. You'd do well to reread that whole chapter now to help prepare yourself to deal better with your partner. Then do the following exercise.

EXERCISE 19–1: RESUMING CIVIL RELATIONS

Time Required: A few minutes a day

Set a goal of one or several days during which you will make no attacks or criticisms and during which you will act civilly. If things have been very bad, don't try to get lovey-dovey—just be polite. This may mean simply saying hello and good-bye, asking about her day or if she wants something from the store. Don't expect anything from her in return. She may not seem to notice your new behaviors, she may react coldly, she may continue to be withdrawn or critical. It is imperative that you not give up or respond angrily because of this. If she says something negative, acknowledge her feelings and ask if there is any way to make amends.

If you have angry feelings that are too strong to shrug off, write them down in a journal or express them to a therapist or friend. But do anything you can to avoid expressing them to her.

When you've reached your goal of being uncritical and civil for a day or more, see how you feel, gather your resources, and then do it again. It may take a week or more before your partner is willing to respond in kind. When she does, one or both of the next two exercises may be appropriate.

If your partner remains withdrawn or angry after you have behaved civilly for a week or two and if she is unwilling to talk about what's wrong, professional help is required. Ask her to go with you; if she won't, go alone.

BEING NICE TO YOUR PARTNER

Psychiatrist Gerry Edelstien makes the point that if you are nice to your partner, she's more likely to treat you well in return than she is if you aren't. We all know this, of course, but we often tend to forget it. So, continues Edelstein, if the man feels ignored or dissatisfied, instead of discussing his feelings in a constructive way, he may deliberately do something to make his partner feel bad—belittle her, deliberately "forget" to do something he had promised to do, pick a fight, withdraw, and so on. The man's actions are understandable—he is upset or angry—but they are also destructive. They will not and cannot get him the attention, support, understanding, time, or whatever else that he wants. Deliberately making your partner feel bad is one of the quickest ways to ruin a relationship. Conversely, making her feel appreciated and loved is one of the quickest ways to improve a relationship.

Couples who have good relationships seem to know at a deep level that it is futile to try to be right or self-righteous, or to pay their partner back. They know that the important thing is to make each other feel as good as possible.

Here's the best exercise I know to start setting things straight. You can do it by yourself without her knowing what you're doing.

EXERCISE 19-2: BEING NICE TO YOUR PARTNER

Time required: Varies
Prerequisite: For the next few days, take a few minutes several times a day to make a list of the kinds of behaviors you know for certain make your partner happy. Stick to everyday, seemingly small things (she likes me to listen carefully when she talks about her work or the kids, she likes me to give her a big hug when we're leaving for work, and she'd like me to finish the work on the back door I promised to do months ago) rather than the occasional big things (she'd love us to go to Japan this summer). When you're finished, go over each item in the list and get a mental image of how you're going to do each one. For instance, imagine yourself walking over to her and giving her a big hug before you leave for work.

Pick several days during which you will do these things that please her. Although it may sound silly, many men have benefited from making

a checklist. They will write down, for example, "Hug when I leave for work; buy screws for door; ask about her day and put down paper and listen when she responds; don't leave briefcase on dining-room table; compliment her artwork; finish door." This helps ensure that they don't forget.

Your primary job during this exercise is to do the things that please your partner, but it is also crucial not to get into any battles with her. Do not criticize or attack, regardless of the provocation. Simply ask questions and acknowledge her feelings when appropriate.

Since life has a way of interfering with the best-laid plans, you should be prepared to deal with interruptions. Say one of your items is to spend at least an hour with your partner every evening. But you can't do that tonight because there is work from the office that absolutely requires your attention. Ask yourself if she has any desires regarding your working at home. You may recall, for example, that she likes to know in advance what time you'll be finished, and she likes to spend some time together talking before you go to sleep. If that's the case, save some time for being together before sleep. Tell her you're sorry you can't spend as much time with her as you'd like, but that you'll be available for a little visit at ten o'clock.

POSSIBLE PROBLEMS

1. You're so angry with your partner that you can't consider being nice to her, maybe because of the "nagging" she's done about the problem.

You should follow the suggestions in Chapter 13 on forgiving and demonstrifying your partner. And also carry out any suggestions and exercises in this chapter that you can. If your feelings don't change in a few weeks, consider seeing a counselor for a few sessions to see if something can be done about your anger.

2. You get upset about her behavior and start focusing on your pain and anger rather than on making her happy. It's easy for this to happen, yet it's crucial that you continue with the exercise. If you simply can't brush your feelings aside, try something else that will allow you to get rid of them or put them in the background. Some men find it helpful to write their feelings down or to say them aloud in a closed room or to talk them into a tape recorder. When I'm seeing a couple in therapy, the man has the option of calling and telling me his feelings. Do whatever works for you.

Another possibility is to ask yourself, "What does she like when she's acting like this?" Maybe she likes to be left alone, or for you to be understanding and nurturing, or simply for you to listen to her. Whatever it is, do it as best you can. That way, you'll be carrying out the exercise despite what she's doing.

3. Your partner asks why you're being so nice to her, or she tells you she feels you're trying to manipulate her. The best response, I think, is the straightforward one: You're being nice because you want the two of you to be closer. And yes, you do want to influence her to work with you to make the relationship better.

FOLLOW-UP

Most men are surprised and happy with the results of this exercise, and they want to do it again immediately for a longer time. That's the idea. If you've done it for a day, try doing it for two days. After that, you can go for three days or more.

Even after your problem has been resolved, occasional use of this exercise can do wonders for a relationship. Some men set aside special times each year to do it: for example, during the week before their partner's birthday, or around an anniversary, or when she's going through a busy season at work.

I realize that this exercise sounds simple-minded and even silly. But what's important is that it often works.

The gamble involved in it—a safe one, with most couples—is that by making your partner happy, you'll end up getting more of what you want from her than you would by using any other approach. But don't expect too much too soon. If your partner has been unhappy for a long time, she probably won't respond to your niceness immediately; it may take several weeks or even longer.

HAVING GOOD TIMES

Having good times together is crucial to the well-being of any relationship. We all seem to know this, at least when we're starting a new relationship. At the beginning, we make sure to have good times. We pick things we know both of us will enjoy, and we're careful about what we say and do. We try not to be offensive, not to pick fights, and to be tolerant and understanding—all of which contribute to having fun.

As couples settle in together, they tend to take things for granted and forget about the importance of planning and having good times. And when problems surface, sexual or otherwise, good times can totally disappear.

The ratio of enjoyable experiences to unpleasant ones is crucial. If the bad times outnumber the good ones, the relationship goes downhill. Bad times build on each other. If things are going poorly, you feel bad and start seeing everything in a negative way. This tends to happen when couples are in a battle about something like sex. The bad feelings spread to all areas, and pretty soon neither person can recall the last enjoyable time they had together.

Before starting to work on making sex better, it's beneficial, perhaps even necessary, to have some fun together. The following exercise can help.

EXERCISE 19–3: HAVING GOOD TIMES

Time Required: Varies

You and your partner agree to take turns setting up a date. Since it's your idea, you might want to go first. Pick something you know the two of you would enjoy—maybe something you enjoyed in the past—and make all the arrangements: buy tickets, make child-care plans if necessary, decide when you have to leave, and so on. Check to make sure she agrees with the plans, then carry them out.

What you do on your date is entirely up to you. You may take a one- or two-hour walk or bike ride, go to a movie or concert or dinner, or take a trip to a nearby city and stay overnight. But one or two days is probably the outside limit. This is not a good time for a three-week trip to Siberia. The only important criterion is that the activity you do is something you both can enjoy. It's not fair to suggest playing tennis if you love the game but she can take it or leave it.

It's important that both of you understand that the goal is to have a good time. A mental trick that works for many people is to pretend that you're on your first or second date. Do whatever is necessary *not* to bring up problems and conflicts. If something does go awry, recover as quickly as possible and get on with the enjoyment at hand.

As an alternative to taking turns arranging dates, you can plan them together if you like. If you get into conflicts doing this, however, try taking turns.

The good times exercise should be done as often as you like, but do it at least once a week for at least a few weeks. If you do it for several weeks and supplement it with other suggestions from this chapter, chances are that your relationship will soon be in better shape.

Now for some other pointers about what you can do for yourself and your partner before you start to work on sex per se.

1. Have a talk with your partner in which you acknowledge the problem and what you are going to do about it—for instance, use the exercises in this book or see a therapist—and what you are going to do in the meantime.

If your partner believes that you have been dragging your feet about resolving the sex problem, this belief needs your immediate attention. You should let her know that her perception is accurate—the problem does need help—and apologize for not realizing it sooner. You should also tell her that you want to get your relationship on a better footing before working directly on sex. Tell her, for example, "You were right all along—this problem really needs attention. I'm sorry I didn't see it sooner. But I'm ready to deal with it now. There are exercises in this book I think would help, but before we do them, maybe we should start having some good times again."

2. Start being more positive about yourself. The worse you feel about yourself and your situation, the harder it is to make your partner happy and have a good relationship with her. It's crucial to keep self-criticism to the absolute minimum. That means you have to take issue with— argue with and change—negative self-statements whenever you catch yourself making them. It also means you need to make as many positive self-statements as possible. Please don't take this advice as an after-thought or as only a small supplement to the "real" change exercises that are to come. The more positive statements and the fewer negative self-statements you make, the better you'll feel. The better you feel, the more clearly you'll be able to think and the greater the return you'll derive from the other change efforts you make. We're talking about very serious and very helpful stuff here. I'll come back to this in more detail in Chapter 21.

3. If you've been staying away from expressing physical affection, get back into it—assuming, of course, that this is acceptable to your partner. Touch, hold, hug, and kiss her when the spirit moves you, and be responsive to her touches and hugs. You can also offer to give her a

massage. Depending on what has been going on with the two of you, it may be advisable to talk about touching first, so she doesn't construe a hug or kiss as meaning you want sex. If she's too angry to engage in physical affection now, try to be understanding of her position and keep on with the ideas and exercises that are acceptable to her.

4. If you've been withholding compliments and words of love, now's the time to start expressing them. If verbalizing is difficult for you, you might want to send a card or flowers.

5. If you haven't been having sex, consider starting again if both of you are willing. If you've been making love but also having fights about it, it's time to start on a new path. After you've started expressing compliments and words of love, and after you've started touching again and had some good times, talk with your partner about sex. Is it okay with her to do something besides intercourse if you lose your erection or come fast? If either one of you isn't sure what the choices are, talk about the sexual options discussed in Chapter 3. Can the two of you agree to use some of the alternatives and not get upset or get into arguments about what's happening? If the answer is yes, then go to it.

6. No more sulking, name-calling, or apologies about the problem. You know about it, and she knows about it—there's no need to belabor the obvious. Don't apologize when it occurs. Just take it into account, and see how whatever you're doing might best be continued so that you both have a good time. And try not to blame her if the problem recurs. Even if it's true that she's somehow contributing to or even causing the problem, blaming and accusing will only make her defensive and make matters worse. The more the two of you can have good times together, sexually and otherwise, and be kind and caring in your interactions, the better the chances that the problem can be resolved.

7. Do your best to see that each sexual encounter ends positively for both of you. For example, if you come fast in intercourse and you know she isn't yet satisfied, say something like, "That was wonderful. Now I want you to feel that good." Then start to stimulate her by hand or mouth, or say, "I want to lick you all over," as you begin to use your mouth. If you don't get an erection or if you lose it, do something similar. One possibility is to say nothing but just start stimulating her in a way you know she likes. Since I assume you've already talked about options, still another possibility is to say, "I don't think I'm

going to get hard. Would this be a good time for me to hold you while you use your vibrator?"

Another way of saying what I've covered in this chapter is this: don't make the problem worse. The more you withdraw from sex and your partner; the more tension that's generated; the more blaming goes on; the greater the sense of failure—the more these things are true, the harder it will be to make positive changes. The worse things get in your mind and between you and your partner, the harder it will be to resolve the problem—it will take longer and will be more expensive (if you're seeing a therapist), and positive change may even become impossible to make. So seriously consider putting the seven principles into practice as soon as you can.

"We can talk and have good times, but sex is still a problem. It's as if the subject is too loaded for us to be able to do anything constructive about it."

This isn't a bad situation at all, actually. Continue with the exercises and suggestions in this chapter awhile longer. And talk to her about doing the sensual exercises in Chapter 14. There's a good chance that doing those exercises, along with the suggestions in this chapter, will in time get you to a better place regarding sex. It's important to keep on talking, as long as the talks are helpful rather than harmful.

"It doesn't work. We can have good times sometimes, but my partner is so angry with me for not taking care of the problem before that she goes into rages whenever I mention doing something without a long-lasting erection."

This situation is common. You should make sure you've acknowledged the problem, apologized for not wanting to deal with it sooner, and assured her that you're going to get help now. Another possibility is to let her express her rage and agree as much as you can with what she says ("I can see why you're so furious. I didn't take you seriously before and it's caused you a lot of pain"), then renew your offer to get help. If that doesn't work, suggest that the two of you see a therapist before any further damage is done to your relationship.

"Nothing works. We've been in a horrible place for months. We can't be civil, we can't have a good time, we can't have a reasonable conversation."

If nothing in this chapter can be applied, then you need professional assistance from a therapist who works with both relationship and sex problems. Get that help now. The longer you wait, the more difficult it will be. Ask your partner if she'll join you, but if she says no, go by yourself.

If she refuses to join you, it doesn't mean the situation is hopeless. I've been involved in a number of cases where the woman refused to go to therapy until after her partner had gone by himself for several sessions. Once she believed he was serious about trying to improve their relationship, she became willing to participate.

20

Getting the Most from Your Self-help Program

"I never thought 'working on sex' could be fun and it sure wasn't the first few weeks. But after I finally admitted to myself that I had a problem and had to work to overcome it, April and I settled in and made the best of it. It wasn't half as bad as I imagined. We made fun and games of it whenever we could and the result is that the problem is largely resolved, we both learned a lot, and we're closer as a couple."—MAN, 41

ONE thing you should do early on is to set one or more goals. Read the whole book first, or at least the chapters that seem relevant. Then set a specific goal for yourself; for example, improving your ejaculatory control to the point where you can usually decide when to come in intercourse, or keeping your erection in intercourse at least 70 percent of the time. If you have a regular sex partner, goal-setting should be a joint endeavor. Make sure the two of you agree on what you want to achieve. If your relationship is in such a place that sexual goal-setting is not possible, follow the suggestions in the previous chapter. When the two of you are in a better place, then you can set goals.

Then go over the sections in the book that are most directly relevant to reaching your goal. If your partner is working with you, she should read the same material. Discuss it together. Does the program make sense? Is anything about it objectionable? Do you have any differences of opinion about what you're going to do that need to be worked out now?

If you're working with a partner, I cannot emphasize enough the importance of getting and keeping her cooperation. It's crucial that you agree about what you're going to do and that you resolve disagreements and conflicts that arise over the program or over anything else as quickly as possible.

A great deal is being asked of your partner, and she has a critical role to play. Her attitude and behavior can make the difference between reaching or not reaching your goals. A supportive, cooperative partner is a blessing, and you need to do everything in your power to help her be this way.

Ideally, your partner has the following characteristics:

• *A positive and lighthearted attitude toward the program.* She does not express anger or frustration at you for having the problem or for the length of time it takes to make changes. Since this is not an ideal world, it's understandable that she might occasionally be frustrated, impatient, or angry. And you may sometimes feel the same. You both need to muster as much empathy and patience as you can to help yourselves and each other get through these times as quickly as possible.

• *A willingness to cooperate to resolve the difficulties and misunderstandings that are bound to occur.* She is also willing to comfort you when you feel discouraged and is open to you comforting her if she feels disheartened.

• *A willingness to be satisfied with nonintercourse sex (sex without an erection) until you are able to have good, long-lasting erections.* This is crucial because virtually every man I've worked with has had to believe that he can give his partner a good time in bed without a hard penis. Without that belief, it's almost impossible to reduce the pressure he feels to have long-lasting erections. That pressure, of course, is at least part of what's causing his problem. If he knows he can satisfy her in other ways, having an erection—or one that lasts a long time—becomes less important to him, thus reducing his anxiety.

Unfortunately, some women find this difficult to accept. Such women are usually orgasmic in intercourse, and either they haven't learned to be orgasmic with other kinds of stimulation, or they have, but they find these other ways not quite good enough. Often these partners convey— sometimes subtly, sometimes almost brutally—that they won't be happy until the man has good erections and can engage in intercourse. (One of the subtle ways is by refusing to allow him to sexually pleasure her. This usually makes the man feel guilty. She's doing all this work for him and giving him pleasure, but he can't reciprocate. This is not a good situation.) The man may not understand why he feels so tense when he's thinking about sex or actually doing the exercises, but he knows something isn't quite right. What he's sensing is his partner's frustration and impatience. Under these circumstances, the chances of resolving his problem are close to zero.

These issues can often be worked out in therapy, but they can be difficult for some couples to resolve on their own. So make sure to discuss them with your partner before you undertake a program. If they can't be settled with good feelings, do not try to do the exercises. Instead, have a consultation with a sex therapist.

Whether you're working with a partner or on your own, you should determine whether now is a good time to undertake the program. Make sure you don't have events on your calendar—such as an extended visit from relatives or an especially busy time at work—that will make it difficult to stay on schedule. It's fine to put off starting the program until a more propitious time. But once you do start, pull out all the stops and go for it.

Plan to make a systematic effort over a period of two to five months. In general, you'll need to devote two to three hours a week to the program, usually in twenty- to thirty-minute segments. This, of course, is an average and it's certainly fine to take a brief vacation from the program. What doesn't work at all is to skip weeks altogether or to do the exercises only on an occasional basis. Learning new skills or habits requires consistency and frequency.

Set up a definite schedule for doing the exercises, such as Monday, Wednesday, and Friday evenings at eight o'clock, and stick to it. If either one of you is not in the proper mood and can't get in one when the appointed time arrives, skip the sexual exercise but do something else that's relevant. For example, review your progress, or deal with problems that have come up, or read or reread a chapter in this book. I guarantee you that regular schedules work better than doing the exercises when the urge strikes you.

The biggest mistake people make is not doing the exercises often enough until they reach the goal. One reason for this that isn't immediately apparent is that although the exercises are fairly simple and easy to do, they can begin to feel like a burden over a long period of time. The people who do best with them are those who find ways of making and keeping them interesting. They keep the goal in mind and imagine how good they'll feel when they reach it, and they approach the exercises in a positive and lighthearted way. They stay disciplined and get through the program as soon as possible.

The closer you stick to your schedule and the faster you move through the program, the better the results will be for you. This is especially true when dealing with a sensitive and private issue like sex. As long as you're doing the program, you've got one too many people in your bedroom: either you and me, or you, your partner, and me. People can quickly get to resent this intrusion. So use me—this book—to get what you want, and then get rid of the unwanted guest.

Please understand that we need prime, unhurried time for the exercises. It doesn't help to do them when you're fatigued. It doesn't help to try to squeeze an exercise in when time is short. You've got to be relatively relaxed and alert to benefit. The time given for each exercise is only for the exercise itself. But you shouldn't just jump into an exercise. Rather, you should start by talking or touching to feel close and get into the proper mood. Then do the exercise. This extra time might be anywhere from one to ten minutes or longer, but make sure you allow for it.

It will help you keep to your program if you make all the necessary arrangements in advance. If you're going to do the exercises in your bedroom, as most people do, you may want to make sure the room is clean and exactly as you want it. Since you're going to need a clock and a lubricant, have them ready. Since you may need to refer to this book, have it on the nightstand, turned to the appropriate page.

Before you do any of the partner exercises, you and your partner should read them over together so you'll both know what is being asked of you. Discuss her feelings, your feelings, what is to come, and work out any disagreements.

One question that comes up a lot is about the amount of flexibility that is allowed in the program. Do you have to do every single exercise? Exactly as it's written? The answer is, not exactly. There is room for selection and creativity. Just take care not to lose sight of what you're doing. When I see a man in therapy for erection problems, for example, I don't necessarily ask him to do every exercise in Chapter 24. It depends on his situation and the results of the exercises he's already done. Doing all the exercises I give in any chapter represents the safest, most conservative route.

Some individuals and couples skip some of the exercises, doing only those they feel are most relevant to them. Others make changes in the given procedures to better suit their own situations. For example, an older man with an erection problem may realize that if he does the exercises three times a week, his own body will be working against him. That is, after an ejaculation, his body isn't ready to produce another erection for two or three days. In his case, it makes sense to do the exercises only twice a week. On the other hand, many men who want to develop ejaculatory control learn that their progress is swiftest when they do the exercises more often than that. They may decide that, say, four or five times a week is best for them.

There is nothing wrong with changing the routine to better suit your needs, provided you are willing to readjust if things don't work out. If, for example, you skip an exercise and then have difficulty doing the next one, you should seriously consider doing the one you skipped. Similarly, if you change an exercise and it doesn't produce the intended results, you should consider doing it in a manner closer to what I've written.

Since the amount of time you'll need to do the exercises is largely a function of how often you do them, you need to reach an agreement about frequency. Your partner should understand that in the majority of the exercises, you are in total control: of the type of stimulation, of when to stop and resume, and of when to end the exercise. You should make clear that you are willing to satisfy her manually or orally either before or after the exercise. Difficulties will arise if she feels she is doing all the work and getting nothing in return. Do whatever is necessary to prevent this from becoming a problem.

One way for you to prevent problems is to take total responsibility for initiating the exercises. Even if the two of you have already planned to get together at nine o'clock on Tuesday evening, it's up to you to initiate the process at that time.

This point is crucial. I can't tell you how many fights I've witnessed because the woman thought the man wasn't initiating the exercises—this fed her fear that he was putting the whole burden of the program on her. The way to avoid this—and it must be avoided—is for you to be very disciplined about initiating the exercises.

Another way you can maximize harmony and effectiveness is to schedule a regular meeting with your partner—say, once a week—to discuss how the program is going, how each of you feels about it, and any changes that may be desired. This is similar to what you'd be doing if you were seeing a therapist. During this meeting, each of you should allow the other to talk without interruption for a few minutes about anything that is relevant. It will pay you to listen with full attention when your partner gives her point of view.

If you're doing exercises without a partner, a once-a-week meeting with yourself is helpful. Use the time to think about how things are going, what needs to be changed, and so on.

Some people object that all this scheduling seems rigid and unspontaneous. They're right—it's supposed to be rigid and unspontaneous, although I prefer the words *disciplined* and *systematic*, because that's what works best when you're learning new skills. If you were serious about learning new sports or business skills, you wouldn't just go to class or practice only when the spirit moved you; you'd probably have some kind of regular schedule. That's exactly what's needed here as well.

Yet scheduling time for being together in advance does not rule out spontaneity. There's nothing wrong with doing an exercise when the spirit moves you, even though your schedule doesn't call for it that day. There's also nothing wrong with occasionally taking a day off from the program and doing whatever the two of you want to do.

It's important *not* to restrict your physical activities with your partner to the exercises. Make sure you do some holding, hugging, kissing, and any other mutually enjoyable expressions of physical affection, in addition to the activities in the exercises. Have fun together in other ways as well.

And learn to be a little patient. Most of the men I've seen with sex problems want the problem resolved yesterday! They wish for a pill, a shot, or some magic words that will straighten things out (literally) this very moment.

One man whom I saw with his wife beautifully exemplifies this attitude. He had been having erection problems for ten years, with all the usual complications. Sex had become almost non-existent, touching had diminished, she had almost given up on ever having good sex again. He had become increasingly de-pressed. I gave them a few assignments to do at home. When they came in for the next session, he said, "We're talking more and we feel closer. And we're doing more touching. But it didn't work. Nothing has changed." What he meant by "it didn't work" was that he hadn't gotten an erection with her that week. After a decade of no erections, he expected to get one after only a week of work.

Even though sex therapy is brief and highly effective, it takes a little longer than a week or two. See if you can accept this fact. Talk to yourself when you feel impatient and start to think that nothing will ever help. Tell yourself, "Hey, I know you're impatient. It's been a long time. But the process takes longer than a few days. Look, in some ways things are already better. We're having fun together. And she's being more cooperative and supportive than before. Things are im-proving and I'm sure the problem will be resolved. Just be a little more patient."

Talking to your partner can also help.

YOU: "I feel so impatient. I'd like this to be over."

HER: "I know exactly how that feels."

YOU: "I know this has been hard on you, and I feel guilty for putting you through it. The sooner it's over, the sooner you'll feel okay, and the sooner I can stop feeling so guilty. I don't know if it's possible, but I'd feel better if you could reassure me in some way. Maybe tell me that it's okay for you to go through this with me. Is that possible?"

Above all, find ways to make the program enjoyable. Some of my clients inject a bit of humor into their activities by saying, "Time to do Dr. Bernie's bidding," or "I wonder if all this hand stuff will cause us to go blind?" Others talk about the hows, whens, and wheres of the sex they'll have once the problem is resolved. Still others remind themselves and one another of all the benefits of undertaking the program. This isn't hard because there are almost always benefits, such as an increased ability to talk about sex, an increased ability to talk about other things as well, new knowledge about sex and intimacy, feeling closer than they have in years, and so on.

I know you wish you didn't have to be doing exercises and that you didn't have the problem. But since you do have the problem and are going to do the program, why not make the best of it?

Getting Your Mind on Your Side

"For the first month, these positive statements were just words. I said them, I heard them, but although they made me feel a lot better than the negative statements I had been making, it's like I didn't really connect with them. And then, about two weeks ago, I started believing. Yes, I really would be a great lover. Yes, I really would show my partner a good time whenever we made love and have a good time myself. Now these statements are part of me."—MAN, 38

IT may be going too far to say that the mind is everything when it comes to sex. But if it's not everything, it's certainly far ahead of whatever is in second place.

Let's look at two men who both had a problem the last time they had sex (say, they didn't get erections). The first one, Bud, was disappointed but not greatly upset. He had a good time anyway. He's eagerly looking forward to making love with his partner again today. He tells himself it's going to be another great experience and imagines kissing and fondling her breasts, which gives him great pleasure. Because he's feeling so good about the prospects, his mind conjures up a picture of her taking his penis in her mouth, which gives him even greater pleasure. When he and his partner get together in bed, his mind will focus on the pleasurable sensations he's feeling, thus maximizing the chances that he will get aroused and that the arousal is translated into an erection.

Art, on the other hand, keeps thinking about what he calls his "failure." He tells himself he may be impotent, that he may not get it up the next time. He, too, has images, but they're different from Bud's. He imagines his wife indicating she's ready for intercourse but himself being totally soft, which makes him feel terrible and hopeless. He's working up a nice stew of defeat and failure. As he gets caught in this muck and mire, he has more depressing thoughts and pictures. Finally, he imagines his wife getting furious and telling him he's not a real man. He gets into such a state of anxiety and despair that he almost jumps out of his skin when she tries to hug him. If he does try to make love, his mind will be busy focusing on the possibility of failure and its consequences rather than on what's going on at the moment, thus helping to ensure that failure is what he gets.

Two men, two minds. One is headed for pleasure and a good time, the other for anxiety and a miserable time. The difference is not in their penises, but in their heads. This fact deserves your attention. The reality is the same for both men: no erection the last time they had sex. But they deal differently with that reality. As psychologist Albert Ellis, the father of what is now called cognitive therapy, has been demonstrating for over four decades, it's not reality itself but rather how you construe or interpret it that makes all the difference.

Your mind can make for beautiful, functional, and satisfying sex, but it can also make sex an agony. Perhaps most important for our purposes, it can create and maintain sex problems and make resolving the problems difficult or even impossible. With your mind on your side, however, it's much easier to solve any problems.

To get the most from your self-help program, it's essential to make sure your mind is working with you rather than against you. In a number of places earlier in the book, I have given examples of using your mind to your advantage, such as mentally rehearsing things you want to say and do, and using fantasies to increase arousal. But now we need to get into more detail.

The mind operates in basically two ways: through thoughts (ideas) and through pictures (images). It's constantly talking to itself with words and images about you. Because these messages are to and about yourself, they are called self-statements. You may or may not be aware of these internal communications, but take it as an article of faith that you spend a good part of every day talking to yourself about you. If you're not aware of what you're saying, you soon will be.

Thoughts and images can be mainly positive or mainly negative. The mind is quite judgmental, much like a child. It knows good and bad, success and failure, and not much in between. In what may be a sad commentary about the state of humanity, a very large proportion of the population goes around making negative statements and showing itself negative pictures. The result is what is called low self-esteem. People who tell and show themselves negative things feel bad much of the time. The bad feelings affect their relationships, behavior, sex life, and everything else.

Men who have had sex problems or who for some other reason don't feel good about themselves sexually do a lot of what Albert Ellis calls "catastrophizing" and "awfulizing." Any disappointment or frustration, any less-than-perfect event—such as a sexual activity that doesn't live up to every single standard in the man's mind—is made into a catastrophe. Lack of erection becomes "impotence" or "I'm over the hill" or "my wife will leave me."

Self-statements have a kind of magnetic quality. They attract other statements of the same kind and build on one another. If you regard your latest sexual activity as positive, your mind will tend to call up supporting positive ideas and images. It may recall another very satisfying sexual event from the past, or some sexual compliments you've received. This will reinforce and heighten your good feelings. Unfortunately, it works the other way as well. Negative thoughts and feelings tend to conjure up other bad experiences, thoughts, and feelings. One bad experience recalls another and another, until you're feeling totally discouraged.

Before going further, it's necessary to say more about images, because there's so much confusion about them. One source of the confusion is the varied terms used to refer to them, including "pictures" and "fantasies." When I use the term "image," I mean *any* nonverbal representation in your mind. It could be sounds (some people can hear things in their head but they don't have pictures), or sensations or senses (for example, you sense in your mind that your partner pulls away from you). But most people have some kind of visual representation (pictures). These can be still, like photographs, or they can be like movies. They can be clear or somewhat fuzzy. Images can also be fragmentary and fleeting (like a quick view of a breast or a fleeting and unclear view of somebody doing something to somebody else).

If you're having a sex problem of any kind, it's probable that you are helping to maintain that problem by the activity of your mind. Such negative thinking makes it difficult for the problem to fix itself and for therapy or self-help materials to work.

You need to get your mind out of your way and on your side. Put differently, you need to think more positively. A negative thought (or image) is anything that leads to negative or bad results for you. A positive thought (or image) is anything that leads to better feelings and helps you do what you want. More positive and helpful thoughts, and fewer negative thoughts, is what you need.

It's crucial to understand that what's important are the effects of telling yourself certain things or having certain images. Whether or not these ideas and images are true is entirely beside the point. People tend to say, "That's not negative thinking, that's reality!" My response is that *it doesn't make any difference if it's true or not; what counts is the effect it has on you.*

In 1989, as he approached the last day of the Tour de France, the world's most prestigious bicycle race, American cyclist Greg Le-Mond knew he had to accomplish something that most experts considered impossible. He was fifty seconds behind and would have to make up more than that on a very short ride. Even his former coach said it was impossible. LeMond didn't deny the difficulty of the task; he simply didn't bother with it. Focusing on how difficult the task was would only make him feel bad. Instead, he focused on riding the race of his life. So intent was he on concentrating on his racing that he told his support crew not to inform him of his times as he went by, a highly unusual request. He would focus only on his position on the bike and his pedaling technique, and what would be would be. Greg LeMond won the race by eight seconds, the closest Tour ever run.

I'm not suggesting you deny reality—facts must be faced—but only that you don't dwell on its depressing and discouraging aspects. Focus instead on the positive aspects of the situation—things that make you feel good, increase your confidence, maintain your ability to think clearly and to take appropriate action—or get away from all evaluations, whether positive or negative, and simply focus on the task at hand. That's what positive thinking is all about, and this is what Greg Le-Mond did so well in the Tour de France.

And LeMond is far from the only world-class athlete who has used mental training, the kinds of exercises I provide in this chapter, to enhance performance. So many athletes use mental training that it would be easier to provide a list of those who don't than those who do, but some of the notable advocates are bodybuilder Arnold Schwarzenegger, diver Greg Louganis, golfer Jack Nicklaus, and football greats Jim Brown, Fran Tarkenton, and O. J. Simpson. Studies done in the United States, the former Soviet Union, and elsewhere support what the players and coaches have been saying. Training the mind is at least as important as training the body. What athletes the world over are doing to increase their performance can be used by you to help you get what you want from sex.

There are several questions you can use to judge what's going on in your head. All of them have to do with how helpful or unhelpful the idea or picture is. I'll use a made-up example to illustrate the use of the questions. The example goes like this. You have the smallest penis in the world. Scientific measurements demonstrate that no one anywhere has a smaller penis than you. To make the example more interesting, let's throw in two more things. One is true, that medical science has no way of providing you with a larger penis. The second is made up, that no woman in the world could have an orgasm in intercourse with your little penis. When you find yourself thinking about your penis, ask yourself these questions:

1. Does this thought or image make me feel better? If telling yourself that you have the smallest penis in the world makes you feel bad, as it almost certainly will, it's not helping you. Without denying the size of your organ, you need to move on. Focus on the assets you have that make you a desirable lover—for example, your genuine liking of women and sex, your sensitivity to the feelings and desires of others, your ability to listen and learn. You keep repeating to yourself that women can be satisfied in many ways, and perhaps you decide that you're going to have the most sensitive fingers and tongue on the West Coast. Focusing on these matters will make you feel better.

2. Does this thought or image help me behave the way I want? If telling yourself that you have a small penis makes you fearful of approaching women for sex, or even of dating, it's not helpful. It's preventing you from behaving the way you want.

3. Does this thought or image help me think productively about the situation? If telling yourself you have a small penis puts you in a funk where you can't think productively, it's not helping you. Negative thoughts often have the effect of stopping all constructive thinking.

4. Does the thought or image reinforce positive images I have about myself? If focusing on your small penis reinforces a larger, more destructive idea—for example, that no one will want to have sex with you or that you'll never have a relationship—it's not helpful. You'll feel even worse, if that's possible, you'll keep focusing more and more on your "handicap," and you'll soon be incapable of any constructive thought or action.

5. Does the thought or image improve my relationship? If imagining your partner joking with her friends about your small penis makes you want to get back at her or withdraw, it's not helpful to your relationship. You need to change the idea or image to help you feel better about the relationship.

No matter what your problem or situation, there are always two ways to go with it. The negative way leads to discouragement, despair, and self-hate. The more positive way leads to useful thinking, good feelings, and solutions.

Some people think the idea of positive thinking is simpleminded and a denial of reality. To be sure, some advocates of positive thinking are simpleminded and do deny reality. But what I'm suggesting is something different. If your sex life is boring, if your ejaculations are very quick, if you and your partner don't agree on how often or what kind of sex to have—if any of these things are true, they are facts and need to be acknowledged. But acknowledging something does not mean dwelling on it; you need to move on. Just because your penis hasn't been working lately doesn't mean it will never work. You can make changes.

One kind of simplemindedness that sometimes accompanies positive thinking is when people advocate doing nothing more than thinking. Just think positive thoughts or imagine yourself having a million dollars and—so this silly theory goes—you'll end up with the million. That's pure bunk. Thinking or imagining will not make you richer or your sex life better. Positive thinking and imaging have to be accompanied by work to make the changes you want.

Changing the thoughts and pictures in your head isn't difficult in principle. You simply argue with and change unhelpful thoughts when they occur to make them more positive and constructive. And show yourself positive images as often as possible. I said this process isn't difficult in principle, and it isn't, but there is a catch: It requires consistent effort over a period of time. We're not talking about changing a negative thought to a positive one once or twice or even a hundred times. We're talking about doing this dozens of times a day, every day, for months. It's simply a matter of repetition and perseverance. There are no brilliant insights to be had and no magical shortcuts. It's by sheer repetition that you change your negative ways to more positive ones.

Consider if you've ever made any of these comments to yourself:

My penis is too small.
I'm not very good sexually.
I'm not a good lover.
Other men are better at sex than I.
I don't know how to satisfy my partner [or women in general].
Sue and I will never have an exciting sex life.
I'll never overcome this problem.

If you've said one or more of these things to yourself every now and then, it probably doesn't mean much. But if you habitually tell yourself things like this, you're going to feel bad about yourself sexually. And that needs to be changed.

The following exercise will help get you started.

EXERCISE 21–1: TRACKING NEGATIVE THOUGHTS

For the next week or two, carry a very small notebook (the kind sold in grocery stores for about $1) or some 3 × 5 index cards in your shirt or jacket pocket wherever you go. Whenever you're aware of having a negative or unhelpful sexual thought or image, jot it down. Obviously, there will be times when you're aware of something but can't write it down; this may happen when you're with others or when you're driving. Jot it down later if you still remember.

If you're unsure if a thought or image is negative or not, use the five questions above, on pages 394–395, to help you decide.

At the end of the week or two, go over all your negative self-statements and pictures. These are the things that you need to change that we'll get to in the next exercise.

Here is what one man, who had erection problems, wrote in his notebook on one day:

"I don't have it together sexually like other men."

"I'm a failure in sex."

An image of not getting it up and a woman making fun of me.

"My dick is defective."

"Sex just isn't my thing."

Recalling Marge [his wife] saying I wasn't a real man.

"I wish sex didn't exist."

An image of Marge passionately fucking another man and afterward telling me that I'm just a limp dick.

These thoughts and pictures are enough to depress anyone. Constantly replaying them is a great example of awfulizing and catastrophizing and will make you feel terrible, as they did this man, and will probably doom any efforts to solve the problem. You have to change them.

How can you change self-statements? Just change them. Here are some examples. The self-statement comes first. The italicized response that follows is an example of what you could say to yourself. My comments are in brackets. You don't need to use my words exactly, but do something to make those statements more positive.

"My penis is too small." *Hey, wait a minute. I measured it and it's the usual six inches, about what most other guys have. It's big enough to give pleasure to me and to Marge.* [If it's true that you really do have a small erect penis, then you need to acknowledge that fact but then focus on your strengths, like this: *OK, so my penis is on the small side, but it's also true that my fingers and tongue are very sensitive and have given orgasms to many women. And don't forget that Kit and Wendy didn't have any problems having orgasms in intercourse with me.*]

"I'm not a good lover." *Let's change that. It's true I've been having some problems keeping an erection, but other than that I'm a good lover. Marge frequently mentions how sensitive I am to her needs. I'm going to take care of the erection problem by using this book and I'll be even better.* [This man isn't lying to himself. He acknowledges the problem, then commits himself to changing it. If, on the other hand, the man had reason to believe that he really wasn't a good lover—maybe his partner had said something to that effect—then he would want to say something like this to himself: *I have more to deal with than just the erection problem. Marge has commented that I don't seem to be aware of where she is or what she needs. I think that's because I'm so focused on how my cock is doing that I forget about her. OK, I have two things to work on. And work on them I will. First I need to pay more attention to Marge. Hopefully, she'll become less critical and that will help take some pressure off of me to get hard. But I also need to start working on getting my penis to function better.*]

"My dick is defective." *Just a minute there. My dick was fine for years, and it's fine now when I masturbate. There has been a problem getting it up with Marge in the last two years. But the doctor says it's not physical and the dick itself is fine. So I just need to focus on what will help it work with Marge.* [Here he is using facts to comfort himself, a subject I'll get into in more detail later on.]

Image of Marge passionately fucking another man. *That hurts, but it's my fantasy, not Marge's. She'd like to fuck like that, but with me, not someone else. I'm going to get some help to make that possible. And right now I'm going to do that movie again, but this time with me and Marge going at it.* [This is a simple technique where you take a negative image and make a more positive one of it. In this case, he runs a series of images, a movie, in his mind of him and Marge making passionate love. Then he tells himself: *That's how it will be.*]

JUST THE FACTS, PLEASE

Although many people view facts as harsh, unyielding, and therefore depressing realities, and although I said earlier it's not necessary to focus on facts, I find that facts are actually often quite comforting and beneficial. The vast majority of human problems would be worked out much more quickly and easily if people stuck to the facts and avoided unwarranted generalizations and moralizing. But most human problems are not worked out by focusing on the facts. People get angry or defensive and jump to ridiculous conclusions and judgments. The facts get lost, and so does a reasonable chance of finding a resolution.

A fact is anything that's true or real. If you want sex once a day, that's a fact. If your partner wants it once a month, that is another fact. The conclusion, yet another fact, is that the two of you disagree. Another fact may also be there: that the disagreement is making both of you feel bad and hurting the relationship. As long as we stick to these facts, we have a good chance of solving the problem. Once we deviate from the facts, we're in trouble. It is human nature to get away from the facts, but the more you know about this, the better the chances of coming back to the facts and solving the problem.

The reasons we don't stay with the facts are twofold: 1) we feel bad—angry, hurt, guilty, rejected, overwhelmed, or something else—and 2) we start generalizing, moralizing, awfulizing, and catastrophizing. Beware when you start using words like "always," "never," "neurotic," "compulsive," "sick," "impotent," "excessive," "undersexed," "oversexed," "frigid," "unloving," "nymphomaniac," "slut," "whore," "too much," "nowhere near enough." These terms are not descriptions of reality but rather good/bad judgments about it. That she wants more sex makes her oversexed and a slut. That you haven't been able to maintain an erection in intercourse for the last year makes you impotent (a very loaded judgment, not a description of the reality) and a sexual flop.

When we were little, we had a saying: "Sticks and stones can break my bones, but words can never hurt me." Like many things we believed as children, this is a lie. **True, sticks and stones can hurt you, but words are the real danger; they can destroy you.** Once you get moralistic and call yourself a failure or impotent, all thinking ends. You enter a downward, destructive spiral with more ugly judgments and more bad feelings. You lose sight of the facts and of any possible solutions. I asked one client to stop his internal name-calling and tell me the facts. Here is what happened:

HIM: You know the facts. I'm impotent.

ME: You *never* have an erection?

HIM: Well, never with Sue.

ME: Never?

HIM: This is stupid. You know I have erections with her as long as we're not trying to have intercourse.

ME: OK, let's look at all the relevant facts. You often wake up with erections. You have erections when you masturbate. You have erections when Sue stimulates you by hand or mouth. Are these things true?

HIM: Of course.

ME: It's clear that your penis is working quite well. Even with Sue, most of the time you get hard. What's bothering you is that in the last five months or so you've been losing your erections when you attempt intercourse. [I notice him smiling.] What's going on?

HIM: It sounds a lot less bad the way you put it.

ME: I believe that's because I'm sticking with the facts and not using loaded terms like "never" and "impotence." The fact we have to deal with is that something is bothering you about having intercourse with her. Let's go over what thoughts you have when you think about having intercourse with her.

This client needed to keep reminding himself that he wasn't a sexual failure or impotent. Each time he used a word like *impotent* on himself, he needed to counter it with something like: "Hey, that's not true. I'm not impotent. I've just been having a problem keeping my erections for intercourse. But I'm working on that."

I had another client who used the terms *mama's boy* and *wimp* against himself. He had to learn to fight these terms and stay with the facts, which, like most facts, were simple and amenable to change: he often did not express his ideas and preferences and that meant he usually didn't come up with activities to do on a date. It's impossible to make someone into the opposite of a mama's boy, whatever that might be, but it is possible to help someone voice more of his ideas and make lists of things he'd like to do on a date.

Moralizing is also used against others, especially the people we love. Here again it's crucial to do as little of this as possible and to stick to the facts as much as you can. It's a lot easier to deal with the situation if you think of your partner as having had more sexual experience than you than it is if you think of her as a slut. It's also easier to deal with if you think of her as wanting sex only once a week rather than as frigid or withholding.

EXERCISE 21–2: CHANGING NEGATIVE THOUGHTS

This exercise is based on the results of Exercise 21–1. Now the task is to take issue with and change your negative sexual thoughts and images into more positive ones, as in the examples above. Whenever you are aware of having a negative thought or image, make the positive changes. If you're too busy at the moment, come back to it later when you have time. It might be hours or even a day later. That's fine. For example: "When driving home yesterday I kept telling myself Marge and I would never work this out. That comes out of my despair, but I don't think it's true. We're going to do the exercises in this book and we're going to make it better."

The words and images you use must be acceptable and believable. Some men have no problem saying, "I will be a great lover" or "I will overcome this problem." For other men, however, such statements are too strong. They might do better with "I will be a better lover" or "I'm working on this issue." Use the kinds of words and pictures that work best for you. And that goes even for what seem like small details. For example, some men prefer in their self-talk to refer to themselves as "you," while others use "I" and still others use "we." As long as you're comfortable with the word you're using, you're on the right track.

Even with acceptable and believable statements, it takes a while, usually months, for them to really sink in. Of course, the more often you talk positively to yourself and the more often you combat negative thoughts and images, the sooner the positive ideas will sink in.

Do this exercise as frequently as possible for as long as necessary, which may well be months, until it becomes your natural way of using your mind.

The previous exercise involves modifying negative thoughts and images of yourself. The next is not dependent on responding to negative mental activity, but simply involves having more positive thoughts and images.

EXERCISE 21–3: HAVING MORE POSITIVE SEXUAL THOUGHTS AND PICTURES

Time Required: Less than 5 minutes a day

Several times a day, take a moment or two to say something positive to yourself about sex and to show yourself a positive picture (or two or more). You'll be more likely to continue doing this if you do it at regular times—as soon as you are awake, while brushing your teeth or shaving, or when you get into the shower or sit down on the bus.

Exactly what to say and what images to have are up to you, as long as they're positive. Some examples:

- Imagining yourself having long-lasting intercourse (if you've been having problems with ejaculatory control).
- Imagining yourself having a firm erection and keeping it during extended sexplay or intercourse.
- Saying to yourself, "I know this program will work and I'll have longer-lasting (or firmer or more frequent) erections."
- Saying to yourself, "I will become less tense and more playful in sex."
- Saying to yourself, "Next time Sue and I have sex, I'm going to focus on the pleasurable sensations and have a grand time."
- Imagining yourself experiencing the problem you have (say, losing your erection in intercourse), but feeling calm about it, hugging or pleasuring your partner, getting aroused again, and getting more sexual stimulation. This is an extremely important image, because the better you feel about setbacks and difficulties, the more easily your problem will be resolved.
- Recalling an experience where you didn't have the problem that's now bothering you. For instance, if you're losing your erection before intercourse, recall in detail a time when you kept your erection and had great intercourse; as you imagine that time, tell yourself, "It will be like that again."

Best of all is to combine an image or fantasy with a statement that reinforces it, as in the last example. Imagining yourself having long-lasting sex and telling yourself at the same time or afterward that "I will learn to last longer" is another example.

There is a group of men, a much larger group than many people would think, who are constantly down on themselves. Women aren't the only ones with low self-esteem. Many of these men aren't able to do Exercise 21–3; or they do it, but the words aren't believable. A different version of that exercise can help.

EXERCISE 21–4: FOCUSING ON YOUR VIRTUES

Time Required: A few minutes a day

This exercise requires that you dwell on your good points (strengths, assets) several times a day. The first step consists of making a list of these points, preferably on index cards, one item per card. One of my clients dubbed these items his "virtues list." Over a period of several days or longer, jot down your virtues on the cards. If you can't think of anything positive, use compliments you've received; if someone thanked you for your generosity, use "generous." One or two words is usually sufficient for each characteristic. A sample list might look like this: "decisive, loyal, good provider, intelligent, understanding, gentle, willing to help, good listener." Try to come up with at least seven to ten items.

Beware of being perfectionistic. No one is always kind, always a good listener, always decisive, or 100 percent creative or intelligent. If you often exhibit the quality or virtue, or if others have complimented you on it, that's sufficient.

The second step consists of going through your list at least twice each day and focusing on one of the items. It should go like this: you read each item and say to yourself, "Yes, I'm quite intelligent" or "It's true, I'm a good listener." Then take a few more seconds to recall an example of one of them ("I remember when Marge told her friends that it wasn't true men couldn't listen, that I was a great listener. This was after I had spent several hours with her, listening to her feelings about her father's death. It's true. I am a good listener.") The next time you go through the list, focus on a different virtue or recall a different example of the same one.

The entire exercise usually takes less than a minute. Twice a day is a minimum; the more often you do it, the better you'll feel. After a week or two of practice, you should also repeat some of your positive points whenever you have a spare moment: While stopped at a red light, or waiting in line someplace.

With a little effort, you'll make this exercise a regular part of your life from now on. You'll find it's a lot easier and more rewarding to focus on positive thoughts than negative ones.

HAVING A TALK WITH YOURSELF

What's this? you ask. We've just been over how to talk to yourself. And to be sure, we have. But here I mean something a bit different. Having a chat with yourself is usually longer than the kinds of self-statements we've been dealing with; whereas a self-statement might take only a few seconds, a chat with yourself might take a minute or longer. It's a gentle, reassuring, supportive talk, even with some cheerleading, designed to calm you down, support your efforts, and keep you on the right track and doing the right things. These are the kind of talks we often get from friends and therapists. I give them to my clients all the time. I don't mind doing it, I see it as part of my job, but the fact is that clients can learn to do it with themselves.

One good time to use these talks is during time-outs (see pages 272–273). Calm yourself and then talk to yourself about what needs to be done. For example:

> Take it easy, take it easy. Take a few deep breaths to get more relaxed. . . . Good. Now let's look at this. You're acting as if Ronnie is your enemy, trying to hurt you. You know that's not the case. It's just that you pushed her button when you mentioned the business with her mother. She tends to lose it when that comes up. What she said doesn't mean anything. She was just very upset. You know she loves you. So what to do? How about apologizing for bringing up her mother? That might help. Fine, let's start with that and then ask if this is a good time to continue talking about our plans for Labor Day. That's the plan. And relax. She loves you. It will be fine.

It's extremely important to have a talk with yourself when you feel discouraged about solving your problem or about how an exercise has gone. I can almost guarantee you will have such feelings sometimes. But don't allow them to interfere with doing the work that will help you reach your goals. The more quickly you can recover from feelings of failure and discouragement, the better you and your partner will feel and the faster you'll make the changes you desire.

The kind of antifailure, antidiscouragement talk you need to be able to have with yourself is so important that I give it a name of its own.

EXERCISE 21–5: SELF–PEP TALK

Time Required: A few moments

Whenever you feel discouraged about your progress or your chances of success, sit down in a private place for a few moments and give yourself a supportive, reassuring talking-to. Do this as many times as necessary over a period of hours or longer to help yourself feel more positive. Several examples follow, but you of course need to make changes in the wording to better suit your personality and situation.

Here's an example of what a man who is feeling discouraged about fixing his problem could say to himself (in a calm, reassuring voice):

> Hey, take it easy. You're letting yourself get carried away. I know you're feeling discouraged, but I don't think there's reason to be. Let's look at the facts. It is true that you've had trouble control-ling your ejaculations with all your partners. But it's also true that you're a good lover; everyone you've been with says so. And it's also true that there are ways to fix the ejaculation thing. You've already got this guy's book, why not do what he suggests. If worse comes to worst and it doesn't help, you can get a referral to a sex therapist here. This problem is solvable, so let's just be calm and get on with it.

This man's self–pep talk is based on looking at the facts of his situation. As I discussed earlier, facts are often comforting, but these talks don't always have to focus on them. You might want to remind yourself of another time in your life when you successfully overcame a problem. Focusing on a past success will almost certainly make you feel better about what's facing you now. Here's an illustration:

> This is one of the toughest situations you've ever faced. It seems like you have so little control. But maybe you can take comfort from the fact that tough situations have always brought out the best in you. Remember the Johnson deal? Now, that was a mess. No one thought you could swing it, and you had plenty of doubts as well. Everything seemed out of control. But you found things you could do something about and you worked on them. And you did it. What you're facing now is similar. You can't directly

control your penis, but you know what you can do. Focus on things you can control, the same way you did with the Johnson deal. Do as well as you can with them, and be forgiving of yourself for the inevitable failures. Yes, this is a toughie, but hang in there. You'll get where you want to be.

Having a talk with yourself is especially important when things aren't going well and when you feel you've blown something and are beating up on yourself.

Hey, you're really beating up on yourself and it's making you feel bad. OK, so you didn't get it up the last two times you and Jane did the exercises. That's not exactly the end of the world. I think the problem is that you're trying too hard. You've been doing the exercises every night the last week. That's asking an awful lot of your penis. Poor guy has to get hard every single night. I'll bet Zilbergeld would agree that's too often and too much pressure. Look, the program has been going well until now and you just got too eager to finish it up. Why don't we back off a bit—say, no more than every other day? And while we're at it, not so late at night, either. Let's do it when we're fresher. I think everything will be fine.

One other function that can be served by these talks with yourself is self-commiseration, expressing compassion for yourself. This is kind of a verbal hug you give to yourself. Men aren't used to doing this. If we get compassion, it's usually from our partners. But you can learn to supply some of it yourself and make yourself feel a lot better. Here's an example of how it could go:

This is so hard for you. You work so hard to handle everything and not have problems. Not being able to solve a problem on your own strikes at everything you hold dear. Makes you feel like less of a man, less of a person. And even though Ann is supportive and understanding, sometimes it feels like you're all alone. It hurts real bad, and you feel so down. It's hard to feel this way, hard to have the problem. You want to deny it, to run away. But there's no place to go, no way of denying it. Try to be kind to yourself, and understanding. It's rough, but problem or not, difficult or not, you're a good person and will get through it. Just be good to yourself, be as generous as you would be if someone else had the same problem and told you about it.

This last example may seem corny as you read it, but many of us receive such expressions of compassion from the women in our lives. And many of us—if we were lucky—got something like it when we were children. Expressing compassion for yourself is healthy and constructive. Why not give it a try when you're in need?

And try not to get discouraged if these self-chats don't have immediate results. You may have to do a number of them, over a period of hours, days, or weeks, before you notice changes.

This completes your introduction to getting your mind on your side. But we are far from done with the subject. In later chapters, I'll suggest other relevant exercises. You'll be far ahead of the game if you've already started doing the exercises in this chapter.

Developing Ejaculatory Control

"I've had dozens of women, and only now do I learn that I've been coming quickly all along. I didn't realize it. I thought what I was doing was normal. I feel bad about all those women I short-changed."—MAN, 26

"Having better control is something I treasure. It's made for better sex and a big difference in how I feel about myself, not only sexually but in all areas."—MAN, 37

LACK of ejaculatory control is probably the most common male sexual problem. The main manifestation of this difficulty is that the men consistently come more quickly than they or their partners want in intercourse; hence the terms "premature" and "rapid ejaculation." Although the complaint is usually stated in terms of time—he comes, say, within thirty seconds of starting intercourse—the issue is really about voluntary control of the ejaculatory process rather than time. The man lacks a vote or influence over when he comes. It happens when it happens, usually quickly and often seeming to sneak up on him.

It has been estimated that about one-third of American men suffer from an inability to control the timing of their ejaculations; that is many millions of men. Though the problem generally affects younger men and tends to improve with age, there are some men in their forties, fifties, and even older who have it. I worked with one man who had very little control over his ejaculations his whole life and still had the problem even though he was seventy. I hope you won't wait as long as he did to develop better control.

WHAT IS EJACULATORY CONTROL?

While ejaculation is a reflex and can't be controlled perfectly, a man who has developed control can enjoy high levels of sexual arousal, whether from oral or manual stimulation or intercourse, without coming, and he usually has a choice when to ejaculate. He can allow his arousal to rise to a high level and then more or less level off until he wants to come, as shown in Figure 8. Don't take the leveling off too literally, however. In reality, his arousal fluctuates, increasing and decreasing, according to his desires and what's going on, until he wants to come. He can also decide to come quickly if that seems appropriate.

In contrast, a man without control tends to go from zero excitement to orgasm without leveling off (Figure 9). He has to come quickly; he has no other choice. He doesn't get to enjoy high levels of arousal for long. He may try various methods of lessening his excitement— thinking of things other than sex is a popular one—but they work neither well nor consistently. And his partner is always in a quandary. She's fearful of stimulating him, because that may bring instant ejaculation. She's fearful of allowing herself to get turned on in intercourse, because it will probably be over before she's derived as much enjoyment from it as she desires. If she has the ability to be orgasmic in intercourse, she at first will try desperately to reach orgasm before he comes, usually a futile endeavor. After repeated failures, she may stop getting turned on. What's the point of getting excited, she wonders, if the only result is to be left hanging and feeling frustrated? Even if she does manage to achieve orgasm in intercourse before he does, it's a hurried and anxious business and often doesn't seem worth the effort.

Lack of ejaculatory control isn't a bad problem to have, because sex therapists have been very successful in resolving it. According to a number of studies and clinical impressions, 80 to 90 percent of men learn better control in therapy, provided they are willing to devote the

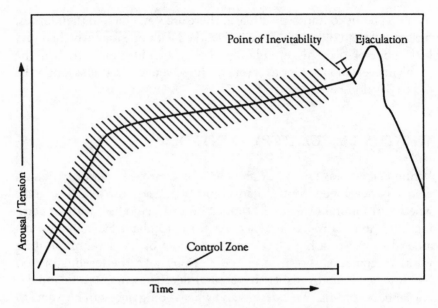

Figure 8: Male sexual experience with ejaculatory control

necessary time and energy. Ejaculatory control is a skill or habit that can be learned in eight to twenty weeks by following the exercises given in this chapter.

Many men without good ejaculatory control have a fantasy, which one of them put this way: "I'd like to be able to screw for an hour—no, make that two or three hours—without coming. I think that would feel great and my wife would love me for it." It's easy to understand how someone who usually can't have intercourse for more than a minute or two would fantasize about the effects of lasting longer. But, as usual, it's important not to get carried away. I've talked with men who do have intercourse for up to an hour, and even longer, and they are not a happy group. They have the problem of not being able to come inside a woman no matter how long they thrust, and their regular bouts of thirty-, forty-, or sixty-minute intercourse really don't feel all that great.

It may seem to you that their partners would be ecstatic, but the reality is somewhat different. Their partners complain about unceasing thrusting and pounding, sore vaginas, and a sense of incompleteness because, although intercourse seems to go on forever, the man never

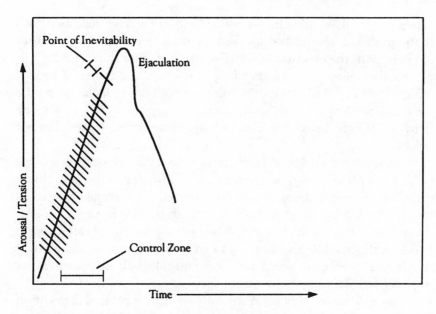

Figure 9: Male sexual experience without ejaculatory control

finishes in "a normal way." A single woman who had an encounter with such a man reported the following: "It's actually not fun. I got a row of coin-sized abrasions down my back from having my vertebrae ground into the carpet for so long." The problem is magnified dramatically, of course, if the couple is trying to conceive. Fortunately, this problem, called "retarded ejaculation" by sex therapists, is far less common than rapid ejaculation. One reason it's fortunate is that rapid ejaculation is much easier to treat.

Lack of ejaculatory control manifests itself in various ways. Some men have very little control regardless of the sexual activity. They come as quickly in masturbation as they do with partner stimulation. Others are OK with themselves but not a partner. Still others, probably the largest group, are fine except for intercourse. There is yet another distinction. Most men without ejaculatory control have had the problem all their lives. But there are some who once had control but no longer do.

Most men without ejaculatory control do not also experience difficulty getting erections. But some men have both problems: Erections are difficult to get and ejaculations are usually quick. **Since many of the** exercises for developing better control require an erection, men with both problems should not attempt to work on gaining ejaculatory control until the erection problem is resolved. First things first.

Sex therapists aren't as knowledgeable about the causes of lack of control as I would like. We aren't sure why millions of males have little or no ejaculatory control, while millions of others do. We aren't sure why control gets better with age and experience for many men, but not for others.

One thing we do know, however, is that unlike erection problems, which are often caused or maintained by physical factors and drugs, rapid ejaculation is almost always due to a lack of knowledge, attention, or skill. Another thing we know is that abstinence hampers control. Even a man who usually has good control may come quickly after several weeks without sex. It also seems to be true that anxiety can cause loss of control. This is seen in men who come quickly with new partners but regain control as they get more comfortable.

In general, men without control simply don't make the adjustments in behavior necessary to stay at high levels of arousal without coming. This may be because these men are not focusing on their own sensations and therefore can't take appropriate action; because they don't know when to make the adjustments in their behavior; or because they don't know what kinds of adjustments should be made.

The benefits of gaining control are many. Better control means longer and usually more-enjoyable sex, especially intercourse. Men who've achieved this feel more confident and better about themselves as lovers, and their partners are appreciative. Also, many men report that their own orgasms feel better: "Fuller" or "more complete" is how they describe them.

It's important, however, not to confuse having better control with the woman having so-called vaginal orgasms (orgasms solely through intercourse without simultaneous clitoral stimulation). There are, of course, some women who can have such orgasms. If your partner is one of these women and you learn to last longer, she may again have such orgasms. But the clear conclusion of a number of surveys is that many, probably a majority, of women are not orgasmic in this way. They require direct clitoral stimulation (by her hand, your hand, your mouth, or a vibrator) to have orgasm, a task for which a thrusting penis is not well suited. Lasting longer will not help these women reach orgasm in intercourse.

It's also important not to assume that lack of control is always a problem. Whether it is or not depends on the couple and the circumstances. There are some couples, for instance, in which the man usually comes quickly but it bothers neither him nor his partner. If they're content, they shouldn't bother to change. There are also many men who have little control with a new partner. The first few times they're together sexually, he comes quickly. But then his control reappears. With a transitory phenomenon like this, there doesn't seem to be much point in doing exercises. The man can explain to his partner that his control will get better over time, or he might want to delay having intercourse with her until he's more comfortable.

As I mentioned earlier, some men have had good ejaculatory control in the past but have lost it. They've lost the control they once had with the same woman, or they no longer have control now that they are separated from their partner. It is difficult to say if these men should do the exercises in this chapter. The exercises certainly won't hurt, and I've seen some cases in which they've done a lot of good. But even there they seemed like supplements. For these men, the main issue is something else. Usually there's something about the current situation (the man is nervous with a new partner, for instance, or he's angry or feels guilty) that needs work before his control can reassert itself. So feel free to do the exercises, but also devote some time to figuring out what's getting in your way. The best way I know to do this is doing the Conditions Exercise in Chapter 6.

One man I worked with had never had great control, but it had gotten much worse in the last two years of his deteriorating marriage. Doing the ejaculatory-control exercises in *Male Sexuality* hadn't helped at all. After his divorce, he came for therapy because he wanted to be a better lover for new partners. It turned out that one of his main conditions for good control was feeling accepted and loved by his partner. This condition was clearly not met as his marriage fell apart. Even when he and his wife weren't in open conflict, he sensed her anger and resentment. Now that she was no longer in the picture, he was able to make rapid progress with the masturbation exercises described later in this chapter. As this happened, he became involved with a woman he had known for years. He felt truly accepted by her and, after two or three sessions in which he came quickly, his control was better than ever before.

A PROGRAM FOR DEVELOPING EJACULATORY CONTROL

My approach for developing ejaculatory control stems from the work of Dr. James Semans in the 1950s. Semans's stop-start technique is the foundation of all the successful procedures used by sex therapists today. Many of them have added variations of their own. I've experimented with most of them and also with some I've developed myself. What follows is the best program of suggestions and exercises for improving ejaculatory control I've come up with in twenty years of dealing with the problem.

Developing better ejaculatory control involves learning two skills. One is the ability to attend more fully to your own sensations of arousal and tension. The other is the ability to make changes in your behavior that will prevent or delay ejaculation.

Let's go back to Figures 8 and 9 to understand in more detail what ejaculatory control means. The shaded area represents the time from the beginning of penile stimulation to just before the point where ejaculation becomes inevitable. I call this area the control zone, because this is where the man can make changes in his behavior to influence when he ejaculates.

The man whose experience is represented in Figure 8—we'll call him Fred—wants to enjoy a long session with his partner. He wants to get to and savor high levels of arousal without coming right away. As he nears the middle and upper ranges of his control zone, he may change his thrusting from faster to slower and maybe he'll even stop moving altogether for a few seconds or longer. Or perhaps he'll move his hips slightly to change the angle of the thrusts, or maybe he'll do some circular movements for a few minutes. He may monitor his breathing and take some slow, deep breaths. If he knows that holding her hips or looking at her face is orgasm-producing, he won't do that until he wants to come. By making these adjustments and avoiding orgasm-producing activities until he's ready, he's able to stay in the shaded area, having a good time and enjoying the sensations. When he wants to come, he'll act differently.

Although Figure 9 represents the experience of a man without much ejaculatory control, it could also be Fred's experience under certain circumstances. Let's say that just as he begins intercourse he recalls that he and his partner have only a few minutes before they have to dress and leave the house. So he wants to come as quickly as possible. His past experiences will guide his behavior to do just that. He will do the kind of thrusting that's most arousing to him, and he may do other things as well: kiss his partner in his favorite way, touch her breasts or hips, look at her face, and perhaps call up his most arousing fantasy. Although Fred's experience in this situation seems similar to that of a man without control, there is a critical difference. Fred is choosing to have a quick orgasm. The other man has no choice. He goes pretty much directly from nothing to orgasm without leveling out. He may be aware of when he's going to come, but he's not aware of the shaded area and what he could do there. Since he's not in the shaded area very long, it's hard to be aware of it. Nonetheless, it exists and can be used. The more it's used, the larger it grows, until this man's experience is similar to that of Fred.

Fred's behavior, whether in trying to lengthen or shorten his sexual encounter, comprises a number of habits carried out automatically and largely outside of conscious awareness. He probably can't tell you what he does to control ejaculation and he might not believe that what I've written has anything to do with him. I once interviewed a number of men with good ejaculatory control and asked how they did it. They not only didn't know, but at first denied that they did anything. Only after they carried out my suggestion to observe themselves during sex did they agree that they were actually doing things to influence when they came. This shouldn't be surprising. Although I've been an avid bicycle rider for many years, I can't begin to describe how I manage to keep my balance on the fool thing. Yet I must be doing something (actually a number of things), because a bike won't stand up alone and neither will one with an inexperienced rider on it.

At the extreme upper end of the control zone is what Masters and Johnson called the point of ejaculatory inevitability, labeled "I" in the diagrams. This is the point at which the man feels he's starting to come. And that's exactly what's happening. The sensations he feels are the contractions of the prostate gland and seminal vesicles; once they con-tract, the ejaculation is on it's way and nothing can stop it. No control can be exercised once the point of inevitability is reached.

The control zone represents either sexual arousal or tension (anxiety). For most men without good control, it's usually a combination of both.

Many men have trouble distinguishing between arousal and tension, but it really doesn't make much difference for those who want to develop better control. Both can make you come quickly. When you're having sex, something in you is increasing or rising, whether you call it passion, tension, or something else. That is what you need to be aware of. The best way to increase awareness is to focus on the part or parts of your body where you most strongly feel the rise in arousal/tension. For most men, this is either the penis or the scrotum. You need to know at what level this anxiety/arousal becomes the point of inevitability. It's before this point is reached that you need to do something to control ejaculation.

Men who have good control have learned that control, usually without knowing they learned anything. And all of us, whether we have ejaculatory control or not, have learned to control other reflexes. Urination is perhaps the closest parallel. At some point when you were very young, your parents let you know that it was no longer acceptable to urinate in your pants. You gradually learned to recognize the sensations in your body signaling that you were about to urinate, and you could tell someone that you had to get to a toilet. You could tell something was about to happen, but you couldn't delay its occurrence.

As time went on, you completed your training. You not only knew when urination was imminent, but you could also exert some control to delay it. If you were in the middle of a game or watching a TV program and had to urinate, you could squeeze some muscles, wiggle around, or literally grab your crotch to hold it back, at least for a while.

All this is many years behind you, or course, and you probably have no memory of it. The processes of control have been under automatic pilot for so long that you may not be aware that you are actually doing anything to control urination, just as many men with ejaculatory control don't realize that they are doing anything to delay ejaculation. If you have any doubts about what I'm saying, just focus your attention on your pelvis the next time you have to urinate but are in a situation that requires you to wait. If you want to see the control mechanisms in vivid detail, watch what you do when you're caught in a long and unexpected traffic jam after leaving work without urinating.

Before getting to the exercises, I need to give some definitions and principles. All of the physical exercises have a similar structure: **While your penis is being stimulated by you or your partner, you will do two things—attend to your arousal/tension level and either stop or do**

something else to maintain ejaculatory control. By doing this repeatedly, you will learn more about your control area and expand it. In doing so, you will achieve control over your ejaculations. And you'll be able to act exactly like Fred.

How Often to Do the Exercises

Therapists differ on how often they ask clients to do the following exercises, from daily to two or three times a week. My experience is that *three or even more times a week is best, provided this is comfortable for you and your partner and you don't have difficulty getting erections.* It is crucial that you not try to force erections during the program; if your penis doesn't easily get hard, just stop and do whatever you and your partner want. Return to the exercise another day. If three or more times a week is too much, or if you sometimes have trouble getting erections, twice a week will be fine. Two or three times, however, is an average. If you do an exercise only once during a week, you might want to see if you can do it three or four times the next week. If you can't, you'll probably still be OK if you get back on track in the following weeks. Less than twice a week over the long run works less well and will almost certainly make the whole training process longer.

Which Exercises You Should Do

Every reader who wants to improve ejaculatory control should do the mind-power exercises and the two masturbation exercises. If you think you don't need to do the masturbation exercises, it's a good idea to do each of them once just to make sure you can easily and comfortably handle them. If you don't want to masturbate, you can skip those exercises and start with the first partner exercise. After the description of the mind-power and masturbation exercises, I discuss exercises you can do with a partner and what to do if you don't have a regular sex partner.

What You Should Focus On

As your penis is being stroked, you need to be aware of your arousal/tension level. For most men, this means focusing attention in their penises or scrotums, the place where they can feel increases in fullness, tingling, or other sensations that mean arousal/tension to them. I guarantee you will get distracted by all sorts of things: fear of coming fast, concern about disappointing your partner, concern about reaching your goals, wondering if your partner really wants to be doing the exercise, and so on. You can't stop yourself from being distracted, but what you can and must do is bring your mind back to where it belongs as soon as you're aware it's elsewhere—what I call refocusing. Just imagine your attention is like a searchlight on a swivel. When it's not where you want it, imagine gently pushing the swivel and the light back where it should be, on your arousal/tension level. Refocusing gets easier and more effective with practice, and you'll be getting a lot of practice with it. Don't get discouraged that your attention wanders: That's natural and expected. Just keep bringing it back, over and over.

When You Should Stop During an Exercise

Many questions come up regarding exactly when during an exercise you should stop stimulation. Anytime you're in the control zone is fine—that is, anytime after stimulation has begun and you're feeling aroused. But you don't want to play brinkmanship, trying to stop just before the point of inevitability is reached. If you do this consistently, you'll find that you often ejaculate before you want. So stop sooner.

If you want something more specific, here's an option. Rate your arousal/tension on a scale of 0 to 10, where 0 represents a total lack of arousal and 10 represents orgasm. As you do the exercises, you'll be able to rate yourself at any time ("I'm about 4 right now, going to 5"). To start, choose a number you're comfortable with in the middle range—say, 4 or 5—and always try to stop when you reach it. But do not choose 9. That's either the point of inevitability or very close to it, and will result in too many accidents. As you proceed through the exercises and feel more comfortable and confident, you can choose higher numbers.

How Long Do You Need to Stop?

When sex therapists were first assigning these exercises in the early 1970s, most of us told men to stop for about a minute, until the urge to ejaculate had completely subsided. This worked well for most men, but an accompanying problem was that without stimulation for a minute or more, many lost all or part of their erections. In order to prevent erection loss, some of my own clients made the stops briefer, anywhere from ten to forty seconds (these are estimates, by the way; you don't need to use a stopwatch). This worked out well for some men, not so well for others. So the answer of how long to stop is this: experiment and find out. You want the stop to be long enough for the arousal/tension level to subside to an appreciable extent, but not so long that you get bored and lose your erection. Stop for different lengths of time between ten seconds and a minute and a half and see what works best. If you need to stop again within a minute or two of resuming stimulation, you need longer stops. If, on the other hand, you're losing most of your erection, try shorter pauses.

What to Do During a Stop

I have found it helps if you do one or more of the following during most stops: 1) talk briefly to your partner just to keep in touch, 2) relax and enjoy the pleasant feelings of decreasing arousal, 3) really experience the control you're exercising over your ejaculatory process, or 4) take several deep breaths to help you relax (see page 422). It may not feel very powerful to be just lying there doing nothing, but it is. You're doing exactly what you need to do to gain control over a reflex that's been giving you trouble for a long time. See if you can experience it that way and remind yourself that you're taking charge of your sex life.

What About Ejaculating While Doing the Program?

You can ejaculate as much as you want when you're not doing the exercises, as long as this does not interfere with your ability to get an erection when it's time to do an exercise. But be careful not to do anything that makes you feel bad about yourself. Some men want to have intercourse at every opportunity, even if this means they come quickly and feel bad. Feeling bad won't help your progress, so think about what is best for you. Of course, it is fine to come quickly when not doing the exercises if there are no negative consequences. Taking a day off from the program now and then can be fun. But keep in mind what you're trying to accomplish and stick to the program most of the time.

If you want to ejaculate at the end of an exercise, you can do so, but keep your mind focused on your arousal/tension level and maintain the stimulation at a moderate pace—that is, don't do fast, hard stimulation. Be aware of reaching the upper reaches of the control region and passing the point of inevitability.

It's important to understand that you will sometimes ejaculate without meaning to, especially the first time or two you do a new exercise. Such accidents are common and nothing to be concerned about. If you didn't have any, you probably don't need to be following the program in the first place. As New York sex therapist Michael Perelman points out, these accidents are even helpful, because they help you to define the boundaries of the control zone. They let you know unequivocally where 9 and 10 are on the rating scale. If, however, you continue ejaculating unintentionally, something is wrong. Perhaps you need to return to the previous exercise and gain greater comfort and control with it.

MIND POWER FOR DEVELOPING BETTER CONTROL

To derive maximum benefit from the physical exercises described below, you need to get your mind on your side, as we discussed in Chapter 21. A man who hasn't had ejaculatory control tends to think of himself as quick on the trigger. This is, for sure, a reflection of reality, but it also becomes a predictor of future behavior and a reinforcer of a self-image you want to change. It will be easier to change your behavior if you also change your view of yourself.

Start right away to apply the material contained in Chapter 21. Imagine yourself as you'd like to be as much as possible and spend as little time as possible imagining how you've been. If you haven't read that chapter and digested its contents, now would be a good time to do so.

Mind Power A: Whenever you're aware of telling yourself that you come fast, or having an image that embodies that idea, argue with it and change it. For example: "It's true, I've always come fast. But I'm going to do this program and change that. I'm going to have good control." When you picture yourself coming quickly, say "That was then," and follow this with an image of having long-lasting sex accompanied by words like "That's the way it's going to be."

Mind Power B: This is an image, really more like a movie, that you should spend thirty to ninety seconds on every day; doing it several times a day is even better. Imagine yourself having long-lasting intercourse with good control, which includes several components. Imagine entering your partner, feeling relaxed and comfortable, and just being still inside her for a moment or two. No movement, just enjoying the feel of being in her. Then imagine slow movements, just taking it easy, still enjoying the feeling of being in her. Then gradually increase the pace of your thrusts. Now slow down again. Now again increase the pace gradually, until you're moving almost as much as you want, still feeling calm and easy. Now imagine slowing down and stopping all movement. Stop thrusting and just experience the pleasure. Then gradually increase the movements, slowly building up until you're moving with abandon, letting your body do what it wants. When you want, and only when you want, imagine a wonderful ejaculation. When you're done with the movie, be sure to end with a statement to yourself of this kind: "As it is in my mind, so it shall be in reality" or "This is how it's going to be."

Mind Power C: Before you do any of the physical exercises, spend a few seconds imagining yourself doing it perfectly, exactly as it is supposed to be done. Be sure to imagine all the parts: for example, asking your partner to do it with you, attending to your arousal/tension level, asking her to stop, asking her to resume stimulation, and so on.

This mental rehearsal takes only a few seconds and can be very helpful. It's exactly what the great diver Greg Louganis did before each dive, imagining himself doing it perfectly, and exactly what the great golfer Jack Nicklaus did every time before he hit a ball. You can do it anyplace. For example, if you and your partner are getting ready to do an exercise, you can close your eyes and do your mental rehearsal right there, or you can go into another room—for some reason, the bathroom has been popular with my clients—and take a few seconds to do it there.

Mind Power D: Every day, preferably just after awakening or just before retiring for the night, take a few seconds to imagine how good you're going to feel once you've achieved ejaculatory control.

Mind Power E: This is the pep-talk exercise given in Chapter 21. Remember to use it whenever you feel discouraged or think you failed in an exercise.

SOME DEEP BREATHS, PLEASE

Proper breathing can help develop ejaculatory control. Put simply, taking a few deep breaths can help dissipate the arousal/tension that leads to quick ejaculations. The kind of breathing that's needed is deep, easy, and relaxing. Unfortunately, many of us don't breathe this way. When I ask clients to take some deep breaths, I notice that many of them actually get more tense. They tense their chest or shoulder muscles, sometimes their neck and even arm muscles as well, and even hold their breath (which will make anyone more tense).

The best kind of relaxing breathing I know is the kind taught in most schools of meditation. There is no obvious tensing of muscles, and while inhaling, the belly (not the chest) swells and protrudes. That is, if you lay one hand on your belly while doing this kind of breathing, you'll notice your stomach pushing out a bit on each inhalation and going down a bit on each exhalation. If you're not used to breathing this way, it will take a little practice to learn it. Keep in mind that the purpose is relaxation, keep a hand on your belly to make sure it's protruding slightly with each inhalation, and try not to tense any muscles. If you have trouble with this, it can help to imagine that your belly is an empty balloon, being gently filled with each inhalation, then being gently emptied with each exhalation. This is a fiction, of course, since the air is always going to the same place, your lungs. Nonetheless, the image is usually helpful.

Once you can do this, it's a good idea to practice it as often as possible. A few deep breaths of this kind are perhaps the quickest way for most people to relax. Experiment with taking a few deep breaths when you stop stimulation in both the masturbation and partner exercises. You can also experiment with taking deep breaths when you're being stimulated or having intercourse. This takes a bit of getting used to, because you'll be going against the grain. The more excited you are, the more likely you'll want to take short, superficial breaths and even pant. But with some practice, most men can overcome that tendency and take deep, relaxing breaths.

If you want to go further with using relaxation to help gain ejaculatory control, you can imagine that the air you take in goes down into your pelvis, relaxing the muscles and the whole region. The more relaxed your pelvis is, the less the chance of ejaculating.

MASTURBATION EXERCISES

As mentioned above, everyone who's willing to masturbate should do these exercises even if you don't think you need them. If you really don't, you only need to do each one once.

These masturbation exercises assume that you masturbate the way most men do, by stroking your penis with one hand moving up and down over the shaft and head. Some men pleasure themselves in other ways— for example, by lying facedown and rubbing themselves against the bed, pillow, floor, or sofa. Unfortunately, these other methods are not well-suited to developing ejaculatory control. You probably should learn to do it the typical way.

EXERCISE 22–1: STOP-START MASTURBATION

Time Required: 15 minutes

Step A: With a dry hand (no lotion or other lubrication), masturbate for 15 minutes without ejaculating. Focus in your penis or pelvic area, as discussed above, so you will know how aroused or tense you are. When you feel you are in the control area, stop all stimulation and 1) attend to the sensations of arousal or tension and 2) take a few deep breaths. When the arousal/tension level has dropped significantly (which can be anywhere from 10 seconds to over a minute), resume stimulation. Stop time, the time when you are waiting for your excitement/tension to abate, is included in the 15 minutes.

You may have to stop a number of times when you first do the exercise. As you continue doing it, you will better learn when to stop and how long to wait, and the number of times you need to stop will decrease.

When you need only one or two stops during the 15 minutes, proceed to Step B.

Step B: Exactly the same as Step A, except that you now use a lubricant such as KY jelly, Albolene, or massage oil on your hand. When you need only one or two stops during the 15 minutes, you are ready to move on to Exercise 22–2.

POSSIBLE PROBLEMS

1. You need to stop again as soon as you resume masturbating. This probably means that you're stopping too late and that your stops are too brief. Try stopping sooner and waiting longer before resuming stimulation.

2. You lose all or most of your erection while stopping. This is not a serious problem, but it probably means you are stopping for too long. Try briefer stops.

We now move on to the idea of subtle adjustments, changes in stimulation more subtle than stopping. There is nothing wrong with stopping stimulation in masturbation, partner stimulation, or intercourse. But there are other alternatives. Years ago I discovered that men with good control don't just bang away with fast in-and-out thrusts for long periods of time. They vary their thrusts to help control ejaculation. They move in certain ways when they want to come and in other ways when they want to delay ejaculation, just like Fred. You will learn these other ways. You can use these subtle adjustments when you want, and of course you can always stop if a stop is required.

EXERCISE 22–2: MASTURBATING WITH SUBTLE ADJUSTMENTS

Time Required: 15 minutes

Step A: Masturbate with a dry hand for 15 minutes without ejaculating and without stopping. When your arousal/tension is anywhere in the control zone, make changes in the stimulation to control your ejaculatory process. Kinds of changes you can make are: slow down the pace; vary the site of maximum stimulation—for example, by stimulating only the shaft of your penis rather than the head; change the type of stroke —for instance, going from longer strokes to shorter ones or using circular motions. Try one change at a time. Find out what works for you and then stick with it.

These more subtle adjustments need to be made a bit sooner than stopping. If you make them too late, you can always stop to prevent ejaculation. When your arousal/tension level has decreased, you can resume the more arousing type of stimulation if you want.

When you can comfortably masturbate for 15 minutes without ejaculating by using only subtle adjustments, go to Step B.

Step B: Exactly the same as Step A, but now you use a lubricant on your hand.

When you can comfortably masturbate for 15 minutes using a lubricated hand and only subtle adjustments, go to the next exercise.

WHAT NEXT?

Readers who have partners willing to do exercises with them to help develop better control should read the section immediately following, and follow the exercises and suggestions that constitute most of the rest of the chapter.

If you don't have a partner, you can wait until you find one and see how your control is. If your lack of control was unique to your last relationship, it may be that you'll be fine after the first few times with a new partner. In the meanwhile, you can continue with the masturbation exercises and spend a few minutes a day fantasizing how you will apply your new understandings and skills with your new partner. Imagine taking your time getting into sex with her, imagine telling her about the problem, imagine stopping the activity when things get too intense during sex, then resuming when you feel more in control. If it becomes clear after a new relationship is established that more work needs to be done on ejaculatory control, you can do some of the following exercises with your new friend. If you prefer professional assistance before then, you can consult with a sex therapist and work with him or her alone or with a surrogate partner (see pages 475–478 for more details).

PARTNER EXERCISES

The following guidelines apply to all the remaining exercises in this chapter unless otherwise noted:

1. Both of you should read and discuss each exercise before you do it for the first time.

2. Both of you should agree what words you'll use to tell her when to stop and start stimulation. Words are necessary because nonverbal signals are easily misunderstood. "Stop," "Hold it," "Start," and "More" are fine, as is anything else that's short, clear, and mutually acceptable.

3. Do whatever is necessary for both of you to feel relaxed and comfortable before beginning an exercise. Some couples like to start right in with penile stimulation. Others prefer to begin with hugging, holding, or massage. And in still others, the man sexually stimulates his

partner before she returns the favor. There is no rule to fit all couples. Do what is right for the two of you.

4. It's essential that your partner take her comfort into consideration in deciding what positions to employ. She's got to last fifteen minutes as well as you. If she's stimulating you with her hand, does she want to sit next to you or between your legs? These details can make a big difference.

5. During the exercise, keep focused on your arousal/tension level, not on your partner. This is crucial.

6. Unless stated otherwise, the goal of each exercise is to last for fifteen minutes without ejaculating. You can come after the fifteen minutes are up if you wish, but go slowly, be aware of your arousal/tension and the point of inevitability, and enjoy.

7. When you are using stops, you should feel confident of your control and need no more than two stops during a fifteen-minute period before going on to the next exercise. If you have a lot of problems with that next exercise and it doesn't get better after a few trials, return to the one before it and practice it until you have further developed your skills.

8. Remember, two or three times a week on average tends to work well for most couples. More is better, provided it's not an effort to get erections or to get your partner to participate.

EXERCISE 22–3: PARTNER STIMULATION OF PENIS

Step A: She stimulates your penis with her unlubricated hand in ways that are arousing to you; feel free to give her instructions on how to stroke you. Keep focused on your arousal/tension level and tell her when to stop. When the arousal/tension level has decreased, tell her to resume.

When you can last for 15 minutes with no more than two stops and feel confident of your ability to do this again, do Step B.

Step B: Exactly the same as Step A, except that your partner now uses lotion, oil, or another lubricant on her hand.

POSSIBLE PROBLEM

You aren't stopping in time because you're focusing on your partner rather than on your arousal/tension. You may be wondering if she is enjoying herself, if she's getting bored or tired. You need to swing your attention back to where it belongs as quickly as possible. You might also want to talk to your lover about your concerns. Maybe she *is* bored some of the time. Can it be OK with you that she is willing to cooperate in this endeavor even though it's not exciting for her? However you work it out, the important thing is that you be able to put your attention on your arousal/tension level.

Now that you're comfortable using stops to delay ejaculation, you're ready for more subtle changes.

EXERCISE 22–4: PARTNER STIMULATION OF PENIS WITH SUBTLE ADJUSTMENTS

Step A: This is exactly the same as Step A of Exercise 22–3, except that this time you'll use changes in behavior other than stopping to control ejaculation. She stimulates your penis with a dry hand and you delay ejaculation by telling her to slow down the pace or change the kind of stroking. Experiment and find out what works best for you, or show her what you learned from the subtle adjustments with masturbation exercise.

Should there be problems with this exercise that don't resolve themselves after a few sessions, consider spending some time mastering the subtle adjustments by yourself, Exercise 22–2.

When you're confident and comfortable using adjustments other than stopping to delay ejaculation for 15 minutes, do Step B.

Step B: The same as A, except that your lover now uses lubricant on her hand.

The following exercise is optional.

EXERCISE 22–5: STOP-START AND SUBTLE ADJUSTMENTS WITH ORAL STIMULATION

If your partner likes giving oral sex and you like receiving it, you can repeat Exercises 22–3 and 22–4 with her, using her mouth rather than her hand. But do not do this exercise if either of you has any qualms at all about it; it will only lead to problems and get in the way of reaching your goals.

Now you're almost ready to enjoy being inside of her without ejaculating. But first you should do the next exercise. It's especially helpful for those men who come before insertion in the vagina or immediately thereafter.

EXERCISE 22–6: PENIS NEAR VAGINA

Time Required: A few minutes
Lie on your back and have your lover sit on your thighs.
Step A: After you have an erection, rub it gently for a few seconds on her inner thighs and see how that feels. Take a few seconds' rest and then do the same in her pubic hair. Take another brief rest. Now rub it gently on the outer lips of her vagina, and see what that's like. Take a pause and then put the head of your penis between her vaginal lips and enjoy that for a moment. And that's the whole exercise.
If you felt any anxiety or any urge to ejaculate, take your time and do the exercise again and again until there is no anxiety and no urge to ejaculate. Remember to take some deep, relaxing breaths before starting it and between each step. When you can comfortably do the whole exercise, move on to Step B.
Step B: Exactly the same as Step A, except now it's her hand that guides your penis.

Starting with the next exercise, your partner's vagina needs to be lubricated before following my suggestions. Natural and artificial lubrication are both acceptable, but the two of you need to agree on what's to be done.

Exercise 22–7 will probably strike you as strange. Here you are, developing your ejaculatory control, and here I am telling you to come as quickly as possible in intercourse. I really do want you to do this. The reason is simple. In the exercises that follow, there will be times when you come quickly by accident, and it's crucial that you and your partner deal with these incidents relatively calmly and harmoniously. By deliberately re-enacting the original problem now and handling it in a way that feels good to both of you, you prepare yourselves to deal with the situation the same way when it happens accidentally.

A word of warning. You and your partner need to read the exercise together carefully before attempting it. Some women feel so hurt and angry by the many quick ejaculations they had to endure in the past that they may not be able to do the exercise or they may need to discharge some angry feelings first. It's crucial that you listen with all the empathy you can muster to what your partner says. If she can't do the exercise, skip it. If she can, but first needs to get some feelings off her chest, see if you can just listen to her.

EXERCISE 22–7: COMING QUICKLY IN INTERCOURSE

When the two of you feel like it, engage in as much sexplay as you like and proceed to intercourse. Your job is to come as quickly as possible and to make sure the experience ends up a happy one. You should use what you've learned about your mind to fight any negative thoughts and pictures, and instead to feel positive about what's happening. And the two of you should go on to do whatever you want and have a good experience. Some possibilities are you stimulating her to orgasm if she so desires, one or both of you getting a massage, cuddling, and talking. When the experience is over, talk and commit yourselves to handle future quick ejaculations (and I guarantee they will happen) in the same constructive way.

How many times you do this exercise depends on how many times you need to, which can be anywhere from once to four or five times. But you shouldn't go on to Exercise 22–8 until both of you are confident that you can handle quick ejaculations with no problems.

Now you're ready to begin a new relationship with your partner's vagina, one that allows more satisfaction for both of you.

EXERCISE 22–8: GRADUAL INSERTION INTO VAGINA

Time Required: Usually less than 5 minutes

The goal is to insert your penis, gradually and in stages, into your partner's vagina so you can develop greater comfort in being there. She needs to understand that this is not intercourse and that she needs to stay relatively still.

Using a position that will be comfortable for both of you, one of you should place your erect penis just at the opening of her vagina. Take a few seconds to get used to having it there. When that feels comfortable, move the penis in a little bit, about an inch. Again, take a few seconds to get used to the feeling. Continue in this fashion until your whole penis is inside of her. Then stay that way for a few minutes and attend to your arousal/tension. See how it feels to have your penis surrounded by her vagina. Be aware of the texture, temperature, and wetness of the vagina. Get used to being there; it's a nice place.

If at any time you feel you are losing control, slow down your breathing by taking several slow, deep breaths.

If you want to ejaculate afterward and it's OK with her, do so, but move slowly and be aware of what's happening to you.

You can proceed to the next exercise when you are comfortable being inside your partner without any urge to ejaculate.

EXERCISE 22–9: PENIS IN VAGINA WITH NO MOVEMENT

Really a continuation of the previous exercise, this one also requires your partner to be still. The goal is to have your penis in her vagina with little or no movement for 15 minutes. Either of you can insert your penis. You don't have to do it in stages, but do go slowly. Once you're fully inside, just be there. It's important that your partner feel comfortable with you doing nothing. Of course, it's fine if the two of you want to talk about what's going on. With no movement at all, you may find your erection waning. If that happens, you can ask her to contract her pelvic muscles a few times or you can move slightly, just enough to keep you hard.

POSSIBLE PROBLEM

The first time or two you do the exercise, you get very excited and come. This is not a problem unless it continues to occur. The solution that works best is to return to the previous exercise and spend several sessions without fully entering her. That is, insert only as far as is comfortable and then spend a few moments there. The next time you do it, see if you can insert a little farther, still feeling comfortable. Continue in this way until you're fully ensconced in her. Then extend the time you can stay in her.

Now we're going to extend your ability to be inside of her with movement. The position usually recommended for these exercises is you lying on your back and her sitting on top of you; this allows you to fully relax, letting the bed support your weight so you don't have to flex any muscles, and works well for many couples. But others prefer something else. So use any position that works best for you; just remember that it has to be sufficiently comfortable for both of you so that changes in it aren't necessary during the fifteen minutes.

EXERCISE 22–10: PENIS IN VAGINA WITH MOVEMENT

Step A: This is similar to the previous exercise, except that now one of you should thrust slowly. Which one moves largely depends on the position you're using. If she's on top, she'll do the moving. If you're on top, it will be you. Regardless of what position is used and who moves, you have to be in charge of how much movement and when to stop and resume thrusting. Use subtle adjustments or stops to delay ejaculation for 15 minutes. It's important your partner *not* start thrusting to satisfy herself. That will come later.

Start with a very slow pace. Make sure you're comfortable with it before increasing movement. Then go a little faster. When that feels fine, no danger of losing control, increase it again. Don't forget to take some deep breaths before increasing the pace.

Continue with this step until the active one is moving at a pretty good pace but not all-out, say about 80 percent of abandoned movement. This will probably not be achieved in one 15-minute session. Use as many sessions as you need. Then do Step B.

Step B: The same as Step A, with the other one moving. This may well require a different position.

Step C: The same as the two previous steps, except both of you move. Start with very slow movements and only increase the pace as you feel comfortable and in control. Use as many sessions as required until you are both moving as fast as you desire.

POSSIBLE PROBLEM WITH ANY OF THE STEPS

You lose control when the movements get faster. This means you are speeding up too much or before you're fully comfortable with a slower pace. Go slower and make sure you're fully comfortable and totally in control before picking up the tempo, and pick it up only slightly. Take your time and some deep breaths.

Now you are ready to experiment with intercourse positions different from the one you've been using.

EXERCISE 22–11: DIFFERENT INTERCOURSE POSITIONS

Agree with your partner on which new position to try; for example, man or woman on top, side-by-side, or rear entry. Your control will almost certainly not be as good in the new position as it was in the old until you have more experience with it. Use the pattern you're now used to: start with only one of you moving very slowly. Gradually increase the pace. Then let the other one move, gradually picking up the tempo as you're comfortable. Then both of you move. Keep in mind that you'll need a number of sessions to feel in good control in each new position.

For many men, no further exercises will be needed. Their control has significantly improved. They and their partners are enjoying sex a lot more and perhaps having more of it as well. But for other couples, there's still a problem.

In couples where the woman is capable of vaginal orgasms, it sometimes happens that the man cannot maintain his improved control when his partner moves with abandon in intercourse—that is, when she starts her drive toward orgasm. These men tend to focus too much on their partner's arousal, and it's as if they get sucked into it. Her arousal becomes their arousal. At first reading, this may sound fine. Her excitement fuels his excitement and they reach orgasm at the same time. Obviously there would be no problem if that is what happened. And it does work that way for some couples.

For others, however, what happens is not so pleasing. To make up some numbers, let's say she needs to move forcefully for twenty seconds to reach orgasm. But he either gets very excited by her excitement or gets nervous for fear of not lasting long enough and he comes ten seconds after she starts her drive to orgasm. If he can't continue thrusting or allow her to continue for another ten seconds, she doesn't have an orgasm. (It's no problem, of course, if he can continue thrusting for a few seconds after his orgasm, until she has hers.) She gets frustrated because she was so close. This may feel even worse to the woman than the old situation where he came before she was anywhere near orgasm. Now she was so close, but still couldn't get there.

I've worked with a number of couples in this predicament, and so have other therapists I've talked to. Interestingly, however, there's been no mention of this issue in the therapy literature. But the complaint exists and requires attention.

One option is to experiment with positions and movements that are more arousing to her than to you. It may be that circular movements of your pelvis or any kind of movement that pushes your pelvis against hers may help her reach orgasm without pushing you over the edge before you want.

The other possibilities I've explored involve helping you to keep some independence from your partner's excitement. You need to recognize her excitement, of course, because it's there and because it can be a source of great joy to both of you. But being aware of it and celebrating it are not the same as becoming part of it. You need to be able to maintain some separateness between what's happening to her and what's happening to you. Several exercises can help. The first one consists entirely of imagery and self-talk.

EXERCISE 22–12: IMAGINING BEING SEPARATE FROM YOUR PARTNER'S EXCITEMENT

To start, you imagine that you're having intercourse with your partner and she is moving slowly and with only a little passion. As the exercise proceeds, you imagine her, in stages, increasing the speed and force of her movements. At each level of the imaging of her movements, you tell yourself "Her excitement is not my excitement. Her passion is not my passion. She's doing her thing, but I have to do my own, focusing on my own feelings." You don't need all these words, but I threw them in so you can get the message. Feel free to change the words to better suit you.

This exercise works even better if you make yourself a tape. The reason the tape works better is that without it you have to do two things: imagine her moving a certain way and tell yourself things. This requires the mind to make a split screen of itself, which is easy for some people and difficult for others. So if you have any problems doing the exercise as written, make a tape of one part of it. That is, you could make a short audiotape (3 minutes or so is plenty) in which you describe your partner's mounting excitement. Be sure to break her behavior into stages, going slowly from one level of arousal and movement to another ("She's breathing more rapidly and moaning with pleasure a bit, and her hips are moving a little faster than before [10-second pause], now her moans are a bit louder, her movements a bit stronger . . ."). Then, as you play this tape, you loudly tell yourself "Her excitement is *not* my excitement. Her arousal is *not* my arousal. I need to refocus on my own sensations, just focusing on sensation and feelings in my body." As you get comfortable doing this for one level of movement and passion on her part (in your mind), imagine her moving a bit faster and with a bit more feeling. When you get comfortable with that, increase her movement and passion again in your mind. Keep on in this way until you're comfortable with her moving with as much abandon and feeling as she's capable of.

An alternate way of doing this exercise is to have her participate. She describes her rising excitement and the behavior she manifests as she moves strongly toward orgasm (even though the two of you aren't really having sex and she's not excited and not moving at the moment), while you repeat the self-talk to yourself and imagine yourself focusing on your own sensations.

Another option requires that you know or learn how to relax quickly. If taking a few deep breaths works, that's all you need. If not, there are a number of good relaxation-training audiocassettes readily available at bookstores. The first thing you should do is listen to the tapes until you can easily and quickly relax when you desire. Then get relaxed and do any or all versions of Exercise 22–12. That is, relax and imagine your partner moving slowly. Hold the image for a few seconds. If you maintain the relaxation, as you probably will, move to a scene of her moving a bit quicker. As you keep progressing in this manner, you will reach a point where the image of her moving disturbs your relaxation; you will get tense. Quickly let go of the image and get relaxed again. Go back to the image before the one that made you tense and spend more time with it, that day and on succeeding ones. Then try the difficult one again. If it again causes you tension, you need to make a half-step or two—add an intermediate image or two—between the one that causes tension and the one that doesn't. I say more about creating half-steps in the next exercise.

The next exercise requires a lot from your partner. In intercourse, she has to gradually increase her movements until she is simulating her behavior when she's close to orgasm. I've done this one many times with different couples, and it's clear that the best results come from the partner acting or pretending rather than actually getting highly aroused. The reason is that you may well have to ask her to stop or slow down, and that's a lot easier done if she's only pretending to be close to orgasm.

EXERCISE 22–13: PARTNER SIMULATION OF INCREASING AROUSAL IN INTERCOURSE

Using an intercourse position the two of you like and that allows her full freedom of movement, she is to start moving slowly; only she is to move. As usual, you are to focus on your arousal/tension. At the same time, you are to repeat your slogan to yourself, about not being part of her arousal, or relax, whichever you prefer. As you feel comfortable, have her increase the pace. If at any time you feel yourself losing control, ask her to stop or slow down. As you regain control by pausing or slowing down, remind yourself several times that her arousal is not your arousal. Have her resume her movements when you feel in control. Continue in this way until you want to stop the exercise or until she's moving as fast and strongly as she would before and during orgasm.

POSSIBLE PROBLEM

You're fine as long as she's moving at a certain pace or in a certain way, but you lose control when she escalates. Try to get a picture of what she's doing differently (same movements, only faster; thrusting more forcefully, although at the same pace; thrusting more forcefully and faster; thrusting faster and harder with accompanying heavier breathing; or whatever) and use this image in doing Exercise 22–12, something you should do many, many times, until the problem is resolved.

With her, you can continue Exercise 22–13, but have her tone down her behavior to somewhere between where you have control and where you lose it. Whether we think in terms of thrusts or breaths per minute, rpms, or whatever, there's always a way of cutting it down a bit. In the next session of Exercise 22–13, quickly get to the highest level of her behavior where you have good control and stay with it a few minutes, then have her increase one relevant feature (breaths, thrusts, or force) by the smallest amount possible. Let's say she increases the pace by a tiny amount. When that feels comfortable to you and your control is good, have her slightly increase the force of the thrusts while maintaining the same speed. You, of course, are to keep relaxing or reminding yourself that your arousal is separate from hers. When you're comfortable with the increased speed and force, she can maintain them while also slightly increasing her breathing rate. Keep on in this fashion (which may take a number of sessions) until she's simulating not only her behavior on the way to orgasm, but orgasm itself.

No couple I've worked with has completed this exercise in fewer than six sessions. Take as much time and as many sessions as you need. Remember, this is the last obstacle. You're almost where you want to be.

If you've done the exercises given, by now you have probably attained good control and are enjoying a more confident, relaxed, and more satisfying sex life.

You have undoubtedly noticed that results come gradually and that it takes a while for the training to sink in and become automatic. Your learning will continue for many months. All you need do to facilitate the process is to stay aware of your arousal/tension and take deep breaths and make other adjustments as needed.

Remember that there is absolutely no way to avoid losing control some of the time. Whether because you haven't had sex for a long time, are extremely excited, are tense or angry, or maybe for some other reason, quick ejaculations will occasionally occur. As time goes on, they will decrease in frequency, but they will probably never disappear. This is simply part of normal male functioning. There is nothing you can do about it and there's no reason for concern.

When you do come quickly, don't fight it. Let it happen and enjoy. There's no need for apology. And no need to think that all your training has been in vain. It hasn't. Just go a bit more slowly the next time, stay focused, and make your adjustments a little earlier than usual.

Keep in mind the effects of tension. Anything that tenses you up or gets you upset—whether trouble at work, conflict at home, money problems, or anything else—will tend to have a negative effect on your control. So be especially aware and careful during tense times. Anything you can do to alleviate the tension will be very helpful.

If you notice yourself slipping back into your old, quick ways, take some time, both alone and with your partner, to determine what's the cause. A brief refresher course with the relevant exercises in this chapter can be helpful. Couples who don't have intercourse during the woman's period find this a good time to practice manual and oral stimulation.

Now that you have better control, please don't assume that every sex act has to last a long time. Exercise your control when and as often as you want, but remember that good sex is not determined by clocks. You can make great love in two hours, in twenty minutes, and even in twenty seconds. The key is not how long it takes, but how good you both feel about yourselves, each other, and what you are doing.

IF YOU NEED FURTHER ASSISTANCE

If you do not progress as much as you want by following the program in this chapter, an obvious next step is to have some sessions with a sex therapist. If progress there also seems difficult, there's something new that you might want to know about. In the last few years, a few sex therapists have been experimenting with medications to help clients develop ejaculatory control. Antidepressants such as Prozac and Ana-franil are the primary kind of drug used. This is not because anyone assumes that people without control are depressed, but rather because certain antidepressants have the side effect of making orgasm difficult to reach. Antianxiety agents such as Xanax and Ativan have also been used, the idea being that reducing anxiety is one way of reducing fast ejaculations.

My experience with using these drugs to treat rapid ejaculation is limited to only a few cases, but I've also talked with several therapists who have used them more extensively. With this background, I have several impressions to impart. First, although the reports so far have been very positive, that is almost always the case with new treatments. At this point, this work has to be considered experimental. Second, drugs are almost always used in conjunction with a regular sex therapy program. I don't know of anyone who recommends simply putting a man on Prozac to help him last longer. Third, these are serious drugs and their use should not be taken lightly. Antianxiety agents can be addictive if taken regularly over a long time. And the antidepressants used can adversely affect other aspects of your sexuality. Some men who've taken Prozac and Anafranil report losing much of their erotic desire and/or developing erection problems.

Nonetheless, if neither the exercises in this book nor work with a sex therapist provides the ejaculatory control you and your partner want, it may be worth talking to a psychiatrist or sex therapist about the possible use of one of the drugs as part of a new program.

23

Resolving Erection Problems: Medical Options

"You want to know how I feel, I'll tell you. I feel like an absolute nothing. I know I can satisfy her in other ways and I do, but that's not the point. I feel like shit, like the center has been taken out of me."—MAN, 51

"I have trouble sleeping and I can't concentrate at work. All I think about day and night is my problem, about how I can't do the job anymore. I feel limp and weak, just like my dick."—MAN, 38

W̲HILE any problem in the critical area of sex is very upsetting to a man, nothing generates as much concern, anxiety, shame, and even terror as an inability to get or maintain erections. Only the loss of his job can make a man feel less of a man. The primary meaning of impotence, the term traditionally applied to erection difficulties, is a lack of power, strength, and vigor, the negation of all that we consider masculine. Men have been taught to tie their self-respect to the upward mobility of their penises and, when their penises do not rise to the occasion, they no longer feel like men.

A man in therapy said it like this: "I've never felt like this before. I just don't feel like a whole person and certainly not like a man." Other men have used terms such as "useless," "hopeless," "fraud," "lost my manhood," and "can't cut it anymore" to describe how they felt when their penises weren't functioning.

Women are often baffled by the agony a man goes through when he fails to get or keep an erection, but they have no parallel experience with which to compare it. A woman can participate in intercourse or any other sexual act without being aroused or even interested. A man is in a more difficult situation. Because of the incorrect belief that sex demands a rigid penis, his "failure" is obvious, dangling in full view. There is no way to fake an erection and, though not impossible, it is difficult to have intercourse without at least a partial erection. So he feels that he cannot have sex; and in his eyes, a man who can't have sex is not really a man.

His partner may be sympathetic and supportive, but he may be so consumed with self-loathing that he can't accept what she offers. Many men distance themselves from their partners after such "failures" and engage in orgies of self-flagellation. The result is usually a miserable time for all concerned.

Given all the feelings men with erection problems have, clear thinking becomes difficult. Yet such thinking is exactly what's needed, because you need to make some decisions about how to deal with your situation. It may help you to feel better to realize that, given the various treatment options available, there is almost certainly a solution for your problem. You can further improve your state of mind by using the material in Chapter 21 to focus on your virtues as a lover and a human being and reminding yourself that you are still a worthwhile man regardless of how your penis has been acting.

There are a number of ways in which penises disappoint men. Almost all men have had at least a few experiences when they wanted an erection and didn't get one or when they lost an erection at some embarrassing point. Some men have problems with getting or maintaining erections at the beginning of a relationship. Then, after they become more comfortable with their new partners, their erections become more reliable. Because these kinds of difficulties are common and transient, it's best to view them as a part of life rather than as problems. A man can explain to a new partner that it takes him a few times to get comfortable enough for his penis to join in the fun or, perhaps better yet, he can put off getting into sex until he feels more comfortable with her.

There are also chronic difficulties. Some men usually have difficulty attaining erections, while others usually have trouble maintaining them. For still other men, the problem is that their erections usually aren't as hard as they would like.

My belief is that if it bothers you, it's a problem. But the solution may not lie where you think it does.

In this chapter I look at what medicine has to offer: whether you should consult a urologist, what tests he might perform, and what treatments he can tender. In the next chapter, I present the sex-therapy exercises and suggestions I have found effective with my clients. If you are certain your problem is not medical and you aren't interested in a medical solution, you can skip this chapter. But if you're not absolutely sure, you might want to read it.

Erection problems can be mainly physical (but almost always with a psychological component because of how men feel about a malfunctioning penis), mainly or totally psychological, or a mixture of the two. While it is helpful to determine what the main cause or contributor is, the nature of the problem does not necessarily dictate the treatment. For example, many men have had penile implants or used other medical treatments despite the lack of evidence that medical problems were causing their erection difficulties. They either preferred a medical solution or were not informed of the option of sex therapy.

On the other hand, there are cases where the problem was clearly physical but the patient didn't want a medical solution and chose sex therapy. Just because there is some physical involvement does not mean that you need medical treatment. There may be, for instance, decreased blood flow to the penis because of arterial blockage; but if the blockage is slight, you may be able to have usable erections provided you are rested and not anxious. With a few sessions of sex therapy, you and your partner may be able to arrange your sexual activity so that your penis usually functions acceptably. And, occasionally, we get a miracle.

One man, close to seventy, had definite physical reasons for his erection problem, but had already had open-heart surgery and wouldn't even consider more surgery. At that time, other medical options such as vacuum devices and penile injections were not in widespread use. His urologist advised him that sex therapy couldn't help but referred him to me when the patient insisted. After talking to the man and reading the urological report, I wasn't hopeful of being able to help, which I told him. But he wanted to give it a try anyway. We did, and much to everyone's surprise, he was functioning very well after only five sessions.

I do not pretend that this outcome is the rule with men who have a physical basis for their erection problems. It isn't. But the fact that it did happen in such an extreme case, and has happened in other, less extreme cases, means there is some hope for those who don't want surgery or other medical treatments. It also offers an option for those who are willing to have surgery or use other medical alternatives but prefer not to. They can try a brief course of sex therapy to see whether it will be enough.

And, of course, there are cases in which sex therapy cannot help and medical treatment is necessary.

A man I saw almost two decades ago had a strong bias against physicians and medicine. Although his penis didn't get stiff or even full under any circumstances, he refused to believe the reason might be physical. Every time he got involved with a woman, the two of them would go to a sex therapist. I was the fourth therapist he tried and, sure enough, he failed with me as well. Only after our absolute failure and continued badgering from me for months was he willing to visit a urologist. A few tests revealed that the problem was indeed medically based. Soon thereafter he had a penile implant inserted and his sex life improved considerably. What is sad is that he could have had a functioning penis five years earlier and saved himself considerable time, money, and energy.

SHOULD YOU SEE A UROLOGIST?

I think it's a good idea to get a urological consultation unless it's clear that the problem is totally psychological. Medical science has been quite active in the sexual arena in the last twenty years, and a number of new diagnostic tests and treatments have been developed and refined. You should know what options are available to you before making any decisions. Even if you choose sex therapy, it's good to know what limits any physical problems you have may put on progress in that therapy.

You should get a consultation from a urologist if there's any possibility that your erection problem may be due to physical causes. Although urologists by definition are specialists in the physiology and pathology of the urinary and genital functions, not all of them are experts in sexuality. You want someone who specializes in sex problems. The best way to find such a person is by getting a referral from your regular doctor or a sex therapist.

If *any* of the following items are true of you, you should see a urologist.

- You never or rarely have erections while asleep or upon awakening. When I say erections in this discussion, I mean of reasonable or satisfactory quality—that is, sufficient for vaginal insertion and intercourse. This does not mean that your penis has to be as hard as a rock.
- You never or rarely have erections in masturbation.
- You never or rarely can maintain an erection until ejaculation.
- You have a consistent pattern of your penis getting hard only a short time before ejaculation.
- You have already failed to improve the quality or quantity of your erections in a sex-therapy or self-help program.

If any of the following are true, you probably don't need a urologist:

- You often have erections while asleep and on awakening.
- You usually get erections with masturbation and maintain them for a comfortable time before ejaculation. If you have erections on awakening or with masturbation, but not with a partner, that almost certainly means that something about you and the partner needs work. It would be a strange physical condition that mani-fested itself only in the presence of another person.
- You have and maintain good erections in certain situations but not others—say, with one partner but not with another, or when you're on vacation but not at home.

If you're going to see a urologist (or a therapist, for that matter), it's important to be a wise consumer. You should review your sexual history, or at least the history of the problem, before seeing the doctor so you can present an accurate and comprehensive picture. You should also make a list of questions you want answered and make sure that you do indeed get the answers. If the doctor doesn't seem comfortable dealing with you and your situation, isn't willing to take the time you want to discuss your case with you, or won't talk to you in language you can understand, go elsewhere. Don't let your fear of looking stupid prevent you from asking all the questions you want. As far as I'm concerned, the only stupid questions are the ones you don't ask.

If your consultation goes beyond tests and into possible treatments, I strongly suggest bringing your partner with you. Even though it's your penis, she's an integral part of your sex life and she should be there to hear the pros and cons of various treatments and to ask any questions she has.

Try not to be overly swayed by the doctor's (or therapist's) authority or certainty about what treatment you should have. Many doctors and therapists are anything but open-minded. They believe that whatever they do is the best treatment for everyone. While you should listen carefully to his or her opinion, remember that's all it is. Every treatment costs money, and most also require time and effort; some, like penile implants, also involve pain and risk. You're the one who will have to live with the consequences. You should get the best therapeutic and medical advice you can, and then determine (with your partner, if you have one) what course of action makes the most sense for you.

WHAT YOU CAN EXPECT FROM A UROLOGICAL CONSULTATION

After a complete urological workup—which may take several visits, depending on the number and nature of tests done—you should have a better understanding of the possible role of medical factors in your difficulty. More specifically:

- Whether there may be physical reasons for your erection problem.
- The nature of the physical reasons and perhaps of their extent. If, for instance, there's a blood flow problem, is it severe, moderate, or slight?
- The medical options for resolving the physical difficulty and the costs and pros and cons of each.

It's a good idea to get copies of your test results from your doctor as well as a summary of your situation. These can then be shown to any other doctors or therapists you consult. When clients of mine have been to urologists, I always ask for a report, and it's surprising to me how many of them can't remember what the doctor said, what tests were done, or even the doctor's name. Getting a written summary from the doctor as well as copies of the test results will save time when you talk to another expert.

Perhaps the best conclusion you could get is negative—that is, that thorough examination has revealed no physical reason for your problem. Then you are free to consider sex therapy with a therapist or by doing the exercises in the next chapter.

THE UROLOGICAL EXAMINATION

A thorough urological exam consists of a number of procedures. Not every doctor does all of them, but I list several of the main ones here for your information.

History-taking: This consists of getting information from you about the problem, and is not much different from what a therapist does. Some of the important questions are: Exactly what is the problem (don't get erections, get them but lose them quickly, penis is full but not rigid)? Under what circumstances do you get erections? Under what circumstances do you not? When did the problem start? Has it changed since then? How is your general health and what medications are you taking? What about alcohol and recreational drugs? These questions are the ones you should address yourself before seeing the doctor (or therapist).

Blood tests: Although hormonal deficiencies account for only a very small percentage of erection problems, most workups include blood tests to determine your level of testosterone, the so-called male sex hormone. The main effect of low testosterone is diminished sexual interest, so if your desire for sex has decreased and you're having erection problems, a series of blood tests will show if your levels are abnormally low.

Your blood sugar may also be checked for diabetes, a frequent cause of erection problems. It's possible that complications of the disease are causing or contributing to your erection difficulty.

Nocturnal penile tumescence (NPT) test: This is a test to determine if and what kind of erections you have while you sleep. Since it's typical for men to have erections during rapid eye movement (REM) sleep, the stage of sleep during which we dream, this is a good way of determining whether the problem is physical or not. NPT monitoring involves a device attached to your penis that records its activity while you sleep. It doesn't sound too appealing, but I assure you it's painless. This test can be done at a medical school or university sleep center (very expensive), or at your home (much less expensive though not quite as reliable). It shows how often you get erections, how full they are, and how long they last. The best NPT monitoring is done with a device called a RigiScan; it measures not only penile fullness but also rigidity.

Although NPT is a reliable test, it's not perfect. If your sleep is disturbed for any reason—because of depression, for example, or discomfort because of having the device attached to you—false readings may occur. Since one's sleep can be easily disturbed by being in a strange place (a sleep center) and having a device hooked up to one's body (at a sleep center or at home), NPT testing is usually done for two or three nights. That way, it can be determined if the readings of the first night are valid or due to sleep disturbances. One limitation of the NPT is that even if it indicates the problem is physical, it doesn't pinpoint what the physical problem is and more tests need to be done. Nonetheless, NPT is very useful in any comprehensive workup.

There are several poor men's versions of the NPT tests. One involves a device called a Snap-Gauge, a strip of plastic with a Velcro closing that is placed around the penis before going to sleep. An erection will break the little plastic bands on the gauge, thus indicating that your penis got full. Unfortunately, it doesn't say anything about how many erections you had, how long they lasted, or how rigid they were. Even less reliable results are achieved with the so-called stamp test. This involves placing a ring of several postage stamps around your soft penis before you go to sleep. A good erection will break the ring. The results of this test depend on a number of things—for example, how tightly you secure the stamps to your penis—and, like the Snap-Gauge, they say nothing about how long the erection lasted or how firm it was. Another problem is that if you move around a lot while you sleep, both the stamps and the Snap-Gauge may break and falsely indicate you had an erection.

Yet another test of nocturnal erections requires no equipment at all and can be done *before* you visit a doctor or therapist. But it requires a willing partner. She has to stay awake all or part of the night to observe what your penis is doing. If you have an erection, she can check it for rigidity and she can also note how long it lasts. Obviously, this requires a great deal from your partner, but the knowledge can be valuable. If she is not a sound sleeper, she may already have this information. A number of women have told me, "I don't know why he can't have an erection when we try to make love. He's always jabbing me with something hard in the middle of the night."

Papaverine or prostaglandin injections: This consists of a relatively painless injection of a drug, papaverine or prostaglandin, into the spongy tissue of the penis. This causes the arteries and smooth muscles to relax and allow increased blood flow into the penis. If you get and maintain a good erection as a result of the injection, this suggests that the blood supply to your penis is in good order and that the problem lies elsewhere, in psychological or other medical areas. Giving yourself such injections is also used as a treatment, which I cover later in this section.

Checking penile blood flow: Several other tests may be done to determine if sufficient blood is getting into the penis. One of them is a radarlike device, called a duplex Doppler, that can help determine how well your penile arteries are working.

Another test, a cavernosogram, involves taking X rays after dye is injected into the penis. This test can give crucial information about whether the blood in your penis is leaking out, thus making it difficult or impossible to maintain an erection.

MEDICAL TREATMENTS

As I indicated above, sexual medicine has made major advances in recent years. A number of new treatments have become available and a number of older ones have been refined. I briefly discuss the most common and promising options now available for erection problems. As you probably suspect, all have pros and cons.

Before getting to them, however, it's important to say that they rarely destroy your existing capacity to experience pleasure or to ejaculate. If you now feel sensation when your penis is stroked, you'll feel sensation when it's stroked after having a penile implant or taking papaverine injections. If you can ejaculate now, you'll be able to ejaculate afterward.

Before deciding on a particular option, especially the more invasive ones like penile injections and implants, it's a good idea to talk to others who have tried it. Your doctor may be willing to give you the names of a patient or two who have had an implant, are using vacuum devices, or are injecting themselves. You'll be getting a skewed sample, of course— it's doubtful he'll give you the name of a dissatisfied patient—but the information you can get by talking to several of these people is still invaluable. Be wary, however, if you get a true believer, someone who talks as if the option he chose is a miracle with no limitations or problems. Try to get both sides. What's good about the treatment, what limitations does it impose, what problems is he having with it?

Testosterone injections: If your testosterone level is low, the urologist may prescribe a series of testosterone injections given every few weeks for several months. Testosterone can also be given orally, but this is less effective than shots and can cause liver damage.

Advantage:

• If low testosterone production is the cause of your erection difficulties, testosterone is exactly what you need and will probably resolve the problem.

Disadvantage:

• Although there is no evidence that testosterone injections cause prostate cancer, they can speed the growth of a tumor that's already present.

Yohimbine: This is a drug in pill form that comes from the bark of an African tree and is commonly given to men complaining of erection problems and low sexual desire. Yohimbine has produced dramatic results in animal studies. In one of them, rats who were injected with large doses of yohimbine engaged in twice as much sex as rats that didn't get the injections. What, if anything, this has to do with humans is unclear. As of this writing, the experts are not in agreement on the effectiveness of yohimbine for men with erection problems. Some claim good results, others don't. Since yohimbine doesn't seem to have any serious side effects for most men, it may be worth a trial if your doctor suggests it. If it helps, fine; if not, look at other options.

Vacuum devices: Several devices have come on the market in recent years that allow you to get an erection by suction. The typical device consists of a plastic cylinder that fits over the penis. You then repeatedly press a lever that pumps the air out of the cylinder. This creates a vacuum that draws blood into the penis, resulting in an erection. When you have a satisfactory erection, you remove the cylinder after placing a specially designed rubber band or tourniquet at the base of your penis; this holds the blood in the penis and keeps it erect during sex. The constrictor band should not be kept in place longer than thirty minutes. Surveys indicate that the majority of men who've tried these devices like them, and so do their partners.

Please note that the bands used with vacuum devices are not the kind you buy in office-supply stores. You can cause serious injury to yourself by using regular rubber bands.

ADVANTAGES:

• These devices, which can be used by most men with erection difficulties, produce serviceable erections when you want them.

• Vacuum devices are relatively inexpensive—a one-time fee of $150 to $450—and have no known side effects or complications, as long as you use the recommended constrictor band and keep it on your penis for no more than thirty minutes.

DISADVANTAGES:

• As with penile injections, you have to stop what you're doing and use the device in the prescribed manner.

• Some users complain that their erections are not as rigid as they want and somewhat wobbly at the base.

• You can cause serious damage to the penis if you leave the band on for more than thirty minutes.

Injections of papaverine or prostaglandin: This consists of injecting the substance into the shaft of your penis, the same as in the diagnostic test mentioned a few pages ago. I realize it sounds painful when you read about it, but it usually is not. A very fine needle is used. In some men, however, the medicine itself, not the shot, does cause pain. This method requires a prescription after your urologist determines the correct dose and teaches you how to inject yourself. When you want an erection, you give yourself a shot. Within fifteen to thirty minutes, you'll have a good erection that will last from thirty minutes to an hour or longer.

ADVANTAGE:

• The ability to have good, long-lasting erections when you want without incurring the cost, pain, and risks of surgery. The erections produced by injections look and feel more "natural"—the size and rigidity are more like what you used to have—than those produced by vacuum devices and implants.

DISADVANTAGES:

• The idea of putting a needle into their penises is not appealing for many men and they won't even consider this option. Or they consider it briefly but turn to other methods before they give it a chance. Others are willing to inject themselves regularly, but they don't like it; one reason, of course, is the pain some of them experience, presumably as a side effect of the drug.

• Injecting yourself can interfere with spontaneity, but this is easily remedied by making the shot a part of loveplay.

• These injections have been used only since 1983, and we don't know a lot about long-term effects. There is some evidence that over time the injections form scar tissue in the penis, making it difficult or even impossible to continue giving them.

• These shots continue to be needed to get erections. It was once thought that many men would regain confidence after a few shots and be able to have erections without them. Unfortunately, this has proven to be true in only a small number of cases.

• Although the risk is small, a few men who inject themselves get priapism, an erection that won't go down. This necessitates a trip to the doctor's office or a hospital emergency room for treatment.

Regarding both vacuum devices and injections, it's well to keep in mind that they can cause some difficulties in the beginning. Most couples, after all, are not accustomed to stopping loveplay in order to do something special to attain erection, and many couples are not accustomed to talking openly about sex. There can be embarrassment, anxiety, and hesitation. One man, for instance, didn't have sex for weeks after he got his injection materials, because he couldn't figure out how to tell his partner that he wanted to go to another room to inject himself. This despite the fact that she had been to the urologist with him and knew full well about the shots. Even though they now have a way to get an erection, some men still feel like failures because they can't get "normal" erections. This feeling makes them hesitant to use their artificial method. Such difficulties can usually be worked out easily if the partners are able to talk openly about their concerns, but in some cases a few sessions with a sex therapist are advisable.

Arterial and venous surgery: There are several types of operations to repair or bypass clogged arteries and to seal leaky veins. I am not going into them in detail here, because as of this writing, the results are not impressive, at least not by my standards. Although the medical literature contains articles by doctors in Europe who claim very high success, the urologists and vascular surgeons I've talked with say they don't get anywhere near these results. This may change in the future, of course, but you should be cautious if your doctor recommends them. Find out what his results have been, especially on long-term follow-up, and insist on talking to several men who've had the operation. You might also want to ask the doctor for references in the medical literature and read the articles about the type of surgery being suggested for you. This reading is rough going, but it may be worth the effort to give you a better idea of what the results might be. Right now the best candidates for arterial surgery are young men whose blood-flow problems stem from trauma such as accidents.

Penile implants: Since as far back as the 1930s, surgeons have been experimenting with ways to produce artificial erections. By now the art of penile implants is highly advanced, and though there are a great many implant models, they can be conveniently put in two groups.

Nonhydraulic (also called semirigid and malleable) implants consist of a pair of silicon rods placed inside the penis. With earlier models, the man always had an erection, and this obviously caused some embarrassment. Newer models are more flexible and can be bent down against the leg. These can still cause embarrassment in locker rooms and public urinals, because the penis is longer than it would be without the silicon rods, but it is easily concealed under clothes.

Hydraulic or inflatable implants come in a variety of styles, but their main distinguishing characteristic is that they mimic the action of a normal erection process. A pair of hollow cylinders is placed inside the erectile tissue of the penis, and when you want to have sex you activate a pumping mechanism, implanted in the scrotum, that inflates the cylinders. Some newer models have the complete mechanism inside the cylinders; when you want an erection, you simply bend or squeeze the head of the penis, and presto—as if by magic—you have an erection.

Hydraulic models have the advantages of seeming more natural, since they mimic what the body does under normal circumstances. The penis is truly soft when it's soft, and only gets hard when you want it to. But hydraulic models are more complex, and the chances of malfunction are greater. They are also more expensive and the surgery more involved.

Surveys show that although many men with implants have some complaints, a large majority of the men and their partners are generally satisfied with the devices.

ADVANTAGES:

• The ability to have a usable erection whenever you want one without having to give yourself shots and without having to go through sex therapy.

• Although implants are expensive (over several thousand dollars), they are covered by many insurance plans.

DISADVANTAGES:

• Implants should be considered irreversible. They can injure or destroy the natural erection system. This will likely mean you can't decide to have an implant taken out and try sex therapy or other treatments.

• The erection produced by an implant is not exactly the same as the ones you had naturally. It is smaller, both in terms of length (as much as an inch or two shorter) and circumference. It is also less rigid, and the head of the penis is softer. This should not be a major problem, because implant erections are certainly rigid enough for vaginal insertion and enjoyable intercourse. However, you need to know that what you get may not look like what you had before.

• Implant surgery can take one to three hours, depending on the kind of implant used, and has the same risks as all surgery. Postoperative pain in the groin typically lasts for four to six weeks, and most patients require medication for pain control during some of that period. The risk of infection is small, but if it does occur after surgery, the implant will need to be temporarily removed.

• Mechanical failure is always a possibility in hydraulic devices. If there is such a failure, further surgery is required. The offending component or the whole device must be removed and replaced.

Since implant surgery may be irreversible, involves the risks of surgery and the possibility of additional surgery to correct malfunctions, and is painful and expensive, it should not be entered into lightly.

Some men have magical expectations of implants, so I want to dispel them right now. An implant at its best will do only one thing: give you a usable erection when you want it. That may be miraculous enough, but some men expect more. An implant will change only the stiffness of your penis, not your personality, behavior, or lovemaking technique. An implant in itself will not make you desire sex more, will not increase your arousal, will not make you a better lover, will not improve sensation or give you a better orgasm, and it most certainly will not save a failing relationship. All these points may seem too obvious to be worth making, but strange things happen with implants. Some men, for example, have had them put in and then never again had sex; some men have had sex only a few times in the years after surgery. Does it make sense to go through all the trouble and pain for something you're not going to use or will use rarely? Make sure you and your partner understand, in both your heads and your guts, exactly what an implant will and will not do for you.

If you have refrained from sex for a long time because of your erection problem, it may be difficult to get started again after the implant is in place. Even though you know you can now get erect, there may be some shyness or hesitation on your part and perhaps your partner's as well. This is especially true if there were bad feelings and ugly words exchanged about not having sex. If this doesn't decrease after a week or two, a few sessions with a sex therapist can help.

Don't forget: An implant is forever (or almost). Make sure you weigh all the options before choosing one.

In considering your options, I think it's sound policy to try the least invasive, least risky, and least expensive alternatives first. For example, since you already have this book, doing the exercises in the next chapter will only cost you some time and energy; and, as far as I know, they have no negative side effects. If you find you don't like doing them or if they don't seem to help, you can consider seeing a sex therapist or choosing an approach discussed in this chapter. But even here it's wise to start with what will cause the least trouble. Vacuum devices are relatively safe, and yohimbine is a close second. While penile injections do have some side effects, they are a much less invasive undertaking than surgery.

Of course, some men don't like the conservative approach I'm recommending because they're in a hurry. They want the problem solved right now, even if they've had it for years and done nothing about it. I have no trouble understanding the impatience—I, too, want all my problems fixed this second—but I've learned it's wise to resist the impulse. With sex problems, as with many of life's difficulties, some degree of patience is a virtue. What's best, I believe, is doing the minimum needed to get you where you want to be, precisely because the minimum involves less complexity and less risk. Instead of thinking of the erection or sex you could have next week or next month, adopt a longer-term perspective. (Actually, even if you decided to get an implant today, it would be more than a month before you could have intercourse.) Think in terms of months rather than weeks, and consider how the alternatives fit your values, your health, and your relationship. And keep in mind that you can always escalate if the method you start with doesn't live up to your expectations.

24

Resolving Erection Problems with Sex Therapy

"Until last year, my penis was always there for me, and I never had to ask what I liked or wanted. Now I find I don't have the foggiest idea of what I like and I feel very stupid, like a kid who doesn't know the answer to a simple question."—MAN, 56

"Although several urologists have assured me there's nothing wrong physically, my penis has always given me trouble. In every new relationship, it's taken me several months before I could have reliable erections. And whenever there's stress because of work, the relationship, or anything else, my penis fails to cooperate."—MAN, 40

"This business of focusing on arousal, sensation, and pleasure is very different from my whole life's experience. All I ever knew and did was perform. Having a good time almost goes against the grain. But I'm getting used to it and have to say there are some good parts to it."—MAN, 43

IF there's no physical reason for your erection problem, the main difficulty may well be in how you think your penis *should* function. A great many men uncritically accept the superhuman standards and myths about penises, then get upset when they discover they are merely human.

456

A married man of thirty-nine called early one morning and virtually demanded an immediate appointment. When he arrived, it was obvious he was in a panic. While still standing at the door to the building, he started talking with great emotion about his "impotence" and his need to know whether he needed a penile implant. I finally got him into my office, but couldn't get a word in for fifteen minutes. After he calmed down a bit and I was able to ask some questions, it turned out that the impotence consisted solely of a failure to have an erection with his wife the night before. Then, in response to my question of how last night had differed from other times he had sex with her, he began to sob. Yesterday, with no warning at all, he had lost the job he had held for fourteen years and that meant the world to him. After wiping his eyes and making an obvious attempt to pull himself together, he smiled weakly and said without a trace of humor, "Other than that, everything was as usual. I just don't understand it." It hadn't occurred to him that his feelings about being fired might have affected his sexual functioning.

Nonmedical erection problems are almost always due to one or more of the following: unrealistic expectations, lack of arousal, absence of the proper conditions, and the anxiety generated by the need for an erection.

• A sixty-year-old man getting upset because his penis doesn't jump to attention when he kisses his partner. He's not taking into account that a sixty-year-old penis differs from a twenty-year-old one and that he's not getting the direct penile stimulation he now requires.

• A man who expects an erection even though he isn't feeling aroused. He just expects his penis to function regardless of how he feels, as if his penis had nothing to do with the rest of him.

• A man who is very tense during sex. He's been criticized by his partner for his "failure to perform" in the past, and he's anticipating more criticism. Because of the way men have been trained, it doesn't occur to him to ask how anyone could get an erection in that situation.

If you are tense or anxious, if you are angry at your partner, if you aren't getting the physical and emotional stimulation you like, if you aren't turned on, if you are preoccupied with other matters—if any of these things are true, what makes you think you should have an erection? The answer, of course, is our sexual conditioning, the nonsense I discussed in Chapter 2.

Recall the example in Chapter 21 of Bud and Art, of how they think differently about sex. If you're having erection difficulties and there's nothing physically wrong, chances are good you're behaving like Art. That is, you're worried about sex even before it begins, you're focusing on how your penis is doing rather than on what you feel.

In order to resolve an erection problem, you need to start thinking and acting less like Art and more like Bud. I know this isn't easy—in fact, at this moment it may seem impossible—but it's necessary and can be done. You need to look forward to sex with positive anticipation, focus on the pleasurable sensations, accurately judge the signs of increasing arousal, and allow them to increase arousal and erection. Another way of saying this is that you need to stop being distracted by negative images and thoughts and to get more focused on the joys, pleasures, and positive cues.

To increase your sexual pleasure and improve your erections, stop stacking the deck against yourself and start stacking it on your side. This means getting your mind on your side; meeting your conditions for good sex; having sex only when you are aroused; and decreasing your anxiety.

I. MIND POWER FOR BETTER ERECTIONS

To derive maximum benefit from sexual activity, you need to get your mind working with you. Men like Art who have had erection difficulties tend to say negative things to themselves and to think of themselves as sexual flops. They run movies in their heads of losing their erections and tend to ruminate over past failures. This is, for sure, a reflection of reality, but it also becomes a generator of anxiety, a predictor of future behavior, and a reinforcer of a self-image you want to change. It will be easier to change your behavior if you also change your view of yourself.

Starting as soon as possible, you need to imagine yourself as you'd like to be as much as possible and spend as little time as possible imagining how you've been. You are going to apply some of the information and suggestions contained in Chapter 21. If you haven't read that chapter and digested its contents, now would be a good time to do so. The following exercises are similar to the ones for rapid ejaculators given in Chapter 22.

Mind Power A: Whenever you're aware of telling yourself that you're impotent or inadequate, or having an image that embodies that idea, argue with it and change it. For example: "It's true, I've had troubles getting it up for the last few months. But I'm going to do this program and change that. I'm going to have good erections again." When you picture yourself not getting or losing an erection, tell yourself "that was then" and follow this with an image of having a good, long-lasting erection accompanied by words like "that's the way it's going to be."

Mind Power B: This is an image, really more like a movie, that you should spend thirty to ninety seconds on every day; doing it several times a day is even better. Imagine yourself having good erections with a partner, which includes several components. Imagine having a good erection, entering your partner, feeling relaxed and comfortable, and just being still inside her for a moment or two. No movement, just enjoying being in her. Then imagine slow movements, just taking it easy, still enjoying the feeling of being in her. Then gradually increase the pace of your thrusts. Now slow down again. Now again increase the pace gradually, until you're moving almost as much as you want, still feeling calm and easy. Now imagine slowing down and stopping all movement. Stop thrusting and just experience the pleasure. Then gradually increase the movements, slowly building up until you're moving with abandon, letting your body do what it wants. When you want, and only when you want, imagine a wonderful ejaculation. When you're done with the movie, be sure to end with a statement to yourself of this kind: "As it is in my mind, so it shall be in reality" or "This is how it's going to be."

Mind Power C: Before you do a physical exercise, spend a few seconds imagining yourself doing it perfectly, exactly as it is supposed to be done. Be sure to imagine all the parts: for example, asking your partner to participate, attending to your arousal and physical sensations, asking her to stop if you get anxious, asking her to resume stimulation, and so on.

This mental rehearsal takes only a few seconds and can be very helpful. It's exactly what many great athletes, entertainers, and businesspeople do to improve their performances. You can do it anyplace. For example, if you and your partner are getting ready to do an exercise, you can close your eyes and do your mental rehearsal right there or you can go into another room and take a few seconds to do it there.

Mind Power D: Every day, preferably just after awakening or just before retiring for the night, take a few seconds to imagine how good you're going to feel once your erections are back on track.

Mind Power E: Whenever the problem recurs, make every effort not to let it get you down. Instead of telling yourself that this is further proof you'll never get it together, ask yourself what you can learn from this experience. Maybe you were too anxious, too tired, too much in a hurry, too little aroused. Then tell yourself something like this: "No reason to get upset. I learned that it doesn't work to have sex when I'm this anxious and tired. Next time I'm this nervous, I'll stop and just talk to Jeannie about what's going on."

Mind Power F: This is the pep-talk exercise given in Chapter 21, on pages 405–407. Use it whenever you feel discouraged or that you failed in an exercise.

II. MEETING YOUR CONDITIONS

You should now turn to and read Chapter 6 to determine the conditions you need to have met for having more or better erections. Consider your desire, arousal, anxiety, mental and physical stimulation, time of day, the state of your relationship, your partner's attitude and behavior, and anything else that seems relevant. Some men need for their partners to be more enthusiastic or aroused. Others need to be less preoccupied and more focused on matters at hand when they have sex.

There are only two important considerations about your conditions:

finding out what they are and fulfilling them. You are who you are and you need what you need. Make sure you get it.

III. INCREASING AROUSAL

As I said in Chapter 16, arousal is basically what powers erections. If there's nothing seriously wrong with you physically, if you are relatively relaxed, if your conditions are met, and if you are aroused, you will get good erections. Since arousal is crucial, you should read or reread Chapter 16 before going on.

Pay particular attention to what I say about focusing on sensation in that chapter. One of the major ways of increasing arousal is to focus on physical sensation, to attend to and fully experience your partner touching, kissing, caressing, and stroking you. Another way of increasing arousal is to ensure that you get the kinds of stimulation that are most arousing to you.

IV. REDUCING ANXIETY ABOUT PERFORMANCE

Since worrying about how your penis will perform is perhaps the major obstacle to good functioning, anything that reduces this worry is helpful. All the methods discussed above play a role in this endeavor, but there are several other things that can help as well.

Since intercourse is the act that causes the greatest anxiety for men with erection problems, *it's best to agree not to have intercourse until you are confident of your erections.* Talk to your partner about this ban on intercourse and see if she can accept it. But this by no means implies no sex. You'll be engaging in lots of enjoyable sexual activity until then.

If you have experience with any relaxation method—meditation, biofeedback, self-hypnosis, yoga, relaxation tapes—I suggest you resume that activity as soon as possible. If you've never done any of these things, you might want to invest in a good relaxation audiotape, many of which are available in bookstores, and listen for ten to fifteen minutes twice each day. Whatever method you use, your goal should be to be able to get relaxed quickly in almost any situation, without special equipment or postures.

JUST PLAY

One effective approach to resolving erection problems involves no exercises beyond those already given. To follow this approach, you do steps I through IV above, and get together with your partner to play sexually as often as both of you desire. You can do whatever you want except have intercourse. When she's stimulating you, you should focus on sensation and try to build excitement as high as possible. Arousal and pleasure, not erection, are the only goals. And that's all there is to it.

This approach is so simple that some men have trouble with it. It seems too easy to them. It *is* simple and easy, but it's also effective.

It will help to keep a few things in mind. One is that the goal really is pleasure and arousal. You will of course note how your penis is doing, but try not to get concerned if it's not acting as you would like. It will in time. Be sure that all your conditions are met, that you have the best stimulation, and that you focus on the pleasurable physical stimulation.

If this approach doesn't work, you may want to do some of the exercises given below.

Which Exercises You Should Do

Everyone should do the mind-power exercises and the two masturbation exercises that follow. If you think you don't need to do the masturbation, it's a good idea to do each of them once just to make sure you can easily and comfortably handle them. If you don't want to masturbate, you can skip those exercises and start with the first partner exercise.

How Often to Do the Exercises

Good results can be achieved by doing the exercises anywhere from every other day to once or twice a week. Masters and Johnson noticed two things about penises that work against doing the exercises as often as you want. The first is what they called a refractory period, a time after ejaculation when your penis will not respond to stimulation no matter how skillfully done and no matter how long it lasts. For many teenagers the refractory period lasts only a few minutes. But it definitely increases with age. Some men in their fifties and sixties can't get another erection until days after their last ejaculation. Masters and Johnson also noticed that many older men can't regain an erection for a day or more after sex even if they don't ejaculate. Take account of these facts in deciding how often to do the exercises.

It is essential that you do the exercises only when you are relaxed and feeling sexy, or believe you can get into a sexy mood with a little time and stimulation. Doing the exercises when feeling under pressure or with gritted teeth will not help at all.

What About Ejaculating While Doing the Exercises?

In general, the less you ejaculate the more easily you will become aroused and perhaps erect the next time you do an exercise. This does not mean you should never ejaculate, only that it is in your interest not to ejaculate unless you really want to.

What About Having Intercourse While Doing the Exercises?

Many men with erection problems develop an understandable but destructive habit. As soon as they notice they have an erection—whether they are engaged in loveplay or not, whether they are doing an exercise or not—they automatically try to stick it in their partners before it goes away. Although this sometimes results in a few thrusts or minutes of intercourse, it usually doesn't because the mind/body tends to interpret the frantic effort to stick it in as anxiety, which it is. This stick-it-in-before-you-lose-it practice causes all sorts of problems. It usually results in lost erections, which makes the man feel more hopeless, and it reinforces the idea that he has a serious problem. It does nothing to alleviate the anxiety that is a large part of the problem to begin with. And it often makes the man's partner upset or angry, because in entering her so frantically he may not notice that she's not ready or interested at the moment.

One woman's account of what happened one morning when she was still asleep is telling:

I was in a rage, but now it seems incredibly funny. I awoke with this horrible pushing feeling inside of my vagina. It took me a few seconds to comprehend what was happening. Frank was behind me trying to shove his cock in me. He didn't even notice that I had a tampon in and his penis was pushing it further into me. I shrieked and fought him off. After an hour or so of yelling and arguing, we finally were able to talk. Turned out that he's been feeling so frustrated because of his lack of erections that when he woke up with one all he could think of was to get it in me. Incredible that he wasn't even aware of the tampon as he pushed against it.

Whether you're with a new partner or an old one, whether you're doing exercises or not, please do not try to put your penis anyplace. Frantic movements will do nothing to help. Anything based on anxiety will only cause more trouble.

WHAT IF YOU DON'T HAVE A REGULAR SEX PARTNER?

If you don't have a partner with whom to do the couples exercises, you should attend to steps I through IV given above and do the two mastur-bation exercises below. When you do get into a relationship, follow the advice about getting into sex very slowly, as per the discussion in Chapter 17. Also consider the discussion in that chapter about telling your partner about your problem. Then, as you desire it, just play as discussed on page 462. If it seems necessary, you can also do the partner exercises in this chapter with your new friend. An alternative is to go through the surrogate therapy discussed later in this chapter before you enter a new relationship.

MASTURBATION EXERCISES FOR BETTER ERECTIONS

If you're willing to masturbate, I recommend doing these masturbation exercises before you begin working with your partner. If you're not willing to masturbate and have a partner, you can begin with the first partner exercise.

EXERCISE 24–1: PLEASURING YOUR SOFT PENIS

Time Required: 15 minutes

The goal is to get comfortable with touching your soft penis and learn what kinds of sensations that produces. Put some lubricant on one or both of your hands and touch your penis in ways that feel arousing. Try different kinds of touches and strokes. You want to focus on the sensations and feel as sexy as possible, but you don't need an erection. In fact, an erection will only get in the way. Don't try not to get hard, just follow the instructions already given. If you find your penis getting hard, just pay attention to the sensations as it does so. But when it's reached what you consider to be about 50 to 80 percent of fullness and rigidity, stop touching it. Enjoy looking at it and let it go down. The session is over for you.

Repeat this exercise two or three times, until you feel comfortable touching your nonerect penis and feel that you've improved your ability to focus on the sensations in your penis.

EXERCISE 24–2: LOSING AND REGAINING ERECTIONS

Time Required: 15 minutes

Stroke your penis with a lubricated hand and focus either on the sensations produced or on an exciting fantasy. When you have an erection, enjoy it for a moment and then stop stimulation. Take your hand away from your penis and let your erection subside completely, which may take from a few seconds to a few minutes. When your penis is soft, resume stimulation and focus on sensation or fantasy. Most of the time your erection will return, in which case you should again stop and let it get soft. Two complete cycles of this sequence—stimulation, erection, stopping, losing erection, stimulation—are sufficient for one session.

If your erection does not return within a few minutes after resuming stimulation, ask if there is anything you can do to get into a more relaxed and more arousing frame of mind. Taking a few deep breaths or looking at some stimulating pictures may help. If the changes you make result in erection, just continue with the exercise. If not, call it quits for now and return to the exercise another time. Whatever you do, don't try to force an erection.

This exercise should be repeated as many times as necessary, with at least one day's rest between repetitions, until you are reasonably confident that an erection can often be regained by proper mental and physical stimulation.

PARTNER EXERCISES

Before starting on the partner exercises, it's a good idea to do Step A of Exercise 14–1 (nongenital body-rubs) in Chapter 14. This will give you some useful experience before you get to genital stimulation in the following exercises.

Exercises 24–3 and 24–4 may surprise you, because in both of them you are asked not to have an erection. You may wonder why after all the travail not having erections has caused you I would be asking you to again not have an erection. My answer is simple. After working with hundreds of men with erection problems, I realized that two of their greatest fears are their partner touching their soft penis (she'll notice I'm still not hard) and losing an erection (here we go again). As long as these fears are unaddressed, they remain in the background or foreground and get in the way of serious progress. Once they are addressed, on the other hand, the other exercises tend to be much easier and proceed more smoothly. Exercises 24–3 and 24–4 are ways of directly dealing with these fears and putting them to rest. Despite what I've said, after reading them you may be tempted to skip them and go to Exercise 24–5. Do what's necessary to resist this temptation.

EXERCISE 24–3: NOT GETTING OR LOSING YOUR ERECTION

Time Required: 5 to 20 minutes

You are to do two things: reenact your old erection problem and handle it differently than you usually did. If your problem was that you did not get an erection while your partner stimulated you, then have her stimulate you and see to it that you don't get an erection. If your problem was getting soft during intercourse, then have intercourse and make your erection go away. Whatever the old problem, re-create it.

There are many ways to not get or to lose an erection. Distracting yourself from the pleasurable stimulation by worrying about a myriad of things can help—anything from whether you'll get or keep hard to whether the kids are listening to how much money the IRS will want from you this year—is probably the best way. Negative thinking about what a terrible lover you are can also help.

After you've managed not to get hard or to lose your erection, deal with the situation in ways that are enhancing to both you and your partner. Acknowledge what's happened but don't apologize. Instead, offer something that sounds good. Here is an example: "I don't think I can get hard again, but I'd love to love you. Anything interest you?" When the two of you agree on something, do it. It can be sexual or not. The only important thing is that you both feel good about yourselves, each other, and what you do.

Repeat this exercise as many times as necessary for you to feel comfortable about losing your erection and dealing with the situation after that. Some men find one or two repetitions sufficient; others can benefit from many more.

Exercise 24–4 is designed to help you feel more comfortable about having your partner touch your unerect penis. Many men are horrified at the prospect. They believe they should be hard before she touches it or, at the very least, should get hard as soon as she touches it. After all, that's the way a real man is. That's the fantasy. The realities are somewhat different. Being comfortable while your unerect penis is being touched is very important. It allows you to enjoy stimulation that might get you erect. Even if you don't get hard, it can still feel very good. The more comfortable you are with her touching your soft penis, the better all the following exercises will go.

EXERCISE 24–4: PARTNER PLAYING WITH YOUR SOFT PENIS

Time Required: 15 to 20 minutes

After making sure you are both in a comfortable position, let your partner play with your soft penis. Try not to get an erection; you want the experience of being touched when soft. If you do get hard, stop for a while until your penis gets soft again, then have your partner resume.

She can explore, caress, stroke, and just generally play with your penis in any ways she wants. Don't let her do anything that's painful or uncomfortable, but, aside from that, keep your hands to yourself and your attention on the sensations produced. Be aware of what it feels like to be touched by her.

Do this exercise at least two or three times, until you are quite comfortable with her touching you when you're soft.

POSSIBLE PROBLEM

You find yourself trying to get an erection or feeling bad because you don't have one. Given what men are taught, this is natural. Use your mind-power techniques to turn negative thoughts and images into positive ones, and resist the temptation to try to get hard. Talking to your partner about the feelings you're having can be very helpful. And keep in mind that you have to keep your penis soft to derive benefit from the exercise. Having an erection interferes with this goal.

The next exercise is optional. It can be very helpful, but should only be done if your partner agrees to it and doesn't feel pressured to perform.

EXERCISE 24–5: SEXY BODY-RUB WITHOUT TOUCHING GENITALS

Time Required: 15 to 20 minutes

Have your partner try to arouse you by touching your body, *but not including your genitals*, with her hands, mouth, hair, or anything else. She can be as creative as she likes and you can give feedback and suggestions.

Your job is to once again focus on the sensations and see what feelings develop. If a sexy feeling develops, follow its progress, then return to focus on sensation. If a positive sexual fantasy appears, feel free to go with it for as long as you want.

If any negative thoughts or images appear, change them into more positive ones.

Do this exercise as many times as you want until you're comfortable focusing on physical sensations and able to bring your mind back easily after it wanders.

EXERCISE 24–6: PARTNER STIMULATION OF PENIS

Time Required: 15 minutes

This time your partner is to touch and stroke your genitals, with a lubricated hand, as you direct her. It's the same as the regular body rub but focused on genitals. Some men prefer to do some touching and kissing before getting to penile stimulation, while others prefer getting to genital stimulation right away. Do whatever feels right to you and your partner.

The goal is to get you as turned on as possible. Arousal, not erection, is what we're interested in. If you get an erection, that's fine, but no finer than if you don't. But if you do get one, don't try to stick it anyplace. Just continue with the exercise.

As in the previous exercises, your job is to focus on sensation and to get as aroused as possible. Give her feedback and directions, using words that turn you on. As you get excited, pay attention to the feelings and feel free to follow them through your body. A feeling may develop in your penis and then you notice differences in the way your chest and stomach feel. Go with these cues of arousal as long as you like. If sexual images or ideas appear, feel free to go with them.

As usual, deal with negative thought and images as per the discussion on pages 397–401.

You can touch your partner, *but only for your own pleasure*. You are not to try to turn her on during the exercise. This is difficult for many men, because they are used to being active and because they want to pay back their partner for the work she's doing and the pleasure she's giving. If it would increase your own excitement to touch her breasts while she stimulates your genitals, it's fine, but touching her breasts only in ways that excite *you*. If you realize you're trying to excite her, change the kind of touching you're doing or stop it altogether.

If you do get aroused and do focus on your sensations, you will probably get an erection some of the time. You can ejaculate, but only if you really want to.

Men vary tremendously in how many times they need to do this exercise. It can be anywhere from three to twenty times, depending on how much time it takes to feel comfortable with it, to get good at focusing on sensation and refocusing when the mind wanders, to turn negative thoughts and images into positive ones, and to be able to give directions to get the best possible stimulation.

POSSIBLE PROBLEMS

You never get an erection in this exercise, or never keep it for long, even after a number of repetitions. Sometimes the problem is obvious. You can't get your partner to stimulate you the way you like, you can't focus on sensation, negative thoughts keep intruding, and so on. If none of these is true, you might want to go on to the next exercise, particularly if you like oral stimulation. If, on the other hand, one of these causes is manifest, you need to determine how to resolve it. Going back and redoing one or more of the earlier exercises may help.

If you usually get erections in masturbation but not with this exercise, there's something in the relationship that's getting in the way. Ask what it would take for you to be able to have an erection with your partner. What issues, attitudes, or behaviors would have to be resolved or changed? See if you can work them out. If not, you may need to seek professional help.

If you respond neither to masturbation nor this exercise, you should definitely see a competent urologist or sex therapist.

If you're like many of the men I've worked with, you are now convinced that things aren't as bad as you had imagined. You may, in fact, think that everything is fine and be in a hurry to get to intercourse. I hope you're willing to resist that temptation for now.

The next exercise is optional. It can be helpful, but not all women are willing to do it. You and your partner need to read and discuss it. If she isn't willing to do it, don't push her. Perhaps, as your sex life becomes more satisfying, she'll be willing to try oral sex.

EXERCISE 24–7: ORAL STIMULATION OF PENIS

Time Required: 15 minutes
This exercise is identical to the preceding one except that now your partner stimulates you with her mouth rather than her hand. Be sure you both assume comfortable positions. Resist the temptation to stimulate her orally at the same time.

The next exercise, like Exercise 24–4, deals with the fear of losing an erection, but it also goes further in demonstrating that lost erections can often be regained, an important lesson for you to learn. Losing an erection is not a catastrophe. If you keep your cool, you can probably regain it. And if not, that's not a tragedy either.

EXERCISE 24-8: LOSING AND REGAINING ERECTIONS

Time Required: 15 to 20 minutes

Have your partner stimulate your penis with her hand or mouth in ways that you like. Your goal, as always, is to attend to the sensations and get as aroused as possible. When you have an erection, enjoy it for a moment, then tell her to stop and allow your erection to go down. You can do anything you want to accomplish this—have a talk, give her a back-rub or a sexual massage, or whatever. Take as much time as you need for your penis to get soft. Then have her resume stimulation. When it gets hard again, repeat the procedure given above. Two or three repetitions of the whole procedure—stimulation, erection, stop stimulation, erection fades, resume stimulation—constitute one session.

You will not always regain your erection and you will not always get one to begin with. When either of these things happens, let her know: ("I guess it's not going to get hard today. I'd like you to stop"). Then talk with her about what the two of you want to do that would be enjoyable. Maybe she'd like you to sexually stimulate her. Maybe one of you wants a back-rub. Maybe you'd both like to talk. Whatever it is, do it.

It's crucial that you master this step. You can be sure your penis will not always respond the way you want. You need to feel comfortable letting your partner know that and talking with her about how to have a good time without an erection.

Do this exercise at least four times, until you are confident that your erection will usually return with proper stimulation and that, when it doesn't, you can still have a good time.

POSSIBLE PROBLEMS

1. You never get an erection. This usually means you haven't yet mastered the previous exercises. Go back to the ones you skipped and do them.

2. Your erection doesn't go down in a reasonable length of time. This isn't a bad problem to have, but it does increase the amount of time it takes to do the exercise. Check to see if what you're doing while waiting

for it to get soft is arousing. If it is, do something else. Getting up and walking around the room or the house will usually do the trick if all else fails.

3. Your erection, once lost, doesn't return in a reasonable length of time. The problem often lies in anxiety about getting it back. In other words, you're forgetting some of the lessons you've learned in this chapter. You might want to reread it and mentally mark the important passages. Try to remember that you don't have to do anything to make your penis hard. It will take care of that itself as long as you focus on sensations
or arousing thoughts or images and build arousal. It might also help to talk to your partner about any concerns you have about regaining the erection.

The exercises that follow require some kind of erection, so care must be taken not to create anxiety or pressure to perform. You can use spontaneous erections or those that occur in loveplay. Say you want to do an exercise and you ask your partner to stimulate you in ways you like. If you get a good erection (meaning one you feel good about, even though it's not 100 percent hard), feel free to go on to the exercise. If you don't get an erection in what seems a reasonable length of time, or if the erection you do get doesn't seem stable, don't try to force it. Do something enjoyable with your partner, sexual or not, and let it be.

These exercises also require that your partner's vagina be well lubricated. Talk with her about whether an artificial lubricant such as KY jelly or Albolene would be helpful.

EXERCISE 24–9: GRADUAL INSERTION INTO VAGINA

Time Required: Usually less than 5 minutes

Using a position that is comfortable for both of you, you are to gradually insert your penis, in stages, into her vagina. First place your erect penis just at the opening of her vagina. Take a few seconds to get used to having it there. When that feels comfortable, move it in a little bit, about an inch. Again, take a few seconds to get used to the feeling. Continue in this fashion until your whole penis is inside of her. Then stay that way for a few minutes and focus on the sensations in your penis. See how it feels to have your penis surrounded by her vagina. Be aware of the texture, temperature, and wetness of the vagina. Get used to being there; it's a nice place.

If at any time you feel your erection start to go down, stay focused and see if you can enjoy the sensations of your erection going down.

If you want to ejaculate after a few moments and it's OK with her, do so, but move slowly and be aware of what's happening to you.

You can proceed to the next exercise when you are comfortable being inside of your partner and can keep your erection for a minute or so without movement.

Now we're going to extend your ability to be inside her with movement. The position usually recommended for these exercises is you lying on your back and her sitting on top of you; this allows you to fully relax, letting the bed support your weight so you don't have to flex any muscles, and works well for many couples. But others prefer something else. So use any position that works best for you; just remember that it has to be sufficiently comfortable for both of you so that changes in it aren't necessary for five to ten minutes.

EXERCISE 24–10: PENIS IN VAGINA WITH MOVEMENT

Time Required: 15 minutes

Step A: This is similar to the previous exercise, except that now one of you thrusts slowly. Which one moves largely depends on the position you're using. If she's on top, she'll do the moving. If you're on top, it will be you. Regardless of what position is used and who moves, you have to be in charge of how much movement and when to stop and resume thrusting. Your job is to focus on sensations and get as aroused as possible. It's important that your partner *not* start thrusting to satisfy herself. That will come later.

Start with a very slow pace. Make sure you're comfortable with it before increasing movement. Then go a little faster. When that feels fine, no anxiety or negative thoughts, increase the pace again.

Continue with this step until the active one is moving at a pretty good pace but not all-out, say about 80 percent of abandoned movement. This will probably *not* be achieved in one 15 minute session. Use as many sessions as you need. Then do Step B.

Step B: The same as Step A, with the other one moving. This may well require a different position.

Step C: The same as the two previous steps, except both of you move. Start with very slow movements and only increase the pace as you feel comfortable. Use as many sessions as required until you are both moving as fast as you desire.

POSSIBLE PROBLEM WITH ANY OF THE STEPS

You lose your erection during intercourse. This happens occasionally to most men, but there are some things to try if you feel it's really a problem. Make sure you are relaxed; if you're not, take some deep breaths and have some positive thoughts and images. If your penis is still in her vagina, you can leave it there and try to get the stimulation you want: moving in certain ways or having your partner squeeze her pelvic muscles may do the trick. Or you can take your penis out and get the kind of stimulation you want, resuming intercourse when you are hard.

If you find that you usually lose your erection at a particular point— say, when your partner is thrusting very quickly—here's something you can do. When you are alone, take a few moments to get relaxed and imagine her moving slowly in intercourse. Continue to relax and imagine her moving a tad faster. Continue in this fashion—relaxing and then imagining her moving at increasingly faster speeds—until you can calmly imagine her moving at full speed. Then do the same thing for real with your partner. Relax and have her move slowly in intercourse. Check to see that you're still relaxed and, if so, have her increase the pace. If at some point you find you are getting tense, get her to slow down immediately to a speed you're comfortable with. Then, in very small steps, have her increase the pace. Always back away from speeds that make you tense and go back to those you are comfortable with. Done consistently, this procedure will allow you to tolerate and enjoy more and more movement.

By fulfilling your conditions, by having sex only when you desire it and are aroused, by making sure you are relaxed, and by getting the kinds of stimulation you like, you are ensuring that your penis will function most of the time you want it to. And when it doesn't meet your expectations or when an erection goes away at an inopportune moment, you no longer have to worry about it. You are prepared to have a good time no matter what your penis does.

As time goes on and your sexual confidence continues to develop, you will not need to be as careful about your conditions. Just don't forget about them altogether. If you should find yourself backsliding, if you notice you're tense in sex, or find that sex isn't as satisfying as it is now, give more attention to conditions, arousal, relaxation, and stimulation, and it probably won't be too long before the situation improves again.

SURROGATE THERAPY

For men who don't have a sex partner but do have a sex problem, perhaps the most effective and certainly the most controversial treatment is what's called surrogate therapy. The word *surrogate*, which means substitute, was chosen by Masters and Johnson to refer to a woman employee who did the sexual exercises that ordinarily a man would do with his partner.

Despite widespread media publicity about surrogate therapy, there is still much confusion about what it is. Some people think that a surrogate is nothing more than a prostitute, because she has sex for money. It's true that surrogates—just like therapists, lawyers, and physicians—like to get paid for their work. But the similarity ends there. A prostitute's goal is to give her customers a good time and get them off, usually as quickly as possible.

A surrogate's role is different. Her job is to teach clients skills they need to be more effective socially and sexually. Reputable surrogates work with therapists—that is, the client has a session with the surrogate and then goes to see the therapist, with or without the surrogate—and function more like the therapist's associate or assistant rather than as a wife substitute. The surrogate's goal is not getting the man off or giving him a good time. Rather, it is therapeutic, helping to diagnose and treat his problem.

A lot of the time the man spends with the surrogate is devoted to talking, which in itself is different than what happens with a prostitute. Talking usually takes up most of the first session, followed by a relaxation exercise or two and perhaps some light touching with both surrogate and client fully dressed. In subsequent sessions, there is a progression to nudity, communication exercises, sensual touching, and finally more direct sexual activity. The physical/sexual activities they engage in, often called body-work, are similar to the partner exercises given in this book. Depending on the surrogate, the therapist, and the nature of the problem, there may or may not be much intercourse. In almost all cases, the surrogate spends a great deal of time helping the client learn ways to reduce the anxiety he feels in sex and increase his confidence.

Surrogate therapy at its best involves the therapist and surrogate working together toward a common goal, with each contributing his or her own strengths. For example, the surrogate may tell me that our client is fine with sexplay as long as there's no thought of intercourse. When intercourse is a possibility, he immediately tenses up and loses his erection. To help prepare him for intercourse, I may do some relaxation work with him, pairing relaxation with scenes of moving toward intercourse. What I do with him in his imagination, she does in reality.

The main advantage of surrogate therapy is that it is highly effective. Although little research has been done on this treatment, the therapists I know who do it agree with me that it is the most effective therapy for men without regular sex partners. It has been almost 100 percent effective with male virgins of all ages. Usually these men have already failed with several women and have felt so humiliated that they refuse to try again until they feel their problem is resolved.

Some people assume that even if surrogate work helps a client function with the surrogate, it won't carry over to other partners. Fortunately, this assumption doesn't seem to be true. The surrogates I've worked with and I are very much aware of the issue and direct our efforts to resolving it. We would view it as an unmitigated failure if a man could function with the surrogate but not with real-life partners. So we always focus on the partner(s) he doesn't yet have. Say a client is able to do something today with the surrogate that he's never been able to do before. When we ask him why, he usually gives credit to the surrogate: "She made me feel so relaxed (or confident) by saying X or doing Y." Then we ask the crucial question: Suppose you're with a woman who doesn't say X or do Y? What could you do to feel as relaxed (or confident)? And then we work on what he needs to be able to do, often involving role-playing with the surrogate and the therapist. In the many cases I've worked with, the ability to function as well with a real-life partner as with a surrogate is over 90 percent.

Surrogate treatment also has some disadvantages. First, it is applicable only for a small segment of the population: those men with sex problems who don't have a regular sex partner and who probably won't find one until their problem is resolved. Second, it is expensive, because two people are being paid. Surrogates generally charge less per hour than therapists, but their sessions are longer, usually two hours. Third, this kind of therapy is not widely available. As far as I know, the main— perhaps the only—places to find it are the major metropolitan centers, especially New York, Los Angeles, and San Francisco. My surrogate and I have had clients from all over the country and from abroad come to us for treatment because it wasn't available closer to home. Men living elsewhere may have to consider coming to one of these cities for two weeks or so of intensive surrogate therapy, which of course involves the additional expenses of travel and lodging.

An important question has to do with sexually transmitted diseases. After all, surrogates have sex with many partners and they seem like prime candidates for contracting one or more of the many common diseases. The fear of spreading or getting AIDS, or of being sued for transmitting it, has caused some therapists who work with surrogates to stop doing surrogate therapy.

I cannot speak for all surrogates, but the ones I have worked with are extremely careful about disease and were this way before the advent of AIDS. As far as I know, not one has ever had any sexually transmitted disease. The surrogate I now work with gets an HIV antibody test every six months and demands two negative test results from every new client. Safe sex is the name of the game, and it is played compulsively. Clients learn just about everything there is to learn about condoms and spermicides.

If you're interested in this kind of therapy, I have a few suggestions:

1. Work only with a surrogate-therapist team, not a surrogate alone. You see both of them and they keep in touch about you. The therapist is crucial: Surrogates are trained in sexuality and surrogate work, but they are not trained psychotherapists. Besides, as many surrogates will be the first to admit, it's often hard to be objective when you're doing body-work with someone. Some therapists refer clients to surrogates and then have nothing further to do with the case. I do not recommend this practice. Both client and surrogate need support and assistance from an experienced therapist.

2. Before making any appointments, ask about safe sex practices and proof that the surrogate has had a recent negative HIV antibody test. If

the surrogate and therapist don't seem concerned about safe sex, if she won't provide the proof, or if she doesn't require similar proof from you, stay away.

3. Work only with a surrogate who respects who you are. Good surrogate work, like any good therapy, requires an understanding of and respect for you and your problem. It should begin where you are and gradually take you to where you want to go. It should not ask you to do what you can't do and it should not humiliate or terrify you. I have heard a number of horror stories over the years about surrogates who work alone. One of them asked a very anxious man with erection problems to undress and masturbate in front of her—after he had known her only half an hour! If he could do that, he wouldn't have needed her help. The only effects were to further embarrass and humiliate him and to convince him that he would never get better.

4. Feel free to bring up any complaints or problems with the surrogate and the therapist. Years ago, a man told me about a difficult session he had just had with the surrogate. In trying to determine what went wrong, we finally hit upon the temperature at her place. He said it was as hot as a sauna and he had felt totally depleted. When I asked why he didn't ask her to turn down the heat or open a window, he answered, "I thought the heat was part of the program." Don't make the same mistake. Anything that bothers you or that makes you uncomfortable should be expressed as soon as possible. This is also good training for what you need to be able to do with your own partners: express what's on your mind.

Since surrogate therapy is expensive ($1,000 is probably the minimum, and it can go as high as $10,000 for a full course of therapy), I recommend trying other treatment options first—for example, the exercises in this book relevant to your problem. If you make some progress but not as much as you want, you can see a surrogate later; the work you've done on your own will probably decrease the number of sessions you'll need with her.

Problems of Sexual Desire and Activity

"I don't know what to do about my girlfriend. I love her and we get along fine, but her idea of good sex is once, maybe twice, a week. I can't survive on such a meager quota."—MAN, 27

"I feel like shit. I just don't want to make love to my wife. She feels ugly and thinks I'm having an affair, which I'm not, and I feel guilty and awful. Why can't I get turned on to her anymore?"—MAN, 44

THE scope of sex therapy as put forth by Masters and Johnson in 1970 included only what were considered functional problems. For men, this meant erection and ejaculation complaints. But sex therapists soon started hearing about a different kind of difficulty, this one having to do with "my partner wants too much (or too little) sex." Michael, for instance, is upset with his lover because "she rarely wants sex. I go around angry at her and horny all the time." Barny, on the other hand, is upset with his lover because "she's always hounding me for sex. It's gotten so I'm almost afraid to come home." Edward and Janet are both upset because they rarely have sex even though they both miss and want it. "It's just that we're too busy and too tired; when one of us is in the mood, the other either isn't or is already asleep."

479

These kinds of problems, having to do with sexual appetite and activity, have become the most common issues brought to sex therapists in recent years. When you first hear about them, they sound easy to resolve. Surely Michael could just make do with less sex than he's used to and Barny could interest himself a little more often in order to make his wife happier. And certainly Edward and Janet could set aside a time each week when they'd both be awake and interested in making love. Of course, some people do come up with these solutions on their own and make them work. Unfortunately, desire problems are often more complex than they seem on the surface and many people cannot work them out on their own. Their egos are involved, their feelings are hurt, and they find it difficult to even discuss the issues constructively with their partners, let alone make any changes. Yet with goodwill and some understanding of the kinds of things that might make one person want more or less sex, most of these complaints can be worked out.

DESIRE PROBLEMS

Problems of sexual desire or appetite basically come up in one of two ways.

1. Within the individual. The man may feel deficient in sexual appetite compared to the amount of desire he believes he should have, that he had earlier in his life, or that he believes other men have. Included in this category is a very small group of men who have absolutely no appetite for sex at all.

There are also men who have more sexual desire than they want. They wish they didn't think about sex and want it as much as they do, because it interferes with other aspects of their lives.

2. Within a couple. The situation here is that while neither partner is totally without interest or totally consumed by sex, one partner wants a lot more sexual activity than the other and they have been unable to negotiate a compromise. This is what I call a desire discrepancy. It's easy to assume that it's the man who wants more sex while his partner is the one with the headache. Although this is the typical pattern, there are also many couples where it's the woman who wants more sex. In my practice, desire discrepancies are by far the most common kind of problem.

A variation on this theme is when both people want more sex but just can't arrange it, as was true with Edward and Janet. Two-career couples and people with children are often in this bind. Both partners want more sex and miss it, but they're usually too busy or too tired, or neither is interested when the other is.

ASPECTS OF DESIRE

Much more is often entailed in desire problems than that term implies, so let's try to define exactly what is involved. There are four key concepts: desire itself, the object or purpose of the desire, the willingness to act on the desire, and the actual sexual frequency or activity.

I take the first concept, **erotic desire,** to mean a physical/emotional interest in engaging in sexual activity. While desire often has cognitive elements (thoughts or images of sex), it is more than a vague intellectual itch. For example, the idea "I should want to make it with such a beautiful woman," if unaccompanied by any feeling or physical sensation, is not desire as I define it. Neither is the idea, "Gee, we haven't made love in several weeks, so I guess it's time." As I use the term *erotic desire*, it is similar to the messages we get from our bodies signifying a desire for food. But just as we don't always eat when we get a message saying "beep, beep, hungry," so, too, we don't always engage in sex when we get a "beep, beep, horny" message. And just as we sometimes eat without having received a "beep, beep, hungry," message, so, too, we sometimes have sex without a "beep, beep, horny" message.

In some people, sexual interest itself is low; they don't have many sexual thoughts, feelings, or fantasies. Seeing or talking to an attractive person doesn't evoke any surges of sexual energy, any thoughts of what they might want to do sexually with these people, or any erotic fantasies. This total or relative lack of interest in sex can be either long-term—and for a few men it's always been like this—or of recent origin. If you've never felt any sexual appetite, you need to consult a specialist. The problem can be mainly physical (for example, a very low testosterone level), mainly psychological, or a combination of both. Or it may come out to be a preference rather than a problem.

Although there are some women who want more sex than the average man and some men who want less sex than the average woman, in general, men seem to have a greater libido than women. The observation of sex therapists and researchers Sandra Leiblum and Raymond Rosen fits my own observations:

> Overall, it does appear that men have a more insistent and constant sexual appetite, which is readily accessed through a large variety of internal and environmental prompts. Women, on the other hand, have less intense and more sporadic sexual desires, which they are more likely to suppress or to ignore if a host of conditions are not met. The pathway between desire and execution seems to be longer—with more byways, detours, and obstacles— for women than for men.

An example of men's more constant appetite is that they think about and want sex regardless of whether they are in a relationship, while many women seem to automatically turn off their erotic interest when they're not connected to someone. As one woman reported: "When I don't have a partner I don't think about sex. And to tell the truth, I don't miss it that much. As soon as I'm in a new relationship, though, and sexually active again, I think about it all the time!"

Women's desire also fluctuates with their menstrual cycles. Very few women, for instance, have much sexual interest just before and during the first two or three days of their periods. And most women do not have much sexual appetite in the last trimester of pregnancy or for a while after giving birth. Although there has been speculation that men have cycles roughly comparable to women's menstrual cycles, at this point there is little evidence to support the idea.

For both men and women, sexual desire decreases gradually with age. The height of sexual interest comes fairly early—in adolescence and the twenties—especially for males. It's like everything reminds you of sex and everything makes you feel sexy. This feeling tends to diminish over the years, although there can be resurgences at various times.

There is no physical reason for sexual desire to entirely disappear with age. The production of testosterone, which largely controls sexual appetite in men, does decline over time, but it never ceases altogether in a healthy male. There are many men in their sixties, seventies, eighties, and older who remain interested in sex and have it when they can, although factors like lack of a partner or medical problems may get in the way. But interest remains, and not only for men. A friend of mine is a doctor who routinely asks her patients about safe sex. One day, without thinking, she asked a ninety-two-year-old single woman patient if she was practicing safe sex. The woman smiled sweetly and said: "No, but I'd like to."

Despite what I've said about the constancy of male libido, it often ebbs and flows over the years, depending on a number of variables. Some men, for instance, look back over the years and report patterns like this:

I was really hot to trot in my early twenties, then seemed to retreat inside myself for a few years. But the motor got revved up again when I hit thirty-one. There was another period of quiet a few years later, even though I was living with a wonderfully sexy woman, and then I got adolescent again when I had my "mid-life crises" in my forties.

The same things affect different men in different ways. Some men, for example, have no interest in sex when they are absorbed in their work. This kind of man might forget about sex altogether for days, weeks, or even longer while he's involved in a big project. Other men are different. They get turned on while working and use sex as a relief from work and as a way of recharging their batteries. Certainly the horrendous job of being President of the United States didn't dampen John F. Kennedy's enormous sexual appetite. And many men's desire, or willingness to act on desire, is heavily dependent on the physical characteristics of their partners. Many men report that their sexual appetites decreased after their partners gained weight or developed stretch marks as a result of pregnancy. Other men are much less affected by such changes. Some men's sexual desire is severely affected by relationship problems. If they feel angry at or rejected by their partners, their libido disappears. But other men barely seem to notice. It's as if their sexual urges are in a separate compartment and are unaffected by other considerations.

A woman I saw in therapy complained that absolutely nothing dented her husband's sex drive. When she was angry with him, he still wanted sex, as he did when he was angry with her. One night, she recalled, she was suffering from the flu, had a temperature of

103, "was coughing and sneezing every minute and, as I noticed later, even had snot running down my face." But she was awakened to find her husband rubbing her breasts trying to turn her on.

As already noted, for a great many men, almost regardless of their age and situation, the appearance of a new partner, especially if she's young and attractive, can greatly increase erotic desire, at least for a short time.

The second crucial concept is the **purpose or object of desire,** which really comes down to the question: desire for what? There are men who desire and engage in sex frequently, but only with themselves. While this can be the result of a block to sex with the partner—for instance, anger at her, feeling that sex with her isn't fun or worthwhile—it can also be a long-standing preference. There are men who get all their erotic needs met in masturbation and, left to their own devices, would almost never have sex with a partner. One European intellectual spoke for these men almost a century ago when he said, "intercourse with a woman is sometimes a satisfactory substitute for masturbation. But it takes a lot of imagination to make it work." While there is nothing specifically wrong with such an attitude, it can wreak havoc in relationships where the partner wants more sex with the man and realizes that although he's unwilling to have sex with her, he's doing it regularly with himself.

The question of desire for what remains even when we talk about partner sex. People don't have sex only to satisfy sexual urges. Many men sometimes or often have sex in the absence of any specific sexual desire; what they do feel, however, is a wish not to disappoint their partners or a desire to live up to their ideals of masculinity or to feel powerful. And certainly some women have sex in the absence of any specific sexual interest in order to please their partners, to avoid hassle or argument, or to avoid feeling guilty. One woman had an appetite for sex that was so ravenous that her husband was fearful of coming home from work. When I asked her why she wanted so much sex, she said, "It's the only time I have his full attention." Another woman in a similar situation said, "Sex is the only time I get the touching I crave." What these women wanted, strictly speaking, was more attention and more touching, not more sex. But they believed sex was the only way they could get what they really wanted.

Many men don't know how to give or get a hug, to express love or feel loved, or to feel strong and masculine except by having sex. Such individuals are often experienced as oversexed by their partners. The way out of this situation is for them to learn to express nonsexual feelings in nonsexual ways.

Just as the purpose or object of the sex that is wanted is an important question, so, too, is the kind of sex. Couples often have arguments about sexual frequency that could be easily resolved if only they could state precisely what it is that they want more or less of. Those who want less sex usually believe that they are being asked to get aroused and go through a lengthy process, when in fact the partner who wants more sex may simply want, or be willing to settle for, a helpful hand or a quickie. And even if this isn't the case at first, a discussion of the menus of possibilities can often bring about a compromise on what at first seemed like an insurmountable problem.

Our third important concept is **willingness,** going along with the desire for sex by engaging in it, or even initiating and having sex in the absence of a specific desire for it. Without willingness, the motor just idles. Willingness is putting the car in gear and stepping on the accelerator.

A pattern of unwillingness in the presence of desire often signifies personal or relationship problems. If you feel desire but are unwilling to do anything about it with your partner, this could mean that you're angry or upset with her or don't find her attractive. Or it could mean that something is getting in the way, something you may not even be aware of, such as a belief that sex is too dirty an activity to have with someone you love. This might explain the behavior of a man who feels desire but instead of approaching his wife either masturbates or goes to prostitutes.

Willingness in the absence of desire could be a problem if it means that you're feeling pressured by your ideas of what a real man should do or by fear of your partner's reaction if you don't have sex. Yet willingness without much desire doesn't have to be a problem, as in this man's case:

Dee wants sex three or four times a week no matter what. It's real important to her. I could be happy with a lot less, but there's no way I'm going to let something like this sour our relationship. So I accommodate her as best I can. Sometimes I don't have much interest, but she gets my penis up anyway and we make love. If we don't get it up, I service her with my tongue and hand. I usually don't get highly aroused with that, but I feel good giving her pleasure. It's a fair trade-off.

The last key concept, **activity or frequency,** refers to how often you actually have sex. It should be clear by now that feeling desire doesn't necessarily lead to sexual activity. The vast majority of times we have sexual thoughts and feelings and even erotic physical sensations, we do *not* have sex. Think of all the times during a day or week when you have erotic thoughts and feelings. Now compare that to the number of times a day or week when you actually do something sexual. What do you find? What do you do with those feelings of desire when you don't act on them?

The question of why people don't act on sexual interest that is present is a fascinating one. It is a fact that many people who aren't having as much sex as they or their partners want do feel sexual desire. They have sexual thoughts, feelings, and impulses. And they may masturbate. What this group is missing is the willingness to have sex with their partners.

Many of us have trouble with the idea of feeling desire but not following up on it. If you're hot, why not have sex with a willing partner? It sounds almost crazy not to. But there are many places in life where interest does not translate directly into behavior. Take a trivial example that comes up all the time. Are you ever interested in a hot-fudge sundae? Let's say you definitely are. You can almost taste it as you imagine yourself eating it. You really want that sundae. But I'll bet you don't get a sundae every time you desire one.

You are more than your desire for ice cream. Other aspects of your being come into play. You may, for example, not get the ice cream because it's too much hassle. You'd have to put your shoes on and walk or drive to the ice cream store. More likely, not getting it has something to do with other concerns—for example, your weight or health. You are also more than your desire for sex.

CAUSES OF DESIRE PROBLEMS

Problems of sexual desire and activity usually stem from one of two factors: different preferences, and either blocks to or intensifiers of desire or willingness.

Difference in Sexual Preferences

Differences in preference for sexual frequency has barely been mentioned in the professional literature, yet I consider it to be crucial to an understanding of desire discrepancies. We assume that couples are or should be well-matched sexually; in the words of another era, they should be sexually compatible. Both partners should want sex about, say, twice a week. If that's not the case, there must be some block or problem. But why should they agree on sexual frequency? Couples disagree on many things: how often to go out or have company in, how to raise children, or even whether to have them, how much money to spend on different things, whether to squeeze the toothpaste from the top or the bottom, and so forth. Why should sex be different?

My impression is that by the time people reach the age of twenty-five or thirty, they have arrived at some natural or preferred level of sexual frequency. Some people really like sex. Almost everything turns them on and makes them desire sex. Most of us can easily think of a man who fits this pattern, but so do some women. Witness the heroine in Peter Benchley's novel *The Deep*:

> To Gail, sex was a vehicle for expressing everything—delight, anger, hunger, love, frustration, annoyance, even outrage. As an alcoholic can find any excuse for a drink, so Gail could make anything, from the first fallen leaf of autumn to the anniversary of Richard Nixon's resignation, a reason for making love.

Gail is very similar to the men I mentioned earlier, who use sex as a way of expressing and experiencing all sorts of feelings, most of them not even sexual. But there are also lots of women and men for whom very few stimuli evoke sexual interest or response.

> Kurt is such a man. Even as a teenager, he noticed that his interest in sex seemed much less than that of his friends. He didn't think or fantasize about sex much and used masturbation only occasionally as a sleeping pill. Although he liked girls and was popular with them, he didn't feel driven to have sex with them. The pattern continued in adulthood. A problem developed in his relationships, because his partners all "wanted more sex than I did and would get

upset when I rejected their overtures." Kurt was evaluated by several doctors and therapists, none of whom could find anything wrong with him. If left to his own preferences, he would have sex with a partner once or twice a month and masturbate two or three times a month when he had trouble getting to sleep. Although he said sex was "enjoyable" and he had no trouble functioning, sex didn't do a lot for him, and having it didn't make him want to have it again anytime soon.

You can get a sense of a person's natural or preferred level of sexual interest and activity by looking at his history. How much sex did he want and have over the years in different relationships? And how much does he desire and have now? People vary considerably in their answers.

Unfortunately, just as people who squeeze the toothpaste from the bottom often marry people who squeeze from the top, people who want sex once a month often marry people who want it twice a week. And that's a real problem. There may be no blocks, no barriers, nothing neurotic, and nothing weird. Just different preferences. This is like a couple in which one person needs physical activity almost every day— whether jogging, swimming, or what have you—and the other is quite sedentary. Neither one is mad or bad; they just have different patterns.

It's important in cases like this to look at both ends, and not just focus on bringing up the desire of the one who wants less sex. It may be just as necessary to decrease the desire of the one who wants more sex. Maybe Gail can find other satisfying ways of celebrating the first day of spring than by having sex. Maybe some of her feelings can be expressed in other ways as well.

Obstacles to Desire or Willingness

Below I discuss some of the things that can inhibit desire or the willingness to act on it.

• Dissatisfaction with partner sex. This category encompasses a number of issues. Perhaps the sex you have with your partner isn't all that great. It seems like too much work compared with what you get out of it. Perhaps your partner isn't that attractive to you sexually; there are things about her looks, attitude, or behavior that make sex with her not appealing. Another possibility is that you're having difficulties functioning as you would like; perhaps you have trouble keeping erections or delaying ejaculations. Avoiding sex is a way of not confronting these problems.

• Dissatisfaction with the relationship. This seems to affect women more than men. A woman may feel, for example, that her partner doesn't pay much attention to her except when he wants sex or that the way he treats her is unacceptable. In short, she feels used or abused. As a result, she isn't interested in having sex with him. But men can also be affected. If the relationship is cold and hostile, the man may feel it's easier to take care of his sexual needs by himself or with another woman than with his partner. By the same token, if he's angry with her, the thought of having sex with her may not occur to him or may not be enticing if it does.

• Drugs. Modern medicine has been quite successful in producing a number of drugs with the unintended and unwanted side effect of decreasing sexual desire. See the appendix for a list of some of the drugs that can cause problems.

• Certain medical conditions. Any acute or chronic medical problem will tend to decrease sexual interest. If someone is chronically ill, a host of variables may affect sexual interest and functioning. Among these are the effects of the disease itself, the effects of treatment and hospitalization, the effects of the patient role, the meaning the patient attaches to the illness, fear of death, fear of rejection by a partner, the demands of coping with a chronic disorder, and so on.

This is a complex area. For example, a man who's had a heart attack may have nothing wrong with him now. His doctors may have pronounced him physically fit. Yet he or his partner may fear that sex will produce more excitement than his heart can handle, a very common fear. So there may be an unwillingness to have sex even though interest is present. Or, as a result of his fears, he may lose interest. If he talks with his doctor, he may learn that sex poses no risk and his interest and willingness will probably return. A woman who's had a mastectomy may fear initiating sex or responding to an invitation for fear of revulsion and rejection by her partner. Yet she may truly want sex. And with some disabilities, those afflicted have feelings of anger or guilt to deal with as well, and these of course can influence sexual interest.

• Depression. Millions of Americans suffer from it, and a great many of them experience decreased desire for sex. If someone has lost interest in sex because of depression, chances of sex therapy working aren't very good unless the depression is treated first. If it's successfully treated, whether by brief psychotherapy or drugs, or both, chances are good that no other treatment will be necessary. One problem to be aware of is that some antidepressant drugs themselves may decrease sexual desire.

• Stress and fatigue. Many people are stressed out much of the time, often because of work pressures. They don't have time or energy for anything, including sex.

• Scheduling problems. Many couples are so scheduled up that they have little time to be together and have fun. The time they do spend together is usually packed with chores and dealing with children, which is not conducive to feeling sexy.

• Beliefs that hinder action. This would be true, at least theoretically, of Catholic clergy. A priest may be sexually attracted to a woman parishioner, let's say, but his beliefs and vows say he shouldn't act on his feelings. This may well put him into a state of great conflict.

Priests and nuns aren't the only ones who hold such beliefs. A small number of desire problems I've seen have been caused by similar beliefs. For example, one man just couldn't allow himself to have sex with his new wife. It turned out that he was raised in a fundamentalist religion that said once married, always married. Even though he was divorced from his first wife, he still felt married to her to the extent that sex with his new wife felt like adultery.

Negative sexual messages from parents and religion have been implicated in a number of sex problems. It certainly doesn't help if you believe that sex is dirty and sinful. Some people are aware of the conflict between wanting to have sex and feeling that it's sinful or wrong, and they struggle with it. Others are not aware and can't understand why they don't want to make love with their partners.

• Fear of too much closeness. Some men and women I have worked with seemed to believe that more sex or better sex would make them too vulnerable. They would end up feeling too close and too dependent on their partners and this would lead to huge problems. This fear caused them to avoid sex with the partner even when they were highly desirous and aroused. They would find a reason not to have sex at all or to masturbate.

• Sexual fears. Millions of Americans, not all of them women, were abused as children both sexually and otherwise. Some of these people have developed fearful reactions to sex and other forms of closeness. Although they may feel turned on and desirous of sex, these feelings come into conflict with the fears and a struggle ensues.

Enhancers or Intensifiers of Sexual Desire and Willingness

Here are some of the things that may cause a person to want and go after more sex than his or her partner desires.

• Heavy rewards for sexual activity. Some men get a great deal from sex. Some get great physical rewards—that is, they seem to feel more than others and derive great pleasure and physical satisfaction. Some get great psychological rewards: they feel much more manly or more at peace. And there are also some who believe that sex is the only thing they are good at or that sex is the only way they can feel good.

• Sex is the solution to too many needs and situations. A man who uses sex to express and experience many nonsexual emotions is going to want sex a lot more than someone who also has other ways of expressing these feelings.

• Fear of closeness and vulnerability. Although such fears can be an obstacle to sexual desire and willingness, they can also have the opposite effect. Some men use sex as a distancer. Instead of engaging in intimate conversation or affectionate touching short of sex, activities that make them feel exposed and fearful, they resort to sex, an activity they feel safe with.

• Inability or unwillingness to control erotic desire. I have known men who felt a lot more sexual interest than that of their partners but it never became an issue. They understood they could never satisfy every sexual impulse and restrained themselves accordingly. Other men, however, seem unable to do this. Whenever they feel a sexual tingling, they try to act on it, and in the process often upset their partners and end up with less sex than would otherwise be the case because the partners feel continually badgered.

• Depression. There is an interesting exception to what I said about depression decreasing sexual desire. In some folks it produces the opposite effect. They want more sex. It's as if sex is the only way they have of gaining relief from the depression, so the more depressed they get, the more sex they want. This can cause huge relationship problems. There he or she is, very morose and hardly an appealing partner, yet wanting lots of sex. And it's hard to turn them down, even though they're not very attractive in this state, because you can see this is the only medicine that works for them.

BEFORE YOU DO ANYTHING ELSE

There are two things to be done before you read the next chapter and start resolving your problem. The first is to determine if there's a physical problem or depression involved. If your desire, or your partner's, is zero or close to it, or has sharply decreased, or if you are taking drugs of any kind or have a serious medical condition including depression, it's a good idea to have a talk with your family doctor or a doctor who works with sex problems.

The second prerequisite is to get yourself into the proper mental/ emotional shape to deal with your problem. When couples can't agree on how much sex to have, things can quickly turn ugly. Both people end up feeling bad. The person wanting more sex (let's say it's you) feels unloved, undesirable, and cheated. All you're asking for is some loving. Why can't she just go along with that? Is it because she finds you unattractive, not sexy, not desirable? Maybe, you think, it's because you're not a good lover. So you alternate between feeling angry and frustrated on the one hand, and doubting yourself on the other. Men, of course, have traditionally been in this fix, wanting more sex than their partners. Unfortunately, it doesn't make any difference how many other men have been and are in the same boat; it still doesn't feel good.

The one wanting less sex doesn't feel any better. She feels always under attack; you're always after her for sex, and that makes her angry. She's afraid to be close to you in any way—holding hands, hugging, kissing, or snuggling—because you might interpret it as a desire for sex. At the same time, she feels guilty. After all, you're not asking for much. Why can't she just go along?

When it's the man who wants less sex, things can get even worse. After all, who ever heard of a man rejecting, even running away from, a willing partner? As one man in this situation put it: "The only word I have for it is crazy. I can't imagine any other man turning down sex, and if I could, I would say he's flat-out nuts. And that's what I think of myself."

Because of the general bias in our society these days that sex in relationships is good, the one who wants less sex will feel the worst and be labeled as the one with problems. Even therapists, who should know better, often hold the same bias and will devote all their efforts to increasing the desire and willingness of the man or woman who wants less.

Whether or not this happens, there are more than enough bad feelings to go around. They do not make for happy people or happy relationships. And, as long as the bad feelings exist, they make resolution of the problem difficult.

You should do what you can about any bad feelings between you and your partner. The material in Chapters 19 and 20 can help in this respect, as can most of the material in Chapters 10 through 13. You are going to need a lot of empathy for your partner.

It is likely that you have been monstrifying her, seeing her as someone who's willfully withholding sex and not caring about your needs and feelings, or as someone who's deliberately demanding far more sex than you can offer, constantly badgering you and making you feel guilty, and not caring about your needs and feelings. You need to try to understand her and her position. Is it that she's willfully withholding, or is something else going on? Can you see her as a person who is as hurt and frustrated by the situation as you are and who is doing her best to deal with it even though her best, like your best, so far hasn't had the desired results? The more you can truly understand her situation and the more you can truly understand that the two of you are stuck, the better things will go. It's extremely rare to find a villain in these situations. Don't create one; doing so is easy but does not help.

You will also need empathy for yourself. You may well have been blaming yourself for being too demanding or not giving enough. Such thoughts, even if based on some truth, don't help. What we have is a problem—you aren't getting what you want and neither is she—which can probably be worked out if both of you can keep cool, remember that you're in this together, and have some tolerance for each other and yourselves as fallible but lovable human beings. Do what you need to get to this place.

Try to keep in mind that more sex isn't better and neither is less sex. The only thing that's better is an arrangement that satisfies the two of you, that makes each of you feel good about yourself, about the other, and about the relationship. With this perspective and with empathy, chances are excellent the problem can be resolved.

26

Resolving Problems of Sexual Desire and Activity

"Ever since high school, I believed the only way I could feel strong and manly was to have sex. This caused no end of problems with the women in my life. It was a revelation to discover that I can feel manly in many ways. Now I only have sex when I truly want sex. It's made my life a lot easier."—MAN, 41

"It was extremely painful to feel I wasn't man enough for my wife because she wanted more sex than I did. But now that I've learned there are lots of ways of being sexual and I don't have to perform all the time, we're much more compatible and having more fun."
—MAN, 36

THE story of a young couple whom I saw only once illustrates most of what is required to resolve issues of sexual desire and activity.

Tam said she could no longer endure the hurt she had suffered for the last three years because of Lincoln's lack of sexual interest. When they were first together, sex had been frequent, although he often came sooner than she wanted and seemed skittish about her being very active. But after a few months, his interest declined to almost zero. She hoped the situation would improve after they married, but it didn't. She tried various ways of seducing him, everything from sexy lingerie to erotic videos, but he rarely responded. She had tried to talk to him several times about what was going on, but the conversations escalated into arguments and nothing really got discussed, let alone resolved.

Lincoln agreed with her account. When I asked what had happened to his interest after the first few months, he became uncomfortable and clammed up. But he agreed that the issue was hurting them and needed to be resolved. And then they proceeded to have their first real conversation about the problem.

TAM: I miss the physical part of sex, but I also miss feeling desired and loved. I know Lincoln looks at other women and masturbates. It's terrible to feel that other women, and even his hand, are more desirable than I am. I'm not particular, I like all kinds of sex. But he doesn't want anything with me. I can't tell you how ugly and unloved that makes me feel.

LINCOLN: I'm sorry you feel so bad. I'm afraid what I have to say is going to make things worse, but I guess it's do or die. There's nothing wrong with my libido. I get turned on to women, including you. But I don't want sex with you, because it's not interesting or fun. You never touch me or try to turn me on. I don't think you've stroked my penis once since we were first dating. And when we have intercourse, you barely move or do anything. My impression is that sex isn't enjoyable for you, and I know you're not making it enjoyable for me. I don't feel good that I'm screwing my hand instead of my wife, but the fact is that my hand is more fun. There . . . I've said it.

TAM: This is unbelievable. When we were first together you didn't want me to touch you or to move in intercourse. If I did, you came immediately and got upset. I'm just doing what you taught me!

LINCOLN: God, that was years ago. The premature ejaculation cleared up after we'd been together a few months. It's not a problem anymore.

TAM: But you never said anything. I've wanted to touch you and stroke you; it's taken quite a bit of effort not to. And I don't like lying there like a log during intercourse. I want to move and express myself. I've been holding back because that's what I thought you wanted.

At that point, they looked at each other and started to laugh. This simple, two-minute conversation cleared up their "desire problem" and would have done so anytime in the last three years.

Although the resolution of Tam and Lincoln's problem was far quicker and easier than most, their case contains most of the elements of dealing with problems of sexual desire and activity. **One step is to *start talking* and to *determine if and when a change in desire or willingness has occurred,*** something they had been unable to do before being in a therapist's office. Another step is to *define what is wanted.* In this case, that was simple. Tam wanted to feel more desired by her husband, a feeling she could get if he wanted more sex with her, virtually any kind of sex. Lincoln also wanted more sex with his wife, but not the kind he had been having. Once it is known what is wanted, the next step is *defining what can be done to make the desire change,* and that was also simple. Lincoln wanted a more active partner than Tam had been. If she were more active, he'd be more willing to have sex with her. The fourth and last step is **negotiating for the change,** which was unnecessary in this case. Tam and Lincoln wanted the same change in Tam's behavior, a change that was no problem once she understood the situation. Notice the heavy dependence on being able to talk and negotiate with one's partner. This is absolutely crucial.

HAS THERE BEEN A CHANGE IN DESIRE OR WILLINGNESS?

What's needed first is to figure out if there's been a change in someone's desire for or willingness to have sex. With Lincoln and Tam, the problem started after they had been together a few months, when Tam started acting the way she thought Lincoln wanted her to. Because this way of being sexual was actually a turn-off to him, even though he had requested it, he lost the willingness to have sex with her. And because they had been unable to discuss the matter, the pattern continued for years. If someone's desire/willingness significantly increased or decreased during the relationship, that change is what needs attention and the following exercise can help.

EXERCISE 26–1: WHEN DID THE CHANGE OCCUR AND WHAT LED TO IT?

Time Required: A few minutes to an hour or more

This exercise can be done alone or with your partner. What you want to do is focus on the time just prior to the changed desire or activity. What happened during that time that may have contributed to the alteration of desire? Consider all the following: changes in physical health or medications; changes in the relationship (your engagement, wedding, trying to have or having a child, an affair, big arguments, and so on) and in other important relationships, such as with your parents; changes in job (hers and yours); changes in living arrangements (moving in together, moving out, moving to another city); changes in finances; changes in how you feel about yourself; changes in friendships. If the answer isn't obvious, get all the help you can. Pull out old calendars, appointment books, and anything else that might jog your memory. If your sexual desire seriously changed in November of 1989, it's probable that something else that happened in November or October had something to do with it. Knowing what that something is can help.

I did a version of this exercise with Jennifer and Chip, who had come to see me after almost a year of tension and bickering because of Jennifer's unwillingness to make love. Her interest hadn't changed, but she didn't want to have sex with Chip. Although at first she said she didn't have any idea why this was the case, she was able to pinpoint the time things had changed; it was the week after she realized that they would have to move once again because Chip had taken a new job. This had been the pattern in their thirteen-year marriage. Chip was a professor and would take a post at a different college every two years or so. Jennifer felt that just as soon as she started making friends and feeling comfortable in a new city, they'd have to move. As we talked about this, she realized that the last time was simply the last straw. She felt that her comfort, security, and feelings weren't even considered. Chip just did whatever he wanted to enhance his career.

Chip was shocked. He hadn't even known she was unhappy about the moves. It's easy to jump to the conclusion that he was an insensitive lout, but Jennifer had never directly voiced her complaints until this therapy session; it's not even clear she had fully recognized how upset she was about them. Chip was deeply concerned about her unhappiness, and the two of them had a series of constructive conversations about what to do. As a result, Chip offered to make no more moves without Jennifer's consultation and agreement.

Although very little was said about sex, Jennifer became more willing to have sex while they were having these discussions. The best explanation I have is that as soon as she was convinced that her wishes were being given the consideration she wanted, she felt free to be sexual with him.

Unless doing Exercise 26–1 resolves the problem, you should do the next three exercises. They have to do with defining the problem more clearly.

EXACTLY WHAT DO YOU WANT MORE OF?

It's a lot easier to get what you want if you first determine exactly what that is. You may feel this is a bit silly. You already know what you want, so why waste time on it? You may be right. But it's also possible that by reading this material and spending a few more moments thinking about it, you'll come up with some new ideas.

Saying you want more sex or less sex is not really as clear as it sounds. You need to get more specific, and sometimes the specifics are surprising, as in the examples I related in the last chapter where one woman wanted more sex because that was the only way she could get the attention she desired and where another woman wanted more touching but felt she could get it only by having sex. There are many aspects of sex that you might want more of, as well as some things that are not primarily sexual or that can be gotten outside of sex. It's crucial to know precisely what you and your partner want more and less of. It helps if both of you do these exercises. Exercise 26–2 may surprise you, because it doesn't mention any sexual acts. That's intentional. It helps to determine first what feelings you want to have.

EXERCISE 26–2: FEELINGS YOU WANT MORE OFTEN

Time Required: Varies

Take a few moments when you'll be uninterrupted and consider which feelings, beliefs, and sensations you'd like more often. Use the following list as a guide, but feel free to add other items and to use your own words.

Attractiveness: The sense that your partner finds you attractive physically and otherwise.

Caring: The feeling that your partner cares for and about you.

Closeness: A sense of closeness, unity, or connectedness with your partner.

Ego Boosts: Feeling really good about yourself. Many men get this from their work, but many also get it from sex. Some require frequent sex in order to feel good about themselves. This can create a problem when the partner doesn't want as much.

Feeling Sexually Desirable: Knowing that you turn her on and she wants you sexually.

Sense of Freedom: A feeling of freedom, not being trapped or tied down.

Sense of Being Important to Your Partner: Knowing that your partner finds you important.

Love: We all define love in our own ways. Though hard to put into words, we know what we mean by it and when we feel loved. Perhaps you want to feel loved more often.

Passion: A feeling of excitement, arousal, zest, or joy.

Sexual Fulfillment: If this is what you want, try to be specific about exactly what you mean by it.

Support: The feeling that your mate, while not always agreeing with you, supports you as a human being, supports your right to grow and develop, your right to have your own opinions and make your own decisions.

EXERCISE 26–3: WHAT CAN GIVE YOU THAT FEELING

Time Required: Varies

Using your list from Exercise 26–2, go back over the feelings that are missing for you. Make a new list of the things that would allow you to have them, or have them more often. Try not to assume that more sex is the only answer. Keep in mind that one can feel love, passion, and many other things without having sex. The acts and events below may help you make your list.

Compliments: Being told you are attractive, manly, competent, loving, generous, successful, and so forth.

Flirting: More teasing and man/woman game-playing.

Genital Play: Genital touches and pressures that do not include intercourse and that may or may not include orgasm. Some examples are petting, dry-humping, and your partner holding or touching your penis. You may want to consult the list of sexual options in Chapter 3 for more ideas.

Intercourse: The experience of having your penis inside your partner is what you want more of. If this is the case, it might be worthwhile to consider exactly what you get from or like about intercourse that's so important. Is it a sense of closeness or unity with your lover? Better orgasms? The sensations produced by your penis moving inside her? Does it make you feel more manly, or give you the sense that she really wants you? Your answer may include one or more of the above or other things. Whatever it is or they are, take a few moments to consider whether the feelings can be generated in some other way than intercourse. For instance, would the feelings be the same with her fingers instead of her vagina around your penis? Could you feel as close or united with her in some other way?

Orgasms: If you love the experience of orgasm and want to have it more often, you need to determine exactly what kinds of orgasm you desire. If you're already masturbating as much as you want, or if masturbation isn't an acceptable option, perhaps what you want is more partner-induced or partner-involved orgasms.

Partner-induced orgasm means that your partner's hand or mouth produces the orgasm. Partner-involved orgasm means that your partner is involved in the experience with you, but your hand is the primary vehicle for reaching orgasm. Your partner may hold you during the experience, kiss you, caress you, talk to you, or do something else that you find stimulating.

Physical Affection: This includes all touching, holding, kissing, cuddling, snuggling, and so on that does not focus on the genitals. This is an issue that you should explore carefully. As I mentioned in Chapter 14, men in our culture have in effect been trained to change their "I want to touch and be touched" button into an "I want sex" button. Many men therefore push for sex when what they really want, if they only knew it, is a hug or some holding or cuddling. Consider whether touching could sometimes satisfy what you've been thinking of as a need for sex.

Spending More Time Alone: You want to be able to spend time by yourself, or with your own friends, without apology or hassle.

Spending More Time Together: Just the two of you being together without distractions or interruptions. This is missing in many relationships, although it's very important in keeping the partners contented. The lack of quality time together makes a number of other activities, such as talking and sex, difficult to get.

Talking Together: Having your partner talk to you about personal issues—hopes and dreams, feelings about you, fears and insecurities—and sharing your own thoughts and feelings.

Verbal Expressions of Love and Affection: Saying or hearing things like "I love you," and "I'm so glad you're in my life."

Take as much time as you like, perhaps over a period of days or weeks, to determine what you want.

The last exercise should have given you a better idea of what you want and also perhaps of some ways of getting it. There is more material on ways of increasing and decreasing desire on pages 507–512. But before looking at that material, it's important to start talking with your partner. It's possible that ways and means will become clearer in these conversations. It's also possible that your goals may change as you understand her perspective and goals.

OPENING NEGOTIATIONS WITH YOUR PARTNER

You may have already talked with your partner regarding how to make sex better, but I wonder if you've done it in the best ways possible, without attacks and counterattacks, and without the bad feelings that so often accompany these conversations. The kind of talk I have in mind is very different. It is based on the information presented in Chapters 8 and 10 through 13. If you haven't already done so, it would be a good idea to carefully study that material before starting discussions with your partner.

If there are already bad feelings between you and your partner about the desire conflict, you may want to write her a note like this:

I feel terrible about the conflicts and bad feelings we're having about sex. It hurts me to see you in pain, and I don't like feeling it myself. I love you and want to make things better.

I'd like us to have a different kind of talk than we've had. I'd like for each of us to get as much time as we want to say exactly where we're at. I'd be happy to go first, but I'd also be happy for you to start. When you talk, I'll just listen to what you have to say. When you're done, I'll summarize what you said to make sure I understand. I'd like you to do the same for me when I talk. At least we'll know we're hearing what the other is saying.

It's not easy being nondefensive about sex, especially after what we've been through, but I promise to do my best not to attack or criticize you, to listen as openly as I can, and to say exactly where I'm at. I hope you'll be willing to do the same.

I'm ready to do this as soon as possible. This Saturday morning might be a good time. Let me know what you think." [This example is basically offering to do the Talk and Listen Exercise in Chapter 13.]

Here's a statement you might want to make if you're not getting as much sex as you want.

YOU: Thanks for agreeing to do this. I think it's important for us. I love making love with you. It's close and loving, and fun. I just wish we did it more often.

I don't mind getting turned down sometimes. I know you're tired or not in the mood or have something on your mind. But when I get turned down five or six times in a row, I feel unloved. That gets me into a real funk, and I withdraw. I know this isn't good for us, but I don't know what else to do. I feel lost and give up. "What's the point of being together?" is what it feels like.

That's my opening statement. I have more things to say, and I have some ideas that may surprise you. Should I go on, or is this enough for now?

HER: So far so good. Keep going.

YOU: I've thought about what you've said so many times, that sex is my only way of relating to you. You're right. I don't have other ways of feeling close. It doesn't occur to me to just lie in bed and hug or to talk about what's on my mind. But I'm trying to be clearer. I want to ask for sex when that's what I want, and to ask for other things when they're what I want. How does that sound?

HER: Great! That would help.

YOU: Do you think you might have more interest in lovemaking?

HER: I don't want to promise, but it's possible.

Now we turn to several examples of what to say when your partner wants more sex than you do. The reason for including all these examples is that the men in this situation I've worked with have had a great deal of trouble expressing themselves.

YOU: I guess I need to be more open than I've been. The reason I turn you down so often when you initiate is that I'm scared. I'm scared I won't be able to get hard and give you what you want. See, when I initiate, that means I'm already turned on and either have an erection or know I can get one. When you initiate, I don't know that. I'm concerned that we'll start and I won't be able to deliver.

Here's another way:

You: After thinking about it, I realize the reason I'm not more interested in lovemaking is that I'm not enjoying it very much. I love you but I feel pressured and burdened in our lovemaking. I'm not sure this is how it really is, but it feels to me that I've got to do a lot of work. Even when you initiate, it seems like I have to spend a lot of time getting you ready and then a lot more time stimulating you to orgasm. Only then can I take my pleasure, and it doesn't feel to me that you do a lot about that. Maybe the way I'm seeing this is unfair and not how it is, but this is my perception and it's affecting my behavior.

Here's another kind of situation:

You: I don't really know why I'm less interested in sex. All I do know is that I don't look forward to making love and don't take advantage of many opportunities. And I know this is making you miserable, which bothers me a lot. I wish I knew more, but I don't. I'd like to get to the bottom of this, but I'm not sure what to do next.

In the last situation, it would help if you could make a distinction between desire and action. That is, apropos of the discussion in the last chapter, is it the case that you don't feel much desire (don't have many sexual thoughts, fantasies, or feelings) or that you do but you are not allowing them to be carried out with your partner? This is a crucial distinction. If you're not having much desire for sex at all, that could indicate a physical or drug-related problem, or maybe high stress. Whatever the reason, your partner may feel a bit better knowing that the lack of feeling is general and not just about her. On the other hand, if your desire is greater than your willingness to have sex with her, you're making a statement about the relationship or how you feel about sex with her. This may not make her feel very good, but it clearly indicates where you need to look for solutions.

And here's another kind of situation:

YOU: I have less interest in sex than before, because I'm feeling exhausted and overwhelmed most of the time, especially in the evenings. I feel totally strung out. It may be different for the two of us. It seems to me that even when you're tired, you're still up for sex. But for me, when I'm tired and overwhelmed, sex just seems like one more burden. I realize that sounds terrible, but that's how it feels.

I would like to change. I miss our lovemaking. But to make a change, something has got to give. If you're up to discussing it, I can go over some of the things I'd like to stop doing or do less often.

HER: Go ahead.

YOU: The first thing is the meals. When you proposed that I cook half the meals, I thought it was a great idea. But now I don't. I'm not good at it, and it's a tremendous strain. After picking up food on the way home, cooking and serving it, I'm a wreck and not up for sex or anything. I want to stop cooking. I'm willing to pick up something already cooked and serve it, but that's all I can do.

Here's one more possibility:

YOU: I never thought I'd be saying this, but I think it's true. As you've pointed out many times, our lovemaking is good when we have it. We both enjoy it. So why don't I want more? The fact is that I'm scared. Often when we have sex, I feel incredibly close to you. All the barriers are down, I'm just fully open. I know that sounds good, and it feels good too, but it's also scary. I don't know exactly why, but it's like I have to draw back from it. There's something threatening there. As long as we don't have sex too often, I can keep the scary part under control. But my fear is that if we have sex more often, I'll lose control of it. That's as far as my thinking has gone so far, but I wanted you to know where I am.

After having a discussion like one of these, the door is open for some kind of action. The man in the last example may want to talk more with his partner. Maybe together they can find out what's frightening him. Or maybe he'll want to spend more time alone trying to figure it out. Another alternative is for him to get professional therapy. And sometimes it happens that just giving voice to the fear resolves the problem.

METHODS TO INCREASE SEXUAL DESIRE OR WILLINGNESS

Most of the following methods with the exception of the first can be helpful whether your concern is to increase or decrease sexual desire or activity. But since they're easier to explain if I take a consistent point of view, I'll take the position of increasing desire or activity. By changing a few words in the exercises, they are equally applicable to decreasing desire.

Simmering

If the reason you're not having much sex is that you are not feeling much desire, and if this lack of interest is *not* the result of depression, drugs, relationship difficulties, or work stress, simmering will help you get your sexual juices flowing again. The simmering exercise in Chapter 16 is an excellent way of doing this, and you should turn to it now.

Conditions for Greater Desire or Activity

There must be certain things that, if they were present or absent, would make you be more willing to have sex. These things are what I call conditions. You should do the Conditions Exercise in Chapter 6, substituting desire for arousal. That is, compare times when you felt greater desire with times when you felt less desire, or imagine what it would take for you to want more frequent sex. Another possibility is to just think about what changes in your life, broadly considered, would make you want more sex. In looking for answers, consider all of the issues mentioned in the last chapter that can negatively affect sexual desire and frequency: fatigue; stress from any source; drugs and alcohol; the quality of the sex you have and any concerns you may have about your functioning; problems with children; negative beliefs about sex; and fear of too much closeness.

If your situation is such that you want to determine what would help you want less sex, adjust the wording of the exercise in that direction. The question in the exercise then becomes something like "What would have to happen for me to want less sex?" What kinds of nonsexual activities might satisfy your desire for sex some of the time? These things can be just about anything: doing something on your own, like relaxing, reading, or working on a hobby; doing something with your partner, such as talking, walking, going out; doing something with others, whether this consists of meetings, sporting events, charity work, visiting with a friend, or what have you.

Men I've worked with have often gasped in horror or disbelief: "Only sex can satisfy my desire for sex!" But almost all found that that's too hasty a judgment. Although it may be true that you desire sex three times a night, or five times a week, that does not mean that only sex can satisfy you. Many people who once thought that certain of their desires could only be satisfied by a cigarette, food, or alcohol have found that other things will do as well, or almost as well.

Improving the Quality of Sex

One reason some people don't want much sex is that the sex they have isn't all that hot. I'm not talking about a dysfunction here; they function fine, but it doesn't seem to be worth the effort. In working with a number of men like this, the problem has usually come down to a lack of assertiveness: They aren't going after what they want.

It took some time and effort before Daniel was able to locate the problem. The best sex he had in his life had been with women he didn't have a lot of feelings for. But now he was married and very much in love with his wife. To help him figure out exactly what he wanted, I had him tell me what went on in sex with his wife and compare it to what had gone on in sex with these other women. With these women, he had been much more forceful, directly going after what he wanted. He did his own thing, to a large extent not even attending to what his partners wanted. This resulted in very high arousal. But he wasn't letting himself go with his wife because he kept thinking about how she was affected by what he was doing. He was much more focused on her than on himself.

One thing that helped was the idea of paying dues. By having lovemaking sessions where he focused totally on her pleasure, he felt he had paid his dues and earned the right to do the same for himself. So in the subsequent "Daniel-focused" sessions, he could focus more on himself and let himself go. Interestingly, and this almost invariably happens in such cases, his wife loved these sessions and didn't think he was being too self-centered. She, too, had been missing his excitement and passion. If being assertive with your partner is a problem, reading Chapter 8 will help.

Improving the quality of sex covers a lot of ground. Perhaps there's something about your partner's behavior that you'd like to be different. A conversation with her—tactful, to be sure—would probably help. Remember to focus on what you want her to do and not on what she is doing that you don't like.

I recall one man who had lost much of his interest in sex and had developed sporadic erection difficulties, which further decreased his willingness to engage in sex. As we talked about how he felt about sex with his partner, he kept mentioning how "enthusiastic and active" she had been when they were dating. When I asked if she was still the same, he thought for a moment and then yelled: "That's it, she isn't. She doesn't fuck me back. I do all the work and she's like a dead person." In the following week, he had several conversations with her about this. She had her own complaints: mainly that he had stopped being romantic and patient after they had moved in together, just wanted to stick it in with a minimum of foreplay, take his pleasure, and then fall asleep. Because of this, she said, she had lost interest. He was able to hear her and change his behavior accordingly. Not surprisingly, her behavior then changed. I got a big charge out of the message he left me one day: "Don't need another appointment. She's fucking back. Feels great."

Resolving Erection and Ejaculation Problems

A major reason that some men lose interest in sex is an erection or ejaculation problem or the fear of one of them. That is, because the men aren't sure they can have erections when required or last as long as their partners want, it seems easier just not to have sex at all.

If you think this might be your situation, take a moment and ask yourself the following: Would you have more sex if the erection or ejaculation problem was solved? It's easy to cavalierly answer yes. But take a moment or two to consider your answer. Imagine yourself being fully functional. Would you want to make love more often to your partner?

If the answer is no, then working on the functional problem is probably not the most important thing to do now. Something else—your feelings about yourself, her, or the relationship, or maybe depression—needs help.

If your answer is yes, ask yourself another question. Suppose the problem wasn't resolved yet, at least not totally, but you knew your partner wouldn't get upset when you didn't get hard or when you came fast. If that were the case, would you want more sex with her?

If your answers to both questions are yes, you'd want more sex, you need to decide whether you want to use the relevant exercises in this book to work on your problem or to see a sex therapist. Then tell your partner what you've found and what you'd like to do about it.

Transition Activities

Work stress and hassles can lessen anyone's desire for sex. Maybe you need to work less, to increase your ability to handle the work you have to do, or to decrease the amount of stress that work is causing you. Many large companies now offer stress-reduction training to their employees, and you may want to look into this. Or maybe you need to be able to say good-bye to work when you're through with it.

One way a number of people handle some of these problems is by engaging in what I call a transition activity between work and togetherness with their partner. They do something—jogging, meditating, taking a relaxing bath, playing with the kids, or some relaxing reading—that allows them to put aside work and get into a more relaxed frame of mind. The exact nature of the activity is unimportant, as long as it achieves the goal of getting you away from focusing on and being bothered by thoughts of work.

In one couple I saw, the transition activity involved more work. Jake was aiming for partnership in a high-powered law firm and simply could not get all his work done at the office. He would bring work home and feel guilty about it, and vacillate between doing the work and being with his partner, Heather. The result was that he never quite did his work and never was fully there with Heather. He felt guilty on both counts and wasn't much interested in sex. The solution we hit upon was that he would get right to his work as soon as he came home and had a snack. Heather wouldn't talk to him, and she would take all phone calls. He would devote up to two hours, but not a minute more, to his work, then take a quick shower and have dinner with her. Because he was now able to devote himself totally to his work before dinner, without having to deal with Heather and without feeling guilty about it, he got a lot accomplished. The shower was his way of leaving all that behind and preparing him to be with Heather.

The solution didn't work perfectly. When Jake was in the midst of a trial, the shower and dinner weren't always sufficient to get his mind off the case and sometimes Heather would tell him to go back to his den. But it worked well enough that his guilt feelings largely disappeared and their sexual frequency picked up enough to satisfy Heather.

Scheduling and Having Time Together

Everyone I know and work with is afflicted by busyness. Some people are so busy that they don't have much time to be together and to have sex. And usually this affects the partners in different ways. One of them still wants the same amount of sex, but the other doesn't. Whatever the exact situation, it may require that both of you look at your schedules and see how to arrange more time for being together. Some couples have more than a little trouble with this. Everything on their calendars is something they want to do. They need to establish priorities. Maybe you can't go to as many meetings as you do or take as many classes or entertain as much and still have the kind of sex life you want. Something has to go, usually several things. If the two of you can talk without getting into arguments, you'll be able to figure out something that's acceptable.

One solution that's worked for some couples is for them both to pull out their appointment books and write in times to be together for the next few weeks and then to keep those appointments as if their lives depended on it. These times are to be considered as sacred. Although there's no rule you have to make love, you should plan to have fun. And there's to be no work done, no calls to make or take, and no chores.

WHEN SHE'S LESS INTERESTED THAN YOU ARE

I think the best thing you can do in this situation is to help your partner talk to you about what's going on with her. In order for that to happen, she needs to feel that she can trust you not to judge her responses or to use them against her. If you've been critical of her comments in the past, you need to apologize and assure her that it won't happen again. You want to hear what's going on with her and you want the two of you to be able to resolve the issue in a way that honors both of you.

You may well hear things you don't like. That may not seem like an enticing prospect, but I assure you it's a good one. I say this in all seriousness, because if it's true that her relative lack of interest or willingness has to do with your behavior (you're not romantic enough, you don't do things she likes, and so on), you're in a great position to change your behavior and therefore to change hers.

What follows is an edited transcript of a conversation that a couple I saw had and recorded.

> HIM: I feel sad that you so often don't want to make love. I'd like to make this better for us. Could you tell me what's going on with you and our lovemaking?
>
> HER: Every time we try to talk about this, you get defensive and we have a fight.
>
> HIM: I know that's the way it's been. But I've decided we've got to talk, so I'm ready to listen. I promise I won't get defensive and won't get angry. I want to understand.
>
> HER: Well . . . OK. But I don't want you to attack me. Promise?
>
> HIM: Yes.
>
> HER: And no answering the phone. Let the machine pick it up.
>
> HIM: Agreed.

HER: Now I don't know how to start. I'm afraid what I'm going to say will sound like I'm blaming you for everything.

HIM: Please don't hold back. I want to hear everything, even if it doesn't feel good.

HER: OK, I'll just say how I see it. When we were first together, you wanted to please me. You were very romantic. You told me what you'd been thinking about me, how beautiful I was, how I turned you on. And you used to enjoy satisfying me. You'd take your time and do what I liked and make sure I had an orgasm before or after intercourse. All this was important to me. But it's changed. This is hard to say, but I feel like you don't care anymore. Or maybe you do, but don't want to take the effort to show it. You rarely tell me nice things and you don't take time to turn me on. You give a quick kiss and a touch or two, then you stick it in me and have your orgasm and that's it. I don't feel included or needed at all. So I've just turned off. And that's it.

HIM: (fighting to keep his composure) Boy, that's really hard to hear. . . . Give me a minute, I'm trying to digest it all without getting uptight. . . . Let's see if I understand. You're saying that I've become selfish. Instead of acting romantically like I used to and instead of making sure both of us are turned on and satisfied, I just do what's necessary to get my rocks off. Because of this, you've lost interest. Is that it?

HER: It sure is.

HIM: I can't say it's good to hear, but I'm glad I heard it instead of not hearing it. Tell you what. I need some time to let this sink in. Could we break this off for now and meet again tonight to continue?

HER: Fine. How about after dinner?

HIM: That's good.

HIM: (later) What you said earlier was hard to hear. But I thought about it and have to admit you're right. I don't know how or why it happened, but it did. And I can see why you're not enjoying sex and not even wanting it.

HER: I'm glad you understand.

HIM: I want to change things. I miss the sex we used to have. Are you up for that?

HER: Sure, that's what I've always wanted. But you're going to have to put more time and energy into lovemaking.

It may also be true that nothing is bothering your partner. She just "naturally" has a lower sexual appetite than you. It's a mistake to assume that everyone else has or should have the same level of interest in sex that you do. If your partner enjoys sex, isn't hung up, yet doesn't want it as often as you do, you're going to have to work out some compromises.

It will not work to make her feel guilty. Many men do this. When their partners turn them down, they sulk for days until the partner gives in because she feels so guilty. This giving in is usually not a joyous event. It's clear she's doing it out of guilt, and with resentment for being coerced. The result is hardly ecstatic sex.

Far better, I think, to go over the list of sexual options with her and see what she's willing to do for you when you're in the mood and she isn't. Here's a way one of these conversations might go.

YOU: I guess I have to accept the fact that you're not as interested in sex as I am.

HER: I think that's true. I enjoy our lovemaking and have no complaints about it, but I don't want it five times a week. That was true before I met you. Twice a week or so is par for me.

YOU: I'm not sure where to go from here. You know me, I always want intercourse. But I read about the other options in the book and I think I could be satisfied with them sometimes. Do you have any interest in that?

HER: I've said many times that I'll be happy to get you off when I'm not in the mood.

YOU: I know. It's just a little hard for me to accept. I'm getting all the pleasure.

HER: I'm not excited the way you are, but why can't you understand it makes me happy to give you pleasure?

YOU: I'm trying, but it's a new idea. OK, next time I'm in the mood and you're not, I'm going to ask you for something else. How about we agree to two things? One is that you accept only if you really want to. I need to know that you're not doing anything you don't want to do. And the second is that I'll try to accept and appreciate what you can do. Is that a deal?

Now let's try a variation. In the following example, the partner isn't as agreeable as the one above. The man has just asked her if she'd be willing to get him off when she's not up for intercourse.

HER: I know the right answer would be yes, I'll get you off whenever you want. But I don't feel that. Sure, I'd be willing to do that sometimes, as I already have. But I'm not going to want to do that every time you want something. We have intercourse once or twice a week, and that's plenty for me. I'm afraid you're going to want something else every day, and I can't honestly say I'd be up for that. I'd rather do something else.

HIM: Like what?

HER: Lots of things. I love to take a walk at night, but I'm afraid to go alone. I think it could be very romantic to take a short walk with you before going to sleep. Or just cuddle. I love it when we lie in bed or on the sofa and just hold each other for a few minutes. Or a short body-rub. You know how much I like them.

HIM: So there are a number of things you'd like to do sometimes instead of sex—like walking, cuddling, and body-rubs. Right?

HER: Sure.

HIM: You'd also be willing to get me off when you're not in the mood for sex, but not every night. Right?

HER: Yes.

HIM: What about this arrangement? I'll ask for what I want and you feel free to answer as you want. If I ask for sex and you don't want that, you say no and also suggest what you want to do. One more thing: you feel free to request a body-rub or a walk when that's what you like. How's that?

HER: Sounds perfect, but I'm worried you'll sulk when I refuse you sex. That's happened so many times. That doesn't make me want to suggest a walk.

HIM: I'm going to have to learn not to do that, to just accept your refusal without taking it personally. You know what would help? If you could make the rejection a little easier. Instead of just saying you're not in the mood, maybe you could say, 'I'm not up for sex now, honey, but I'd love to be with you. What about some cuddling?' That would soften the blow.

HER: You're asking me to show I care even though I don't want sex. I'll try to remember to do it.

MIND POWER FOR DESIRE PROBLEMS

Getting your mind on your side is an important part of resolving desire and frequency complaints. These complaints often involve one or both partners feeling discouraged ("We'll never find a solution"), so it's important to combat these discouraging thoughts with positive statements. I've given a number of examples of using positive self-statements in Chapter 21 and will not repeat them here. You should reread that chapter at your convenience and develop a number of positive statements to use. The more hopeful you feel about finding a solution, the better your chances of finding one.

The partner who wants less sex often feels inadequate or guilty ("I should want to make love more often" or "It's not fair to deny her the lovemaking she wants"). When you're aware of telling yourself things like this, argue with the statement and change it. For example: "I'm not a bad person and I'm not denying her. We just have different appetites. But we're working on it and will come up with something better."

Since monstrification of partners frequently happens in couples with desire/frequency differences, it's important to remind yourself as often as possible that your partner is not a demanding or withholding bitch. She's not a bad person, and neither are you. You just have some differences that need to be worked out.

Another helpful technique is mental rehearsal. In a number of the examples above, people promised to do or not to do something—for example, to ask for sex when they wanted sex, to ask for something else when that's what they wanted, and not to get upset when they were turned down. Since these promises may be easier made than kept, mental rehearsal—rehearsing in your mind doing what you promised to do—can help. The more often you imagine asking for sex when you want it, for example, the better the chances you will actually do it.

A tougher issue for many people involves not expressing a certain feeling. An example is the man in the dialogue on page 515, who told his partner he wouldn't sulk when she rebuffed his sexual advances. But how does one *not* sulk? Not doing something is much harder to conceptualize than doing something, so we need to turn the question around. How would he like to act when she says no? Let's say he answers, "I'd like to come across as feeling that it's no big deal, that we can always have sex another time, and I'd like to be open to doing something else with her."

This is a good answer, because it includes not only his actions but also the thought "It's no big deal." This will allow him to feel better about the rebuff and enable him to be open to doing something else.

One thing he can do, as often as possible, is to imagine her saying no to sex and then tell himself, "It's no big deal. We can always have sex another time." When he's comfortable with this, he can add a second element to his fantasy: his being interested in doing something else with her, whether from her suggestion or from his.

The whole movie in his head might go like this:

• He makes a sexual advance
• She says she's not interested in the way he wants her to say this
• He tells himself, "It's no big deal"
• He's open and interested as she suggests something else to do

After he's comfortable with the whole movie, he should add some variations—for example, she saying she's not interested in her old way (because she may not always remember to do it the way he wants) and he making a suggestion about doing something else without waiting for her to make one.

When the typical frequency problem recurs, and you can be sure it will, make every effort not to let it get you down. Instead of telling yourself that this is further proof that you'll never resolve the problem, ask yourself what you can learn from the experience. Maybe you need to do more mental rehearsal of how you want to react when she turns you down, or maybe you need more practice in new ways of initiating sex. Then tell yourself something like this: "No reason to get upset. We tried, but were both tired and just got back into old habits again. I have to be careful about initiating when I'm tired and I need a lot more rehearsal on not getting upset when she says no."

And last, don't forget the self–pep talk exercise in Chapter 21 (pages 405–407). Use it whenever you feel discouraged or that you failed in something you said you would do.

The suggestions in this chapter have been helpful to many couples with complaints about sexual desire and frequency. If you find you can't put them into practice or that they don't work for you and your partner, make an appointment with a competent sex therapist. The sooner you do this, the better the chances you'll achieve the results you want.

What You Can Do for Your Son

"No one ever talked to me about sex. The word was never mentioned in our house. I'd like it to be different for my boy."—MAN, 28

"When I was about fifteen, my father gave me a pamphlet to read. It was mainly about male and female plumbing and how babies are made. It had nothing to say about the questions that were troubling me at the time. I hope to be more sensitive to my sons' concerns."—MAN, 33

"I had lots of questions in high school about girls, love, dating, and sex. I wished I had someone older to talk to. But I could never talk to Dad about anything. I could talk to Mom but it didn't seem right to go to her about these subjects. How can I make it so my kids will feel free to approach me?"—MAN, 37

"I'm still angry about it. The Church taught me nothing but crap about sex and my folks didn't say anything. That's no way to prepare people for living in the world. I deserved better. Everyone deserves better."—MAN, 51

MANY men have asked for guidelines to provide a better sex education for their children than they themselves received. Although much of the material in this chapter is relevant to both girls and boys, and although mothers have an important role to play in the sex education of their male children, because of time and space considerations I focus on what fathers can do for their sons.

It's a noble desire to want your sons to have a better introduction to sex and related subjects than you had. But doing something about it is a bit more complicated than it seems. Some men have told me that they want to have better man-to-man talks with their teenage sons about sex. As far as I'm concerned, adolescence is a little late to begin sex education, and those famous talks are useless at any age.

If you desire to do better by your sons, the most important thing to consider is that a good sex education requires a loving, respectful relationship between father and son. A far greater tragedy than the absence of a good sex education is the absence of any kind of human relationship between father and son. I used to do workshops called "Man to Man," for heterosexual men who wanted to explore closer relationships with other men. One thing that happened in every workshop, with no prodding from me, was that the participants started talking about their fathers, always in a sad way. Their stories were invariably about what wasn't there: Many men couldn't remember a hug or kiss from their fathers; many couldn't remember their fathers ever saying they loved them; many said their fathers weren't interested in them and didn't respect or like them; and almost all concurred they couldn't talk to their dads. It is difficult to convey the depth of the sadness, frustration, and anger these men expressed. And their reports and feelings have been echoed by most of the men I've seen in therapy and had as friends. This is the subject that makes grown men cry.

I know that things are changing, that fathers are taking a larger role in child-rearing, but I think even more may be needed. If you want to do better by your son than was done to you, the first thing is to ensure there is a connection between the two of you, that you are a father in fact as well as in name.

Connection covers a lot of ground. At the very least, it means spending time together, really listening to your son, acknowledging his inclinations and feelings, sharing your interests and feelings and, yes, even biases, and expressing your love and appreciation for him. Underlying and supporting these behaviors is an attitude of respect for this small, naïve, and fragile human being.

It's not unusual for a three-, four-, or five-year-old boy to say that his feelings are hurt, that he's shy or nervous, or that he loves you. We need to acknowledge and accept those feelings. What we don't need to do is tell him he shouldn't feel that way or indicate that only girls talk about feelings. In response to "I'm scared a monster might eat me," it's far better to say "You're really afraid a monster might get you" (perhaps followed by a comment indicating that he, or the two of you, can fight the monster off) than "That's silly, there's nothing to be afraid of." In response to "Do you love me?" it's crucial to reassure him of your love rather than dismissing his question with "What kind of stupid question is that?"

Little people have many fears. The other day, for example, the local television news featured a kindergarten class on the first day of school. A number of the children were scared, and one very frightened boy got under a desk and refused to come out. I don't know what was done about him, but I've seen fathers in such situations berate a boy for his timidity, call him a sissy (or say that others will consider him so), or order him to shape up. A better way is to acknowledge his feelings, stay with him, and see what can be worked out. If you're open to him and the memory of your own childhood, it shouldn't be hard to understand his fears. Leaving home and going to school involve entering a whole new universe, and the prospects don't seem bright. There are a zillion strange kids all over the place—how is he going to get the kind of attention for himself that he's accustomed to?—and for all your boy knows, the teacher could be Dracula's mother. No wonder he's under the desk. What's amazing is not what he's doing but the fact that *all* the kids aren't hiding under their desks. The boy under the desk needs understanding and support.

But boys in such situations often don't get what they need. After being admonished hundreds of times to be strong, to shape up, to stop acting like a sissy, boys learn to hide their feelings and to act tough regardless of how they feel. The result is adult males who are always pretending to be someone they're not and who are fearful of letting anyone know what's going on inside.

Little boys, like little girls, like to touch, hug, and kiss, but parents, especially fathers, stop touching their boys early. Although affectionate touching is a general problem in our culture, especially for males, something needs to be done about it if we want our children to be better prepared for intimate relationships than we were. Physical affection is an essential way of conveying love and support. Let's hope your son won't show up at a "Man to Man" workshop twenty years from now and cry that his father never kissed him. While I'm on the subject of physical affection, it's important to add that no one ever outgrows the need for it. What's wrong with hugging and kissing your son, even though he's fifteen or twenty or forty? Despite all the sexual titillation, our culture is one of the most touch-deprived in the world, and our males are the most touch-deprived people in it. Why not touch your son, whatever his age?

Almost all the men I've talked to complained that their fathers didn't have time for them. Dad was rarely home and, when he was, he was too busy talking on the phone, working in the yard, or watching television to be with his boy. Here is how one man described it:

> It's amazing. I grew up thinking a man was someone who was gone most of the time, then showed up and ordered people around and, aside from that, never said a word. I don't want my sons to have to deal with that kind of situation.

Don't kid yourself. A real relationship requires time: time spent doing things, talking, and just hanging out together. Without the time, there can be no relationship.

Children are extremely sensitive to how much time you give them. When my friend Ian was three, both his mother, a physician, and I were quite busy and not seeing much of him. One day his mother explained to him how demanding her work was and said she hoped he wasn't upset that she couldn't be with him more. His angry answer was gut-wrenching: "And I hope you won't be upset when you come home and I don't have time to play with you. I'm a very busy person." His mother and I quickly decided to be home more.

Divorced fathers represent a special group when it comes to spending time with their children. Studies have shown that most divorced dads spend minuscule amounts of time with their sons (and daughters as well). No amount of rationalization about the quality of that time can change the fact that this is not good for the child. I realize it's often tough. Your ex-wife may not make it easy to see the kids and it can be difficult trying to balance your work, your own social life, and time with them. There may also be a desire to avoid the child because contact can bring up sad or ugly memories about the marriage, feelings of missing the child, and so on. Nonetheless, there's a boy who probably wants your attention and love more than almost anything in the world, although he may not be able to show it in ways that are immediately clear to you.

It is up to you, not the child, to maintain contact. Some divorced fathers go the other way. When the mother of a five-year-old told her former husband that their son missed seeing and hearing from him, the father's response was: "If he wants to talk or see me, tell him to call." It is not the responsibility of a child to establish or maintain contact with his father. The very idea boggles the mind.

The divorced father who wants to be a real father can be one. It may be difficult, it may mean making peace with your ex, it may mean less time for other activities you like, it may mean extra expense, but it can be done. The rewards can be immense, to both father and son.

Many of the men I've talked to complained bitterly about their fathers' lack of tolerance for who they were. Many said they never could do anything good enough or fast enough to suit their dads. By definition, children are undeveloped in many ways. Their physical strength and coordination fall far short of adult standards, as do their vocabulary and thinking abilities. Too many fathers demand too much from their boys, rationalizing it as setting high standards. High standards are fine, as long as they take into account the age, ability, and interests of the child. But many fathers don't understand just how limited their son's abilities are. Two-, three-, and four-year-old boys can't throw a ball very well, and when you throw one at them, even a soft one, they get scared and are more likely to try to protect themselves than try to catch it. That's just the way it is. Constantly criticizing and belittling a little boy for not being what he can't be is nothing but cruel and destructive.

What needs to be done comes up in small, seemingly trivial ways. Heroics are not what's required in child-rearing. Rather, what's needed is attention to the little details of life. One such trivial detail is the seat belt in cars. Sooner or later, your child is going to want to buckle himself in and unbuckle himself unassisted. And many parents bungle it right there. It's understandable, of course; you're in a hurry and it takes the child what seems like an hour to get the belt on or off. So the parent often takes over, against the protestations and rage of the child, doing the belt himself, and accompanies this with denigrating remarks about the child's slowness. Once or twice won't hurt, but repeated application of the same treatment will eventually do marked damage to the child's self-esteem and sense of competence.

You also need tolerance for your son's interests. Not every boy is interested in sports and other "manly" things. What's wrong if a boy is more interested in playing house than in throwing balls, more interested in the family cat or dog than in hitting his sister, or more interested in coloring books than riding a bicycle? And what's wrong if a teenage boy is more interested in drama or dance than in football or basketball? This is a difficult issue for many men because of their concern about how other children will react to a boy who doesn't seem masculine enough. But you have to weigh that concern against the risks of pushing the child to give up his genuine interests and spend time in pursuits that he doesn't care about and may never be good at. To be sure, a boy with none of the traditional masculine interests will have trouble with some of his peers and will often feel left out. But a boy who's unhappy because he's not doing what he wants and who's learned not to trust his own instincts and inclinations will also have problems.

We need to give our kids countless strokes, to appreciate and praise their small accomplishments, to give them the space and support to explore their own interests and desires.

Some readers may think that I'm too biased toward the child's perspective. After all, they say, the world does impose real limits. Parents do have to work, and children can't get everything they want. I couldn't agree more. Children can't have everything they want nor should they. They have to become socialized into the ways of the family and the world, and one of the most important lessons they need to learn is about limits: They can't have Daddy or Mommy all to themselves; they can't stay up all night; they can't make messes and leave the cleaning up for someone else.

Spending more time with your son does not mean spending all your time with him. Acknowledging his feelings does not mean he can do whatever he desires. The boy under the desk in kindergarten sooner or later is going to have to come out and join the class. The boy who delights in hitting his baby brother or sister must be made to stop, no matter how disappointing that may be to him. But there are different ways of accomplishing these things, and that's the point. The boy who is constantly belittled will learn different things about himself and the world than will the child who is treated with greater respect—not equality, because children are not equal, but simply respect.

So when should you have that famous man-to-man talk about sex? With a little luck, never. Needing to have that talk suggests to me that something is terribly wrong. Kids don't suddenly have an impulse to know all about manhood, women, love, and sex. They're curious about many aspects of all these subjects at different times. Effective education is almost totally informal, just dealing with the subjects as they come up.

For example, Ian started asking questions about "womens" when he was three. One of the first things he asked was why womens didn't wrestle. He occasionally watched wrestling on television and had seen only men participate, so he assumed there were no women wrestlers and wanted to know the reasons. Later on came questions based on other observations and information: Why didn't womens have pee-pees? Why couldn't he marry his mother? Would his pee-pee be as big as mine when he grew up? Why couldn't he or I have a baby? Where do babies come out of a woman's body? Could a girl be a pal? And so on. While none of these questions had to do with the mechanics of sex (most children have far less interest in glistening vaginas and thrusting penises than parents imagine), they all related to his developing ideas about gender roles and sexuality.

One time when he was about three, he said he wanted a pee-pee as big as mine (of course any adult penis looks very large to a small boy). When I asked why, he was surprised by my failure to see the obvious: "So I'll be able to pee more, silly." A few days later he announced that his pee-pee must be getting bigger because he had just peed a whole lot. This, by the way, is a good example of the concrete and logical (but inaccurate) way that young children think. I could have used his statement as an opening to explain what else penises are for, but I let it pass.

This is the best kind of education, where information is given many times in ways relevant to the child, the situations, and the questions raised. I think it would have been irrelevant and inappropriate to explain to Ian at this point that bigger penises aren't necessarily better.

To a three-year-old boy, everything bigger, taller, faster, and older looks better because it means being grown-up and in charge of one's own life or, as Ian put it, "being the chief." It's crucial always to remember that there are vast differences between an adult mind and the mind of a three-, five-, ten-, or twelve-year-old. When information is given and questions are answered in relevant ways over the years, there is no need for the Big Discussion later on unless, of course, the child requests it.

Although I said earlier that there can be no good sex education without a decent human relationship between father and child, it's also true that, whether intended or not, whether labeled as such or not, sex education goes on all the time. And it's a very broad education, encompassing not only sex itself but also sex roles, love, and what it means to be a man. It's also broad in the sense that children learn at least as much, if not more, from what they see as from what you tell them.

If your son observes that you like women, in the person of his mother, he learns something crucial that he can't learn another way. If he sees you being physically affectionate with his mother, that's another important lesson. If he hears you expressing feelings to her, to himself, and to others, he's learned another lesson about what it means to be a man. If you don't express feelings, he learns a different lesson. Virtually every man I've talked to who has trouble expressing himself said that his father was the same way.

Your son learns another crucial lesson if he sees and hears you and his mother talking things out, especially when the two of you don't agree. If, on the other hand, he sees the two of you shrieking, calling each other names, using or threatening violence, or one of you storming out, he also learns something. He's learning how one behaves with a person one loves, and you can be certain those lessons will leave an indelible mark on him.

He also learns from how you treat his sister, if he has one, and other females. And you can bet your marbles that he'll learn something if you go around making comments like "Women are weird," "What do women want?" and "There's no satisfying a woman." The same idiocies will spout from his own mouth within a few days.

Without knowing it, a great many men, including many of our fathers, display contempt for and fear of women. Children always learn from such exhibitions. So take care about what you say about females and how you treat them. If a rape case is reported on the news, for instance, what you say and imply will be well noted by your son. Many men report that their fathers' attitude was always that "she was asking for it" or that "she helped bring it about." Be careful as well about what you say and imply about women's aptitudes, abilities, and behavior. "What do you expect? She's on the rag"—that's not something you'd like to hear yourself say, but a great many men heard it from their fathers. It's also good to be aware of any comments about weakness or fear, two qualities men often attribute to women. Just remember, your son is also weak and fearful, and he knows it. He will tend to apply to himself the denigrating statements you make about other people's fear and weakness.

A lot of men's sillier comments about women are made in groups of men. How you treat other men and what you and they say about women will also be noted by your son. One thing that men in groups often do is to use the words girl, lady, or pussy to refer to a man who acts weak or frightened or even makes a mistake. This is guaranteed to generate contempt for women and for the expressive, vulnerable side not only of the man who is being denigrated but of all the males present. If you use these terms in this way, you might want to consider what you're doing and what effect it will have on your son.

But suppose you were raised with traditional and negative ideas about women and haven't yet succeeded in escaping that heritage? One thing to do is explain that to your son. You might, for example, refer to a derogatory comment you made about women and say why you wish you hadn't said it and why you did. Children often enjoy hearing how attitudes, sexual and otherwise, have changed since their parents were children. This can open the door to the huge and important issues of changing societal views of men and women and sexuality.

Some men who've read what I've written above have sadly said that it all sounds good, but they haven't done it and now their sons are ten, fifteen, or older. Is there anything they can do now? The answer is yes. It's never too late. But again I emphasize that what's needed is not a lecture about sex but the establishment of a relationship. Children of all ages dislike lectures and usually don't listen to them anyway. If you'd like to spend time with your son and get to know him, then by all means do so. Here is one man's story about doing this:

I was horrified when I realized what had happened. I had been so busy building my company that Rob was now fourteen and I didn't know him at all. For all practical purposes, the boy didn't have a father. I resolved to make it different.

I started asking him to do things with me, but he rejected my offers, saying he was too busy. After consulting with my wife and a therapist, I had a talk with Rob. This was one of the most difficult things I've ever done. I told him the whole story, about how I had made a mistake being so wrapped up in work, about feeling sad because I hadn't spent more time with him, and about wanting to make up for it. I poured my guts out and even started crying while talking. I can't say he jumped for joy, but he seemed open to me.

Thus began a slow process of getting acquainted with him. His schedule was as packed as mine, but we started setting aside time to be together. I took him to my office and showed him what I did. I took more of an interest in his studies, his ball games, and his friends. Talking wasn't easy for him at first. Like he didn't quite trust me. But he gradually opened up.

As he did, I found out some surprising things. I always thought he was socially adept. He seemed to have lots of friends and there were always girls calling him. He finally confided in me that he was very shy and felt very uncomfortable in groups and alone with girls. He was afraid to approach the girls he liked and was just as afraid of saying no to the ones who called him. It took everything I had to stop myself from telling him what to do, but I did; just listened and acknowledged what he said. It must have worked, because he talked to me about it at other times and sometimes even said that it was good to talk to me.

As this story indicates, it's not always easy. Your son may have been desperately hoping for your attention and approval, but if he hasn't had it for a long time he may well be suspicious and guarded at first, and perhaps angry as well. It will probably take a while. You need to persist.

Not only is it never too late, but it also doesn't matter if your father didn't do well by you. You can be a good father no matter how poorly you were fathered. An example is martial arts champion and movie star Chuck Norris, whose own father was an alcoholic and far less than a positive role model.

Having grown up without a strong father image . . . I wanted my two sons to know that I was there, that I cared, and that I was always in their corner. I am very close to my sons. I have played with them, listened to their problems, held them in my arms when they were hurt, and shared most of the major events, crises, and successes of their lives. One of my biggest gratifications today is that my grown-up sons aren't embarrassed to kiss me hello or goodbye in front of anyone and that they come willingly to me for advice or help if they have problems.

And neither they nor I have ever been ashamed to say, "I love you," three simple words that mean so much and are so rarely said between parents and their children. I never told my father that, and to this day it bothers me that he died alone, not knowing that I loved him despite his faults.

Being a real father has many benefits for men. One is that it can make for more closeness between you and the boy's mother and for the whole family. Another is that, in the truest sense, it's a real learning experience, one that mothers take for granted and that many fathers know little about. My experience with Ian has enriched me in more ways than I can recount. It's deepened my understanding of what it means to be a human being and in many ways has made me a better therapist and more sensitive person.

When angry, women are likely to complain that men are just little boys in business suits. I think there is truth in that statement and I think it applies equally to women. There's a little Ian or a little Bernie or a little Diane in each of us, often not too far beneath the surface. Being with kids gives a good look at not only who they are, but also who we are. It demonstrates with eloquent clarity just how frail and vulnerable we all are and how much we need love, understanding, and support.

Being with them also gives the clearest picture I know of just how difficult everything is and, at the same time, how much persistence and practice pay off. Watching Ian learn to walk, after falling thousands of times, and learn to kick a ball in a straight line, after hundreds of times when it went everywhere but straight, and learn to tell a b from a d, after months when he almost always got them confused, gave me a new respect for the abilities of people and a greater understanding of the importance of not giving up but persevering as long as it takes to achieve success.

Helping to raise Ian has also given me a profound lesson in humility, a lesson I needed and that many men could use. No matter how hard I tried, no matter how careful I was, hardly a day went by when I didn't blow it with him in some way. I said or did the wrong thing or reacted in a way I later regretted. It's not that I was intentionally trying to wrong him; it was usually a conflict of demands, as with the seat belt. Yes, I admit I more than once grabbed the seat belt out of his hands and buckled it myself because we had to be somewhere at a certain time. I knew I was right—we were already late—but I couldn't forget his wails of rage and the sad look on his face, as if I had betrayed him. I learned something I already knew, that you can't satisfy everyone, but I also learned about the importance of letting others down as gently as possible. At the very least, not to criticize him for being slow with the belt.

And then there were those horrible times when I realized I had just said something unbelievably stupid to Ian that my father had said to me when I was young, word for word, and that I had always hated. Although I apologized and resolved to do better next time (no more quotes from Bernie's childhood book of sayings-definitely-not-worth-repeating), it was an important lesson on how difficult it is to avoid repeating the errors of past generations.

Being a good father is also important for men because it demands that we behave in ways that are crucial for the maintenance of adult love relationships as well. Children are the real teachers of intimacy. You can't be a good father without being expressive, supportive, sensitive, nurturing, and loving. There is no good fathering without the ability to cuddle, to soothe real and imagined hurts, to apologize for things done and things not done, to express love and caring in a variety of ways. The traditional male hero—silent and tough—can be neither a good father nor a good lover. It's fascinating to me that the requirements of being a good father are precisely the things that women want most from us and that the experts tell us are necessary for stable, loving adult relationships. Maybe there's a moral here.

When do you talk to your son about sex? My answer is the same as it would be to the questions of when do you talk about family matters, education, or money. Whenever you want, whenever he wants, whenever it's appropriate, and starting from as early an age as possible.

It's fascinating to compare the amount of time and energy parents spend with their children on other important issues such as responsibility, schoolwork, choice of adult work, and dealing with money with the amount of time and energy they spend on the important issue of sex.

With regard to money, we early on teach them the value of coins and paper bills, we give them piggy banks, allowances, and later real bank accounts, we let them pay for smaller and later larger items at the store, and when they're older we may give them a credit card. Over the years we have hundreds if not thousands of discussions with them about making and spending money, the value of money, responsibility about financial obligations, and the like.

We'd all be better off if we just added sex to the list of crucial things we have to prepare our children for and tried to discuss it as relevantly, frequently, and clearly as we do the other items on this list. This may seem to be a cold way of dealing with sex, but I don't think it is. Although sex certainly does include personal and family values, so do the other issues. You should feel as free to pass on your values about sex and love as you do about personal responsibility, honesty, schoolwork, money, and the rest.

One time you should definitely deal with sex is when your son wants to. You want him to feel safe in asking you about sex (or anything else, for that matter). This is easier said than done because his questions may well come at the wrong time and in the ways that may make them difficult to hear, let alone answer. What do you do, for example, when your seven- or eight-year-old asks over dinner, in front of the rest of the family and perhaps the neighbors as well, "What's a blow job?"? Questions like this come up all the time when children feel free to ask. If you respond critically or harshly, there'll be no more questions and you will have lost a world of opportunities. If, on the other hand, you can appreciate the fact that your son feels safe in asking you and put together a satisfying answer—and it's certainly acceptable to tell him you'll be happy to discuss the matter with him after dinner, as long as you do remember to do so—you'll hear more questions as they occur to him.

It can help to keep four things in mind. The first is that you should ensure you understand both the question and the child who's asking it. A joke I heard many years ago shows what can happen when such understanding is absent. After a day in school, six-year-old Johnny comes to his father and asks, "Where do I come from?" Dad has been dreading this moment but also preparing for it. Full of tension, he launches into his rehearsed speech, complete with diagrams, about eggs and sperm and birds and bees. He rattles on for a long time (which, for a six-year-old, can be anything over thirty seconds) and barely notices Johnny. Finally, speech concluded, he asks Johnny if he answered the question. Johnny responds: "Not exactly. One of the kids in my class said he came from New York and I just wanted to know where I came from."

Dad would have been spared his long lecture had he gotten more information about what his son wanted. A simple statement like "I'd be happy to tell you, but could you first tell me how this question came up" would have put Johnny's father on the right path.

A second thing to keep in mind is that no one expects you to give the world's ultimate answer on everything pertaining to sex (or even blow jobs); what you say doesn't have to be all-inclusive and doesn't have to be perfect, and the less it's like a lecture, the better it will be received.

A third consideration is that sex education does not refer only to the mechanics of the sex act. Sex acts are always seen in some kind of context, and these contexts are of great interest to children of all ages: what it means to be a man, how to treat women, what love is, how one goes about getting to know girls, shyness, what's right and wrong, and so forth. It's of no benefit to the boy to know the importance of the clitoris, for instance, if his general feeling about women is that they are merely objects put here to gratify his erotic desires.

In answering the blow job question, I think it's necessary to talk about the mechanics (a woman sucking a man's penis to give him pleasure) because that's what defines the act, but it's also entirely appropriate to say that this is most often done when two people really care about each other and that there's something similar a man can do for a woman. You can go into the mechanics of that act (licking her clitoris) if your son seems interested and even give one of the slang labels he's already heard or soon will (going down on her or eating pussy, for instance).

It's often easier and less embarrassing at first for both parent and child to talk about some of the contexts than about sex itself. But once you've established the habit of comfortable talking, it's easier to get to more difficult subjects.

The last thing to keep in mind in dealing with your son's questions, and sex education generally, is that you want to find a middle road between ignoring the subject altogether and pushing it at him or overwhelming him. It's impossible to stay the middle course perfectly—at times you will err one way, at times the other—but if you guide yourself by your son's reactions, you'll do fine.

Most men, and women too, are not very comfortable discussing sex with their children. That is to be expected, given the way our society deals with sex. And the children don't necessarily make it easy. Euphemisms about storks, birds and bees, and putting Daddy's car in Mommy's garage will not satisfy them after they reach four or five, but at the same time they may be put off by the truth. Ian asked about sex when he was six, and after I explained briefly in simple, down-to-earth terms and was about to congratulate myself on the good job I had done, he exclaimed, "You just made that up and it's not even funny!" And I heard "That's gross" from him many times in our discussions about sex.

Overcoming our discomfort in dealing with the sexuality of our children isn't easy for many parents, but it can and should be done. One of the best ways I know is to start talking about sex with your partner (or a therapist or a trusted friend), especially about the discomfort you feel with your children. It can also help to tell the children about your uneasiness ("When I was growing up no one ever talked to me about sex, so it's a little hard for me to do it") and then go on to answer their questions or tell them what you want to say.

Parents aren't the only ones uncomfortable discussing sex. As already indicated, children sometimes find it hard to understand or accept what they hear from you. And after the advent of puberty, something else can happen. A previously open boy can shut down. He no longer asks questions about sex and seems uninterested in and sometimes totally dismissive of what you say. Assuming that there is a basically decent relationship between the two of you, this usually occurs because of the boy's concerns about privacy and vulnerability.

It's important not to give up under these circumstances. The boy hasn't lost interest—to the contrary, chances are his interest has skyrocketed—but he's just protecting himself. You should still feel free to say what you want and try not to get upset when he doesn't respond the way you'd like. You might check how you've been talking to him about sex to make sure it hasn't been lecturing or in a way that makes him feel inadequate.

In addition to talking, you might occasionally give him something to read. If you run across an article or a chapter in a book that addresses sex in a useful way, you might leave it for your son along with a short note: "Wish I had something like this when I was younger. Thought you might find it interesting."

If you do leave something for him to read, you can mention it a week or so later, but try not to do it in a way that could make him feel bad. Instead of asking "Did you read that article?"—which could cause him to feel guilty if he has not—it might be better to say something like, "I liked the point the author made about sex being for pleasure rather than performance. It took me a long time to see it that way." If your son responds, fine. If not, let it go. Don't pester him to talk if he doesn't want to.

Here are several possibilities for discussion, dealing with both contexts and sex, that have worked for some fathers:

- While watching someone like Barbara Walters or Diane Sawyer on TV, you could mention that it's good to see a woman like her in an important position, something that was unheard of when you were a teenager. This can easily lead to a discussion of the many ways in which women were restricted then and even now.
- At an appropriate time, you could say something about how it was for you growing up, dating, being interested in girls, and so on. It's best if your story has to do with your ignorance, questions, concerns, or embarrassment. Bragging of any kind is a definite no-no.
- When superhuman or supermacho men are portrayed on TV or in the movies—someone like Rambo, for example—you might mention how destructive and silly they are and the kinds of harm that can result from trying to emulate them. You could mention the supermacho men of your childhood and how you wanted to be like them. You might also want to say something about the destructive competition among men that the media delight in portraying.
- You can also comment about other harmful male values. When five-year-old Ian was about to go to his first soccer practice, we had a little talk because he was nervous. As a farewell, I said, "Have a good time. That's the important thing." Much to my surprise, he exploded, "Bernie, you know that's not true. In sports, the only important thing is winning!" Where he got this Vince Lombardi philosophy was beyond me. His mother had never said any such thing and neither had I. He hadn't yet met his soccer coach, so it couldn't have been from him. We never did figure out where the idea came from, but we had a number of discussions in the following weeks about the purpose of sports and the idea of winning. And I became much more careful about what I was conveying when he and I played soccer.

- Since a great many children, especially teenagers, feel terminally shy (their expression), any opportunity to dive into the subject of shyness should not be passed up. Often the child will simply tell you he's shy or act in ways that give you the message. A number of parents have found that confessing their own feelings of shyness made their sons feel more comfortable and better able to talk not only about shyness but also about other fears as well.

- When watching an appropriate show on TV or in the movies, you could mention how much more openly sex is portrayed now than when you were growing up. Young people are fascinated by my story of how a movie I saw in high school was put on the Catholic Church's proscribed list because an actress in it said the word *virgin*. You might mention that you wish sexuality had been more openly discussed when you were growing up. Because it wasn't, you developed many mistaken ideas (and you might want to say what one or two of those were).

- When there's news about AIDS or other sexually transmitted diseases, you could note that sex has certainly become more risky than it used to be and the importance of using protection against disease and conception. You could continue with what the major risks of sex were for you and how you dealt with them.

- Although it has nothing to do with the mechanics of sex, the issue of fathering should be discussed. Children of all ages seem interested in how their fathers were raised. Letting your son know how you were treated as a child, what was good and what wasn't, will give him crucial information about yourself and help him start thinking about what it means to be a good dad. Letting him know how you're trying to improve on your father's efforts is also important, as is eliciting information on what he wants from you and what complaints he has.

Let me emphasize that none of what I'm suggesting is easy. You will feel frustrated, annoyed, angry, and like an absolute failure many, many times. Being a good parent is one of the most demanding and difficult tasks in this world. But it is also one of the most rewarding. One of the biggest rewards is that despite all the difficulties and screwups, you can be a father that both you and your son will be proud of.

Although this book focuses on heterosexuality, of course not all children of heterosexual parents are heterosexual. If your son is homo-sexual or show signs that he might be, he will have great need of your understanding and support. And you may well be in conflict and in need of help for yourself. This is a difficult situation for all concerned because of the way our society, even these days, regards homosexuality. Many fathers, because of the way they were raised, don't do a good job of dealing with it. Berating your son and bringing in "experts" such as teachers, coaches, and religious authorities to straighten him out will not help. Such actions will only make him feel worse about what he already may not feel good about.

Exactly how to deal with yourself and your son if confronted with this predicament is beyond the scope of this work, but I mention it because it certainly will come up for some readers. Fortunately, there are now many therapists and counseling services, as well as some teachers and schools, that are sensitive to the issue and that can help both of you. It helps to keep the larger scheme of things in mind. He's still the same son you've known and loved all these years and you're still the father he's needed and may now need more than ever. Your love may be sorely tested, but let it bring out your best and guide you to act in ways that honor both father and son.

If you want to go further in this question of how to best be a father to your sons (and your daughters as well), here's a useful exercise. Just take some time reviewing your childhood and ask yourself what you disliked about the way your father treated you. Then ask yourself how you would have wanted him to be, how you would have wanted him to father you. If you come up with concepts like more loving, more attentive, more approachable, or more sensitive, get specific by asking how you would have liked him to express these qualities. By the time you're finished with this, you'll probably have a very good idea of how you want to be toward your children.

Be the father to your children that you wish you had had. It will mean the world to them, and to you as well. Sex education will be just a small but integral part of this loving human connection. And come to think of it, maybe that's what sex itself should be: a small but integral part of a respectful, understanding, supportive, loving human connection.

Appendix

The Effects of Drugs on Male Sexuality

THE issue of drug effects on sexuality is complex, and the following discussion and charts are intended to be suggestive rather than exhaustive. The charts comprise three major categories: prescription drugs that may cause adverse sexual side effects; street drugs, including tobacco and alcohol; and prescription drugs that may have beneficial effects on sex. Some medicines could not be included because there is no information about their sexual effects. (Sex is not a high priority of drug researchers.) Just because a drug is absent from the list does not mean it is without sexual side effects. And just because we don't list negative effects for a particular drug on the list does not mean it doesn't have such effects for some people. Bad news can take a long time to be made public.

In dealing with drugs, prescribed or not, it is crucial to understand that they are not innocuous substances. Any drug you put into your body, regardless of the amount and how you take it, can have serious effects. **All drugs should be considered powerful and potentially dangerous.** Even widely used over-the-counter medicines may cause distressing side effects for some people. Exercise caution.

It is also important to understand that hardly any drug in any of the categories has the same effects on all the people who take it. A drug that is known to have adverse effects, for instance, may only have these effects on 10 to 15 percent of the men who take it. So even if you have an erection problem and are taking a medicine known to produce this result in some people, this

537

does not mean the drug is the cause of your erection problem. It may be, and then again it may not be.

Some detective work is needed to determine what is going on. *Such work should always be done in conjunction with a physician.* Perhaps a different dose of the same drug will help, or a different drug in the same category. Or perhaps the drug is having the adverse sexual effect only in conjunction with other drugs you are taking. And there is also the possibility that the drug has nothing to do with your sexual problem. If, for instance, you are having trouble getting or keeping an erection with your partner, but not with masturbation, it's doubtful that the drug is what needs changing. Sex therapy, either with a qualified professional or by using the appropriate exercises in this book, may help.

Prescription Drugs with Adverse Effects: The main thing that needs to be said about these drugs is that **under no circumstances should you fiddle with dosages or stop taking them without the consultation of a physician who is knowledgeable about drugs and your medical and sexual situation.** Some antidepressants and other drugs should not be discontinued abruptly, but need to be tapered off. Other drugs may not have the intended main effect unless taken in certain strengths. If you think a prescribed medicine you are taking may have something to do with a sex problem you are having, talk the situation over with the physician who prescribed it or with a physician who specializes in sexual problems.

In a few cases, what looks like a negative side effect can also be seen from a different perspective. As I mentioned in Chapter 22, several antidepressants and antianxiety agents have been used in conjunction with sex therapy to help men learn ejaculatory control precisely because they have the side effect of making ejaculations more difficult to achieve. Unfortunately, some of these drugs also have the side effect of making erections more difficult to achieve.

Street Drugs: People have been looking for aphrodisiacs since antiquity and every substance imaginable has been tried: all sorts of barks and herbs, rhinoceros horns, bugs (like Spanish fly), turtle eggs, the testicles of many animals, oysters, and just about everything else. The word *honeymoon* comes from the former European custom of drinking honeyed wine to promote sexual desire during the first moon (month) of marriage.

Although a reliable and safe aphrodisiac has yet to be found, a number of common drugs do have beneficial effects for some people. But, as indicated in the charts, the amount you take is usually crucial. Many men find that small amounts of alcohol make them feel sexier and function better. But alcohol is a central nervous system depressant and too much can lead to difficulty with erections. How much is too much depends on the individual, and you need to figure this out on your own. So it may be fine if you like one drink to relax, but you may find that three or four drinks is too much. If you are using street drugs, including alcohol, it is fine to experiment with decreasing the amount or giving them up altogether.

A caveat regarding street drugs. The charts only indicate *sexual* effects, both positive and negative. But there can be nonsexual side effects you should take into account. The volatile nitrites, including the popular amyl nitrite, are used to increase the intensity of orgasm and are usually thought not to have adverse sexual effects. But if you pop one even a few seconds too early, your erection may disappear. More important, amyl nitrite and its chemical cousin butyl nitrite—sold under such names as Locker Room, Rush, and Climax—can cause headaches and fainting, can increase the risk of stroke, and occasionally have led to death. I assume it's not necessary to comment on the general negative effects of other street drugs such as cocaine, heroin, and PCP.

The famous Spanish fly didn't make it into the charts, but I should say something about it. Made from beetles ground into a powder, it irritates the urinary tract and therefore leads some people to think they want sex. What they really want is a way to scratch their urethra. Nonetheless, they may experience increased erotic desire. Spanish fly, however, is not user-friendly. It is a dangerous potion and people have died from it.

Prescription Drugs with Beneficial Effects: This chart, unfortunately the shortest one, lists prescription drugs that have positive sexual side effects in some users. If you are already taking one of these medicines and aren't experiencing the positive sexual effects noted, or if you'd like to consider trying one of them, talk with a knowledgeable physician.

The following charts were prepared by John Buffum, Pharm.D., based on research he has been conducting since 1978. Dr. Buffum is a leading expert on the effects of drugs on sexual functioning and has published a number of important papers on this topic in professional journals. He has consulted research studies, case reports, and letters in medical journals, and also the personal reports of sex therapists such as myself and physicians who regularly prescribe the drugs in question. The information in the charts is considered valid through December 1991. Dr. Buffum is Associate Clinical Professor of Pharmacy, University of California, San Francisco, and Clinical Pharmacist, VA Medical Center, San Francisco.

PRESCRIPTION DRUGS WITH ADVERSE EFFECTS ON MALE SEXUAL FUNCTION

Drug	Decreased Desire	Erection Problems	Anorgasmia/ Delayed/Dry Ejaculation	Priapism or Other
ANTIHYPERTENSIVES				
Diuretics				
Bendroflumethiazide (Naturetin)	0	2	0	0
Chlorothiazide (Diuril)	0	2	2	0
Chlorthalidone (Hygroton)	0	2	0	0
Furosemide (Lasix)	0	0	0	0
Hydrochlorothiazide (Hydrodiuril)	1	1	0	0
Indapamide (Lozol)	0	0	0	0
Spironolactone (Aldactone)	2	2	0	0
Adrenergic Inhibitors: Beta-Adrenergic Blockers				
Atenolol (Tenormin)	0	1	0	0
Metoprolol (Lopressor)	0	0	0	0
Nadolol (Corgard)	0	1	0	0
Pindolol (Viskin)	0	1	0	0
Propranolol (Inderal)	1	2	0	0
Timolol (Blocadren)	1	1	1	0
Central-Acting Adrenergic Inhibitors				
Clonidine (Catapres)	0	2	0	0
Guanabenz (Wytensin)	0	1	0	0
Methyldopa (Aldomet)	2	3	2	0
Peripheral-Acting Adrenergic Antagonists				
Guanadrel (Hylorel)	0	1	2	0
Guanethidine (Ismelin)	2	3	3	1 (P)
Reserpine (Serpasil)	2	2	2	0
Alpha-Adrenergic Blockers				
Prazosin (Minipres)	0	1	0	1 (P)
Phenoxybenzamine (Dibenzyline)	0	0	3	0
Combined Apha- and Beta-Adrenergic Blockers				
Labetalol (Normodyne)	0	2	2	0

0 = No reports in medical literature
1 = Scattered cases, personal communication, or less than 10% occurence in studies
2 = 10–50% occurence in studies
3 = Greater than 50% occurence
P = Priapism—very serious when it occurs
EP = Ejaculatory pain

Drug	Decreased Desire	Erection Problems	Anorgasmia/ Delayed/Dry Ejaculation	Priapism or Other
ANTIHYPERTENSIVES (continued)				
Vasodilators				
Hydralazine (Apresoline)	0	0	0	1 (P)
Minoxidil (Loniten)	0	0	0	0
Angiotensin-Converting Enzyme Inhibitors				
Captopril (Capoten)	0	0	0	0
Enalapril (Vasotec)	0	0	0	0
Lisinopril (Zestril)	0	0	0	0
Slow Channel Calcium-Entry Blocking Agents				
Verapamil (Isoptin)	0	1	0	0
Nifedipine (Procardia)	0	1	0	0
ANTIDEPRESSANTS				
Amitriptyline (Elavil)	1	1	1	0
Amoxapine (Asendin)	1	1	1	1 (EP)
Bupropion (Wellbutrin)	1	1	0	0
Clomipramine (Anafranil)	1	2	3	1 (EP)
Desipramine (Norpramin)	1	1	1	1 (EP)
Doxepin (Sinequan)	1	1	1	0
Fluoxetine (Prozac)	1	1	2	0
Imipramine (Tofranil)	1	1	1	1 (EP)
Isocarboxazid (Marplan)	0	1	1	0
Maprotiline (Ludiomil)	1	1	1	0
Nortriptyline (Aventyl)	1	1	1	0
Phenelzine (Nardil)	0	2	2	0
Protriptyline (Vivactil)	1	1	1	1 (EP)
Sertraline (Zoloft)	0	0	2	0
Tranylcypromine (Parnate)	0	1	1	0
Trazodone (Desyrel)	0	0	1	1 (P)
Trimipramine (Surmontil)	0	0	1	0
ANTIMANIC-DEPRESSIVE AGENTS				
Lithium (Eskalith)	1	2	0	0

PRESCRIPTION DRUGS WITH ADVERSE EFFECTS ON MALE SEXUAL FUNCTION

Drug	Decreased Desire	Erection Problems	Anorgasmia/ Delayed/Dry Ejaculation	Priapism or Other
ANTIPSYCHOTICS				
Butaperazine (Repoise)	0	0	1	0
Chlorpromazine (Thorazine)	1	1	1	1 (P)
Chlorprothixine (Taractan)	0	0	1	0
Clozapine (Clozaril)	0	0	1	1 (P)
Fluphenazine (Prolixin)	0	2	3	1 (P)
Haloperidol (Haldol)	0	1	0	1 (P) 1 (EP)
Mesoridazine (Serentil)	0	0	1	1 (P)
Molindone (Moban)	0	0	0	1 (P)
Perphenazine (Trilafon)	0	0	3	0
Pimozide (Orap)	0	1	1	0
Trifluoperazine (Stelazine)	0	0	1	1 (P) 1 (EP)
Thioridazine (Mellaril)	0	3	3	1 (P) 1 (EP)
Thiothixine (Navane)	0	1	0	1 (P)
ANTIANXIETY DRUGS				
Alprazolam (Xanax)	1	1	1	0
Buspiron (Buspar)	0	0	0	0
Diazepam (Valium)	1	1	1	0
Lorazepam (Ativan)	1	0	1	0
HORMONES				
Androgens				
Testosterone	0	0	0	0
Other anabolic steroids (e.g. methandienone, norethandrolone)	3	3	0	0
Estrogens	3	3	0	0
Corticosteroids	0	0	0	0
Antiandrogens				
Cyproterone (Androcur)	3	3	0	0
Ketoconazole (Nizoral)	3	3	0	0
Medroxyprogesterone	3	3	0	0

0 = No reports in medical literature
1 = Scattered cases, personal communication, or less than 10% occurence in studies
2 = 10–50% occurence in studies
3 = Greater than 50% occurence
P = Priapism—very serious when it occurs
EP = Ejaculatory pain

Drug	Decreased Desire	Erection Problems	Anorgasmia/ Delayed/Dry Ejaculation	Priapism or Other
CARBONIC ANHYDRASE INHIBITORS				
Acetazolamide (Diamox)	1	0	0	0
Dichlorophenamide (Daranide)	1	0	0	0
Ethoxzolamide (Cardase)	1	0	0	0
Methazolamide (Neptazane)	1	0	0	0
ANTIEPILEPTIC DRUGS				
Carbamazepine (Tegretol)	2	2	0	0
Phenobarbital	2	2	0	0
Phenytoin (Dilantin)	2	2	0	0
Primadone (Mysoline)	2	2	0	0
MISCELLANEOUS DRUGS				
Aminocaproic acid (Amicar)	0	0	2	0
Amiodarone (Cordarone)	1	0	0	0
Cancer chemotherapy agents	2	2	0	0
Cimetidine (Tagamet)	0	2	0	0
Digoxin (Lanoxin)	2	2	0	0
Disopyramide (Norpace)	0	1	0	0
Disulfiram (Antabuse)	0	1	0	0
Metoclopramide (Reglan)	1	1	0	0
Naproxen (Naprosyn)	0	0	1	0
Ranitidine (Zantac)	0	0	0	0
Thiabendazole (Mintezol)	0	1	0	0

EFFECTS OF STREET DRUGS ON MALE SEXUAL FUNCTION

	Acute, Low-dose	Acute, High-dose	Chronic	Withdrawal	Recovery
Alcohol	Increased desire Delayed ejaculation Decreased tumescence	Erection problems Delayed ejaculation Decreased orgasmic intensity	Decreased drive Erection problems Ejaculation problems	Decreased desire Erection problems; fewer nocturnal erections	Return of normal sexual desire and erections for most, but damage to erections and sex drive may be permanent in some cases of severe alcoholism
Dissociative Anesthetics (PCP)	Sexual enhancement	Erection problems Ejaculation problems Decreased orgasm intensity	Erection problems Ejaculation problems Decreased orgasm intensity	Depression Decreased desire	No information
Opiates and Opioids (e.g., heroin, morphine, methadone)	Orgasmlike subjective effects	Erection problems Ejaculation problems Pharmacogenic orgasm	Decreased desire Erection problems Ejaculation problems	Increased nocturnal emissions, morning erections, and sex dreams	Return to normal sexual functioning
Stimulants (e.g., cocaine, amphetamine, methamphetamine)	Increased desire Delayed ejaculation	Increased desire Delayed or total ejaculatory inhibition Erection problems	Dose-driven desire Erection problems Ejaculation problems	Decreased desire Increased erectile ability	Return to normal sexual functioning
Psychedelics (LSD, MDMA, MDA)	Increased intimacy Heightened genital responsiveness Delayed ejaculation	Ejaculation problems	No information	No information	No information

Drug				
Nitrous Oxide				
Increased arousal Increased orgasm intensity	No information Probable decreased sexual function due to anesthesia	Erection problems due to myeloneuropathy	No immediate improvement in erectile function	Erection problems slowly reversed
Tobacco				
Possible decreased erection (Greater with increased age and diabetes)	Erection problems	Dose-driven erection problems	Possible return to baseline function, but erection problems may be irreversible with long-term use	Possible return to baseline function, but erection problems may be irreversible with long-term use
Volatile Nitrites				
Increased desire Enhanced perception of orgasm Facilitated anal sex Erection problems	Increased desire Erection problems	No reported chronic negative effects	None reported	None reported
Marijuana				
Increased desire Increased sensuality Delayed ejaculation	Decreased desire Erection problems Anorgasmia	Dose-dependent increased/decreased desire Delayed ejaculation Erection problems Anorgasmia	Return to preexisting function (May include sexual boredom and premature ejaculation)	Return to normal sexual functioning
Sedative Hypnotics (e.g., benzodiazepines, methaqualone, barbiturates)				
Enhanced arousal Decreased anxiety Delayed ejaculation	Enhanced arousal Erection problems Anorgasmia	Decreased desire Erection problems Ejaculation problems	Return to preexisting function	Return to normal sexual functioning

PRESCRIPTION DRUGS WITH BENEFICIAL EFFECTS ON MALE SEXUAL FUNCTION

Drug	Increased Desire	Increased Erectile Function	Increased Coital Frequency	Comments
Drugs Used for Reversal of Sexual Dysfunction Due to Illness				
Zinc salts	3	3	3	Reverses zinc deficiency due to renal failure
Bromocriptine (Parlodel)	3	3	3	Reverses hyperprolactinemia in parkinsonism
Testosterone	3	3	3	Reverses low testosterone in hypogonadism
L-dopa (with carbidopa—Sinemet)	2	1	0	May cause hypersexuality during treatment for parkinsonism
Selegiline (Eldepryl)	1	0	0	Treatment for parkinsonism
Pergolide (Permax)	1	0	0	Treatment for parkinsonism
Lisuride	3	0	3	Reversal of hyperprolactinemia
Drugs Used Specifically for Reversal of Erectile Dysfunction				
Yohimbine (Yocon)	0	2	0	
Apomorphine	0	3	0	
Quinelorane (LY163502)	0	3	0	Experimental use only
Luteinizing hormone releasing hormone (LHRH)	0	1	0	
Naloxone (Narcan)	0	3	0	
Naltrexone (Trexan)	0	3	0	
Nitroglycerine 2% topical (Nitropaste)	0	3	0	Applied to penis
Minoxidil 2% topical (Rogaine)	0	3	0	Applied to penis for treatment of nerve-related erection problems
Trazodone (Desyrel)	1	3	0	Increased frequency of erections during sleep

0 = No reports in medical literature
1 = Scattered cases, personal communication, or less than 10% occurence in studies
2 = 10–50% occurence in studies
3 = Greater than 50% occurence

References

Although space considerations preclude listing all the materials that have been helpful in working with men and writing this book, I list those works that are of particular interest for further reading, and also document quotations and information taken directly from other sources.

Introduction

2. The modern view of sex, including our adamant sense of entitlement about it, is well portrayed in L. Rubin, *Erotic Wars* (Farrar, Straus, Giroux, 1990).

5. The new consciousness among men has received a great deal of media coverage and is the subject of a number of recent books, including H. Brod (ed.), *The Making of Masculinities* (Allen & Unwin, 1987); W. Farrell, *Why Men Are the Way They Are* (McGraw-Hill, 1986); P. Garfinkel, *In a Man's World* (Mentor, 1985); S. Keen, *Fire in the Belly* (Bantam, 1991); M. Kimmel & M. Messner (eds.), *Men's Lives* (Macmillan, 1989); and A. Kipnis, *Knights Without Armor* (Tarcher, 1991).

7. On the prices men pay, see the references for p. 5 and also J. Balswick, *The Inexpressive Male* (Lexington, 1988); H. Goldberg, *The Hazards of Being Male* (Nash, 1976); M. Miedzian, *Boys Will Be Boys* (Doubleday, 1991); K. Thompson (ed.), *To Be a Man* (Tarcher, 1991).

8. "Boys are far more likely than girls. . . ." A. Moir & D. Jessel, *Brain Sex* (Lyle Stuart, 1991), 65.
   "Boys must travel a more torturous route. . . ." L. Rubin, *Intimate Strangers* (Perennial, 1983).
   On violent crime against men, "in the world today, for every woman who is violently assaulted, there are three or four men; for every five thousand U.S. female homicides in 1987, there were fifteen thousand male; and for U.S. males between fifteen and thirty-four throughout the 1980s, homicide was the second most likely cause of death, exceeded only by fatal

547

accidents." R. Miles, *Love, Sex, Death, and the Making of the Male* (Summit, 1991), 23.

9. On life expectancy and related issues, see J. Doyle, *The Male Experience*, 2nd ed. (Wm. C. Brown, 1989), 62–63.

10. " 'zipless fucks'. . . ." coined by E. Jong, *Fear of Flying* (Signet, 1974).

Chapter 1

20. On manly characteristics, see D. S. David & R. Brannon (eds.), *The Forty-nine Percent Majority* (Addison-Wesley, 1976), and J. Doyle, *The Male Experience*, 2nd ed. (Wm. C. Brown, 1989).

21. H. Robbins, *The Adventurers* (Pocket, 1966), 8; S. Sheldon, *The Sands of Time* (Warner, 1989), 353; C. Schuler, *Sophisticated Lady* (Harlequin, 1989), 8–9.

22. "Nature had different purposes. . . ." Sociobiologists are the people who most strongly, and in my mind most cogently, make the case for genetic differences between males and females. A good place to start is the outstanding book by D. Symons, *The Evolution of Human Sexuality* (Oxford, 1979).

23. "little girl burst into tears. . . ." J. Kellerman, *Time Bomb* (Bantam, 1990), 1.

24. On the differences between girl-girl and boy-boy friendships, see M. Caldwell & L. Peplau, "Sex Differences in Same-Sex Friendships," *Sex Roles*, 1982, 8, 721–731; P. Erwin, "Similarity of Attitudes and Constructs in Children's Friendships," *J. Experimental Child Psychology*, 1985, 40, 470–485; L. Kraft & C. Vraa, "Sex Composition of Groups and Pattern of Self-disclosure by High School Females," *Psychological Reports*, 1975, 37, 733–734; M. Waldrop & C. Halverson, "Intensive and Extensive Peer Behavior," *Child Development*, 1975, 46, 19–26.
    "face-to-face intimacy" and "side-by-side intimacy." These terms were coined by P. Wright, "Men's Friendships, Women's Friendships, and the Alleged Inferiority of the Latter," *Sex Roles*, 1982, 5, 1–20.
    N. Mailer, *The Armies of the Night* (Signet, 1968), 36.
    D. Gilmore, *Manhood in the Making* (Yale, 1990), 11.

25. "got rid of these rituals. . . ." To those who might argue that the Jewish Bar-Mitzvah remains, let me suggest that it is no longer a rite of passage. The thirteen-year-old boy still can't work in the adult world, still can't support himself, still can't vote, drink, or drive. There is no substantive way in which his life changes. Despite the ceremony, he remains a boy.
    On the relationships between fathers and sons, of over seven thousand men

respondents to Shere Hite's questionnaire, "almost no men said they had been or were close to their fathers." *The Hite Report on Male Sexuality* (Knopf, 1981), 17. As extreme as this finding seems, it doesn't differ that much from those in other surveys: S. Osherson, *Finding Our Fathers* (Fawcett, 1986), 6–8.

25. R. Heckler, *In Search of the Warrior Spirit* (North Atlantic, 1990), 38–39.
26. T. O'Connor, "A Day for Men," *Family Therapy Networker* (May/June 1990), 36.
28. J. Lester, "Being a Boy," *Ms.* (July 1973), 112.
    A. Pines, personal communication.
    Because of the emphasis on competition, strength, and self-reliance, men have a difficult time forming close friendships. On the basis on his research, D. Levinson states, "close friendship with a man or woman is rarely experienced by American men." *The Seasons of a Man's Life* (Knopf, 1978), 335.
29. D. Tannen, *You Just Don't Understand* (Morrow, 1990).
    "They are slow to admit to illness. . . ." A. Kipnis, *Knights Without Armor*, (Tarcher, 1991), 38–43.
31. J. Lester, "Being a Boy."
    "He was, after all. . . ." C. Schuler, *Sophisticated Lady*, 87.
32. B. Cosby, "The Regular Way," *Playboy* (December 1968), 288–289.
34. "Her hands left my neck. . . ." J. Kellerman, *Time Bomb*, 121.
    I. Wallace, *The Guest of Honor* (Dell, 1989), 223.
35. L. Barbach & L. Levine, *Shared Intimacies* (Bantam, 1981), 33.
    "For women, sex is intertwined. . . ." J. Carroll, et al., "Differences Between Males and Females in Motives for Engaging in Sexual Intercourse," *Archives Sexual Behavior*, 1985, *14*, 131–139; M. Brown & A. Auerback, "Communication Patterns in Initiation of Marital Sex," *Medical Aspects of Human Sexuality*, 1981, *15*, 107–117.

Chapter 2

39. "magical instruments. . . ." S. Marcus, *The Other Victorians* (Basic, 1966), 212.
40. "She was a month away. . . ." J. Higgins, *Season in Hell* (Pocket, 1990), 52.
    J. Gardner, *The Secret Houses* (Jove, 1990), 58.
    "That's right, honey. . . ." H. Robbins, *The Adventurers* (Pocket, 1966), 251.
41. H. Robbins, *The Betsy* (Pocket, 1972), 101–103.
44. L. Rubin, *Erotic Wars* (Farrar, Straus, Giroux, 1990), 9.

550 References

"A man in a research study. . . ." M. E. McGill, *The McGill Report on Male Intimacy* (Perennial, 1985), 194.

45. "A woman in the same study. . . ." *McGill Report*, 190.

45. The classic study of touching is A. Montagu, *Touching* (Perennial, 1971).

47. "Ike Vesper. . . ." R. Gorton, *The Hucksters of Holiness* (Bart, 1989), 128.

"Now all Alexis wanted. . . ." R. Latow, *Three Rivers* (Ballantine, 1981), 113.

On the difficulty men have saying no to sex, research indicates that men actually have more unwanted sex than women. Unlike women, however, most men who have unwanted sex aren't forced into it. Rather, they go along largely because of the fear of being thought less than men if they refuse. C. Muehlenhard & S. Cook, "Men's Self-reports of Unwanted Sexual Activity," *J. Sex Research*, 1988, 24, 58–72.

49. E. Jong, *Parachutes and Kisses* (Signet, 1985), 340–341.

50. "She reached inside. . . ." B. Sassoon, *Fantasies* (Pocket, 1991), 461.

"She swears. . . ." S. Sheldon, *If Tomorrow Comes* (Warner, 1986), 202.
M. Puzo, *The Godfather* (Fawcett, 1969), 28.

50. H. Robbins, *Dreams Die First* (Pocket, 1978).

"She wailed. . . ." D. Morrell, *The Covenant of the Flame* (Warner, 1991), 406.

"She captured. . . ." H. Robbins, *The Adventurers*, 475.

51. "The lingering kiss. . . ." I. Wallace, *The Guest of Honor* (Dell, 1989), 226.

"With Dax it's like having. . . ." H. Robbins, *The Adventurers*, 427. "She looked at him. . . ." 386.

53. The original description of orgasm experienced as the earth moving is in Hemingway's *For Whom the Bell Tolls* (Scribner's, 1940), 160. The earth moved for Robert, but his lover Maria died each time she came. Since then, everything in between moving the earth and leaving it altogether has been used to portray the cataclysmic effects of fictional sex.

"Then Jeff rolled. . . ." S. Sheldon, *If Tomorrow Comes*, 369.

S. Filson, *Nightwalker* (New American Library, 1989), 176–177.

54. "Alix felt as if. . . ." E. Lustbader, *French Kiss* (Fawcett, 1989), 119.

"You're good, Ezra. . . ." I. Wallace, *The Guest of Honor*, 226.

55. "Deeper, harder. . . ." C. Schuler, *Sophisticated Lady* (Harlequin, 1989), 82.

"With three violent thrusts. . . ." B. Sassoon, *Fantasies*, 428. "Within seconds. . . ." 411.

56. "No wonder that faking orgasms. . . ." C. Darling & J. Davidson, "Understanding the Feminine Mystique of Pretending Orgasm," *J. Sex &*

Marital Therapy, 1986, *12*, 182–196. See also S. Carter and J. Sokol, *What Really Happens in Bed* (Evans, 1989), 315, who claim that "almost every women has faked orgasm." Many men refuse to believe that women fake orgasm. The audience reaction to the film *When Harry Met Sally* is instructive. I've seen the faking orgasm scene (where in a restaurant Meg Ryan demonstrates to Billy Crystal how she can fake it) many times in classes, workshops, even twice in movie houses. The women always laugh sympathetically in unison—they know exactly what's going on—but a large proportion of men seem puzzled and some, like Billy Crystal, are adamant that such things can't happen in real life, at least not in their lives.

57. "He pressed me. . . ." Anonymous, *The Pearl* (Grove, 1968), 411.

N. Mailer, *American Dream* (Dell, 1965), 49 and 51.

D. H. Lawrence, *Lady Chatterley's Lover* (Bantam, 1968), 268.

58. "One study found. . . ." I'm not citing the original study because it was presented at a psychology meeting and never published. A similar study with college students is G. J. Fischer, "College Student Attitudes Toward Forcible Date Rape," *Archives Sexual Behavior*, 1986, *15*, 457–466.

"Given the double messages. . . ." Even though it is true that some women, some of the time, do say no when they mean yes—C. Muehlenhard & L. Hollabaugh, "Do Women Sometimes Say No When They Means Yes?," *J. Personality and Social Psychology*, 1988, *54*, 872–879—I think a man who is concerned with his own well-being should guide himself by the principle that no always means no. Any another assumption can get you into a great deal of trouble.

59. J. Collins, *Lucky* (Pocket, 1986), 344 and 352.

61. "The reality is that men. . . ." For estimates of the extent of male sex problems, see Chapter 5.

Chapter 3

65. W. Brinkley, *The Last Ship* (Ballantine, 1988), 452–453.

67. Carol Ellison, "Intimacy-based Sex Therapy" in W. Eicher & G. Kockott (eds.), *Sexology* (Springer-Verlag, 1988), 234–238.

70. "women were given permission and encouragement. . . ." See, for example, L. Barbach, *For Yourself* (Doubleday, 1975).

72. "Other things can be fun. . . ." These objections, which I use in a number of places in the book, are the exact words spoken to me by men in therapy or elsewhere.

78. M. Brenton, *Sex Talk* (Stein & Day, 1972), 61–62.

Chapter 4

84. The exercise of writing a letter from the point of view of your penis is given in my *Male Sexuality* (Bantam, 1978), 89.

85. "The producers of these films. . . ." Not only do they use the largest penises they can find, they also give them some help. E. McCormack, "Maximum Tumescence in Repose," *Rolling Stone* (Oct. 9, 1975), 56–71.

89. "The parts and how they work. . . ." A useful book is J. Gilbaugh, *A Doctor's Guide to Men's Private Parts* (Crown, 1989).

91. W. Masters & V. Johnson, *Human Sexual Response* (Little, Brown, 1966). Much of our current understanding of sexual anatomy and physiology stems from this important work. The sexual response cycle is another matter entirely. See L. Tiefer's devastating critique, "Historical, Scientific, Clinical and Feminist Criticisms of 'The Human Sexual Response Cycle' Model," in J. Bancroft (ed.), *Annual Review of Sex Research*, vol. 2 (Society for the Scientific Study of Sex, 1991), 1–23.

92. A. Kinsey, et al., *Sexual Behavior in the Human Female* (W. B. Saunders, 1953), 594.

95. Masters and Johnson discuss the sense of ejaculatory inevitability in various places in *Human Sexual Response*.

97. For men raped by women, see P. Sarrel & W. Masters, "Sexual Molestation of Men by Women," *Archives Sexual Behavior*, 1982, *11*, 117–132.

98. Two good books for laypeople on the medical aspects of erection problems, as well as medical treatment options, are R. Berger & D. Berger, *BioPotency* (Rodale, 1987), and I. Goldstein & L. Rothstein, *The Potent Male* (The Body Press, 1990). R. Berger and Goldstein are prominent urologists.

99. Performance anxiety, now almost a household term, is a relatively new concept in sexology. It was first used by the founder of behavior therapy, J. Wolpe, in *Psychotherapy by Reciprocal Inhibition* (Stanford, 1958), and later popularized by Masters & Johnson, *Human Sexual Inadequacy* (Little, Brown, 1970).

101. On the role of the clitoris in women's sexual pleasure, see S. Hite, *The Hite Report* (Macmillan, 1976), and Masters & Johnson, *Human Sexual Response*, Chapter 5.

103. "While a significant minority of women. . . ." L. Barbach and C. Ellison, personal communication.
    On women who can orgasm solely via fantasy, see S. Wilson & T. Barber, "The Fantasy-Prone Personality," in A. Sheikh (ed.), *Imagery* (Wiley, 1983), 340–387.

104. "Three researchers. . . ." A. Ladis, B. Whipple, & J. Perry, *The G-Spot*

and *Other Recent Discoveries About Human Sexuality* (Holt, 1982).

"the evidence for an anatomical structure is shaky. . . ." W. Schultz, et al., "Vaginal Sensitivity to Electric Stimuli," *Archives Sexual Behavior*, 1989, *18*, 87–95.

106. On the physical similarities between male and female orgasm, see Masters & Johnson, *Human Sexual Response*. Regarding emotional similarities, the classic study is by E. Vance and N. Wagner, "Written Descriptions of Orgasm," *Archives Sexual Behavior*, 1976, *5*, 87–98. So similar were the experiences of orgasm that a panel of physicians and psychologists could not reliably determine which had been written by which sex.

107. Masters & Johnson, *Human Sexual Response*.

108. J. Lester, "Being a Boy," *Ms.* (July 1973), 113.

110. L. Schover, personal communication.

Chapter 5

113. "Similar nonsense was promoted. . . ." I have relied heavily on two excellent sources, from which come all the quotes. R. Deutsch, *The New Nuts Among the Berries* (Bull, 1977), and J. Money, *The Destroying Angel* (Prometheus, 1985).

114. On the efforts to prevent masturbation, see A. Comfort, *The Anxiety Makers* (Delta, 1967), an excellent historical survey.
"one-third of births in colonial America. . . ." J. D'Emilio & E. Freedman, *Intimate Matters* (Harper, 1988), 22–23. This work is probably the best history of sex in America.

115. "A majority of boys. . . ." According to a report that became available after the text of this book was in press, a large majority of boys (76 percent) and a majority of girls (67 percent) have had intercourse before they were out of high school. "Sexual Behavior Among High School Students," CDC, MMWR, Jan. 3, 1992, 885–888.
On the incidence of oral and anal sex, see M. Hunt, *Sexual Behavior in the 1970s* (Playboy, 1974), 198–200.

116. J. Brown, *Out of Bounds* (Zebra, 1990), 205.
S. Carter & J. Sokol, *What Really Happens in Bed* (Evans, 1989), 310.

117. S. Hite, *The Hite Report on Male Sexuality* (Macmillan, 1976), 340–358.
I. Spector & M. Carey, "Incidence and Prevalence of Sexual Dysfunctions," *Archives Sexual Behavior*, 1990, *19*, 389–408.
S. Carter & J. Sokol, *What Really Happens in Bed*, 311.
S. Hite, *The Hite Report on Male Sexuality*, 1097–1098.

118. "Research indicates that a fairly large number of men. . . ." Kinsey reported that 37 percent of the thousands of men he interviewed had at least one sexual experience leading to orgasm with another man. *Sexual Behavior in the Human Male* (W. B. Saunders, 1948). Regarding fantasies, Masters and Johnson reported that "some form of homosexual imagery was the fourth most frequently reported fantasy pattern" among heterosexual men they studied. *Homosexuality in Perspective* (Little, Brown, 1979), 182.

119. "Estimates are that about 70 percent. . . ." M. Hunt, *Sexual Behavior in the 1970s,* and R. Levin & A. Levin, "Sexual Pleasure," *Redbook* (Sept. 1975), 51–58.

122. Kinsey's definition of a nymphomaniac is given in W. Pomeroy, *Dr. Kinsey and the Institute for Sex Research* (Signet, 1972), 317.

124. "A controversy has raged. . . ." Feminist viewpoints are given in L. Lederer (ed.), *Take Back the Night* (Morrow, 1980), and a wide range of men's opinions are in M. Kimmel, *Men Confront Pornography* (Crown, 1990).

128. "Studies of sexual fantasies. . . ." C. Crepault & M. Couture, "Men's Erotic Fantasies," *Archives Sexual Behavior,* 1980, 9, 565–581; M. Hunt, *Sexual Behavior in the 1970s;* D. Sue, "Erotic Fantasies of College Students During Coitus," *J. Sex Research,* 1979, 15, 299–305; D. Zimmer, et al., "Sexual Fantasies of Sexually Distressed and Nondistressed Men and Women," *J. Sex & Marital Therapy,* 1983, 9, 38–50.

Chapter 6

135. J. Brown, *Out of Bounds* (Zebra, 1990), 205.

Chapter 7

152. "Having the kind of relationship. . . ." The finding of an intensive study of couples says it all: "When the nonsexual parts of couples' lives are going badly, their sex life suffers." P. Blumstein & P. Schwartz, *American Couples* (Morrow, 1983), 203.

On the importance of communication, see S. Metts & W. Cupach, "The Role of Communication in Human Sexuality," in K. McKinney & S. Sprecher (eds.), *Human Sexuality* (Ablex, 1989), 150–161, and A. Pines, *Keeping the Spark Alive* (St. Martin's, 1988), 171.

156. The issue of sex differences is complex and extremely sensitive. When I first decided to address it in the book, I assumed I would simply adopt a list or discussion from another source. After an extensive search and correspondence with a number of experts, I was surprised to find that

such a list did not exist. A number of the people I talked to warned that the reason was because the subject was too controversial and that I would be severely criticized if I created one. After all, since about 1965 there has been a huge effort in certain academic, feminist, and intellectual circles to deny almost any differences between the sexes aside from the obvious anatomical ones. But there is some evidence that a new era is imminent. A good example is the work of psychologist Eleanor Maccoby. In 1974 she coauthored a book with Carol Jacklin summarizing the work that had been done on sex differences and basically concluded that hardly any existed (*The Psychology of Sex Differences*, Stanford U. Press); her book was used by many others to buttress their arguments against sex differences. But in a 1990 article ("Gender and Relationships," *American Psychologist*, 45, 513–520) she acknowledged that the conclusion was erroneous and there were indeed important differences between males and females in social behavior. Likewise, researcher Dan McAdams notes that a countervoice is being heard among his colleagues, a voice suggesting that, "especially when it comes to intimate relationships, sex differences may be more deeply ingrained than we initially thought." *Intimacy* (Doubleday, 1989), 167.

Of the few authors who have undertaken to explore the differences between men and women, I have relied most heavily on the seminal work of D. Symons, especially *The Evolution of Human Sexuality* (Oxford, 1979). Another useful book is A. Moir & D. Jessel, *Brain Sex* (Lyle Stuart, 1991), although it suffers from some unwarranted generalizations.

157. "If the first space visitor. . . ." Quoted in F. Pittman, "The Masculine Mystique," *Family Therapy Networker*, (May/June 1990), 42.
     V. Barbieri, personal communication.
158. On men's style of loving, see F. Cancian, *Love in America* (Cambridge, 1987). Cancian is one of the few writers I found who treats men's style as something of value, rather than as an inadequacy.
159. The story of the man who washed his wife's car is in T. Wills, et al., "A Behavioral Analysis of the Determinants of Marital Satisfaction," *J. Consulting and Clinical Psychology*, 1974, 42, 802–811.
162. On the reactions of boys and girls to the first experience of intercourse, see J. DeLamater, "Gender Differences in Sexual Scenarios," in K. Kelley (ed.), *Females, Males, and Sexuality* (SUNY, 1987), 127–140. The best survey I know of girls' first sexual experiences is S. Thompson, "Putting a Big Thing into a Little Hole," *J. Sex Research*, 1990, 27, 341–361. Many of the girls describe the experience as painful, boring, or disappointing, and many of them talk about it as just sort of happening without any intention on their part.

On the differences between the sexual thoughts, fantasies, and activity of women and men, see R. Coles & G. Stokes, *Sex and the American Teenager* (Harper, 1985); DeLamater, 1987, cited above; A. Hass, *Teenage Sexuality* (Macmillan, 1979); J. Jones & D. Barlow, "Self-reported Frequency of Sexual Urges, Fantasies, and Masturbatory Fantasies in Heterosexual Males and Females," *Archives Sexual Behavior*, 1990, *19*, 269–279; R. Knoth, et al., "Empirical Tests of Sexual Selection Theory," *J. Sex Research*, 1988, *24*, 73–89; and S. Hite, *The Hite Report on Male Sexuality* (Macmillan, 1976), 599–615.

163. "In one study. . . ." J. Carroll, et al., "Differences Between Males and Females in Motives for Engaging in Sexual Intercourse," *Archives Sexual Behavior*, 1985, *14*, 131–139.

"a study of responses of college students. . . ." R. Clark & E. Hatfield, "Gender Differences in Receptivity to Sexual Offers," *J. Psychology & Human Sexuality*, 1989, *2*, 39–58.

164. "Men sexualize all sorts of situations. . . ." In a review of the research literature, C. Muehlenhard concludes that "men are generally more likely than women to interpret a variety of behaviors as signals that the other person is interested in sex." " 'Nice Women' Don't Say Yes and 'Real Men' Don't Say No," in E. Cole & E. Rothblum (eds.), *Women and Sex Therapy* (Harrington Park, 1988), 96.

"Male fantasies include more visual content. . . ." B. Ellis & D. Symons, "Sex Differences in Sexual Fantasy," *J. Sex Research*, 1990, *27*, 527–555. This is probably the best study yet done on the subject.

166. "over 80 percent of the lesbians. . . ." P. Blumstein & P. Schwartz, *American Couples*, 570–571. JoAnn Loulan, a lesbian therapist who works with lesbians, agrees that lesbian lovers find it difficult to initiate sex and have it on a regular basis. "Research on the Sex Practices of 1566 Lesbians and the Clinical Applications," in E. Cole & E. Rothblum, *Women and Sex Therapy*, 225.

167. Regarding the importance of touching to women, perhaps the most dramatic evidence comes from the answers of 100,000 women to a question asked by advice columnist Ann Landers. The question was: "Would you be content to be held close and treated tenderly and forget about 'the act'?" Seventy-two percent of the respondents said "Yes," and 40 percent of them were *under* forty years old. "What 100,000 Women Told Ann Landers," *Reader's Digest* (Aug. 1985), 44–46.

"study of sexual fantasies. . . ." B. Ellis & D. Symons, 1990.

168. "Only a small number of men have problems. . . ." These men are called retarded ejaculators by sex therapists and they certainly do exist. But theirs is by far the least common of the male sexual problems.

"Men don't necessarily want to be . . . close after sex." N. Denny, et al., found that women wanted to spend more time in foreplay and afterplay than did men. "Sex Differences in Sexual Needs and Desires," *Archives Sexual Behavior*, 1984, *13*, 233–245. J. Halpern and M. Sherman also found that women wanted more physical affection after sex than did men. *Afterplay* (Pocket, 1979).

169. Regarding men's interest in sexual variety, I have never seen a study that indicated the contrary. Kinsey seemed on the mark when he said: "There seems to be no question but that the human male would be promiscuous in his choice of sexual partners throughout the whole of his life if there were no social restrictions." *Sexual Behavior in the Human Male*, 589.

The study of college students is the previously cited B. Ellis & D. Symons.

Chapter 8

173. On what assertiveness is and is not, the best source is R. Alberti & M. Emmons, *Your Perfect Right* (Impact), any edition. This is the book that started that whole assertiveness movement.

177. Yes's and No's: L. Barbach, *For Yourself* (Signet, 1976), 50–51.

179. C. Tavris, *Anger* (Touchstone, 1989).

Chapter 9

199. Regarding oral sex, P. Blumstein and P. Schwartz found that men who give and receive oral sex are happier with their sex lives and relationships in general. *American Couples* (Morrow, 1983), 231.

Chapter 10

202. D. Tannen, *That's Not What I Meant!* (Ballantine, 1986), 16.

203. Regarding the physical and emotional consequences of not expressing emotion, see S. Jourard, *The Transparent Self* (Van Nostrand, 1964); J. Balswick, *The Inexpressive Male*; H. Goldberg, *The Hazards of Being Male*. Also see the fascinating work by J. Pennebaker, *Opening Up* (Morrow, 1990). His research indicates that the prolonged inhibition of important thoughts and feelings is unhealthy and, further, that expressing these feelings—confessing, as he puts it—promotes physical and emotional well-being.

S. Hite, *Women and Love* (Knopf, 1987), 5.

204. "25 percent of husbands were surprised. . . ." E. Hetherington & A. Tryon, "His and Her Divorces," *Family Therapy Networker* (Nov/Dec 1989), 58.

205. D. Tannen, *You Just Don't Understand* (Morrow, 1990).

206. On the difficulties men have talking in personal terms to one another and

therefore being close friends, see D. Sherrod, "The Bonds of Men," in H. Brod, *The Making of Masculinities* (Allen & Unwin, 1987); and S. Miller, *Men and Friendship* (Houghton Mifflin, 1983).

211. War games is my own way of categorizing some of the main ways in which partners hurt each other and themselves. Men are not always enthusiastic about dealing with relationship and communication issues, but in my experience the war games label gets their attention better than anything else.

214. The classic work on how we dehumanize political enemies before and during war is S. Keen, *Faces of the Enemy* (Harper, 1986).

Chapter 11

My ideas about listening, talking, and dealing with conflict have been significantly influenced by informal conversations over the years with psychologist Dan Wile. His book, *After the Honeymoon* (Wiley, 1988), is not easy but can be very helpful to couples willing to put out some effort. Two other useful works are J. Gottman, et al., *A Couples Guide to Communication* (Research Press, 1976); and J. Creighton, *Don't Go Away Mad* (Doubleday, 1990).

228. On nagging, a study of divorced men and women had some interesting findings. Half of the women complained that lack of communication and affection was the main problem in their marriages. But the most common complaint of the men "was their wives' nagging, whining, and faultfinding." Hetherington & Tryon, "His and Her Divorces," *Family Therapy Networker* (Nov/Dec 1989), 58.

230. As difficult as I myself find it to believe, fifteen years is no longer the record for not being willing to face up to a problem. After this book was in press, I saw a man who had been a very quick ejaculator for thirty-three years and during that whole time had resisted his wife's pleas to get help. As he and I talked about the situation, he mentioned that she was "a bit angry." I couldn't imagine why.

Chapter 12

240. The research indicating that our emotions are generated and maintained by our thoughts has been conducted by cognitive psychologists and therapists. A good introduction, and a useful self-help book as well, is D. Burns, *Feeling Good* (Signet, 1980).

248. A. Pines, *Keeping the Spark Alive* (St. Martin's, 1988).

Chapter 13

264. On forgiving others, a useful work is S. Simon & S. Simon, *Forgiveness* (Warner, 1990).

268. D. Wile, personal communication.

Chapter 14

277. "A number of observers. . . ." I cite again A. Montagu's classic *Touching* (Perennial), 1971. Also useful is H. Colton, *The Gift of Touch* (Seaview, 1983).
278. A. Montagu, *Touching*, 192.
281. R. Heinlein, *Stranger in a Strange Land* (Berkley, 1961), 175.
284. These body-rubs are similar in some ways to the sensate focus exercise Masters and Johnson give in *Human Sexual Inadequacy* (Little, Brown, 1970), 71–75.

Chapter 15

292. "78 percent of the women said music was a turn-on. . . ." L. Wolfe, *The Cosmo Report* (Arbor, 1981), 73.
297. "95 percent . . . like their partners to undress them. . . ." *The Cosmo Report*, 79.

Chapter 16

302. Many people, including some sex therapists, use arousal as a synonym for erection. But then they are faced with the problem of what to call the feeling or experience of excitement. Confusion is the inevitable result when they use the same term to refer to both. Clarity seems best served if we use separate terms for separate phenomena.
310. B. Apfelbaum, personal communication.
312. "Simmering. . . ." B. Zilbergeld & C. Ellison, "Desire Discrepancies and Arousal Problems," in S. Leiblum & L. Pervin (eds.), *Principles and Practice of Sex Therapy* (Guilford, 1980), 79.
315. "collections of erotica written by women. . . ." A good one is L. Barbach (ed.), *Erotic Interludes* (Doubleday, 1986).
319. Dr. Arnold Kegel started using this exercise with women who were incontinent after childbirth, and they told him their sex lives had improved. "Sexual Function of the Pubococcygeus Muscle," *Western J. Surgery*, 1952, 60, 521–534.

Chapter 17

325. "Surveys show that many men. . . ." "Sex Partners Can't Be Trusted for AIDS Protection, Study Says," *San Francisco Chronicle*, Aug. 12, 1989, A-5; S. Cochran & V. Mays, "Sex, Lies and HIV," *New England J. Medicine*, 1990, 322, 774–775.
326. The tragic story of Magic Johnson shows why using condoms is necessary

for sexually active singles. The woman he got the HIV virus from didn't tell him she had the disease either because she feared the consequences of sharing this information or because she didn't know she was infected. And he in turn didn't tell subsequent partners because he didn't know he was infected.

327. "A recent survey. . . ." S. Cochran & V. Mays, "Sex, Lies and HIV."

329. "men also report feeling 'empty,' 'hollow'. . . ." L. Rubin, *Erotic Wars* (Farrar, Straus, Giroux, 1990), 98.

Chapter 18

344. E. Jong, *Fear of Flying* (Signet, 1974), 8.
C. Lamont, "How to Be Happy—Though Married," *The Humanist* (May/June, 1973), 16.
When I use marriage in this discussion, I mean any long, committed relationship, including people living together without a marriage license.

345. "The results of a number of surveys. . . ." L. Barbach & L. Levine, *Shared Intimacies* (Bantam, 1981); M. Hunt, *Sexual Behavior in the 1970s* (Playboy, 1974); L. Levine & L. Barbach, *The Intimate Male* (Doubleday, 1983); C. Tavris & A. Sadd, *The Redbook Report on Female Sexuality* (Delacorte, 1977); L. Wolfe, *The Cosmo Report* (Arbor, 1981). The *Playboy* study is the one by M. Hunt.
"sex in many marriages leaves a lot to be desired. . . ." When columnist Ann Landers asked her readers, "Has your sex life gone downhill after marriage?" an astounding 82 percent of her 141,000 respondents said yes. The adjectives most frequently used were "boring, dull, monotonous, and routine." *San Francisco Examiner*, Jan. 23, 1989, B-10.
G. Wilson, *The Coolidge Effect* (Morrow, 1982).

354. On the effect of children on a couple's sex life, see P. Blumstein and P. Schwartz, *American Couples* (Morrow, 1983), 204–205; C. Botwin, *Is There Sex After Marriage?* (Little, Brown, 1985), 37–46; J. Cuber, "The Natural History of Sex in Marriage," *Medical Aspects of Human Sexuality*, 1975, 9, 51–73; J. Mancini & D. Orthner, "Recreational Sexuality Preferences Among Middle-Class Husbands and Wives," *J. Sex Research*, 1978, 14, 96–106.

356. A delightful guide for parents is A. Mayer, *How to Stay Lovers While Raising Your Children* (Price Stern Sloan, 1990).

357. On the effects of age and illness, two fine works are R. Butler & M. Lewis, *Love & Sex After 60*, revised edition (Perennial, 1988), and L. Schover, *Prime Time* (Holt, 1984). For clinicians, nothing compares to L. Schover & S. Jensen, *Sexuality and Chronic Illness* (Guilford, 1988).

360. "Men are more likely. . . ." P. Blumstein and P. Schwartz, *American Couples*, 279.

"The consequences of extramarital sex. . . ." Although I do not seek to encourage extramarital sex, I give several examples where the results were not disastrous to counter the dominant bias in the other direction found in the popular media and professional journals.

Chapter 19

374. G. Edelstien, personal communication.

Chapter 20

383. J. LoPiccolo's discussion of "good prognostic indicators" for sex therapy is similar in several ways to my list of ideal partner characteristics. He places particular emphasis on both partners holding realistic views of sexual functioning, on the woman being able to accept nonintercourse sex during treatment, and on the man believing that he can fully satisfy her without an erection. "Post-Modern Sex Therapy for Erectile Failure," in R. Rosen & S. Leiblum (eds.), *Erectile Failure: Assessment and Treatment* (Guilford, 1992).

Chapter 21

391. A. Ellis has published so many works it's difficult to know which to cite. Two of the most important are *How to Stubbornly Refuse to Make Yourself Miserable About Anything—Yes, Anything!* (Lyle Stuart, 1988) and *A New Guide to Rational Living* (Wilshire, 1975), coauthored by R. Harper.
393. On getting your mind on your side, there are a number of useful books. Among those I like are D. Burns, *Feeling Good* and *The Feeling Good Handbook* (Morrow, 1989); almost anything by A. Ellis; M. Maltz's classic, *Psycho-Cybernetics* (Wilshire, 1967); M. Seligman, *Learned Optimism* (Knopf, 1991); and one I wrote with A. Lazarus, *Mind Power* (Ballantine, 1988).

My summary of Greg LeMond's victory in the Tour de France is taken from two articles in *Sports Illustrated*: F. Lidz, "Vive LeMond!," July 31, 1989, 13–17; and E. Swift, "Le Grand LeMond," Jan. 1, 1990, 55–72.

Chapter 22

408. "It has been estimated. . . ." I. Spector & M. Carey, *Archives Sexual Behavior*, 1990, *19*, 389–408.
409. "According to a number of studies. . . ." A few years ago P. Kilmann and I estimated that 75–85 percent of men develop better ejaculatory control

in therapy: "The Scope and Effectiveness of Sex Therapy," *Psychotherapy*, 1984, *21*, 319–326. My current estimate—based on my own results, on reading the therapy literature, and on discussions with colleagues—is a bit higher, but it applies only to men who stay in therapy for at least eight sessions and who are willing and able to do the homework exercises, including exercises with a partner.

412. "rapid ejaculation is almost always due to. . . ." In fairness, I should say that there may be a physical component for a small number of men. Some clients seem to be extremely sensitive to penile stimulation—that is, the same amount of stimulation that another man might describe as simply nice takes them very close to orgasm. One man like this who had the problem for many years and had given much thought to it said, "It's as if my arousal system is always in hyper-drive." My experience with such men is that although they need to spend more time than other men on the beginning exercises, they often do develop very good control.

Regarding the issue of how women have orgasms, S. Hite, *The Hite Report on Male Sexuality* (Macmillan 1976), and L. Wolfe, *The Cosmo Report* (Arbor, 1981) come up with almost identical figures: Only about a third of women reliably orgasm in intercourse and the rest, the large majority, require direct clitoral stimulation.

414. J. Semans, "Premature Ejaculation," *Southern Medical J.*, 1956, *49*, 353–358.

420. M. Perelman, personal communication.

Chapter 23

I could not have put this chapter together without the kind assistance of four excellent urologists who provided information and made comments on various drafts. My sincere thanks to Sumner Marshall, Richard Reznichek, Ira Sharlip, and Steve Taylor.

446. R. Schiavi, "Nocturnal Penile Tumescence in the Evaluation of Erectile Disorders," *J. Sex & Marital Therapy*, 1988, *14*, 83–97.

449. L. Sonda, et al., "The Role of Yohimbine for the Treatment of Erectile Impotence," *J. Sex & Marital Therapy*, 1990, *16*, 15–21.
On vacuum devices, there are three important articles in *J. Sex & Marital Therapy*, 1991, *17*. R. Witherington, "Vacuum Devices for the Impotent," 69–80; L. Turner, et al., "External Vacuum Devices in the Treatment of Erectile Dysfunction," 81–93; R. Villeneuve, et al., "Assisted Erection Follow-up with Couples," 94–100.

450. S. Althof, et al., "Sexual, Psychological, and Marital Impact of Self-Injection of Papaverine and Phentolamine," *J. Sex & Marital Therapy*, 1991, *17*, 101–112.

S. Althof, et al., "Why Do So Many People Drop Out from Auto-Injection Therapy for Impotence?," *J. Sex & Marital Therapy*, 1989, *15*, 121–129.

452. L. Tiefer, et al., "Psychosocial Follow-up of Penile Prosthesis Implant Patients and Partners," *J. Sex & Marital Therapy*, 1988, *14*, 184–201; J. McCarthy & S. McMillan, "Patient/Partner Satisfaction with Penile Implant Surgery," *J. Sex Education & Therapy*, 1990, *16*, 25–37.

453. L. Tiefer, et al., "Follow-up of Patients and Partners Experiencing Penile Prosthesis Malfunction and Corrective Surgery," *J. Sex & Marital Therapy*, 1991, *17*, 113–128.

Chapter 24

462. W. Masters & V. Johnson, *Human Sexual Response* (Little, Brown, 1966), 7, 252.

475. W. Masters & V. Johnson describe their work with surrogates in *Human Sexual Inadequacy* (Little, Brown, 1970), 146–154.

476. "Although little research has been done. . . ." One report of a very large number of cases seen by a therapist-surrogate team is B. Apfelbaum, "The Ego-Analytic Approach to Individual Body-Work Sex Therapy," *J. Sex Research*, 1984, *20*, 44–70. Apfelbaum estimates that 90 percent of the cases were successful.

477. "this kind of therapy is not widely available. . . ." One indication is that in a survey of the kinds of methods used by almost 300 sex therapists, surrogate therapy was employed in less than 2 percent of the cases treated and was therefore the *least* used method. P. Kilmann, et al., "Perspectives of Sex Therapy Outcome," *J. Sex & Marital Therapy*, 1986, *12*, 116–138. My impression is that this is simply because the vast majority of sex therapists don't work with surrogates.

Chapter 25

479. In 1977, Helen Kaplan criticized Masters and Johnson's sexual response cycle for not including a desire phase ("Hypoactive Sexual Desire," *J. Sex & Marital Therapy*, 3, 3–9), and Harold Lief reported that desire problems had become the most common presenting complaint in sex therapy clinics ("Inhibited Sexual Desire," *Medical Aspects of Human Sexuality*, 7, 94–95).

482. S. Leiblum & R. Rosen, "Introduction," in Leiblum & Rosen (eds.), *Sexual Desire Disorders* (Guilford, 1988), 12–13. This important professional book contains chapters by many of the leading sex therapists who work with desire problems.

484. "One European intellectual. . . ." The man was Karl Kraus and the quote appears in T. Szasz, *Karl Kraus and the Soul-Doctors* (Louisiana St. U., 1976), 154.

485. The willingness or motivation to act on sexual desire with one's partner is also part of the thinking of therapist Stephen Levine. His work is complex, subtle, and important. "An Essay on the Nature of Sexual Desire," *J. Sex & Marital Therapy*, 1984, *10*, 83–96; "Intrapsychic and Individual Aspects of Sexual Desire," in S. Leiblem & R. Rosen (eds.), *Sexual Desire Disorders*, 21–44.

486. Although sexual frequency is what makes for headlines, I hope it is now clear just how superficial it is. It is simply a kind of body count—so and so has sex four times a week—but says nothing of desire, motivation, or satisfaction. Not only is it true that people often don't have sex when they'd like to, it's also a fact that many men and women do have sex when they don't necessarily want to, or when their reasons have little to do with erotic activity. Muelenhard & Cook, *J. Sex Research*, 1988, *24*, 58–72.

487. P. Benchley, *The Deep* (Bantam, 1977), 63.

489. Relationship dissatisfaction and conflict—whether about things erotic or not—seems to be one of the most important reasons for desire problems. H. Lief, "Foreword," in S. Leiblum & R. Rosen (eds.), *Sexual Desire Disorders*, xii.

491. On sexually abused males, a subject one doesn't hear much about, see two books by M. Hunter: *The Sexually Abused Male* (Lexington, 1990) and *Abused Boys* (Lexington, 1990).

Chapter 27

519. On talking with and listening to children, an invaluable guide is A. Faber & E. Mazlish, *How to Talk So Kids Will Listen & Listen So Kids Will Talk* (Avon, 1982). This book can also be used to improve conversation among adults.

521. "Studies have shown. . . ." F. Furstenberg, et al., "The Life Course of Children of Divorce," *American Sociological Review*, 1983, *48*, 656–668.

527. C. Norris, *The Secret of Inner Strength* (Charter, 1989), 163–164.

533. On winning: I'm sure Ian had no idea who Vince Lombardi was, but I later realized that he sure knew about Joe Montana. And here's what his favorite quarterback had to say on the subject: "Vince Lombardi supposedly said, 'Winning isn't everything, it's the only thing,' and I couldn't agree more. There's nothing like being number one." Quoted in M. Messner, "The Meaning of Success," in H. Brod, *The Making of Masculinities* (Allen & Unwin, 1987), 193.

Acknowledgments

M<small>Y</small> heartfelt gratitude to the many people who made this book possible:

- The clients I've worked with over the last twenty years, with special thanks to those who read and made comments on earlier drafts of the chapters.

- The many people who've written to me about my earlier book, *Male Sexuality*, and those who attended my talks and workshops. By sharing their concerns and problems, asking questions, and just talking, these people and my clients provided the raw material on which the book is based. Many of the stories they told me are recounted in the book, although their names and other identifying information have been changed.

- The thirty women who allowed me to interview them about what makes a man a good lover.

- The colleagues and friends who were kind enough to read through the whole manuscript in one of its versions and give me their suggestions: Robert Badame, Victor Barbieri, Sandy Caron, Marsha and Allen Goodman, Jackie Hackel, Jo Kessler, Diane Morrissette, Ayala Pines, Rebecca Plante, Howard and Barbara Ruppel, Dan Wile, and Robyn Young.

- The colleagues and friends who read and commented on various chapters or discussed the ideas in them with me: Bernard Apfelbaum,

Lonnie Barbach, Dawn Block, David Bullard, Jill Caire, Isabella Conti, Gerald Edelstien, Albert Ellis, Carol Ellison, Suzanne Frayser, Joshua Golden, Susan Hanks, Harriet Jacobs, Michael Kimmel, Arnold Lazarus, Sandra Leiblum, Joe LoPiccolo, Sumner Marshall, Michael Perelman, James Petersen, Jackie Persons, Richard Reznichek, Ray Rosen, Carolyn Saarni, Leslie Schover, Ira Sharlip, Deborah Tannen, Carol Tavris, Steve Taylor, Leonore Tiefer, Carol Wade, Anne Weiwel, and George Zilbergeld.

• John Buffum for preparing the charts in the Appendix and Marsha Goodman for helping with the illustrations.

• My agent of many years, Rhoda Weyr, always there with a sympathetic ear and good advice; my wonderful and tireless editor, Toni Burbank, and her equally indefatigable assistant, Linda Gross; and copy editor Mike Mattil, who once again helped to improve the quality of my writing.

Index

R

rape, 4, 162, 165, 526
  by acquaintances, 58
  of males, 97
  partner's reports of, 235–37
rapid eye movement (REM) periods, erections
    in, 96, 446
rejection, sexual, 6–7, 56–59, 189, 192,
    195–96, 290, 298–300
relationships, 11–13, 343–68
  affairs and, 345, 359–65
  communication as central to, 12, 152–54
  differences in sexual desire in, 13, 156–70
  feelings as basis of problems in, 213
  long-term, 343–68
  men as unprepared for, 26
  mother-son, 7, 8, 25
  non-sexual aspects of, 190
  in problem-solving process, 372–81
  responsibility and, 194
  separate time in, 349–50
  sexual satisfaction in, 345
  single men and, 321–42
  women's emphasis on, 35, 162–63, 168,
    360
  see also father-son relationships; marriage
relaxation methods, 461
"report talk," 205–6
"riding high," 103
RigiScan, 446
rituals, as proof of manhood, 25
Robbins, Harold, 21, 40, 43, 49, 50, 54, 141
role-playing, 315–16
romance, 198–99, 350
"romantic lust," 343–44
Ronstadt, Linda, 32
Rosen, Raymond, 482
Rush, Benjamin, 113

S

safe sex, 477–78, 483
Sartre, Jean-Paul, 218
Schover, Leslie, 110
scrotum, 31, 89, 91, 416
seduction, 288–301
  definition of, 288–89

  as invitation, 290–93
  kissing and, 292
  mistakes in, 294–97
  music in, 292
  rejection and, 298–300
  by women, 300–301
self-criticism, 378
self-esteem, 392
self-expression, 238–56
  dangers of lack of, 239–40
  exercises in, 244–45, 246–47, 249–50
  getting in touch with feelings and, 241–46
  of negative feelings, 247
  of positive feelings, 247–48
  see also communication
self-hypnosis, 461
self-statements, 391–92, 397
Selleck, Tom, 44
Semans, James, 414
semen, 94
seminal vesicles, 89, 94, 415
sensitivity:
  assertiveness and, 154–56, 172, 176
  passion inhibited by, 78
"servicing," 54
sex, sexual activity:
  agreement as necessity in, 67, 80, 121,
    131, 132
  anger expressed with, 80
  anticipation of, 350–51
  committed vs. casual, 9–10
  as compulsion, 131
  conditions (requirements) and, 134–47,
    151–70, 460–61, 507–8
  as demonstration of love, 163–64
  discomfort with, 42–44
  as escape, 30
  ever-readiness for, 47–48, 134, 140
  extra-marital, *see* affairs
  fantasy model of, 37–61, 65, 83, 95, 116,
    134, 140, 344
  feelings as paramount in, 67, 72, 139, 191,
    213
  feelings expressed in, 77–81, 297, 352
  female initiation of, 3, 165, 186, 300–301,
    333, 335
  feminization of, 9–10
  illegal acts and, 130–31
  intercourse equated with, 51–53, 68–72